James Chrystal

Authoritative Christianity

The third world council which was held A.D. 431, at Ephesus in Asia

James Chrystal

Authoritative Christianity
The third world council which was held A.D. 431, at Ephesus in Asia

ISBN/EAN: 9783744754491

Printed in Europe, USA, Canada, Australia, Japan

Cover: Foto ©Suzi / pixelio.de

More available books at **www.hansebooks.com**

AUTHORITATIVE CHRISTIANITY.

THE SIX SYNODS OF THE UNDIVIDED CHURCH, ITS ONLY UTTERANCES, "THOSE SIX COUNCILS WHICH WERE ALLOWED AND RECEIVED OF ALL MEN,"
SECOND PART OF THE CHURCH OF ENGLAND HOMILY AGAINST PERIL OF IDOLATRY WHICH IS APPROVED IN ITS ARTICLE XXXV.

THE THIRD WORLD COUNCIL;
THAT IS THE THIRD COUNCIL OF THE WHOLE CHRISTIAN WORLD, EAST AND WEST, WHICH WAS HELD A. D. 431, AT EPHESUS IN ASIA.

VOL. II.,
WHICH CONTAINS ALL OF ACTS II. TO VI. INCLUSIVE, WITH MATTER BETWEEN THE ACTS,

—TRANSLATED BY—

JAMES CHRYSTAL, M. A.

The first six Acts of this Council and the matter between them are on the Nestorian controversy, and show incontestably that the third Council of the *"One, Holy, Universal and Apostolic Church"* expressly or by necessary implication condemned, once for all, all denial of the Incarnation, all invocation and worship of any thing but the Substance of the Triune Jehovah, all relative worship, and all forms of Consubstantiation and Transubstantiation on the Lord's Supper; and the Seventh and last Act condemns all claims of Rome, even when it was sounder, to Appellate Jurisdiction outside of Italy. Now by other Ecumenical decisions it is idolatrous and no part of the Universal Church, but doomed to perish, Rev. xvii. and xviii. *"If he neglect to hear the Church, let him be unto thee as a heathen man and a publican,"* Matt. xviii., 17.

JAMES CHRYSTAL, PUBLISHER,
2 Emory Street, Jersey City, New Jersey, U. S. A.
1904.

DEDICATION.

TO THE GREEK RACE EVERYWHERE, WHICH HAS GIVEN THE
CHURCH AND THE WORLD THOSE GREAT CHAMPIONS
FOR THE INVOCATION OF THE TRIUNE GOD ALONE,
AND FOR THE SYMBOLIC, THE FIGURATIVE
DOCTRINE ON THE EUCHARIST, SAINT
ATHANASIUS AND SAINT CYRIL
OF ALEXANDRIA, AND
FURNISHED THE
BULK OF
THE
BISHOPS WHO SAT IN THOSE SOLE UTTERANCES OF THE WHOLE
CHURCH, EAST AND WEST, THE SIX ECUMENICAL SYNODS,
A. D. 325—680, AND WHICH HAS SO NOBLY STOOD UP
FOR 800 OR 1000 YEARS AGAINST THE AT-
TEMPTS OF ROME, THE HARLOT OF
THE REVELATIONS (REV. XVII.,
18), TO SUBJUGATE
AND ENSLAVE
IT.

MAY IT SOON DO AWAY ALL THE ABUSES AND IDOLATRIES
CONDEMNED BY NECESSARY INCLUSION IN THE DECISIONS
OF THE SAID SIX COUNCILS, BUT FOSTERED NEVERTHE-
LESS BY THE IGNORANT CLERGY AND PEOPLE IN
THE MIDDLE AGES, AND BOUND ON IT TYRAN-
NICALLY BY THE FOLLY OF WOMEN, THE EM-
PRESSES IRENE AND THEODORA, AND
THEIR SUCCESSORS, AND MAY IT AND
THE WHOLE CHURCH, EAST AND
WEST, BE REUNITED AGAIN
ON ALL NEW TESTA-
MENT AND ORTH-
ODOX SIX
SYNODS BASES, AND MAY CHRIST'S CHURCH EVERYWHERE
SOON BE "A GLORIOUS CHURCH, NOT HAVING SPOT
OR WRINKLE OR ANY SUCH THING" (EPH. V.,
27) AND REGAIN ALL THAT IT
LOST IN DEGENER-
ATE TIMES.

PREFACE.

Nearly nine years have passed since the issue of Volume I of *Ephesus*. Lack of sufficient means to publish with has been the cause of the delay. Works of this kind appeal mainly to scholars, and hence their patronage is limited for the most part to a small, but select class, and hence they do not pay in money, and need help to defray the necessary expense of putting them before the people.

On the first volume the translator sunk about half his small capital; on the second the generosity of friends saved him from loss, and the same generosity enables him to put out this whole Volume II., and it is proposed to publish in this way the volumes which remain of the VI Councils so long as means come in to do so. The work is the only one in English which gives the Acts in full. A late work by the creature-invoker Percival gives Definitions, but I think that it will be generally deemed by sound Anglicans that a man of his creature worshipping type, condemned as he is by the Six Synods, and by necessary implication, deposed and anathematized by the decisions of Ephesus is unfit to edit it or any other Ecumenical utterance. Even his fellow-idolatrizer of *The Church Quarterly Review* for Jan. 1901, confesses that *"the execution of his work is by no means so good as it ought to have been;"* that *"the attempts at supplying the historical setting of the Councils; their constitution and proceedings are most inadequate,"* and that *"a lack of exact scholarship is often evident, and in matters of detail, there are actual blunders."* Furthermore, he does not cover the field of this work, because he does not give the Acts, that is, Minutes, in full. And they are necessary to a complete understanding of the Definitions. He is since dead in his sins.

There are still at least eight or ten volumes more of the set, and next to the Bible they are the most indispensable works in the World to the theological student. The translator has spent much time on them since 1864, and can put a volume to press every year till they are all out. But he is nearly 72. These facts, it is hoped, will induce some to come forward and furnish the necessary means to pay printers and binders. Otherwise they may never see the light. The subscription list does not pay half the monetary cost even.

Certain facts must be remembered :

1. These documents, next to the Bible, are the chief and all sufficient support of the English Reformers in their contention against Rome, against her idolatries, and her claim to jurisdiction in Britain or elsewhere.

2. But, except so far as the published volumes of this set of what the Second Part of the Church of England *Homily against Peril of Idolatry* approved in its Article XXXV., calls well, "*those Six Councils which were allowed and received of all men,*" have been circulated, the great bulk of the Bishops and clergy and people are almost utterly ignorant of some of their decisions which favor their Church. For example, Newman, Pusey, and Keble died utterly ignorant of the fact that they condemn all their traitorous worship of saints and images, and their new-fangled heresy of Two Nature Consubstantiation, all errors against their own Anglican Formularies. An instance of their dense ignorance is the fact that Keble and Pusey in their works on the Eucharist so mistook one or two utterances of Theodoret, the chief champion of Nestorianism, in favor of one nature Consubstantiation in the Eucharist as to make them favor their heresy of Two Nature Consubstantiation in the Eucharist; and besides they seem to have been ignorant of the fact that Theodoret's errors on the Eucharist were condemned by the Third Synod of the whole Church, Ephesus, A. D. 431, and were among the bases of his deposition by it.

3. As a result of that ignorance of the utterances of the Universal Church by its leaders, the Oxford Movement of A. D. 1833, has been in doctrine, discipline, rite, and custom, a merely Latinizing, Romanizing, Anti-Catholic, Anti-Anglican, Anti-Reformation movement, which has carried hundreds of the clergy and thousands of the laity to Rome, and, as Cardinal Vaughn has lately testified, has resulted in such anarchy that to-day nearly every doctrine of Rome is preached and practised in the Church of England by its own clergy. Aye, "The Church Review," an organ of the Romanizing party in England, itself, according to the Romanizing *Churchman* of New York of October 27, 1900, page 504, openly testifies :

"This land [England] is, *so far* as concerns *eighty per cent. of its vitally important population*, either indifferent to any kind of practical religion or given up to some form or other of our Protean

Protestantism." The poor people seeing their Churches again filled with idols, the idolatrous worship of the Host brought in again, and Rome's abominable Paganizings and spiritual Harlotries restored, and their clergy become the agents for perverting their wives and daughters to Rome's errors, have left by the hundred thousand or million, some going to other Trinitarian Protestant Communions more loyal to Christ and to the Reformation, while others having come to look upon the Bishops and clergy as traitors, shirkers, and corrupters have forsaken the Church till a better day comes, and others, alas! in their utter disgust with such evils and with their toleration by the unworthy so-called Bishops have gone over to stark infidelity.

4. To make clear therefore what the profession in the Creed of belief in the "*One, Holy, Universal and Apostolic Church*" means, and binds us to, and to recall clergy and people from Rome's mere *localisms* to the *Universal Church* doctrine, discipline, rite, and, custom, and roll back forever the torrents of idolatry and infidelity, these documents must see the light, for in them alone has the whole Church East and West spoken. Will you not give us your aid by helping to publish them and that at once, for to-morrow may be forever too late; and will you not also do what you can to circulate them? For $500. a year for his own support while giving himself wholly to this work, and $1500. a year to publish with, the translator offers the plates, the income from the works, and all else belonging to them, on one condition, that not one thing in them be changed, and so things fathered on him which he abhors as contrary to Christ and his Church, and lest on the other hand, any of the truths taught by him be weakened or negatived, or omitted.

To all the contributors on pp. V, VI and VI, A, I have this Commo- '04, sent gratis and prepaid where marked in margin of said pages, 1 copy each of vol. 2 of Epl-, 1904 edition, with a letter of gift, and besides, written or circulars to most of them.

A MEMORIAL OF GRATITUDE TO BENEFACTORS TO CHURCH AND STATE,

For the state has been made by pure Christianity, and falls without it.

NAMES OF THE THIRD VOLUME CONTRIBUTORS TO THE FUND TO PUBLISH THE SIX ECUMENICAL SYNODS,

that is in the period 1895-1904, since vol. 2, of Ephesus was issued; those sole utterances of what the Second Part of the Church of England *Homily Against Peril of Idolatry*, well calls, "*Those Six Councils which were allowed and received of all men.*" The same Part II. of that Homily rejects the image-worshipping and saint invoking and Host-worshipping Conventicle, the Second of Nicaea A. D. 787, which Romanists and Greeks call the Seventh Ecumenical, so that the Church of England holds to the Six Ecumenical Synods only. And she makes this fact still clearer when in her Articles and Offices she condemns the forespecified idolatries of that abominable Conventicle of A D. 787, which contradicts the Third Synod and the Fifth. In the *Homily Against Peril of Idolatry*, which is approved by her XXXVth Article, she condemns that conventicle of Nicaea, of A D. 787, as idolatrous.

The translator again expresses his heartfelt gratitude to those who have helped him on the first two volumes of the set of the VI Great Synods of the Christian world, and to those who have given on this the third volume, the Second of *Ephesus*. And he blesses that God who has given him strength and will to labor so many years for the good of His Church and of all who call themselves Christians, and has raised up for him such valuable and generous helpers and co-workers, and prays that their numbers and gifts may be increased, and that they themselves may be most richly rewarded, and that he may finish this great task before he dies, and so that we may have for the first time, the entire Acts of the Six Synods in English, that the plainest man may know what alone the Universal Church, which he confesses in the Creed, has said.

GIVERS OF SUMS TO PUBLISH VOLUME II. OF EPHESUS, ETC.:

ARCHBISHOPS.

THE LORD ARCHBISHOP OF DUBLIN, (Lord Plunket, since fallen asleep in Christ)..£5

BISHOPS.

RIGHT REV. HENRY CODMAN POTTER, D.D., L.L.D., Bishop of New York...$25 00

RIGHT REV. THOMAS U. DUDLEY, D.D., D.C.L., Bishop of Kentucky... 20 00

Names of Contributors.

RIGHT REV. OZI W. WHITAKER, D.D., Bishop of Pennsylvania...... 20 00

THE LORD BISHOP OF LICHFIELD, England, (THE HON. AND RIGHT REV. AUGUSTUS LEGGE, D.D.) £2 2s

RIGHT REV. GEORGE F. SEYMOUR, D.D., L.L.D., Bishop of Springfield $10 00

RIGHT REV. WM. F. NICHOLS, Bishop of California.................. 10 00

RIGHT REV. D. S. TUTTLE, Bishop of Missouri......................... 15 00

A BISHOP OF THE CHURCH OF IRELAND, (Anglican) 10 00

RIGHT REV. EDWIN G. WEED, S.T.D., Bishop of Florida............ 10 00

RIGHT REV. GEORGE W. PETERKIN, D.D., L.L.D., Bishop of West Va.. 10 00

RIGHT REV. CHAUNCEY B. BREWSTER, Bishop of Connecticut..... 10 00

RIGHT REV. THOMAS A. JAGGER, D. D., Bishop of Southern Ohio.. 6 25

RIGHT REV. JOHN WILLIAMS, Bishop of Connecticut, (since departed) 5 00

RIGHT REV. THOMAS MARCH CLARK, Bishop of Rhode Island, (departed)... 5 00

THE LORD BISHOP OF ELY, (LORD ALWYNE COMPTON)........... 5 00

RIGHT REV. ELLISON CAPERS, D.D., Bishop of South Carolina..... 5 00

RIGHT REV. BOYD VINCENT, D.D., Bishop Coadjutor of Southern Ohio.. 5 00

RIGHT REV. FREDERICK D. HUNTINGTON, D.D., L.L.D., L.H.D., Bishop of Central New York... 5 00

RIGHT REV. WM. W. NILES, D.D., L.L.D., D.C.L., Bishop of New Hampshire 5 00

RIGHT REV. ROBERT A. GIBSON, D.D., Bishop Coadjutor of Va.... 5 00

A BISHOP OF THE AMERICAN CHURCH 5 00

RIGHT REV. JOHN F. SPAULDING, D.D, Denver, Col. (deceased) 5 00

PRESBYTERS.

REV. EUGENE AUGUSTUS HOFFMAN, D.D., L.L.D., Dean of the General Theological Seminary, N. Y, (deceased).................. 200 00

REV. JOHN W. BROWN, (deceased), N. Y............................ 50 00

REV. DAVID H. GREER, Rector of St. Bartholomew's Church, N. Y., now Coadjutor Bishop of New York. 40 00

REV. AUGUSTUS VALLETTE CLARKSON, Croton, N. Y............. 30 00

REV. W. ALLEN JOHNSON, Professor Emeritus in Berkeley Divinity School, Middletown, Conn.. 20 00

REV. E. WINCHESTER DONALD, D.D., Boston, Mass................ 10 00

Names of Contributors. VI.A

Rev. WM. N. DUNNELL, D.D., N. Y.	10 00
Rev. W. R. HUNTINGTON, D.D., D.C.L., L.H.D., N. Y.	5 00
Rev. GEORGE R. VAN DE WATER, D.D., N. Y.	5 00
Rev. E. A. BRADLEY, (deceased), N. Y.	5 00
Rev. A C. KIMBER, D.D., N. Y.	5 00
Rev. ARTHUR BROOKS, (deceased), N. Y.	5 00
Rev. I. NEWTON STANGER, D.D., Philadelphia	5 00
Rev. G. F. WILLIAMS, D.D., Washington, D. C.	5 00
Rev. P. G. ROBERT, D.D., St. Louis, Mo	5 00

OF THE LAITY.

FRANCIS G. Du PONT, Esq., Wilmington, Del	100 00
A FRIEND	1200 00
MR. AND MRS. ISBISTER, Jersey City, N. J.	5 00

OLD CATHOLIC PRESBYTER.

E. R. KNOWLES, Worcester, Mass	20 00

CONTRIBUTIONS SINCE RECEIVED.

RIGHT REV. W. A. LEONARD, Bishop of Ohio	$ 5 00
THE LORD BISHOP OF LICHFIELD	£2 2s
RIGHT REV. O. W. WHITTAKER, Bishop of Pa	$ 5 00
RIGHT REV. D. S. TUTTLE, Bishop of Mo	5 00
RIGHT REV. ROBERT A. GIBSON, Bishop of Va	5 00
REV. AUGUSTUS VALETTE CLARKSON, New York City	10 00
REV. CANON W. WIGRAM, Watling House, St. Alban's, England	£1 8d
MR. FRANCIS G. Du PONT, Wilmington, Del	100 00
MR. JAMES RUTHERFORD, Carbondale, Pa	25 00
MR. W. H. ISBISTER, Philadelphia, Pa	5 00

Without counting anything for the support of the editor and annotator for nine years, about $1,500 were needed for the cost of the whole volume, including the pay of the printers, electrotypers, paper makers and binders. A volume of this set, of 500 pages, costs about $1,500, for much of the type is fine print, and the Greek costs extra, and the translator needs and asks about $500 a year on which to live while giving himself wholly to this work. And at his death the set will be given into the hands of any society which may be formed before to continue their publication without addition or subtraction or any other change. And he earnestly asks that such a society be formed at once and that he be advised of it.

Certain facts must ever be borne in mind.

1. Because of the lack of accurate knowledge of the contents of these priceless documents, the leaders of the Oxford Movement of A. D. 1833, Pusey, Newman and Keble, fell into the idolatry of invoking saints and the worship of the Host and favored the worship of images, and, not heeding the command of God in Revelations XVII, 18 and XVIII, 4, to come out of Rome, they led hundreds of the clergy and thousands of the laity back into her sins and brought the Church of England into such disrepute that hundreds of thousands, aye millions of the English people are no longer with her, and she is threatened with disestablishment. If she is to be saved therefore her clergy and people must know these sole decisions of Christ's "*one, holy, universal and apostolic church.*" And this is the only translation of them into English.

2. If ever orthodox Protestants, and indeed all Christians, are to be united, it must be on these former bases of union, its sole possible way to godly unity, for since the church forsook them in the eighth century and the ninth, and became idolatrous, it has split into East and West and remains divided till this hour and will till it all reforms; just as the Israelitish church before it, was split for like idolatry into Judah and Israel, as the blessed Reformers teach in the *Second Part of the Homily of the Church of England against Peril of Idolatry.*

3. Of nearly 1,000,000 immigrants who came to us last year, perhaps not more than 150,000 were Protestants. And if this land of ours is to be saved from being swamped by a vast influx of Christ-hating Jews, Romanists, Mohammedans and other non-Christians or rather Antichrists or Antichristians, the Protestants must get together on the basis of the VI Synods of the Christian World, A. D. 325-680, and, on matters not decided by them, on the Scriptures as understood in the pure period of the church, the first three centuries—that will be to perfect and crown our Reformation of the sixteenth century by a perfect Restoration, as the reformed Jews perfected their Reformation made in Babylon, by a complete Restoration at Jerusalem in the days of Ezra and Nehemiah. Some facts necessary to a full Restoration were not well known then. They are now.

TABLE OF CONTENTS OF THIS VOLUME II. OF THE THIRD ECUMENICAL SYNOD, WHICH WAS HELD AT EPHESUS A. D. 431.

It embraces Acts II. to VI. inclusive. They set forth the final decisions mentioned on the title page as theirs.

	PAGE
UTTERANCES OF THE THIRD ECUMENICAL SYNOD BETWEEN ITS DEPOSITION OF NESTORIUS AND ITS SECOND ACT	1

These are:

1. Its Letter to the Clerics and Stewards of Constantinople, as to the Deposition of Nestorius, and as to the Church property of his late see 3
2. Its Report to the Emperors 14
3. Epistle of the Synod to the Clergy and People of Constantinople 16
4. In this place, following Coleti, we put the Archimandrite Dalmatius' Letter to the Ecumenical Synod, because it bears on the utterance of the Synod given next below 16
5. Copy of an Epistle sent by the Holy Synod to the Archimandrite Dalmatius 17

SUMMARIES OF DOCUMENTS WHICH ARE NOT UTTERANCES OF THE THIRD ECUMENICAL SYNOD, BUT WHICH ARE FOUND IN EDITIONS OF THE COUNCIL BETWEEN ITS ACT I. AND ITS ACT II.; PUT THERE FOR MERE INFORMATION'S SAKE 21

They are:

1. A Letter of Cyril to Two of his Bishops then acting as his agents at Constantinople, and to some other Clerics there 21
2. A Letter of Cyril of Alexandria to the Clergy and Laity of Alexandria, translated in full . . . 25

3. Another Letter of Cyril to the Presbyters [that is Elders], Deacons and Laity of Alexandria . . 26
4. A Letter of Cyril to the Fathers of the Monks in Egypt and to the rest of the Monks . . . 27
5. "A Homily of Rheginus, Bishop of Constantia in Cyprus, delivered in Ephesus after the Deposition of Nestorius" 27
6. "A Homily of Cyril, Bishop of Alexandria, delivered in Ephesus when the gatherings were concluded and Nestorius had been deposed 28
7. A Spurious Homily, fathered falsely on Cyril . . 29
8. A Protest of Nestorius' partisan, Count Candidian, against the First Act of the Third Ecumenical Synod, addressed to the Nestorians at Ephesus . . 40
9. Another Protest of the same Candidian against the First Act of the Third Ecumenical Council addressed to them 41
10. Report of Nestorius and of his few partisans at Ephesus to the Emperors 42
11. Action of John of Antioch after his arrival at Ephesus, and his small faction, in which they presume to depose Cyril and Memnon and to excommunicate all the rest of the Bishops of the Third Ecumenical Synod . 46
12. Impudent Letter of John and his small faction of Nestorians in which they inform the Third Ecumenical Synod that they have deposed Cyril and Memnon, and excommunicated the rest of them till they repent of their Orthodoxy and embrace their heresy . . 56
13. Report of John of Antioch and his "Conventicle of the Apostasy" to the Emperor Theodosius II., against the Third Synod 56

14. A Letter of John of Antioch and the same Conventicle to the Clergy of Constantinople, to maintain Nestorius as their Bishop, notwithstanding his deposition by the Ecumenical Synod 58
15. Epistle of John of Antioch and the same Apostatic Conventicle to the Senate at Constantinople for Nestorius 59
16. An Epistle of John of Antioch and his Apostatic Conventicle to the Laity of Constantinople for Nestorius . 60
17. A Report of John of Antioch and his "Conventicle of the Apostasy" to the Empresses, for Nestorius . 61

WORK OF THE THIRD ECUMENICAL SYNOD.

ACT SECOND OF THE THIRD ECUMENICAL SYNOD. "A Copy of the Record of what was done in the presence of the Bishops and Presbyters" [that is Elders], "who came from Rome" 67

In this Act and in the one following, Rome, and what of the West she represented gave assent to Act I. of the Third Ecumenical Synod—so that with the vote of the East in Act I. and with the assent of Carthage already given there, it was thus made Ecumenical

An Epistle of Celestine, Bishop of Rome to the Ecumenical Synod, was read in this Act Second . . . 72

ACT THIRD OF THE THIRD ECUMENICAL SYNOD   94

This contains the completing of the approval of the Act by Rome and its local Synod, the East having spoken before.

It contains besides a Letter or Report of the whole Synod to the Emperors, page 114; and a Letter of theirs to the Clergy and Laity of Constantinople . . . 124

A warning on Philip's haughty and boastful Roman
    language on page 99 above . . . 128
FOURTH ACT OF THIRD ECUMENICAL SYNOD . 138
FIFTH ACT OF THE THIRD ECUMENICAL SYNOD . 153

{ In these Acts IV. and V. the Third Synod pronounces the action of the "Conventicle of the Apostasy" against Cyril and Memnon null and void; and suspends its members, John of Antioch and the rest, from communion and from all exercise of ministerial functions. In the Vth Act the Council report their action in one Document to the Emperors, page 163; and in another to Celestine, Bishop of Rome, page 168. In the latter Document they approve the action of Rome and the West in deposing Celestius, Pelagius, Julian, and others for Pelagianism, and record themselves as "co-voters" with Rome and the West against them and their heresy.

MATTER PUT BY SOME BETWEEN ACTS V. AND VI.
OF THE THIRD WORLD SYNOD.

1. [A Homily] of Cyril, Archbishop of Alexandria, against
    John of Antioch who separated [from the Synod] . 183
ACT SIXTH OF THE THIRD ECUMENICAL SYNOD .
This deals with the Man-Serving, relatively worshipping,
    Nestorian Creed attributed to Theodore of Mopsuestia
    and condemns it. 185

MATTER WHICH FORMS NO PART OF THE ACTS OF THE
THIRD ECUMENICAL SYNOD BUT WHICH IS PUT
BETWEEN ITS ACTS FOR INFORMATION. . . 235

1 "A Homily of Cyril, Bishop of Alexandria, against the
    Nestorian Worship of Christ's humanity, delivered in
    Ephesus before he was arrested by the Count, and committed to be kept under their guard." . . 235

MATTER ON THE APOSTATIC SANHEDRIM PUT FOR INFORMATION'S SAKE BETWEEN ACTS VI. AND VII. OF THE THIRD ECUMENICAL SYNOD THOUGH NONE OF IT IS IN THE ACTS: PART OF IT IS FROM THE SYNODICON OF MONTE CASINO	241
Prefatory Note on that Synodicon	241
Document 1. An Emission of the Apostatic Conventicle of John of Antioch and Count Candidian against the Third Ecumenical Synod	247
Document 2. An Epistle of John of Antioch's Nestorian Conventicle to the Clergy and People in Hierapolis in Euphratesia	249
Document 3. A Report of the same Conventicle against the Third Ecumenical Synod and its Action in sustaining Cyril and Memnon	250
Document 4. A statement of the same Conventicle against Cyril and Memnon, against the Third Synod and against Cyril's XII Chapters	253
Document 5. Letter of the Emperors to the Third Synod, through Palladius of Magisterial rank. This favors the Nestorians and attempts to bully the Ecumenical Synod and to undo its work	257
Document 6. Report of John of Antioch and his Nestorian Conventicle to the Emperor, "which they wrote in reply," through the same Palladius. They claimed to be the Synod, few as they were	260
Document 7. An Epistle of the same John and his little gathering to the Prefect and the Master of the Imperial Household	266
Document 8. An Epistle of the same John and his small following at Ephesus to the Praepositus and the Scholasticus; or "to the Praepositus even Scholasticus"	267

Document 9. A Report of the same John and his Conventicle to the Emperor to show again that they had deposed Cyril and Memnon 268

Document 10. Report of John and his little fragment of the Synod to the Emperor given to their friend Count Irenaeus with the forewritten Report . . . 271

Document 11. Epistle written by the Count Irenaeus to John of Antioch and the Nestorian Conventicle at Ephesus concerning the Actions on the Business after his entrance into Constantinople and the Delivery of the Report . , . . . 273

Document 12. A Letter of Nestorius to Scholasticus, the Chamberlain of the Emperor Theodosius the Second . 277

Document 13. A most unwise Letter of the Emperor in which, though he wisely admits the Action of the Third Ecumenical Synod in deposing Nestorius, he neverthless unjustly admits the Action of John and his Nestorian Conventicle in deposing Cyril and Memnon, and urges them to compromise, in effect to the sacrifice of God's truth, and tells them that he sends to them Count John to carry out his wishes . . 285

Document 14. "Copy of an Epistle of John, Count of the Imperial Treasury, written from the City of Ephesus to the Emperors" 288

Document 15; A. and B. A Letter of John of Antioch and twelve other Nestorian Prelates "to the Presbyters and Deacons and the rest of the Clerics, and the monks" and the laity of Antioch 292, 293

Document 16. Another bad Letter of the Emperor to the Third Synod, in which he dismisses them to their homes, refuses to regard the disciplinary action of the Third Synod against the Nestorians of John of Antioch's Conventicle at Ephesus as valid, and

Table of Contents. xiii

persists in regarding the deposition of Cyril and Memnon by the Nestorians as valid. In brief he nullifies, so far as he can, all the Work of the Ecumenical Synod 294

Document 17. A Letter of Nestorian Bishops at Ephesus of John of Antioch's party to Acacius of Berrhoea . 302

Document 18. Letter of Instructions of the Nestorian Conventicle at Ephesus to their Delegates to the Emperor at Constantinople 306

Document 19. First Petition of the Nestorian Delegates aforesaid which was sent from Chalcedon to the Emperor 309

NOTE: What do the seven Bishops of the Apostasy mean by charging, on page 311, in the Document last above, upon Cyril of Alexandria and the Third Ecumenical Synod, the design to "*adulterate*" the worship offered by the angels above to God (evidently to God the Son as that alone was involved in the discussion), and by accusing them of "*really taking away that worship and establishing*" Cyril's Twelve "*Chapters,*" the eighth of which, by the way, forbids worship to Christ' humanity, and confines it to His Divinity?
When the Father said (Heb. i: 6), "*And let all the angels of God worship Him*" (by bowing as the Greek shows) did he mean worship both natures in Christ, not only the Uncreated and Eternal Word but the Man also, that is, the creature put on; so serving a creature contrary to the prohibition in Matt. iv: 10; or, did He mean to serve God the Word alone in accordance with Matt. iv: 10?

Answer to those Questions and Explanation of Passages above specified in the last Document above. . . 317

Document 20. Another Petition of the Nestorian Delegates

to the Emperor Theodosius the Second . . 335
Remarks on a Statement of the Seven Bishops of the Apostasy that Ambrose, Bishop of Milan, had opposed the Orthodox Dogmas of Cyril, one or more, which had been approved by the Third Ecumenical Council . 344
Document 21. Third Petition of the same Delegates to the Emperors 355
Document 22. An Epistle of the same Delegates to their own at Ephesus 358
Document 23. "An Epistle of Theodoret, Bishop of Cyrus, written from Chalcedon to Alexander of Hierapolis" . 359
Document 24. "Part of a Homily of Theodoret, Bishop of Cyrus, delivered at Chalcedon," where he was as one of the Nestorian Delegates to the Emperor . . 365
Document 25. "A Sermon of John of Antioch which he delivered in Chalcedon after the Sermon of the Presbyter Aphthonius and of that of the Bishop Theodoret" 370
Document 26. Another Epistle of the Nestorian Delegates from near Constantinople to their own at Ephesus, "in which they boast too soon of their victory" . . 373
Document 27. An Epistle of the Nestorian Delegates to Constantinople to Rufus, Bishop of Thessalonica . 375
Document 28. An Epistle of the Nestorian Conventicle at Ephesus to their Delegates at Constantinople . . 387
Document 29. A Report of the Nestorian Conventicle at Ephesus to the Emperors 392
Document 30. An Epistle of the Delegates of the Apostasy, from Constantinople to their own at Ephesus . . 394
"WRITINGS OF THE ORTHODOX BY WHICH THE PRECEDING CRAFTY FABRICATIONS OF THE SCHISMATICS ARE REFUTED" . 399

Document 1. Copy of a Report of the Third Ecumenical Synod sent by Palladius the Magistrian to the Emperors on July 1, 431	399
Document 2. An Answer of the Bishops found in Constantinople to the Memorials from the Synod	405
Document 3. Copy of an Epistle written by the Clergy of Constantinople to the Holy Synod	418
Document 4. "Copy of a Report of the Holy Synod in response to that imperial Letter which was read by John the most magnificent Count of the Imperial largesses"	419
Document 5. Copy of an Epistle of Cyril, Archbishop of Alexandria, written to the clergy and people of Constantinople	424
Document 6. Copy of an Epistle written by Memnon, Bishop of Ephesus, to the Clergy of Constantinople	428
Document 7. Report of the Holy Synod to the Emperors for the Restoration of Cyril and Memnon; and urging the Emperors to receive the Synod and its work	433
Document 8. A Synodical Epistle to the Clergy of Constantinople	437
This includes, or is followed at once by "A Monition" [or "Reminding"] "sent to the Constantinopolitan Clergy with the Report"	441
Document 9. Copy of an Epistle written by the Archbishop Cyril to the most religious Bishops in Constantinople, Theopemptus and Potamon, and Daniel, in regard to the intrigues from which he suffered from the trumped up charges in the Letters of Nestorius and John	444
Document 10. Copy of a Letter written to the Holy Synod in Ephesus by the Bishops found in Constantinople, August 13, 431	446
Document 11. An Answer of the Holy Synod to the same Bishops who had been found in Constantinople	448

Document 12. A Prayer and Supplication by the Clergy of Constantinople for the Holy Synod in Ephesus, addressed to the Emperors 452

Document 13. "A Mandate made by the Holy Synod for the most religious Bishops who were sent by the Holy Synod itself to Constantinople to plead its cause against those from the [Diocese of the] East," that is, against the Nestorian party of John of Antioch . . . 458

Document 14. Copy of a Report to the Emperors sent through Juvenal, Firmus, Flavian, Arcadius, Theodotius, Acacius, and Evoptius, Bishops, and through Philip a Presbyter, that is, an Elder, the Synod's Delegates to Constantinople 461

Document 15. Epistle of Alypius to Cyril . . . 467

Document 16. "An Imperial Letter to the Holy Synod in Ephesus, releasing all the Bishops and dismissing them to their own homes, and reinstating the most holy men, Cyril and Memnon, in their own Churches" 470

End of Act VI. 472

UTTERANCES OF THE THIRD ECUMENICAL SYNOD BETWEEN ITS FIRST ACT AND ITS SECOND, THAT IS, BETWEEN ITS DEPOSITION OF NESTORIUS AND ITS SECOND ACT.

These are:
  I. ITS LETTER TO THE CLERICS AND STEWARDS OF CONSTANTINOPLE, AS TO THE DEPOSITION OF NESTORIUS AND AS TO THE CHURCH PROPERTY OF HIS LATE SEE.
  II. ITS REPORT TO THE EMPERORS.
  III. EPISTLE OF THE SYNOD TO THE CLERGY AND PEOPLE OF CONSTANTINOPLE.
  IV. In this place, following Coleti, we put THE ARCHIMANDRITE DALMATIUS' LETTER TO THE ECUMENICAL SYNOD because it bears on Document V. below. It is DOCUMENT IV.
  V. COPY OF AN EPISTLE SENT BY THE HOLY SYNOD TO THE ARCHIMANDRITE DALMATIUS. This is UTTERANCE IV.

DOCUMENT I.
UTTERANCE I. OF THE COUNCIL AFTER ITS ACT I.

A LETTER SENT TO THE CLERICS AND STEWARDS OF THE CHURCH OF CONSTANTINOPLE ON THE SAME DAY ON WHICH IT (1) WAS SENT TO NESTORIUS HIMSELF ALSO.

The Holy Synod by God's grace (2) gathered in Ephesus in accordance with the decrees of our most religious and dear-to-God Emperors, to the most illustrious Eucharius to the most religious Presbyters (3), and to the Stewards (4), and to the rest of the most

---

(1). That is, the Sentence of Deposition, or this Letter.
(2). Greek, χάριτι Θεοῦ, that is, "*by God's favor.*"
(3). That is, as *presbyters* (πρεσβυτέροις) means, *elders,* as the Greek term here used is translated in the New Testament. In Smith and Wace's *Dictionary of Christian Biography,* under "*Eucharius (2),*" we are told that he was ' the head of the clerical body at Constantinople after the deposition of Nestorius.'
(4). Greek, οἰκονόμοις·

religious Clerics of the holy Church of God in the Christ-loving City of Constantine (5) wisheth joy.

Let your Piety know [hereby] that the blasphemous Nestorius, on account of his impious preachings (6) and of his disobedience to the Church Canons, was on yesterday, which was the twenty-second of the present month of June, deposed by the Holy Synod in accordance with the behests of the Church Canons, and is an alien from every ecclesiastical grade (7). Guard therefore all the ecclesiastical possessions, as those who are also soon to render an account to him who according to God's will, and with the approval of our most pious and Christ-loving Emperors, shall be ordained for the Church of the Constantinopolitans (8).

---

(5). That is, Constantinople.

(6). Greek, διὰ τὰ δυσσεβῆ αὐτοῦ κηρύγματα, the κηρύγματα, *preachings*, being a reference to the 20 Extracts in Act I., pages 449–481, vol. 1 of Ephesus, from Nestorius' Sermons, for which and for his disobedience to the Canons he was condemned by the Universal Church in this Council in its Act I., pages 486–504, vol. 1 of Ephesus.

(7). See the reference in the note last above.

(8). By Canon XXVI. of the Fourth Ecumenical Synod every Bishop is required to manage the property of his Parecia by a steward taken out of his own clergy. This is commanded by four local canons which were made Ecumenical by Canon I. of Chalcedon, namely, Canons XXIV. and XXV. of Antioch and Canons VII. and VIII. of Gangra. These are the Ecumenical decisions on that point and are still unrepealed by any Council of the whole Church, and are therefore binding. Compare the so-called Apostolical Canons XL., XLI. and compare Bingham's *Antiquities of the Christian Church*, Book II., Chapter IV., section 6. Yet the Bishop could not alienate the revenues of the Church against the will of his clergy, but must get the consent of his Metropolitan and his coprovincial Bishops. See Bingham, Book V. chapter VI., section 7, and the Canons above. The present anti-Christian management of the temporalities by mere laymen, or even by unbaptized men, who are independent of the Bishop and not responsible to him in the strict sense in which his clerical Stewards are, leads sometimes to great evils. Take a few instances out of many: the Protestant Episcopal Church of the Annunciation, a fine stone building, on West 14th Street, New York City, in a neighborhood where it might have done vast good was alienated by a vestry when it had a debt of less than $100,000 and, after it had been sold for between $200,000 and $300,000, the proceeds were given to endow a chair in the General Theological Seminary in the same city for its clergyman, so that he with his vestry became the destroyers of a parish! Another instance: a parish in Jersey City, N. J., had the affliction once upon a time to choose a rector who turned out to be an idolater, that is, a worshipper of the Host, and he scattered

Document II.

Utterance II. of the Council After its Act I. and Before Act II.

Report to the Most Religious Emperors Concerning the Deposition of Nestorius, From the Holy Synod.

"To the most religious and most dear-to-God Theodosius and Valentinian, Victors, Trophy-bearers, ever August Ones, the Holy

---

many of his congregation, and so diminished his salary about one half. He finally left and was succeeded by another of similar type, who induced the vestry to move the Church from four lots which they had owned, and to put it on two which they did not own. He still further scattered the flock, but after two requests from the vestry to leave he did so. After him came a sounder man, who gathered some of the scattered again, but through illness he soon left. After him came another Romanizer who scattered part of what still remained in the way of a congregation, and so left the parish unable to pay his salary. So the treasurer advanced the money to pay it, and the cleric left, and the said treasurer then seized the Church property for the debt, and the parish name disappeared. As a matter of fact and experience the Bishop who does not control the Church property of his Parecia and does not place and remove his own clergy is not a Bishop. I have known of a church lent to Romanists for them to defile with their idolatry. And any vestry may permit heretics to occupy their Church, and may cling to and support a heretic and take the church building along with them: that was done in the case of King's Chapel, Boston, now an Anti-Trinitarian conventicle. The present anti-Episcopal control of Church temporalities is merely the product of windbagism, rights of the people against God and His faith, (really rights of a clique, a secret society, etc.), and is absolutely destructive of the minister's freedom to proclaim God's full truth. The control of the temporalities by the highest order of the ministry, the Apostolate, that is, the Episcopate (compare Acts I, 20, with Acts I, 25), is Scriptural, for when property was given it was "*laid* . . . *down at the Apostles' feet; and distribution was made unto every man according as he had need,*" Acts IV., 34, 35. And the Apostolate founded the Diaconate to be the channel of their ministration to the needs of the poor (Acts VI., 1-7). And as Christ founded only one order, the Apostolate, and gave them the fulness of power, they must have founded the Presbyterate, which we find possessing what must therefore be a delegated power over "*the possessions,*" that is, "*the inheritances,*" τῶν κλήρων, which is implied in the exhortation not to "*lord it over*" them, as the Greek is in I. Peter V., 3. There was of course the danger that a married Bishop's children or widow or a single Prelate's heirs might grab the Church property after his death. That was guarded against, so far as might be, in Canons XXIV. and XXV. of Antioch which are of Ecumenical authority, and Canons XL. and XLI. of the Apostles, so-called, which, whatever their origin, once had and have still in parts of Christendom, the force of law.

Synod gathered together by Christ's favor (9), and by the command of your Mightiness (10) in the Metropolis of the Ephesians [sendeth as follows]:

Your Piety, O Christ-loving and most dear-to-God Emperors, which received the true faith from your ancestors and increases it daily, makes a special care of the dogmas of the truth, and when trouble arose regarding them not only in that great city (11) but also in all the inhabited world, because of the dogmas both preached and taught by Nestorius, which are alien to the tradition of the holy Fathers, and that of the most holy Apostles and Evangelists, your Mightiness did not overlook the trouble of the Churches and the adulterations made in the dogmas of the faith and in those of true piety; but your Piety commanded to be gathered together the most God-revering Metropolitans out of every Metropolis, and [for them] to bring on Bishops [with them], and it commanded certain Bishops of the other cities also [to come], and it decreed that the period before Pentecost would suffice to assemble them. And so we were all assembled together in the Metropolis of the Ephesians (12) on the day pre-appointed in the decree, but it turned out that the most holy John, the Bishop of Antioch, delayed. But we, supposing that the difficulty of the way was the cause of his delay, postponed the hearing [on the matters involved] for sixteen days' time after the day before appointed in the decree of your Mightiness. And some of the holy Bishops pressed by old age were not able to endure the stay in a strange place; others were in peril in sickness, and furthermore, some had ended their lives in the Metropolis of the Ephesians; while others under the binding pressure of [their] poverty, kept coming to us and urging the hearing. So after sixteen whole days, numbered from the holy Pentecost (13),

---

(9). Greek, χάριτι Χριστοῦ·

(10). Greek, τοῦ ὑμετέρου κράτους· The singular is used, for the Empire was still considered as one, especially in religion, though one of the Emperors reigned over the East and the other over the West.

(11). Constantinople, where the Nestorian controversy burst forth.

(12). That is, Ephesus, the above being a common form of expression in ecclesiastical Greek.

(13). That is, what is commonly called in English defectively, *Whitsunday*, which was the day appointed in the decree of the Emperor for the Council to meet. The ancient Christians did not among themselves, commonly call the

had passed, we began (14) the hearing. And forasmuch as the most holy Bishop of the Antiochians, John, had signified to us through the most God-revering Bishops Alexander of Apamea and Alexander of Hierapolis, who had arrived before him, to take hold of the business, and as his non-appearance was a burden to the Holy Synod by subjecting it to still more delay, we were therefore gathered together on the twenty-second day of the month of June, according to the Romans (15), and on the day before we had besought, through most religious Bishops, the admirable Nestorius both to co-sit with us and to take part in the investigation concerning both piety and faith. But we received no answer from him, for he stated through those who had been sent this only, *I am considering, and if I shall approve I will go and meet with you.* On the morrow therefore (16) we were assembled in the holy and great Church which is called Mary (17), the holy Gospel lying forth on the throne which was most exactly in the middle, and showing that Christ Himself was present with us (18); and in accordance with the order and sequence of the Canons, we again sent to him three other most holy Bishops to beseech him to come to the Holy Synod and to make his defence of his teaching. But he had prepared soldiers to encircle his house, (though at that time there was no uproar in the city, nor, moreover,

---

first day of the week Sunday but the Lord's Day. Sunday is a heathen appellation and comes from them. In the older Christian Churches *Pentecost* and not *Whitsunday* is used. That is the better custom. The number of days between Pentecost, the day appointed for the opening of the Council, and the day of its actual opening is given above as 16, that is, according to the Roman way of reckoning. But according to ours it was 15. See note 102, vol. I. of *Ephesus*.

(14). Greek, συνεκροτήσαμεν, literally *clapped together*, or *gathered*.

(15). That is, according to their way of computing time. There were several ways of computing it among the ancients. The Egyptians had one, the Romans another, etc.

(16). That is, "sixteen whole days" after Pentecost, the day when the Synod opened, that is, 15 days in our time.

(17). Of this Church we treat in a Dissertation elsewhere. It has been supposed that it was so called because Mary was buried there. The primitive Christians did not generally name their Churches after saints, but after God.

(18). They did not know of the later Romish doctrine of Christ's *own divine Substance* being present in the Eucharist, or they would have had that *Personal* presence instead of a mere inspired book.

had there been any), and he did not deign to give any answer to those who were sent [by us]. But inasmuch as the Canons command that the disobedient (19) shall be summoned three times (20) we again sent to him other Bishops, and we found him disobedient (21), and he sent away our messengers (22) with much shame and insult through the soldiers who were standing before his house.

But inasmuch as it was not behooving that so great a Holy Synod should have come together and yet continue to do nothing, [simply] because he had an evil conscience and would not meet with us, we therefore necessarily began to treat of the dogmas on the faith and on piety, and decreed that the dear-to-God Letter of your Piety shall shine forth in front of the Acts (23); after which we set forth the Exposition (24) of that pious faith which was at first handed down to us by the most holy Apostles, and afterwards set forth by the Three Hundred and Eighteen holy Fathers gathered in the Metropolis of the Nicaeans by Constantine who is [now] among the saints (25), whose right faith your Mightiness has exhibited more clearly and

---

(19). Or "*contumacious.*"

(20). Literally "*by the third call,*" τῇ τρίτῃ κλήσει·

(21). See last note but one above.

(22). Greek, τοὺς ἀπεσταλμένους·

(23). See it on pages 32-41, vol. I. of *Ephesus* in this Set. It is not the one in which the Synod are, in effect, forbidden to depose Nestorius, to which the Council gives here a silent go-by, to avoid trouble, and lest the truth should be hindered by the Emperor if angry. This last decree is on pages 8-13, vol. I. of *Ephesus*.

(24). Or, *Forthset*, that is, the Creed of the First Ecumenical Council, not that of the Second which is commonly called now among us the Nicene, for it is the Constantinopolitan with an unauthorized and wrong addition, the words "*and the Son,*" (the *Filioque*), and with three other changes, that is, "*of the Virgin Mary,*" where the Greek means "*and the Virgin Mary,*" and the insertion of "*God of God*" before "*Light of Light,*" and the omission of "*holy*" between "*one*" and "*Catholic.*" There are other inaccuracies also.

(25). This is remarkable language to use of a man who, though he had done vast good, came to some extent under the influence of Arian Bishops at the last. But some of the Fathers were prone to take the charitable side and to hold that he did not share their heresy, and this merciful view is that of the Council, and is defensible on the ground that all the departed are entitled to the benefit of the doubt in their favor. Even the Arian, Eusebius of Caesarea, (page 340, vol. I. of *Nicaea* in this Set, and note 519) confesses that the Emperor had been

brightly (26). And we first compared with that Exposition (27) the Epistles of the most dear-to-God and most holy Archbishop Cyril concerning the Faith, and we found them in harmony both with its dogmas and its thoughts, and that his teaching is in no respect alien from that pious Exposition (28). And inasmuch as it remained to examine and to test [next] thereafter the dogmas preached by the most admirable Nestorius, [we began to do so]; for they were not obscure, but were distinctly proclaimed in his epistles, and in books, and are clearly heard in his public discourses, and were plainly spoken by him in the [very] Metropolis of the Ephesians itself to some of the most religious Bishops, for he did not cease to say: *It does not behoove to say that he who became man for us was God*, and he reproaches Divinity for having put on the human things, which He put on, not on account of [any] infirmity [of His own] but because of His Man-lovingness towards us, and he derides as it were, our august and divine mystery, by daring to say in conversation with the most religious bishops, *I do not say that God is a two months' old and a*

---

decidedly in favor of the expression "*of the same Substance*" at Nicaea, and there is no proof that he ever denied it, or took it in an Arian sense as Eusebius alleges.

(26). This may mean that the Emperor's faith was clearer and brighter than Constantine's because of Arian influence over the latter.

(27). Or, *Forthset*, or *Statement*, that is, the Creed of the First Ecumenical Synod.

(28). Page 548 of tom. V., Paris., 1644 of the *Collectio Regia Concil.*, and Coleti *Conc.*, tom. 3, col. 1100: Καὶ τῇ ἐκθέσει ταύτῃ πρότερον μὲν τὰς περὶ τῆς πίστεως ἐπιστολὰς τοῦ θεοφιλεστάτου καὶ ἁγιωτάτου ἀρχιεπισκόπου Κυρίλλου συγκρίναντες, συμφώνους εὕρομεν τοῖς τε δόγμασι καὶ νοήμασι, καὶ κατ᾽ οὐδὲν ἀπηλλοτριωμένην τὴν αὐτοῦ διδασκαλίαν τῆς εὐσεβοῦς ἐκείνης ἐκθέσεως· If we ask what Epistles of Cyril are meant here, we shall find on examining Act I. above that two only of Cyril's Epistles were read in it, first his *Shorter Epistle* to Nestorius on which the Council took a vote and by that vote approved it, and second the *Long Epistle* of Cyril and of his Diocesan, that is, as we now say, Patriarchal Synod, which has the Twelve Anathemas. Though no vote is recorded as having been taken on it, nevertheless the words above vouch for its orthodoxy. Hefele was right therefore in stating that the Third Synod approved that second letter, as he does on page 48, note 2 in vol. 3 of his *History of the Councils of the Church*, English translation. I have quoted it on pages 205, 206, vol. I. of *Ephesus*, note.

three months' old (29); and these things [he kept saying] three (30) whole days before the Holy Synod, as the good faith of the Minutes (31) also has it, and we necessarily compared those things [of Nestorius] with the Exposition of the holy Fathers, and we found them hostile and contrary in every respect to our Universal and Apostolic Faith. So that Nestorius did not even ask any defence, but he became his own accuser on each matter, and persisted in his dogmas, which are corrupt and entirely contrary to our Universal and Apostolic Faith.

For that reason therefore we have caused him to cease from the priesthood and from corrupt teaching, and have made a canonical deposition of him, and we have praised the most dear-to-God and most holy Bishop of the Great Rome, Celestine, who, before our vote, (32) condemned the heretical dogmas of Nestorius, and, before us put forth his vote (33) against him for the sake of the safety of the

---

(29). Greek, ἐγὼ τὸν διμηναῖον καὶ τριμηναῖον Θεὸν οὐ λέγω· The Bishops of the Council deemed this language a proof among others that Nestorius did not believe that the Eternal Substance of God the Word dwelt in the infant, but that he deemed that infant merely a human being in whom God the Word dwelt by His Spirit only as He dwelt in the prophets and in the apostles and in other inspired men. And let us remember that they knew Him better than men do in these later days, and they had known of how He had expressed Himself in conversation, as well as in documents some of which are no longer extant. And it is fair to suppose that they were not a set of scoundrels to do him injustice, but acted justly and in the fear of God when they condemned him as a denier of the Incarnation, a Man-Server, and an advocate of the cannibal view on the Eucharist.

(30). Greek, ποὺ τριῶν ὅλων ἡμερῶν τῆς ἁγίας συνόδου· See πρὸ in Sophocles' Greek Lexicon.

(31). Coleti *Conc.* tom. 3 col. 1100: Greek, καθὰ καὶ ἡ τῶν ὑπομνημάτων περιέχει πίστις·

(32). Coleti as above; Greek, πρὸ τῆς ἡμῶν ψήφου·

(33). Greek, τὴν κατ' αὐτοῦ ψῆφον· Celestine cast "*his vote*" against him, but that represented only a part of the whole Church. Hence to make his condemnation final the vote of the Orient was necessary also, and that was given in this Third Synod, and so Nestorius was *Ecumenically* condemned. Neither part of the Church had power to condemn him for the whole Church, though it might for its own part, and then wait for the rest to do the same. Compare vol. 1 of *Ephesus*, page xxxi.—lii., and note 94, page 38, id.; Celestine's Epistle was that of a local Synod of a part only of the West. See under *Celestine* on page 577,

Churches and of the pious and saving faith handed down to us both

id. The idolater, the Romish Latin priest, Luke Rivington, in the *Dublin Review* ingeniously and perversely tries to make out that Celestine was absolute monarch over the decisions of the Council. The English *Church Review* well replies to him. That Rivington, on page 375, of the April, 1895, number of the *Dublin Review*, tells us that in two articles in that Review, April and July, 1892, he had considered the bearings of the history of the Ecumenical Council of Ephesus (A. D. 431) on the Anglican appeal to the Primitive Church, and had enlarged his positions there maintained, and had embodied them in a work on the Primitive Church, entitled *The Primitive Church and the See of Peter*, by the Rev. Luke Rivington, M. A.; Longmans & Co., 1894. He states further that an answer had been made to him in the *Church Quarterly Review*

The Second Part of the *Church Quarterly Review's* answer is in its number for January, 1895. The First Part is found in the number for October, 1894. Rivington abounds in misstatements and misrepresentations, and while endeavoring to make out that the Third Synod admitted Celestine's infallibility and merely obeyed him, is evidently ignorant of the facts which prove the contrary, and ignorant also of the fact that it condemned anticipatively the present Romish view on the Eucharist, and all Rome's worship of creatures, as is shown in vol. I. of *Ephesus* in this Set. Rivington, like all other Romanists, tries to make out an absolutism in the Church for Rome, not from the Canons of the first four Ecumenical Councils, which by necessary implication condemn such a claim, but out of his own private Romish opinions on certain matters in the past which he does not understand. Aye, he seems not to know that this Holy and God-guided Synod decided in its noble Canon VIII. against the claim of the Bishop of Rome to Appellate Jurisdiction in Latin Africa, and any where else outside of Italy, and that it approved in that memorable Canon the contention of the great Metropolitan of Carthage (Patriarch of Carthage, as we would now say), and the 217 Bishops of his Council that Rome's claim to Appellate Jurisdiction outside of Italy is forbidden by the Canons of the Holy-Ghost-led First Ecumenical Synod held at Nicaea, A. D. 325. See especially its Canons IV., V. and VI. In the *Church Journal* of N. Y. 1870, I have translated the documents on that controversy in which the Africans rejected that very claim of Zosimus, Boniface, and this very Celestine, when they either ignorantly or with design to defraud them of their rights, tried to palm off on them local canons of Sardica as being those of Nicaea. Those documents will, God willing, appear in this Set. And yet men as contemptible as this creature Rivington can always be found to turn traitors to the Ecumenical Canons and to their Fatherland, and to help a foreign and now anti-Six Synods and idolatrous prelate to conquer and degrade their own flesh and blood and to damn their souls to the idolaters' hell, (Rev. xxi., 8; Galat. v., 19-22). It was the wicked wretch Apiarius, whose Appeal to Rome after he was justly convicted of crime in Africa, gave Celestine and his predecessors in the See of Rome an occasion to try and subjugate the Africans. He afterwards confessed his shameful iniquity. Alas! he was not the last Appellant to Rome. He has

by the holy Apostles and Evangelists and by the holy Fathers, which [faith] he had attempted by corrupt discourse to pervert. And though he is [now] condemned, [nevertheless] there is a great mass [of stuff] which he has poured forth (34) and we beseech your Mightiness to command that all his teaching be removed from the most holy Churches, and that his books wheresoever found be committed to the fire, for by those things he tries to do away the grace (35) of God's having become man for us, which grace he himself (36) considered to be not Man-lovingness but as an insult to Divinity. And if any one shall despise the Decrees let him fear the indignation of your Mightiness. And so the apostolic faith will continue unwounded (37) being strengthened by your Piety. And we will all make earnest prayers for your Mightiness, for by it Christ (38) is glorified, and the faith is strengthened and the grace (39) of God becomes well known to all men (40). And in order to the clearer

---

successors in Rivington and others, though an Appeal to Rome now is worse than then, for then she was not idolatrous but is now and is condemned by the Six Synods for her creature worship. Alas! the English and Irish and Scotch and Welsh Churches do not excommunicate such Appellants. Surely they might learn to imitate the worthy action in so doing of the Latin Patriarchate of Africa. Its stand on that matter was afterwards adopted by the whole Eastern Church in the Trullan Synod of A. D. 691 or 692, and it remains their law till this very hour. Let the English Church first restore fully the VI. Synods and all primitive doctrine, discipline and rite and custom, and then do so.

(34). Greek, Καὶ πολὺ τὸ πλῆθος, ὁ καταγνωσθεὶς ἐξέχεε· Perhaps this refers to persons, though the Latin in Coleti does not so render it. If it does, it may be translated: "*And though he is* [now] *condemned,* [nevertheless] *there is a great multitude whom he has scattered* [from the Church]."

(35). That is, "*the favor.*"

(36). Nestorius.

(37). Or, "*invulnerable,*" ἄτρωτος·

(38). Χριστός, literally "*the Anointed* One."

(39). Greek, ἡ χάρις Θεοῦ·

(40). Here we have a specimen of what the Universal Church as, under God, the great source of all blessings to the State in spirituals and temporals, its great preserver by its moral teachings from evils domestic and foreign, may justly demand of a Christian State which is composed of her children as the Roman Empire then was. She asks: 1. That the State shall accept and protect her decisions on faith and discipline, and enforce her decisions in both, and for the silencing of heretical, anti-Incarnation, creature-invoking, and Host-wor-

and more perfect knowledge of what has been done (τῶν πεπραγμένων)

shipping teachers and their removal from the Churches, and from all control of her spiritualities and temporalities, and that the secular rulers shall enforce against them her depositions and anathemas. Of course the Emperors as her children, were bound to hold to her faith and obey her canons and discipline and leave her perfectly free. For at this time they and the whole Church had been made members of it fully by receiving at the same time, the three initiatory rites, baptism by the trine dipping, confirmation, and the Eucharist, whether they were baptized in infancy or in later years, and so Church and State were one. That was the universal custom everywhere for at least 800 years after Christ. God grant that that primitive and Scriptural system, which is absolutely necessary to the true idea of Church and State may be restored speedily everywhere, and may the isms and changes of the middle ages, and of modern days opposed to it pass away forever! That system prevails among the Greeks till this very hour. We must all restore it among ourselves.

2. That the secular powers shall burn the books of Nestorius and his fellow heretics to the end that their soul-destroying infidelizings and paganizings may be removed forever.

As the civil magistrate is God's minister, deriving his whole power and authority from Him (Rom. xiii., 1-8) and not from the people, though they are bound to see to it in a Christian State that no other than a Christian shall be a magistrate or exercise civil or military authority, the chief duty of the civil ruler is not to do the people's will when they oppose God, but to do God's will always, and, according to His will, to seek the best good of the people in material and in mental things and especially in spiritual and moral Christian things, by maintaining the Six Synods forasmuch as the sole source of blessing is that true Christian Six Synods religion, that is, New Testament religion as defined by Christ's agent thereto authorized and appointed, the Universal Church in said Six Synods. For it is the fullest manifestation of that *righteousness* which alone *exalteth a nation* (Prov. xiv., 34), and is that *godliness* which alone *hath promise of the life that now is as well as of that which is to come* (1. Tim. iv., 8); aye, it is the very basis of the State, and is the most important and most precious thing in the State, for it makes good citizens, and it is the only thing that can, and the history of God's people under the Old Testament teaches us infallibly that when the civil power, as in the persons of the pious kings, David, Hezekiah, and Josiah, crushed creature-worship and all false religions, and fostered and cherished sound religion only and made it supreme in the State, all was prospered in the nation and blessed; and that, on the other hand, when the civil power was in the hands of wicked kings, that is, in the persons of Ahaz and Zedekiah for instance, and did not keep God's religion pure and supreme, but tolerated the false, or mingled the false with the true, all went ill in the State; weakness, poverty, defeat, or slaughter, or subjugation, and at last captivity came on it, on its rulers and its armies. All these things should teach the Christian magistrate his bounden duty not to tolerate for one moment any thing opposed to the Six Councils of Christ's Universal Church, but to maintain them to the fullest extent, their two Creeds, their Definitions, the Normal Epistles approved by them, their Canons, their depositions, their anathemas, and every iota of theirs against all deniers of the Trinity, against all deniers of the Incarnation, against all invokers of creatures, and against all worshippers of crosses, pictures, graven images, relics, and other things not God's Substance, Which alone may be worshipped, and against all who contend that the Sixth Ecumenical Synod erred in condemning Honorius, Pope of Rome, as a Monothelite heretic.

And God's people should see to it that no idolater, no Mohammedan, no Jew, no creature-invoking, or image-worshipping, or Eucharist-worshipping so-called Christian, should be allowed to rule us, or to be among us to corrupt us, by teaching error, or marrying among us. We should live the spirit of the prayer which Christ Himself teaches us, "*Thy kingdom come. Thy will be done on earth as it is in heaven,*" Matt. vi., 10. Is it to live the spirit of that prayer to admit into *your country* pagans, Mohammedans, Jews, and the idolatrous votaries of Rome, who are troubling you now and will trouble you more as the years roll on, who on battle fields, by massacres and by the Inquisition have slaughtered hundreds of thousands of your brethren as they will slaughter many of you yet, who trouble your common schools, and raise religious and strike riots in your cities and mining districts, and compel you to pay for the property which they destroy? Universal suffrage in the hands of such means, as in New York and many other of your cities, the rule of the grog-shop and the Romish Church, and the ignorant and superstitious mob, and of the degraded Anti-Christian, usurious, cheating and lying or Nihilistic Jew, who will always remain a Jew and will never be thoroughly an American, with whom you are forbidden by your Christian law to marry (II. Cor. vi., 14), and whom you are forbidden to receive into your house or to bid *God speed* to (II. John 11), who is driving you out of business and getting your houses and lands and wealth into his possession, who will not go back to his country, which is now open to him, but will come to us in millions, and fatten on us till we become poor and his underlings, aye, even now he can give the casting vote in our elections, because contrary to the New Testament and to common sense and patriotism we have suffered him to enter our country and to remain in it, and to vote in it and to share the rule over a Christian people. To Rome and the Jew we have lost our cities, and we are losing our country, and we are subjected and tyrannized over by them. And our vile press and low politicans cater to them and betray us, aye, and Christ's Six Synods Religion. And we will not unite on those Synods the sole basis of help.

How bitter a curse the Jew was to Spain, how thoroughly Anti-Christian and Anti-Spanish he was, how well he requited Spain by aiding her Mohammedan invaders, and how thoroughly the Jews remained "*a nation within a nation*" there and elsewhere the incontestible facts of history tell.

And how bitter a curse, how thoroughly anti-national the Roman, the national Italian Church, has been in other lands in promoting idolatry and superstition, in raising rebellions and exciting civil wars, and other wars, and

the Minutes also are [herewith] conjoined, and all the most religious

all for her own ends, on the old Roman principle, *Divide them and, so rule them*, and in hindering the development of a native literature and of national progress and civilization, let Germany and Holland for example, with their long and bloody struggles for God's word and truth, and for nationality against Austria and Spain answer. Let England with her long and heroic struggle for the worship of God alone, and for her very life against Romish Spain and France, and against Rome's stirrings up of trouble in Ireland, answer. Let the Protestants of Ireland answer, diminished as they are in numbers by the fearful massacre of A. D. 1641, in which from 40,000 to 200,000 of them were slaughtered at the instigation of a foreignized and Anti-Six Synods and creature-invoking priesthood which denationalized and degraded their Romish countrymen and made them their fanatical dupes and tools, willing to serve in alien Romish armies against the best interests of their own land, aye, against every thing Evangelic and uplifting. And let the Fleming of to-day, who prefers for the sake of a foreign prelate at Rome to separate from his fellow Teutons and to join men of another race and another tongue, let him answer. Moreover let us notice how to-day the denationalized Irish Romanist is using the power given him in Parliament to destroy the very Protestant Religion and the very Protestant government which has given it to him, and how the German Romanist of the Centre Party is using his power in the Reichstag, against his own race and against German, Reformed, God alone serving Christianity, and for Rome, and her Church so alien in speech and in spirit from the German people, for the Latin Language in the service, and against German in it, and for Rome's idolatry, and for a foreign Prelate in preference to his own native ruler. Surely the statemanship which admits the Jew and the devotee of anti-national Rome to rule or to share in the rule of a God-alone-invoking Christian people is idiocy and ruinous. Well might the King of England who signed the misguided bill which gave that power to a denationalized, a Latinized mob, and a denationalized and Latinized, idolatrous, so-called priesthood their leaders, dread the result of his own signature to it, as he did.

God's word teaches that before the judgment *the kingdoms of this world are to become the kingdoms of our Lord and of his Christ* (Rev. xi., 15). Are we working to that end when we admit to our shores and our suffrage men alien to us in faith and in blood, who are going to reward us for that crime by doing all they can not to make our country God's country, but to make it the country of the unbelieving and Christ-hating Jew and of the idolatrous Romanist, and of the Christian-hating and Christian-murdering Mohammedan?

A false so-called liberalism, opposed to the Bible and to common sense, has been our bitter curse. The Scriptures taught the Israelite not to allow the pagan to own any of his land, not to allow him to build places for his heathenism in it, not to permit him to intermarry with God's people. We are doing the very contrary to all that. The New Testament teaches us *not to be unequally yoked together with unbelievers* (II. Cor. vi., 14), and to admit only one cause

Bishops, who are mentioned before in order in the Minutes, have subscribed " (41).

Document III.

Utterance III. of the Council:

"Epistle of the Synod to the Clergy and People of Constantinople.

'To the most religious Clergy and the Laity of Constantinople from the Holy Synod:

No one who has dared to oppose his own Maker, has remained without just punishment from God, but straightway, as men can see, is requited [though only] in part, because the more perfect requital is reserved against him for the future world. Wherefore Nestorius also, the renewer (42) of impious heresy, having from the start alienated himself in the city (43) of the Ephesians, (where John, the advocate of the Divinity of God the Word (44), and the Virgin

---

for divorce, adultery on the part of the wife (Matt. xix., 9), and we make many. And the Anti-Christian law made by our lawyers, many, alas! prefer to Christ's law by which alone we shall be judged. But in a godly union of Church and State we shall all be members of both. The Church's law will in all things be supreme as being Christ's law in His word, or by His Universal Church which we are all commanded *to hear*, (Eph. vi., 17 and Matt. xviii., 17). And the Church will be managed not by infidels or idolatrizers but by its own Bishops sound and true to the Six Synods. Then we shall be a happy and prosperous people. Jews will no longer drive our people out of business and deprive many of them of their bread and take it for themselves, and the devotees of superstition and of idolatry will no longer control us. Our country will be our own again.

But I hope to treat of this whole question of a Christian Church in a Christian State in a special work, and therefore here leave it with the above, which I pray we may not forget to our detriment but remember to our profit.

(41). The list of Bishops present at the opening of the Council is in vol. 1. of *Ephesus* in this Set, pages 22–29; the second, of those present at its close, is on pages 489–503.

(42). Greek, ἀνακαινιστής. The Synod by using this expression seem to hint at the fact that Theodore of Mopsuestia and Diodore of Tarsus were the originators of the heresy; but that Nestorius gave it new life.

(43). Or, "*the Metropolis.*"

(44). Greek, 'Ο θεολόγος Ἰωάννης. On this term θεολόγος, Sophocles in his Greek Lexicon states that,

"As an epithet, it is applied to John the Evangelist, and to Gregorius of Nazianzus, because they stand at the head of the assertors of the divinity of the

Bringer-Forth of God (45), the holy Mary, [*are buried*, or, *once dwelt* (*46*)]), from the assembly of the Holy Fathers and Bishops (47), and not having dared, because he had an evil conscience, to meet with them, after he had been summoned three times, was, by the just decree (48) of the Holy Trinity, and of their (49) God-inspired judgment (50), condemned and cast out, as is stated in writing in the Minutes of the Act (51), from every hieratic Dignity.

Rejoice ye therefore in the Lord always, and again, I will say, rejoice.' For the stumbling-block (52) has been removed and the tares (53) have been rooted up out of the field of the spiritual

---

λόγος·'' It is sometimes rendered into English "*by Theologian*," but defectively, for we do not commonly confine that expression within such bounds, but make it cover the whole field of Christian knowledge. Its exact equivalent is "*God-the-Worder.*" John the Evangelist treats of God the Word in the first chapter of his Gospel.

(45). Greek, ἡ θεοτόκος παρθένος ἡ ἁγία Μαρία.

(46). As a note in the margin here in Coleti (*Conc.*, tom. 3, col. 1102) informs us, some understand here "*are buried*" or "*once dwelt*," which I have supplied, for some thing of that kind has evidently been omitted by mistake or intention. If "*are buried*" are the omitted words, as Alban Butler the Romanist seems to imply, it looks as though it was done to get rid of that testimony against the myth of her Assumption. The Greek verb *buried*, or whatever Greek verb was there, is omitted. The Greek, as now found, is as follows: ὁ τῆς δυσσεβοῦς αἱρέσεως ἀνακαινιστὴς, φθάσας ἐν τῇ Ἐφεσίων ἔνθα ὁ θεολόγος Ἰωάννης, καὶ ἡ θεοτόκος παρθένος ἡ ἁγία Μαρία, τοῦ συλλόγου τῶν ἁγίων πατέρων καὶ ἐπισκόπων ξενώσας ἑαυτὸν, etc. Some verb is lacking after ἔνθα.

(47). The Third Ecumenical Synod.

(48). Greek, ψήφῳ.

(49). This refers to the Third Ecumenical Synod.

(50). This is a strong expression as to the judgment of the Third Synod against the Man-Service of Nestorius, but it is justified by the Word of God. For it makes all religious service prerogative to God.

Besides, he so corrupted the Eucharist as to make it a cannibal and a creature-serving act! See under "*Eucharist*" in the *General Index* to vol. 1. of *Ephesus* in this Set, and Εὐχαριστία in the *Index to Greek Words* in it.

(51). Act I. of the Third Synod, where the condemnation and deposition of Nestorius were both affected.

(52). Greek, τὸ σκάνδαλον.

(53). Greek, τὸ ζιζάνιον.

husbandry. And take heart, and having taken the shield of the Faith, drive away the workers of the foul and profane novelty (54). For [if ye do] your reward will be not less than that of those who have labored here (55). All the genuine (56) brethren who are here with us, greet you.' " (57).

Document IV.

"Epistle sent to the Holy Synod in the City of the Ephesians from Dalmatius, the Most Holy Archimandrite:

' I received the Epistle sent to me by the Holy Synod (58), and, having ascertained its contents, I was, in the first place, exceedingly grieved because of the circumstances and the afflictions which have happened to you; for it is written in the Epistle, that some of the

---

(54). Greek, τῆς μιαρᾶς καὶ βεβήλου καινοφωνίας. This is a strong and yet a warningly necessary and just expression concerning the Anti-Incarnation, and creature-serving heresy of Nestorius, for creature-service is an error on fundamentals, as was also its heresy of the real presence of the substance of Christ's body and blood in the Eucharist, and the cannibalism of eating that substance of flesh there and the drinking the substance of blood there; and the worshipping of them there is plainly what Cyril called it, *Man-Worship*.

(55). This is a blessed and Ecumenical encouragement given by the "One Holy, Universal and Apostolic Church," to all who contend against the invocation of the Virgin Mary, angels, archangels, and other creatures, and against image worship of every kind, and against all relative service and, in brief, against any thing and every thing but the direct and absolute worship of God Himself, the consubstantial Trinity. It is an encouragement also to all who contend for the Incarnation and against Cannibalism in the Eucharist.

(56). This implies that the Nestorian Man-Servers are not "*genuine brethren*," and that only those are who give every act of religious service, be it bowing, prayer, prostration, incense, and every other act of service mentioned in the Scriptures, and every other which may be devised, to God alone, the Father, His Co-eternal Word, and His Co-eternal Spirit, and that Cannibalizers on the Eucharist, and deniers of the Inman are not "*genuine brethren*."

(57). Coleti *Conc.*, tom. 3, col. 1101. The " I " before "*will say*" does not mean that the above Epistle represents one alone, for it and the sentence in which it stands is a quotation from Philippians iv., 4.

(58). Compare the title of St. Cyril's Epistle XXIII., *Eph.* I. p. lxxi., above. Dalmatius' name is in it. With the reference above to the death of Bishops at Ephesus, compare what is said on page 4 above in the Synod's *Report to the Emperors*.

Epistle of Dalmatius, the Archimandrite, to the Synod. 17

holy Fathers, who were sojourning there, have died from the difficulties connected with the place. And, furthermore, know ye, that I hold myself in readiness to fulfill your every command, and that in no way have I overlooked, nor do I overlook, nor am I careless [in regard to your wishes], and especially because the matter is both for the Orthodox Faith and fitly pertains to God. For no one can apostatize from the living God, and devise any other things [than He allows], (59). For those who *rightly divide the Word of the Truth* (60) of God have life (61) both in this world and in that which is to come. But those who apostatize from God's grace are accursed and cast into the outer darkness; as is both Nestorius and, with him, those who are of the same mind with him (62). For the God and Father of our Lord Jesus Anointed, cheered and edified all the Holy Synod, and has accepted our wearisome toils and sweating labors (63) [for Him]. We thank therefore God, who has so prospered your course, and given you the victory for the Faith. Pray for me, I beseech your Holiness,' " (64).

DOCUMENT V.

UTTERANCE IV. OF THE COUNCIL:

"COPY [OF AN EPISTLE] (65) SENT BY THE HOLY SYNOD TO THE LORD DALMATIUS (66), [or "to Mr. Dalmatius"].

---

(59). In the Canons of the Third Ecumenical Synod Nestorianism is spoken of again and again as *an apostasy*, and it was such because it was a denial of the Incarnation and a return to creature-service, for Nestorius and his fellow heretics worshipped the separate humanity of Christ, a mere creature, both in heaven and in the Eucharist.

(60). II. Tim. ii., 15.

(61). Or, " *Those who rightly divide the Word of the truth*, have life of God."

(62). This refers to the truth taught in Holy Writ that those whom the Apostolate, that is, Episcopate (compare Acts 1, 20 and Acts 1, 25), bind on earth, if rightly done according to God's will, are bound in heaven, Matt. xviii., 15-19. This language applies to all who hold to any of the errors of Nestorius on the Incarnation or on Man-Worship.

(63). Greek, τοὺς κόπους ἡμῶν καὶ ἱδρῶτας.

(64). A collective title of the Council.

(65). The words in brackets, though not in the original, must be supplied in an English translation in order to make the sense clear. The Latin translation in the parallel column in Coleti well supplies them therefore.

(66). Greek, τὸν Κύριον Δαλμάτιον.

18   *Ecumenical Documents Between Acts I. and II.*

The Holy and Ecumenical Synod, assembled in the Metropolis of the Ephesians, in accordance with the command of Theodosius and Valentinian, the most religious and Christ-loving Emperors, having received the Letter (67) sent by Dalmatius the most holy Archimandrite and Father of the Monks, and having found that he was so moved by zeal as after forty-eight years to go out of his little cell, and to go away to the most religious and Christ-loving Emperor, and that he instructed him as to all things as they followed in due order and were done by the Holy Synod in regard to the Deposition of the unholy (68) Nestorius, we thanked Christ our true God, Who so moved you, to take up for the right dogma of our faith and to make clear our wearisome toils and our sweating labors, not only to the most religious Emperors but also to the most holy Archimandrites and to all the Christ-loving Clergy and the Laity. For what other man helped us but your Holiness only? For through no other was the truth made manifest than by you, that is, [by] the Lord Dalmatius. For that reason we all stretch out our hands to the man-loving and good God for the well-living and safety (69) of our most religious Emperors and of your Holiness. We therefore beseech you to put forth your efforts for us still further, and to fill our place in the matters which rise there (70) regarding the Faith. For we have learned that even before Nestorius went to stay in Constantinople, God revealed to thee the things which were in his (71) heart, and

---

(67). Or, "the Epistle," τὴν ἐπιστολὴν.

(68). Greek, τοῦ ἀνοσίου Νεστορίου. Nestorius was unholy as being a denier of the Incarnation of God the Word, and as a chief advocate of Man-Service and of the real substance presence of Christ's humanity in the Eucharist, and the cannibalism of eating it there, and the worship of that humanity there before eating it. Surely every one who entertains any of those God-cursed heresies is unholy enough.

(69). Or, "for a happy life, (or "for the well being") and salvation of our most religious Emperors," etc., (ὑπὲρ εὐζωίας καὶ σωτηρίας τῶν εὐσεβεστάτων ἡμῶν βασιλέων, etc. For ὑπὲρ εὐζωίας, the Latin translation here in Hardouin's *Concilia* has " pro felici vita."

(70), That is, Constantinople.

(71). That is Nestorius'. Did the Council mean that Dalmatius knew nothing of the Anti-Incarnation, Man-Worshipping and Man-Eating doctrine of Nestorius, and that God miraculously revealed it to him in a vision, as he revealed to Peter, by the Vision of the clean and unclean animals, that he must receive Cornelius without circumcision?

that thou wast wont to say to all those who went into thy little cell,
'*Guard yourselves, brethren, because a wicked wild beast has come to stay in this city and has many to injure by his teaching*' (72).

The holy and Same-Substance Trinity keep thee safe and strong in soul and body hymning Christ (73) our God. Pray for us, most holy brother.'"

Or did they mean that God had revealed it to him in a non-miraculous manner through others or by Nestorius himself? We can not say. But we can say that Nestorius' errors and paganizings were so dangerous to the Church and to souls that, if ordinary means did not suffice, the occasion was worthy of a miracle. We must not reject miracles which favor the truth, but we must reject all so-called miracles which favor false doctrine and error. For it is absurd to suppose that the error-hating God will work a miracle to attest any error whatsoever. Hence we must reject as spurious all alleged miracles which favor the worship of creatures, of relics, of images, and of anything in the Eucharist. For it is impious even to entertain such an insult to the Jealous God who commands us to serve Him alone (Matt. iv., 10, and Luke iv., 8; Isaiah xlii., 8), and who was about to wipe out Israel for worshipping Him through a calf in the wilderness, and who actually sent Israel into exile for that sin (Exod., chap. xxxii., and I. Kings xii., 25 to I. Kings xiv., 17, and II. Kings, chap. xvii.

(72). Nestorius injured many by leading them in his lifetime into a denial of the Incarnation and into making Christ a mere man, and into worshipping that mere man in heaven and in the Eucharist, and into eating him in the Eucharist, and during it he gave occasion for the establishment of the heretical sect of the Nestorians, and the creature-worship (ἀνθρωπολατρεία) and cannibalism (ἀνθρωποφαγία) which he taught have, *in a modified form*, spread into the Greek and Roman Communions. For while they reject some of the Nestorian errors regarding Christ, as, for instance, the denial of the Incarnation, they nevertheless hold with him to the cannibalism of eating the substance of Christ's humanity in the Eucharist, and, besides, Rome holds to his error of worshipping Christ's mere humanity, as for instance in her worship of the Sacred Heart, and both Rome and the Greeks even worship other creatures less than Christ's humanity, that is, saints, etc., and in image worship are far worse than the Nestorians, though on the details of such errors they quarrel endlessly. It should be added that both Nestorius' and Kenrick's worship of Christ's humanity was *relative* to God the Word. The facts on that are told in vol. I. of *Ephesus* in this Set, pages 332-343, note 679.

(73). Greek, Χριστόν, that is, the "*Anointed One.*" Hefele, in his *History of the Church Councils*, volume 3, pages 59, 78, thinks that the Emperor Theodosius II. sent to "Dalmatius and other Monks and Clergy of Constantinople" the letters which the Synod had addressed to them immediately after the deposition of Nestorius . . . and so he [the Emperor] must have received the account [that is, he means the Synodal Report] which had been addressed to him. He refers in proof to an Epistle of "Dalmatius and other Monks and Clergy of Constantinople to the Synod." And therefore on page 59 he concludes that though,

"It is generally assumed that Candidian anticipated the legitimate Synod with his information, and did not allow their account to reach Constantinople," yet "this was not the case."

In response, I would say: 1, the "*Answer of the Epistle written by the Bishops who were found at Constantinople to the Commonitory from the Holy Synod*," shows that every thing from the genuine Council was prevented from reaching the Court or the Clergy of Constantinople, or the monks, till the beggar there mentioned brought the letter of Cyril in a reed.

2. The place which Hefele relies on in a letter of Dalmatius and others to the Third Ecumenical Council (in Mansi's *Concilia*, tome IV., col. 1431) proves only that at a later date, that is, after Dalmatius and the monks on getting that letter, which had been smuggled in a reed, went to the Emperor's palace, and Dalmatius with the rest of the Archimandrites were invited in, and Dalmatius informed the Emperor that all representatives of the Synod were prevented from going to him, and the letter in the reed was read to him, then he was persuaded of the injustice done the Synod and removed the obstructions and let its missives go to those to whom they were sent. See further on that matter volume I of *Ephesus* in this Set, pages lxxii-lxxvi.

DOCUMENTS WHICH ARE NOT UTTERANCES OF THE THIRD ECUMENICAL SYNOD, BUT WHICH ARE FOUND IN EDITIONS OF THE COUNCILS BETWEEN ITS ACT I. AND ITS ACT II. WE MERELY EPITOMIZE OR NOTE IMPORTANT THINGS IN THEM.

The aggregate of Documents bearing on the Council, though no part of it, would fill many volumes. The amount of such matter on Ephesus is several times greater than its Acts. It is impossible to do more here therefore than to epitomize them.

Of these there are, exclusive of Document IV. above, no less than XVII. at least. But, as has just been said, they are no part of *the Decisions* or of the Minutes of the Synod, though as materials for history they serve to throw light on them. And furthermore, as has just been said, they are only a small part of what is found of that kind. But inasmuch as we are concerned with translating into English, only the *Decisions* and *all the Minutes* of the Synod proper, we here give a mere Epitome of the most noteworthy things in them, as follows:

INDEX OF THE CONTENTS OF THIS PART.

1. A Letter of Cyril to two of his Bishops then acting as his agents at Constantinople, and to some other Clerics there.
2. A letter of Cyril of Alexandria to the Clergy and Laity of Alexandria, translated in full.
3. Another Letter of Cyril "*to the Presbyters, Deacons, and Laity of Alexandria.*"
4. A Letter of Cyril to the Fathers of the Monks in Egypt and to the rest of the Monks.
5. "A Homily of Rheginus, Bishop of Constantia in Cyprus, delivered in Ephesus after the Deposition of Nestorius."
6. "A Homily of Cyril, Bishop of Alexandria, delivered in Ephesus when the gatherings were concluded and Nestorius had been deposed."
7. A spurious Homily, fathered falsely on Cyril.
8. A Protest of Nestorius' partisan, Count Candidian, against the First Act of the Third Ecumenical Synod, addressed to the Nestorians at Ephesus.
9. Another Protest of the same Candidian against the First Act of the Third Ecumenical Synod, addressed to them.
10. Report of Nestorius and of his few partisans at Ephesus to the Emperors before the arrival of John of Antioch.

11. Action of John of Antioch after his arrival at Ephesus, and his small faction, in which they presume to depose Cyril and Memnon and to excommunicate all the rest of the Bishops of the Third Ecumenical Synod.
12. Impudent Letter of John of Antioch and his small faction of Nestorians, in which they inform the Third Ecumenical Synod that they have deposed Cyril and Memnon, and excommunicated the rest of them till they repent of their Orthodoxy and embrace their heresy.
13. Report of John of Antioch and his "*Conventicle of the Apostasy,*" to the Emperor Theodosius II., against the Third Synod.
14. A Letter of John of Antioch and the same Apostatic Conventicle, to the Clergy of Constantinople, to maintain Nestorius as their Bishop, notwithstanding his deposition by the Third Ecumenical Synod.
15. Epistle of John of Antioch and the same Apostatic Conventicle to the Senate at Constantinople, for Nestorius.
16. An Epistle of John of Antioch and his Apostatic Conventicle to the Laity of Constantinople, for Nestorius.
17. A Report of John of Antioch and his "*Conventicle of the Apostasy*" to the Empresses, for Nestorius.

Document I.

The first document is an important Epistle of Cyril of Alexandria to some of the Clergy then at Constantinople. Its title is:

"Cyril, Archbishop of Alexandria, to Comarius and Potamon, Bishops, and to the Archimandrite of the monasteries the Lord Dalmatius, and to Timothy and Eulogius, Presbyters, beloved and most desired and sanctified in Christ, wisheth very much joy."

Cyril begins by stating that they were expecting Nestorius to repent of his blasphemies uttered by him since his ordination, and to seek pardon of the Holy Synod, though it would have been very perilous to grant it to a man, "*who by breaching such things,*" he adds, "*had perverted all the world and had undermined* [or, "*paralyzed*"] *the faith religiously observed by the Churches.*" For if he who utters a single infamous expression against the Emperors is justly punished by the laws, much more does he deserve punishment who has denied the saving mystery of the Incarnation, by which and its results we are saved. But, he continues, that they had wondered at the man's hardness of heart for he had not repented, nor had he wept over the expressions which he had dared to utter against the glory of Christ, the Saviour of us all, but on the contrary, even after he came to Ephesus he had again shown that he held the same perverted sentiments. And then Cyril adds,

"*And so when certain of the celebrated Metropolitans and most God-revering Bishops justly disputed against him, and then shut him up by the inspired Scripture, and taught him that He who was born according to the flesh out of the holy Virgin is God, he used the following impious expression and said,* I do not call God a two-months old and a three-months old. *And, furthermore, he uttered other expressions besides, which do away with the Inman of the Sole-Born*" [Word].

This part of Cyril's Letter shows that the above language of Nestorius found in the First Act of the Synod, and in its Report to the Emperors elsewhere given in this work, was not judged of without the circumstances attending it which show that it was understood by the men then on the ground as a denial of the Incarnation. And they knew the facts better than any others.

Cyril continues by stating that the First Edict of the Emperors, which, I would add, is found translated on pages 33–41 of vol. I. of *Ephesus* in this Set, (compare pp. 5–8), had appointed Pentecost (A. D. 431), for the opening of the Synod, that, as it was not fitting that their mandate should be treated contemptuously, they [the Synod] had arrived at Ephesus before the day set; that inasmuch as they had heard that John, Bishop of Antioch, was coming, they had waited sixteen days for him, *"though"* he adds *"all the Synod cried out and said that he did not wish to co-sit with them, for he feared lest the most honored Nestorius, (who had been taken out of the Church under himself* [John]), *might have to endure deposition, and that naturally it would be disgraced by the matter (1), and the result showed that the suspicion was true, for he put off his coming.* For certain *of the most religious Bishops of the East* [that is, John's Patriarchate], *who were with him but had arrived before him*, said, 'The Lord John the Bishop charged us to say to your God-worshippingness, If I delay, do what you [are to] do.' "Then Cyril narrates the events told in Act I. on the meeting of the Synod, and the Deposition of Nestorius, only with a few additional details. For he writes that the Synod had met on the twenty-second day of the Egyptian month Paunus, in the great Church called Holy Mary, and that, *"It had sent certain most religious Bishops to summon him to come and to stand for himself, and to make his defence in regard to those things which he had taught and written*," which, while it includes probably all of Nestorius' heretical writings, especially refers probably to the twenty citations from him, most of which Cyril had answered already in his *Five-Book Contradiction of the Blasphemies of Nestorius*, which work was probably well conned by the assembled Prelates in their fifteen days of waiting for John of Antioch if not before. Then Cyril states that Nestorius answered the summons by saying only, "*I am considering and will see*," that afterwards he was summoned a second time by the Synod, but that he had done a thing which was out of place by getting soldiers from the Count Candidian (2) and by causing them to stand before his house with clubs to hinder any one from entering to him, that the Bishops who had been sent by the Synod had therefore to remain outside but had told him, " *We have not come to say or*

---

(1). Or, "*would feel shame as to the matter*."

(2). This was plainly an act of interference against the Orthodox by Candidian and shows with other facts how much they were troubled by those in secular power and how up hill their work was, and how much they were willing to imperil to maintain God's truth against Nestorius' denial of the Inman of the Word, against his worship of a Man, and against his Cannibalism on the Eucharist.

hear any thing harsh, but the Holy Synod summons him," that he made use of different excuses because he was not willing to attend, for his conscience rebuked him, that afterwards they gave him the third citation by Bishops of different Provinces, but that he again made use of the violence of the soldiers, and did not suffer the Bishops who had been sent, to reach him, that, " *Therefore the Holy Synod had sat down, and had followed the ecclesiastical Canons and had read his Epistles and his Explanations* [of Scripture and of dogmas involved] *and had found them* FULL OF BLASPHEMIES ; and, moreover, noted most religious Metropolitan Bishops had testified that in the city of the Ephesians itself, and in argument against us, he had said plainly that *Jesus is not God*, that accordingly the Synod had deposed him, and had put forth a just and lawful sentence by vote against him."

Cyril states further that he had sent these facts to Comarius, Potamon, and the rest to whom he is writing, that they may tell them to those especially who should know them, so that neither Nestorius nor his party should deceive any one in regard to them. He then adds the important fact that here follows:

"*And, moreover, we have an Epistle of the most God-worshipping and most dear-to-God Bishop John written to him* [Nestorius] *throughout which he very much chides him for bringing new and impious dogmas into the Churches and paralyzing the preaching which had been handed down to the Churches out of the holy Evangelists and Apostles. And because Nestorius could say nothing for his impieties, by way of evasion he begged a delay of four days till the Bishop of the Antiochians might arrive, and they* [the Synod] *did not grant it, and that because the aforesaid most holy Bishop John had declined to come. For if he had wished to be present, why did he state through the Bishops subject to him,* [or, "*under his hand*"], '*If I delay, do what you* [wish to] *do?*' *For, as I have said, he was not willing to be present, for he knew that the Holy Synod would pronounce by vote Nestorius' deposition, on the ground of his having spoken irreligious and impious things against Christ the Saviour of us all. Since therefore, as I have learned, reports have been borne up* [to Constantinople] *from the most magnificent Count Candidian, be wary and vigilant, and show that the Minutes of the things done in regard to his* [Nestorius'] *Deposition are not yet perfectly committed to paper, and that therefore we have not been able to send the Report which should be sent to our pious and Victor-Emperors, but say that with God's help, the Report shall be received* [by them] *with the Minutes if only it be permitted us to send one who can bear them* [to them]. *If therefore the arrival of the Minutes and the Report be delayed, know ye that we are not permitted to send them. Fare ye well.*" (1).

And so Cyril's Letter ends.

---

(1). Coleti *Conc.*, tom. 3, col. 1089. See the same Epistle in Migne's *Patrologia Graeca*, tom. 77, col. 132 and after.

DOCUMENT II.

In the next document of his Cyril gives such an interesting account of the concluding events of the day when the First Act of the Council ended, that I here translate it in full:

"EPISTLE OF BISHOP CYRIL TO THE CLERGY AND THE PEOPLE OF ALEXANDRIA.

'Cyril to the Presbyters and Deacons and People of Alexandria, beloved and most desired, wisheth joy in the Lord:

Though the things which have been done should have been made more fully known to your God-worshippingness (1), nevertheless because the bearers hence of the letter are in haste, I write briefly. Know therefore that on the twenty-eighth of the month Paunus the Holy Synod assembled in Ephesus, in the great Church of the city, which is called *Mary Bringer-Forth of God* (Μαρία Θεοτόκος) (2), and we continued in session all the day, and the blasphemous Nestorius having at last been condemned, and not having dared to present himself in the Holy Synod, we have subjected him to deposition and cast him out of the Episcopate. And we, the Bishops, who had come together, were about two hundred, less or more. And all the people of the city stayed by from early in the morning till evening, waiting for the judgment of the Holy Synod. And as soon as they heard that the wretch had been deposed, all with one voice began to praise the Holy Synod and to glorify God because the enemy of the Faith had fallen. And when we went out of the Church they escorted us with torches to our lodging (3) for it was then evening. And there was much gladness of heart and lighting of lamps in the city; so that even women having censers went before us (4). And the

---

(1). The ancient Greeks of the Fourth Century were fond of titles, fonder than accords with Christian simplicity, and therefore should not be imitated by us, but it is observable that the above title used often of Bishops is not confined to them but is here given to the Presbyters, Deacons, and even the Laity. It is not well for us in the West to use such expressions, for their common use leads to insincerity and deceitfulness, which is practically lying, which God hates and which damns the soul eternally in the lake of fire (Rev. xxi., 8).

(2). It has been thought that she was buried there: see note 22, page 21, vol. I. of *Ephesus* in this Set. And yet the experience and result of the use of other titles than God's in relation to Churches has been so accursed in the way of creature-service, that the next Ecumenical Synod, the only true Seventh, should by all means forbid creatures' names to be used of a Christian Church, School, or College. Indeed that use of saints' names for Churches among the Latins has led them to speak of St. Peter's Church, for instance, as dedicated "*under the invocation of St. Peter,*" and the same language is used of other saints.

(3). As the singular "*lodging*" is here used I do not feel sure that the reference is to any more than Cyril of Alexandria himself. He certainly deserved honor after his long and self-sacrificing labors before the Council to defend the doctrine of the Church and of the Scriptures on the Incarnation, and against serving any but God, and against Cannibalism in the Eucharist.

(4). Incense is used in the East for secular uses such as giving a better odor where there is a corpse at a funeral, etc. I have known it to be presented to a Sultan of Turkey by a Christian woman when he visited Smyrna, not at all as an act of worship, but, as one would present a nosegay. I do not, however, presume such to have been its use here, for Cyril was not the man to suffer it. It may have been swung up to perfume the air, as I saw, not long ago some of the attendants in the funeral procession of a late Patriarch of Constantinople kept sprinkling rose water to perfume the atmosphere, etc., as the cortege moved along on its way to the grave, and so to make a pleasant smell. Such a use of incense was much more common in the streets of the East than among us.

Saviour showed to those who had spoken ill of his glory (1) that He can do all things. We are about therefore to complete the papers which are made out on his Deposition, and then to hasten on to you. By God's mercy we are all in good spirits and in health through the grace (2) of the Saviour. I pray that you may [all] be strong in the Lord, beloved and most longed for.'" (3).

Document III.

In the third document, which is a Letter addressed "*to the Presbyters, and Deacons, and People of Alexandria,*" Cyril their Bishop, speaks of the great labor that they had undergone in defending God's truth, but is comforted by the hope of heavenly reward for it. And he rejoices that God had humbled "*a most foul heresy which had already tried to lift up itself against all under heaven, and had exalted its horn on high and spoken iniquity against God, and that though like a flame it had wished to burn up the right dogmas of the Church, the Sole-Born Word of God* (4) *had quenched it, and that He had brought to nought its contriver and father and had caused from the Priesthood by a vote of the Holy Synod,* "*so that,*" he adds, "*We rejoice and say,* 'The Lord hath magnified His action with us, and we have been made glad (5).' *For there is joy for the teachers and the leaders of the peoples, because the right Faith has prevailed and because the God and Saviour of all is glorified everywhere, and because Satan has been brought to nought, and the scandals raised by him have been done away, and because the dogmas of the Truth have overcome the lie* (6)*; so that we may all say harmoniously as from one mouth,* 'One Lord, One Faith One Dipping (7).' *And I write these things now as to my children and recount*

From the fact that "*women*" alone are mentioned as going before Cyril and his friends, it seems most likely that the incense was used to perfume the air with, for if it had been used as an act of worship to God, it would seem most natural to expect men to offer it. For though, as an act of worship, women may offer it as they offer other acts of worship, such as prayer, bowing, kneeling and prostration, directly to God in private, not in Church, where the clergy alone can offer it, nevertheless they would hardly have done it in the presence of the clergy.

(1). That is, by giving the glory of God the Word to a creature, even to the mere separate Man united to Him. For they bowed to that creature in the Eucharist, in heaven, and elsewhere, and that in direct contradiction to the two passages against *creature-service* which Cyril so often quotes, namely, Matt. iv., 10, and Isaiah xlii., 8, ayc, Psalm lxxx., 9, Sept., our lxxxi., 9.

(2). Greek, τὴν χάριν, that is, "*the favor,*" literally.

(3). Coleti *Conc.*, tom. 3, col. 1101. See the same Epistle in tome 77 of Migne's *Patrologia Graeca*, col. 137.

(4). See the Nicaean Creed which guided Cyril and the Orthodox who were defending its true sense, where the expression "*Sole Born*" of God is explained to mean his birth out of the Substance of the Father before all the worlds. The words are "*the Son of God, born out of the Father, Sole-born, that is, out of the Substance of the Father, God out of God,*" etc.

(5). Psalm cxxv., 3.

(6). The lie of *creature-service*, and of denial of the Incarnation. On the use of the terms, *the lie*, for creature service, compare Romans i., 25, where the Greek says literally "*the lie*" as here.

(7). Eph. iv., 5.

the wonderful works of the Saviour, in order that ye may make more earnest prayers, that by God's will, we may be restored rejoicing to you rejoicing and with strength. I pray that ye may be strong in the Lord." (1).

DOCUMENT IV.

This is a Letter written from Ephesus by Cyril of Alexandria after Act I., to the Fathers of the Monks in Egypt, and to the rest of the Monks, in which he refers to the fact that the Jews maltreated Christ, and applies to His case the words of Psalm lxix., 20, "*I looked for some to take pity, but there was none; and for comforters, but I found none,*" and that so there were some then even of the Priesthood, by which he means John of Antioch and the Bishops of his party, who were setting Christ at nought by co-operating with the heretic Nestorius and with those who were making war on Christ. But Christ had removed from the ministry such men and their blasphemies, and he asks the Monks to pray for him and for the truth against their hostility and their efforts and to uphold the hands of the Orthodox Fathers, as Joshua, the Son of Nun, had upheld the hands of Moses at the time of the conflict with Amalek (2).

And so the Letter ends.

DOCUMENT V.

This, as its title states, is a "HOMILY OF RHEGINUS, BISHOP OF CONSTANTIA IN CYPRUS, DELIVERED IN EPHESUS AFTER THE DEPOSITION OF NESTORIUS."

It is an eloquent and glowing portraiture of the wickedness of Nestorius in attempting to corrupt the faith, and his ingratitude to God for His saving mercy in the Incarnation, and, referring to the fact that Nestorius had divided Christ into a separate God, and a separate Man; God the Word's Substance not being in the Man, but in heaven, and the Man being on earth with mere inspiration and God's grace only like a prophet or an apostle, he tells Nestorius, "*For God the Word, who is parted by thee* [from His humanity], *and who humbled Himself to be born in flesh out of Mary the Bringer-Forth of God, will decree to thee the unavoidable chastisement of the torment in the day of judgment.*"

And then, at the close, he brings out the fact that the Orthodox Council worshipped God the Word, not a mere man, when he says :

"*But let us, following the divine commands, bow to* GOD THE WORD (3) *who deigned to live with flesh among us, though He did not cease to be of the*

---

(1). Coleti *Concilia*, tome 3, col. 1104. The same Epistle is found in Migne's *Patrologia Graeca*, tom. 77, col. 137 and after.

(2). Coleti *Conc.*, tome. 3, col. 1105. The same Epistle is in Migne's *Patrologia Graeca*, tom. 77, col. 140 and after.

(3). Greek, προσκυνήσωμεν τὸν Θεὸν Λόγον.

Father's Substance, being 'Radiance of His glory, and Character of His Subsistence (4), and upholding all things by the word of His mouth.'" (5), (6).

DOCUMENT VI.

This bears the title:

"*A Homily of Cyril, Bishop of Alexandria, delivered in Ephesus when the gatherings were concluded and Nestorius had been deposed.*"

This use of the plural "*gatherings*" here might be taken to imply that there were one or two or more gatherings of the Orthodox Bishops for conference and action before the First Act; and there may have been several informal ones during the fifteen days of waiting for John of Antioch, after Pentecost, A. D. 431, the time appointed by the Emperors for the Synod to open. That would certainly be a natural thing, for all hearts would be eager to know whether the assembled Prelates would be on the side of God's truth or not, and every zealous man would try to sound the rest and enlighten them if he found them ignorant of the merits of the questions involved, and to strengthen any one who might be wavering, and to confirm and unite and organize the sound. There were such informal meetings before the Formal Session of the First Ecumenical Council at Nicaea in A. D. 325. For the Bishops met on May 20 of that year, but owing to the fact that the Emperor Constantine was to be present but could not till the 19th of June, no formal session was held till then: see vol. 1 of *Nicaea* in this Set, pages 258-267. Probably both waits were Providential, for the Bishops had well discussed matters during them. But to return to Cyril's Homily. It sounds thoroughly Cyrillian. For it is a noble defence of the Incarnation of God the Word, and a denunciation of the Nestorian error of worshipping a mere man. I quote a part where he contrasts the *God-worshipping* disposition of the saints with the *Man-Worshipping* error of the Nestorians. His reference to the preceding Action of the Synod refers also to their condemnation of Nestorius for denying the Incarnation, for Cannibalism on the Eucharist, and for Man-Worship. I quote:

"It was behooving indeed to be content [or "You should have been content"] with the Explanations of Mysteries by the teachers preceding, and to have honored the satiety [to be found] in those sacred and full floods. But since I see that you are yet unfeignedly disposed towards love of hearing, come and let us say a few things *in consonance with those which have gone before.* There is then no doubt in any quarter that the illustrious choir of the saints take pride in praises for Christ, and make a genuine boast of their love for Him. And so the blessed prophet Isaiah says somewhere to Him, '*Lord my God I will glorify*

---

(4). Greek, χαρακτὴρ τῆς ὑποστάσεως αὐτοῦ. It is wrongly rendered in our Common English Version. The "*of one Substance*" of the Nicene Creed is based on this text.

(5). Heb. i., 3. The use of the expression here "*word of His mouth*" instead of "*word of His power*" is noteworthy. As I do not find the lection "*mouth*" in Tischendorf's last Greek text, I suppose that Rheginus is quoting from memory only and makes a slip.

(6). Coleti *Conc.*, tom. 3, col. 1108.

A Homily of Cyril of Ephesus—A Spurious Homily. 29

Thee, I will hymn Thy name, for Thou hast done wonderful things* (7). And the blessed prophet David says, '*My tongue shall rehearse Thy righteousness, and Thy praise all the day*' (8). And this indeed is the aim of the saints. But the wicked and guilty, not knowing the great and august and profound mystery of the Inman of the Sole-Born (9), unguardedly blaspheme and open an uncontrolled and gateless mouth. Therefore let them hear the prophet Isaiah saying to them, '*Draw near hither ye lawless sons,* [the] *seed of adulterers and of a whore, why have ye acted wantonly* (10), *and against whom have ye opened your mouth? Are ye not children of perdition, a lawless seed?*' (11). For those who have *denied the Lord who bought them* (12) are in truth children of perdition and a lawless seed. *For we are bought with a price, and not with corruptible things, as silver or gold, but with the precious blood of Christ as of a Lamb without fault and without spot* (13). But how could the blood of a common Man, and of one like us, be an equivalent for the inhabited world? (14). And how did one [mere man] die for all to save all? Why have we become his [the mere man's], we, who are even enrolled under the name of Him who is very God by Nature? WHY ARE WE TO SERVE HIM [the Man], 'WE, WHO REFUSE TO BOW TO THE CREATURE CONTRARY TO THE CREATOR?'" (15), (16).

The rest of the Homily is of the same tenor, and is well worth reading.

DOCUMENT VII.

This bears the title :

[A Homily] *of the same* [Cyril] *to* [or, "*against*"] *Nestorius when the seven came down to the Holy Mary* (1), though it contains not a word of any such event. The words in brackets, moreover, are not in the Greek.

It addresses Nestorius as present and as hearing this denunciation of him-

---

(7). Isaiah xxv., 1, Septuagint Greek Version.

(8). Psalm xxxiv., 28, Sept., Psalm xxxv., 28, English Version.

(9). God the Word, the "*Sole-Born out of the Substance of the Father;*" see the Nicene Creed.

(10). Greek, ἐν τίνι ἐτρυφήσατε.

(11). Isaiah lvii., 3, 4, Sept.

(12). II. Peter ii., 1.

(13). I. Cor. vi., 20, I. Peter i., 18, 19.

(14). St. Cyril of Alexandria in his Anathema X., which was approved by the Third Ecumenical Council, dwells much on the absurdity of supposing that a mere Man, the Nestorian Christ, could redeem us by his blood, and that a mere man separate from God the Word can be our Intercessor on high, or be worshipped. See it on pages 339-346: see also notes 682-688 inclusive on it, and especially note 688. Those notes are on pages 363-406.

(15). Rom. i., 25. Compare Matt. iv., 10.

(16). Coleti *Conc.*, tom. 3, col. 1108 and after.

(1). Coleti *Conc.*, tom. 3, col. 1112. Τοῦ αὐτοῦ πρὸς Νεστόριον, ἡνίκα κατῆλθον οἱ ἑπτὰ πρὸς τὴν ἁγίαν Μαρίαν. The same document and title are on pp. 992-996, vol. 77 of Migne's *Patrologia Graeca*. It is Homily IV. there. In passing I would say, that Stephen, an image-worshipper, a deacon of Constantinople in A. D. 808, wrote a life of a paganizer named Stephen Junior, who is said to have been put to death in A. D. 766 under the Iconoclast Emperor Constantine V. abusively called Copronymus (tome 100 of Migne's *Patrologia Graeca*, col. 1067, 1068, C.) In it, in column 1144, D, in the same tome 100, he says that the Third Ecumenical Council was held in the Church of St. John the Theologian, that is, of the Apostle John, at Ephesus. But this could not be unless that and the Church called *the Mary* were the same, and they certainly were not. But that writer constantly blunders as to facts like all his ignorant party.

There are several Homilies in Migne's *Patrologia Graeca*, tome 77, which are said to have been delivered at Ephesus. But we should find external evidence that they are Cyril's before admitting them to be his. Some of them may be sermons written long after his century for later established holidays of the Virgin, or for commemorations of the Third Ecumenical Synod, and ascribed to Cyril of Alexandria to make them bring more money. That would be the easier because as most men never put their names on their Sermons or festival addresses, it would not be necessary to erase any author's name but only to write Cyril's name on them and call them his, and so at once, lo! the copper coin has become a gold piece, and the dealer makes a much larger amount on his sale. There are tricks in all trades, and some sharpers and cheats in all markets. And the Jewish seller of manuscripts in the middle ages, or the Christian, lived in an evil time when the type of morality was low, and some of them were not more honest than many now-a-days who mark butter "*Orange County*" which has never been in Orange County, or mark goods as imported from England or elsewhere which were made here, and have never crossed the sea. These facts should be remembered by every one who tries to study Patristics and Conciliar matter; or, otherwise he will be liable to be misled and lose his own soul by relying on lies, as men in the middle ages relied on alleged passages of Athanasius and others for image worship which all now admit to be spurious. Witness also how the forgery of the False Decretals of Isidore deceived nearly all or all Western Christendom from the ninth century till David Bloudel exposed the imposture in the seventeenth, a period of about 800 years. And works on Patristics show many more of such instances, too many to enumerate a tithe of in this note. And there are documents in editions of the Fathers' writings which are admitted as theirs, for which there is no certain proof. Almost no, or no edition of the Fathers or Councils is perfect in all respects. That is especially true of those of Cyril, for some of his genuine works have been interpolated by the Monophysites, while others which he never wrote have been fathered on him.

As an aid to those who are about commencing the study of Patristics I would recommend the following rules:

1. Remember that most editions of Fathers are by Romanists, who are naturally prone to prefer such readings and changes as favor their errors, as, for example, a well known utterance of an African Father, Augustine, where he speaks of its being proper to appeal "*to the Apostolic Sees*" that is to the Church Universal, is changed by Romish editors, against nearly all the manuscripts as is confessed by men of that faith, to "*the Apostolic See*" to make it favor an appeal to Rome alone.

2. Separate all the writings of an author into three classes:

A. Those which are attested as his by external testimony and by internal from about the time of their production till now, and see that they are not interpolated. You cannot judge well regarding the internal testimony of a work till you have carefully read all the genuine works of the author to whom it is ascribed.

B. Writings alleged to be his, which however are never said by any ancient writer to be his, but which contain nothing which disagrees with the doctrines of his other writings, or with his known style. Under this head may be put one or more alleged Homilies of Cyril. Put these down as *not proven to be his*, or *doubtful*.

C. Writings alleged to be his which lack both external and internal proof.

Put these down as *spurious*.

In Romish editions some of Class B and some of Class C are put in the genuine class.

3. As a matter of chief importance, before attaching any value whatsoever even to any genuine utterance of any ancient writer, or of any mediaeval writer, or of any modern writer,

self and this argument against himself (2). It mentions him as *deposed* and *cast out* of the Church (3). But we know that Nestorius was not present at any time before Cyril and the Ecumenical Council.

Moreover, the Minutes of the First Act do not mention any utterance of Cyril or any one else after the deposition of Nestorius, nor do they mention any thing of this alleged address of Cyril at all. Cyril is here represented as having addressed Nestorius in "*short letters*" (4), whereas the fact is that the letter which has the Twelve Chapters is quite long, and the other letter of Cyril to Nestorius which was approved by the Third Synod is not notably short, but is of some length making between two and three columns of printed matter in the large tome of Coleti (5). Such representations therefore seem to have been the

---

see whether it agrees with the Six Ecumenical Synods, or whether it disagrees with any thing approved by the whole Church, East and West, in them. If it agrees with them respect it; if it disagrees with them reject it at once and forever. For Christ commands us to "*hear the Church*" if we would not be accounted "*as a heathen man and a publican*" (Matt. xviii., 17.) For its highest order, which alone can sit in a Synod, the Apostolate, that is, Episcopate (Acts i., 20, compared with Acts i., 25), was alone empowered by Christ Himself to teach (Matt. xxviii., 19, 20). All the teaching power possessed by the Presbyterate and the Diaconate is delegated by the Apostolate. The Apostles founded the Diaconate (Acts vi., 1-7), and the Presbyterate also, for Christ did not. To the Apostolate alone did He promise the Holy Ghost *to be with them forever* and to *guide them into all truth* (John xiv., 16, 17; John xvi., 13, and Matt. xxviii., 20). Therefore the Church in the Six Synods, in which the Apostolate alone sat, was "*the pillar and ground of the truth*" (I. Tim. iii., 15). We are not told in the New Testament to hear any individuals or any later consensus of individuals against the Church. Next to the New Testament in authority is the Universal Church and it alone is the authorized interpreter and expounder of Holy Scripture. It is supreme. And it has spoken in the VI. Synods alone. The great curse of the middle ages was that then men substituted for them mere local, Anti-Six Synods Councils, like the creature-invoking one of A. D. 787 at Nicaea, like the Trullan of A. D. 691, and like all those Western Councils after the Sixth Ecumenical Synod, which the merely local Roman Communion terms wrongly Ecumenical, such, for example, as those of the Lateran, that of Trent, that of the Vatican, and the rest of them; and Books of Sentences from the Fathers and systems of theology made up largely of the utterances of mere individuals, like that of the Syrian idolater, John of Damascus, that of the Italian idolater, Thomas Aquinas, and others. The consequence of that evil substitution was that the utterances of the Universal Church in its six Councils were largely forgotten for long centuries, and idolatry and creature-worship opposed to them spread like a pall over the East and the West, and the papal monarchy rose in the West on the ruins of the Ecumenical Canons, and Transubstantiation took the place of the discarded and despised doctrine of the Holy Ghost at Ephesus; and God's curse came upon the Church, and wiped out large parts of it by the Arab, the Tartar, and the Turk, in Asia, Africa, and to some extent even in Europe. The Lesson from all this may be put reverently and fitly in Christ's own words "*Hear the Church*," as in its Six Synods, and your local National Church next, and only so far as it agrees with the Six Councils and with all Ante-Nicene doctrine, discipline, universal rite, like trine immersion for example, and universal custom, like standing on the Lord's Day and from Pask to Pentecost in prayer. But where a custom was merely local in the Ante-Nicene period, we must as Westerns prefer Western local customs, and the Orientals must prefer Oriental local customs

(2). Coleti, id., col. 1113, 1116.

(3). Id., col. 1113, E, and 1116 E.

(4). Greek, γραμμάτων βραχέων.

(5). It is in col. 868 and after in tome 3 of Coleti's *Concilia*.

work of some ignorant fellow of later times who supposed that Nestorius was arraigned in the presence of the Council and condemned by it, and that Cyril after that made this speech to him before the Synod.

The work is therefore evidently spurious, as is another entitled, *"An Encomium on the holy Mary, the Bringer-Forth of God"* (6), (which, however, is not put by any editor of the Councils between Acts I. and II.), for both abound in worse creature-service than is attributed to Nestorius himself. The former, moreover, teaches Anti-Cyrillianism, if it calls upon its hearers to worship the Unity of the Natures in Christ (7) instead of worshipping God the Word alone, which is Cyril's doctrine (8), and it makes the blasphemous statement that Christ is named *blessed* through Mary which is a plain pagan utterance, and it ascribes to her the peculiar works of God such as being *" the sceptre of Orthodoxy"* (9), the putting of demons to flight, and the giving of holy baptism, and caps the climax of to be shuddered at blasphemy by saying that *" the Trinity is sanctified"* or *" hallowed"* (10) through her. It also speaks with approval of the idolatry of bowing to the cross (11).

I would put the date of this forgery, made by some paganizer, some centuries after Cyril's death (12) in corrupt and evil times.

---

(6). Migne's *Patrologia Graeca*, tome 77, col. 1029: 'Ομιλία ια΄, 'Εγκώμιον εἰς τὴν ἁγίαν Μαρίαν τὴν θεοτόκον. This is, *" Homily XI., an Encomium* ('Εγκώμιον) *on the holy Mary, the Bringer-Forth of God"* in columns 1029-1040 of tome 77 of Migne's *Patrologia Graeca*.

(7). Coleti *Concil*., tom. 3, col. 1116: γένοιτο δὲ ἡμᾶς τρέμειν καὶ προσκυνεῖν τὴν ἑνότητα.

(8). See in proof Cyril's words in note 183, page 79, and indeed all of that note, and note 582, page 225, and Cyril's Anathema VIII. on pages 331 and 332, with the notes on it, and Nestorius' Ecumenically condemned profession of relative worship of Christ's humanity on page 221, text, and what there follows on pages 221, 222, and 223. See that same evil profession of mere Man-Worship, that is, Creature-Worship, on page 461, and the notes on it there. Compare others of his heretical expressions there, namely, Passages 6, 7, 10, 14, 15, and 16, on pages 459, 460, 464, and 466-470. Flavian of Philippi pronounces those Passages of Nestorius *" horrible and blasphemous,"* and he adds, " Let every part of his *blasphemy* be inserted in the Acts, for an *Accusation* against him who has taught those things," id., pages 479, 480. On pages 486-504, the God-guided Council of the Universal Church deposes Nestorius for those and his other *" blasphemous"* utterances. All these references are to vol. 1 of Chrystal's *Ephesus*.

(9). Id., col. 1113, where it calls the Virgin Mary, τὸ σκῆπτρον τῆς ὀρθοδοξίας.

(10). Coleti *Conc*., tom. 3, col. 1113: δι' ἧς [the Virgin Mary, that is,] Τριὰς ἁγιάζεται. In Coleti the Synod is said to be assembled *for* [or *"on behalf of,"* (ὑπέρ)] the Virgin; in Migne *by* (ὑπό) the Virgin. See the Homily at the beginning in both. This is in Mansi's *Concilia*, tome 4, col. 1253, A.

(11). Coleti, ibid. Greek, δι' ἧς [that is, the Virgin Mary] σταυρὸς τίμιος ὀνομάζεται καὶ προσκυνεῖται, δι' ἧς δαίμονες φυγαδεύονται. This is in the same place in Mansi as the passage in the note last above. Hardouin does not give this Homily here. It is Homily IV. of Cyril in col. 992-996 of tome 77 of Migne's *Patrologia Graeca*.

(12). The spurious document which is found in Coleti which is attributed to Cyril of Alexandria there, and which claims to be an oration of his when the seven came down, is not given by Hardouin in his arrangement of the matter between Acts I. and II. of the Third Ecumenical Synod. It is however given between those Acts by Mansi in his *Concilia*. One can readily

I am not aware that any part of the sound things in it was taken from any writing of Cyril, though forgers sometimes take a few words from an Orthodox writer and then add their own stuff. The worse than Nestorianized creature-server who was the author of this document, seems to have made it all out of his own head to sell as Cyril's, and by pleasing creature-invokers with its spurious additions make it sell for more. It would naturally so sell; for, some centuries after Cyril, the glorious protest of the Synod against creature-service was ignored and forgotten by creature-servers, and from its use of the expression *Bringer-Forth of God*, the ignorant came at last to think that the Council was held to sanction her worship.

This writer approves of "*hymning the ever-Virgin Mary*," which of course is an act of worship to a creature, which Cyril impliedly curses in his Anathema VIII. (13), and which Christ Himself forbids in Matt. iv., 10.

Another mark of spuriousness in this Document is that it represents the Emperor as Orthodox (14), whereas Cyril had abundant evidence in a letter to himself from the Emperor before the Synod (15) and from his course at the beginning of the Council and for some time after that he was on the side of Nestorius against Orthodoxy.

The other homily referred to above, that is, the Encomium (*Homily XI*. of Cyril in col. 1029-1040 of tome 77 of Migne's *Patrologia Graeca*, Aubert tells us

---

see therefore that every editor of the Councils sandwiched between the Acts whatever genuine or spurious writing he happened to meet with outside of them, if it pleased his Romish fancy. So one of them stumbles upon this bastard production of centuries long after Cyril, and claps it between Acts I. and II., though most plainly it is simply one of many sermons or rhapsodies for some festival of the Virgin, on which some cheating manuscript seller had written St. Cyril's name to make it bring vastly more money. Besides, its flowery swollen style is plainly not Cyril's, for he is argumentative, calmer and plainer. Yet with external and internal evidence against this wretched rhapsodical trash it has been fathered on poor persecuted Cyril, cruelly persecuted by such fathering. The more ignorant Romanists have accepted such stuff as Cyril's, and even Protestant writers not understanding him, and prone to receive without examination Romish misstatements regarding him, have sometimes accepted such forgeries as his, or in other cases, have not so strongly denounced them as they should. For an example of this latter class, see in Dr. Bright's article *Cyrillus* in vol. I. of Smith and Wace's *Dictionary of Christian Biography*, page 767, outer column: he writes there:

"The encomium on the Virgin, included among his [Cyril of Alexandria's] works as delivered at this time [the fifteen days of waiting at Ephesus before the Council opened] is perhaps spurious."

Now that is not strong enough. It is *undoubtedly* spurious.

(13). Coleti *Conc.*, tom. 3, col. 1116, 1117, γένοιτο δὲ ἡμᾶς . . . . . σέβειν τὴν ἀδιάστατον Τριάδα· ὑμνοῦντας τὴν ἀειπαρθένον Μαρίαν, δηλονότι τὴν ἁγίαν ἐκκλησίαν, καὶ τὸν ταύτης Υἱὸν, καὶ Νυμφίον ἄσπιλον. This is found in col. 1257, tome 4 of Mansi's *Concilia*. It is found also in col. 996 of tome 77 of Migne's *Patrologia Graeca*.

(14). Coleti, id., col. 1116.

(15). It is Document XLIV. in the volume of *Forematter* to the Third Ecumenical Synod, to be published hereafter, if God affords us the means and strength to do so. Compare also the Second Imperial Decree summoning the Council and what is said of it on pages 8-18 of vol. I. of *Ephesus* in this Set.

he had copied from "*a most faulty codex of the Royal Library*," and that he had "*amended it, so far as it was permitted him, by conjectures*," (16). This leaves the question as to the original text of this spurious document more uncertain still. There is a lacuna in it as it is in Migne. Both purport to be uttered at Ephesus *on behalf of the Virgin* (17) in such a way as to make that chief; whereas Cyril always makes the defence of the Incarnation and the prohibition of creature-worship and of Cannibalism on the Eucharist the chief things. And he expressly disclaims in his *Five-Book Contradiction of the Blasphemies of Nestorius* any worship to the Virgin as a slander: see the Oxford translation, Book I., sections 9 and 10, and the *General Index* in vol. I. of *Ephesus* in this Set, under *Mary the Virgin*.

And I would add that there is not a single syllable in favor of the sin of worshipping the Virgin Mary in any of the Acts of the Council, nor in any genuine writing of Cyril of Alexandria, but on the contrary it is impliedly condemned in the condemnation by the Third Ecumenical Synod of the *Man-Service*, that is, *Creature-Service* of bowing to the Man put on by God the Word, for surely if I may not give that act of religious service to that perfect humanity, that highest of all creatures, I may not give it or any other act of religious service to any lesser creature such as the Virgin Mary, the apostles, archangels, angels or any other. See vol. I. of *Ephesus* in this Set, pages 221, 222, 223, 238 239, 331, 332, and the notes on those places, especially note 183, pp. 79-128, and note 677, and note 679 on pages 331-363.

Nor does the Third Ecumenical Synod state its object to be to struggle *on behalf* of the Virgin, but *on behalf of God the Word*. The notion that its chief object was to struggle on her behalf belongs to the creature-servers who are deposed and anathematized by the Synod for that very sin of creature-service by bowing to the creature, the mere Man, who was all there was of the Nestorian Christ.

Whoever forged these lies which have so misled many regarding the faith of the Third Ecumenical Synod and of Cyril its chief leader, richly deserves, if he died impenitent, the terrible penalty which God denounces in Rev. xxi., 8, against *all liars*. For such lies have led many into worshipping the Virgin Mary and other creatures to the angering of that awe-inspiring and *Jealous* God, who forbids us to bow to any but Himself (Matt. iv., 10; Luke iv., 8), and who told ancient Israel that He would not give His glory to another (Isaiah xlii., 8), and what is there dearer to the "*Jealous*" God (Exod. xx., 3, 4, 5, and xxxiv., 12 to

---

(16). Migne's *Patrologia Graeca*, tom. 77, col. 1029, note 1: Ex mendosissimo Reginae Bibliothecae codice hanc homiliam exscripsimus, et quantum conjecturis licuit, emendavimus.

(17). See Coleti *Conc.*, tom. 3, col. 1112, where the first document professes to have been delivered in the Church of St. Mary, and Migne's *Patrologia Graeca*, tome. 77, col. 1032, for the second. In the former place the gathering addressed is said to have been "*called together in behalf of the holy and ever Virgin Mary, the Bringer-Forth of God*," (κεκλημένων ὑπὲρ τῆς ἁγίας καὶ θεοτόκου Μαρίας τῆς ἀειπαρθένου. In the latter place, the Synod are spoken of as "*wise avengers of Mary the Bringer-Forth of God*." σοφοὶ ἔκδικοι τῆς Θεοτόκου Μαρίας.

18; Deut. iv., 24, and vi., 15; Joshua xxiv., 19, 20, and Nahum. i., 2), in the way of glory than worship? And not only have they been lured into that sin of creature-service but into the eternal damnation which is, by God's word, its sure punishment (Matt. iv., 10; I. Cor. vi., 9, 10; Galat. v., 19–22).

I would add that there is much of resemblance in parts of these two spurious documents. Indeed a few expressions, are, word for word, the same, and though the *Encomium* is much longer than the other, and in some things fuller, yet the arrangement of the matter is so similar that I judge that the forger of one may have had the other before him, or that the same forger may have written both.

Since writing the above I have found some excellent remarks of the, in some respects, ablest and soundest Anglican Theologian of our time, Rev. J. Endell Tyler, on the last two documents above, which he also regards as spurious and as productions of an age later than Cyril. His remarks are found in his work against "*The Worship of the Blessed Virgin Mary*," page 360, and Appendix D, pages 408–410. I quote both places.

On page 360, Tyler, after showing how free St. Cyril is from any trace of worshipping the Virgin Mary, adds:

"And yet, even to the testimony of this Cyril we are referred for proof that the Virgin is invoked, and '*that to her, in some sort, the works of Christ are attributed*' (18) The Homily (19) quoted in evidence was for the first time admitted among the works of Cyril by Aubert, and in the second part of the fifth volume of his edition of Cyril's works is entitled, "*An Encomium of the same Cyril upon Holy Mary, the Theotocos* ' (20).

This is one of those works which make us more especially regret that the Benedictine editors left Cyril of Alexandria without undergoing their examination. This homily cannot, in any point of view, be regarded as genuine; it carries its own condemnation with it, and evidently is the corrupt version of a rhapsody composed in a much later age than the Council of Ephesus. Our remarks upon it will be found in the Appendix."

I quote here also Tyler's *Appendix D*. in that work, pages 408–410. It is as follows, text and notes:

APPENDIX D.—*Cyril of Alexandria.*

" That the two homilies referred to in the text [in the passage just quoted from page 360 of it], and now ascribed to Cyril, (palpably different versions of the same original), are the productions of a later age, can scarcely admit of the least doubt. That the homily quoted by Dr. Wiseman is a corrupt copy, whoever was its author, we learn even from Aubert himself, who first added it to Cyril's works. That editor informs us that he copied it out from a most faulty (mendacissimo) manuscript in the King's Library (Paris), and emended it as

---

(18). "Dr. Wiseman's Remarks on Mr. Palmer's Letter. 1841, p. 25."

(19). "Vol. V., part 2, p. 379."

(20). "There is, in the same volume, another version of the same homily, entitled ' Of the same against Nestorius, when the Seven went down to the Holy Mary,' p. 355."

well as he could, by guesses. He tells us, also, that it will prove itself to any one at a glance to be the genuine offspring of Cyril; assigning, as his proof, 'that the author of the homily inveighs against Nestorius; and also, by a most clear testimony, calls Celestinus Archbishop of THE WHOLE WORLD.'

Celestinus was Bishop of Rome when the Council of Ephesus was convened; and among the monuments of that Council many letters are recorded, some from Cyril to Celestinus, some from Celestinus to Cyril, and some from each of those Bishops to others, with the epistles of other Bishops to them. Now, so far from Cyril acknowledging Celestinus to be Archbishop of the whole world, in his letter to Nestorius he speaks of Celestinus as Bishop, indeed, of Great Rome, but still as his fellow-minister, and brother, and fellow-bishop (21); and he addresses him just as he does the Bishop of Constantinople: 'Cyril, to the most holy father and most dear-to-God, Celestinus;' 'Cyril to the most holy and sacred lord archbishop and father, Maximianus.' And Cyril is thus addressed by Celestinus: 'Celestinus, to his beloved brother, Cyril.' Celestinus, in one letter, adds, 'The same we have written to our holy brothers and fellow-bishops, John [Antioch], Juvenal [Jerusalem], Flavian [Constantinople],' etc. And he urges Cyril to induce Nestorius to confess the same faith 'which the Roman Church holds, and the Church of your holiness [Alexandria] holds,' etc. Paul, Bishop of Emesa, thus addressed Cyril: 'To my lord, the most holy and sacred Archbishop, Cyril.' And John, Bishop of Antioch, addresses in the same terms Xystus, Bishop of Rome, Cyril, Bishop of Alexandria, and Maximianus, Bishop of Constantinople, as 'his most holy brethren.'

But whoever was the author, the homily in point of evidence is of no value. It might with equal reason be cited by a pagan in defence of his addressing an invocation to a thing that never had life. 'Hail, thou City of the Ephesians— rather, Goddess of the Sea (22); because, instead of earthly harbours, angelical and heavenly harbours are come to thee! And hail, thou thrice-blessed John, Apostle and Evangelist! and hail, thou too, Mary, who didst bear God!' In the body of the homily, the preacher certainly 'attributes to Mary the works of Christ;' ascribing to her, among other works of the only Saviour, the salvation of every believing soul: 'Hail Mary, parent of God, through whom every spirit that believes is saved!' The close of the other version of the same homily, which is found also in vol. IV. of the General Councils, p. 1251, as it now stands, is a mass of confusion; in which, nevertheless, whatever be the author's meaning, he declares that when he praises Mary, it is the Church he is praising: 'Praising the ever-Virgin Mary, that is to say, the holy Church and her Son, and her spotless husband, because to him is glory forever. Amen.' (23).

---

(21). "ἀδελφοῦ καὶ συλλειτουργοῦ ἡμῶν: again, συνεπίσκοπον ἡμῶν."

(22). "It is difficult to know how to render this expression μᾶλλον δὲ θαλασσοθέα. The Latin of Aubert renders it, 'Novo maris prospectu ornatior.' Mr. Palmer (Letter V. to Dr. Wiseman, p. 27), translates it, 'more than sea-beholding.' It has been rendered, 'Spectacle of the sea;' but nothing turns upon the meaning of the word."

(23). "Vol. VI., p. 358."

A Spurious Homily Fathered on Cyril.   37

Cardinal Bellarmin (24) seems not to have been at all aware of the existence of such a homily (25)."

A word or two on the above of the learned and able Tyler:

1. He states that, "*among the monuments of that Council many letters are recorded.*" Only a part of the letters to which he refers are in the records proper, or belong at all to the Council. In the editions of the Synods of the whole Church, East and West, it is common to include matter which merely serves as information regarding the Councils, but is no part of them. So such matters are often referred to as belonging to the Synod of Ephesus, but do not. Only the Acts, that is, the Minutes, and its Letters belong to it. Five letters, however, are found included in Act I. They are two of Cyril to Nestorius, one of Nestorius to him, one of Celestine to Nestorius, and one of Capreolus of Carthage to the Council. Four utterances of the Synod are on pages 1–20 above.

2. While the Homily is of no value, for it is spurious, the expression ἀρχιεπίσκοπος, literally *chief Bishop*, in the sense of *first Bishop* would imply only what was then admitted, that Rome was the first See of the Christian World, as Constantinople was the second, (Canon III. of the Second Ecumenical Synod, and Canons IX. and XXVIII. of the Fourth; compare Canon VI. of the First); but it would not imply that the Bishop of Rome had any right of Appellate Jurisdiction outside of Italy, or that the Bishop of Constantinople had any right to such Jurisdiction outside of the Eastern Empire. See those Canons. Rufinus, an Italian of the Fourth Century, the very century in which the First Ecumenical Synod was held, limits in his translation of its Sixth Canon the sway of the Bishop of Rome to "*the suburbicarian Churches*," which included nothing outside of Italy. On that matter we will treat more fully when we come to Canon VIII. of Ephesus. See, on Canon VI. of Nicaea, Hammond on the *Canons of the Church*, and Dr. Bright in his *Notes on the Canons of the First Four General Councils*. On the term *Archbishop*, see under the word ἀρχιεπισκόπου on page 697 of vol. I. of *Ephesus* in this Set. It is there applied to Cyril in a specially honoring sense. He is there called by Bishops outside of his own jurisdiction "*our Archbishop Cyril,*" that is, *chief Bishop* of the whole Ecumenical Council, as being its moving spirit, head, and teacher. For Alexandria was the Third See of the Universal Church, being preceded in rank by Rome and Constantinople only. But he was chief here because he represented two sees, Rome and Alexandria, and because the Archbishop of Constantinople, Nestorius, was not in the Council but accused of heresies. But especially was Cyril the *chief Bishop* as being the greatest teacher of Orthodoxy then in the world, or before or since, against denial of the Incarnation, against Man-Worship, and against Cannibalism and all Real-Substance-Presence in the Eucharist.

We must remember three all important facts against the genuineness of any such creature-serving document when ascribed to Cyril. They are:

---

(24). Vol. VII., p. 50.
(25). See Concilii Ephesini Acta; Ingolstadt. 1576. Concilia Generalia; Florence, 1761, Vols. IV. and V."

1. The lack of any early authority for ascribing it to him.

2. Its flat contradiction of his constantly expressed and characteristic and Ecumenically-approved opinions against all service to creatures.

3. It is ascribed to him first by some creature-server in later times.

Does the expression "*when the seven came down*" in the title of the homily or rhapsody in praise of the Virgin Mary found among the documents between Acts I. and II. of Ephesus, and ascribed to St. Cyril, really refer to the *seven Iconoclast Bishops coming down* to image-worship and to the worship of the Virgin in Act I. of the Iconodulic Conventicle of Nicaea, A. D. 787, as mentioned in Migne's *Dictionnaire des Conciles*, col. 103? That is the only mention of a *Seven Bishops coming down* to the worship of Mary which I can find. There is nothing of that exact number specified in any undisputed document which relates to the Third Ecumenical Synod and which belongs to its date. But there are discrepancies. The spurious rhapsody is represented as being delivered "*when the seven came down to the Holy Mary*," whereas, according to Migne's *Dictionnaire des Conciles*, tome 2, col. 102, Act I. of the Image-worshipping Conventicle of Nicaea in A. D. 787, the coming down of the seven took place in the Church of Holy Wisdom there. If we take "*to Holy Mary*" therefore to mean the Church of that name at Ephesus, there is certainly a contradiction here.

If any one understands "*when the seven came down to the Holy Mary*" to mean that the Iconoclasts came down to her worship, and asserts that though in the records of the Image-Breaking Council of A. D. 754 at Constantinople, we find approval of the worship of Mary and of other saints in the present text, nevertheless there is reason, according to Crakanthorpe on page 392 of his "*Defensio Ecclesiae Anglicanae*" (Oxon., Parker, 1847), to think that many or at least some of the Iconoclastic party were opposed to the invocation of the Virgin, and that therefore an Image-worshipper could speak in triumph of the seven as *coming down* to it, we let those statements go for what they are worth. It looks very much as though the forger of this rhapsodical nonsense lived after A. D. 787, and while he bases his spurious trash on an event which occurred in Act I. of the Synod of A. D. 787, he seems to have written other things in the document to represent or rather to misrepresent Cyril and Ephesus at least 356 years before. Or, perhaps, the original of this forgery had reference in that coming down of the seven in the Image-worshipping Conventicle of A. D. 787 in the Church of Holy Wisdom at Nicaea, and may have at first been written as a sermon to commemorate that fact on the First Lord's day in the forty days of Lent, that is, on Orthodoxy Lord's Day as the Greeks call it, which commemorates the overthrow of the Iconoclasts (26), or for some other Lord's Day, or holiday; and afterwards some image-worshipper and Mary-worshipper merely altered the title to make it refer to the Third Ecumenical Synod, and perhaps changed the body of the Homily a little in places to make it fit the occasion. The Greeks commemorate

---

(26). Smith and Cheetham's *Dictionary of Christian Antiquities*, vol. II. page 1055, outer column.

in their service at special times the VI. Ecumenical Councils, and alas! the so-called Seventh, that is, the Anti-Six Synods Conventicle of A. D. 787 at Nicaea.

Sometimes a late sermon or homily on a festival of the Virgin would be written by some one, and then committed and spoken on such festivals by him as one of her worshippers, and, becoming popular with them, would be copied by other such preachers, each, as is often the case, making alterations and additions to suit himself and the particular festival of Mary on which he held forth to the creature-worshipping crowd. This would account for the changes in such documents. The same thing would occur in the case of such trash on other saints. Such a use by preachers of good homilies also was not unknown, for Gennadius of Marseilles tells us, in Chapter LVII. of his work *On Ecclesiastical Writers* that "the Bishops of Greece committed St. Cyril of Alexandria's Homilies to memory to declaim them." (27).

This same thing may occur in our day. Years ago, for instance, I lent a clergyman several of my manuscript sermons, and I learned that he had preached them, and when they came back to me I found interlineations and interpolations in them in places, which I had to erase. That would be much more the case when the interpolator had bought and owned the sermon himself.

To sum up. As to *external evidence:* there is no proof in the Acts that St. Cyril of Alexandria ever said a word of the above spurious creature-worshipping *Encomium.* It is in tome 77 of Migne's *Patrologia Graeca,* Homily XI., col. 1029 and after (28).

As to *internal evidence:* it seems strange that the Romanist Aubert should have so little acumen as to ascribe it there to St. Cyril of Alexandria, when,

1. Cyril impliedly anathematizes all such pagan creature-serving trash in his famous Anathema VIII. For surely if he anathematizes every one who bows to Christ's mere humanity above, *because that is an act of worship to a human being,* much more does he by necessary implication anathematize every worshipper of the Virgin Mary, a lesser human being as compared with the perfect humanity of Christ which is confessedly the highest of all mere created things.

But as this *Encomium* is not in the Acts of the Council and is plainly spurious we here dismiss it. Indeed there was no need to mention it at all. But as the former Document, the Homily " *when the seven came down,*" is admitted by Mansi into the matter between Acts I. and II., it was seemly to dwell a little on it, lest those unaccustomed to Patristics and imperfectly acquainted with Cyril might be deceived and harmed by it.

---

(27). Migne's *Patrologia Latina,* tome 58, col. 1091, Gennadii Massiliensis *de Scriptoribus Ecclesiasticis,* cap. lvii., CYRILLUS, Alexandrinae Ecclesiae episcopus, edidit variarum hypotheseon tractatus. Homilias etiam composuit plurimas, quae ad declamandum a Graeciae Episcopis memoriae commendantur.

(28). Migne's *Patrologia Graeca,* tome 77, col. 1029, 1030, where, on the above Homily XI., we find the following: " Ex mendosissimo Regiae Bibliothecae codice hanc homiliam exscripsimus, et quantum conjecturis licuit, emendavimus. Genuinum esse porro Cyrilli fetum vel eam intuenti statim patebit. Nam et invehitur in Nestorium, et Coelestinum archiepiscopum totius orbis luculento sane testimonio nuncupat; denique omni ratione se prodit. AUBERTUS."

Document VIII.

The number of these Documents between Acts I. and II. of the Third Ecumenical Synod is not the same in all the Collections of the Councils. The next two below are not here in Mansi nor in Coleti.

They were both set forth on the day after the First Act of the Third Ecumenical Synod, and therefore before the arrival of John of Antioch.

From the solemn invocation of the Trinity in the first, which is addressed to the handful of bishops with Nestorius, one might suppose that some of them were shaky, or else that the strong language was used for effect with the Emperor Theodosius should he doubt in his anger the zeal of his representative Count Candidian.

Hardouin gives before the Acts of what the Greek calls "*The Apostatic Council*" that is, the Nestorian Conventicle of John of Antioch and his party at Ephesus, between Acts I. and II. of the Third Ecumenical Council, two documents, but in Latin only, "*Ex Synodico Casinensi,*" as it reads in his margin, col. 1448, tom. 1, of his *Concilia*, that is from the Latin translation preserved at Monte Casino, of a Nestorian work, the original of which was in Greek.

The first document is a "*Contestatio*" directed to the few Bishops of Nestorius' party who had not been part of the Ecumenical Synod in that Act, by the Count Candidian, after that First Act, in which he states that he had learned that some Bishops who were in that First Session were there by necessity, of whom he says several "*were said to have subscribed*" to what had been done in that First Session. Then he adds a statement which implies that the Emperors should be final judges. I translate:

"*Another* (1) *calling to witness by the most Magnificent Count Candidian after the* [First Act of the Third Ecumenical] *Synod:*

. . . . . . For that reason, I write by [this] letter to all those who would by no means come together on that same day, adjuring [you] by God

---

The Greek title of this document on page 1029 is, Ἐγκώμιον εἰς τὴν ἁγίαν Μαρίαν τὴν Θεοτόκον. The Latin heading in the parallel' column, (col. 1030), is, "*Encomium in sanctam Mariam Deiparam.*" The Greek is given in columns 1029-1040. The above quoted criticism by Aubert shows how wofully unfit he was to edit Cyril's writings and how incapable he was of separating the genuine from the spurious. There is no well grounded and sure external proof for ascribing the above spurious *Encomium* to Cyril, and the internal evidence is utterly against so doing.

(1). Count Candidian, the friend of Nestorius, had received powers from the Emperor Theodosius II. to control, practically, the business and decisions of the Third Ecumenical Council: see in proof vol. I. of *Ephesus* in this Set, pages 8-18, and note 107, page 42. But the Council at the risk of losing their honors and of imprisonment at the will of an absolute monarch, refused to let him control them, and though he protested against their going on with their work at the opening of their Act I., they nevertheless after waiting fifteen days according to our time beyond the time set for the opening of the Council, (sixteen days according to the Roman), by the Emperor himself, went on with their work, and in Act I. regularly, canonically, and righteously and most Orthodoxically deposed him. But Candidian would not cease his attempt to control their decisions in favor of Nestorius, which really meant to make their

Almighty and by His Christ (2) and by the Holy Ghost, and by the safety of the Lords of the World, that ye do nothing besides those things which are commanded by our most pious Lords, the Emperors; but that ye wait for the whole Synod and the presence of the most holy Bishops, and besides, for the judgment of our Lords, the most pious Princes. Let your Religiousness know therefore that due information has been given to you in regard to all things." (3).

The statements of Candidian, like those of the other favorers of Nestorius, were probably exaggerated or false. Very few if any of the Bishops who subscribed to the Decisions of the Third Ecumenical Synod's First Session were afterwards so weak-kneed and so weak-headed as to retract their good action in so doing.

Document IX.

The second Document is an "*Edict of the most Magnificent Candidian to the Synod,*" in which he complains to the Orthodox Council of what they had done on the preceding day in their First Act. He warns them that he had told them often that all must meet and "*discuss the question as to the exactness of the pious and Orthodox Faith, in accordance with the commands which are given by the divine and inviolable head,*" that is, the Emperor. And he warns them that what they do without John of Antioch and those who were expected from the West would be invalid for that reason, and he adds significantly "*and because it has been done contrary to the commands of the Lords of the World.*" (1).

As has been said, Mansi does not give these two Documents here, nor does Coleti.

---

decisions favor his denial of the Inflesh and the Inman, and his Man-Worship, and his Cannibalism on the Eucharist, and all his other errors, and so to corrupt and destroy the Christian Church and the Christian Religion, and so to make Christ's death of no value and to ruin the souls for whom He died.

Glory be to God that He gave the Bishops of the Synod His Spirit to resist that assumption of their Christ-given functions, and to do their bounden duty and to save the Faith and the Church from infidelity and from paganizings which destroy the soul forever (Rev. xxi., 8). We cannot be too grateful to God for what He wrought for us by them. Men should understand the soundness and necessity of their work and they will bless God for the Third Synod.

(2). Literally, "*and by His Anointed One.*"

(3). Harduini *Conc.*, tom. 1, col. 1447: *Acta Conciliabuli: caput 1. Contestatio alia magnificentissimi Comitis Candidiani post Synodum* . . . . . Ob hoc universis qui eodem die minime convenerunt, per epistolam scribo; conjurans per Deum omnipotentem, et per Christum ejus, et per Sanctum Spiritum, et incolumitatem Dominorum mundi, ut nihil praeter illa quae a Dominis nostris piissimis Imperatoribus praecepta sunt faciatis; sed expectetis Universalem Synodum et sanctissimorum Episcoporum praesentiam, nec non et judicium Dominorum nostrorum piissimorumque Principum. Cognoscat ergo Religiositas vestra eis relatum fuisse de omnibus.

(1). Harduini *Conc.*, tom. 1, col. 1447, 1448.

DOCUMENT X. IN ALL.

(*Document VIII. in Coleti.*)

This and the documents which next follow are utterances of the Conventicle at Ephesus which favored Nestorius, or of part of it. Its title as in Coleti is:

"*Report of Nestorius and of the Bishops with him to the Emperors, in regard to the things done in the Holy Synod, written before the arrival of John of Antioch in Ephesus.*"

In the text of Coleti, the names appended to it are as follows:

Nestorius, Bishop of Constantinople.
Fritilas, Bishop of Heraclea in Thrace.
Helladius, Bishop of Tarsus.
Dexianus, Bishop of Seleucia, in Isauria.
Himerius, Bishop of Nicomedia.
Alexander, Bishop of the Metropolis, Apamea.
Eutherius, Bishop of Tyana.
Basil, Bishop of Thessaly.
Maximus, Bishop of Anazarbus.
Alexander, Bishop of Hierapolis, in Euphratesia, and
Dorotheus, Bishop of Marcianopolis, in Mysia: eleven in all. But in a note there it is stated that another catalogue gives six more names, as follows:

Berinianus, Metropolitan Bishop of Perga.
Maconius, Bishop of Sardis.
Dalmatius, Metropolitan Bishop of Cyzicus.
Peter, Metropolitan Bishop of Trajanopolis.
Julian, Bishop of Sardis.
Cyrus, Metropolitan Bishop of Aphrodisias: and after Dorotheus it adds, "*and all the others*" which of course would make the document the work of the whole Conventicle as it was constituted before John of Antioch came. At any rate it professes to speak for all there was of it at that time.

It commences by telling the Emperors that they had come without any delay, in accordance with their command to Ephesus, and that in obedience to their edicts they wished to await the arrival of the Bishops from every quarter, and especially John of Antioch and his Metropolitans, and the Bishops from Italy and Sicily, and so make a Synod in common, and confirm by a common vote the Faith of the holy Fathers who had assembled at Nicaea. Nestorius and his friends by this language meant that they wished in such a sense to confirm the Faith or Creed of Nicaea as would favor their own heresy, that is, their own false Anti-Incarnation sense of it, and so work against Cyril and Orthodoxy. And evidently from the tone of Theodosius' censorious letter to Cyril just before the Council and his last edict on it, his mind had been so warped and twisted by Nestorius or some of his party as to regard Nestorius and his errors as sound and Cyril and his Orthodoxy as wrong.

And they continue in such a way as to imply that they held to the Faith of
Nicaea, and that Cyril and the Orthodox were endeavoring to change it. And
they say further that after they learned that "*the Egyptian Bishops*" were
vexed and believed that they [Nestorius and his party] were merely delaying
in craftiness, they promised to co-sit with them whensoever the most magnificent Count Candidian of the devoted household troops or body-guards, might
wish to call them together, who, they said, had been sent by the Emperor for
that very purpose, and that they had so stated to him by Bishops; but that
because Candidian knew that John of Antioch and those with him were near,
for that had been stated by his agents, and because other Bishops were coming
from the West, Candidian had commanded them to await the arrival of all in
accordance with the decree of the Emperors, though nothing of the kind was
commanded in either decree of the Emperors; and that thereupon Nestorius and
his party had such a love for peace that they obeyed the decree of the Emperor.
There is much of adroitness and cunning in these statements, For they write as
though the Egyptians only, Cyril and his Suffragans, were vexed at their delay,
whereas the vexation was felt by all the Orthodox as the facts mentioned by the
same Orthodox show. And they write as though they felt sure of the Emperor
being on their side, as probably they well might when Nestorius departed from
Constantinople, for either he or some one of his party had taken pains to pervert
the Emperor Theodosius the Second's mind on this whole matter, as his letter
to Cyril of Alexandria just before the Council and his last edict show. And
Candidian acted thoroughly in accord with Nestorius. So that all the Imperial,
the secular government influence, was on his side, and against the Orthodox
Cyril.

They continue by adding that the Egyptians, and the Asiatics, (meaning by
this last expression the Bishops of the whole kirk diocese of Asia), would not
admit the aim of the Emperor's decrees, and that they had trodden under foot
the ecclesiastical and imperial sanctions by refusing to make an orderly and harmonious confession of the faith (which really meant that they had refused to
agree with them on the faith), but wished to burst the bond of the Church's
union and to hold a Synod by themselves, and so they had done what is foreign
to ecclesiastical order and to the edicts lately put forth by the Emperors; for,
they add, the Emperors had in those decrees charged that one harmonious faith
should be set forth by all, a thing, I should add, plainly impossible. till oil and
water will mix, for Orthodoxy can never be one with heresy, and least of all
with creature-service. They then accuse the Orthodox of exciting tumult in the
city, and of shutting the Churches and monasteries and the Apostle's [John's]
memorial against them. Then they ask that they be protected, for Nestorius was
then deposed, and practically excommunicated, and those who harbored him and
sided with him, a condemned and deposed heretic, were justly liable to the same
punishments, and those they wished to avoid. They ask further that the Synod
be lawfully convened, and thereafter they add what shows much craft and guile,
that is, that no more Bishops sit in the Council than the Metropolitans with two
Bishops besides from each province; and they demand that the Suffragans thus.

selected must be men capable of knowing such questions. The trick in all this lay here : Antioch, the Patriarchal See of Syria, the chief seat of the creature-serving Nestorian heresy, where its authors, Diodore of Tarsus, and Theodore of Mopsuestia, had flourished, and whence had come Nestorius himself, had many Metropolitans. Bingham assigns to Antioch no less than twelve, exclusive of Cyprus.

This would give therefore twelve Metropolitans, plus twenty-four Suffragans, thirty-six votes in all at least, or, as the three Provinces of Palestine were not yet cut off from Antioch, Antioch would at this time claim fifteen Provinces, and including Cyprus, sixteen, which with thirty-two Suffragans would be forty-eight votes in all, and she could be sure of thirty-six of them for Nestorius. (1).

Whereas, Alexandria had fewer Metropolitans. Bingham in his *Antiquities*, Book IX., Chapter ii., Section 6, tells us that,

'The Egyptian patriarchate was sometimes divided into three provinces, sometimes into six, sometimes into nine . . . Carolus a Sancto Paulo . . makes seven provinces in Egypt."

Wiltsch in his *Geography and Statistics of the Church*, English translation, vol. I., page 192, states that,

"Several Metropolitan seats arose at the beginning of the fifth century. Thus Synesius was raised, about 410, by the Patriarch Theophilus, to the dignity of Metropolitan of Ptolemais, and in the imperial proclamation, at the Second Synod of Ephesus, in 449, Dioscurus received the command to appear with ten Metropolitans."

On the same page he adds,

"As the Metropolitans in the Alexandrian Diocese never subscribed themselves as such at the Councils, it is not certain what cities were their seats."

Even if Alexandria had ten Metropolitans in Cyril's day at Ephesus, its whole number of votes would be eleven Metropolitans, plus twenty-two Suffragans, making only thirty-three votes in all. But from what is said above by Wiltsch it is not clear that the Nestorians might not deny that it had any Metropolitans at all in the strict sense with Suffragans under each.

Then there was an opportunity to pack the Synod still further by taking advantage of the clause as to the *two Suffragan Bishops able to know such questions*, from each province. The thirty-six of Antioch, including Nestorius' friend, John of that See, and Nestorius himself with those whom he might cause to be chosen as possessing those qualifications, might really in effect decide against any would be Orthodox Suffragan in their Patriarchate having any place in the Synod, for, according to them, no such man would be *able to know such questions*, because he would not agree with them and their heresies. And so they might decide in favor of their errors in what they are pleased to call *peace and harmony*, but their paganizing and denial of the Incarnation would not have been God's peace nor in harmony with God.

---

(1). See Bingham's *Antiquities*, Book IX., chap. 1, sect. 6: and id., Book IX., chap. 2, section 9. In the former place he makes out fifteen provinces, and indeed that number did belong to Antioch till the Fourth Ecumenical Synod set off the three Palestines from it.

And at the end they make the singular request that if the Emperors will not do as they request above, that then, "*they command them without peril* [the deposed Nestorius and his partisans in error] *to go to their own things without danger*" (2), which certainly may mean, and was intended by them to mean, (for they did not regard Nestorius' deposition as valid), that they might be allowed to return to their own episcopal sees and to discharge their former functions in them, though Nestorius their leader was deposed, and the rest of them as maintainers of his heresy were justly liable to the same penalty. "*For*," they add, "*they threaten to deprive us even of life itself*." (3). They certainly, as warring against fundamental doctrines of the Christian Church, could not expect it to support them for teaching against it. And there is no proof that any of the Orthodox threatened their lives or their persons, though their brethren had been deprived of *their own living* as clerics in Constantinople by this same Nestorius, and persecuted by him, as laics also had been. So that both Celestine of Rome and before him, St. Cyril of Alexandria, had been compelled, as a matter of Christian duty, to write that they would not admit such depositions, and such suspensions from the Communion or excommunications. Moreover, Nestorius had misrepresented and slandered the persecuted as Manichaeans. Aye, he had asserted that they were of Cyril's *disposition of mind*, which implied that he also was a Manichaean, a wanton falsehood and insult. See on those matters vol. I. of *Ephesus* in this Set, pages 165, 183, 191, 192, and 212.

If it be said by some that the Third Ecumenical Synod should have permitted Nestorius and his partisans of the Nestorian Conventicle at Ephesus to go back to their sees and waste and ruin souls by their errors, I answer the fact that the Council wished just the opposite by the leading of the Holy Ghost, is enough for me. See pages 8, 9 and 10 above. And all history shows that no Christian Orthodox Six Synods people can ever be fully blessed unless they crush all idolatrous and creature-invoking episcopates, and banish all teachers of error, and close their places of worship and burn their books as Ephesus demands on pages 8, 9 and 10 above. We have suffered teachers of Rome's idolatry, Mormons, and Mohammedans, to enter our land to spread Anti-Six Synods heresies, and we are suffering from it now, and will suffer more from it hereafter. The most precious thing in any State is Christ's sound religion. It is the sole source of blessings, and therefore should be most jealously safe guarded, and all its interests. The greatest, aye, the chief and only source of evil to any people is false doctrine, and it therefore should be expelled at once, that we may act the spirit of Christ's prayer, "*Thy kingdom come, Thy will be done on earth as it is in heaven*," for why should we pray in one way and act in another? Would not that be inconsistent? We must do all we can to hasten the day when *the kingdoms of this world shall have become the kingdoms of our Lord and of His*

---

(2). Coleti *Conc.* tom. 3, col. 1096: Δεόμεθα οὖν τῆς ὑμετέρας Εὐσεβείας . . . . . ἢ κελεῦσαι ἡμᾶς ἀκινδύνως τὰ οἰκεῖα καταλαβεῖν· ἀπειλοῦσι γὰρ καὶ αὐτῆς τῆς ζωῆς ἡμᾶς ἀποστερεῖν. Instead of "*go to their own things*," we may render "*keep their own things*."

(3). See the last note above.

Christ (Rev. xi., 15). And surely a Christian people and a Christian State have power to do all that.

Nestorius did not deny that it is the duty of the civil magistrate to suppress heresies. For he had from the beginning of his episcopate exerted himself to shut up all Arian, Novatian, Quartodeciman, and Macedonian places of worship in his jurisdiction, as the (seemingly) Novatian Socrates (4) tells us. Indeed he aimed to purge the Eastern Empire of all heresies (5). But now that he had himself become a heretic, and the Universal Church had deprived him in consequence of all clerical honor and pay, he and his partisans began to cry *persecution*, though his rough soldiers had threatened the messengers of the Council, the respected Bishops who had gone to summon him to make his defence before them.

And so Nestorius, and ten Bishops with him, end and subscribe this document.

DOCUMENT XI. IN ALL.
(*Document IX. in Coleti.*)

The next document comes from what the Canons of the Orthodox Council of Ephesus call the Synod "*of the Apostasy.*" It is headed by the name of one of Cyril of Alexandria's chief opponents, John of Antioch, and the name of another of them, a Suffragan of John, Theodoret, Bishop of Cyrus, appears as the twenty-eighth of the forty-three names appended to it as subscribers; even that Theodoret whose writings against Cyril's Twelve chapters were afterwards to be condemned by the Fifth Ecumenical Synod. Nestorius' name, presumably because it is the work of his friends for him, is not among them. As there were often cities of the same name, we can not tell exactly where some of these sees were, but of the rest, at least twenty-six, more than half of all, were of the Patriarchate of Antioch, as we now term it, and probably more, for six of the doubtful sees bear names found under Antioch, though as they occur elsewhere also, we cannot surely say they belonged to Antioch, though probably most of them did. There were a few only from the Asiatic Diocese, two being from Bithynia, from Moesia three, from Thrace one, so that there were very few from that part of Europe which was under Constantinople, a fact that points to the unpopularity of Nestorius' heresies in his own jurisdiction of Thrace, three from Pontus, one from Thessaly, and the rest from localities not so precisely defined as to be without doubt. So that the Apostatic Conventicle may be called an *Antiochian* body with a few odds and ends from hither and yon. And as Nestorius had been a Presbyter of that see, his errors seem to have been derived

---

(4). See the references to him under "Nestorius" in the Index to Socrates' *Ecclesiastical History*, Bagster's edition of the English translation.

(5). Socrates' *Ecclesiastical History*, Book VII., chapter 29, "Nestorius . . . having been ordained [Bishop of Constantinople] on the tenth day of the month of April, in the consulship of Felix and Taurus, he at once uttered that much talked of expression to the Emperor, in the presence of all the people when preaching: '*Give me,*' saith he, '*O Emperor, the earth purged of the heretics, and in return I will give thee the heaven: help me to put down the heretics and I will help thee to put down the Persians.*'"

from the prevalence there of the heresies of Diodore of Tarsus and of Theodore of Mopsuestia—Mopsuestia is not represented, but it is a curious fact that we find Helladius, Bishop of Tarsus, among the forty-three signers of the Apostatic Document which we are about to epitomize or quote; so that St. Paul's birthplace was but illy represented, as well as St. Peter's See of Antioch as it is called in the Acts of the Fourth Ecumenical Synod.

The heading of these Acts of the Apostatic Assembly of the forty-three Bishops reads as follows:

"*Minutes of* [the Acts done by] *the Oriental Bishops, in which they depose the most holy Cyril and Memnon, and excommunicate all the Bishops of the Holy Synod.*"

The Minutes then state that John of Antioch and the Bishops of the Synod, (of the forty-three, that is), had met in his lodging in Council, that Count Candidian stated to him that he had wished to deliver the Letter of the Emperors to the whole Synod so that they might do what it enjoined, but that five (or four) days before their then meeting, Cyril, Bishop of Alexandria, and Memnon, Bishop of Ephesus, had assembled, with the Bishops who were of their party, in a Church, and were hindered by him from co-sitting by themselves contrary to the decree of the Emperors, and that they were admonished to wait for the arrival of all then assembled; and that they had asked him to read the Emperors' Letter, that he, on the contrary, did not wish to do any thing because John of Antioch and his Bishops had not all arrived, and that many other Bishops and Metropolitans had not yet arrived, (a remark which must not however deceive us into forgetting that four-fifths were on the ground); that he was under compulsion from them because they said that they did not know what had been written by the Emperors; that therefore when they had been assembled and he was forced in order not to give any pretext for disorder, he had read to them the Emperors' Decree, and that while he was still present and about to go out he had protested to them to do nothing hasty, as many Bishops who had gone in with him to them knew, but that not even after all that would they stop, but did what pleased them. But Candidian's "*many*" can not include one-fifth of all the Bishops in Ephesus, for even after John of Antioch's arrival, they numbered only about one to five of the Orthodox. By "*many*" here I presume he may mean some Nestorians who were afterwards thrust out, seemingly for aiding the attempt of Candidian to hinder the Ecumenical Council from assembling and acting. See below.

The Letter of the Emperor referred to is not that which was read in Act I, and is found on pages 32–41, vol. I. of *Ephesus* in this Set. That was the first Decree convoking the Council and ordering it to assemble on Pentecost, A. D. 431. The other Letter of the Emperors is found on pages 8–18 of that volume. Cyril confirms the statement of Candidian above that he had read the Second Letter to the Council. It was done just before they began their First Act, seemingly. For the Minutes make no mention of it there. A little further on, however, Cyril refers to it, but then, at the suggestion of Theodotus of Ancyra, the Synod postponed the consideration of it to a later time; see pages 42-44 of vol. I. of *Ephesus* in this Set.

The absurdity of the Nestorian party in this whole matter lay here; the Emperors, or rather the Emperor Theodosius II. who was the chief manager of the whole business, being in sympathy with Nestorius, had called a certain number to come, and had commanded the meeting of the Synod to commence at Pentecost, and had sent Candidian, a friend of Nestorius, thither, and had practically forbidden the Synod to depose Nestorius, but to deal with matters of faith alone, as though there could be justice done without deposing the leader and poison-spreader himself and his friends. The idea of Theodosius in issuing such an edict was about as wise as the old woman's utterance to her boy that she was willing that he should learn to swim, but that he must not go near the water. Besides, his action was an outrageous usurpation of the rights of the Episcopate, that is, Apostolate (Acts i., 20, 25). For Christ gave to the Apostles alone the power of binding and loosing. It was for them therefore to state when it should be used and when not; whether Nestorius and his fellow-heretics deserved to be and should be bound for their errors or not.

Furthermore, as to the plea that all the Bishops had not yet assembled, the fact was that about one hundred and sixty had come on the Orthodox side as against perhaps twelve or twenty on the Nestorian side, that is, about, say eight to one. And when all did arrive there were two hundred of the Orthodox as against forty-three of the Nestorian party, that is, about five to one, so that Orthodoxy had always an overwhelming majority of the Council with it, and the Deposition of Nestorius was signed by about four-fifths of all who came. And they were so firm for the truth that nothing in their after trials changed them. Besides, John of Antioch had sent on word to proceed with the business of the Council if he tarried, though, as we see from Documents above, the Council suspected him justly of purposely delaying to favor Nestorius who had belonged to his Church, (see pages 4, 5, 23 and 24 above). And let us remember that they waited for him fifteen days over the time set for the opening of the Synod. So that no man could accuse them of unseemly haste.

After all that has been said therefore it is clear that from the start the Orthodox party always had a clear majority of the whole with them. Even if John had come and all his forty-two friends, there would still at the opening have been about one hundred and sixty of the Orthodox as against forty-three of the Man-Servers, and Deniers of the Incarnation, and Real Substance Presenceites, and Worshippers of Christ's separate humanity in the Eucharist and elsewhere.

And let us remember also that delayers in any other Council, or in any legislative body in the State, have no right to fault anybody but themselves if, when they are clearly warned of the day of opening, they are fifteen days behind time; and least of all when they are as only about one to four or five of the other party can they blame them, if, when they have waited fifteen days for them beyond the appointed day, they go on with business without them.

John of Antioch, at the conclusion of Count Candidian's statement before the Conventicle, asks him to tell what was done after he had read the Emperors' Decree, one part of which in effect precluded Bishops, the deposing power in the

Action of the Apostatic Conventicle Against the Third Synod. 49

Church, from deposing Nestorius. The Decree meant is the Second; see it on pages 8–18 in vol. I. of *Ephesus* in this Set.

Then Count Candidian states that all the Bishops of the Council with Cyril and Memnon had applauded at the close of the reading of the Emperors' Decree, so that he thought that they would really obey all the injunctions of those civil rulers, and he rejoiced with them; but that afterwards when he was exhorting them all to obey the Letter in those matters, no one was willing to permit him to do so, but thrust out with ignominy the Bishops who had been sent by Nestorius and those who were with them, and that when he again attempted to exhort the Synod, at great length, they had thrust him also out (1), as if he ought not to take part in their Decisions. The Nestorian Bishops, we shall soon see, were afterwards invited to be present, so that their being thrust out now is to be ascribed to their making nuisances of themselves by trying to hinder the Synod from acting; and as to thrusting out Candidian, a mere laic, the Synod were right, for the Church from the beginning never allowed the laity to take part with the Bishops in formulating dogma, and this was, in effect, what Candidian asked. He goes on to state that they would not permit a warning to be read to them which had been sent through the Bishops of Nestorius' party, who, I will add, were a mere handful, and he refers to those Bishops as able to verify his statements, and he adds further that he had reported all those things to the Emperors, and had shown them that the Synod should have waited for John of Antioch and the Bishops who were with him.

Next John of Antioch puts the question to the Apostatic Council of the Forty-three, whether it had been in conformity with the Canons and the Ecclesiastical Sanctions and the Imperial Letter, to discuss matters in the presence of all and after proper questions and answers to arrive at the same result by proofs, or to condemn Nestorius by default in his absence.

This was a deceptive way to put things; for there was no Canon or Church Sanction which commanded the great majority of the Council to wait fifteen days after the day set, for about one-sixth of all the number of Bishops who came, and it was the Imperial Letter which set Pentecost as the day of the opening, and if the Emperor usurped the power of the Bishops and, in effect, forbade them to depose Nestorius, he had done wrong; and how little Nestorian question and Orthodox answer or Orthodox question and Nestorian answer would have changed the Orthodox Bishops was clear from the result. For they remained as firm as they came.

And it was in strict conformity with the Canons for four-fifths of a Synod to condemn a contumacious and thrice-summoned heretic who refused to appear.

---

(1). The Bishops applauded as a token of *loyalty* to the Emperor, not to express assent to all that was in his Second Letter which, as we show on pages 8–18 of vol. I. of *Ephesus* in this Set, might have hindered their work; hence they did not allow it to be read to them a second time in it, when they had learned its true character, though they heard his other letter which was better, with favor in that Act: see pages 32–44, vol. I. of *Ephesus*. This circumstance shows us how we are to understand complimentary actions or utterances as to some other documents in Acts of Councils. Sometimes they may be understood as entire praise, at other times as only partially so, for collateral facts compel us so to believe.

See the so-called Apostolic Canon LXXIV., which had much prevalency, whatever be its origin.

In response to John of Antioch's question, Candidian answers: "*All the most God-fearing Bishops* [the Nestorians, he means] *who were present with me, know that their Decisions* [those of the one hundred and sixty or two hundred Orthodox Bishops of the Ecumenical Synod] *had been passed without any judgment and* [without any] *investigation;*" an assertion manifestly false as the Acts show. For in the first place they had ordered one of the Decrees of the Emperor convoking the Synod to be read, and omitted the other because it tried to hinder them from doing their God-given duty, then they had canonically summoned Nestorius, and inasmuch as their three summonses had failed to bring him before them, (a thing which was his fault, not theirs), they had proceeded in the next place to examine the errors of Nestorius. First they read the Nicaean Creed as a guide, then approved an Epistle of Cyril to Nestorius as Orthodox; then they condemn an Epistle of Nestorius to Cyril of Alexandria as heretical; both those Epistles had been judged by the touchstone of the Nicaean Creed. These Epistles contain much of the whole controversy on the Inflesh and on Man-Worship. Next they read an Epistle of Celestine and a local Council of Rome, representing part of the then West, which condemned Nestorius as a heretic. They then read the celebrated Epistle of Cyril of Alexandria and the Synod of Egypt which has the celebrated Twelve Chapters and which condemns and anathematizes the errors of Nestorius. That covers the whole controversy on the Inman, Man-Worship and the Eucharist.

Then proof is given by those who had conversed with Nestorius as to his errors. Then passages are quoted from twelve Fathers of the East and the West against those errors and for the truth. Then twenty heretical passages are given from Nestorius' own writings, and they are inserted in the Acts as proofs of his heresy against the Incarnation, for Man-Service and for Cannibalism in the Eucharist, etc.

Then another Patriarchate in the West is heard from, by the letter of Capreolus of Carthage, who was in sympathy with the Synod.

Then with the proofs all in and abundant, they justly condemn Nestorius, the notorious heresiarch, on the points above, and depose him; and one hundred and ninety-eight Bishops subscribe making with those who came later more than two hundred in all, nearly five-sixths of all who were at Ephesus. Besides, as the Orthodox Synod state, many of the Bishops of the Synod of the Apostasy were Coelestians, that is, Pelagians, and for that reason deposed (2). Hence of the Bishops with a clear right to sit in an Ecumenical Synod, probably more than five-sixths at Ephesus were Orthodox. So that Candidian in stating that the Decisions of the true Synod had been enacted without judgment and without investigation had stated what the facts prove to be a downright falsehood, as the marginal note here in Coleti, in effect teaches.

---

(2). Hefele's *History of the Church Councils*, vol. III., (English translation), pages 98 and 56 and the original documents there referred to.

John of Antioch then complains that on their arrival at Ephesus, Cyril and the Synod with him had not greeted them in a brotherly manner, and had not treated them kindly while dusty with traveling, and that he had not refreshed them with a brotherly disposition, but had troubled them and raised clamors against them and manifested their usual disorderliness, but that nevertheless he [John] and his Synod did not even endure the hearing of them; and he calls upon his Synod of the Forty-three, humorously enough, as though they were the majority of all, whereas they were only about one-sixth of all, to decide what should be done with the other five-sixths, whose decisions he speaks of as an unlawful and tyrannical troubling of all things. He omits, skilfully enough, to state why Cyril and the Orthodox Synod gave no better reception to these sympathizers with a deposed and anathematized man, whom by Christ's law they should have regarded "*as a heathen man and a publican*" (Matt. xviii., 17), and with whom they were now by their action classing themselves, and therefore rendering themselves liable to the same penalties. Cyril and his friends as maintainers of God's truth could do no less than ask them whether they received the Decision of the Synod against Nestorius. If they had, they would have welcomed and treated them as brethren. If they did not, they should have been treated as they were as enemies of Christ and of His pure worship, and warned that by failing to admit the Decision of the Synod they were siding with heresy on the Incarnation, on the Eucharist, and on Man-Service; and that therefore the Orthodox Synod must depose them also as was its right and duty. And this John and his friends would style *troubling* them! And he tells us what proves that he and his little gathering would not even hear the threats of canonical punishment and the clamors against his attempts to infidelize and idolatrize the Church.

Then Candidian, knowing his men quite well, and feeling sure of the result, goes out, and the duet between him and John of Antioch here ends, and a new duet takes its place; that is, between John and the other forty-two Bishops of this Apostatic little Synod.

John harps on the same string about the Emperors having wished them to meet together and examine matters quietly by question and answer, without trouble, forgetting that there is ever trouble to maintain God's truth against error, that Christ came in that sense to send a sword on the earth and to set members of the same family at variance (3); that it was his fault and the fault of the small minority, the Conventicle, of which he was one, that the Ecumenical Council had gone on, as was its duty, without him, when he was fifteen days late, and when it was not clear that he wished to be present at all, when it was even suspected that his absence was intentional to delay and hinder the Synod, and to defeat any action being taken against Nestorius or his heresies. He continues that the Emperors had commanded that no accusation should be made before the exact setting straight and confirmation of the pious faith of the holy and blessed Fathers who had met at Nicaea in Bithynia. But whatever might have been the desire of the Emperor Theodosius II., deceived as he seems to

---

(3). Matt. x., 32-40.

have been by Nestorius and his party to save him from just accusation, it was not right for Cyril and the Orthodox to hear the Emperor, for to leave him undeposed and his fellow heretics would have left them to poison men's minds and finally to do away the Orthodox Synod's Decisions themselves. And Theodosius II. should have known that the two Ecumenical Synods before Ephesus had always enforced their Decisions by deposition and excommunication.

And the Synod of the Orthodox had done exactly what John mentions, that is, they had approved by vote Cyril's sense of it in his Shorter Epistle, that is, they had defined the true sense of the Nicaean Symbol and faith to be for the Incarnation and against Creature-service, and they had condemned by vote Nestorius' Anti-Inflesh and Man-Worshipping sense of it in his *Epistle to Cyril;* see pages 52-178, vol. I. of *Ephesus* in this Set, where those Epistles and the voting on them, and on the agreement of Cyril's with the Nicaean Creed, and on the disagreement of Nestorius' with it, are found. Aye, they had received and been instructed by Cyril's *Long Epistle,* in which he explains that Creed at greater length still; see id., pages 204-358, text. That the *Long Epistle* has Ecumenical Sanction is shown in the same volume in the notematter, on pages 205-208. And on account of Nestorius' Epistle to Cyril, in which he perverts the sense of the Creed of the 318, and on account also of his perversions of it and of Scripture, in his XX. Blasphemous passages he is deposed by the Third Council in their Act I.; see vol. I. of *Ephesus* in this Set, as above, and pages 449-480, 486-504 of it.

John's whole interrogation at this point is as to the way that the Orthodox had treated the Emperors' First, and especially their Second Decree, that is, Letter, for the Nestorians felt sure of his support, and wished to flatter him, and they were willing to ignore the fact that Bishops have a God-given right to decide dogma, and to bind and to loose. And so John of Antioch asks of his little opposition Conventicle at the close here:

"*What, therefore, does your God-fearingness agree ought to be done, on account of so great a contempt for the pious Letter?*" that is, for the Second Decree of the Emperor, John means.

To this the Apostatic Conventicle reply that Cyril of Alexandria and Memnon, Bishop of Ephesus, had acted together against them, that the latter had shut them out of the sacred edifices of the Church in Ephesus, and had not permitted them to celebrate Pentecost, that is, Whitsunday, as it is called in English; that he had brought a multitude of rustics into the city and troubled it; that he had sent his own clerics to the houses of the Bishops of Nestorius' party and threatened them with irreparable loss (perhaps he means deposition and excommunication, which the Synod, I should add, had a right to inflict), unless they would meet with their Council and approve what the Conventicle calls its *disorderly Decisions. The Apostasy* then accuse the Orthodox Council of having an evil conscience in every respect, and of confounding all things, and of filling Church matters with uproar, a favorite cry of their Creature-Serving kind against Orthodox Reformers, and, they add, "*of despising the pious Letter,*" that is, the Emperor's wrong Decree—and then they

Action of the Apostatic Conventicle Against the Third Synod. 53

show still more clearly and unmistakably their doctrinal virus by accusing the Orthodox Synod, as follows:

"*They trample under foot the Ecclesiastical Sanctions, so that their heretical misbelief may not be inquired into; which misbelief we have found in the Chapters sent some time ago to the imperial city by the most religious Cyril, the Bishop; the most of which agree with the impiety of Arius, and of Apolinarius, and of Eunomius.* It is, therefore, necessary that both thy Holiness and we all should fight courageously for Piety, so that no persons may be deceived by the heretical Chapters of the most dear to God Bishop Cyril, and that the faith of the holy Fathers be not corrupted, and that the Synod condemn by a vote worthy of such lawlessness, the authors of the heretical way of thinking, and of the disorder which exceeds all description, and that the most religious Bishops who have been deceived by them, and swept away by them be subjected to ecclesiastical punishment.

John, the most dear to God Bishop, said: It was my wish (4) that no one of those who have been separated to be priests to God, should be put outside the ecclesiastical body, but since the cutting off of the members which cannot be healed is necessary for the health of the whole body, it behooves that Cyril and Memnon be subjected to deposition as authors of the lawlessness which has occurred, and of the treading under foot of the Ecclesiastical Sanctions (5), and of the pious Decrees of our most religious Emperors (6), and on account of the heretical sense of the aforesaid Chapters, and that those who have been deceived by them be excommunicated (7) till they recognize their own fault (8) and anathematize the heretical Chapters of Cyril, and promise to stand by the faith put forth by the holy Fathers who were gathered together in Nicaea, and to add to it nothing else, nor any thing foreign to piety, and that, in accordance with the pious Letter of our most pious Emperors, they will meet with us, and make the examination, in a brotherly manner (9), of the matters to be investigated, and confirm the pious faith (10.)

---

(4). Or, *it was a matter of my prayer*, or *of my wishing*, εὐχῆς μοι ἔργον ἦν.

(5). Greek, ἐκκλησιαστικοὺς θεσμούς. No such thing had been violated by Cyril and the Orthodox.

(6). Harping on the old string again, the right of a layman to usurp the functions given by God to Bishops alone, and this to flatter the Emperor.

(7). Greek, ἀκοινωνήτους γενέσθαι; which may also be rendered "*suspended from communion.*"

(8). Or, "*so that they may recognize their own fault,*" ὡς ἂν, etc.

(9). That is, the Nestorians would have Cyril and the Orthodox to be brotherly with men who had denied the Incarnation, brought Man-Service into the Church, and the error of the real presence of the substance of Christ's human flesh and blood in the Eucharist, and the Cannibalism of eating and drinking them there, and the creature-worship of worshipping them there. But the New Testament forbids us to have anything to do with such infidels and idolaters and cannibals. Yet such notions of liberalism and of brotherliness are common among heretics till this hour.

(10). In plain English and without any verbiage, John would have Cyril and the Orthodox admit *their sense* of the pious faith, which, according to them, includes the heresies of denial of the Inman, of Man-Worship, and of Cannibalism on the Eucharist.

The Holy Synod said, Thy Holiness hath spoken lawfully and justly. It behooves, therefore, that by a common writing, proclamation be made of the deposition of Cyril and of Memnon, and the excommunication of the rest, and that it be ratified by the subscriptions of us all.

The most dear to God Archbishop John said, The things which seem good to you shall be done.

John, Bishop of the Antiochians, pronounced [the]

VOTE [or "SENTENCE"] (11.)

The Holy Synod gathered by God's grace in Ephesus in accordance with the Letter of our most religious and Christ-loving Emperors, has pronounced as follows:

We did, indeed, wish that the Synod might be held in peace, in accordance with the Canons of the Holy Fathers (12), and in accordance with the Letter of our most pious and Christ-loving Emperors (13). But since ye have made use of audacity and disorder, and a heretical mind, and have held a Session by yourselves, although we were at the doors in accordance with the Letter of our most religious Emperors, and since ye have filled the city and the Holy Synod with all trouble, in order that the Chapters which agree with the misbelief and impiety of Apolinarius (14) and Arius and Eunomius be not examined into, and since ye did not wait for the arrival of the most holy Bishops from every quarter who had been summoned by our most religious Emperors, and inasmuch as the most magnificent Count Candidian had told you these things in writing and by word of mouth, not to dare to do any such thing but to wait for the common sitting of all the most holy Bishops; therefore, know ye that ye are deposed, and aliens from the Episcopate, [that is], thou Cyril the Bishop of Alexandria, and Memnon the Bishop of this city, and that ye are aliens from all ecclesiastical ministering, as authors and leaders of all the disorder and transgression of law (15), and that ye have been the causes of the treading under foot of the Canons of the Fathers (16), and of the imperial Decrees (17), and all ye the rest who agreed with those who were disorderly and transgressed

---

(11). Greek, ψῆφος.

(12). More misrepresentation of the Orthodox Synod as though it had violated any Canons of the Church. No such thing had been done.

(13). More holding up of a layman's Letter as an authority on a matter where the faith was concerned, though it in some respects interfered with the God-given and peculiar rights of Bishops. That was mere demagogueism unworthy of any true self-respecting Bishop.

(14). The above is the Greek spelling of the name. The common Latin one is *Apollinaris*.

(15). No just law had been transgressed by the Orthodox, but the Man-servers had transgressed God's law by their heresies, and their leader Nestorius had justly been stripped of the Episcopate for it.

(16). The constantly recurring misrepresentation again. No such Canons had been violated.

(17). When the imperial decrees are in harmony with God's laws, they are to be obeyed; when not, not. And the Council had obeyed the two Imperial Decrees, that is, Letters, so far as it was in accordance with God's law to do so, and had disobeyed the Second of them only where it violated God's law.

Action of the Apostatic Conventicle Against the Third Synod. 55

the law against the Canons and against the imperial Decrees, are excommunicate (18) till ye recognize your own fault and change your minds, and receive the faith of the holy Fathers who assembled in Nicaea, and introduce nothing else foreign to it, and anathematize the heretical Chapters which have been put forth by Cyril, the Bishop of Alexandria, which oppose the Evangelic and Apostolic doctrine, and abide by the Letter of our most religious and Christ-loving Emperors which commands the examination of matters of the Faith to be made quietly and accurately" (19.)

Then follow the names of forty-three, the first of whom is "*John, Bishop of Antioch*," who so signs, whereas Metropolitans, subject to him, sign themselves *Metropolitans*, as for instance, John of Damascus, who calls himself "*John, Metropolitan of Damascus.*"

The reader will see in the above the hatred of the Nestorian party against Cyril's Twelve Chapters—for the Conventicle asserts that "*most of them agree with the impiety of Arius and of Apolinarius and of Eunomius,*" and further on they call them, "*The heretical Chapters of the most dear to God Bishop Cyril,*" and speak of their duty to contend against them, as a corruption of the Faith of the Fathers, and call upon John of Antioch to depose Cyril, and suspend from communion the rest of the Ecumenical Synod who had sided with them.

John, in reply, agrees that Cyril, their author, should be deposed with Memnon, and that all who had sided with Cyril, that is the rest of the Ecumenical Synod, should be excommunicated or suspended from communion "*till they anathematize the heretical Chapters of Cyril,*" and in the same address, just before, he mentions "*the heretical sense of the aforesaid Chapters*" as one of the reasons why Cyril and Memnon should be deposed.

And so the *Vote* or *Sentence* of the Conventicle of the Forty-three speaks of Cyril and Memnon as using "*a heretical mind,*" and asserts that those Chapters "*agree with the misbelief and impiety of Apolinarius and of Arius and of Eunomius,*" and gives this as one of the reasons for the deposition of their author and his chief co-worker, Memnon. For, I would add, Memnon had agreed with Cyril and been his great helper under God; and this Vote or Sentence excommunicates all the rest of the Ecumenical Synod "*till * * * they anathematize the heretical Chapters put forth by Cyril, the Bishop of Alexandria, which oppose the Evangelic and Apostolic Doctrine.*"

And throughout these Acts, so full of misrepresentation and heresy, it is always taken for granted, or implied, that the Twelve Chapters are opposed to the faith of Nicaea and its Creed. In place after place it is taught that the Nestorian, the Man-Serving and Incarnation-denying sense of that Creed is right, and the Orthodox sense of it is wrong.

There was great danger to the Church, therefore, in this gathering, small as it was, for it represented what the Court of Constantinople wanted in the

---

(18). Or, "*suspended from Communion.*"

(19). As though it had not been: and as though the Nestorian heresies of denial of the Incarnation, of Man-Worship, and of Cannibalism on the Eucharist were the *accurate* faith!

beginning as to the non-deposition of Nestorius; and the Emperor's representative and adviser, Count Candidian, was strongly on its side. And it knew its secular strength, and hoped through it to win victory in the end for its soul destroying errors—which, on the Incarnation, were Jewish, and on the worship of Christ's *humanity, a creature*, were *pagan*, as they were on the Eucharist also.

DOCUMENT XII. IN ALL.
(*Document X. in Coleti.*)

This is a remarkable piece of brazen-faced impudence, in which the Apostatic Conventicle of the Forty Three inform the Two Hundred of the Orthodox Synod that they (the 43) have excommunicated them, on account of their co-operation with Cyril and Memnon, who, it tells them, are deposed, because when they, the 43, had left the door of kindness open to them, the 200, they had not run forward and entreated to be delivered from the bonds of excommunication—but still held with Cyril and Memnon. They warn them, therefore, that unless they quickly repent, and withdraw from Cyril's society, and promise to hold fast the faith (1) of the blessed Fathers who met at Nicaea, and unless they be willing to make up a Synod with them quietly and without any uproar, they will have to blame themselves, and not the one-sixth of the Synod who were with John of Antioch (2), who, by the way, mean by all this, that unless they accept their perverted interpretation of the Nicaean Creed and renounce Cyril's Twelve Chapters read in their First Act and go over to the erring course of these sympathizers with Nestorius, the Man-Server, they will induce the secular government to override the Decisions of five-sixths of the Synod canonically and regularly expressed. This, stripped of high sounding and deceptive wording, is the gist of this unworthy Document. It is an illustration of the principle of a ridiculously acting minority, making themselves the whole, as for instance, in the proclamation of the three tailors of Tooley Street, London, "*We, the people of England.*"

DOCUMENT XIII. IN ALL.
(*Document XI. in Coleti.*)

This is a Letter of the Apostatic Council of the Forty Three in sympathy with the unbeliever and creature-server, Nestorius, to the Emperor Theodosius II., in which they tell him what they have done, and give the cause of the lateness and slowness of the arrival of John, Bishop of Antioch, at Ephesus.

They state that in conformity with the Emperors' Letters they arrived at Ephesus and found Church affairs full of confusion and of intestine war by the plotting of Cyril and Memnon, that they had assembled a multitude of rustics, an assertion which may not be true, but if true, is easily explained by the fact that as the sympathizers with the Man-Server Nestorius were aiming to put

---

(1). Greek, τὴν . . . πίστιν.

(2). Coleti *Conc.*, tom. 3, col. 1129.

Memnon of Ephesus, Cyril's strong and efficient right hand man, out of his see for his stand for God's anti-creature serving faith against heresy, and as they had, seemingly, the power to do it, because Count Candidian with the troops under his orders were certainly on their side, the people rose for their Bishop, and for the worship of God alone, which he represented, as the English people rose for their Bishops and for the same tenet in 1688, and drove James II. out of England for actions similar to those of John of Antioch and Candidian. And, as is the wont of infidelizing and paganizing heretics, they lay on the contenders for God's truth the commotions, which, they themselves, by their own evil conduct had stirred up, and which were necessary to resist their wicked errors. James II. and his friends gave similar accounts of the conduct of the English people and the English Bishops who resisted him. Then John and the Forty Two with him complain that the Orthodox would not help them to celebrate the Pentecostal festival, which was the ordinary treatment given to sympathizers and co-workers with heresy, when they wished to make a minority Synod, or were likely to do so, and represent it as the voice of the whole. Then they complain, as before, that they had been shut out of the Churches and martyries, which, by the way, being sympathizers with a condemned heretic, they had by Church law no right to use. Furthermore, few of them were in Ephesus at Pentecost, certainly not John of Antioch.

Then they complain further that the Orthodox party had held a Synod, which they brand as contrary to the Canons, which is a falsehood; and as contrary to the Emperor's Decrees, notwithstanding the efforts of Count Candidian to stop them, and to induce them to await the arrival of the rest of the Bishops and then to hold the Synod in accordance with the Emperor's Letters, to which they seem never tired of referring, as though Emperors had power to make Bishops, who had waited sixteen days beyond the time set by themselves, wait still longer, when the great bulk were on the ground already, and while it was by no means certain that John and his party were not purposely delaying in order to break up the Council. Then they state in effect that Cyril had sent word to John of Antioch two days before the Session of the Orthodox Synod was held that all the Synod were awaiting his arrival, as, it may be added, they certainly were; but as he did not come, and as he himself had sent word to Cyril to go on without him if he delayed, a fact which John finds it convenient to say nothing about here, Cyril and four-fifths of the Synod did so. Then they go on to say that they have deposed Cyril and Memnon, because of these alleged faults, and have excommunicated the rest of the Ecumenical Synod till they should condemn the Twelve Chapters, which were evidently a sore thing for them, for they write against them constantly. I quote this place in full:

"*Wherefore, we have deposed both the aforesaid, Cyril and Memnon,* and have made them aliens from every ecclesiastical function, and have excommunicated the rest who shared that transgression with them *until they reject and anathematize the Chapters sent forth by Cyril, which are full of the misbelief* of Apolinarius, and of Eunomius, and of Arius, and, in accordance with the Letter of your Piety, sit together in common with us, and quietly and accurately examine with us the questions [agitated] and confirm the pious doctrine of the Fathers" (1.)

Then, John of Antioch, who here, as in one other place of this document, speaks of himself in the singular, gives his reasons for being late at the Synod. They are, 1, the distance which he makes forty stopping places or lodgings,— though he avers that he had travelled without cessation to be there. The marginal annotator in Coleti accuses him of exaggerating the length of the distance. The next, 2, were circumstances of various kinds, namely, the famine at Antioch, the troubles among the people there, and the copious rains and the danger to it from the torrents, which had detained them in that city not a few days (2.)

Neither Cyril nor the Ecumenical Synod seem to have regarded John's statements as sincere and entirely trustworthy, but rather as evasive and delusive. See above.

DOCUMENT XIV. IN ALL.
(*Document XII. in Coleti.*)

This is a Letter of John of Antioch and his Synod of the Forty Three to the Clergy of Constantinople, in which they in effect teach them that Nestorius is still their Bishop, for they regard all done in Act I. of the Third Ecumenical Synod, the only one yet held, as null and void and criminal.

The Document commences by saying to them that they doubtless have learned of what they term the things against right and against law, which had been done by Cyril the Alexandrian and Memnon the Ephesian, and those with them, in their Session contrary to the Letter of the Emperors, and that, therefore, they had deemed it necessary to inform them, that all their audacious doings were, to use a prophet's language (1), *a spider's web;* and that Cyril and Memnon, who had dared to do those things, as having been authors of the disorder and transgression of law, had been deposed by John of Antioch and his Synod, and made aliens from the Episcopate, and then they add:

"*And we have excommunicated* those who chose to co-sit with them, until they see their own fault, and anathematize the heretical Chapters of Cyril the Alexandrian, and sincerely accept the faith of the holy Fathers, who were gathered at Nicaea in Bithynia. Let no one, therefore, of those who are wont to do such things trouble your Piety, for, as we have already said, their audacious acts contrary to law, have no force. And we have made this known to our pious and Christ-loving Emperor, and to the most magnificent and most glorious Archons (2)."

(1). Coleti *Conc.*, tom. 3, col. 1132.
(2). Ibid.

(1). Isaiah lix., 5.
(2). Coleti *Conc.*, tom. 3, col. 1132: ἄρχουσι, translated in the parallel column by "*principibus.*" We may render it "rulers."

DOCUMENT XV. IN ALL.
(*Document XIII. in Coleti.*)

This is an Epistle of John of Antioch and the rest of the Apostatic Synod of the Forty Three to the Senate in Constantinople.

They tell the Senate, perhaps somewhat hypocritically, that they did not wish to cut off any bad members of the body, such as they deemed Cyril and Memnon to be, but they had been compelled to do so, in order to preserve the sound parts of the body; that Cyril of Alexandria and Memnon of Ephesus had done countless and terrible things against the Church of God, that they had filled the city and the holy Synod with uproar and trouble, that they had made use of Egyptian seamen and Asiatic rustics as ministers of their tyranny, that they had not suffered the Letter of the Emperors (an allusion, probably, to their refusal to read in Act I. that Second Letter of the Emperors, which, in effect, forbade them to depose Nestorius), that they had not obeyed the admonitions nor the commands of Count Candidian (as though in matters of faith they were bound to obey that sympathizer with Nestorius); that they had brought confusion into the venerable things of religion, that though *they had come from afar with a strong desire to clasp* [or *to embrace*] *all the chests or coffins of the holy martyrs* (1), (which, by the way, shows that they were relic worshippers), they were not allowed to do so, but had been shut out of the Churches and martyries; and that, therefore, they had deposed the aforesaid Cyril and Memnon, and excommunicated the Bishops of the Synod who had acted with them until they should "*feel their fault, cease from their heretical misbelief, and admit the faith of the holy Fathers, who had met at Nicaea in Bithynia,*" and co-sit with them in accordance with the Letter of the Emperors, which, by the way, I would add, forbade the deposition of Nestorius; in other words, these sympathizers with creature-service and with error this about one-sixth of the Synod asked the other five-sixths of it to regard their noble action in Act I. of the Ecumenical Synod as null and void and criminal, and it anathematized the five-sixths till they should accept their heretical sense of the Nicaean faith—in which case they gravely add that they are disposed to be merciful to the said five-sixths of the Synod!! They hoped that the strong leaders, Cyril and Memnon, being out of the way, they could drive the rest of the Bishops like a flock of sheep, over to heresy, as had been the case, I would add, in the Arian controversy when the Arian creature-servers had, by the aid of the imperial power, driven for the time being one or more Councils

---

(1). Coleti *Conc.*, tom. 3, col. 1133, where John of Antioch and the rest of the Forty-three, speak of themselves as ἐφιεμένοις δὲ πάσας τὰς τῶν ἁγ.ων καὶ καλλινίκων μαρτύρων περιπτύξασθαι λάρνακας.

The Second Canon of the First Council of Carthage in A. D. 348, is golden on that point, for it commands the bodies of martyrs to be buried and forbids to worship them. Alas! that superstitious and creature-serving Africa brought the curse on itself by not keeping to it. The penalties by that Canon were for clerics deposition; for laics, being brought to penance, evidently much as those who had fallen away to idolatry were by the Canons of the First Ecumenical Synod.

composed mainly of the Orthodox, as for example, Ariminum, into what was practically the Arian fold. And so they end. See Athanasius *on the Councils at Ariminum and Seleucia in the Oxford translation*, pages 125, 158.

DOCUMENT XVI. IN ALL.
(*Document XIV. in Coleti.*)

This is an Epistle of John of Antioch and of his little Council to the laity, that is, the people of Constantinople. It has the wearisome and slanderous complaints against Cyril of Alexandria and Memnon of Ephesus of making trouble, whereas John's friend, Nestorius, had done that by corrupting the faith and by bringing in error on the Incarnation, and by Creature-Service, and by Cannibalism in the Eucharist; and Cyril and Memnon merely did their duty as God's watchmen against it. It tells the Constantinopolitans, evidently with the intention to bolster up the justly deposed Nestorius and to get them to look upon him still as their Bishop, as to its writers, John's party, as follows:

"*Therefore we deemed it necessary to prepare your souls, by a letter, that ye should not be deceived by vain rumors and lose heart, and take trouble in your thoughts.*" Then it falsely accuses Cyril of Alexandria, whom it calls, somewhat spitefully, "*the Egyptian,*" of being actuated in what he had done by a desire to screen his Twelve Chapters from investigation; and it charges Memnon with recklessness.

"*For,*" say these false accusers, "*they feared, the Egyptian, lest we might investigate the Chapters of his heretical misbelief, which agree with the impiety of Apollinarius, and condemn him as a heretic; the other* [Memnon, *feared*] *in regard to common reports as to the rest of his recklessness which were repeated throughout the city.*" Then they say that Cyril had fifty Egyptian Bishops and Memnon more than thirty Asiatic Prelates, for we are to remember that Ephesus was at this time the chief or Exarchal (Canon IX. of Chalcedon for the East) or Patriarchal See of the civil Diocese of Asia Minor, and that it was not till the Fourth Ecumenical Synod, about twenty years later, that that Diocese was subjected to Constantinople, by its XXVIIIth Canon; this Document adds that there were some others with Cyril's Synod: there certainly were, I will add right here, for when the First Session of the Orthodox Synod commenced there were one hundred and sixty Bishops present, and, at the close of that First Act, one hundred and ninety-eight, but the fact that about five-sixths of the Bishops were present at the regular Synod is not stated in full; and then they accuse Cyril and Memnon of deceiving the Bishops and terrifying them, of not being willing to wait for the arrival of all the Bishops, though they leave out of sight the fact that they had waited fifteen days of our time, beyond the time set in the Emperors' decree, and that it was not their fault that John and his were not on hand, and that those of the heretical party in Ephesus and on the way thither were not, all told, more than about a sixth of the Synod, and that the unjust appeal to fear and the deception were wholly on their own side, for they had the Emperor and Candidian; then comes the same worn and threadbare falsehood that Cyril and Memnon had despised the Church's Canons and acted in a way out of place and against the law; that they had sent Egyptian seamen and clerics and Asiatic rustics to the abodes of the Bishops and threatened them with ruin, and had terrified the more unsound, and written on the outside of houses so as to make them conspicuous for attack, and had compelled them to agree with what had been lawlessly done by them, from which last expression we see that it can not refer to any of the one hundred and sixty who were at the beginning of the Synod, but to some who were not so present, but came after its close to subscribe: but the lie is given to these falsifications and special pleadings of a Creature-Serving coterie by the fact that through thick and thin the Orthodox Bishops stuck to Cyril and Memnon, even when they were cast into prison, and if they threatened ecclesiastical ruin in the sense of deposition and excommunication to such of the heretical Prelates as refused to sign their manly vindication of the Incarnation, and their condemnation of Man-Service and of Cannibalism in the Eucharist, they did only what it was their duty to do and as the Universal Church in its sound period thereafter ever did, and as it should do now to every such false apostle (1). Then the Synod of the Apostasy tell the laity of Constantinople that they had deposed Cyril and Memnon and excommunicated the rest of the Bishops who held with them, till, they add, *"they may be willing to anathematize the Chapters sent forth by Cyril and those things which are alien to the Apostolic and Evangelic teaching, and to return to the faith of the Holy Fathers who met in Nicaea in Bithynia,"* and in accordance with the Letter of the Emperors, which, I will add, forbade Nestorius to be deposed, meet with John and his fellow-heretics and in effect, to strip the matter of all verbiage, agree with their errors. And so they end this precious barefaced Document of the One-sixth against the Five-sixths, of the false against the true.

DOCUMENT XVII. IN ALL.

(*Document XV. in Coleti.*)

This is the last of the Documents found between Acts I. and II. of Ephesus, in the arrangement of Coleti. Act II. of the Orthodox Synod immediately follows it.

It is a report of John and his fellow-heretics of "*the Apostatic Synod,*" as the heading terms it, of the Forty Three, to the Empress. It commences with the old threadbare and senseless complaints against Cyril, Memnon, and five-sixths of the Ecumenical Synod for not waiting for John and his fellow sympathizers with Nestorius in his errors. It falsely asserts that they were bound by the Church Canons to do so, and then it adds that the Decrees of the Emperors bound them so to do, though it fails to mention the fact that the Orthodox had waited sixteen days, fifteen in our time, after the day set, for John of Antioch and his friends; that they had held a Synod by themselves when they had learned that John and his party were only about three days' journey off, which is a deceptive statement, for Cyril and the Orthodox, five-sixths of the Council, show that they did not know for sure that John would ever come, and

(1). II. Cor. xi., 13; Galat. i., 7, 8, 9; II. Peter ii., 1-22, and Rev. ii., 2.

they suspected that he would not, in order to defeat any Council being held, for the Bishops of the Five-Sixths were clamoring against the delay, and some had died, others were sick, and others who had come in time and had expected the business to be attended to punctually, had been kept in idleness by the fault of John and his, and so had spent their money in waiting, and from motives of poverty must soon return and leave only a small number present, not enough to represent the whole Church. John and his fellow sympathizers with heresy fail also to state another fact of much importance and which makes against him, and that is, that he had sent word himself, as is shown above by Cyril, to go on with the business of the Synod if they did not arrive (1). Then John and his little Synod accuse the Ecumenical Synod of having in their First Act done things reckless and lawless and out of place ; and that too when "*Count Candidian, who,*" it adds,"*had been sent for the sake of keeping good order by our most pious and Christ loving Emperors, had commanded* [or "admonished"] *them both by word and by writing to wait for the most dear-to-God Bishops who had been called together, and not to make any innovation regarding the pious faith, but to obey the Decrees of our Emperors who hold the godly opinions.*" (2). The "*good order*" here referred to was to favor Nestorius, the Emperor Theodosius' own Bishop, and oppose Cyril whom he had already censured before the opening of the Council ; and the opinions which the heretic John would deem "*godly*" were pronounced heretical in the First Act of the Third Ecumenical Synod. But John and his little company evidently thought that by means of *the secular power* they would override the Ecumenical Synod and by going through the unauthorized farce of deposing Cyril and Memnon and excommunicating the rest of the Five-Sixths scare them, and force their necks under the yoke of their unbelief and Man-Service and Cannibalism.

"*But,*" they continue, "*notwithstanding their*" [the Orthodox Synod] "*hearing the Imperial Letter and the counsels of the most magnificent Count Candidian, they thought but little of good order, but 'they hatch cockatrices' eggs and weave the spider's web,' as the prophet says, ' but he who was about to eat one of their eggs, has found it rottenness when he has broken it ; and there is a basilisk in it;' wherefore we boldly cry out, 'Their web shall not be for a mantle, nor are they clothed with the works of their own hands.'*" (3). These doleful prophecies of sympathizers with fundamental errors came true, not as they wished of the work of the Orthodox, but of their own.

Next they repeat the complaint that they had been shut out of the Churches and martyries, which is not wonderful considering that they were aiding and abetting a condemned heretic, and really held some if not all of his heresies : and it is difficult to see how Memnon could have let them use any of them for the purposes of their heresy without incurring fearful guilt himself, undoing his own work and that of the Synod, exposing the souls of his people to their corrupting influence, and rendering himself liable to deposition as an

---

(1). See vol. I. of *Ephesus* in this Set, pages l., li. Compare id., page 41, note 102.
(2). Coleti *Conc.*, tom. 3, col. 1137.
(3). Isaiah lix , 5, 6, Septuagint.

enemy of God and of the Universal Church which had already condemned their errors. And it was absurd in them to expect him so to do. And let us remember that by the Canons as well as by the New Testament, the Bishop alone had supreme control over all the possessions of the Church. See Canon XXVI. of the Fourth World Synod, and Canons XXIV. and XXV. of Antioch, which are approved by it. Compare Apostolic Canons XL. and XLI.

Then these condemned heretics make the complaint that they had not been permitted to celebrate Pentecost, but they could not expect to be allowed to do that in their collective capacity, which is meant, in Memnon's Orthodox Churches, while themselves on trial for heresy. Moreover there were laws against heretics, and no one had been more fierce in enforcing those enactments than Nestorius himself, as the Ecclesiastical Historian Socrates (the Novatian?) tells us (4).

And when the Nestorian party got power in Persia they invoked the aid of the unbelieving secular powers, and almost utterly exterminated Orthodoxy there (5), and many were put to death by those powers thus stirred up by them (6).

Then they repeat the complaint that persons had been sent to the houses of Bishops and had threatened them with ruinous things, (perhaps they mean the canonical punishments of deposition and excommunication usually enforced against Bishops of the Church who did not come up *to the help of the Lord against the mighty* (7) but sympathized with heresy), and so they "*had compelled*" some "*to subscribe to their unlawful and daring doings;*" (this seems to refer to some few, if there be any truth in it at all, who subscribed after the one hundred and ninety eight had subscribed to Act I. of the Ecumenical Synod.)

Therefore, they say, they had deposed Cyril of Alexandria and Memnon, and they had furthermore excommunicated the rest of the Bishops who sided with them, "*till,*" they add, "*they come to a sense of their own wounds, and repent sincerely, and anathematize the heretical Chapters of Cyril which agree with the impiety of Apolinarius* (8), *and of Arius, and of Eunomius, and reinstate the faith of the holy Fathers who had been gathered in Nicaea,*" and hold a Synod with them "in accordance with the pious Decrees of our Christ-loving Emperors," which, in effect, forbade the deposition of Nestorius, and, in effect, agreed with them in formulating their heresies as truth. And so they end (9). This is cheek with a vengeance! A comparative handful, whose heresies are condemned in Act I. of Ephesus, and whose leader, Nestorius, was deposed there for his heresies, presume to judge and condemn the Third Ecumenical Council

---

(4). Socrates' *Eccl. Hist.*, Book VII., chapters 29 and 31.
(5). See under *Nestorians* in *McClintock and Strong's Cyclopaedia*, and in *Murdock's Mosheim's Eccl. Hist.*, under *Nestorians* in the index to vol. I.
(6). See under "*Barsumas the Nestorian*" in *Smith and Wace's Dict. of Christian Biogr.*, and the reference to Gibbon there.
(7). Judges v., 23.
(8). This is the ordinary spelling of this name in the Council of Ephesus and in the Documents foregoing. A more common spelling among us is Apollinaris.
(9). Coleti *Conc.*, tom. 3, col. 1137 and after.

because it will not accept his Anti-Incarnation sense of the Nicene Creed and their heresies of Man-Worship and Cannibalism. Cyril's Orthodox sense of that Symbol is set forth in his two Epistles received by the Council and approved by it (vol. I. of *Ephesus*, pages 50-154, and pages 204-358). Nestorius' perversion of the sense of that Creed, and the Third Synod's condemnation of it are in id., pages 154-178.

I would add as to the foregoing Documents from John of Antioch and his "*Apostatic Synod*,"

1. That none of them ever mentions the expression *Bringer-Forth of God* (θεοτόκος), a thing which implies, what we shall see more fully developed hereafter, that they were not all agreed as to it.

But, 2, they oppose with might and main Cyril of Alexandria's Twelve Chapters and the doctrines which they contain, which they slanderously accuse of agreeing with the misbelief and impiety of Apolinarius, and of Arius, and of Eunomius. These were their great bugbear. One of their number, Theodoret, Bishop of Cyrus, at the instance of his Patriarch, John of Antioch, had already written against them. And Cyril had replied to him. It was plain that Cyril was opposed to serving the mere humanity of Christ or any thing but God, and he would serve Him *absolutely only*, *not relatively* (10), whereas it was equally clear that Theodoret and the Orientals of his, the dominant party East, were servers of that separate humanity *relatively* by bowing, the most common act of religious worship, (for we bow in prayer, etc. (11),) and probably by other acts of religious service such as prayer, thanksgiving, kneeling, etc. Besides, on the Eucharist, that is, on the Thanksgiving, a wide difference had developed itself, Theodoret holding to the real presence of the substances of the human body and blood of Christ in the Eucharist and to worshipping them there, and to the Cannibalism of eating human flesh and drinking human blood there, even the human flesh and blood of Christ's humanity; and Cyril denying all three, and advocating the spiritual "*energy*" view. Besides he denied the eating of Christ's Divinity in the rite, and he denied also the real presence of the Substance of Christ's Divinity in the Eucharist at all, and admitted only His grace by His Spirit which however he deemed effective, blessed and saving. In other words, Cyril held that there is no real substance either of Christ's Divinity or of His human flesh and blood in the Lord's Supper. But the bread and wine remaining unchanged as to their substances after consecration, become by it a peculiar flesh and blood, not of Christ's humanity at all, but of God the Word, who indwells them as instruments of grace and pledges of salvation, not by the Substance of His Divinity, but by His quickening and sanctifying grace only so that there is nothing at all to worship in the rite.

3. On the Incarnation, judging from the differences among the Orientals of John's Patriarchate as to receiving the expression "*Bringer-Forth of God*,"

---

(10). See vol. I. of *Ephesus* in this Set, page 79, note 183; page 295, note 582; note 679, pages 332-362; pages 404, 405, note, and pages 459-467 and especially note 949, pages 461-463.

(11). Ibid.

there was a division ; for while some might admit it, others were moved by the authority of Diodore of Tarsus and Theodore of Mopsuestia, whom they deemed great teachers, and of whom as being of their Patriarchate they were proud. And so they were inclined to deny that doctrine of salvation. See in proof vol. I. of *Ephesus* in this Set, pages 637-639 under "*Nestorius and his Heresies, 1*," and see in the same *Index* under *Diodore of Tarsus and Theodore of Mopsuestia*.

All those heresies,

A, of denial of the Inman ;

B, of Man-Worship, and

C, of the real presence in the Eucharist of the substances of Christ's humanity,

D, of their being worshipped there, and

E, of their being eaten and drunk there, are condemned and anathematized in Cyril's XII. Chapters and in his *Long Epistle* of which they form part. They are all condemned also in his *Shorter Epistle*, except the heresy of the real substances presence, and the Cannibalism of eating them there, which are not treated of in the *Shorter*.

They are all asserted by Nestorius in his Ecumenically condemned XX. "*Blasphemies*" on pages 449-504, vol. I. of *Ephesus* in this set. Compare Note F on pages 529-551.

For example, he denies the Incarnation in his Blasphemies 1, 2, 3 and 4, on pages 449-458.

He asserts the relative worship of Christ's humanity in Blasphemies 5, 6 and 7, on pages 458-460, id., by applying the name *God* to that mere creature because of his relation to God the Word, and in Blasphemies 8, 10 and 14, pages 461-467, by bowing to that mere creature; and, in Blasphemy 18, pages 472-474, he, in effect, asserts the eating of the substance of Christ's human flesh and the drinking of the substance of His human blood, and, of course, of their real presence for that purpose. And as we see in the note on pages 280, 281, 282 and 285, Nestorius' chief champion, Theodoret, affirms the worship of Christ's human flesh and blood. And such, I presume, was Nestorius' view also. And Cyril, in his two Epistles which were adopted by the whole Church in the Third Ecumenical Council, teaches that Christ's mere humanity, being a creature, can not be worshipped. See in proof the *Shorter* of those Epistles, in vol. I. of *Ephesus* in this Set, pages 79-85, text, and the notes there, especially note 183, and see also the *Longer Epistle*, id., pages 221-224, text, and the notes there, and Cyril's Anathema VIII. on pages 331 and 332, where we see that it also forms part of Cyril's *Longer Epistle*. And those Epistles, being approved by the Universal Church at Ephesus, A. D. 431, their utterances against Man-Worship, and against all Real Presence views on the Eucharist, and all Cannibal views on that rite, and against Nestorius' denial of the Incarnation, are now as much a part of the Universal Church's faith as the Nicene Creed is, or the Constantinopolitan, for they all rest for their authority on the same basis, that is, on their approval and adoption by the whole

Church in an Ecumenical Council defining with the Christ-promised aid of the Holy Ghost (John xiv., 16, 17; Matt. xxviii., 19, 20, and I. Tim. iii., 15; Matt. xvi., 18; Eph. ii., 20, compare Rev. xxi., 14, and see Matt. xviii., 15 to 19.) All are bound on us under pain of deposition and anathema. On pages 205-208, vol. I. of *Ephesus*, I have shown how thoroughly the Universal Church has approved Cyril's *Long Epistle* of which the XII. Chapters form part.

And Nestorius was deposed for his "*Blasphemies*" against them, including those just mentioned: see vol. I. of *Ephesus*, pages 449, 486-488, and 503 and 504.

4. As we see by page 59 of this volume, John of Antioch and his *Apostatic Synod* had descended so low in the relative worship of creatures as to worship relics!

5. As to the complaints of John and his fellow-heretics against the Orthodox, it will suffice to say that their statements are evidently made for a purpose and are exaggerated, and some of them are contradicted by the Orthodox Documents above and are evidently false. They abound in that form of deception which is called *suppression of truth* (suppressio veri).

There is no proof that any one of them suffered any violence, but there is proof in their own documents above that they wished to defeat the utterance of the great majority of the Synod, and, by the aid of the secular power, force them to embrace their heresies. And after this we shall find them bringing about the imprisonment of Cyril and Memnon. Nestorius' party had discourteously treated and threatened the Bishops who went to him as the messengers of the Council. And if some of them with Candidian were thrust out of the Ecumenical Synod for persistently trying to hinder it from doing business, it was their own fault, for no legislative body permits such conduct. There does not appear to have been any actual violence, as yet, but they were appealing to it themselves in order to tyrannize over the faith of about five-sixths of the Synod. And we shall find them after this barring the approach to the Emperor's ears in order to get a snap judgment from him against them and so to undo their holy and blessed work.

ACT SECOND.

A COPY OF THE RECORD OF WHAT WAS DONE IN THE PRESENCE OF THE BISHOPS AND PRESBYTERS (1) WHO CAME FROM ROME.

In the time of (2) the consulship of our Masters, Flavius Theodosius, Consul for the thirteenth time, and Flavius Valentinian, Consul for the third time, the ever August ones, on the sixth day before the Ides of July (3), which is the sixteenth of [the month] Epiphi according to the Egyptians, the Synod being assembled in the Metropolis of the Ephesians by the decree of the most religious and Christ-loving Emperors, and there having taken their seats in the episcopal residence of the most dear to God Bishop Memnon, the most dear to God Bishops, Cyril of Alexandria, who also managed the place of Celestine the most holy and most devoted Archbishop of the Church of the Romans, and Juvenal of Jerusalem, and Memnon of the City of the Ephesians, and Flavian of Philippi who held also the place of Rufus the most religious Bishop of the Thessalonians, and Theodotus of Ancyra in the First Galatia, and Firmus of Caesarea in the First Cappadocia, and all the fore-arranged Bishops in their standing in the Minutes, and Besula a deacon of Carthage; there came in from the West and co-sat down, the most dear to God, and most God-revering Bishops and Ambassadors (4), Arcadius and Pro-

---

NOTE 1.—As there was only one Presbyter, Philip, this looks like an error for "and the Presbyter."

NOTE 2.—Τοῖς μετὰ τὴν ὑπατείαν τῶν δεσποτῶν ἡμῶν· On this idiom see a note above at the beginning of Act 1, (note 19, page 19, vol. 1, of Chrystal's translation of *Ephesus.*)

NOTE 3.—That is July 10, 431. The first session had been held on what moderns term June 22, 431.

NOTE 4.—Greek, πρεσβευτῶν· The Latin in Harduin. Conc., tom 1, col. 1466, for this is "*legatis.*"

jectus, and the most dear to God Philip a Presbyter (1) of the Apostolic Throne (2) and Legate (3).

Translation of the Statement:

Philip a Presbyter and an Ambassador (4) of the Apostolic

NOTE 1.—The word "*Presbyter,*" that is *Elder*, is lacking in Coleti but is in the *Collectio Regia.*

NOTE 2.—Rome is here called "*the Apostolic Throne*," according to its title among Westerns, because it was the only Apostolic Throne in the West. There were quite a number in the East, as for instance, Corinth, Thessalonica, Ephesus, Smyrna, Jerusalem, Antioch, etc.

NOTE 3.—Greek; ληγάτου.

NOTE 4.—Greek, πρεσβευτής· This *translation* and those following were evidently made from the Latin into Greek, which seems to have been understood by all the Orientals present. The Greek here uses two words, πρεσβευτής, and ληγάτου, the latter evidently a Grecized form of the Latin *legati.* But the Latin translation uses *legatus* as the rendering for both Greek terms. However, as the Greek is the form approved by the Synod here, and therefore authoritative, and as it makes a distinction and uses two Greek terms where the Latin does but one, we here follow it by rendering πρεσβευτής, by *ambassador* and ληγᾶτος, by *legate.* But πρεσβευτής may be rendered *deputy* also, as well as *intermediary.* Many things in the way of titles in these Acts are Byzantine and stilted, and so different from the New Testament! We here mention it but cannot stop to refer to all such trash; but the reader can see it often elsewhere for himself. In a future Seventh Synod this should be corrected and conformed to God's Word, which is given for correction, II. Tim. iii., 16. We repeat what we have said elsewhere that what we prize in the Six World Councils is not such evils, but *the final Decisions themselves* which, amid all that was human and faulty and condemnable, were guided by the Holy Spirit. See *Titles* in *Ephesus* in this set, vol. I, page 659, and under θεῶς in Sophocles' Greek Lexicon, and in his Glossary of Later and Byzantine Greek. Among the Greeks of Cyril's day, the eternal Spirit of God is only the "*Holy* Ghost," but mortal, sinful men like Bishops as above are "*most holy*," etc.; God is *divine*", and the sinful Emperor is "*most divine,*" and his palace and his letters are "*divine*". See Sophocles as above. When any such flattering and wicked titles are used of Rome she has made the most of them. and perverted them to bolster up her pretensions to sway which are forbidden in the Canons of the first Four Ecumenical Councils, and to infallibility which are condemned by the Sixth Synod. We must use no title except it be in the New Testament. Flattering titles are forbidden in Scripture (1. Thess. ii., 5; Job xvii., 5; Job xxxii; 21. 22; Psalm xii., 2, 3; Prov. xxvi., 28), and lead to insincerity, more flattering, and lying, and scandal, and everlasting ruin (**Rev.** xxi., 8).

Throne said: We thank the Holy and August Trinity, that it hath deemed unworthy us worthy of your Holy Assembly.

Accordingly our most holy and most blessed Father Celestine, the Bishop of the Apostolic See, put forth a Decision by his own letter to the holy and most religious man Cyril, the Bishop of the Church of the Alexandrians, which letter has been brought to your Holy Assembly; (1) and now, furthermore, he hath sent through us a letter to the Piety of you all to strengthen the Universal Faith (2), which having [already] been fitly shown by us privately, command to be read to the Holy Synod and to be incorporated into the ecclesiastical Minutes.

NOTE 1.—That Epistle of Celestine to Cyril bears date August 11, A. D., 430, and is number XI., in Tom. 50, of Migne's *Patrologia Latina*, col. 459-464. It commits to Cyril his place, and asks him to co-join his authority to Cyril's own, and like Celestine's Letter to Nestorius read in Act I., of *Ephesus* (pages 197-203, vol. 1, of Chrystal's translation) it commissions Cyril to warn him that unless within ten days after that warning reaches him (Nestorius), he condemns by a written confession his own evil preachings, and gives positive assurance that he himself holds fast to the faith on the birth of Christ our God, which both the Church of the Romans and the Church of thy Holiness, and the whole body of those consecrated to God's service holds fast to, that he (Cyril) should at once make provision for his (Nestorius') Church, and know that he (Nestorius) is to be by all means removed from our body, because he is unwilling to receive the treatment of [spiritual] physicians, and because he is pestilential and is wickedly hastening to his own perdition and the perdition of all who have been entrusted to him

NOTE 2.—Greek as in Harduin.Conc., tome I, col. 1465: Πάλαι μὲν οὖν ὁ ἁγιώτατος καὶ μακαριώτατος πάπας ἡμῶν Κελεστῖνος, ὁ τῆς ἀποστολικῆς καθέδρας ἐπίσκοπος, περὶ τῆς παρούσης ὑποθέσεως δι' ἐπιστολῶν ἑαυτοῦ πρὸς τὸν ἅγιον καὶ εὐλαβέστατον ἄνδρα τῆς Ἀλεξανδρέων ἐπίσκοπον ἐκκλησίας Κύριλλον ὥρισεν· ἅ τινα γράμματα τῷ ἁγίῳ ὑμῶν συλλόγῳ πεπόρισται· καὶ νῦν δὲ πρὸς βεβαίωσιν τῆς καθολικῆς πίστεως πρὸς τὴν πάντων ὑμῶν εὐλάβειαν δι' ἡμῶν γράμματα ἐξέπεμψεν, etc. In tome 50 of Migne's *Patrologia Latina*, are found two Epistles of Celestine to Cyril, one, Epistle XI., in Latin with the Greek in columns 459-464, which is genuine, and one, Epistle XVI., in columns 501-504, in Latin without the Greek, as to whose genuineness and authenticity I doubt. As the term ἐπιστολῶν, though plural, is sometimes used for the singular, as Liddell and Scott in their Greek Lexicon under ἐπιστολή inform us, I have deemed it safest to render it by the singular above in the text. Celestine in his *Epistle to Nestorius* read in Act I., of *Ephesus*, refers to his genuine Epistle to Cyril. See the reference on pages 197-203, vol. 1., Chrystal's translation of *Ephesus*, and the note last above.

Translation of the Statement:

Arcadius, Bishop, and Ambassador (1) *of the Church of the Romans said:* Let your Blessedness command that the Letter which has been brought to you from the holy and with all bowing named Father Celestine, Bishop of the Apostolic See, be read, from which your Blessedness will be able to know, what sort of care he has for all the Churches.

Translation of the Statement:

Projectus, Bishop and Ambassador (2) *of the Church of the Romans, said:* Let your Blessedness command that the letter brought to you from the holy and with all bowing (3) named Father Celestine, Bishop of the Apostolic See, be read, from which your Blessedness will be able to know what sort of care he has for all the Churches.

And after Cyril, the most holy and most dear to God Archbishop of the Church of the Alexandrians, had spoken as it reads next below, Siricius, a notary of the holy Universal Church of the City of the Romans, read [it].

Cyril, Bishop of Alexandria, said: Let the Letter received from Celestine the most holy and in all things most devoted Bishop of the holy Apostolic See of the Romans, be read with suitable honor, to the Holy Synod.

Siricius, a notary of the holy Universal (4) *Church of the City of the Romans, read* [it].

NOTE 1.—Greek, πρεσβευτής; its Latin translation in Hardouin here is *Legatus*.

NOTE 2.—Greek, πρεσβευτής.

NOTE 3.—καὶ μετὰ πάσης προσκυνήσεως ὀνομαζομένου πάπα Κελεστίνου· Alas! for such extravagant titles as we find used by all parties contrary to God's Word. The Byzantine and imperial compliments were anything but Christian simplicity. Celestine did well for the faith, but like a tyrant, tried to subjugate the Latin African Church to his See but failed; See Chrystal's Articles in *the Church Journal* (N. Y.) for 1870 on his attempt to get Appellate Jurisdiction there. And his Legates err against Christian simplicity in using flattering titles here.

NOTE 4.—The Roman Siricius, according to the custom of his local Church and of the whole West afterwards, uses the term καθολικῆς, that is *Universal* here in the sense of *Orthodox*. The Orientals generally used it in its strict Greek sense of *Universal*. Yet in translating Latin documents they sometimes preserved the Latin use of terms in them. Moreover, in section XVI., of the

And after it had been read in Latin, *Juvenal, Bishop of Jerusalem*, said,

Let the Letter which has been read, from Celestine, the most holy and most devoted Bishop of the Great Rome, and which contains what is pious and orthodox, be embodied in the Minutes.

All the most religious Bishops asked that the Epistle be translated and read.

Translation of the Statement:

Philip, a Presbyter of the Apostolic See and an Ambassador, said: Sufficient has been done to satisfy the custom of reading the Letter of the Apostolic See in Latin at first; and now likewise, since your Blessedness (1) demands that it be read in Greek also, it is necessary that sufficient be done to gratify the desire of your Holiness, and we have taken care to do that very thing, that is to say to have the Latin speech translated into Greek (2); command therefore that it be received and put into your ears.

Translation of the Statement :

Arcadius and Projectus, the most religious Bishops (3) *and Ambassadors said :*

Forasmuch as your Blessedness (3) has commanded that the Letter which has been brought shall come to the knowledge of all, because there are many of our holy brethren and Bishops, who do not know Latin, for that reason the Letter which has been brought

---

Martyrdom of Polycarp, he is called "*Bishop of the Universal Church in Smyrna*," ἐπίσκοπός τε τῆς ἐν Σμύρνῃ Καθολικῆς Ἐκκλησίας. According to Salmon's Article on Polycarp in Smith and Wace's *Dict. of Christ. Biogr.* this *Martyrdom* was written about A. D. 156. Compare Καθολικῃ, page 713, vol. 1, of Chrystal's translation of *Ephesus*.

NOTE 1.—More Anti-Scriptural titles.

NOTE 2.—The translation below of Celestine's letter was done therefore before Philip spoke, but *where* is not said, whether at Rome or at Ephesus or elsewhere, nor do we know exactly *when* it was done. The language however would seem most probably to indicate that it was done at Ephesus at the wish of the Easterns, and probably by Greeks.

NOTE 3.—More complimentary and extravagant titles contrary to the simplicity of the New Testament. Indeed that is a characteristic of these Acts. No wise Christian approves it or similar *obiter dicta* (things incidentally said) but only the final decisions as wrought with the promised guidance of the Spirit.

has been translated into Greek also, and if ye command, it shall be read.

Flavian, Bishop of Philippi, said: Let the translation which has been brought of the Epistle from the most dear to God and most holy Bishop of the most holy Church of the Romans (1) be received and read.

Peter, a Presbyter of Alexandria and Chief of [the] *Secretaries, read: Celestine to the Holy Synod, gathered in Ephesus, beloved and most longed for, wisheth joy in the Lord* (2).

NOTE 1.—More superlatives and flattering trash.

NOTE 2.—It does not appear that this letter of Celestine ever was read in any alleged local Roman Synod of A. D. 431, held before the Third Ecumenical. The Romanist Abbé Peltier in his "Dictionnaire des Conciles," under "Rome (Concile de) l'an 431," indeed states that Celestine assembled a local council at Rome in A. D. 431, confirmed what had been done in that of 430, (the outcome of which was his letter to Nestorius, which was read in its First Act); and then sent the two Bishops and the one Presbyter who represented him in Acts II. and III., of the Ecumenical Synod. But He says nothing of this second letter of Celestine's having been read in that second local Roman Council.

The Ecumenical Council, however, in their report to the Emperor at the end of the Third Act, speaking of the Roman legates, Arcadius, Projectus, and Philip, who arrived in time for the Second Act, say that they "*have made clear by the Letter the judgment of all the holy Synod in the West to the Synod here held,*" etc. This would imply that the Roman legates had told them that it represented the mind of all the Synods of the West, though it does not assert that it was written in any Western Synod. That it did represent the West on the Incarnation and on the great facts and doctrines involved is clear from the statement above and from all the facts. But as such Letters as to *their wording*, at Carthage and Rome were left after the Bishops of the Synod had expressed themselves in favor of Orthodoxy, to the Patriarch of each see, and were sometimes written by him after the council, we must not ascribe to them rashly any such *obiter dicta* as Celestine's wrong language on the worship of relics in this second Letter, which must have been offensive to the Ecumenical Synod, for they condemned the relative worship even of Christ's humanity. And its form was altered for the better before it was read in that Synod. It does not appear that all Bishops of the West had met at Rome at any time. I have found no proof that Abbé Peltier is right in asserting that Celestine gathered a council of Bishops at Rome in A. D. 431. On the contrary the above mentioned Epistle of Celestine was *individual* and *personal, not Synodical,* as is clear from its whole tone and especially its conclusion. It does not profess to be Synodical; and neither Mansi in his edition of the Councils, nor Hardouin in his, mentions any Council at Rome in A. D. 431. Indeed neither of them mentions any

The Synod of the Priests (1) makes clear (2) the presence of the Holy Ghost. For what is written is true, because the Truth cannot lie, for the following utterance is in the Gospel, [namely], '*Where two or three are gathered together in my name, there am I in the midst of them*' (3). As this is so, since the Holy Spirit is not absent even from so small a number, how much more do we believe that It (4) is "*in the midst*" now, where so great a multitude of the saints are gathered together, in one place? For a Synod in which we can see piety, as we read of the piety of that greatest Synod of the Apostles, is holy by the very fact of its own religiousness (5). For never as yet at any time does the Teacher, preached by them, fail

---

Council there on the Nestorian Controversy in A. D. 430, or 431, except the one in A. D. 430, whose decisions Celestine had uttered in his Synodal Epistle to Nestorius which was read in Act I., of Ephesus. Happily therefore we must not credit the Roman local Italian Council with the relic worshipping passage in the Epistle to the Bishops of this Council of *Ephesus*, but Celestine only himself. Furthermore, we know not the name of even one Bishop, except Celestine, who was present at the Council of Rome, A. D. 430 on the Nestorian heresies, nor a see there represented except Rome itself, nor whence even one of them came except Celestine himself.

We conclude therefore that the expression in the Report of the Council to the Emperors, "*All the Holy Synod of the West*," does not mean that all the Bishops of the West had gathered in one Synod, but that it means that all the Bishops of all the provincial Councils of the West so far as known to Celestine and his Legates had approved Orthodoxy. Perhaps also *Synod* is a copyist's error for the plural *Synods*.

Celestine's Epistle to the Synod of Ephesus, in Mansi, Hardouin, and in tome 50, Migne's *Patrologia Latina*, columns 505-512, is entirely without any signature, or any sign of one, except Celestine's own name at the beginning. We will show more fully further on the meaning of the expression "*All the Holy Synod of the West*" when we come to speak of the Report in which it stands, and that it favors no claim of Rome to dominate the Occident.

NOTE 1.—That is here, *Bishops*, for as all Christians are priests, (1. Peter ii., 5, 9, and Rev. i., 6), the Bishop is so also, and, by virtue of his office, so in an excellent sense.

NOTE 2.—Or "manifests," ἐμφανίζει.

NOTE 3.—Matt. xviii., 20.

NOTE 4.—That is, the Holy Ghost.

NOTE 5.—Καὶ γὰρ ἅγιόν ἐστι κατὰ τὸ οἰκεῖον σέβας συνέδριον ἐν ᾧ, καθάπερ ἐκείνης τῆς μεγίστης τῶν ἀποστόλων συνόδου, ὡς ἀνέγνωμεν, ἐστὶν ὁρᾶν τὴν εὐλάβειαν· *Coleti Conc. tom. iii., col. 1144.*

them. The Lord and Teacher was always with them. Aye, those taught were never deserted by their own Teacher. He Who sent them, was [ever] teaching them. He who said what they are to teach, was teaching them. He Who manifests Himself to His own Apostles was teaching them. Let those things be heard by all in common, Lords [and] Brethren, which the care for the entrusted doctrine has justly transmitted to us as an inheritance. By that care are bound those everywhere, even throughout all the world, who are in the succession from them, and who preach the Lord's name as it was enjoined on them to do, [in the following words], '*Go, disciple all the nations*' (1). Your Brotherliness (2) ought to notice, that it (3) has received a general (4) commandment: and He Who gave charge to them all concerning the faith and service, wished us all ourselves to do that thing. It is necessary that we should fitly follow our own Fathers, for we have all entered into their work; and let us who have succeeded to their honor, exhibit care for their teachings, after which, as the Apostle warns us, we are commanded to add no doctrine (5). The keeping of the things handed down is a not less honor than their ministry for the Teacher [Himself]. They sowed the seeds of the Faith. Let your care guard them and keep them safe, in order that the Advent of our Lord may find the fruitage uncorrupted and multiplied; the Lord by whom alone the coming to maturity of the fruit [of the labor] of the Apostles is manifested. For Paul, speaking to his own elect, said that it was not enough for himself to plant and to water, unless God gave the increase (6) and the fulness. Therefore we must be very earnest and labor that we may guard, by the common toil, the things entrusted to us and held together until now by apostolic succession. For we are asked to walk in accordance with the Apostle (7). For now it is not any person, but our faith which is put on trial. We must arm

---

NOTE 1.—Matt. xxviii , 19.
NOTE 2.—Greek, ἡ ὑμετέρα ἀδελφότης.
NOTE 3.—"*Your Brotherliness.*"
NOTE 4.—Greek, γενικὴν ἐντολήν.
NOTE 5.—Galat. i., 8, 9; Rom. xvi. 17; 1. Tim. i., 3.
NOTE 6.—1. Cor. iii., 6, 7.
NOTE 7.—Rom. viii , 4; Philip iii., 17-21.

ourselves with spiritual weapons, because the wars [now] stirred up concern souls, and the darts now shot forth (1) are those of words, in order that we may stand fast in the faith of our King. The blessed Paul now warns all engaged in this conflict (2), where he gave charge to Timothy to stand fast (3). Therefore the same place, the same matter, even now demands the same ministry. And let us now act and be earnest in this duty which it was enjoined on him to perform, that no one hold any other opinion, and that no one prolong questions arising from the present very great verbosity. As he himself commands (4), let us abide of one soul and have the same one mind, for that profits. Let us wish to do nothing from love of strife, nothing for the sake of foolish vain opinionatedness (5). Let all have [but] one soul, and one heart, for the faith which is [but] one is falsified and counterfeited (6). Let all the Synod, in common with us, be in affliction or rather lament on account of that fact. He who judges all the inhabited world is summoned into judgment (7)! He who shakes all the earth is made subject to [human] correction (8). The Redeemer is made subject to slander (9). Let your Brotherliness put on the whole armor of God (10).

NOTE 1.—Or "hurled."
NOTE 2.—Literally "*all there*, (ἐκεῖσε)
NOTE 3.—I. Tim. iv., 16; II. Tim. iii., 14.
NOTE 4.—Philip. ii., 2; Rom. xv , 6. Compare 1. Peter, iii., 8.
NOTE 5 —Philip. ii., 3.
NOTE 6.—Nestorianism, as being infidel on the great and essential tenet of the Incarnation, as well as from its other heresies is a most dangerous counterfeit of Orthodox Christianity.

NOTE 7.—That is, is treated like a person accused of the crime of deception, for He claimed to be God incarnate, and His disciples in the New Testament speak of Him as God incarnate; but Nestorianism denied all this, and practically put Him upon His trial as a liar! Christ said, "*I came out of God*" (ἐκ τοῦ Θεοῦ ἐξῆλθον), John viii., 42. Compare John i., 1, 2, 3, 14, and John xvi., 28, "*I came out of the Father;*" Rev. xix., 13, 16; 1. John v., 7, etc.

NOTE 8.—That is, Nestorianism in effect attempted blasphemously to correct His statements and those of the New Testament that He is the Word incarnate, by contradicting them. Compare John i., 1, 2, 3, 14; John xx., 28; John xvi., 28, etc.

NOTE 9 —The Nestorian heresy slandered Him, in effect, by impliedly teaching that He lied when He claimed to be God incarnate.

NOTE 10.—Ephes. vi., 13.

Ye know the helmet which guards the head (1). [And] what a breast-plate (2) walls our breasts! The ecclesiastical inclosures have not now, for the first time, received you for teachers. No one should doubt that, with the cooperation of God who makes both one (3), arms will be laid aside, and peace will follow when this very matter vindicates (4) itself. And let us again consider the words of our Master, which He used for the sake of His own Bishops especially, when He admonished and said as follows; ' *Take heed unto yourselves and to all the flock over which the Holy Ghost hath made you overseers (5) to rule (6) the Church of God which He hath purchased with His own blood*' (7). So we read that the Ephesians who heard those words were called such: [*Overseers to rule, etc.,*] where now your Holiness (8) has come together. Therefore let your vindication [of the Faith] be made known to those to whom the doctrine also of the Faith is well known. Let us show (9) to them by our own mind and thought the force and sense of that [true] religion (10) of which they are worthy. And let those doctrines which the continuous peace has preserved in their pious sense, remain superior to evil utterances. Let those things which were before preached (11) by the Apostles be proclaimed by you; for never have the utterances of the King of Kings been made less by [any]

NOTE 1.—Eph. vi., 17: "*the helmet of salvation.*"

NOTE 2.—Eph. vi., 14; "*the breastplate of righteousness.*"

NOTE 3.—Eph. ii., 14.

NOTE 4.—Coleti *Conc., tom.* iii., col. 1145: ἐπειδὴ αὐτὴ ἡ ὑπόθεσις ἑαυτὴν ἐκδικεῖ. Or "*because this matter is vindicating itself.*"

NOTE 5.—Greek, ἐπισκόπους, literally, " *overseers.*" It is rendered "*Bishops*" in several places in our Common English Version.

NOTE 6 —Greek, διοικεῖν, *manage* or *rule*. It is not given in Tischendorf's *Novum Testamentum Graece, Editio Octava Critica Major*, Lipsiae, 1872. Ποιμαίνειν is. Perhaps Celestine did not mean to quote literally this passage, Acts xx., 28.

NOTE 7.—Acts xx., 28.

NOTE 8.—A collective title of the Synod.

NOTE 9 —Greek, παράσχωμεν.

NOTE 10.—Greek, προσκυνήσεως.

NOTE 11.—Προκηρυχθέντα, which is sometimes translated simply "*preach.*"

tyrannical attempt (1), nor have they been able to suffer by falsehood. Let the power of the truth, most honorable brethren, impel you; let that judgment be respected which is in accordance with the utterance of John, the Evangelist, whose remains ye, being present, have honored (2). Let there be prayer in common to the Lord. And we know what will be the power of His divine future presence when so great a multitude of the priests (3) beseeches [Him,], with the same soul. For He, by Whom, we read, the Twelve Apostles were of one judgment (4) can move you (5). [And] what was the request of the Twelve when they prayed? [Why], plainly, that they might get [the power] to speak the word of God with boldness,

---

NOTE 1.—A reference to Nestorius' tyrannical and persecuting treatment of his Orthodox clergy for maintaining the true faith.

NOTE 2.—See the Chapter on this in this work elsewhere. The above language is too dangerous to be imitated, even if Celestine meant no worship of relics. If used in the sense of relic worship it is impliedly condemned by the Council. The Synod, however, seem not to have understood him to use it in that wicked sense. Yet God used Balaam and Caiaphas. And why not Celestine?

NOTE 3.—*Priests* here is evidently used for *Bishops*, because they are *Priests in an excellent sense*, as being Apostles in order and rank, and so the source, under Christ, of whatsoever priestly power is delegated to Presbyters and Deacons. The Greek of the above as in col. 1469, tome 1 of Hardouin's *Concilia*, is as follows: 'Ἐκείνη μόνη περισκοπείσθω ἡ γνώμη [πρὸ ἀγάπη, marginal note in the same column of Hardouin] κατὰ τὴν φωνὴν Ἰωάννου τοῦ Εὐαγγελιστοῦ, οὗ τὰ λείψανα παρόντες τετιμήκατε· The Latin in col. 1470, tome 1, of Hardouin's *Concilia* for the above Greek is, Respiciatur illa sola dilectio, in qua utique, secundum vocem Joannis Apostoli, cujus reliquias praesentes veneramini, manere debemus. It is noteworthy that Celestine's idolatrous expression, "*ye venerate*," or "*ye worship*" is toned down to "*ye have honored*" which however savors of idolatry, though it was not, surely, so intended. Hardouin in the margin of col. 1467, id., tells us that the Latin from which the above is taken is "*From a translation which is in the Cresconian collection in the edition of Ant. Coutius,*" etc. The Monitum on the above Epistle in col. 503, tome 50, of Migne's *Patrologia Latina*, tells us in effect that it was originally written in Latin, then translated into Greek for the Council of *Ephesus*, and then translated back from that Greek into Latin again thus involving changes. The Greeks seem purposely to have changed some of the Latin expressions in it and other Papal utterances to meet their own views better before they came before the Council.

NOTE 4.—Greek, ὁμογνωμόνως· Compare Acts iv., 32.

NOTE 5.—Greek, τούτους, referring to the Synod, the use of the third person for the second.

and to energize (1) by the same power (2), and they had [already] received the authority to do those things, for Christ (3) our God gave it [to them]. And what other thing is there now for your Holy Synod to ask than that ye may speak the Word of Christ (4) with boldness? And He has given [you] to keep those things as He has granted [you] to preach [them] also. And do ye, filled with the Holy Ghost, as it is written, transmit harmoniously to all those of [spiritual] nerve, though your mouths be different, nevertheless the but one thing [5] which the Spirit Itself taught and sent forth, for, as the Apostle says, *I speak to those who have knowledge* (6), and *I speak understanding* (7) *among those who are perfect* (8). Contend for the regular faith, (9) and plead for the peace of the Churches, for it is so said both to those in the past and to those in the present, and to those of the future; beseeching, and preserving the things which favor peace for Jerusalem (10).

By way of maintaining our care we have sent our holy brethren and fellow ministers, of the same soul with us and approved, Arcadius and Projectus, Bishops, and Philip our Presbyter, who will be present at the Actions and will present (11) the things decided by us some time ago (12); to which, we do not doubt, co-assent will be given by your Holiness (13); because, as ye may know, that which

NOTE 1.—Or *"to work miracles,"* Greek, ἐνεργεῖν.
NOTE 2.—Acts iv., 29-32.
NOTE 3.—Greek, Χριστοῦ, literally, *"Anointed."*
NOTE 4.—Greek, τοῦ Χριστοῦ, literally "the *Anointed One.*"
NOTE 5.—Greek, ἕν.
NOTE 6.—1. Cor. x., 15; 1. Cor. viii., passim.
NOTE 7.—Greek, σύνεσιν.
NOTE 8.—1. Cor. ii., 6. The Greek, τοῖς τελείοις, means also *complete*, that is in the sense of having full faith in the Gospel.

NOTE 9.—As in the Scriptures, as interpreted by the writers of the Church from the beginning, on the Incarnation, etc., and defined by the two preceding Ecumenical Synods

NOTE 10.—Psalm cxxii., 6. A note in Coleti informs us that two manuscripts, have *"Israel"* instead of *"Jerusalem."*

NOTE 11.—Or *"will execute."* See a deposition in this Act II., below.
NOTE 12.—That is, in the Council at Rome, in A. D. 430.

NOTE 13.—A collective Byzantine, non New Testament title given to the Council. Such often occur in these Acts.

has been decided, seems good for the security of all the Churches (1). *All the most religious Bishops shouted out together.* That is a just judgment! All the Synod thanks Celestine a new Paul (2);

NOTE 1.—Coleti Conc. tome III., col. 1148, οἱ τοῖς πραττομένοις παρέσονται, καὶ τὰ παρ' ἡμῶν πάλαι ὁρισθέντα ἐκβιβάσουσιν· οἷς παρασχεθῆναι παρὰ τῆς ὑμετέρας ἁγιότητος οὐκ ἀμφιβάλλομεν συγκατάθεσιν ἐπειδὴ τοῦτο, ὅπερ ἂν γνῶτε, δοκῇ ὑπὲρ τῆς πασῶν τῶν ἐκκλησιῶν ἀμεριμνίας κεκρίσθαι.

NOTE 2.—In Mansi we read in a note here on the first "*Celestine*" above (*Conc. tome iv., col. 1288*), "In MSS. fere semper scribitur *Celestinus.*" "*In the manuscripts it is nearly always written Celestinus.*" According to this the Latin would force us to render instead of "*All the Synod* thanks Celestine *a New Paul; thanks Cyril a new Paul,*" as follows:

"*Celestine is for the New Paul! All the Synod thanks Cyril a New Paul.*"

But Mansi does not say that the Greek manuscripts have "*Celestinus,*" but only the Latin. Did the Latin translator have the Greek Κελεστῖνος before him? We can not say, but we do know that Mansi in the Greek, like Coleti, gives the dative, νέῳ Παύλῳ Κελεστίνῳ. Of course if the Greek has not the dative, but the nominative for "*Celestine,*" the probabilities are that we should give the English rendering which is in this note, not that in the text. Yet I have translated from the Greek as it stands. For I am not sure as to the Greek, indeed I am not sure whether this is the only place in these acclamations where the nominative for Celestine occurs. We desire fuller information on those points. Since writing the above I have examined Hardouin in this place, and find that he gives the note in his margin which I have translated from Mansi above. And as Hardouin simply places it by no less than the first three mentions of Celestine's name, in the above exclamations in the Latin text I am not sure whether the nominative form of *Celestine's* name occurs only in the first place above or in other places in those exclamations. If he means it for the first three, the passage would read, "Celestine is for the new Paul, for the new Paul Cyril! Celestine is for the Guardian of the Faith! All the Synod thanks Celestine who is of one soul with the Synod! All the Synod thanks Celestine! One Celestine! One Cyril! One faith of the Synod! One faith of the inhabited world!" But his Greek here is the same as Mansi's text.

If the reading "*Celestine is for the New Paul,*" be accepted, then the meaning is, *the* MAJORITY *is on the side of Cyril and Orthodoxy,* because not only is that true of the Orientals assembled in the Third Ecumenical Synod at Ephesus, but also of the West represented by its two greatest sees, Carthage in Act I., and now Rome. Similarly joyful expressions occur in different voting bodies when one side gets a clear majority by the count of votes, even before the President announces the result, and this is most apt to be the case when very important questions are being voted on, and when there is intense feeling and anxiety as to the result.

thanks Cyril a new Paul, thanks Celestine, the Guardian of the faith, thanks Celestine who is of one soul with the Synod! One Celestine! One Cyril! One Faith of the Synod! One Faith of the inhabited world!

Translation [in Greek from the Latin original] *of the statement* [following]:

Projectus, the most pious Bishop and Ambassador [of Rome] said, Let your Holiness (1) consider the type of the Letter (2) of the holy and reverend Father Celestine the Bishop, who exhorts your Sanctity (3) not as though he would teach the Synod as though it were ignorant, but he reminds it as itself possessing knowledge; in order that those things which he also some time since decreed (4) and has now deemed it proper to

---

NOTE 1.—A collective title of the Synod.

NOTE 2.—Or *"letters,"* τὸν τύπον τῶν γραμμάτων.

NOTE 3.—Another collective title of the Ecumenical Council.

NOTE 4.—The reference is especially to the letter of Celestine to Nestorius which was read in Act I, of the First Ecumenical Synod, in which Celestine, as holding what was then the first see of the Church, and as having gathered the sense of part of the West, and of part of the East, in a Synodal Letter tells Nestorius that unless within ten days after that Letter reaches him, he agrees with the doctrine of the Roman Church, the Alexandrian Church, and the Constantinopolitan before him, on Christ our God, and condemns his misbelief in a plain and written confession he should be cast out of the communion of the whole Church. It is on pages 178-203, vol. 1, of *Ephesus* in this set. No action was taken on it by the Ecumenical Synod at that time, farther than to order its enrolment in the Minutes. It was not final at all. Afterwards the Long Letter of Cyril and his Patriarchal Council of Egypt which denounces the same penalties on Nestorius is read, id., vol. 1, of *Ephesus*, pp. 204-358.

Then *Peter, a Presbyter of Alexandria*, states to the council that, before its Act I, Celestine's Letter, and the Long Letter of Cyril of Alexandria and his Egyptian Synod had been sent by certain Bishops to Nestorius, and he asks that two of them then present be questioned as to the result. Both of them testified that he refused to comply with the demands of both Epistles that he renounce his heresies within ten days. Then at the suggestion of *Fidus, Bishop of Joppa*, and approved by Cyril of Alexandria, two other Bishops, Acacius and Theodotus, then present, were asked to state the results of their discussions with Nestorius. They both testified that he continued obstinate in his denial of *the Incarnation* and of the doctrine of *Economic Appropriation*. Then at the suggestion of *Flavian, Bishop of Philippi*, the Council having ascertained the facts regarding Nestorius' impiety proceeds to further facts which help to put the case fully, that they may judge intelligently. Accord-

remind you of, ye may command to be brought to a most complete

ingly certain passages of Fathers, as an orthodox basis of interpretation and decision, are read and inserted into the Acts. Then quite a number of passages from the writings of Nestorius are read to prove his heresies; then a letter of Capreolus Patriarch of Carthage favoring Orthodoxy and exhorting the Synod to maintain it is read; and then after all this evidence, and after all these minor decisions. decisions that is of individual Bishops and of local Churches, that is to say of Rome and Alexandria, the Ecumenical Synod as the *sole supreme Authority*. pronounces the final and irrevocable decision; and, the East and Carthage of the West having acted in the first Act in proper person in this second Act the Bishop and Synod of the then chief city of the West and capital of the Western Empire adds its suffrage. that the decision may be made universal. All this shows that though local Synods, one at Rome and another at Alexandria in the documents read in Act I, of the Third Council had agreed to regard Nestorius as an alien to the episcopate and as excommunicate within ten days, their decree did not get "*effect*," to use the language of the above document further on, till the whole Church had examined the whole testimony and given its decision about six months afterwards in Ecumenical Synod. We see besides from those documents that Rome and Alexandria both agree that Cyril's two warnings to Nestorius and Celestine's one shall be deemed three summonses to him to amend before pronouncing sentence on him. Yet in Act I of the Third Synod the three regular summonses are sent to him, as though he had never been summoned before. So much superior is the authority of an Ecumenical Synod of the Church to its greatest sees!

To such a Synod does Christ subject every Apostle and every one of their successors: Matt. xviii , 15 to 19; Matt. xxviii., 16 to 20 inclusive: John xx., 22, 23; John xiv., 16, 17; John xv , 13, 14. All these promises are given to the whole Apostolate alone, not to Peter alone, as the Harmonies of the Gospels show. And so the *teaching* part of the "*Church* ' in Matt. xxviii , 16-20. is *the whole* apostolate as is clear by comparing the above texts. And the faith and the practice of the whole Church from the beginning, as well as the practice and decisions of the Six Ecumenical Councils are in perfect accordance with that view. Indeed it is not a mere *view*, it is a *dogma* taught by every Ecumenical Synod, *impliedly* in some places, *expressly* in others. Aye such an Ecumenical tribunal has in the exercise of that supreme and Christ delegated authority condemned as heretics, occupants of all its chief sees, namely, Honorius Bishop of Rome condemned by the Sixth Ecumenical as a heretic and as an instrument of the Devil in raising up a heresy to the Orthodox people; and his predecessor Vigilius, was forced to profess Orthodoxy against his will by the Fifth Ecumenical Synod; for he was heretical himself. Nestorius Bishop of Constantinople was condemned as a heretic by the Third Ecumenical Synod, Macedonius of the same see by the Second Ecumenical Synod, and Sergius, Pyrrhus, Paul, and Peter of the same see by the Sixth; Dioscorus Bishop of Alexandria by the Fourth, and his successor, Cyrus, by the Sixth; John of

termination according to the rule of the common faith and for the benefit and usefulness of the Universal Church (1).

Firmus, Bishop of Caesarea in Cappadocia said, The Apostolic and holy Throne of the most holy Bishop Celestine put forth, before this, both a vote and a form on the matter (2) by letters to the most

Antioch by the Third, and his successor Macarius by the Sixth. And when that most august assemblage of the not remote future, a true, Orthodox Seventh Ecumenical Synod is held, which shall represent ten times as many Christians as the largest of the ancient Ecumenical Synods did, it will follow their same processes and mode of deciding and with the same supreme power over Rome, Constantinople, Alexandria, Antioch and every other local Church; and will anathematize such of their Bishops as have died in creature service and in idolatry with the same supreme and infallible authority as the Ecumenical Synods before it anathematized the dead heretics, Honorius of Rome, Sergius, Pyrrhus, Paul and Peter of Constantinople, and Dioscorus and Cyrus of Alexandria, and John and Macarius of Antioch.

NOTE 1.—This Roman ambassador uses the expression *"most complete"* here because, until an Ecumenical Synod had gathered up the sense of the whole Church and expressed it, the case and controversy were not brought to a complete termination. Peter had not been absolute nor Master over the whole of the Apostolate. Neither was his successor Celestine. The Universal Church had never regarded any one see as autocrat of the Faith. It had spoken as final Judge in two Ecumenical Synods alone in its *collective* capacity. And Projectus speaks of this *"most complete termination,"* this settlement of the whole controversy as *"according to* THE RULE OF THE COMMON· FAITH," words which we may well understand as referring to the common faith on the Incarnation as the *Criterion matter,* and also to the common faith as to the supreme authority of an Ecumenical Synod as the *Criterion mode* of determining what that faith is.

NOTE 2.—Greek, ψῆφον ἐπέσχε, καὶ τύπον τῷ πράγματι, ὁ ἀποστολικὸς καὶ ἅγιος θρόνος, etc. The article is not used before ψῆφον or τύπον here. The Romanist Hefele, page 63, vol. 3, of the English translation of his *"History of the Church Councils",* is guilty of most gross perversion of facts here; for he translates ψῆφον καὶ τύπον here *"the sentence and direction;"* whereas there is no article at all in the Greek, and the Greek literally means " *a vote and a form,"* that is a vote and a decision of Rome and of that part of the West represented in the Synod at Rome of which Celestine's letter is the outcome. Hefele's idea that the question as to Nestorius was settled by that local Synod at Rome or by Celestine without the Third Ecumenical Synod is refuted by all the facts in the Synod, and savors of the art of the flatterer of Rome to get honor and profit. The East gave its ψῆφον καὶ τύπον that is its vote and statement of decision in that Ecumenical Synod, and then the aggregates of all these votes and decisions settled the matter in the Ecumenical Council, those of Rome by Celes-

dear to God Bishops, I mean to Cyril, the Bishop of Alexandria, and Juvenal the Bishop of Jerusalem, and Rufus, the Bishop of the Thessalonians, and to the holy Churches, the Church in Constantinople, and that in Antioch; and we, following him, when the set day

---

tine and its Synod and legates, those of Alexandria by Cyril and its Synod and representatives, those of the Bishops of Pontus by their votes and decisions, those of Asia Minor, such as Memnon and others by their votes and decisions, those of Macedonia by their votes and decisions, those of Cyprus by their votes and decisions, those of Palestine, such as Juvenal of Jerusalem and others, and those of the other parts of the Christian world represented by their votes and decisions. Some of those votes and decisions were twice given; as for instance, Celestine's and his Council of part of the West at Rome, and afterwards in the Ecumenical Synod; and Cyril's and his Egyptian Synod at Alexandria, and afterwards in the Ecumenical Council: and that thing occurred in other instances with those and other sees, where local councils were gathered and voted before an Ecumenical Synod, and each local council gave its local conciliar vote and decision, and another afterwards in an Ecumenical Council and so assisted to make up the aggregate of votes which made the Ecumenical vote and decisions, as, for example, in the Pelagian controversy, which was finally settled in the Third World Synod; or sometimes individual prelates gave their individual vote and decision before the Ecumenical Council, as, for example, Alexander Bishop of Alexandria against Arius, and afterwards gave them in an Ecumenical Synod to help make up that aggregate of all individual votes and decisions which made the Ecumenical vote and decision. Projectus, the Roman legate, does not claim that Rome's local decision was final but represents Celestine as deferring to the judgment of the Synod; see above.

Furthermore, I would add that τύπος is used 16 times in the New Testament, according to the *Englishman's Greek Concordance of the New Testament;* and is translated:

2 times by *"print."*
1 time by *"figure."*
1 time by *"figures."*
1 time by *"fashion."*
1 time by *"manner."*
1 time by *"form."*
2 times by *"pattern."*
7 times by *"example,"* or its synonym *"ensample,"* some times used in the singular number, at other times in the plural.

The word came sometimes in the case of the Emperors' *forms* to mean *decree*, since they had that force, but that use is not found in the New Testament. That follows more the literal meaning of the word, which is *impression, form, pattern, example*. It is cognate with τύπτω, which means to *strike*, and so to strike off *an impression, a sample, a form,* or *a pattern.*

granted Nestorius to amend had passed, and much time had elapsed, after we came to Ephesus, in accordance with the command of the most religious Emperor, and we had spent not a little time here, so that the day appointed by the Emperor [for opening the Synod] had passed; after we had summoned Nestorius and he would not obey [our citations], we [we repeat] gave effect to the form, considering the judgment against him to be canonical and Apostolic (1).

NOTE 1.—Coleti *Conc. tom.* iii., *col.* 1148, ἐπειδὴ προσκαλεσαμένων ἡμῶν Νεστόριον, οὐχ ὑπήκουσε, τὸν τύπον ἐξεβιβάσαμεν κανονικὴν καὶ ἀποστολικὴν αὐτῷ κατανοήσαντες κρισίν. Coleti has here by a misprint ὑπήκουσι. The *Collectio Regia* gives it correctly as above. I have several times found it useful in correcting the mistakes or misprints in Coleti.

As to the words "*gave effect*," see the third note above.

Wonderful is the Romanist Hefele's perversion of facts here. For on page 63, vol. III., of the English translation of his "*History of the Councils of the Church*," he writes on this part of Act II., of the Council.

"The papal legate Projectus then directed closer attention to the contents of the papal Letter, and especially to the point that the sentence which had already been delivered by the Pope should be carried into effect for the use of the Catholic Church, and in accordance with the rule of the Catholic faith; that is, that all the Bishops should accede to the papal sentence, and so raise it to the position of a judgment of the whole Church. In this matter, according to the Pope's opinion, the Synod had no longer to examine whether Nestorius taught error; this was quite settled by the Roman sentence, and it was only incumbent upon the Synod to confirm this by their accession. The Synod had in their first session practically taken a different view, and had introduced a fresh examination as to the Orthodoxy of Nestorius; nevertheless they now gave, partly in silence and partly expressly, their adhesion to the papal view, whilst Archbishop Firmus of Caesarea, in Cappadocia, declared '*that the former Letter of the Apostolic See to Cyril had already contained the sentence and direction* (ψῆφον καὶ τύπον) *respecting the Nestorian question, and they (the assembled Bishops) had, by ordering themselves accordingly, only fulfilled this direction, and pronounced the canonical and apostolic condemnation against Nestorius.*'"

On this we remark:

1, that Hefele gives an utterly wrong impression here as to the facts. For Projectus speaks modestly, more so indeed than papal legates often have since, defers to the council, disclaims any assumption of superior or sole knowledge on the points involved, as well he might, so inferior was he and Celestine his leader in dogmatic ability to Cyril its leader, and in effect merely states that as the Roman See, which was the chief See of the then only partly Christianized West, had condemned Nestorius, and as it was necessary according to the custom of the Church from the beginning that both parts of it, the West and the

Translation [in Greek from the Latin original] *of the Statement* [following]:

East, should pronounce and agree on the same verdict to make it Universal, therefore he asks them to agree.

Firmus, Bishop of Caesarea in Cappadocia, speaking for the Council, which in the First Act had been wholly composed of Easterns, states again that Celestine had put forth *a vote* that is of his See and the Bishops under it, or, as we would now say, of his Italian Patriarchate, and a *form* that unless Nestorius recanted his errors and made profession of Orthodoxy within ten days after that warning reached him, he should be deposed; and that he [Celestine] had sent that form to Cyril, the Bishop of Alexandria, and Juvenal, the Bishop of Jerusalem, and Rufus the Bishop of Thessalonica, and to the Church of Constantinople and to that of Antioch; that accordingly summoned by the Emperors to the Council they met, summoned Nestorius, and on his refusal to appear for trial, *"they gave effect to the form;"* But how? Why by deposing him as it proposed. But why? He replies, *"considering the judgment against him to be Canonical and Apostolical."* Act I., shows the different steps by which in their examination they reached that conclusion. We have specified them in note 4 on pages 80–82 above. All this most plainly shows that the East had the right by its own vote to make the verdict of Celestine and his local Roman Synod Universal by their adhesion, or to make it merely local and Roman by rejecting it, that is by refusing to give effect to the merely local *vote and form* of Celestine and the prelates of his jurisdiction, in Italy. They had approved only, as Act I., shows, because after listening to two Epistles of Cyril of Alexandria and approving them as Orthodox, and after listening to one of Nestorius and condemning it as heretical, and after hearing from the two then greatest Western Sees, Rome and Carthage, and after examining passages of Fathers, East and West, to show the faith which had been hitherto held in the whole Church on the Incarnation, and other passages from Nestorius which prove his opposition to it and its sequences, they pronounce him deposed, not merely because one See, Rome, had voted against him but because the whole Church East and West had. These are the plain facts. And stilted and assuming as is the language of the Papal legates there is not a word in them or in Firmus which contravenes it. Nor did Firmus give the impression that the East had approved Rome's vote and form merely because its Bishop and his Synod gave them, but because they were sound and just.

2. What is very important, Firmus does not say that the former Letter of Celestine to Nestorius, (translated on pages 179–203, vol. 1, of *Ephesus* in this set), "contained *the sentence* and direction respecting the Nestorian question," but "*a vote and a type*" (ψῆφον καὶ τύπον), as the Greek here means, that is a vote of Celestine in connection with a local Roman Council in A. D., 430, on the guilt of Nestorius and a *type* or *form* to the effect that unless within ten days after that document of Celestine and his local council reached him he would renounce his errors and preach on the Incarnation not the faith of Rome

Arcadius, the most religious Bishop and Ambassador [of Rome]

only but also that of Alexandria, Constantinople and the Universal Church he should be cast out, or to put it exactly as Celestine and his Synod write to Nestorius," "Unless thou preach those very doctrines, concerning our God Anointed, which both the Church of the Romans and the Church of the Alexandrians, and all the Universal Church holds fast, and as the holy Church in the great city of Constantine" [that is Constantinople] "very well held fast until thee, and unless within the tenth day, reckoned from the time that this admonition comes to thy knowledge, thou put away by a clear and written confession that unbelieving novelty and innovation of thine which attempts to separate the very things which the Holy Scripture joins together," [Christ's Divinity infleshed within His humanity] "thou art cast out from" [all] "the communion of the Universal Church " (Chrystal's *Ephesus*, vol. I, pages 200-202).

Here the demand to Nestorius is not as Hefele seems to intimate, Thou, Nestorius, must accept as infallible and final the vote of Celestine, Bishop of Rome, one Prelate and his local Council, but thou must accept the faith of Rome, of Alexandria as expressed by Cyril its Bishop, who has written against thy errors, the faith of Constantinople prior to thee, and *of the whole Universal Church*, that is not the faith of one Church, Rome alone, but the faith of the whole Church East and West.

To that was added, as we have shown above, Cyril's summons to Nestorius and that of his Patriarchate of Egypt, Libya, and Pentapolis (Canon VI., of Nicaea), in which he does not assert any personal infallibility of Celestine, but only the weight and vote of himself and his local Roman Synod, equally with the vastly abler vote and Letter of himself and his Egyptian Synod. Cyril's words are:

"Behold therefore, that we, together with the Holy Synod which was collected in great Rome in which our most devout and most God fearing brother and Fellow-Minister Celestine, the Bishop, was President, do hereby, even for the third time, by this Letter "[Cyril's *Long Letter to Nestorius* which was approved by the Third Ecumenical Council of which the above quotation is part] "protest against thee, and counsel thee to forsake those dogmas so sinister and perverted which thou holdest and teachest, and to choose instead the correct faith which has been handed down to the Churches from the beginning through the holy Apostles and Evangelists, who *were* also *eye-witnesses and ministers of the Word* (Luke i, 2, and Acts i., 20-23). Or if thy Piety will not do that before the day specified in the Letter of the aforesaid most devout and most God-fearing brother, our Fellow-Minister, Celestine, Bishop of the Church of the Romans, [then] know [hereby] that thou wilt have no lot with us, nor place nor reckoning among the Priests of God and Bishops," (Chrystal's translation of *Ephesus*, vol. I, pages 209-212).

Here is no admission of any claim of Celestine to any personal infallibility in the decision of himself and his Synod. Nestorius is as much required to accept the decision of Cyril and his Synod as that of Celestine and his, aye

said, Though slow sailing and contrary and tempestuous wind kept us back most of all, and hindered us from arriving at the place ap-

and the XII Anathemas at the end of their Epistle, which are not in Celestine's, and which so far as appears he had not even seen or understood.

3. In the sentence pronounced on Nestorius at the end of Act I., of the Council of Ephesus, the Synod base their action of deposition against him,
    A. On his disobedience to their summons.
    B. On his refusal to receive the Bishops sent to him by the Council
    C. On the proof of his impieties in *" his letters and writings."*
    D. On the duty of the Synod to enforce the Canons against him.'
    E. On the Epistle of Celestine and his Synod which represented, of course, a part of the Church against him, and
    F. On *"other things."*

This does not look as though the Council were moved by any one of these 6 things to the exclusion of the other five. If they had not admitted into their examination Celestine and his Roman Synod they would not have treated him and them as well as they did Cyril and his, for one part of the Church had as much right to be heard as another. And they certainly followed Cyril in that Act.

4. When Rome's Legates were present in Act II., and after, the Council discussed and determined matters, giving them the place of one See only, Rome, not of the whole Church, and decided matters without any more consulting of them than of Cyril of Alexandria, Memnon of Ephesus, and Juvenal of Jerusalem. Indeed Cyril himself, as all admit, was the leader under God of the Synod, and the formulator of the doctrines approved by it. Celestine's influence in it was not equal to his.

5. Letters and other utterances of Bishops of Rome were approved or condemned in other Ecumenical Councils on the merits of the Orthodoxy or the heresy contained in them. That was the case with Leo the First's *Epistle to Flavian, Bishop of Constantinople,* which after examination and questioning as to parts of it which were deemed to need further elucidation was approved in the Definition of the Fourth Ecumenical Synod, which Council approved also three Epistles of Cyril of Alexandria with less questioning. And so the Sixth Synod approved a Letter of Agatho, Bishop of Rome, and at the same time followed *"the Synodical Letters which were written by the blessed Cyril against the impieties of Nestorius."*

And on the other hand the Fifth Ecumenical Synod condemned by necessary implication all the writings of Vigilius, Bishop of Rome, against those who condemned the Three Chapters; and the Sixth not only rejected two Letters of Honorius, Bishop of Rome, to Sergius, Bishop of Constantinople, but anathematized him on the basis of them. I quote here part of what Barmby writes on that in his Article *"Honorius (15),"* in Smith and Wace's *Dictionary of Christian Biography.*

"When in the 6th general Council (680), the doctrine of two wills and two

pointed [for the Ecumenical Synod] at the very time on which we

energies was finally asserted, Honorius was anathematized by name among other former upholders of heresy. 'And with them *we anathematize, and cast out of the Holy Catholic Church, Honorius who was Pope of the elder Rome, because we have found through* HIS LETTERS TO SERGIUS THAT HE FOLLOWED HIS OPINION IN ALL RESPECTS, AND CONFIRMED HIS IMPIOUS DOGMAS' (*Synod. Occum* VI., Actio XIII., Mansi, XI , 556). The same anathema was repeated in Act XVI., and Act XVIII., (Mansi XI., 622, 655). The acts of the Council were signed by the legates of Pope Agatho, and it was accepted as œcumenical both in the East and West. Further, Leo II., the successor of Agatho, in his letter to the Emperor Constantine, in which he confirms the Council, writes, '*We anathematize .... and also Honorius, who did not purify this apostolic Church by the teaching of the apostolic tradition, but by profane treachery endeavored to pollute the undefiled*,' (Mansi XI., 731). See also his letter to the Spanish Bishops (Mansi XI., 1052), and to Evagrius, King of Spain (ib, p. 1057). Also in the profession of faith, subscribed by subsequent popes on their accession, they anathematized "Sergium, etc......una cum Honorio, qui pravis eorum assertionibus fomentum impendit, [In English this Latin is, "*We anathematize Sergius*, etc., ... together with Honorius who furnished material to aid their evil assertions."], *Lib. Diurn.*, cap. 11., tit. 9, professio 2)."

Whatever therefore may have been the stilted language of Celestine and his Legates, it is clear that the Council regarded him only as "*first among his equals,*" as Peter was among the Apostles, and that they looked upon his Epistle read in this Second Act as an utterance of but one of the great Bishops of the Church and his local Roman fallible Non-Ecumenical Council and nothing more. It contained paganism in the form of relic-worship and it is noteworthy that they did not approve it by vote, as in Act I. they approved the Shorter Epistle of Cyril to Nestorius, Bishop of Constantinople, against Man-Worship, but changed Celestine's erring language in it and in his Epistle read in Act. I., (Chrystal's translation of *Ephesus*, vol. 1, pages 129-154). Indeed so far as explanation of doctrine is concerned it is so vastly beneath Cyril's two Letters which were approved by the Council as to be hardly deserving of notice. The best that can be said of him and his local Roman Council is that they voted and acted on the side of Cyril and of Orthodoxy. Put in no less than three places the Council seemingly altered his Latin, in two cases at least to get rid of errors broached by him, that is that the Apostles wrote the Roman Creed, and that men should worship relics, see on these points under "*Celestine,*" page 577, vol. 1. of Chrystal's *Ephesus*. So little confidence had Cyril in him that at first he was very chary of having him know the full controversy, (id., pages 31. 32, and the notes there).

6. The Council went further and, by necessary implication, condemned the attempts of Celestine and two of his predecessors to gain Appellate Jurisdiction in Africa, aye, and anywhere else outside of Italy; see it, Canon VIII., and Chrystal's Articles in the Church Journal of New York City of

had hoped to come, nevertheless by God's governance, and [by that of] your Blessedness' (1) our Mediocrity has arrived [here]. And we thank Him because we have found your Blessedness (2) remaining in one place and in one faith and full of care for the *Church of God which the Lord Jesus Christ purchased with his own blood* (3). Therefore we ask your Blessedness (4) to give command that we be taught what has been decreed by your Blessedness.

Aug. 10, 17, 31, Sept. 7, Nov. 30, and Dec. 7, 1870. They are entitled *"Defence in Centuries V., and VI, by the Diocese of North West Africa of its Rights, as guaranteed by Oecumenical Canon, against the claim of Rome to Appellate Jurisdiction there."*

I would add that Hefele's work on the Councils is one of the most dangerous to the faith of an unlearned man that I know of. For he brings in his Romish prejudices instead of the full truth and often perverts the facts. Furthermore, we must remember that the present unbaptized, idolatrous, and Ecumenically condemned Bishops of Rome, have not even the limited power of the former sound Bishops of that See, nor indeed any power at all, for, as all the rest of the Apostolic Sees hold and indeed all sound men, they are not even laymen. And we must well remember that in discussing the question as to what powers the Universal Church in its Canons gave to Orthodox Bishops of that See in ancient times, we are not admitting the Ecumenically condemned absurdity that an idolatrous, condemned, and deposed, and anathematized so-called Bishop of that See in modern times has any power in the Church at all. These questions so entirely different are often confounded by the Harlot's (Rev. xvii., 18) champions and alas! even by unlearned or unskilful Protestant writers or speakers. The Greeks with all their faults do better and wiser in their conflicts with her, for they insist on dogma first, then orders. It is a fundamental principle that we must never even for a moment admit any prelate's claim to any See or power in the Church if he worships images, relics, or saints, or any thing in the Eucharist, or in any other way opposes any decision of the VI. sole Synods of the Christian world. This is the way of the Scriptures (Rev. ii, 2) for which Christ commends the Ephesian Church, (ibid), and this is embodied in the Canons and decisions of the Six Councils of the Universal Church. We beg the reader to remember the facts of this note regarding the modern invalid prelates of Rome as ever understood, though we may not repeat them.

NOTE 1.—A collective title of the Ecumenical Synod. The Greek is, ὅμως κυβερνῶντος θεοῦ, καὶ τῆς ὑμετέρας μακαριότητος.

NOTE 2.—The Ecumenical Synod

NOTE 3.—Acts xx., 28.

NOTE 4.—The Ecumenical Synod.

Translation [into Greek from the Latin original] *of the Statement* [following]:

Philip, a Presbyter and an Ambassador of the Apostolic See (1) *said:* We confess our thanks to the Holy and Reverend Synod, because when the Letter of our holy and blessed Father (2) was read to you, ye added your holy and harmonious assents to our holy utterances (3) and responded with your holy exclamations to the holy head (4). For your Blessedness (5) is not ignorant that the blessed Peter the Apostle [was] the head of the whole faith (6) or even of

NOTE 1.—Rome, the only Apostolic See in Western Christendom and therefore so called there commonly; and sometimes, by imitation and courtesy, in the East also.

NOTE 2.—Celestine, Bishop of Rome. The Letter is contained in this Second Act above. Celestine's Letter read in Act I. of the Synod was Synodal, that is the outcome of a local Synod at Rome, and was dated Aug. 11, 430.

NOTE 3.—The Letter of Celestine read in the Second Act which, as being the words of their own Bishop, these Roman Legates might speak of as *"our holy utterances."*

NOTE 4.—Celestine, occupant of the then first See in the Church. We must remember however that like all the other Patriarchs and autocephalous Metropolitans he had no right to claim Appellate Jurisdiction or any other jurisdiction outside of his own Patriarchate, which is lawfully and canonically only seven of the fourteen provinces of Italy, and the islands Sicily, Sardinia, and Corsica, as Bingham shows in chapter 1, book ix., of his *Antiquities*. The Canons of the First Four Ecumenical Synods, the only ones which made Canons, settle this matter. This is often lost sight of by those who do not know the Canons, but attempt to make Rome absolute in the whole Church contrary to them.

NOTE 5.—A title of the Synod.

NOTE 6.—The reference may here be to Peter's making the first distinct confession of entire faith in Christ as the *Son of God*. It is recorded in Matt. xvi., 13 to 21. For it Christ blessed him by giving him the power to use the Keys of the Kingdom of heaven by opening it by his sermon on Pentecost to the Jews, for then was the Kingdom of heaven first opened, and then took place the first baptism into it. The other powers there mentioned were given to the other Apostles afterwards as we read in the New Testament, the privilege of being *foundation stones* of the Church (Eph. ii., 20; Rev. xxi. 14, Matthias being put into Judas' place, Acts i., 25, 26); and the power of *binding and loosing* (given to the Eleven by Christ Himself in John xx., 23, and exercised by an Apostle not of the Eleven, Paul, in I. Cor. v., 3 to 6; and II. Cor. ii., 10, 11; I. Tim. i., 19, 20, etc., which shows that the peculiar power of dis-

the Apostles (1). And forasmuch as our Mediocrity has now arrived later than we would, owing to many tempests and much trouble,

cipline was not to perish with the first Twelve, but was to remain in the hands of an Orthodox Apostolate, that is Episcopate, forever).

NOTE 1.—Greek, ἢ καὶ τῶν 'Αποστόλων· Persons blunder wonderfully in supposing that if Peter were head of the Apostles therefore he alone could order them about, rule them as inferiors in rank, control all ordinations to the Apostolate, exercise Appellate Jurisdiction over them all, and in brief be as absolute lord and despot over them as the so-called Bishop of Rome now is over all the Prelates subject to him; and they blunder furthermore when they think that if he were head of the Apostles, then he was not only an absolute monarch over them, but that his monarchical power also has descended, not to St. Peter's See of Antioch as it is called in the Acts of the Fourth Ecumenical Synod, and as it has been termed by at least one of the Bishops of Rome, Gregory I., but to Rome exclusively, and that she exercises all the powers mentioned in this note above as prerogative. See Gregory I., in Coxe's Guettée's *Papacy*, page 228 and after, and for the Latin, Gieseler's *Church Hist.*, vol. 1., p. 409, note 18.

But the reply to all this inexcusably ignorant trash is that the Church has forbidden all such autocracy of Rome and of every other See in the whole Church and has limited the exercise of rule and sway of every Patriarch, Rome included, and every autocephalous Metropolitan, to his own Patriarchate or Metropolitical territory whichsoever it be. And if a man will not hear the Church's decisions on all such points in the Canons of the First Four Ecumenical Synods but persists in talking wind and gas to violate and outrage the Ecumenical Canons, he must be treated as Christ commands us to treat him in Matthew xviii., 17, "*as a heathen man and a publican.*" Such partisans have done too much harm to the Church's faith and discipline to the damnation of souls by subjecting them to a paganizer and a creature server, whose orders and baptism are rejected as invalid by every Apostolic See in Christendom except Rome itself, not to be punished as Christ commands. They have torn the Church to pieces, rent nations asunder, and set those who professed to be Christians to cutting each others throats and making widows, orphans, desolation and ruin, to the rejoicing of Mohammedans and other foes of the Christian name.

But what shall we say of the assertion of the Roman Legate here that Peter was the head of the Apostles?

I answer, 1, that it is a *theoretical* rather than a *practical* question so far as Rome's rank in the Church is concerned, since the Universal Church has decided in Canon III., of the Second Ecumenical Council and Canon XXVIII., of the Fourth Synod, that Rome inherited no peculiar privileges in the Church such as they gave Constantinople except by the fact that it was then the imperial city. Constantinople is made the second See because it became the second capital of the Empire, and therefore was then put before St. Peter's See of Antioch, which

we therefore beg that ye command that the things done in the Holy Synod before our arrival be made known to us; in order that in accordance with the mind of our blessed Father (1), both the present

had always even before that, been placed after St. Mark's See of Alexandria; so that the Eastern half of the Church had, from the beginning gone on the principle that the Ecclesiastical precedences of cities should be determined by and follow the civil precedences. And they hold that principle to this very hour. Indeed it is enacted in Canon XVII, of Chalcedon.

2. Peter was prominent among his equals, sat as coordinate with them in the gatherings at Jerusalem, and was rebuked by Paul at Antioch, who spoke of himself as *"in nothing .... behind the very chiefest apostles,"* (see his language in II. Cor. xi., 5, and xii., 11), all which facts show that Peter was not their lord but their colleague.

And, as has been shown above, the Universal Church in the above mentioned Canons, teaches that no right of Appellate Jurisdiction over the whole Church has descended from Peter to Rome or to any other See. Compare Canons V. and VI., of *Nicaea*, Canons II. and VI., of the Second World Synod, Canon VIII., of the Third and Canons IX. and XIX., of the Fourth.

3. The words of this Legate on Peter's being the head of the Apostles are mere *obiter dicta, passing words, incidental utterances*, on side points which as having been sufficiently settled already, and as not bearing specially on the points under discussion, that is the Incarnation, etc., are passed by.

4. This very Synod in its Canon VIII. impliedly condemns the tyrannical attempt of Rome to usurp *Appellate Jurisdiction* over Carthage and Latin Africa, and anywhere else outside of that part of Italy where Rome had jurisdiction from the beginning. Moreover, it vindicates the Metropolitan and the Bishops of Cyprus against the claim of St. Peter's See of Antioch to jurisdiction over them, and its language in that Canon VIII., impliedly forbids any claim of Rome to jurisdiction outside of Italy, where alone it had been exercised *"from the beginning,"* to use the words of that enactment, in the seven provinces of South Italy, and the three Islands, Sicily, Sardinia, and Corsica. He might not interfere in *"the other Dioceses,"* be it Britain, Gaul, Spain, Italy, Africa, or any other, (Canon II., of the Second Ecumenical Council). And at no time did Rome have jurisdiction over any part of the Eastern Church.

5. Any privileges recognized by Canon III., of the Second Synod, and Canon XXVIII., of the Fourth, as conferred on the Bishop of Rome because it was the capital of the Western Empire, have long since passed away with that Empire. So Greeks hold; (note, p. 228, vol. 2, *Smith's Gieseler's Church Hist.*)

6. The present Bishop of Rome being an Ecumenically condemned idolater (condemned and deposed and excommunicated antecedently by the Third Synod and the Fifth) is not a member of the Christian Church at all, and therefore has neither primacy nor any other place in it. Indeed the Greeks assert that he is both unbaptized and unordained.

NOTE 1 —Celestine.

Holy Assembly, once more, and we likewise may confirm their Statement (1).

Theodotus, Bishop of Ancyra said: The God of the Universe (2), by the arrival of the Letter (3) of the most God-revering Bishop Celestine and by the presence (4) of your God-Reveringness (5) has shown that the vote of the Holy Synod was just. For ye have shown both the zeal of the most holy and most devout Bishop Celestine and his earnestness regarding the pious faith. And, moreover, inasmuch as your God-Reveringness (6), has, with reason, asked to thoroughly learn what has been done, your Piety shall be fully assured by (7) the Minutes of the Actions themselves as to the justice of the vote on the deposed Nestorius, and as to both the zeal of the Holy Synod and its agreement with the faith, which the most God-revering and most holy Bishop Celestine also preaches with a great voice; that is to say after that full information is given to you and the things which are lacking [and which you wish to know] are added to the present Action, (8).

NOTE 1.—The Statement is the Deposition of Nestorius, which is now to be confirmed by the part of the West which was under Rome, as well as by the East, and by Carthage, so making it Universal. The Greek of this place in Hardouin is as follows: ἵνα κατὰ τὴν γνώμην τοῦ μακαρίου πάπα ἡμῶν ἔτι γε μὴν καὶ τοῦ παρόντος ἁγίου συλλόγου καὶ ἡμεῖς ὁμοίως τῇ αὐτῶν καταθέσει βεβαιώσωμεν

NOTE 2.—Greek, ὁ τῶν ὅλων θεός.

NOTE 3.—Greek, τῶν γραμμάτων, which may be rendered *"letters"* also, in which case it would include both the one read in this Second Act and that in the First.

NOTE 4.—Or, *"by the coming."*

NOTE 5.—Greek, καὶ τῇ παρουσίᾳ τῆς ὑμῶν θεοσεβείας. This seems to refer to the Roman Legates and to be a collective title for them.

NOTE 6.—The Roman Legates, a collective title for them.

NOTE 7.—Or *"from the Minutes,"* etc.

NOTE 8.—This Second Act is in Coleti *Conc., tom.* III., *col.* 1140 to about the middle of col. 1149. The Greek of this last part in *Harduin. Conc., tom.* I, col. 1473, is as follows: δηλαδὴ μετὰ τὴν ὑμῶν πληροφορίαν, καὶ τῶν ὑπολοίπων τῇ πράξει τῇ νῦν προστιθεμένων. This Greek is the same in *Mansi, Conc., tom.* iv., col. 1289.

ACT THIRD.

In the time of (1) the Consulship of our Masters, Flavius Theodosius, Consul for the thirteenth time, and Flavius Valentinian, Consul for the third time, the ever August Ones, on the fifth day before the Ides of July, which, according to the Egyptians, is the seventeenth of Epiphi (2), on the day after [the Second Act of the Ecumenical Synod], the same Holy Synod came together in the same place, and the most dear to God and most God-revering Bishops having sat down, *Juvenal, Bishop of Jerusalem, said* to Arcadius and to Projectus, most religious Bishops, and to Philip, a most religious Presbyter: Yesterday when this Holy and Great Synod was sitting together, your God-Reveringness (3) was present, and after the reading of the Letter of the most holy and most devout Bishop of the Great Rome (4), Celestine, asked that the Minutes composed on the deposition of the heretic Nestorius be read. Accordingly the Holy Synod ordered it to be done (5). If therefore your Holiness has read and learned their sense and force, your Holiness will deem it a worthy thing to state (6) it.

Philip, a Presbyter and Ambassador of the Apostolic See, said, The things decreed in your holy Assembly against Nestorius have indeed been made clear to us from the reading of the Acts, in which

NOTE 1.—Greek, Τοῖς μετὰ τὴν ὑπατείαν τῶν δεσποτῶν ἡμῶν. On this idiom see a note at the beginning of Act I., page 19, vol. 1, of *Ephesus* in this Set.

NOTE 2.—That is July 11, 431. The Second Act or Session, as we see by page 67 above, was on the day next preceding, that is July 10, 431.

NOTE 3.—A collective title of the Roman Ambassadors to the Synod.

NOTE 4.—A title of the old Rome from long before Christ's birth in flesh. It is so called in Revelations xvii., 5; Compare Rev. xvii., 1 and Rev. xvii., 18; which explains what city is meant. The description, *"that great city which reigneth over the Kings of the earth,"* in the last mentioned verse was true of Rome only, in John's day.

NOTE 5.—This reading seems to have been done informally, for, beyond the command of the Synod to have it done, nothing is said in Act II. above. Below the Roman Legates ask that it be done formally in this Act III. that they may formally confirm it for Rome by their formal vote. That accordingly is done.

NOTE 6.—Literally, "*Your Holiness will deem it worthy*" [or "*deign*"] "*to teach as to that.*"

Minutes we have ascertained that all things were judged and decided canonically and in accordance with Church discipline (1); but we ask now also of your crown (2), even though it be superfluous, (3) that the same things which were read in your Synod (4) be read to us again, in order that we, following the form of the most holy Father Celestine, who put this care into our hands, may be able still further also to make firm (5) the Decisions of your Holiness (6).

A translation of the [following] *statement* [from its Latin original into Greek]:

NOTE 1.—Greek, καὶ κατὰ τὴν ἐκκλησιαστικὴν ἐπιστήμην, literally "*in accordance with Church Science,*" that is in accordance with the mode of procedure of the Universal Church, that is by consulting all parts of the Church, by the three regular citations of the accused, the giving him time and opportunity to defend himself, the fair examination of his writings and acts when he refused to appear, and his just deposition after proof given.

NOTE 2.—This looks like a reference to what was called "*a crown of Presbyters,*" which was a body of Presbyters in the apse of the Church, the Bishop being in the middle, and they sitting apse wise to his right and left in curves frontwards. They were back of the Holy Table. Perhaps the chief Bishops so sat in the Church at Ephesus. Or the allusion may be merely complimentary.

NOTE 3.—Greek. εἰ καὶ ἐκ περιττοῦ.

NOTE 4.—In Act I

NOTE 5.—Or, "*to confirm,*" τὰ κεκριμένα βεβαιῶσαι. Cyril, acting not only for Alexandria, but as placeholder for Rome also, might be said to have cast the votes of those two great Sees and so joined so much of West and East to condemn Nestorius' heresies. But now that the Roman legates are present, they desire to add their own confirmation, as themselves Westerns representing the then great Western Rome, of the Actions of the Synod, so making it the voice of the whole Church by uniting the local decision of the greatest Western See to the East and to Africa. For the East being only a local Church could never hold an Ecumenical Synod nor pronounce an Ecumenical decree without the assent of the whole Church, West as well as East. In a future genuine Seventh Ecumenical Synod there will be several Western Sees greater than Rome, even if she shall then have a right to be represented by becoming Orthodox before it.

NOTE 6.—A collective title of the whole Synod. In Greek it is τῆς ὑμετέρας ἁγιωσύνης. The last part of the above as in Greek in Coleti is as follows: ὅπως ἡμεῖς ἀκολουθήσαντες τῷ τύπῳ τοῦ ἁγιωτάτου πάπα Κελεστίνου, τοῦ ταύτην ἡμῖν τὴν φροντίδα ἐγχειρίσαντος ἔτι γε μὴν καὶ τῆς ὑμετέρας ἁγιωσύνης, δυνηθῶμεν τὰ κεκριμένα βεβαιῶσαι. The τύπῳ means, I presume, the decision in the Letter of Celestine and the Western Synod as to deposing Nestorius unless he renounced his heresy within ten days after notification.

Arcadius, the most religious Bishop and Ambassador of the Apostolic See, said, We confess [our] thanks to your Blessedness (1) because ye satisfied our desire and request by the Acts. And now let your Blessedness decree [them to be read] that we who have followed the Decision (2) of your Holiness, may be able to be taught the things decreed by you (3).

Memnon, Bishop of the Ephesians, said, Nothing hinders that in accordance with the request of the most holy and most devout Bishops, Arcadius and Projectus, and of the most religious and most dear to God Presbyter Philip of the Apostolic See of the Great Rome, (4) the things done regarding the deposition of Nestorius the heretic be again read, that is even a second time. Wherefore let them be read even again.

Peter, a Presbyter of Alexandria and chief of the Secretaries read:

"*In* (5) *the time* (6) *of the consulship of our Masters, Flavius Theodosius, Consul for the thirteenth time, and Flavius Valentinian, Consul for the third time, the ever August ones, on the tenth day before the Calends of July; which is the twenty-eighth of* [the month] *Pauni according to the Egyptians* (7), *the Synod was assembled in the metropolis of the Ephesians in accordance with the decree* (8) *of the most*

NOTE 1.—The same sort of a title. In Greek it is τῇ ὑμετέρᾳ μακαριότητι.

NOTE 2.—Greek, τῷ τύπῳ Here this Roman Legate in the name of all the Roman Embassy professes to follow the Decision of the Council.

NOTE 3.—Greek, τὰ ὁρισθέντα παρ' ὑμῶν.

NOTE 4.—On this expression see a note above.

NOTE 5.—Here begins the quotation from Act I.

NOTE 6.—Both the *Collectio Regia* and *Coleti* have in this place Τοῖς μετὰ τὴν ὑπατείαν, but in both the Τοῖς is lacking at the beginning of Act I. of this Synod. As to μετά see a note on the beginning of Act I.

NOTE 7.—That is June 22, 431.

NOTE 8.—Greek, ἐκ θεσπίσματος, literally "*by the oracle, by the decree,*" for according to Liddell and Scott, in their Lexicon, on θέσπισμα, its first meaning anciently was "*that which is given as an oracle, an oracle,*" and then seemingly to flatter the Roman Emperor in pagan times it was applied to his decrees and also to those of the Roman Senate. For as is shown in note 20, pages 19-21, vol. I. of Chrystal's translation of *Ephesus*, the pagan Romans worshipped their Emperors and their images, and the sin of worshipping their images and using flattering titles to those monarchs and of them continued into Christian

dear to God and Christ-loving Emperors, and there sat down in the most holy Church which is called Mary, the most God-reverencing and most dear to God Bishops, namely Cyril of Alexandria, who was charged with and managed the place of Celestine also, the most holy and most devout Archbishop of the Church of the Romans, and Juvenal of Jerusalem, and Memnon of the [metropolis of the] Ephesians, and Flavian of Philippi, who held also the place of Rufus the most religious Bishop of the Thessalonians, and Theodotus of Ancyra in the First Galatia" (1), (2).

After the things which follow in order, [in the First Act of the Third Ecumenical Synod, most of which Act had been read] "*The Holy Synod said*, [at the end of that same Act I.,] (3): *Forasmuch as in addition to the other things the most impious Nestorius was not willing to obey our summons, and besides, did not admit the most holy and most dear to God Bishops sent by us, we therefore necessarily proceeded to the examination of those things which had been impiously said by him; and inasmuch as we found out in regard to him, both*

---

times and brought ruin. The Synod however use the word here in the sense of *decree* only. For that had come to be its common meaning.

NOTE 1.—Though the above professes to be a part of Act I., translated in vol. 1, it is singular how many changes have been made by the copyists, or somebody else. They are as follows, as in both the *Collectio Regia* and *Coleti's edition of the Councils*:
  1. The words, "*In the days*," or "*times*" (Ταῖς), are lacking in Act I.
  2. "*Flaviou*" (Φλαυίου) is lacking before "Valentinian" in Act I.
  3. A Greek, τῇ, "*the*" is lacking before "*tenth day before the Calends of July*" in Act I.
  4 "*Which is the twenty-eighth of*" [the month] "*Pauni, according to the Egyptians,*" is lacking in Act I
  5. "*And*" (καί) before "*there sat down*," is lacking in Act III.
  6. Act I. has "*most dear to God and most devout Bishops*," where Act III. has "*most God-reverencing and most dear to God Bishops*."
  7. Act I. has the word τῆς, "*the*" referring to "*metropolis*," "*church*" or "*city*" before "*the Thessalonians*," which is lacking in Act III. Our English idiom differs so much from the Greek, that it is not always possible well to make the lesser of these differences clear in our English translations.

NOTE 2.—The above is found in Chrystal's *Ephesus*, vol. 1, page 19 and after.

NOTE 3.—What follows is in Chrystal's *Ephesus*, vol. 1, pages 486–488. The intervening parts are on the intervening pages.

from his Letters and from his Writings which were read, and from the things lately said by him in this very metropolis (1) and testified to in addition, that he thinks and preaches impiously, and forasmuch as we are necessarily moved both by the Canons and by the Epistle of our most holy Father and fellow-minister Celestine, the Bishop of the Church of the Romans, we have [therefore] *come* [though] *often weeping, to the following sad sentence against him: Therefore Our Lord Jesus Anointed who has been blasphemed by him, has decreed through the present most holy Synod that the same Nestorius is an alien from the Episcopal dignity and from every Priestly assembly"* (2).

And the subscriptions of the most religious Bishops followed in [due] order (3).

NOTE 1.—Ephesus.

NOTE 2.—As has been said already, this sentence is from Act I., of the Third Ecumenical Synod translated in vol. 1. See it there. But either by the fault of copyists or others, those two places differ. The variations as in *Coleti* and the *Collectio Regia* also are as follows:

1 Act I. has *"most God-revering Bishops,"* where Act III. has *"most dear to God Bishops"*

2. Act I. has *"did not receive"* δεξαμένου, where Act III. has *"did not admit"* προσδεξαμένου.

3. Act I. has *"the impieties committed by him,"* (τῶν δυσσεβηθέντων αὐτῷ), where Act III. has *"those things which have been impiously said by him,"* τῶν δυσσεβῶς λεχθέντων παρ᾽ αὐτοῦ.

4. Act I. has *"from his letters and writings,"* where Act III. has *"from his letters and from his writings which were read."*

5. Act I. has *"pressed,"* (κατεπειχθέντες) where Act III. has *"moved"* (κινηθέντες).

6. Act I. lacks the expression *"following"* or *"this"* (ταύτην) before *"sad sentence,"* which we find in Act III.

NOTE 3.—They are translated on pages 489-503, vol. 1, of Chrystal's *Ephesus*. Perhaps the other matter on page 503, and the end on page 504 was read also.

From the foregoing parts of this Act III., it is clear that *all* the First Act was read to the Legates of Rome, including not only its decision on the Incarnation, but also on *Man Worship* (ἀνθρωπολατρεία), that is *the worship of a human being*, and on *Cannibalism* (ἀνθρωποφαγία) in the Eucharist, *Economic Appropriation*, and everything else in Act I. And what follows shows that the Roman Legates formally and most clearly accepted the decisions of the Council in that Act on those topics and on every other, so that Rome did most plainly commit herself then to a condemnation of the worship by bowing, invocation, or in any other way *of Christ's mere humanity*, the highest of all mere creat-

A translation of the [following] *statement* [from its original Latin into Greek.]

Philip, a Presbyter, and an Ambassador of the Apostolic See, said,

It is doubtful to no one, but rather has been made known for all the ages, that the holy and most blessed Peter, the leader and head of the Apostles, the pillar of the Faith, the foundation of the Universal Church, received the keys of the Kingdom from our Lord Jesus Anointed the Saviour and Redeemer of the human race, and that authority to bind and loose sins was given to him, who until now and always lives and exercises judgment in his successors (3). Therefore his successor in order and place-holder, our holy

ures, as all admit, and much more to the condemnation by necessary implication of the service by bowing, invocation, or in any other way of *any lesser creature,* be it the Virgin Mary, any other departed saint, or any angel or archangel, and much more to the condemnation of the worship, by bowing, kissing, incensing, or in any other way of *mere inanimate things,* such as crosses painted or graven, pictures, graven images, relics, altars, communion tables *and all other mere inanimate things;* and also to the condemnation of *Cannibalism* in the Eucharist, and hence also, by necessary implication, to the condemnation of Transubstantiation and Consubstantiation both which assert said Cannibalism, and include it as a part of their real substance presence dogma.

NOTE 3.—The Roman Legates did not for the first time put on airs and use stilted language in this Council. They tried it before in the African Council in the days of this same Celestine, when in his name they tried to pass off on the Africans Canons of the local Council of Sardica for those of the Ecumenical Council of Nicaea in order to get Appellate Jurisdiction in Africa, as is shown in Chrystal's Articles on that matter in the *Church Journal* of New York City, for 1870.

The words in the text above may mean nothing more than a claim that the Bishop of Rome, like Peter, was only first among his equals, without implying any claim to Appellate Jurisdiction outside of Italy; and that such a limited primacy is of divine right (*jure divino*). If that was the view of the local Roman Church and of some in the West, it certainly is not that of Canon III. of the Second Ecumenical Council or that of Canon XXVIII. of the Fourth, for both agree in basing its claim to a primacy and privileges on the fact that it was the imperial city. That was, if not the Ecumenical, at least the local Eastern view; and the Eastern local view is as weighty as the local Western or Roman; and to day a large part of the West is Protestant and rejects the local Roman claim, as firmly as the Greeks. Peter, we know, was at Antioch, and in the Acts of the Fourth World Synod it is called a See of Peter, yet it always ranked after Alexandria, a See of Mark, Peter's disciple. (1 Pet. V., 13).

and most blessed Father Celestine, the Bishop, has sent us as repre-

If Philip meant to imply that Peter's Roman See had any right to jurisdiction outside of Italy, his idea has no foundation in the Canons of the first Four World Synods. Indeed it is forbidden by them. See above, page 80, note 4, page 84, note 1, page 90, note 4, and page 91, note 1.

We must remember moreover, that Cyril of Alexandria had assisted the Africans to expose the ignorance or deceit, and the ambition of this very Celestine of Rome, by furnishing them with the genuine Canons of Nicaea, and that Ephesus in its Canon VIII., in effect decided against his unrighteous claim to Appellate Jurisdiction in Latin Africa. Yet, probably from prudential considerations, the Council bears with the not humble language of Rome's Legates, though it took care at the proper time to show its own mind in that Canon. I here add the Greek of the above as in *Harduin. Concil.*, tome 1, col. 1477: Φίλιππος πρεσβύτερος, καὶ πρεσβευτὴς τῆς ἀποστολικῆς καθέδρας εἶπεν· Οὐδενὶ ἀμφίβολόν ἐστι, μᾶλλον δὲ πᾶσι τοῖς αἰῶσιν ἐγνώσθη, ὅτι ὁ ἅγιος καὶ μακαριώτατος Πέτρος, ὁ ἔξαρχος καὶ κεφαλὴ τῶν ἀποστόλων, ὁ κίων τῆς πίστεως, ὁ θεμέλιος τῆς καθολικῆς ἐκκλησίας, ἀπὸ τοῦ Κυρίου ἡμῶν Ἰησοῦ Χριστοῦ τοῦ Σωτῆρος καὶ Λυτρωτοῦ τοῦ γένους τοῦ ἀνθρωπίνου τὰς κλεῖς τῆς βασιλείας ἐδέξατο, καὶ αὐτῷ δέδοται ἐξουσία τοῦ δεσμεῖν καὶ λύειν ἁμαρτίας ὅστις ἕως τοῦ νῦν καὶ ἀεὶ ἐν τοῖς αὐτοῦ διαδόχοις καὶ ζῇ, καὶ δικάζει. On Philip's language above perhaps sufficient is said in this work on page 80, note 4, page 82, notes 1 and 2, page 90, notes 4 and 6, and page 91, note 1. Yet I may add as to the words, "*Peter, the leader and head of the Apostles,*" that the matter is discussed in note 1, page 91 above. Peter was not "*the pillar of the faith,*" but only "*a pillar,*" that is one of many. Peter was very fallible, for in a brief space on one night he committed a triple apostasy from Christ and his faith. He not only denied Him thrice as Christ had forewarned Him (Matt xxvi., 34; Mark xiv., 30, Luke xxii., 34, John xiii., 38), but had added viler features of crime still. Aye, after he had twice denied that he was one of His disciples (John xviii., 17, 25), he went so far in his base cowardice as to commit the frightful sin of perjury by swearing with an oath that he did not even know the man (Matt xxvi., 72,), and when accused the third time of being a follower of Christ he began to curse and to swear (Matt. xxvi., 73, 74; Mark xiv., 70, 71, 72), and he lied a third time (Luke xxii., 59-61); and at Antioch afterwards he denied, in effect, the faith again, for by his conduct he taught that the Mosaic Law is still binding and therefore was justly rebuked by his fellow Apostle Paul (Galat. ii., 11-21). And we must remember that Paul in that scathing rebuke condemns him for very grave crimes, such as "*dissimulation,*" (it is "*hypocrisy*" in Greek, ὑποκρίσει). And whereas, we should expect him to set the newer Apostle Barnabas a good example and to strengthen him, he did not but became to him an occasion of falling, for Paul expressly writes, that because he feared the Jews he would not eat with the Gentiles, but "*withdrew and separated himself*" (Galat. ii., 12), which was a teaching by example *contrary to known duty* in that matter, regarding which God had taught him by a vision at Joppa that Jewish dietary

sentatives of his own presence to this holy Synod, which holy Synod laws, and Jewish exclusiveness were abolished, and by a further miracle at Caesarea in the case of Cornelius (Acts x., 1–48). And to show his guilt the more, that he was committing wilful sin against light, he had defended at Jerusalem his conduct in receiving Cornelius by baptism without the abolished rite of circumcision, and in eating with Gentiles, by appealing to those miracles when the Jewish only partly enlightened, abolished-Law-ridden brethren had said to him, "*Thou wentest in to men uncircumcised, and didst eat with them*" (Acts xi., 3, and the context). And yet now again like a poltroon he refuses to stand up for Christ and his sound doctrine, but horribly enough, he, an Apostle, Judaizes and by his evil example and teaching leads Barnabas to commit the same sin. "*For before that certain came from James*" (the Bishop of the still abolished-Law-ridden and only partly enlightened Jerusalem Church, Acts xxi., 10–27), "*he did eat with the Gentiles*" (as he had confessed that God had taught him to do, Acts x, 14, 15, 28, 34, 35, and the context); "*but when they were come, he withdrew and separated himself, fearing them which were of the circumcision. And the other Jews dissembled likewise with him*" (literally "*played the hypocrite with him*," Greek, καὶ συνυπεκρίθησαν αὐτῷ) "*so that Barnabas also was carried away with their dissimulation*" (literally "*so that Barnabas also was carried away with their hypocrisy*"). And Paul adds that he "*withstood*" Peter "*to the face, because he was to be blamed*," because he "*saw*" that he and the rest of those dissemblers "*walked not uprightly according to the truth of the Gospel*" (Galat. ii., 11, 14), and so he rebukes him for teaching for the abolished Mosaic Law and against Christ and the Gospel: to put it in Paul's own words;

"But when I saw that *they walked not uprightly according to the truth of the Gospel, I said unto Peter before them all,* If thou, being a Jew, livest after the manner of the Gentiles" [that is free from the abolished law of Moses], "and not as do the Jews, *why compellest thou the Gentiles to live as do the Jews?*" [the very thing forbidden by the Holy Ghost in the gathering at Jerusalem in Acts xv., 1–32, so that Peter's fault was against light. He did not act as Paul had, "*ignorantly in unbelief*" (1. Tim. i., 13, compare Acts xxvi., 9, and Acts iii., 17). Then Paul goes on to show Peter that he was in fact inconsistent, a Judaizer, *a sinner and a transgressor* by his hypocrisy, and that we should not charge such sins, as though done by a wicked Economy or dispensation, on Christ, but on ourselves. For he adds] "We were by nature Jews and not sinners" [that is *idolaters*] "of the Gentiles, and having learned that a man is not justified by the works of the Law, but by the faith of Jesus Christ, even we believed in Jesus Christ, that we might be justified by the faith of Christ and not by the works of the Law, for by the works of the Law shall no flesh be justified. But if, while we seek to be justified by Christ, we also are found sinners, is Christ therefore the minister of sin" [that is, canst thou charge Him with the fault of thy sinful and hypocritical and harmful inconsistency?] "God forbid! For if I build again the things which I destroyed," [the errors of the Judaizers who

the most Christian and most man-loving Emperors decreed [should

would have bound the Law on Gentile Christians but who were condemned for that heresy, for example in Acts X., XI., and XV.], "I make myself a transgressor. For I through the Law [*or through a* [new] *law* [of Christ]] died to the [Mosaic] Law, that I might live to God. I have been crucified with Christ. Nevertheless I live, yet not I, but Christ liveth in me, and the life which I now live in the flesh, I live by the faith of the Son of God, who loved me, and gave himself for me. I do not set aside the grace of God," [as thou, Peter, dost], "for if righteousness come by the Law" [as thou Peter impliest by thy Judaizing conduct] "then Christ died in vain," Galatians ii., 14-21. So nobly and warmly did Paul rebuke his erring brother Apostle Peter, and it was necessary, for his conduct at least was an apostasy from Christianity to Judaism, and a man may teach as well by his example as he can by his lips, for as the old proverb has it, *Actions speak louder than words*. In short as though God would antecedently warn us against papal infallibility, His book tells us more of the fallibilities of poor erring Peter than of all the rest of the Apostles put together, except Judas Iscariot. So that if Peter were *"the pillar of the faith,"* and not merely *"a pillar of the faith,"* the Church would have fallen in New Testament times. But it did not because the rest of the Apostles were, each of them *"a pillar of the faith,"* and they stood when Peter fell. For, in Acts xv., 1-32, they and Peter with them forbade the Judaizing error which he followed at Antioch, when *he compelled the Gentiles to live as do the Jews* (Galat. ii., 14). And when in his self-sufficiency, Peter, the first of the Apostles, *first that is among his equals*, (primus inter pares), professed that he would not deny him, Christ told him he would, and he did most shamefully deny Him thrice in one night, and yet the rest of the eleven did not, but stood to their faith though they fled. And when Liberius, Peter's Roman successor, gave way in the Arian persecution and fell, Athanasius, the successor of Mark, stood firm, and, as some one writes, slightly altered, of another, "He was a strong man in the high places of the field, and hope shone in him like a pillar of fire when it had died out in the hearts of most other men." And when in the Fifth Ecumenical Council, A. D. 553, Vigilius, Peter's sorry enough Roman successor, twisted and turned from truth to error, and from error to truth again and again, the rest of the successors of the Apostles stood like *pillars*, censured him, went on without him, saved the faith and the Church, and he was finally forced, much against his will, to come around to the faith which they had defined. And, at the time of the Monothelite controversy in the seventh century, Peter's Roman successor, Honorius, fell into that heresy and was condemned in the strongest terms and anathematized for it by the whole Church, East and West. Rome included, in the Sixth Ecumenical Council, A. D. 680. We must never therefore for a moment agree with the Roman gasconade of Philip the Roman Presbyter that Peter was *"the pillar of the faith,"* but must be guided by the facts which show that like all the rest of the Apostles he was only *"a pillar of the faith,"* a poor pillar at times, for

assemble], because they were mindful of the Universal Faith and that pillar fell on the night when he thrice denied his divine Master Who was delivered up for us all, and he fell at Antioch again: and he needed to be set up again, at first by Christ himself at the lake of Galilee, (John xxi., 1-24), and the next time by Paul's rebuke (Galat. ii., 11-21). Others are mentioned as *pillars* besides him, for example, James and John with him in Galatians ii., 9; and in Rev. iii., 12, Christ promises, *"Him that overcometh will I make a pillar in the temple of my God."* And in I. Timothy iii., 15, Paul the Apostle shows that it is not one Apostle, but the whole Apostolate and ministry and people of the Church which constitutes the fulness of *the pillar*, for he writes that *"the house of God, which is the Church of the living God,"* is *"the pillar and ground of the truth."*

Philip goes on, and pompously calls Peter *"the foundation of the Universal Church."* Here is more Roman bumptiousness and arrogance in these *things passingly said (obiter dicta).* But it is easily refutable from Scripture as well as from the VI. Councils of the whole Church. For while Peter is *a part* of the foundation he is not *the whole foundation* nor is he *the chief corner stone.* For the Holy Ghost by Paul teaches, that we are *"built upon the foundation of the Apostles and prophets, Jesus Christ Himself being the chief corner stone*, in Whom all the building fitly framed together, groweth unto a holy temple in the Lord, in Whom ye also are builded together for a habitation of God through the Spirit,"* Eph. ii., 20, 21, 22. And in the *foundations* of the wall of the New Jerusalem are found *"the names of the twelve Apostles of the Lamb"* (Rev. xxi., 14), not Peter's only. Peter therefore was not *"the* foundation of the Universal Church," but only a part of it, for we are "built upon the foundation of the *Apostles* and *Prophets, Jesus Christ Himself being the chief corner stone,"* (Eph. ii., 20).

Philip adds further that Peter had *"received the keys of the Kingdom,"* which is admitted by all to be true in the sense that as he made the first full confession of Christ's Messiahship and Divinity, he therefore as a reward should be the first after the New Testament had become of force by Christ's death, and the Church, the Kingdom of heaven upon earth, had been established by that act, to admit men into it (Matt. xvi., 16-20). And he did put the keys into the lock of the new Kingdom of heaven, so to speak, by his sermon on the day of Pentecost and by the baptism which followed it by which about three thousand souls were added to the Church (Acts ii., 1-47). But those were all *"Jews and Proselytes"* (Acts ii., 5, 10). As even after that when the Christian religion had become established we find even Jewish Christian brethren demanding that convert Gentiles must be circumcised, and contending that they could not be saved without it, (Acts xv., 1), and that they must *"keep the law of Moses"* (Acts xv., 5, 24), and as they condemned Peter for *going in to men uncircumcised and for eating with them* (Acts xi., 1-4), though those men were believers in the true God, that is Cornelius and his, it seems quite possible that the *"proselytes"* of Acts ii., 5, 10, were proselytes not of the gate, but of righteous-

guard it perpetually; and they have guarded and still guard the

ness, that is they had not only believed in God like the former class, but like the latter class had been circumcised and had absolutely renounced their own nationality and become Jews, and bound themselves to keep the whole law of Moses. Such a proselyte may have been, many think probably was, the Eunuch whom Philip converted and baptized (Acts viii., 26-40). Peter had therefore opened the doors of the Church of the New Covenant, the Kingdom of heaven on earth and above to the Jews.

But the doors of the new Kingdom must be opened to the uncircumcised Gentile also. And God made choice of Peter to do that work, when he gave him that vision on the house top at Joppa and taught him that what He had cleansed he must not count common; and when he gave, just before, another vision to the uncircumcised Gentile Cornelius, and ordered him to send men to Joppa and to *"call for one Simon whose surname is Peter,"* who should *tell him what he ought to do* (Acts. x., 1-7), and he did so. And Peter, prepared by his vision just mentioned, receives Cornelius' messengers, hears from them the story of Cornelius' vision, and of God's order to him to send for Peter, and goes with them to Caesarea, and, contrary to what the narrow Jewish brethren deemed a law, he *went into* the home of the Gentile Cornelius and found many that were come together, and then, referring to the vision at Joppa which had told him that what God had cleansed he should not count common, he tells them he had come: "*And he said unto them, Ye know how that it is an unlawful thing for a man that is a Jew, to keep company, or come unto one of another nation; but God hath showed me that I should not call any man common or unclean.*" Therefore came I unto you without gainsaying, as soon as I was sent for. I ask therefore for what intent ye have sent for me.

And Cornelius said, Four days ago I was fasting until this hour, and at the ninth hour I prayed in my house, and, behold, a man stood before me in bright clothing, and said, Cornelius, thy prayer is heard, and thine alms are had in remembrance in the sight of God. Send therefore to Joppa, and call hither Simon, whose surname is Peter; he is lodged in the house of one Simon, a tanner, by the seaside, who, when he cometh, shall speak unto thee. Immediately therefore I sent to thee, and thou hast well done that thou art come. Now therefore are we all here present before God, to hear all things that are commanded thee of God" (Acts x., 28-34). Here everything shows that *it was Peter who was chosen to open the Kingdom to this uncircumcised Gentile fearer of God.* And at the beginning of his sermon he falls back again on the lesson taught him in a vision that he should not call the Gentile unclean, but that the Christian religion is for all impartially. For we read:

"Then Peter opened his mouth, and said, Of a truth I perceive that God is no respecter of persons, *but in every nation, he that feareth Him and worketh righteousness is acceptable to Him,*" Acts x., 34, 35. Then he preaches the doctrine on Christ to them, and ends with a proclamation of its salvation to all men, for he says, "To Him give all the prophets witness, that through His

Apostolic teaching, which has been handed down to them till now

name *whosoever believeth in Him shall receive remission of sins*" (Acts x., 34-44). "While Peter yet spake these words. the Holy Ghost fell on all those who heard the word. And those of the circumcision who believed were astonished, as many as came with Peter, because that on the Gentiles also was poured out the gift of the Holy Ghost For they heard them speak with tongues, and magnify God. Then answered Peter, Can any man forbid water that these should not be baptized who have received the Holy Ghost as well as we? And he commanded them to be baptized in the name of the Lord."

Here then it is Peter who puts the keys into the lock of the door of the Kingdom of heaven, for by a sermon and by baptism he puts them into it, and opens the doors of the Kingdom of heaven on earth and above to the uncircumcised Gentile.

But Peter was to meet with opposition, for we read after that:

"And the Apostles and the brethren who were in Judaea heard that the Gentiles also had received the word of God. And when Peter came up to Jerusalem, they that were of the circumcision contended with him, saying *Thou wentest in to men uncircumcised, and didst eat with them*". (Acts xi., 1-4). Then Peter falls back on the authority of God in the vision to him which taught him the impartiality of the Gospel and in the corresponding one to Cornelius, and to His attestation of the work by pouring out the Holy Ghost on Cornelius and his.

Then seemingly in wonder at such an unknown and unexpected thing as such a mercy bestowed on the uncircumcised believer, they glorify God. For we read "When they heard these things, they held their peace, and glorified God saying, *Then hath God granted repentance unto life unto the Gentiles also*" (Acts xi., 18).

Afterwards when in Acts XV., the narrow Jewish Christian party wished to make trouble again for the uncircumcised Gentile brethren, and to bind on them the peculiarly Jewish law of circumcision, Peter in the gathering at Jerusalem on that matter refers to the fact that he had already opened the doors of the Christian covenant, the kingdom of heaven, to them. For he said, "Men and brethren, *ye know that a good while ago God made choice among us that the Gentiles by my mouth should hear the word of the Gospel and believe.* And God who knoweth the hearts, bare them witness, *giving them the Holy Ghost, even as He did unto us, and put no difference between us and them, purifying their hearts by faith.* Now therefore why tempt ye God, to put a yoke upon the neck of the disciples, which neither our fathers nor we were able to bear. But we believe that *through the grace of the Lord Jesus Christ, we shall be saved in the same way they also are*" (Acts xv., 7-12).

Peter therefore by the keys of preaching and baptism opened the New Covenant, the Christian Church on earth and in heaven, the kingdom of God, to the Jew first and afterwards to the Gentile, and those doors never can be closed. Paul gathered into them the Jew and the Gentile; so did the other

from their most religious and most man-loving grandfathers (1) and

Apostles, and so have all sound Christian ministers of every order been doing since, and so will they do by preaching and baptism till the end of the world. Peter's only peculiar glory in the matter was that, because of the priority of his confession, he had the glory of first putting in the keys of preaching and baptism which opened it first and forever. For up to Christ no man had ascended into heaven, John iii., 13. Now every saved soul so far as we know goes thither at death, "*absent from the body,.....present with the Lord*," who, we know is in heaven (Acts iii., 20, 21, Acts i., 11; Rev. iv., 1 to v., 14, vii., 9-17, etc., 1 Peter iii., 21, 22; where also all his departed brethren are, for there are the elders, Rev. iv, 1, compared with Rev. v, 6, 9, 10, and the souls under the altar, Rev. vi., 9, 10, 11, compared with Rev. xi., 19, and Rev. viii., 1-4, Rev. ix., 13, and Rev. xiv., 17, 18; and the 144,000 are before the throne of God which is in heaven Rev. xiv., 3, compared with Rev. iv., 1, Rev. v., 7, and there is the "*great multitude*" of the saved "*whom no man could number*," Rev. vii., 9-17. For heaven is the intermediate place of the soul only, till it comes thence with Christ at the beginning of His 1000 years reign on this earth to be reunited to its then to be raised body, and to reign with Him during that time on this earth, after which all the saved dwell in the New Earth and its capital the New Jerusalem (1 Thess. iv., 13-18; 11 Peter iii., 13; Rev. xx., xxi., xxii.,), according to the primitive Church belief in Justin Martyr of the Second Century, etc.

Philip's assertion that Christ gave the Apostle Peter "*authority to bind and loose sins*" is admitted by all. He gave it to him in Matt. xvi., 19. It is admitted also by all that afterwards in John xx., 23, the Redeemer gave it to all the rest of the Eleven Apostles, and that it was exercised by the Apostle Paul who was not of the Eleven, for in I. Cor. v., 1-13, he binds, and in II. Cor. ii., 1-12, he looses the same person on his repentance. And in 1 Timothy, i., 18, 19, 20, he binds. That shows that those powers did not perish with the Twelve but rest in the hands of the highest order of a sound ministry forever for the preservation of Orthodoxy, and discipline. There was therefore no power in the hands of Peter in binding and loosing which was not in the hands of every other Apostle, and which is not in the hands of every sound Bishop to-day, for all such powers, the property of all, are valid because they come from Christ, and it matters not whether as in Jerusalem, they are derived through James, or as in Corinth through Paul, or as in Rome through Peter and Paul, or through any other Apostle.

Lastly, Philip's assertion that Peter the Apostle "*until now and always lives and exercises judgment in his successors,*" is as true of every other successor of Peter, and so Paul is in his successors, and John in his, and James and Barnabas in theirs, and so of any other Apostle. So much for Philip's buncombe which is amply refuted by Holy Writ followed and attested by the Canons of the first four Ecumenical Synods, and the Decisions of the whole Six.

NOTE 1.—Or, "*ancestors*," (πάππων).

fathers of holy memory. Therefore swayed by that care, as we have said before, they ordered the [assembling of the] Synod, in order that the Universal Faith which has been kept till now during the ages, may so remain, and be unshaken perpetually. Nestorius therefore the author (1) of the new perversity and head of the evils was summoned and warned, as has been made clear to us from the Acts of the Synod, in accordance with the forms (τοὺς τύπους) of the Fathers, that is in accordance with the discipline of the Canons, but spurned coming to trial; whereas he should, of his own accord, have presented himself to so great a holy Assembly to get health by spiritual treatment. But because he had a seared conscience, though warned, as I have said before, canonically, even in strict accordance with the discipline of the Canons, he was unwilling to come and make his appearance. And not only had the period of delay (2) granted [him] by the Apostolic See passed by, but also many [other] intervals of time. Therefore the sentence put forth against him who with hostile spirit and with impious mouth dared to bring in blasphemy against our Lord Jesus Anointed (3), is valid and unshaken, [for it is] in accordance with THE FORMULATED DECISION

NOTE 1.—Greek, Νεστόριος .... ὁ τῆς καινῆς διαστροφῆς ἀρχηγὸς. Nestorius was not the originator of all the Nestorian heresy, but seemingly of parts of it only, for, as Cyril of Alexandria shows in his writings against Diodore of Tarsus and Theodore of Mopsuestia, parts of it at least had been advocated by them. Still in its entirety the heresy was Nestorius'. At least he attempted to make it *Universal*, though, before that, it or parts of it had to a great extent infected the Patriarchate of Antioch, as is evident from the great sympathy for him there. For both Diodore and Theodore were of that Patriarchate and by their writings had perverted many into what were later known as Nestorian heresies. So was Nestorius of the same Patriarchate and had learned his heresies from them. In the Oxford translation of "S. *Cyril of Alexandria on the Incarnation against Nestorius,*" page 321, note a, end, we find Cyril quoted as saying, in his first Epistle to Successus, of Diodore as follows: "*His disciple Nestorius became, and darkened by Diodore's books, feigns,*" etc. And in note "a," page 337, id., the annotator writes that Theodore was a disciple of Diodore and a comrade of Chrysostom, and in a note on page 363, Liberatus states that "*he was Nestorius' master.*" It is a question which will bear discussion, whether Chrysostom, though in the main sound, was not at least on the Eucharist affected somewhat by the school of Diodore and Theodore.

NOTE 2.—Greek, τὴν ὑπέρθεσιν.

NOTE 3.—Greek, Ἰησοῦ Χριστοῦ.

OF ALL THE CHURCHES, SINCE THE PRIESTS BOTH FROM THE EASTERN CHURCH AND FROM THE WESTERN CHURCH, ARE PRESENT AND STAND TOGETHER IN THIS PRIESTLY ASSEMBLY, EITHER IN PERSON OR BY THEIR AMBASSADORS (1) For that reason therefore the present Holy Synod also following the forms (2) of the Fathers has put forth a sentence (3) against that blasphemous and reckless (4) man, so that he who was so shameless as not to amend, shall have his part with him of whom it is written, *"His Bishoprick let another take"* (5). Wherefore let Nestorius know that he himself is an alien from the Communion of the Priesthood (6) of the Universal Church.

A translation of the [following] *statement* [out of the original Latin into Greek]:

Arcadius, the most reverent Bishop, and Ambassador of the Apostolic See, said, Very much spoken of by us, and full of tears is the grief and trouble [which comes] from the Formulated Decision of our Priesthood and from Nestorius (7), who though warned by the Letter of the Apostolic See, and moreover by your Blessedness (8), wished nevertheless to go astray both because of his own evil

---

NOTE 1.—*Coleti, Conc.* tom. iii., col. 1156: κατὰ τὸν τύπον πασῶν τῶν ἐκκλησιῶν, ἐπειδὴ συνεστήκασιν ἐν τούτῳ ἱερατικῷ συλλόγῳ διά τε τῶν παρόντων, διά τε τῶν πρεσβευτῶν, τῶν ἀπὸ τῆς ἀνατολικῆς τε καὶ δυτικῆς ἐκκλησίας οἱ παρόντες ἱερεῖς. Philip, though a Latin, brings it as an argument for the validity of the Decisions of the Ecumenical Synod that they were uttered not by Rome only, but by the voice of *the whole Church East* (which he courteously places first,) *and West.*

NOTE 2.—Greek, τοῖς τύποις τῶν πατέρων, that is the Canons of the Fathers, in accordance with which Nestorius had been thrice summoned, etc.

NOTE 3.—Greek, ἀπόφασιν.

NOTE 4.—Greek, προπετοῦς.

NOTE 5.—Acts i., 20.

NOTE 6.—Greek, ἱερωσύνης

NOTE 7.—Or, according to the Latin translation in Coleti, *"from the Formulated Decision of your Priesthood."* The margin in Coleti proposes *"against Nestorius,"* instead of *"and from Nestorius."* The Greek is, ἀπὸ τοῦ τύπου τῆς ἡμετέρας ἱερωσύνης καὶ Νεστορίου. The Latin in the parallel column in Coleti is, Sacerdotii vestri sententia, et ipse Nestorius nobis attulit.

NOTE 8.—Greek, ὑμετέρας μακαριότητος, a title of the Synod.

dogma and his evil-willed judgment (1), as also the sentence put forth against him has made clear [to us], and he did not consider that it was time for him to amend and to set himself straight, and he did not receive the decision formulated by the Apostolic See, and the warning and exhortation of all the Holy Priests (2), by which he might have become sound; for he proceeded to so great [a depth of] impiety that he dared to bring in teaching full of blasphemy against his own Maker and Redeemer, our Lord Jesus the Anointed One (3) and Saviour of the human race, so that, like the old Serpent, he crept in stealthily and perverted those beliefs of the human race which were well regulated and in accordance with God, and as he was unmindful in the first place, of his own salvation and of eternal life, and had the disease of ignorance of the Fathers' Traditions (4); and as he was, moreover, unmindful of the preaching of the prophets, and, besides, of the Gospel and Apostolic Traditions (5), he there-

---

NOTE 1.—Greek, γνώμης.

NOTE 2.—*Priests* (ἱερέων) is here used as often elsewhere among the ancients for "*Bishops*," because the Episcopate is the sole source of ministerial authority. For Christ founded no order except the Apostolate which is the Episcopate. Compare Acts i., 20, 25, etc.

NOTE 3.—Greek, τὸν Χριστὸν.

NOTE 4.—Greek, τῶν πατρικῶν παραδόσεων, that is the Fathers' Transmissions. But what transmissions are specially referred to here?

I answer, Probably the passages of the Fathers on the Incarnation, etc., which were read in Act I., of this Council, to show what their doctrine had all along been and that of the Universal Church. Yet the other writings of the Orthodox Fathers might well be included.

NOTE 5.—Greek, καὶ τῶν εὐαγγελικῶν καὶ τῶν ἀποστολικῶν παραδόσεων. These are written in the New Testament, and in the Apostolic Fathers. Yet the ancients did believe that such customs as had been from the beginning in the whole Church were Apostolic traditions though they be not in Scripture, such, for instance, as the chrisming of the baptized, standing on the Lord's day in prayer, etc. All those customs are right, proper, and should be observed always. None of them is opposed to Scripture. Standing on the Lord's Day and during the whole period from Pask to Pentecost is a law of the whole Church, set forth in Canon XX of *Nicaea*, and the chrisming is found as early as Tertullian as the established custom. It beautifully teaches the Scripture truth that every Christian becomes by his baptism and full initiation by all the rites a priest and a king (1. Peter ii., 5, 9, and Rev. i., 6). On those matters see Bingham's *Antiquities* under proper terms.

fore precipitated himself into his own [peculiar] unbelief. And since, of his own judgment, he has made himself an alien and an exile to us, for that reason we also [for our part] following the Decisions (1) handed down from the beginning from the holy Apostles and the Universal Church, (for they taught that which they had received from our Lord Jesus Anointed); and following also the Decisions (2) formulated by the most holy Father of the Apostolic See, Celestine, who deemed us right for this business, and sent us as his own executors (3), [that is, of his sentence]; and following also the decrees (4) of the holy Synod; [we therefore say], let Nestorius know that he has been stripped of the dignity of the Episcopate, and that he himself is an alien from all the Church Universal and from the Communion of all the Priests.

 A Translation of the [following] *Statement* [from its Latin original into Greek].

 Projectus, Bishop, Legate and Ambassador of the Church of the Romans said: From the reading of the things done in this Holy and most dear to God Synod of so many and so great (5) Priests of God, Nestorius is very clearly cognized as an ungrateful person, who though he had experienced so much forbearance both from the holy Father Celestine, the Bishop of the holy and Apostolic See of the city of the Romans, and, besides, from the [here] present most reverent Fathers and brethren, the Lord's Bishops, [nevertheless] started (6) that unbelief and that blasphemy to his own destruction. Wherefore since he dared to bring in the perversity of his own heresy, against the Gospel Faith and the Apostolic Teaching, which has been confirmed through the Universal Church everywhere, therefore, as a matter of course, I also decide by the authority of an embassy (7) of

---

 NOTE 1.—Greek, τοῖς ὅροις.

 NOTE 2.—Or *"types,"* Greek, τοῖς τύποις.

 NOTE 3.—Greek, καὶ ἐκβιβαστὰς ἑαυτοῦ ἐξαπέστειλε; *Coleti Conc.* tom. III., col. 1157.

 NOTE 4.—Greek, τοῖς δόγμασι.

 NOTE 5.—Greek, τοσούτων καὶ τηλικούτων τοῦ θεοῦ ἱερέων.

 NOTE 6.—Or, *"has taken in hand,"* ἐπικεχειρηκέναι.

 NOTE 7.—Greek, πρεσβείας. As has been shown above, in note 4, page 68, sometimes the word *Ambassador* (πρεσβευτής) is used of Celestine's representatives in these Acts, sometimes *Legate*, (λεγάτος).

Cyril asks that the Roman Legates subscribe the Acts. 111

the holy Apostolic See, inasmuch as with my brethren (1) I am an executor of its sentence (2), that the aforesaid Nestorius, the enemy of the truth, the corrupter of the Faith, as guilty of those crimes of which he is accused, is outside of the grade (3) of the Episcopal honor, and outside of the communion of all the Orthodox Priests.

Cyril, Bishop of Alexandria, said: The statements made by the most devout and most God-revering Bishops, Arcadius and Projectus and, besides, by the most God-revering Presbyter Philip stand clear to the holy Synod. For they have made those statements as filling the place of the Apostolic See, AND ALSO OF ALL THE HOLY SYNOD OF THE MOST DEAR TO GOD AND MOST HOLY BISHOPS IN THE WEST (4). AND THEREFORE THEY HAVE EXECUTED THE THINGS

NOTE 1.—His fellow Legates, Arcadius and Philip.
NOTE 2.—Greek, τῆς ἀποφάσεως ἐκβιβαστὴς ὑπάρχων.
NOTE 3.—Greek, τοῦ βαθμοῦ, *the grade.* The sentence of the Synod on Nestorius in its Act I., has ἀξιώματος, *rank, or dignity.* Arcadius above has ἀξίας, *honor.* The episcopate is often called τάξις, *an order,* also. Compare Chrystal's *Ephesus,* vol. 1, pages 488, 504.

NOTE 4.—On the expression "*all the Holy Synod of the ....Bishops in the West,*" see a note below. The West of to-day was not the West of Cyril's day. Then Germany, Denmark, Norway, Sweden, and other large parts of it were heathen. Latin Africa was no part of Rome's jurisdiction. Nor were Spain, Portugal, and Gaul, and, besides they were of minor account in the ecclesiastical Notitia. The West at that time was mainly Italy, (at least to one living in the remote East), as distinguished from Africa, which was represented by Besula, one of its own clergy, who bore with him a Letter from his own Patriarch, the Bishop of Carthage, which was read in the Synod. And so Cyril means that Italian Synod here. Britain was then little known, and it may well be doubted whether that London which to-day with its 5,000,000 of inhabitants is more than twice the size of Rome in its palmiest days was known even by name to Cyril.

But it is observable how Cyril makes the validity of the Action against Nestorius hinge on the fact that it represented the East, and the West, and not merely the East, and Celestine's See alone. And when there is another Ecumenical Synod what great Sees and Countries will be represented, London the capital of an Empire of about 380,000,000, Paris of the populous land of France, Berlin, the head of powerful Germany, Vienna of many tongued Austria, Moscow or St. Petersburg of the vast empire of Russia, Brussels with Belgium, the Hague with Holland, Copenhagen with Denmark, Stockholm with Sweden, and Christiana with Norway, Washington and New York with the United States, Ottawa with British America, Mexico with Mexico, and so every other nation of North America, and

ALREADY DECREED BY THE MOST HOLY AND MOST DEAR TO GOD BISHOP CELESTINE (1). And, moreover, they have agreed with the vote put forth against the heretic Nestorius by the Holy Synod which is assembled here in the metropolis of the Ephesians. Wherefore let the Minutes of the Acts done yesterday and to-day be joined to those of the Acts done before (2), and let them [all] be presented those of South America, of Australia and of all Oceanica, and the vast array of Christian Asia, and of Christian Africa, most of which were not Christian in Cyril's day. God grant a perfectly sound Synod of them all, and only blessed results.

NOTE 1.—Coleti *Conc.* tom. III., col. 1157. Κατεθέντο γὰρ τὸν τόπον ἀναπληροῦντες τῆς ἀποστολικῆς καθέδρας, καὶ ἁπάσης δὲ τῆς κατὰ τὴν δύσιν ἁγίας συνόδου τῶν θεοφιλεστάτων καὶ ἁγιωτάτων ἐπισκόπων· ὅθεν καὶ τὰ ἤδη ορισθέντα παρὰ τοῦ ἁγιωτάτου καὶ θεοφιλεστάτου ἐπισκόπου Κελεστίνου ἐξεβίβασαν. The sentence of Celestine, even with the approval of Cyril of Alexandria and his large Patriarchate was not final. It was a threat of what would be done to Nestorius unless, within the days specified in it, he amended That time had passed even before the Council met, and it is a significant fact that Nestorius' case was not then considered settled. It needed the positive action of the sole tribunal of the Universal Church, an Ecumenical Synod, against him before that was reached. The East and the West were represented in it in its Act I., in which it deposed Nestorius. For the East was there with its many Bishops, and the West was represented by Cyril for Rome and by Besula for Carthage. And besides each of those two great Western Patriarchal Sees had sent a Letter. The East then pronounced its own Sentence of Condemnation and Deposition on Nestorius, and Cyril spoke for Rome, and Besula for Carthage. But so great was Cyril's care to have the whole Church represented in the verdict for the truth that on the arrival of the Ambassadors of Celestine and of what Cyril here calls "*all the Holy Synod of the most dear to God and most holy Bishops in the West,*" when they wished to have the Acts read to them, and it was done, then Cyril wished them to approve in person the Decisions of the Ecumenical Synod in its First Act which had settled the business of Nestorius and his heresy, and they did so. They pronounced, however, not the verdict of the whole Church, but of their own part of it, and they executed it by pronouncing it.

"*And moreover,*" adds Cyril, "*they have agreed with the vote put forth against the heretic Nestorius by the Holy Synod which is assembled here in the metropolis of the Ephesians.*" This was another thing They first executed Rome's local sentence against him, that is, that in its judgment he should be excommunicated from the whole Church, as they excommunicated him from their part of it and from the whole of it so far as they could do it. Compare Chrystal's *Ephesus*, vol. I., pp. xxxvi-xlix. Then, secondly, they agreed with the way that the Synod some time before had done that very thing.

NOTE 2.—That is Acts II. and III. should be joined to Act I.

The Synod calls on the Roman Legates to subscribe. They do.

to their God-reveringness (1), that they may by their own signature, in the usual manner, make manifest their (2) canonical agreement with us all.

A Translation of the [following] *Statement* [from its original Latin into Greek.]

Arcadius, the most reverent Bishop, and an Ambassador of the Church of the Romans said: In accordance with the things done in this Holy Synod we necessarily confirm their teachings with our own subscriptions.

The Holy Synod said: Inasmuch as the most reverent and most God-revering Bishops and Ambassadors, Arcadius and Projectus, and Philip the Presbyter and Ambassador of the Apostolic See, have expressed their agreement [with us], it is next in order to make good their promise and to confirm by [their own] signature the things done. Let the Minutes of the Acts be therefore presented to them.

A translation of the [following] *Statement* [from its Latin original into Greek].

I, Philip, Presbyter and Ambassador of the Apostolic See, have subscribed to the Minutes.

I, Arcadius, Bishop and Ambassador of the Apostolic See, have subscribed to the sentence put forth against Nestorius the author of the schism and heresy, [and] of all [the] blasphemy and impiety.

I, Projectus, Bishop and Ambassador of the Apostolic See, following out in all things the righteous judgment (3) of this Holy and Ecumenical Synod, as we have learned [them to be] from the Acts, have subscribed to the deposition of the impious Nestorius (4).

NOTE 1.—The Roman Embassy.

NOTE 2.—They were to show their agreement with Cyril and the Synod that it might represent all and so be really Ecumenical, and its decision Ecumenical and final.

NOTE 3 —Greek, κρίσει.

NOTE 4.—Cyril here demands an approval of all the first Act, not of a part of it; and the Roman Embassy here give it, excepting nothing. So that it is clear that they approved not only the condemnation of Nestorius for his denial of the Incarnation, but also for his worship of Christ's mere humanity in the Eucharist and elsewhere and for his Cannibalism in that rite. See on that whole topic note 3, page 98.

A copy of the Report (1) *to the most reverent Emperors regarding the Bishops and Ambassadors who came from Rome. It was sent by the Holy Synod through the Deacon Eutyches.*

To the most religious and most dear to God Theodosius and Valentinian, Victors, Possessors of Trophies, ever August Ones, the Holy Synod assembled by the favor (2) *of Christ* (3) *and the decree* (4) *of your Mightiness, in the metropolis of the Ephesians* [send greeting].

The God of the Universe, O Christ-loving Emperors, has accepted your care and earnestness regarding piety, and He has stirred up the souls of the holy Bishops in the West with zeal to avenge Christ because he has been outraged. For although the very great length (5) of the way seemed at first to hinder all this multitude of the most holy Bishops from coming, nevertheless they have been assembled here, and Celestine the most devout and most dear to God Bishop of the Great Rome is present (6), and now with much harmony they have preached up our sense of the Faith, and they have decreed that those who think otherwise (7) shall be utterly aliens

NOTE 1.—Greek, διαφοράς, *Coleti Conc.* tom III., col. 1160.

NOTE 2.—Greek, ἡ ἁγία σύνοδος, ἡ χάριτι Χριστοῦ, καὶ νεύματι τοῦ ὑμετέρου κράτους συναχθεῖσα ἐν τῇ Ἐφεσίων μητροπόλει, *Coleti Conc.* tom. III., col. 1160.

NOTE 3.—See the last note.

NOTE 4.—See the last note but one.

NOTE 5.—Greek, τὸ πλεῖστον τῆς ὁδοῦ διάστημα.

NOTE 6.—That is by his Legates, as is explained below.

NOTE 7.—Literally, *those who think* [or *"who have thought"*] *outside of that sense*" [of the Faith.] τοὺς ἔξω τούτο φρονήσαντας. It will be noticed that Cyril dwells on the fact that not merely Rome, but what he takes to be *"all the Holy Synod in the West,"* as he writes just below, were on the side of the Orthodox Council of *Ephesus*. And it is very probable that in A. D. 431, in the two parts of the Church of the West represented in the Synod, Rome for Italy, and Carthage for the whole Diocese of Latin Africa, there were many more Bishops than in Gaul, Spain, and Britain, the other Christianized parts of the Occident. Wiltsch in his *Geography and Statistics of the Church*, English translation, vol. I., pages 138-145, gives a list of about 500 sees in the six provinces under Carthage, not to mention 12 other Cathedral Churches which had no Bishops. Bingham makes a total of about 561, not to include a list of 189 more. (Bingham's *Antiquities* "*Appendix on the Six African Provinces*" after Book ix, chapter viii). Bingham thinks that in the 17 Provinces of Italy "there were about three hundred episcopal dioceses," id., Book ix, chapter v., Sect. 1. Of these 17 provinces, 10 were under the Bishop of Rome, and 7 under the Bishop

from every priestly lot and grade. And indeed even before this most holy Synod was assembled, Celestine also the most holy Bishop of the Great Rome had already indicated these things by his own

of Milan. In those under the Bishop of Rome Bingham reckons about 200 episcopates. If the local Council of Rome represented only the jurisdiction of the Bishop of Rome, in South Italy, it, with Africa represented by Besula, would give a Western representation in the Ecumenical Council of A. D. 431, amounting to about 700 or 760 sees. If all Italy were represented in the Roman Council of A. D. 430, it would give a Western representation of about 800 to 860 sees.

Now as to the rest of the West. Bingham (Book ix., chapter vi., Section 10), reckons only about 122 or 132 sees in all Gaul; in Spain he reckons at the most 74 or 76, (book ix., chapter vi., Section xi.). Ireland in A. D. 431 was yet pagân. So was the bulk of Scotland. In what is now England we find before this date three British Bishops in a Council at Arles A. D. 314, but exactly how many there were in A. D. 431 we know not.

Now if we add together all the Western Bishops outside of Italy and Africa in 431, we find only about 200, which is less than were in Italy alone, and in the aggregate only about a fifth of the then known sees of the West. Besides Gaul, Spain, and Britain were then ravaged by the barbarians, and in the two former Arian powers largely predominated; so that Cyril and the Synod are nearly right when they reckon that *"all the Holy Synod in the West"* were in favor of Orthodoxy. Yet it seems clear that when Cyril and the Synod say that the Roman Legates had arrived *"and made clear by the Letter"* [of Celestine] *"the judgment of all the Holy Synod in the West"* to the Ecumenical Council, they do not refer to all the West, nor even to Africa, but only to what was then the dominating country of the West, that is Italy, or the part of it which was ecclesiastically subject to the Bishop of Rome; just, for example, as when men spoke of the Synod of the East they often meant not the whole Episcopate of the Eastern Empire, but only that part of it which belonged to the Church Diocese of the East, and was ecclesiastically subject to Antioch. So we find the term *Asia* used for the whole Diocese of Asia, and sometimes only for the small part of it called also Proconsular Asia.

Or as is stated in note 2, page 72 above, the expression *"all the Holy Synod in the West"* may mean the whole Episcopate of the West so far as known to Celestine and his Legates. Compare furthermore note 1, page 84, and note 4, page 90. It is noteworthy that while the Roman Legates, blow aloud their trumpets regarding Peter's See of Rome, Cyril says little or nothing on that but emphasises the fact that they represented *"the Holy Synod of the West,"* the chief thing when the Synod of Ephesus was to gauge their importance, for that meant not the vote of the Bishop of Rome alone, which was that of one man only, but hundreds of Western votes in favor of the Ecumenical Council and against Nestorius and his partisans, John of Antioch, Peter's Eastern See, and seemingly nearly all the Bishops under it. In other words the talk of the Legates represented Rome's localism and bumptiousness, Cyril's the system in

Letter, and had turned over the holding of his own place to the most holy and most dear to God Bishop Cyril, the Bishop of the Great City of the Alexandrians (1), and now again, and that by another Letter (2), he has made these things clear to the Holy Synod which your Mightiness ordered to be gathered in the metropolis of the Ephesians, and he has sent that Letter both by the most holy Bishops, Arcadius and Projectus, and by the most dear to God Presbyter Philip of the Great Rome, who supply the presence of the most holy and most dear to God Bishop, Celestine. BECAUSE THEREFORE those men have arrived and have made clear, by the Letter (3), THE JUDGMENT (4) OF ALL THE HOLY SYNOD IN THE WEST TO THE SYNOD HERE HELD (5), (6), and because they have shown

---

the Ecumenical Canons, which give every Bishop one vote and no more, and limit Rome's Jurisdiction and give her no eminence except what comes to her from being the imperial city, a reason long vanished and with it her claim to be *"first among her equals."* See in proof Canon VI. of Nicaea and Canon III. of the Second Ecumenical Council, and Canons IX. and XXVIII., of Chalcedon. And at the most she never had any Ecumenically Canonical jurisdiction outside of Italy. For a *primacy of Honor* is one thing and *jurisdiction* another and very different thing. And we must remember that only a few years before *Ephesus*, this very Cyril had aided the Africans against this very Celestine and the Roman attempt to usurp Appellate Jurisdiction over them by trying to palm off on them the local Canons of Sardica as being the Ecumenical Canons of Nicaea. Cyril had exposed the cheat by sending to the Africans the genuine Canons of Nicaea.

NOTE 1.—See Celestine's Synodal Letter of August 11, 430, addressed to Nestorius, pages 202, 203, vol. I, of Chrystal's *Ephesus*. See on it in this volume, page 69, note 1.

NOTE 2.—That is Celestine's Non-Synodal Letter of A. D. 431, addressed to the Third Ecumenical Council.

NOTE 3.— It is found on pages 72-79 above.

NOTE 4.—Greek, τὴν γνώμην.

NOTE 5.—That is the Third Ecumenical. Celestine's Letter is regarded as being not his *mere individual work*, or as conveying his mere single judgment, but what was of vastly greater importance, *"the judgment of all the holy Synod in the West,"* as is specified below. Hence it was regarded not as representing one vote, but the votes of the scores or hundreds of Bishops whose faith it represented. The Letter of Celestine in which he threatened Nestorius with alienation from the Universal Church used justifiable language, for it spoke the language of a Synod of part of the West and agreed with the Egyptian Patriarchate, whose Bishop had stirred up the West and East to this step, and that their understanding both on piety and on the Faith is in harmony with all the Orthodox in the Orient. As the first Bishop of the Church Celestine as "*first among equals*" and as Bishop of the then chief See of the West, uttered in connection with his Roman Synod of A. D. 430, the verdict of his local Church, and, subject to an Ecumenical Synod, what he deemed ought to be the verdict of the whole Church. In other words the controversy between Cyril and Nestorius had become not merely an Eastern question but an Ecumenical one. The Appeal had been made not merely to the great Oriental thrones, but to the West as well, that is to the whole Church everywhere. The great Sees of the Orient had taken sides, Jerusalem and Ephesus and others for Cyril, Antioch for Nestorius. And Rome and Africa of the West answer separately as they were separate Churches, Occidental indeed but independent of each other. The rest of the Occident was reachable only to a small extent, for its episcopates, hardly more than two hundred in prosperous days as compared with the about 300 of Italy, were either wiped out or under the barbarian or Arian harrow. And Rome herself had subject to her own Bishop more than half of the whole Episcopate of the West, outside of Africa, which at this time was ravaged by the Arian Vandals, and, as Capreolus' Letter expressly states, its Bishops were unable to be present at Ephesus (Chrystal's *Ephesus*, vol. 1, pp. 481-486). In other words, Rome and her local Italian Council with the rest of Italy were the only parts of the West then capable of meeting in Council. And it or all Italy had met and decided against Nestorius. But that verdict not satisfying all parties, for the Patriarchate of Antioch and Nestorius of Constantinople, and his partisans here and there, opposed, resort was had to the court of highest, of supreme and final appeal, and the majority of the two great branches of the Church, the East and West, overwhelmingly decided in favor of Cyril and of Orthodoxy and against Nestorian denial of the Incarnation and against its Man Service, that is against its creature service, and besides against its Real Presence doctrine, and its Cannibalistic heresies on the Eucharist. See on the expression "*All the Holy Synod in the West,*" note 7, page 114 above and the note next below.

NOTE 6.—In note 2, on Act II., page 72 above we have shown that Celestine's Epistle to the Synod of *Ephesus* which was read in its Act II., was *not Synodal* but *individual*. We come now to ask therefore what this Report means by the statement that this Letter makes clear "*the judgment of all the Holy Synod in the West*."

It is equivalent to *all the Bishops in the West*, so far as known to the informants of Cyril when he wrote the above Report. It does not mean that there was a Synod held of all the West.

• For there never was a permanent Synod or Council of the whole West. But in accordance with the Canons of Nicaea, it had many Provincial Councils, all of which, outside of Italy, were independent ecclesiastically of Rome according to said Canons, They were not of its Patriarchate. Bingham has shown that very ably in his *Antiquities of the Christian Church* book ix., chapter 1, sections 9, 10, 11, 12.

Furthermore *the circumstances of the time prevented the gathering of a Council of the whole West*, even if it had been desired.

Indeed a large part of it was still pagan. And of the parts which had received the Gospel, Britain was forsaken by the Romans about A. D. 410, and at this period, A. D. 431, was ravaged by barbarians, the Scots and the Picts. And its prelates would have found it difficult to go to Rome.

And the history of the struggle between Hilary of Arles and Leo I of Rome even after this, when the latter tried to get Appellate Jurisdiction in Gaul shows that the Gallic Provincial Councils were not gathered at Rome, and that they were not the same as the Roman Council nor under it. And Gaul and Spain at this time were not subject to Rome, and were so worried by barbarian Arians who had conquered all of Spain and much of Gaul that they could not merge their Synods in the Roman, even if they would. And they certainly would not wish to be slaves to it. And from the records of the struggle of the African Council under Carthage, and its 217 Bishops against the attempts of this very Celestine and his immediate predecessors, Zosimus I. and Boniface I., to secure Appellate Jurisdiction there, it is most clear that the African Bishops were no part of the Roman Council but of the Council of Latin Africa, and that they were entirely independent of Rome, and that *they held that they were and should be by the Canons of Nicaea*, and that they did not receive any Canons of the local Council of Sardica which gave power to any Bishop of Rome. And so it is clear that though, as the Report of the Ecumenical Council to the Emperors states, though the Roman Legates to it may have claimed that this Letter of Celestine *"made clear....the judgment of all the Holy Synod in the West to the Synod"* of Ephesus, nevertheless it can not be said that all the Western Prelates outside of Italy met at Rome, in A. D. 431 nor indeed that any one of them did. In other words Celestine's Letters represent no Council outside of Italy. Rome was wont to misrepresent where it was for her selfish interest to do so, as, for example, her Bishops and Legates, this very Celestine among them, had attempted, only a few years before the Ecumenical Council of Ephesus met, to palm off upon the Latin Africans the Canons of the local Council of Sardica as being those of the Ecumenical Council of Nicaea, See Chrystal's Articles on that struggle between Rome and Carthage in the *Church Journal* of New York for 1870. In all this we wish to show, not that all the Westerns did not approve of Orthodoxy on the Incarnation, which might be safely assumed, but only that there was no such thing in existence then as a Synod of the whole West. Such a thing of course, might be held when there was a reason for it, though mentioned or authorized in no Ecumenical Canon. But there is no proof that it was held in A. D. 430 or 431. In brief, the only Ecumenical Canons, those of the first four Ecumenical Synods, recognize only three sorts of Councils, namely:

1. *That of the Province*, Canons IV., V., VI., and VII., of the First Ecumenical Synod; Canon VI. of the Second, and Canons IX. and XIX. of the Fourth.

2. *That of the whole Civil Diocese*, Canons VI., of the Second World Sy-

nod, and IX. of the Fourth. Where the people of the civil Diocese were in the main of one race and nation and tongue, as for example in Syria, Egypt, Latin Africa, and probably Britain, the Diocesan Council was really a National Council.

3. *The Ecumenical Council* composed of all the God alone-invoking and sound Bishops of the Christian World, and no others.

4. There was also another kind of Council, *that of the whole of the West*, or of *the whole of the East*, but it was very seldom gathered, and then by the Emperors alone or for the most part. It was extraordinary and is not provided for in the Ecumenical Canons. Examples of it are the Council of Ariminum (Rimini) in Italy, gathered by the Arian Emperor Constantius in A. D. 359 to represent the whole West, and that of Seleucia in Isauria, gathered by him in the same year to represent the whole Eastern Episcopate. But both Councils failed to Arianize the Church, for they were finally rejected, and the decisions of the Ecumenical Council of Nicaea stood. Yet the decisions of the local Synod of Constantinople, A. D. 381, which at first represented the Eastern Empire only, finally became Ecumenical by its acceptance by the West. Such a Council was of *an Empire* consisting of *many nations*, whereas the Council of a Diocese was often *National*, as consisting of *the Bishops of one race and nation only*. But no Council representing the whole East, and its many nations, Syrians, Egyptians, etc., seems possible again unless Russia gets it all, in which case, as in the case of the Council of Constantinople A. D. 381, it would be possible for its Emperor, imitating Theodosius the Great, to gather a Council of the whole of Eastern Christendom.

In the middle ages when the Roman Harlot of the Revelations (Rev. xvii., 18) had all the West in her grasp, she held local Councils, composed of the whole West, sometimes with a few prelates from the East whose assent to Rome was always condemned and cancelled by the Greeks. Rome falsely terms such conventicles of idolaters and creature invokers General and Ecumenical, but the Greeks have always rejected them and always will, and they are now rejected by the about 160,000,000 of Protestants of Western Christendom.

A Council of the whole West will never be possible again, till all Occidentals are reformed and meet on the basis of the Six Ecumenical Synods, and on all the doctrine, discipline, rite, and custom which accords with the New Testament and has come down from the beginning there among all.

It should be added that Canon XXXIV. of the so called Apostles recognizes in effect the *National Council*, which corresponds to the *Council of the Diocese* of Canon VI., of the Second Synod of the Christian World, in other words it recognizes each Diocesan that is National Church, such as that of Brittania should be, and the rights of its Exarch, that is Patriarch. It reads as follows:

"The Bishops of each nation must recognize him who is first among them, and account him as [their] head, and do nothing of consequence without his judgment; but each may do those things only which concern his own parish and the [country] places under it. But let not him [who is the first] do anything without the judgment of all: for so there will be unanimity, and God will be glorified through the Lord Jesus Christ by the Holy Ghost."

That Canon and indeed the first 50 of those 85 Canons were received by the Roman Church, and the whole 85 are by the Greeks, (Chrystal's *History of the Modes of Baptism*, pages 89-94). Consequently the first 50 have had Ecumenical Sanction, including of course, the above Canon XXXIV., so that National Churches and the rights of the first Bishop in each are guaranteed by Ecumenically approved enactments.

There were four Appeals allowed and provided for and ordered in the Ecumenical Canons:

1. To the *Synod of the Province* from the decision of any single Bishop of that Province against any of his clergy or people. Canon V., of the First World-Synod, VI. of the Second, and IX. and XIX. of the Fourth.

2. To the *Synod of the* (civil) *Diocese*, Canon VI., of the Second Ecumenical Council, and Canon IX. of the Fourth. Canon II. of the Second forbids the interference of the Bishops of any such Diocese with the affairs of another.

3. *To the Chief Bishop of the Eastern Empire*, that is to the See of Constantinople from any Metropolitan in the Eastern Empire, Canon IX. of the Fourth; he decided it with the few Bishops of his Synod, not with the Synod of all the Bishops of the Orient.

No Canon of any Ecumenical Council authorizes any such Appeal from any Diocese outside of Italy to the Bishop of Rome. On the contrary it is forbidden by Canon II. of the Second Synod.

Yet it was favored by Emperors of the West, who would, so far as they might, concentrate at Rome not only the secular dominion and rule of the Empire of the West, but also the Ecclesiastical. Notable among such tyrannical acts is that of Valentinian III., Emperor of the West, who crushed Hilary, Metropolitan of Arles, who tried to defend his rights and those of Gaul guaranteed by the Canons of Nicaea, against the unjust and unworthy and ambitious attempt of Leo I., Bishop of Rome, to get Appellate Jurisdiction there. For the absolute monarch, and in this case *tyrant*, issued on July 8, A. D. 445, an edict which gave Leo I. Appellate Jurisdiction over what remained of his Empire, for he had lost Britain, Spain, and part of Gaul and Africa. Of course even the imperial power which made that edict became utterly ineffective when the Western Empire passed away in 476. Valentinian the Third's edict is addressed to his general Actius, and he orders it to be enforced by the secular powers under a severe penalty. Migne's *Patrologia Latina*, tome liv., col. 636-640. No Bishop could oppose that. Consequently all had to submit to force, and to tyranny, and the Ecumenical Canons were trampled under foot in all the remnant of Valentinian's Empire. And after the fall of that Empire the same sway of Rome largely prevailed in the West, owing to the ignorance and superstition of Bishops and secular rulers.

By the second sort of Appeal, an Appeal would lie from any part of England to its Exarch, that is Patriarch at London.

mony with us, and have become of one soul [with us] (5), both by those Epistles, and by the commands given them (6), which commands they have stated in written form; therefore we, necessarily and in the performance of those things which are right and proper have made [this] Report concerning their agreement with us (7)

By the third sort of Appeal, an Appeal would lie to the Patriarch of London from any part of the British Empire.

By the second sort of Appeal, an Appeal would lie to the Bishop of any civil Diocese in the United States to the Bishop, that is Patriarch of its chief See, as for example from all the Diocese of New England to Boston, from all New York to Albany or to New York, etc. For there is room for about 8 or 10 such civil, that is Ecclesiastical Dioceses in the United States.

By the third sort of Appeal, an Appeal would lie from any such Diocese against any Metropolitan to the chief Bishop of the nation at Washington.

But unless the Empire is of one race, nationality and speech, this third sort of Appeal will fail as it has in the case of Constantinople, where alone the Greeks are satisfied because it is a Greek See, the other Eastern Church nations, like the Bulgarians for example, not. Of course, it could be enforced by the Imperial power, as was done by the Eastern Emperors till they fell.

Of course two other sorts of Appeal have ever been allowed on great doctrinal questions, namely:

4. To the whole Orthodox Episcopate of the Christian world, in its local Councils which often by its unanimity settled questions without bothering an Ecumenical Synod, and

5. To an Ecumenical Synod, composed of God-alone-invoking, and anti-image-worshipping Bishops alone.

When the 4th sort of Appeal failed as it had on the Arian Controversy, then the 5th and final must be used. The appeal to Alexandria, Antioch, Rome, etc., from both parties at Constantinople was the 4th sort. It failed and then Appeal 5th became necessary.

NOTE 5.—According to the marginal reading in Coleti we may read here ὁμόψηφοι, that is "*of one vote*" with the Synod. This seems the preferable reading because they were of "*one soul*" with the Orthodox Orientals before they voted.

NOTE 6.—Given "the Legates", Greek, καὶ τῶν ἐντεταλμένων αὐτοῖς.

NOTE 7.—"*Their agreement with us.*" Here the Ecumenical Synod insists again that the dogmas put forth by it in its First Act, when there was no Bishop present *in person* from the Occident, (for Rome was represented by Cyril, an Oriental, and Carthage only by the Letter of its Bishop Capreolus and by its Deacon Besula,) were now the dogmas not of the Oriental Bishops alone who had approved them, but by the coming of the Embassy from the West and by their approval of them by their own subscriptions they had become the voice of *the whole Church*, of the East and of the West in effect, for the northern

that your Piety may be able to know that the decision (1) lately set forth by us HAS BECOME (2) THE ONE AND COMMON VOTE OF ALL THE INHABITED WORLD (3): and your zeal for the Faith and for piety has prepared the way for its being better stated in doctrinal form and for its being made plain (4). *Since therefore the matters of*

parts of the West not represented were as yet little more than barbarous, and were ignorant, and of small account. The Synod, in other words, insists that now the doctrine enunciated by the Synod is *Ecumenical*, and not *local*, as it would, they admit in effect, have been, had it been the utterance of the East alone, or of the West alone.

NOTE 1.—Greek, κρίσις· That decision was given in Act I., and it had condemned Nestorius and all his heresies.

NOTE 2 —Before, by the action of the Egyptian Patriarchate, and Rome, and the assent of the great bulk of the Church to whom the Appeal to the Whole Church every where had been made, the decision had been given against Nestorius. This, as has been said, not satisfying Nestorius and the part of the Church sympathizing with him, the final appeal had been taken to an Ecumenical Synod, in the first session of which, though Rome and Carthage were represented nevertheless all the Bishops present were Orientals, and they with Cyril for Rome and Besula for Carthage, had condemned Nestorius and his errors. Now by the coming of two Bishops and a Presbyter from Rome and by their representing in person the Roman Patriarchate in Italy and by their subscriptions in Ecumenical Synod it had become the voice and decree not only of the East and of Africa but also of the whole Church. Yet as one of the Legates implies above, when he speaks of the action of the Roman Embassy which came in at the Second Act, their subscription might seem superfluous, because, that is, Rome had really been represented by Cyril and Carthage by the Letter of its Bishop Capreolus and by its deacon Besula. Yet for greater surety it was deemed wisest to have Rome subscribe again by her own Western Legates. This would better satisfy the Roman Patriarchate which, of course, had the common right of casting its own vote and would be a better proof of the Ecumenicity if the Synod, if the Nestorians should deny it.

NOTE 3.—This was practically true of those parts of it which were then Christian, which, of course, are alone meant, for the greater part of it was still pagan, and the Christian parts which had sent no representatives, such as Britain, Gaul and Spain, were hardly in a position, harried and oppressed as they were by barbarians or Arians, to gather each a Council of its own Diocese, or national Church and to send them. And that was true of Africa as Capreolus, Metropolitan or Patriarch of Carthage, attests in his *Epistle to the Ecumenical Council* (Chrystal's *Ephesus*, vol. 1, pages 481-486) and therefore he sends only his Deacon, Besula, with his Letter.

NOTE 4.—The Ecumenical Council does not profess to make a new doctrine, but to state the old more clearly and more plainly, and by the highest

the business have received AN END (1) both well desired by your Piety and most safe and unerring for all the Churches, and since that end has given the greatest firmness to the Faith, we beg your Piety to release us therefore both from that care and from farther sojourn in this foreign city (2), for some are bound fast by poverty (3), others are held fast by disease, and others are bent over with old age, and are unable to endure a longer stay in this foreign city, and to such an extent is this true that some of us, Bishops and Clerics, have died; and this we have asked, so that we may as a sequence cease from such anxiety" [regarding dogma], "and bestow care upon the Church in the Great City (4). And we earnestly entreat that the court of *the whole Church*, the court of final appeal, representing the whole Apostolate to which alone Christ gave the right, the power and the duty to define doctrine and all else.

NOTE 1.—This expression implies, of course, that the matters of the Nestorian controversy had not *"received an end"* by the decision of Celestine and his Roman Synod in A. D. 430, nor by his Letter to the Ecumenical Council read in its Act II., but by the action of the whole Church, East and West in the Ecumenical Synod. And that indeed is the whole tenor of this Report written by St. Cyril and subscribed by all the rest of the Bishops, and therefore authoritative, aye vastly more so than the special pleaders, like Hefele and other Papists and creature invokers, for the Roman Harlot (Rev. xvii., 18), and for her spiritual whoredom of image worship and saint worship and relic-worship, and wafer-worship which damn the soul forever (Rev. xxi., 8; Rev. xviii., 4; I. Cor. vi., 9, 10, and Galat. v., 19-22.)

NOTE 2.—Or *"strange city."* To Cyril, the writer of this Report, Ephesus was what had formerly been to an Egyptian, or to an inhabitant of Pontus, or of Thrace or of Greece a foreign city. Roman military force alone had made all these and other lands parts of one Empire, not of one nation.

NOTE 3.—Coleti *Conc.* tom III., col. 1160. Greek, Ἐπεὶ οὖν οἱ ἄνδρες παραγενόμενοι τὴν γνώμην πάσης τῆς κατὰ δύσιν ἁγίας συνόδου φανερὰν τῇ ἐνταῦθα γενομένῃ συνόδῳ πεποιήκασι διὰ τῶν γραμμάτων, σύμφωνόν τε ἡμῖν τὸ φρόνημα καὶ τῆς εὐσεβείας καὶ τῆς πίστεως ἔδειξαν, καὶ ἡμῖν ὁμόψυχοι [margin in Coleti ὁμόψηφοι] διά τε τῶν ἐπιστολῶν, καὶ τῶν ἐνταλμένων αὐτοῖς, ἃ καὶ ἐγγράφως κατέθεντο, γεγένηνται, ἀναγκαίως καὶ περὶ τῆς αὐτῶν πρὸς ἡμᾶς συμφωνίας πράξαντες τὰ εἰκότα, ἐπὶ τὸ ὑμέτερον ἀνηνέγκαμεν κράτος. ὡς εἰδέναι ἔχοι ἡ ὑμῶν εὐσέβεια, ὅτι μία καὶ κοινὴ ψῆφος ἁπάσης τῆς οἰκουμένης, ἡ παρ' ἡμῶν ἔναγχος ἐξενεχθεῖσα κρίσις γεγένηται· ἣν ἀναδιδαχθῆναι, καὶ φανερὰν γενέσθαι, ὁ περὶ τὴν πίστιν καὶ τὴν εὐσέβειαν ὑμῶν ζῆλος παρεσκεύασεν· ἐπεὶ οὖν τὰ τῆς ὑποθέσεως πέρας εἴληφεν εὐκταῖόν τε τῷ ὑμετέρῳ κράτει, καὶ ταῖς ἐκκλησίαις ἁπάσαις ἀσφαλέστατον, καὶ τῇ πίστει τὸ βέβαιον παρέχον, δεόμεθα τῆς ὑμῶν εὐσεβείας, ἀνεῖναι λοιπὸν ἡμᾶς τῆς τε φροντίδος, καὶ τῆς ἐν τῇ ξένῃ διαγωγῆς, τοὺς μὲν πενίᾳ σφιγγομένους, etc.

NOTE 4.—Constantinople, the capital city of the East, whose throne was

Letter also which it has been threatened will be sent to the" [secular] "rulers (1) in every place be forbidden and prevented, lest some difficulty be again brought into the Churches (2), or lest some affliction rise up for the most holy Bishops in their own places. For [what true] piety [is] has been declared, and ALL THE INHABITED WORLD HAS SET FORTH A VOTE (3) IN AGREEMENT WITH IT, except a few who preferred the friendship of Nestorius to piety. We ask [therefore] a righteous favor when we beg your Mightiness that we may be therefore released from the care [imposed on us] and may devote our attention to the ordination of the future [Bishop of Constantinople], and thereafter delight ourselves in the fact that both the Faith and Piety have been made firm, and that we are permitted also to send up pure and sincere prayers for your Mightiness to Christ the Lord of the Universe (4).

Cyril, Bishop of Alexandria, drew up the Report (5), and all the most reverent Bishops, who are mentioned in the order of the Minutes, subscribed.

Copy of an Epistle written by the Holy Synod to the Clergy and Laity of Constantinople regarding the deposition of Nestorius.
The Holy and Great and all the World Representing (6) *Synod,*

vacant owing to the deposition of Nestorius; and for which they would appoint an Orthodox Bishop in place of Nestorius deposed. They refer to that below again.

NOTE 1.—Greek, τοὺς .... ἄρχοντας.

NOTE 2.—This letter was evidently in Nestorius' interest; and as a matter of fact the misguided Emperor, Theodosius II., did use the secular power after this for Nestorius, as he had before.

NOTE 3.—This expression "*Vote*," ψῆφον, so often used by Cyril and the Ecumenical Synod refers to the Church way of deciding in Ecumenical Synod, that is by giving each Bishop a vote and letting him use it under the influence of the invoked Holy Spirit, and accepting such a verdict in its purer ages as final.

NOTE 4.—Literally *"to the Anointed Lord of the Universe,"* τῷ Δεσπότῃ τῶν ὅλων Χριστῷ.

NOTE 5.—Greek, Κύριλλος ἐπίσκοπος Ἀλεξανδρείας ἀνήνεγκε. Καὶ ὑπέγραψαν πάντες οἱ ἐν τῇ τάξει τῶν ὑπομνημάτων εὐλαβέστατοι ἐπίσκοποι.

NOTE 6.—Greek, οἰκουμενική.

Epistle of the Synod to the Clergy, and Laity of Constantinople.

gathered by God's grace (1) in the metropolis of the Ephesians, to the most God-revering and most religious fellow-Presbyters (2) and Deacons, and to all the Clergy and the Laity of the holy Church of God which is in Constantinople, wisheth joy in the Lord.

We have come to the very mournful announcement; and though we have first wept at what has come to pass, nevertheless we have been forced by the very necessity [of the case] and to save more from being caught by the plague of his impiety to cut off the author of that disease. For Nestorius who was the appendage of his own impiety has been made to cease from the priesthood (3). Of that impiety ye are witnesses from those discourses which he often audaciously addressed to you; and his blasphemy here was a further addition to those wickednesses. For neither the announcement of the assembling of the Holy Synod nor the multitude of those who assembled restrained him from his rashness; but he added more unendurable blasphemies by saying that he did not bow (4) to a God only two months old, and to a God who had been fed on milk, and that

---

NOTE 1.—Greek, χάριτι, which literally means *"favor"*.

NOTE 2.—Greek, συμπρεσβυτέροις. Here the Ecumenical Synod following the example of the Apostle Peter in 1 Peter v., 1, use the same term that he does to the Elders. It is used in the sense of *age*, not of *rank and order*. For the *"elders"* were probably elders in age at first, and probably the majority of the Ecumenical Synod and of the *"fellow Presbyters,"* that is *"fellow-Elders"* whom they here address were *"fellow-Elders"* in years. See a good note on this in Wordsworth's Greek Testament, who writes on ὁ συμπρεσβύτερος: "' *Your co-Presbyter*'. The *Apostle* St. John calls himself the *Presbyter* (II. John i , III. John 1), and in the third century S. *Hippolytus* calls his master, S. Irenaeus (who was *Bishop* of Lyons), the blessed *Presbyter* (Philos. pp. 202, 222). A Presbyter is not called a Bishop by ancient Ecclesiastical writers, but a Bishop is often called a Presbyter." Yet in Acts xx., the *Elders* (πρεσβυτέρους) of verse 17 are called *Bishops* (ἐπισκόπους), in verse 28.

NOTE 3.—Greek, τῆς ἱερωσύνης, here used as often for the Episcopate, the highest order in the Universal Priesthood of Christian people, and therefore a Bishop is a Priest in a high sense to offer *"spiritual sacrifices,"* the highest of all sacrifices, precisely because they are spiritual, *"acceptable to God by Jesus Christ,"* (1. Peter ii., 5). See on that Chrystal's *Nicaea*, vol. 1, pages 3, 6, and his *Ephesus*, vol. 1, pages 508, 512, page 39, note 95: page 195, note 491, and under *Priest* and *Priesthood* in that volume, and compare note 599. pages 229-238.

NOTE 4.—That is, that he did not worship.

he did not name Him God who fled into Egypt (1). So that as a consequence [of his utterances] nearly all the Economy wrought by the Saviour for us has become a matter of doubt to the more simple. So let it be your work of prayer, to beseech God earnestly to make known a man worthy of the throne of the Great City (2), to Bishop your affairs. For if the imperial City (3) be well governed and directed, the work (4) becomes a common gain to the holy Churches of God every where.

I Cyril, Bishop of Alexandria, wish (5) you to be strong in the Lord, beloved and most desired brethren.

Philip, Presbyter of the Church of the Apostles.
Juvenal Bishop of Jerusalem (6).
Arcadius, Bishop, Legate.
Projectus, Bishop, Legate.
Firmus, Bishop of Caesarea.
Flavian, Bishop of Philippi.
Memnon, Bishop of Ephesus.

NOTE 1.—Certainly when we consider how long the discussion on the Incarnation had been going on, and how plain and clear the Orthodox had made their meaning to be, and all the other circumstances, they were right in deeming this blasphemous language of Nestorius taken in connection with other utterances of his, to be a denial that God the Word was in the babe of two months old, and in effect an assertion that Christ was a mere human being, a creature, who fed on milk, and that he who fled into Egypt was a mere creature alone; in other words all this taken together with his other utterances does show that Nestorius denied the Incarnation, and held that the wise men from the East were guilty of the sin of worshipping a mere creature (Matt. ii., 1-12), contrary to Christ's own holy and immutable law in Matt. iv., 10, "*Thou shalt bow to the Lord thy God, and Him only shalt thou serve.*"

NOTE 2.—Constantinople, the capital of the Eastern Empire.

NOTE 3.—The same city.

NOTE 4.—Coleti Conc. tom. III, (from whose edition I have taken the above Greek where it is not specified otherwise), Col. 1164, gives in the margin κέρδος for the ἔργον of the text. According to that we should translate, "*the gain becomes common to the holy Churches of God every where.*"

NOTE 5.—Or, "*pray,*" (εὔχομαι; the Latin for it in the parallel column in Coleti is "*opto*" "I wish").

NOTE 6.—The arrangement of some of these signatures looks a little queer, for Cyril of the Third See of the Church signs first though Rome's own Western Legates were now present; he is followed by a Presbyter of the First See,

Epistle of the Synod to the Clergy, and Laity of Constantinople. 127

Theodotus, Bishop of Ancyra.
Berianus, Bishop of Perga (1).
Inasmuch as those who deposed Nestorius were above Two Hundred [in number], we are satisfied with the subscriptions herein [above].

---

or of the Second ; and he is followed by Juvenal, Bishop of a See which about twenty years later at Chalcedon gets the fifth place, and he is followed again by the two Episcopal Legates of the First See. Juvenal claimed, as we shall see, the highest rank, and was very prominent in the Council of Ephesus.

NOTE 1.—The order of names here is not exactly the same as in the list of these Bishops at the beginning of Act I. of *Ephesus*, nor is the order there the same as at the end of that Act. See Chrystal's *Ephesus*, vol. I, pages 22, 23, 489, 490, 503. It seems queer to find Juvenal of Jerusalem's name directly after Philip the Presbyter's and before the two Episcopal representatives of Rome. We shall see hereafter how thoroughly ambitious Juvenal was, and how after claiming higher rank he finally agreed with the Patriarch of Antioch to accept the three Provinces of Palestine, a sway and rank much higher than that given him by the Seventh Canon of Nicaea, which had recognized him not as a Metropolitan at all, but as a mere Suffragan. See sessions vii., x., and xiv., of the Fourth Synod of the Christian World. What Hefele writes on Juvenal on page 77, vol. III, seems to be in part based on very doubtful documents.

The Presbyter Philip who signs second above, was probably, Daniell thinks, the same Philip, who was present at the Council of Carthage in A. D. 419 as a legate of Zosimus, Bishop of Rome, when he tried to get the power of Appellate Jurisdiction in Latin Africa, by passing off on the Africans canons of the local Council of Sardica, A. D. 347, as being those of the Ecumenical Council of Nicaea. See *Philippus* 12 and 14 in Smith and Wace's *Dictionary of Christian Biography*. Hefele, though a Romanist, admits the fact of Rome's misuse of Sardican Canons; see in proof the English translation of his *History of the Church Councils*, vol. II, pages 462-478, 480, 481, compare pages 172-176. And as he shows on pages 128, 129, id, Rome has gone even beyond what the merely local Sardican Canons gave her, and in the middle ages by the spurious Isidorean Decretals she got and still has absolute control of all the Western Romish Bishops, clerics, and people.

A WARNING ON PHILIP'S HAUGHTY AND BOASTFUL ROMAN LANGUAGE
ON PAGE 99 ABOVE.

The remarks of Philip the Roman presbyter and ambassador or legate as to the rank and authority of the Apostle Peter and of the transmission of his rank to the Bishops of Rome are not on the great themes for which the Council was gathered and which had been discussed by Cyril of Alexandria in his *Five Books Contradiction of the Blasphemies of Nestorius*, namely, the Incarnation, service to Christ's humanity, and the Eucharist. On the contrary Philip's utterances on Rome are mere *obiter dicta*, utterances that is on things aside from the main things, mere *Passing* incidental *Sayings*. And the Council rightly and wisely gave them the go-by, and fastened only on what was of chief importance, the adherence of the then greatest see of the West, the first see of the whole Church, to the Orthodox Decisions of the Synod.

Philip's assertions may be viewed in three aspects, according to men's opinions:

1, as a claim of Rome to a *jure divino* that is *a divine right Primacy* in the whole Church, but with no *jurisdiction* out of the Roman patriarchate in that part of the West then subjected to it.

Or, 2, it may be looked at as a claim of Rome to a *jure divino* that is a *divine right Primacy* in the whole Church, and also as a claim to *jurisdiction* over the whole of it, East and West.

Or, 3, they may be viewed as a claim for all under No. 2, and also as an assertion of *infallibility* for the Roman successors of the very fallible Peter, who denied his Master and his Christian faith and indeed his being a Christian at all, and all, as Christ told him, in one night before the cock crew twice (Matt. XXVI., 34; Mark XIV., 30: Luke XXII. 34: John XIII., 38. Compare on Peter's denial of the faith and of even knowing Christ, Matt. XXVI., 69 to 75 inclusive: Mark. XIV., 66 to 72 inclusive: Luke XXII., 56 to 62 inclusive: John XVIII., 17, 19 to 28). Compare his betrayal of the faith at Antioch afterwards, and the rebuke given him by Paul for it in Galat. II., 11 and after.

I will speak of these in reverse order, beginning therefore with No. 3; and shall state *what the Six Synods of the whole Church have decided on them.*

Philip of course made no claim of *infallibility* for his Master, the Bishop of Rome. That absurdity was not invented till long after this, not indeed till after the whole Church in the Sixth Ecumenical Synod, A. D. 680, had settled the whole question forever by condemning, in its Definition, Pope Honorius as a Monothelite heretic and an instrument, as it reads, of *"the author of evil."* In that verdict the Universal Church has said not only that a Bishop of Rome *may err* but that a Bishop of Rome *has erred*, and not only that he *has erred*, but also that he has been *Ecumenically condemned* for it. The Romish attempts to dodge and evade that decision are simply repetitions of old and crafty heretical devices such as any one may make against the condemnation of any other Ecumenically condemned heretic. If the Council has not made it clear in its Definition and in its Acts it is impossible to make anything clear. It is illogical and wicked and contemptible to reject the utterances of a Universal Synod deciding with the Christ-promised aid of the Holy Ghost as all believe, and to accept instead the merely local conventicle of the Vatican of A. D. 1869, 1870. Not a single Bishop of the Eastern Church proper, including the Greek Church, the Russian, the Roumanian, the Bulgarian, and the Servian was present, for they all look upon Rome as heretical and as without valid orders, and all of the four Oriental Patriarchates, Constantinople, Alexandria, Antioch and Jerusalem, deny even her baptism. It was an Italian Council in its management and results. The article *Vatican Council* in *McClintock and Strong's Cyclopædia* states on that:

"Of those present a large majority were Italian, while the French and German were least in number, although strongest in learning and importance of the dioceses they represented. The management of the Council was entirely in the hands of the pope and his cardinals and advisers."

According to the Papal Almanac [*Annuario Pontifico*] for 1870, Italy had then 275 episcopates, and the article *Italy* in *McClintock and Strong's Cyclopædia* states the following very important facts which seem not to be well known to most of Rome's dupes in other lands:

"The dioceses of Italy, in point of territorial extent, are smaller than in any other country; and while the (nominally) Catholic population is no more than one eighth of the Roman Catholic population of the World it has more than one fourth of all the dioceses. Thus the Italian bishops have an undue preponderance at every council; and as they generally hold the most ultramontane views, they have considerably contributed to the success of ultra papal theories within the Catholic Church." For *Roman Catholic* and *Catholic* above read the vastly more accurate *Romish* or *Latin*, and the facts are as represented.

Besides, as Dr. Schaff page 141, vol. 1 of his *Creeds of Christendom* tells us, nearly one half of the bishops were entertained during the Vatican Council at the expense of the Pope. They would naturally under the circumstances feel that they could not vote against him. Indeed as every Romish Bishop is at best a mere appointee, a mere vicar of the Pope, and liable to be removed by him at once, there was no such thing as real independence among them.

God seemed to rebuke the giving the lie by this merely local conventicle to the doctrine of the Universal Church in the Sixth Synod that the Bishop of Rome, so called, is fallible. For, as Dr. Schaff adds on page 159 of the same volume:

"The days of the two most important public sessions of the Vatican Council, namely the first and the last, were the darkest and stormiest which Rome saw from December 8, 1869," [the date of the opening of the Synod], "to the 18th of July, 1870", [the day of its close]. "The Episcopal votes and the Papal proclamation of the new dogma were accompanied by flashes of lightning and claps of thunder from the skies, and so great was the darkness which spread over the Church of St. Peter, that the Pope could not read the decree of his own infallibility without the artificial light of a candle."

Quirinus, a Romanist, quoted in a note there, states that after the Council had gone through with "*the Litany of the Saints*," which by the way is the worship of creatures by invocation, condemned by Matt. IV., 10, and by the whole Church at Ephesus, and after chanting the *Veni Creator*, a hymn to the Holy Ghost, to assist them, I would add, in trying to undo the work of the Holy Ghost by the Sixth Ecumenical Synod in condemning Pope Honorius as a Monothelite heretic and an instrument of the devil, then followed "the voice of a secretary reading in a high key the dogma" of the infallibility of the Bishop of Rome, that is the formal contradiction of the Sixth Synod of the whole Church, East and West by this local conventicle of Idolaters.

"At its conclusion the names of the Fathers were called over, and *Placet* [*I agree*] after *Placet* [*I agree*] succeeded *ad nauseam*. But what a storm burst over the Church at this moment! The lightning flashed and the thunder pealed as we have not heard it this season before. Every *Placet* [*I agree*] seemed to be announced by a flash and terminated by a clap of thunder. Through the cupolas the lightning entered, licking as it were, the very columns of the Baldachino over the tomb of St. Peter, and lighting up large spaces on the pavement. Sure, God was there—it was a remarkable coincidence and so it struck the minds of all who were present. And thus the roll was called for one hour and a half, with this solemn accompaniment, and then the result of the voting was taken to the Pope. The moment had arrived when he was to declare himself invested with the attributes of God—nay, a God upon earth. Looking from a distance into the hall, which was obscured by the tempest, nothing was visible but the golden mitre of the Pope, and so thick was the darkness that a servitor was compelled to bring a lighted candle and hold it by his side to enable him to read the formula by which he deified himself."

On page 160 Schaff goes on as to the results of investing with an attribute of God, an unbaptized idolater, deposed and excommunicate by the decisions of the Third Ecumenical Synod for his *worship of human beings* (ἀνθρωπολατρεία) and of the wafer in his alleged Lord's Supper, and for his *Cannibalism* (ἀνθρωποφαγία), and by its Canon VIII. for his usurpation of Appellate Jurisdiction outside of Italy, and for his denial and rejection of the work of the Sixth Synod in condemning his predecessor Honorius as a heretic. He there states:

"And behold, the day after the proclamation of the dogma, Napoleon III., the political ally and supporter of Pius IX., unchained the furies of war, which in a few weeks swept away the Empire of France and the temporal throne of the infallible Pope. His own subjects forsook him, and almost unanimously voted for a new sovereign [Victor Emmanuel, King of Italy] whom he had excummunicated as the worst enemy of the Church. A German Empire arose from victorious battlefields, and Protestantism sprang to the political and military leadership of Europe. About half a dozen Protestant Churches have since been organized in Rome, where none was tolerated before, except outside of the walls, or in the house of some foreign ambassador; a branch of the Bible Society was established, which the Pope in his Syllabus denounces as a pest; and a public debate was held in which even the presence of Peter at Rome was called in question. History records no more striking example of swift retribution of criminal ambition. Once before the Papacy was shaken to its base at the very moment when it felt itself most secure: Leo X. had hardly concluded the fifth and last Lateran Council in March, 1517, with a celebration of victory, when an humble monk in the North of Europe sounded the keynote of the great Reformation."

We come now to the 2nd point above: namely, to consider whether Philip meant to claim for the see of Rome *appellate* or *other jurisdiction* in the whole Church, East and West.

On this matter it will suffice to say that the Canons of the first Four Ecumenical Synods, the only Ecumenical Synods which made Canons, utterly forbid such an error. For Canon VI. of Nicaea tells us definitely who are the rulers of particular parts of the Church, that is, Metropolitans. For it assigns *"Egypt, Libya and Pentapolis,"* to *"the Bishop of Alexandria."*

It makes the assertion that that sort of thing, metropolitical power, was then customary to the Bishop of Rome, and Rufinus, an Italian of the fourth century, on this Canon explains this by stating that the *suburbicarian churches* were subject to him, which, as Bingham in his Antiquities of the Christian Church, Book IX., Chapter I., Sections 9, 10, 11 and 12, shows, include at the farthest ten provinces of Italy, that is, seven on the mainland and the three islands, Sicily, Sardinia and Corsica. See on this *Bright's Notes on the Canons* also. Antioch is mentioned in the same Canon as having a peculiar jurisdiction, which we know from history to have been the civil diocese of the East: a part of which, that is, the three Palestines, was erected as a separate patriarchate under Jerusalem by the Fourth Ecumenical Council in A. D. 451, as we see by its Acts.

Further the same Canon VI. of the First Synod orders that not only in *"Antioch,"* but *"in the other provinces"* also *"the privileges are to be preserved to the Churches,"* which guards the rights of all other metropolitans and their provinces against the claims of Rome or any other see to appellate jurisdiction over them.

And under this very Canon Carthage and all Latin Africa maintained against the very Pope Celestine, who sent this Philip, their rights and rejected his claim to appellate jurisdiction there. And the Fourth Ecumenical Council gave definitely to Constantinople as its jurisdiction the three civil dioceses of Thrace, Pontus and Asia Minor.

And Canon VIII. of this very Synod of Ephesus guards Cyprus against the tyrannical claim of Antioch to jurisdiction there. So that we see from the Ecumenical Canons that jurisdiction was limited in every case; Alexandria's being confined to Egypt, Libya and Pentapolis; Rome's to the Suburbicarian Churches in part of Italy; Antioch's to the civil diocese of the vast region termed the East, which included Syria, Phœnicia, Arabia, Euphratensis, Osrhoene, Mesopotamia, Cilicia and Isauria; and Constantinople's to the three civil dioceses of Thrace, Pontus and Asia Minor, and Carthage's to the six provinces of North Africa under her sway; and that the other provinces which are not specified have their rights guarded in the words in the canon which follow, namely: "*In the other provinces the privileges are to be preserved to the churches.*"

And we are to remember that the patriarchs, that is, Rome, Constantinople, Alexandria, Antioch, Carthage and all other bishops of great sees were as yet only greater metropolitans; and so are the metropolitans of Canons IV. and VI., of the Second Synod, the term *patriarch* not yet being in use to any extent at least, if indeed at all. And if any doubt be entertained as to whether this Canon VI. of Nicaea was meant to guard Western sees, as well as Eastern, from the claim of Rome to *appellate jurisdiction* there, let us remember that we have the best sort of commentary in the resistance, successful to the last, of Carthage and the six provinces of North Africa under it against the claim of Rome to exercise that very jurisdiction there. Among those resisting bishops was Augustine of Hippo, who died in his faith on that point. I have translated and published in the Church Journal of New York City for 1870 some of their documents. They will appear in this work later on.

And what is vastly important is the fact that the Trullan Synod of 691, representing the whole Oriental Church and what of the North African was then left, adopted as its own and as the voice of the whole Church so far as it could make it universal that resistance on the basis of Canon VI. of Nicaea of the Western see of Carthage to any jurisdiction of Rome in its six provinces or any where else where there was a Metropolitan and a province not under Rome, in A. D. 325, when that Canon VI. was made. Seven of the provinces of Italy and three Italian islands as aforeshown were lawfully under Rome as being its original jurisdiction by that same Canon VI., and they alone were. Indeed, some, for example Gothofred and Dr. Cave, held that only a part of that territory was originally under her; see in proof *Bingham's Antiquities*, book ix, chapter 1, section 9. Each of the greater Metropolitans, who was the Bishop of the chief city of one of the 13 or 14 civil dioceses of the Roman Empire, was made a Patriarch by Canons II. and VI. of the Second Ecumenical Synod in A. D. 381, as *Socrates* tells us in chapter 8, Book V., of his *Ecclesiastical History*, and was forbidden to exercise jurisdiction out of it, which prohibits Rome from exercising sway outside of Italy. Bingham in chapter 1 of his ninth book shows how the Church for convenience and better government followed in her provincial and diocesan system those divisions of the Empire. The civil dioceses were largely national divisions, as for example, Britain, Gaul, Egypt, etc., and their churches were generally both Patriarchal and National. And by that system and the Ecumenical Canons the Bishop of London and not he of Canterbury should be Patriarch of all England and Wales.

May not the fact that this very Third Ecumenical Synod in its eighth Canon guarded the rights of Cyprus and all "*the other dioceses and the provinces everywhere*" as it reads, (and by Diocese here must be understood, one or more provinces), against any who had subjugated them or might subjugate them, have something to do with the fact that Carthage had for some years been struggling to maintain its rights by resisting the claims of successive bishops of Rome there, (among them the very Celestine whose legates talk so big at Ephesus in its Acts II and III,), and that the representative of Carthage would naturally speak of such anti-canonical and usurping attempts of Rome against Latin Africa, when the Cypriot bishops mentioned the similar attempts of Antioch against them? Those attempts of Rome as well as those of Antioch may well have led the Synod to forbid such attempts of Antioch in Cyprus, and also as the general and universal wording of the Canon means, to forbid the attempts of Rome in Africa or anywhere else outside of those places which *"from the beginning"* had been *"subject to"* her. See that canon further on. The same prohibition is in Canon II. of the Second Ecumenical Council, and in effect in Canons IV. and V. of Nicaea, and in Canons IX. and XVII. of the Fourth World-Synod, the Appeal to Constantinople there never having been understood to refer to the West, but to the East only.

And the probability that the Synod had the dispute between Rome and Carthage in mind also is vastly increased by the fact that this very Cyril of Alexandria had been appealed to by Carthage for information as to what the Canons of Nicaea were, in regard to the claims of Rome for Appellate Jurisdiction in Latin Africa for which she attempted to palm off Canons of the merely local Synod of Sardica on the Africans as those of the Ecumenical Synod of Nicaea, and Cyril had helped them by sending them the genuine Canons, as had Atticus of Constantinople; and both of these prelates from the tone of their letters and their regard for the laws of Nicaea were evidently in sympathy with Carthage. And this was years before the Third Synod of the Christian World met at Ephesus, for Atticus died in A. D. 426. And Peltier in his *Dictionnaire des Conciles,* places the Council of Carthage, which gave the snub direct to Celestine's attempts to get for his see *appellate jurisdiction* in Latin Africa, in A. D. 426. The Africans in that Synod wrote to Celestine and told him that they had heard from Cyril of Alexandria and Atticus of Constantinople, to both of whom they had sent to get the true Canons of the First Ecumenical Synod, and that the information received had shown them that the Canons alleged by Rome as those of that Synod were not found in it. So well had our Cyril and Atticus helped them to maintain the liberty wherewith Christ had made them free! And Cyril, in all probability, as a theologian would remember the messenger sent by Carthage to him on that very important matter and the attempt to pass what now we know to have been the Canons of the merely local Council of Carthage on the Africans as those of the World-representing Council of Nicaea, and what must have appeared to him either the astounding ignorance of Rome in so doing, or its utter scoundrelism if the fraud was intentional. And he could see that the assault on Carthage was in reality an assault on himself and on every head of a patriarchal or metropolitical see. The assault of Antioch on Cyprus was of the same kind. And hence he had not only oppressed Antioch and Carthage in mind, when in that canon he not only forbids such interference and tyranny in Cyprus, but adds what has sometimes been overlooked, the all-important law, that *"the same thing shall be observed both in the other dioceses and the provinces everywhere."* So that this very valuable law forbids Rome to exercise appellate jurisdiction out of that part of ancient Italy which originally belonged to her, hence not in Africa, not in France, or

Spain, or Portugal, or Great Britain or Ireland or elsewhere, out of those seven provinces of the mainland of Italy and its three islands which belonged to her, namely, Sicily, Sardinia, and Corsica.

The present episcopate of Rome judged not by mere private opinion but by the decisions of the VI. World-Synods is heretical and idolatrous by worshipping relics and images, and by invoking saints, and angels, by wafer worship and wine worship, and by cannibalism in the Eucharist, and by rejecting the decisions of the Sixth Ecumenical Council against the absurd heresy of Papal Infallibility, and is therefore deposed and excommunicate by those ecumenical decisions, aye, is unbaptized and without the slightest claim to exercise jurisdiction anywhere. The Greek episcopate is guilty of idolatry in relatively worshipping relics, pictures, and crosses, and by invoking saints and angels, and by worshipping bread and wine in the Eucharist, and is guilty also of Cannibalism in the Eucharist, and is therefore deposed and excommunicate but not unbaptized, and its prelates, if they cast away those errors and restore all the doctrine, discipline, rite and custom of the Ante-Nicene Church and of the VI Synods, are then deserving of honor as sound Bishops. But, alas! episcopally governed, unreformed Churches are the most idolatrous and worst of all. Hence God's people leave them in strict accordance with Revelations xviii, 4, and 1 Corinthians v, 11, and with the decisions of the VI Synods. Even the Bishops of the Anglican Communion, the best of the Communions claiming succession in the Episcopate, are so criminally remiss in the discharge of their duties as to tolerate idolatry among their clergy, and move not a finger to save their people from it and hell, and five-sixths of them are a curse and deserve deposition and excommunication, and have not the slightest claim to respect or honor. Their sons, the presbyters, make themselves vile by leading unsuspecting and innocent women into spiritual whoredom, the sins of invoking creatures, worshipping relatively altars and crosses and images, and worshipping the Host, as it is called, and to the idolater's hell, and therefore of every such Eli God may well say, as He said of one whose guilt was less because against less light, that *his iniquity shall "not be purged with sacrifice nor offering forever."*

Let us cease to denounce our non-episcopal reformed Trinitarian brethren till we can show them an Anglican Church which does not allow idolatry, and which therefore they may safely join and to which they can entrust their women and children, and till that is done the Ecumenical Canons forbid them to join it. They are safer as they are. For, alas! it is only too true that those who are sending a constant stream of perverts to Rome are not the Romish clergy, but traitorous Anglican Bishops and Presbyters and Deacons who are paid and supported by their own church.

I come now to consider No. 1, that is to consider whether Rome has any claim to a *jure divino primacy* in the whole Church, as distinguished from *appellate jurisdiction* over it. In other words has it *jure divino*, that is *by divine right*, the mere "Privileges of Honor" as they are termed in canon III. of the Second Ecumenical Synod? See also canon XXVIII. of the Fourth Ecumenical Synod.

I answer, No! For these very Canons settle that very question by putting the possession of such privileges by Rome not on the ground of its being a see of Peter at all but simply and only on its civil rank, as the old capital of the Empire, for which reason both those canons give *"equal privileges"* to Constantinople which was not a see of Peter at all. (1.) Indeed it was merely suffragan to Heraclea, the metropolis of its province at first, but afterwards got *"equal privileges"* with Rome because it had become the capital of the Eastern Roman Empire.

That settles it.

Since therefore the Universal Church has settled the question as to *the transmission of any alleged headship of Peter over the other Apostles to the Bishop of Rome in the negative,* by condemning it at Chalcedon in passing its celebrated twenty-eighth Canon in the very teeth of the Papal legates there who could see that it was aimed against their view, and against their opposition and Protest, it will be useless to discuss the question as to whether Peter was the leader and head of the Apostles; for even if the Universal Church had settled the question in the affirmative it would not help Rome a bit, because it has in effect, *plainly denied the transmission of any privileges to Rome from its being a see of Peter.* But the Church has never in any Canon or formal Definition of any Ecumenical Synod sanctioned the Roman notion that Peter was ever the head of the Apostles, though that view has been held by individuals.

And as to the power of binding and loosing, though given to Peter first because he made the first confession of Christ (Matt XVI., 19;); nevertheless it was afterwards given to all the Apostolate (John XX., 22;), and was exercised afterwards by an Apostle not of the Twelve, I mean Paul, for he bound the incestuous member of the Church of Corinth by excommunication (I. Cor. V. 3, 4, 5), and loosed him on his repentance (II. Cor. II., 5 to 12); and he binds Hymenaeus and Alexander (I Tim. I; 20.) for heresy and for opposing the Gospel for they had *made shipwreck of their faith* (I. Tim. I., 19, 20; and II. Tim. II., 16, 17, 18; II. Tim. IV., 14-19, and Acts XIX., 33, 34).

And as to Philip's assertion that Peter is *"the foundation"* (ὁ Θεμέλιος) that is false, though he is *"a foundation"* [stone] in the same sense as the other Apostles, as for instance, James and John and Andrew, and Matthew and the rest. For this is set forth by Paul, an Apostle himself, in Ephesians II., 20, who

---

NOTE. 1.—Hence the Greeks of Centuries XI., XII., XIII., and XIV., maintained that since the Western part of the Roman Empire has perished, and Rome has ceased to be its capital, it has lost its position as the first see, for it was based on its civil rank alone. See in proof *Smith's and Gieseler's Church History,* vol. II., page 228, note—That position is logical and right. But as the Eastern Empire has now perished, and Constantinople has also ceased to be its capital it also has lost the rank given it in Canon III. of the Second Synod and XXVIII. of the Fourth. In a future Seventh Synod there will come a new order of the sees of the Christian World. The Roman Empire is dead beyond resurrection, but the ecumenical principle that in every nation the ecclesiastical rank of every city must follow its rank in the civil notitia will be maintained forever as most rational and most convenient, so that each national capital shall be a Patriarchal see, and each capital of a province shall be a Metropolitical one.

says that *we are built upon the foundation* ('ἐπὶ τῷ θεμελίῳ) (this very word used by Philip) "*of the apostles and prophets*, JESUS CHRIST HIMSELF BEING THE CHIEF CORNER STONE." So that though the privilege of being one of the foundation stones was given to Peter before the others because he first confessed Christ's full divinity, nevertheless the same privilege was given to all the twelve apostles afterwards, though Matthias is now in the place of Judas owing to the latter's apostasy, (Acts I., 15 to 26 inclusive.).

And so we find John telling in the Revelations not that Peter is the whole and sole foundation of the new Jerusalem, but that in its "*twelve foundations*" are "THE NAMES OF THE TWELVE APOSTLES OF THE LAMB," (Rev. XXI., 14).

To Philip's wrong assertions as being mere *obiter dicta*, that is mere *Passing Utterances*, utterances on side matters not then before the Council, the Synod wisely make no reply. The whole Church had already replied in the Third Canon of the Second Ecumenical Synod, as far back as A. D. 381. It was about to reply at the proper time to such egotistic Roman claims in Canon VIII. of this very Third Synod, and in the Twenty Eighth Canon of the Fourth Ecumenical Synod.

And in that eighth Canon of this very Third Council it forbade all claims of Rome to Appellate Jurisdiction in any place except the seven provinces of South Italy and the three Italian islands, Sicily, Sardinia and Corsica. We will, God willing, show that when we come to that enactment. In that it followed Canons II. and VI. of the Second World-Synod.

Moreover, the Third Ecumenical Synod in a quiet but clear way rebuked the seeming idolatry of Celestine in an Epistle which he wrote to it. For, first, whereas his Latin original has regarding the relics of John the Evangelist, the words "*whose remains ye being present, venerate*" or "*worship*," the council did not approve that expression, but the words in the Greek translation, which reads, "*whose remains ye being present have honored*," which does not mean any act of worship, relative or absolute, be it bowing, kissing, or any other; see above, page 77, and note 2 and 3 there.

For, secondly, that the Synod did not understand the terms "*have honored*" in the sense even of *relative worship* is clear from the fact that they condemned and deposed Nestorius, the chief bishop of the Eastern Church, for bowing as an act of relative worship to the highest of all mere creatures, the spotless humanity of Christ; see in proof his Blasphemy 8, page 461, volume I of Chrystal's translation of *Ephesus*, and note 949 there, where further condemnations by the Universal Church of Nestorius and the sin of relative worship are found, and in pages 449, 486-489, and 503, 504. Several others of the *Twenty Blasphemies* of the arch-heretic and creature worshipper on the basis of which he was condemned and deposed contain the same sin of ἀνθρωπολατρεία, that is of "*worshipping a human being*" as Cyril the Orthodox leader of the Council calls it. It was done by applying the name *God*, *Son*, or other names peculiar to God the *Word* to his humanity, or co-bowing to that humanity or co-glorifying it with God the *Word*, that is, co-worshipping that humanity, a mere creature, contrary to Matthew IV., 10 with the uncreated God the Word all which is anathematized in Cyril's Anathema VIII. which was approved by the

Council in its Act 1; see in proof Chrystal's *Ephesus*, vol. 1, pages 331, 332, 221, 222, 223, and for proof of the ecumenicity of the Epistle, id., page 204, note 520.

Furthermore, all opponents of the decisions of the Third World-Council, if Bishops or clerics are deposed, if laics are anathematized: see in proof its first six canons, especially Canon VI.

Consequently, if Celestine in the Latin and not ecumenically approved form of his *Epistle to the Third Synod*, meant to teach even the relative worship of a dead apostle's bones, he is by necessary implication condemned and anathematized in Cyril's Long Epistle to Nestorius which was approved by the whole Church East and West in that Council and others after as is shown in note 520, page 204, vol I. of Chrystal's *Ephesus*.

One other matter shows that the Synod thought so little of his credulity in believing that the Apostles made a Creed that they refused to translate his allusion to it in his *Epistle to Nestorius*, section 4, and approved a Greek translation of that letter without it. It was read in Act 1 of the Council. I have shown that matter in note 444, page 185, vol., 1 of *Ephesus*, where see.

Another instance of the *things incidentally said (obiter dicta)* on the part of one of Cyril's co-laborers for Orthodoxy in the Third Ecumenical Synod, which he did not notice at the time probably because it was not necessary and might have imperilled the truth by turning Juvenal against it, but which he did condemn some time after the Synod is given by Bright in his note on Canon VII. of the First Ecumenical Synod in his "*Notes on the Canons of the First Four General Councils*" as follows:

"Juvenal * * * went so far as to assert, in the fourth session of the Council of Ephesus, that the bishop of Antioch himself (with whom the Council was then at feud) ought to be subject to the '*Apostolic see of Jerusalem*' (Mansi, IV., 1312). Cyril of Alexandria said nothing at the time, but afterwards wrote to Leo, before he became Bishop of Rome, against this pretension (Leo, Epist. 119, 4.)"

ACT FOURTH.

Booklets (1) *offered to the Holy Synod by the most holy Bishops, Cyril of Alexandria and Memnon of Ephesus* (2).

In the time of the consulship of our Masters, Flavius Theodosius, Consul for the thirteenth time, and Flavius Valentinian, Consul for the third time, the Ever August Ones, the Synod being assembled by the decree of the most dear to God and Christ-loving Emperors, on the seventeenth day before the calends of August (3) in the metropolis of the Ephesians, the following sat down in the most holy Church, which is called *Mary*, namely the most dear to God, and most God-revering Bishops,

Cyril of Alexandria who managed the place of *Celestine* also, *the most holy Archbishop of the Church of the Romans*, and

Arcadius, Bishop and Legate of the See of the Romans, and

Projectus, who himself was also a *Bishop and Legate* of the Church of the Romans, and

Philip, a Presbyter and Legate, and

Juvenal of Jerusalem, and

Memnon of the [Church (4)] *of the Ephesians,* and

Flavian of Philippi, who held the place of *Rufus,* the most religious *Bishop of the Thessalonians,* and

Firmus of Caesarea in the First Cappadocia, and

Acacius of Melitene, and

NOTE 1.—Λίβελλοι, *Little Books*, or, as we would say, *Papers*, probably done up like a little book, or pamphlet instead of being on a roll. *Complaint* or *Petition* is a good rendering here.

NOTE 2.—In Harduin. Conc. is here added in Greek what translated is as follows:—" In the Seg. Codex the following words are subjoined, '*Records of the Acts done at Ephesus in which* [Acts] *it decreed excommunication against the Orientals.*'" "*Orientals*" means here those who belonged to the Diocese of the Orient as it was termed, which included the whole Patriarchate subject to Antioch, consisting of Syria and other countries, with the exception perhaps at this time of Palestine, and with the exception of it certainly after the Fourth Ecumenical Synod, A. D. 451. Of course all with John's Orientals are included by Ephesus in their condemnation of *the Apostatic Conventicle.* But the Orientals are mentioned because they were the bulk of that gathering. On the same page in Harduin. we read that "In the Bellov. MS. the title is, '*Acts of Excommunication against John, Bishop of Antioch, and the Bishops who were with him.*'" This is given in Latin in Harduin. in the margin to col. 1486, tom 1, of his Concilia.

NOTE 3.—This was July 16, 431.

NOTE 4.—τῆς, with ἐκκλησίας, πόλεως, or μητροπόλεως understood, I cannot say which; so below several times.

Theodotus of Ancyra in the First Galatia, and all the rest [of the Bishops], and

Besula (5) a Deacon *of Carthage;* and

Hesychius (6), *A Deacon, said,* The in all things most holy and most devout Archbishop of the Church of the Alexandrians, Cyril, and the most holy and most God-revering Bishop of the Church (7) of the Ephesians, Memnon, have offered a Booklet (8) to the most holy and Ecumenical Synod, which is assembled in the metropolis of the Ephesians in accordance with the decree of our most dear to God and Christ-loving Emperors, and we have it in our hands, and will read it, if your Holiness (9) so command.

Juvenal, Bishop of Jerusalem said, Let the Booklet offered by the most holy and most devout Bishops, Cyril the Bishop of the Church of (10) the Alexandrians, and Memnon the Bishop of the Church (11) of the Ephesians, be read, and inserted in the Acts.

Hesychius, the Deacon, read [as follows]:

To the Holy Synod gathered together by the grace of (12) *God and the decree of the most dear to God and Christ loving Emperors, in this metropolis of the Ephesians, Cyril, Bishop of the Alexandrians, and Memnon, Bishop of the Church* (13) *of the Ephesians.*

A pious decree commanded both us and your Holiness to run

NOTE 5.—Besula, being only a Deacon, not a Bishop, had no right *by virtue of his own rank* to have a place in the Synod, but he had as the representative of the Bishop and Patriarch of Carthage. So Philip, being a Presbyter only, had no place in it by any virtue of his own order but he had as a representative of the Bishop and Patriarch of Rome.

NOTE 6.—As Cyril now comes before the Synod as a complainant, his notary or secretary, Peter of Alexandria, no longer leads the reading. That is reserved for a Deacon of his Orthodox friend Juvenal of Jerusalem. The prominence of Juvenal in this Synod is an indication of what was to take place in the Fourth Ecumenical Synod, about twenty years after the Third, when, with the approval of that Council, his See was lifted out of the place assigned to it at Nicaea A. D. 325 in its Canon VII. of suffragan to Caesarea, and made what is now called a Patriarchate. But this was a case in illustration of the Oriental principle from the beginning that Ecclesiastical precedences should follow those of the civil Notitia.

NOTE 7.—See note 4, above.

NOTE 8.—λίβελλον.

NOTE 9.—A collective title of the Synod, but Byzantine and anti-New Testament.

NOTE 10.—See note 4, above.

NOTE 11.—See note 4, above.

NOTE 12.—Χάριν, literally, "*favor.*"

NOTE 13.—See note 4, above.

together in this very metropolis of the Ephesians, that the correct Definition (14) of the Apostolic faith might be strengthened by a common vote, and that the heresy recently brought in by Nestorius might be examined, and put to the test. And your Holy Synod doing all things rightly and canonically, sat together in the holy Church in this very metropolis, and commanded the aforesaid Nestorius to come into the Synod, and to make his defence concerning the blasphemies which he had uttered both in [his] Expositions and in his own Letters, for he had put forth impious and sinful expressions against the Anointed Saviour (15) of us all: and after he had been thrice summoned and could not bear to come and meet us, because he was smitten by an evil conscience, the Synod following the Church's established laws (16) subjected him to deposition; having accurately investigated the charges against him, and having fully ascertained that he is both a heretic and a blasphemer. After these things had been so done and been borne up to the knowledge of our most religious and beautifully victorious (17) Emperors, John, the Bishop of the Antiochians, arrived late, and reluctantly (18), and when he wished, in the metropolis of the Ephesians, and gathered together, as we have learned, certain persons who hold the errors of Nestorius, some of whom have been long deposed, and others of whom have no cities but are Bishops in name alone (19);

NOTE 14.—I think that this refers to the Creed of the First Ecumenical Synod, for that of the Second does not appear in the Acts of the Third. And, so far as the incarnation is concerned, a chief point of dispute between Cyril of Alexandria and Nestorius was as to the teaching of that Symbol on it.

NOTE 15.—Τοῦ . . . . Σωτῆρος Χριστοῦ·

NOTE 16.—What laws are referred to here are not clearly specified. The reference may be to Paul's course towards the incestuous brother in the Church of Corinth, or to the false teachers, Hymenaeus and Alexander (I Corinthians v., 9-13, and I Timothy, i., 20; II Timothy ii, 16, 17, 18, and iv. 14-19), or to the so-called Apostolic Canon LXXIV., if it was in use then. See also the Canons of Ephesus against the Nestorians. Or the reference may be to many local Canons on the trial of Bishops which have since perished, or to general enactments against persons accused.

NOTE 17.—Καλλινίκων ἡμῶν βασιλέων·

NOTE 18.—μόλις, which often means "*scarcely*" or "*hardly*", and seems to be best rendered here by "*reluctantly*."

NOTE 19.—These facts must be remembered in judging of the Apostatic Council of Nestorius. Those who were not under accusation before they came to Ephesus, had placed themselves in the same category of heretics with Nestorius by taking his part and opposing the Orthodox leaders and Synod for justly and necessarily condemning him for his heresies. See the statement regarding them all further on in this document of Cyril and Memnon.

and just as though he were angry that Christ has been glorified by the fact that he (20) who blasphemed against Him has been made to bear a just deposition, he has, we know not why, if indeed the common talk (21) is altogether true, trodden under foot every ecclesiastical law and has outraged all ecclesiastical order by drawing up an impious and unlawful paper; and, supposing that he was able to strike us [with terror] by the [mere] name of deposition, he has committed an unendurable outrage; and that too when the Holy Synod which deposed Nestorius has holy Bishops over two hundred in number—whereas he [on the other hand,] gathered of heretics and others who were accused of crimes only some thirty in number (22). And indeed he had no authority either by ecclesiastical laws or by imperial decree either to judge any one of us, (23), or indeed to attempt any such thing at all, especially against a greater throne (24), and even though he had been permitted (25) to judge, he would have been bound to follow the Church Canons and to give warning to those who had been outraged, and to summon them with all the rest of our Holy Synod to make their defence. But now having made no account of those

NOTE 20.—Nestorius.

NOTE 21.—τὸ θρυλλούμενον.

NOTE 22.—*Harduin-Conc.* tom. I. col. 1487, margin, here adds: "*Below in the Report of the Synod to the Emperors they are said to have been thirty-seven, more or less.*'"

NOTE 23.—Every Metropolitan had his rights guaranteed by the canons of the First Ecumenical Synod and by those of the Second. See especially canons V. and VI. of Nicaea under which the Metropolitan of Carthage in the fifth century and in the sixth defended his rights and those of his provinces against the claim of the Metropolitan of Rome to appellate jurisdiction there. And Canon VI. of the Second Ecumenical Synod is equally strong. I made the chief Metropolitan of a civil Diocese an Exarch or Patriarch.

NOTE 24.—μάλιστα κατὰ μείζονος Θρόνου· Alexandria, though only a see of St. Mark, had always ranked before St. Peter's see of Antioch, because the Eastern Church had always from the beginning, acted on the principle that the ecclesiastical rank of sees should follow the rank of their cities in the civil Notitia. But Alexandria, being more populous than Antioch, always for that reason outranked it in the civil Notitia, and hence in the Ecclesiastical. This is the principle promulgated as Orthodox and Ecumenical in canon III of the Second Ecumenical Synod and in Canon XXVIII. of the Fourth. Rome struggled against it because, after the seat of empire had passed to Constantinople it would give the Bishop of that city a position too much like what she claimed for herself, and because after the fall of the Western Empire altogether in the last half of the fifth century, when Rome ceased to be the chief capital of the Empire, it would cause her to lose her place as the first see of the Church so long as she was in the Roman Empire at least, and so long as Constantinople was the largest capital city of Christendom.

Some of the Greeks were prone to draw that inference. See some of them in *Smith's Gieseler's Church History*, vol. 2, page 228, note. Some of them went as far as to deny that

things, nor having admitted the fear of God into his mind, at the very hour that he came secretly into the Metropolis of the Ephesians, and while no one of us all knew of his audacious deed, he made a mock at his own head, not to say at the laws (26) of the Church, and insults and outrages by a vote (27) of deposition those who up to this day knew nothing [of his audacity]. And indeed what sort of a pretext had he for that thing? Since therefore it is not right for the established laws of the Church to be so trodden under foot, nor for him to bear himself recklessly against greater [numbers], or even for his audacious deeds to pass by unnoticed, which deeds he would not have perpetrated even against one of those who have the lowest grade (28) in the churches and who officiate under his own hand, and since he is here with those who co-perpetrated that thing with him, we necessarily present these very Booklets (29) to your God-reveringness (30), adjuring (31) you by the Holy and Same Substance Trinity, to send for both that John himself and those who got up and performed that drama with him, to come to the Holy Synod and to make their defence regard-

---

Rome is any part of the Church at all, and so denied its baptism and orders, as they do still. See id., Vol. 2, pages 226 and 227, notes.

Rome herself afterwards at Florence in 1439, in what she calls an Ecumenical Synod admitted that Constantinople has the second place, though she would not admit the Eastern principle above mentioned on which it was based by the Ecumenical Synods. She was always forced to treat Constantinople as the second see in fact, from the date of the Fourth Ecumenical Synod, A. D. 451, if not from soon after the Second in A. D. 381. See *Guettee on the Papacy* on that matter and the Pope's letters, etc.

NOTE 25.—Or, "*and even though it had been possible for him to have pronounced judgment,*" εἰ καὶ ἐξῆν αὐτῷ δικάσαι, Coleti Conc. tom. III, col. 1165.

NOTE 26.—τῶν τῆς ἐκκλησίας θεσμῶν·

NOTE 27.—ψήφῳ.

NOTE 28.—τελευταῖον · · βαθμόν· He had dared uncanonically to treat a Bishop of a see which ranked before Antioch, and the Bishop of highest rank in Asia Minor worse than he would one of the lowest grade of his own clerics.

NOTE 29.—Greek, τάδε τὰ βιβλία, ὁρκίζοντες, etc. The Booklets were merely this statement of Cyril and Memnon done up like a little book.

NOTE 30.—A collective title of the Synod, τῇ ὑμετέρᾳ Θεοσεβείᾳ· Whoever wrote these minutes forgot Christian simplicity and lugged in Byzantine title after title. They should never be imitated among us. The Council should be blamed, for it it was guilty of it, because Scripture so far blames it. And it is supreme.

NOTE 31.—That is "*swearing you,*" or "*putting you on your oath.*"

ing their own audacity; for we hold ourselves in readiness to show that he himself has made an unholy and an unlawful attempt to perpetrate an outrage and an insult upon us.

Acacius, Bishop of Melitene said, Both the mere suspicion regarding the men accused is a matter [now] superfluous (33) even if it be true: and the accusation made against the most holy and most dear to God Bishops Cyril of Alexandria and Memnon of the metropolis of the Ephesians is a matter of no account (34). For it was not within the power of those who had apostatized (35) from the Holy Synod and had joined and connected themselves to the wicked opinions of Nestorius, and who were under so great an accusation, to dare to effect any thing against the Presidents of this Ecumenical Synod, nor did they have any authority at all. But since it has been pleasing to your Holiness (36) that they shall be brought to judgment on these matters also, John, the President of such an Apostasy (37) as that, and Bishop of the Church of the Antiochians shall be warned and summoned through the most religious Bishops, Archelaus, and Paul, and Peter, and shall make his defence regarding those things of which he is accused, [and shall tell] for what reason he dared to do such things.

And after Archelaus, Bishop of Myndus in Caria, and Paul, Bishop of Lampe in Crete, and Peter Bishop of Parembola in Palestine had departed and come back, Firmus, Bishop of Caesarea in Capadocia said, Let the most God-revering Bishops who were charged to serve the notice on the most religious Bishop John teach (38) us what sort of an answer they happened to get from him.

NOTE 33.—Greek, Περιττή; literally "*superfluous,*" or "*trivial,*" or "*of no account.*"
NOTE 34.—Greek, Περιττή.
NOTE 35.—ἀποστατήσαντας.
NOTE 36.—A title of the Synod.
NOTE 37.—ἀποστασίας. Nestorius, John of Antioch, and some of the others with them had originally been invited by the Emperor's command to the Ecumenical Council, though most or all of them had refused to sit in it or to obey its decisions in favor of Orthodoxy, but maintained heresy against them on fundamental points of faith and so were justly reckoned as Apostates. Nestorius was an apostate to creature service and to a denial of the Incarnation of God the Word, and to Real one nature Substance Presence and Cannibal views on the Eucharist. And John of Antioch and Theodoret held some or all of those errors of Apostasy, as did probably all or nearly all those with them.

Paul, Bishop of Lampe, said, Having been sent by your Holy Synod to the most religious John, Bishop of the Church of the Antiochians, and having come near his house, we beheld a multitude of soldiers, and some others, bearing arms and swords, and they would not give way for us to get near the gateway (39). But we did get near with difficulty and many things were said by us, to the following effect : We are peaceful, for we are not a multitude. We who have been sent are three [only]. Receive us. The Holy Synod has sent us with pacific utterances, (40) on account of a canonical matter, to the most religious Bishop John. While many therefore stood about us, he knowing, as is likely, the cause of our being sent, did not receive us. And many things were said by many, among which also were abusive (41) words against the Holy Synod and against the Orthodox Faith, which we are not able to serve you by stating with exactness on account of the uproar that was made there.

Archelaus, Bishop of Myndus, said, Though there was a great uproar, and though we came within a little of having to endure peril, we nevertheless came to the house of the most religious Bishop John, while soldiers stood about us with drawn swords, and held clubs, and threatened us, and while a multitude of others stood around ; and [though] we besought many that we be announced, we were not received, we know not for what cause.

Peter, Bishop of Parembola, said, I myself went also together with the most religious Bishops to the house of the most religious Bishop John, and many soldiers brought in weapons, and had them bare and unsheathed, and surrounded us, and many others together with them made an uproar there, and threatened us (42) and uttered blasphemous words against the Orthodox Faith and your holy and dear to God Synod. We begged to be announced and serve the utterances [even the summons] from the Holy Synod on the most

NOTE 38.—διδασκέτωσαν· This is a courteous expression for, " *let them tell us.*"

NOTE 39.—Or portal (τῷ πυλῶνι).

NOTE 40.—Literally, "*sent us having pacific utterances,*" that is, "*sent us who have pacific utterances.*"

NOTE 41.—Or "*blasphemous,*" δύσφημα·

NOTE 42.—The Collectio Regia has ἡμῖν here but Coleti gives ὑμῖν, but the Latin for it in the parallel column in each is "*nobis.*" I have therefore preferred to render by "*us*" instead of."*you.*"

religious Bishop John, [but] we were not admitted, the same most religious Bishop having ascertained, as we suppose, for what cause we were sent: for some of his clerics were present, to whom we said that we were indeed sent by the Holy Synod, but no one permitted us to be received.

Cyril, Bishop of Alexandria, said, Your Holy Synod all see that I indeed and the most religious and most dear to God Fellow-Bishop Memnon are here, and have a good conscience, and are well prepared to defend our reputations. But, as seems likely, both the heretic Nestorius, and John Bishop of the Antiochians who throws the defence of his shield over his dogmas (43) have but one care and aim, which is both to rage senselessly against the laws of Holy Church, and when they are summoned to make their defence in regard to their transgressions, to fence their houses round with arms, and to show that they are inaccessible to those who canonically summon them to make their defence on matters on which they stand accused. Since therefore the aforesaid most religious John fears in regard to his own error, and contrives various pretexts for his own delay, as can be seen from what the most religious Bishops have stated, and still more, as I have been saying, by the fact that he made his own house inaccessible to those who were sent by the Holy Synod, he is clearly casting a vote of condemnation against himself, and accusing his own audacities, on account of which [audacities] he suspects and fears as to his coming to this holy and great Synod. Let therefore your Holiness (44,) which does not lend its ears to vain rumors, and looks into the nature of the affair, cause to disappear, by most lawful votes his unholy and au-

NOTE 43.—Coleti Conc. tom 3, col. 1109: καὶ τῷ ὑπερασπίζοντι τῶν αὐτοῦ δογμάτων Ἰωάννῃ τῷ τῆς Ἀντιοχέων ἐπισκόπῳ.

NOTE 44.—A title here given to this Ecumenical Synod.

NOTE 45.—Coleti Conc. tom 3, col. 1109. Καταξιωσάτω τοίνυν ὑμῶν ἡ ὁσιότης, ἀσυνάρπαστον τὴν ἀκοὴν ἔχουσα, καὶ τῇ φύσει τοῦ πράγματος ἐνορῶσα, τὰ μὲν καθ' ἡμῶν ἀνοσίως παρ' ἐκείνου τετολμημένα ταῖς ἐννομωτάτοις ἀφανίσαι ψήφοις, ὁρίσαι δὲ τὰ δοκοῦντα κατ' αὐτοῦ, τοιαύτην ὕβριν ἐπενεγκεῖν ἡμῖν τολμήσαντος.

The Council proceed to this further on in the Act. Cyril was careful to fortify every point so that no just cause should be given the creature-serving enemy to fault the Synod or its holy work—which was blessed in its results and will be still more so in the future. For those decisions will guide a true Seventh Ecumenical Council.

dacious action and utterances against us, and decree what shall seem good against him who has dared to inflict such an outrage on us. (45)

Juvenal, Bishop of Jerusalem, said, John, the most religious Bishop of Antioch, ought to have considered this Holy, and Great and Ecumenical Synod and straightway to have run to it to make his defence in regard to the charges brought against him, and to have considered the apostolic throne of the Great Rome (46) sitting together with us, and he ought to have obeyed and to have honored the Apostolic Throne of God's holy Church of Jerusalem, at which it was certainly a custom arising from apostolic order and tradition that the throne itself of the Antiochians should be set straight and judged (48). But since in the exercise of his usual

---

NOTE 46.—Rome on the Tiber, as distinguished from Constantinople, which was called New Rome.

NOTE 47. In Hardouin's Concilia tom. 1, col. 1489, margin, is the following reference to a stupid remark of some Romanized Scholiast or Romish Scholiast on this place:

"*Scholion Graec.* διὰ τὸ κακοσύντακτον καὶ ἀνακόλουθον, ἴσως σύνοδων ταύτην, καὶ τὸν ἀποστολικὸν θρόνον συνεδρεύοντα ἡμῖν τῆς μεγάλης Ῥώμης σὺν τῷ ἀποστολικῷ τῆς Ἱεροσολύμων ἁγίας τοῦ Θεοῦ ἐκκλησίας εὐθέως εἰς ἀπολογίαν τῶν ἐπαγομένων αὐτῷ δραμεῖν, ὑπακοῦσαι καὶ τιμῆσαι).

[ἐν ᾗ (παρ᾽ ᾧ μάλιστα ἔθος) δηλαδὴ τῷ τῆς Ῥώμης. Ἐκεῖ γὰρ καὶ τὰ τοῦ Σαμοσατέως ἐξηλάσθη, καὶ ἡ Παυλίνου πρὸς Μελέτιον ζυγομαχία διεγνώσθη.

There is not a word in Juvenal's remarks which favors any appeals to Rome. But the class of Romanizers forgetting canons and facts against their absurdities bring in their follies and misrepresentations where they will.

NOTE 48.—*Coleti Conc.* tom. III, col. 1169: Ἰουβενάλιος, ἐπίσκοπος Ἱεροσολύμων εἶπεν· Ἐχρῆν μὲν Ἰωάννην τὸν εὐλαβέστατον ἐπίσκοπον Ἀντιοχείας, ἐνθυμούμενον τὴν ἁγίαν καὶ μεγάλην καὶ οἰκουμενικὴν σύνοδον ταύτην, εὐθέως εἰς ἀπολογίαν τῶν ἐπαγομένων αὐτῷ δραμεῖν, καὶ τὸν ἀποστολικὸν θρόνον συνεδρεύοντα ἡμῖν τῆς μεγάλης Ῥώμης, καὶ τῷ ἀποστολικῷ τῆς Ἱεροσολύμων ἁγίας τοῦ Θεοῦ ἐκκλησίας ὑπακοῦσαι, καὶ τιμῆσαι· παρ᾽ ᾧ μάλιστα ἔθος αὐτὸν τῶν Ἀντιοχέων θρόνον ἐξ ἀποστολικῆς ἀκολουθίας καὶ παραδόσεως ἰθύνεσθαι, καὶ παρ᾽ αὐτῷ δικάζεσθαι. Ἐπειδὴ δὲ τῇ συνήθει ὑπεροψίᾳ χρώμενος, etc.

Juvenal refers by "*custom*" here probably to what is related in Acts xv. of an appeal being taken to the Twelve Apostles at Jerusalem from Antioch on the question of circumcising the Gentile Christians. And by "*The Apostolic Throne of God's Holy Church of Jerusalem*", he may, perhaps, mean that Jerusalem is Christ's own See, and therefore higher than any other. But though so openly made in the Council, Juvenal's claim was treated like the claims for a *jure divino* Primacy in the whole Church for Rome on the basis of its having it

haughtiness, he has fenced round his house with arms by soldiers, as the most God-revering Bishops sent by this Holy Synod have

from Peter its founder, by succession : that is they were passed by. And the whole Church never admitted the claim of either Rome or Jerusalem. By the Seventh Canon of the first Ecumenical Synod the Bishop of Jerusalem was subject to his Metropolitan at Caesarea. But by the time of this Third Synod, Jerusalem had become the civil capital, and so its Bishop had become superior to him of Caesarea, and in the Fourth Synod definite limits formerly under Antioch were assigned to it. They were the three Palestines. At the Fifth Ecumenical Synod it got in addition Arabia from Antioch. See Bright's note on that Canon VII. of Nicaea in his "*Canons of the First Four General Councils*," and more fully still in the English translation of *Wiltsch's Geog. and Statistics of the Church*, vol. I., page 214, and after. But nevertheless it always ranked, even after that, after Antioch, for it was the Fifth of the Patriarchal thrones, whereas Antioch was the fourth.

And if Juvenal meant to base any claim of Jerusalem to obedience to it from Antioch on the appeal in Acts XV., he was unfair, for that, as the context shows, was to all *the Church Teaching and Governing*, that is to the *whole Apostolate, not to James of Jerusalem alone.*

A humorous fact in this connection is that in response to the Non-Jurors certain Greek prelates who presumed on their theological verdancy and folly proposed to them brazenfacedly to sobject themselves to Jerusalem. That must have been too heavy a joke, for the correspondence came to an end not very long after it.

If it be asked why Cyril and the Synod suffered the claim of Rome to a *jure divino* Primacy in the whole Church, and why it suffered the other extravagant claim of Juvenal, which it might logically enough, from his false basis, extend to a claim of Jerusalem to direct the whole Church, and to its obedience, for the reason he gives for its superiority to St Peter's See of Antioch would apply to Rome, Alexandria, Constantinople and every other See: if this question be asked, I say, the reply is easy. The Canons of the Church in the first two Ecumenical Synods, settled the whole matter against the claims of both. And, moreover, the Eighth Canon of Ephesus made by this same Synod further on, adds still more bulwarking against the claims of both those Sees.

Furthermore, it would have been very unwise on the part of Cyril and the rest of the Council to alienate Rome and Jerusalem unnecessarily from the Synod by wasting time on mere side questions to which the whole Church in its two Ecumenical Synods before the Third, in that, and in the three following, has always given a most emphatic and decided No! Such a course might have resulted in playing into the hands of the Nestorians by dividing the forces of those in favor of Orthodoxy by unnecessary discussions to the neglect of the great questions which they had come to settle, and might have broken it up altogether. Afterwards, as Bright as above shows, Cyril expressed his disapproval of Juvenal's claim, and Rome and the West never for one moment admitted it. Nor has the East at any time admitted the claims of the Roman legates. As it opposed them in the Third Canon of the Second Ecumenical Synod, so it opposed them afterwards in the twenty-eighth Canon of the Fourth, and it has ever maintained those laws and their sense till this very hour.

Leo I., Bishop of Rome, in an Epistle to Maximus, Bishop of Antioch, of June 11, 453, sympathized with Antioch against the claim of Juvenal of Jerusalem to obtain the sway or the chief place in the province of Palestine (ad obtinendum Palestinae provinciae principatum), and speaks of his "*insolent ventures*" to that end "by *spurious writings*" which looks like an unjust charge. He states further that Cyril, Bishop of Alexandria, had been horrified at them and had written to him, Leo, and had pointed out Juvenal's *daring cupidity*, and had asked him to give no assent to unlawful attempts. The Fourth Ecumenical Synod had given Juvenal the headship of Palestine, but Leo here protests against it as a violation of the Canons of Nicaea, that is doubless of its Canon VI. which preserved to all Metropolitans their old and then established jurisdictions, which would make all Palestine, as before for some time, subject to Antioch ; and a violation of Canon VII. also which distinctly made Jerusalem suffragan to Caesarea. Cyril of Alexandria of course had not

stated and made known to us, we therefore, following the Canons, and preserving the usual consecution and order (49), decree that he be summoned again, for the second time. Other most God-revering bishops therefore shall go with the same gentleness as before and summon him to come to the Holy Synod and answer the charges which are brought against him.

And after Timothy, Bishop of Termesus and of Eudocias, and Eustathius, Bishop of Docimium, and Eudoxius, Bishop of Choma in Lycia had departed on that mission and come back, Eudoxius Bishop of Choma, in Lycia, said, In accordance with

---

expressed himself against the arrangement made at the Fourth Ecumenical Synod, for he had died some years before it met, nor is it likely that he would have resisted that decision, for the principle common to all Orientals was that Ecclesiastical precedences should follow the civil precedences, and as Jerusalem had now gotten back its old rank as the head of all Palestine in civil matters, it was fitting it should in those which were Ecclesiastical. And as Leo's opposition never received any backing for any great length of time in the East, and as what there was of it in Antioch soon succumbed to the Fourth Synod, and as furthermore, the Bishops of Rome themselves afterwards admitted the Patriarchal jurisdiction of Jerusalem and do at this very hour, Leo's opposition is now a mere record of a protest which was soon universally disregarded. The Epistle which contains it is in the 119th in Migne's *Patrologia Latina*. See it there, tom. 54, col. 1044, 1045. He says there, with reference to the action of his legates at Chalcedon, that if any thing had been done by them beyond what pertained to matters of faith it had no validity, and with reference to the decision of that Synod of the whole Church, in giving Jerusalem jurisdiction over Palestine, which he deemed a violation of Canons of Nicaea, that for that reason "*it will never be able to obtain the consent of the Apostolic See*" (Apostolicae Sedis numquam poterit obtinere consensum). Nevertheless it did and has it now.

Leo and other Bishops of Rome seemed to fear after the removal of the seat of Empire to Constantinople, or after Constantinople was made the capital of the Eastern half of the Empire, and after it became evident that the Western Empire must fall under the repeated invasions of the northern tribes, and that Rome must then sink into a secondary place, and that its then Primacy, on the Eastern principle, that the ecclesiastical must follow the civil precedences, would pass to its rival, Constantinople. Hence they so often kick against that principle when, in accordance with it, Constantinople ceased to be suffragan to Heraclea, and became the chief see of the Orient and when Jerusalem became the chief see of Palestine. Probably the dread of losing its Primacy by that principle had much to do with their repeated utterances against it, and their unavailing attempts to hinder its application in the East. It was always a dominant fear, and was not without foundation, for some of the Orientals were afterwards, at least, disposed to take away the primacy from Rome on that principle. See *Smith's Gieseler's Church Hist.*, vol. 2, page 228, note.

NOTE 48.—See the last note above.

NOTE 49.—καὶ τὴν ἀκολουθίαν φυλάττοντες· The reference is to the order mentioned by Christ in Matt. xviii., 15 to 19, and laid down as a rule regarding the Apostolate at least. See some harmony of the Gospels on this last point. It was spoken to the Apostolate alone, which is continuous in that Episcopate which invokes God alone, (Acts i., 20 compared with 25). These citations must always be given, according to the general practice of the Church from the beginning.

the command of your God-fearingness (50) we went to the house of the most religious *John, Bishop of the Antiochians*, and we found about his house soldiers with drawn swords, and some clerics, and we besought the clerics, saying, We have been sent by the Holy Synod to tell some words to the most religious Bishop John; and deign ye to announce us. And they went in and signified these things and returned and gave us a reply, saying, The Bishop John said, We make no reply to men deposed by us and who are excommunicate. And when we asked, By whom we had been deposed and are excommunicated, they said to us, By John, the Bishop of the Antiochians. And when we sent to learn more exactly, they said, We do not refuse to say these things before the public Registrars.

Timothy, Bishop of Termesus and of Eudocias, said, As your God-reveringness commanded, we went to (51) the house of the most religious Bishop John: and finding clerics standing before the doors we announced ourselves, and asked to be admitted, and that we might in person tell the words which we had been charged to deliver. And after they had gone in, they gave us this reply, namely, We make no reply to men excommunicated and deposed. Let them not weary themselves by continually summoning us.

Eustathius, Bishop of Docimium, said, In accordance with the command of your Holiness (52) we went to the house where *John*, the most religious *Bishop of the Antiochians*, stays. And we begged of the clerics there found that it might be announced that we must meet personally the same most religious *Bishop John*, and tell him the things declared to him by this Holy Synod. And they went in, and came back to us, and said, We have both deposed and made [them] excommunicate, and let them not weary themselves by summoning us. But we tried to learn the names of those who

---

NOTE 50.—A title here given to the whole Synod.

NOTE 51.—The Greek here Παρεγενόμεθα ἐν τῇ οἰκίᾳ, would in classic times be rendered "*we were in*," or "*we came in*," but Sophocles in his *Lexicon of Later and Byzantine Greek* informs us that in later Greek ἐν is equivalent to εἰς which means both "*to*" and "*into*." The circumstances here would incline us to take the ἐν here therefore in the sense of "*to*," for it does not appear that the two messengers of the council went into the house at all.

NOTE .52—A collective title given to the whole Synod.

had gone in to announce [us], and they were unwilling to tell or to signify them, saying, We are Clerics Public Registrars (53).

Cyril, Bishop of Alexandria, said, Our Lord Jesus Anointed, who also is now present with the Holy Synod (54), laid down [a principle as to] the plain nature of things when he said, *Every one who doeth evil things hateth the light, and cometh not to the light lest his deeds may be reproved* (55). And your Holiness (56) and Sobriety (57) certainly sees that *John*, the most religious *Bishop of the Antiochians*, is even now in that evil position, (58). For if he were conscious to himself that he had done any thing which is canonical and pleasing to God against us, why should he not have come willingly to this Holy and Ecumenical Synod, so that his attempt might be confirmed by your vote (59) and so have more force against us, that is to say if it were in accordance with the ecclesiastical laws? But because he fears this Holy and Great Synod's hatred of wickedness and knows that he has impiously and lawlessly insulted and outraged us, he refuses to come, so as not to have to suffer punishment and wrath most fit for him, for he hides his errors, and is ashamed to make plain his own lawlessness before you (60) [as] judges. Wherefore also we beg this Holy Synod to declare that now and henceforth his audacious actions against us (61) have no validity nor force, and that he be summoned

---

NOTE 53.—Greek, κληρικοί ἐσμεν, καὶ οὐ ταβουλάριοι·

NOTE 54.—Ὁ Κύριος ἡμῶν Ἰησοῦς Χριστός, ὁ καὶ νῦν τῇ ἁγίᾳ συνόδῳ παρών, etc. This belief is in strict consonance with the belief that Christ is with his Apostolate to the end of the world by his guiding Spirit and good providence—a belief founded on his own utterances and promises in the New Testament, but only when they teach in accordance with it, not against it. He was not with Peter in his error, Gal. i., 1-21.

NOTE 55.—John iii., 20.
NOTE 56.—A title given the whole Synod.
NOTE 57.—A title given the whole Synod.
NOTE 58.—Literally "suffers that thing," τοῦτο παθόντα·

NOTE 59.—Literally *"sealed by your vote,"* that is by the vote (ψήφῳ) of the whole Synod. Voting was the most solemn and deliberate way for the Council to act, though sometimes a *viva voce* expression of sentiment in cases of unanimity answered every purpose.

NOTE 60.—The Ecumenical Synod.

NOTE 61.—Or *"against you."* The *Collectio Regia* has *us* (ἡμῶν), but Coleti gives *"you"* (ὑμῶν). The Latin translation in both has however only *"against us"* (in nos).

once more regarding those things which he has unholily done, and subjected to a lawful and most righteous sentence from you and from the Canons.

Memnon, Bishop of Ephesus, said, The uncanonicity of the judgment of the most religious John, Bishop of the Church (62) of the Antiochians, and of certain persons easily counted (63) together with him, have become clear to your Holiness (64), from the INNOVATIONS (65) which he has made and from his disorderly action against the Church Canons. Wherefore also we have stated to your Holiness by means of a Booklet that (66) person's audacious actions against us, and ye, being canonically moved, have summoned him by most devout Bishops to answer for his sins against the Church laws, and [much] more against ecclesiastical order and sequence (67) and to make his defence in regard to those things which he has audaciously done against the canons, but he, following his corrupt conscience, was not willing to obey after being summoned. For that reason we besought your (68) Holy and Ecumenical Synod that the things unlawfully done by him (69) and by those with him who are easily counted (70), some of whom are heretics, and some of whom have no cities, and others [of whom] are under many accusations (71); that those things I say, though without effect and invalid in themselves, be swept away (72) by a vote of the Holy and Ecum-

---

NOTE 62.—Or, "city of the Antiochians."

NOTE 63.—εὐαριθμήτων, that is, there were very few of them.

NOTE 64.—A collective title of the Ecumenical Synod.

NOTE 65.—Greek, ἀφ' ὧν ἐνεωτέρισε· This shows Memnon's idea of the lateness of Nestorius' errors.

NOTE 66.—Greek, τὰ ἐκείνῳ τετολμημένα καθ' ἡμῶν· This may be rendered "*his audacious actions,*" etc.

NOTE 67.—Greek ἀκολουθίας.

NOTE 68.—Or, "our Holy and Ecumenical Synod." Coleti has "*our*," but the *Collectio Regia* gives "*your*." The Latin translation in both has "*your*."

NOTE 69.—John of Antioch.

NOTE 70.—That is, they were very few in number, (εὐαριθμήτων)·

NOTE 71.—Or, "liable to many accusations," πολλαῖς αἰτίαις ὑπεύθυνοι ὄντες.

NOTE 72.—καταλυθῆναι καὶ ψήφῳ τῆς ἁγίας καὶ οἰκουμενικῆς συνόδου·

enical Synod, and that ye approve your (73) stand regarding the Orthodox Faith, which we have received from the Holy Fathers, and that ye decree what is proper against them (74).

THE HOLY SYNOD SAID, IT HAS BEEN MADE CLEAR BY THOSE THINGS WHICH HAVE BEEN DONE (75) THAT JOHN WAS UNCANONICALLY MOVED IN EVERYTHING, AND THAT HIS ACTIONS POSSESS NEITHER VALIDITY NOR ORDER NOR EFFECT. FOR SURELY, IF HIS ACTIONS HAD ANY REASONABLE ORDER, HE WOULD HAVE HAD THE COURAGE TO DEFEND HIS INNOVATIONS (76) WHEN SUMMONED BY THE HOLY SYNOD. WHEREFORE, INASMUCH AS THOSE ACTIONS HAD NO VALIDITY NOR FORCE AT THE BEGINNING, AND WERE NOT DONE FOR CANONICAL REASON, THE HOLY SYNOD DECLARES THEM INVALID AND WITHOUT FORCE, AND THAT THEY CAN WORK NO PREJUDICE TO ANY ONE OF THOSE INSULTED AND OUTRAGED [by them] AND THE [most] HOLY (77) SYNOD DOING THAT WHICH IS A SEQUENCE AND WHICH BELONGS TO ITSELF, WILL BRING THE THINGS DONE [by it] TO-DAY TO THE KNOWLEDGE OF THE MOST RELIGIOUS AND CHRIST-LOVING EMPERORS, SO THAT NOTHING OF THE AUDACITIES OF JOHN'S IMPUDENCE DONE IN INSULT AND OUTRAGE AGAINST THE HOLY SYNOD MAY BE UNKNOWN TO THEM, AND AFTER THE MOST RELIGIOUS BISHOP JOHN HAS BEEN SUMMONED BY A THIRD CITATION, UNLESS HE COMES AND MEETS US. THEN IN ACCORDANCE WITH THE CANONS, THE HOLY AND ECUMENICAL SYNOD WILL VOTE TO HIM THE PUNISHMENT WHICH IS DUE TO HIM (78).

NOTE 73.—Or, "*our stand regarding the Orthodox Faith.*"

NOTE 74.—John of Antioch and his conventicle.

NOTE 75.—That is from what John and his conventicle had done.

NOTE 76.—ἀφ' ὧν ἐνεωτέρισε· This shows that the Church looked upon John's actions and that of his Synod as novelties as they certainly were, for they were against the canons and doctrine of the whole church. But he and Nestorius had put their trust in princes, that is in the secular power, to aid them in their uncanonical course, and in their anti-incarnation, Man-worshipping and cannibalizing heresies.

NOTE 77.—The *most* is lacking in the Latin translation in both Coleti and the Collectio Regia, but is found in the Greek of them both. As "*holy*" is a term commonly used of the Synod in these Acts. I think it likely that it was used here, but that some copyist, used to the high-sounding titles of the Orient, has changed it for "*most holy*" by mistake. Still it is not certain.

NOTE 78.—I have translated Act IV. from the Greek as given in the *Concilia* of Coleti, tom. III., col. 1164-1170, but have compared in places the *Collectio Regia*, tom. V., pages 613 625, and Mansi tom. IV., and Harduin, tom. 1; from the last of whom I have taken some marginal matter which is in Mansi also.

Act Fifth.

In the days of the consulship of our Masters, Flavius Theodosius, consul for the thirteenth time (79), and Flavius Valentinian, consul for the third time, the Ever-August Ones, on the sixteenth day before the calends of August (80), on that same day, after the Holy Synod itself of the most dear to God and most God-revering Bishops had sat down in the same Church, which is called Mary (81), *Cyril, Bishop of Alexandria*, said :

Yesterday, while your Holiness (82) was sitting here, and while the legates, that is the place-holders, of the most holy and most dear to God Bishop Celestine, who have been sent from the Great Rome (83) were also present, both I and the most dear to God Memnon, Bishop of this very metropolis of the Ephesians, presented booklets, (84) and asked that the most religious Bishop John of the episcopate of the Antiochians, and those who together with him contrived the outrage and insult against us and dared to fore-decree

---

NOTE 79.—The Greek here as in Mansi's *Concilia*, tome 4, col. 1317, is Τοῖς μετὰ τὴν ὑπατείαν τῶν δεσποτῶν ἡμῶν, Φλαυίου Θεοδοσίου τὸ τρισκαιδέκατον, etc.

The Latin translation in the parallel column 1318, is "Post consulatum dominorum nostrorum semper Augustorum Flavii Theodosii xiii., etc.

NOTE 80.—That is, in our way of reckoning, July 17, 431.

NOTE 81.—See what is said on the use of the term *Mary* for a Christian Church in Chrystal's translation of Ephesus in this set, volume I, page 21, note 22. There is no proof that I have seen for Hefele's assertion that it was dedicated to her (*Hefele's History of the Church Councils*, English translation, vol. 3, page 45). Some assign as the reason for the name that Mary was buried there. It is not called St. Mary's Church in the Acts of Ephesus. That was later. No church should be named after a creature, but after God only as the wont of the earliest Christian centuries was, and as was the case of the Jewish temple. The New Testament never names churches after dead saints or angels: see the simple way they are spoken of in Rom. xvi, 5; I Cor. xvi, 19; Colos. iv, 15; Philemon, 2. And they are named after cities, as for example, I Cor. 1, 2; II Cor. 1, 1, and often, or after countries as in I Cor. xvi, 1, 19; II Cor. viii, 1; Gal. i, 22, and again and again. Bingham in his *Antiquities of the Christian Church*, book VIII, chapter 14, section 8, shows that anciently all churches were dedicated to God, never to saints or to any creatures; and we must change all saints' names for churches to the Triune God's alone, and so honor Him, never even to one Person of the Trinity, for they all belong to all Three. For it is prerogative to the Triune Jehovah to have all churches named after Him. As a mark of distinction and convenience the name of the street or quarter of the city, where they are, may well be added, as in Athanasius' day in Alexandria.

NOTE 82.—The Ecumenical Synod : more Anti-New Testament Byzantinism.

NOTE 83.—As the original seat and then capital of the Western Empire, and for long the largest city of the whole Roman Empire ; Constantinople, New Rome, being the second, and then Capital of the Eastern Empire.

NOTE 84.—βιβλία, That is *statements*. See the two in one above.

the [empty] name of deposition [against us], might be summoned to this Holy and Ecumenical Synod, in order that they may be present and make their defence and plead for their unbridled utterances, that is to say for their lawless attempts [against us]. And your God-reveringness doing all things in due order and canonically, summoned them by a first summons, and by a second, by sending [to them] most religious and most dear to God Bishops, as the faith of the Minutes also has it [and shows.] But they were not able to find reasons fit for their bold and presumptuous actions, nor could they find ways for making their defence, for [if they had], they would certainly have run straightway to this holy and Great Synod in order to support their deeds. They have done a thing both disgraceful and befitting a vagabond, and loafers about a market place. If they wished to make anything clear to this Great Synod it was behooving them to come rather with good order and with that decorum which befits Christians, and to say what was necessary and to hear, and surely there was no one to hinder them. For soldiers did not stand before the Holy Synod, as they did before the houses in which they are. But they drew up a paper full of madness and ignorance, and put it forth publicly, and stirred up all the city to tumults, or rather to the condemnation of their own ill-counsel. If indeed therefore they did that thing in order that we might be grieved when we saw the reputation of brethren behaving itself indecently and by seeing it laughed at by all (85), we have [certainly] been sufficiently grieved ; for, because of their doing that, they have been very often laughed at. But if they are really able to prove, as it reads in the paper put forth by him (86), that we have become leaders of the heresy of Apolinarius, or indeed that we have ever yet held his errors, let them come forward even now. Let them prove us heretics, if they can, and not merely insult us with empty expressions ; let them keep in mind the divine indignation· For God, the Judge of all, has said, *"A false witness shall not be unpunished"* (87). And by the voice of the blessed David [He adds]

NOTE 85.—Or, *"when we saw brethren of reputation behaving themselves indecently and by seeing them laughed at by all,"* etc. This would be the English idiom ; that is the text is one of the Greek idioms.
NOTE 86.—John of Antioch.
NOTE 87.—Proverbs xix., 5.

Thou sattest and spakest against thy brother" (88). For we have never yet held the errors of Apolinarius (89), nor those of Arius (90), nor those of Eunomius (91), but from the time when we were little we have learned the sacred Scriptures, and have been brought up in the hands of orthodox and holy fathers. And we anathemize Apolinarius, and Arius, and Eunomius, and Macedonius (92), Sabellius, Photinus, Paul (93), and the Manicheans, and every other heresy, and, besides them, Nestorius the contriver of the new blasphemies, and those who commune with him and agree with him, and those who hold the errors of Celestius, that is of Pelagius. We have never held the errors of those men. Nor have we now by a change of mind become willing to hold the right doctrines; but, as I have said, we have been brought up in the right and apostolic dogmas of the Church. Moreover, since it is necessary that those who have been once ordained to the priesthood should be true to see, and to speak those things which they know to be so, we now also beseech this Great and Holy Synod to canonically send for the most religious John himself, the Bishop of the Antiochians, and those who together with him put together the false accusation against us, for it is a thing rational and necessary that they should come and show that we are heretics, and hold the errors of Apolinarius as they assert; or if they refuse to come and shrink from presenting their proofs, they

---

NOTE 88.—Psalm L., 20.

NOTE 89.—This is the common spelling among the Greeks for the name which ordinarily the Latins and ourselves spell Apollinaris.

NOTE 90.—His great heresies were 1, his denial of the counsubstantiality and coeternity of God the Word with the Father; and, 2, *his worshipping him as a creature* and hence attempting to bring the ancient sin of *creature worship* into Christ's sound church, which holds to his law in Matt. iv, 10, "*Thou shalt worship the Lord thy God, and Him only shalt thou serve.*" How Athanasius and other Orthodox Champions denounced those sins is told in their own words in Chrystal's translation of *Nicaea*, vol. I, pages 213-255. See also Arius' own statements on pages 163-212, of the same volume.

NOTE 91.—He held that the Word is unlike in Substance to the Father, and changed the form of words in baptism, into the death of Christ only, instead of in the name of the Father Son, and Holy Ghost, and the mode of triue immersion into but one dip, on account of which his alleged baptism is rejected as invalid in canon VII of the Second Ecumenical Synod. See on these points the testimony of Theodoret and Sozomen, page 76 of Chrystal's *History of the Modes of Christian Baptism.*

NOTE 92.—He made God the Spirit a creature, and hence tried to degrade the Church's worship of Him to the sin of creature worship, the sin of the heathen.

NOTE 93.—Paul of Samosata.

are condemned by that very fact, especially because, as it is written besides in the paper put forth by them, they have carried cold and stale false accusations to the ears of the most religious Emperors. And it especially behooves your Holiness (94) to take the greatest (95) care that the pious ears of the rulers (96) be not deceived by any persons, for your Holiness knows what is said by the godly Scripture, *Let no lie be said by any tongue to the King, and let no lie go out of his mouth* (97).

The Holy Synod said, The present request also of the most dear to God and most devout Bishops Cyril of Alexandria and Memnon of the Church of the Ephesians, is reasonable. And therefore, this day, the most dear to God Bishops, Daniel, and Commodus, and Timothy, shall go with a summons and warn the most religious Bishop John, the Bishop of Antioch, to come with those who are under the same accusation with himself and make their defence in regard to those things of which they are accused. And the most religious Bishops Daniel of Colonia, and Commodus of Tripolis in Lydia, and Timothy of Terma in the Hellespont, departed with Musonius, a Notary, with the summons, the contents of which were as follows:

Since the Holy Synod has wished to decree pacifically what shall be in accordance with the canons, it has summoned thy Piety by a double summons, and thou hast not obeyed, so as either to make a defence in regard to the outrage and insult which thou didst commit (98), or to correct thyself [as to it], the Holy Synod therefore does not for the present permit thee to perform any episcopal act of thy own determination, nor does it permit it to any of those with thee. And if thou do not obey this the third summons and come into their presence, those things which seem in consonance with the canons shall be decreed against you.

And when they came back, Daniel Bishop of Colonia, said, We went to where your God-Reveringness commanded, that is to

---

NOTE 94.—This is a collective title for the Ecumenical Council again.
NOTE 95.—Literally, *"the most care."*
NOTE 96.—The Emperors.
NOTE 97.—Proverbs xxiv., after verse 22, in Van Ess' Septuagint.
NOTE 98.—That is, against Cyril of Alexandria, Memnon of Ephesus, and all the Ecumenical Synod.

the house of the most God-revering Bishop John. And a long way off from it, we got down from the animals which we rode, and with much entreaty made known to the clerics that we had come as messengers sent by your Holy Synod. And we found there standing Asphalius the presbyter, who is indeed of the church of the Antiochians, but at Constantinople defends and manages the affairs (99) of the same church (100). He led us nearer the house in which the most God-revering Bishop John stays, and he stood by us and hindered those who were coming on [against us]. And we acknowledge our gratitude to the soldiers; for because they knew the in all respects most God-revering Bishop Commodus, from their having been in garrison in his city, they stopped all the clerics who

---

NOTE 99.—Or *interests*, (τὰ πράγματα)·

NOTE 100.—῎Ος ἐστι μὲν τῆς Ἀντιοχέων ἐκκλησίας, ἐκδικεῖ δὲ ἐν Κωνσταντινουπόλει τὰ πράγματα τῆς αὐτῆς ἐκκλησίας·

Bingham (*Antiq.* book III., chap. xi, section 5), expresses the opinion that the Greek ἔκδικοι and the Latin *Defensores* were the same. The existence of such a class of men from a great see like Antioch at the seat of civil government suggests the inquiry whether Antioch and the other great autocephalous sees of the Orient did not keep Defenders at Constantinople because they were afraid that, if they did not, they might practically lose their independence, and become as subject to Constantinople as all parts of the West finally became to Rome. For the growth of the power of Constantinople had been rapid from the epoch in the fourth century when it became the seat of civil empire for the East; and by canon XXVIII. of Chalcedon it secured power over the three great civil and ecclesiastical Dioceses of Thrace, Asia, and Pontus. Besides at times it practically subjugated other Oriental Patriarchates, though against the canons; and extended its Patriarchal power over large parts of Europe outside of Thrace, including, among the rest, the vast extent of the Russia of the middle ages. The imperial power of Constantinople was prone to lend a listening ear to the Bishop of its own chief city, and to be very partial to him against the Ecumenical canons; as the Emperor of the West was prone to be very partial to the Bishop of his chief city, Rome. This influence of the Patriarch of Constantinople has never been wholly lost even under the Turks, for he still has much influence and power as the head of the Oriental Church. The causes of this influence were, I, the relation existing between the chief pastor of the Empire and his chief parishioner the Emperor. They would, as residents in the same city naturally become much better known to each other than strangers; and the pastor of the Emperor would naturally have much more influence with him than stranger Bishops a long way off. Wiltsch in his *Geography and Statistics of the Church*, English translation, vol. I., pages 145-154, 434-458, shows how, from the fourth century on, the Bishop of Constantinople exercised authority in the East outside of the great civil dioceses granted him by Canon XXVIII of Chalcedon, and how he even wrested from the Roman Patriarch part of his territory in Italy. Indeed in the middle ages, after A. D. 1000, the Patriarch of Constantinople ruled more territory than the Roman Bishop. But in modern times moved by race and national feeling, the Bulgarians have stricken off his yoke as that of a Greek and an alien, and though their Bishops have been deposed and excommunicated for it by him in his lust of power over them, nevertheless their people and all the Slavic Churches of Russia, Servia.

were rushing against us. And Asphalius and other clerics having informed him (101), *his Archdeacon* came down to us: his name we do not know, but the man has very little natural beard, is sallow, and short of stature—and he brought a paper which he offered to us and said, *The Holy Synod* (102) has sent you this that ye may receive it.

We said, We have been sent to utter the message of the HOLY SYNOD, but not to receive a letter. For we have not brought a paper, nor do we receive a paper. But we have brought a peaceful notification. For the Holy Synod exhorts the lord John (103) to cosit, and to come to the Holy Synod.

The Archdeacon answered us, Then wait in order that I may make those things known to the Bishop. He went away, and came back, and brought us the same paper again, and said as follows—

Montenegro, and elsewhere, stick by them and condemn the Greek Patriarch's action, so that he is practically to-day the spiritual ruler mainly and almost only of the Greek race in Europe, Asia and Africa.

2, The convenience of communicating with the whole church in his Empire through its chief prelate.

Hence the wisdom of having *Defenders*, that is *Advocates*, to maintain the rights under the Ecumenical Canons of the other Patriarchates, and Autocephalous sees. This custom has not been wholly lost even to this day.

In the above remarks I would not however assert that the only duty of the Defender was to protect the rights of his Patriarchate or other chief see at the imperial court, but only that it was one of his obligations. A number of Patriarchates, as for example, Syria, Egypt, Gaul, Britain. etc, were nations and in effect national churches. As Socrates tells us in chapter 8, book V, of his *Church History*, the Second Ecumenical Synod, A. D. 381, instituted the Patriarchs by raising the Metropolitans to that rank: see its Canons II and VI. Indeed some had it practically before. London should be the seat of an English Patriarch, and we should have several for our wide land, the chief one at Washington.

NOTE 101.—John of Antioch.

NOTE 102.—John of Antioch's little Nestorian Incarnation-denying, Man-Worshipping, One nature Consubstantiation and Cannibalizing conventicle. Their attempt to condemn the whole orthodox Synod was bumptious and laughable enough. It reminds us of the utterances of the three tailors of Tooley Street, London, "We, the people of England," and of the ignorant prattle of the effeminate, idolatrous clergy in the Anglican Communion to-day, who have changed the New Testament and primitive communion tables of their churches into closed Roman altars, and brought in again worship of creatures by invocation, and of altars, and of the cross and other images by bowing and kissing and genuflecting, and not merely one-nature, but, what is still worse, even two-nature Consubstantiation, and the Nestorian Man-Worship, and Host-Worship and Cannibalism, things unknown to the primitive church of the Ante-Nicene times and condemned by the Third Synod of the whole church East and West, and yet such ignorant paganizers laughably enough, speak of such heresies as *Catholic*, for *Catholic* to them means Rome, and mere mediaevalisms, and Westernisms! aye, even mere modernisms, like, for example, the new-fangled Romish Benediction of the Wafer God, called the Benediction of the Blessed Sacrament, which even the idolatrous Greeks have not yet.

NOTE 103.—John of Antioch.

Send ye not to us, and we will not send to you; for we await an edict from the Emperor, since we have once reported to him what seemed good to us. And when we said, Then hear also the message from the Holy Synod, he leaped away, saying Ye have not received the paper. I will not hear the message of the Synod. Those words he said.

But we said to Asphalius who escorted us, and to Alexander, Presbyters, as follows: *The* HOLY SYNOD declares to the Lord John its inner heart of peace and of love and of kindness; and especially, since he has been twice summoned, and has refused to appear, it has deemed it right that he should do no priestly act, and it entreats him by the third summons to come with us, in order that it may not be compelled to put forth any canonical sentence against him.

Commodus, Bishop of Tripolis in Lydia said, We both saw and state the same things as those reported by the most God-revering and most devout Bishop Daniel.

Timothy, Bishop of Terma in the Hellespont, said, We both saw and tell the same things as those reported by the most God-revering and most devout bishop Daniel.

The Holy Synod said, The warning and summons are now performed by the most God-revering Bishops Daniel and Commodus and Timothy, and they have made known the cause of their being sent, and have given the notification to those of priestly rank, so that the most religious John is ignorant of nothing in the notification, and he can not make use of any pretext as a defence by pleading ignorance.

Cyril, Archbishop of Alexandria said: And I am yet present, together with the most religious *Bishop Memnon*, and demand apologies in regard to those things which the most religious John, Bishop of the Church of the Antiochians, has wrongly committed against us in violation of the laws of the Church, and contrary to all reason. Your Holy Synod all see and there is no doubt, that if we had feared refutation from him, we would not have used such bold confidence (104) as to beg that the aforesaid [John] be urged by that

NOTE 104.—τοιαύτῃ παῤῥησίᾳ

third summons to come, and to make use of whatsoever arguments he might wish against us. But since he contrives various delays, at one time inventing one set of pretexts and at another, another set, (for as it is written, *He swims in words* (105), it is in order that this Holy and Ecumenical Synod pronounce what is in accordance with the Church laws.

The Holy Synod said, It was behooving indeed that this Holy Synod should be canonically moved at the insults and outrages wrought against the most holy and most God-revering Bishop Cyril and the most dear to God and most devout Fellow-Bishop Memnon, by both John, the most religious Bishop of the Church of the Antiochians, and those with him, [and especially that it should be so moved] after that third summons has been given by us, which they have in no wise suffered themselves to obey, nor moreover to come to the session of the Holy Synod, and to render clear the reasons for which they have burst forth into such revolutionary innovation, contrary to the laws and the canons of the Church, and have passed their sentence, which befits such madness, against both him (106) and those who are with him. But inasmuch as we reckon it to be a work of episcopal kindness to bear with long suffering those things which have been done, for the present, in accordance with what has been already decreed by us, let the following persons be aliens from Church communion, namely,

Both John himself, and the following who got up that drama with him, [that is],

John of Damascus,
Alexander of Apamea,
Dexianus of Seleucia,
Alexander of Hierapolis,
Himerius of Nicomedia,
Fritilas of Heraclea,
Helladius of Tarsus,
Maximinus of Anazarbus,
Dorotheus of Marcianopolis,
Peter of Trajanopolis,

NOTE 105.—Job xi. 12, Septuagint Greek translation.
NOTE 106.—Cyril of Alexandria.

Suspension of John and his Conventicle.

Paul of Emisa (107),
Polychronius of the city of the Heracleans,
Eutherius of Tyana,
Meletius of Neocaesarea,
Theodoret of Cyrus (108),
Apringius of Chalcis,
Macarius of Laodicea the Great,
Zosys of Esbus,
Sallustius of Corycus in Cilicia,
Hesychius of Castabaia in Cilicia,
Valentinus of Mustublaca,
Eustathius of Parnassus,
Philip of Theodosiana (109),
Daniel,
Julianus,
Cyrillus,
Olympius,
Diogenes,
Theophanes of Philadelphia,
Palladius,
Trajanus of Augusta,
Aurelianus of Irenopolis,
Musaeus of Aradus (110), [and]
Helladius of Ptolemais;

and they shall have no permission as from priestly (111) authority to be able to injure any persons or to help them by it, until they condemn themselves and acknowledge their own fault. And they are to know that unless they do that quickly, they will draw the complete and

---

NOTE 107.—This place is spelled, as above, in Coleti, and some times, elsewhere, Emess, and Hemesa.

NOTE 108.—This is the noted opponent of Cyril of Alexandria, of the Third Ecumenical Synod, and of Orthodoxy.

NOTE 109.—The Latin translation for this in Coleti would show that Theodosiopolis is meant. So it is in the *Collectio Regia*.

NOTE 110.—The Latin for this in Coleti would show that Arcadiopolis is meant.

NOTE 111. As every Christian is a priest in the highest and noblest sense (I Peter ii, 5, 9; Rev. i, 6; compare Rev. v, 9, 10), because he offers up not *carnal*, that is *fleshly sacrifices*, like those of the Jews, which were *imposed on them till the time of Reformation only* (Heb. ix, 10.) that is till spiritual Christianity should come, but *spiritual sacrifices acceptable to God*

entire sentence in the canons on themselves. And it is evident from the start, that what has been already done by them unlawfully contrary to the canons in insult and outrage against the most dear to God and most holy Bishops and Presidents (112) of the Church, Cyril and Memnon, has no force nor validity, against what is now declared and what was declared yesterday. And all that has been done shall be reported to the pious and Christ-loving ears of the most dear to God Emperors, that their godly (113) ears may know what has occurred.

Translation of the Subscriptions following:

I, Juvenal, Bishop of Jerusalem, have subscribed (114).

I, Arcadius, a Bishop, and an ambassador of the Apostolic See, have subscribed.

I, Projectus, a Bishop, and an ambassador of the Apostolic See, have subscribed.

I, Philip, a Presbyter, and an ambassador of the Apostolic See, have subscribed.

And all the rest subscribed also.

---

through Jesus Christ (I Peter ii, 5, 9,), therefore every Christian minister is also a priest as well as every Christian layman, woman and child, for we all offer the same spiritual sacrifices. See on that whole theme more fully under *Priest, Priestly* and *Priesthood*, page 650, vol. I of *Ephesus* in this set, and under *Bishops* on page 575, and under *Priesthood* on page 462, vol. I of *Nicaea* in this set.   Only this must be remembered that in public services the Bishop, if he be orthodox, is the leader and the clergy under him are leaders subordinate to him. In closet and family prayer every laic is a priest.

NOTE 112.—Greek, καὶ ἁγιωτάτων ἐπισκόπων, καὶ προέδρων τῆς ἐκκλησίας, Κυρίλλου καὶ Μέμνονος, (Coleti Conc. tom. 3, col. 1184.

NOTE 113.—τὰς θείας ἀκοάς, literally "*divine* ears" a reprehensible relic of old Roman paganism which deified their Emperors, and called them *divine*. See *Ephesus*, vol. 1, page 19, note 20, in this set. A future Seventh Synod must condemn such wicked titles.

NOTE 114.—It is remarkable that Juvenal, the Bishop of what afterwards was elevated to be the fifth of the great sees signs before Rome, the first. This should be remembered in connection with his extravagant claims above. As his subscription, according to the heading above, was translated into Greek it must, of course, have been written in some other tongue. The legates of Rome would, of course, use their native Latin. Venables in his article on *Juvenalis*, that is this Juvenal, in Smith and Wace's *Dictionary of Christian Biography* states "At the Council of Ephesus, in 431, he asserted for '*the apostolic see of Jerusalem the same rank and authority with the apostolic see of Rome,*' Labbe, Concil III., 642." That is more than he could expect or the Universal Church would allow, because Rome was the old capital of the Empire. But Venables is too severe in blaming Juvenal for desiring to do away Canon VII. of Nicaea which made Jerusalem suffragan to its metropolis Caesarea, according to the usual principle that the Ecclesiastical precedences should follow the civil. On that principle, when Jerusalem became the capital of the province, Caesarea should become suffragan to it; as when Constantinople became the capital of the province of Europa, Heraclea, the former metropolis

Copy of a Report (115) from the Holy Synod to the most Religious Emperors Regarding the Orientals (116).

To the most religious and most dear to God, Theodosius and Valentinian, Victors, Trophy-bearers, ever August Ones, the Holy Synod gathered by God's favor and your Mightiness' decree (117) in the Metropolis of the Ephesians [sendeth greeting]. Those things which were enjoined on the Holy Synod by your Mightiness (118) have been brought to a fitting end, and we have made it known to your Mightiness (119). And the Apostolic faith which the Three Hundred and Eighteen also who were gathered together at Nicaea put forth, we have explained to your Piety (120). And Nestorius who held opinions hostile to it, we have deposed from the sacerdotal ministry and have taken from him liberty to preach his own impiety. But since some few who had before been corrupted in judgment by the teaching of Nestorius, adhered to him, and in addition took with themselves those who were under accusation, and the most religious John, Bishop of Antioch, joined himself to him, either through contentiousness or through human friendship (121); all of

---

to which it had been suffragan, became in ~~since its~~ suffragan. It appears that Thalassius of Caesarea took no umbrage at his former suffragan being preferred before him; see "*Juvenalis* 2," in Smith and Wace as above. He must have known the Eastern principle of precedences and acted on it. But by Canon II of the Second Synod of the whole Church in 381, no Patriarch or other Bishop has any jurisdiction outside of his own civil diocese except he of Constantinople, which by Canon XXVIII of Chalcedon had in three Eastern ones there mentioned.

Note 115.—As this Report is not mentioned in the minutes of Act V., I presume that it was drawn up by Cyril and the chief Bishops between Acts V. and VI. But the signatures of all the Bishops appended to it vouch for its being the work of the Synod.

Note 116.—The Orientals here are the Bishops of the Diocese, that is Patriarchate of the Orient, the capital of which was Antioch. They were John of Antioch and the Bishops of his jurisdiction who formed the bulk of the Apostolic Conventicle.

Hardouin, *Conc.*, tom. 1, col. 1502, margin, says of the above heading: "So it is in two manuscripts. In the MS. Bellov. it reads, '*Report* of the *Holy, Universal Ephesian Synod to the Emperors on the excommunication of John and those who are with him.*'"

Note 117.—Literally "nod," νεύματι·

Note 118.—A collective title for the Two Emperors, for in a certain sense the Empires were still one.

Note 119.—The same sort of a title. The Synod refer to their Report to the Emperors after the First Act. See it page 3, above. They refer also to their Report to them after the Third Act. See it page 14, above.

Note 120.—A collective title for the two Emperors.

Note 121.—Human friendship had much to do with John's conduct and that of his Bishops. For Nestorius was from their Patriarchate. Still there was much of heresy among them, though perhaps a few would not go so far as Nestorius did.

them [together] being only thirty, (122) before they had made a
defence of themselves in regard to those faults concerning which each
was accused, they called themselves a Synod, as though your Piety
had commanded two Synods to be celebrated—as though it had not
commanded only one, the duty of which was to confirm and
strengthen the Gospel faith and to cast out of the Church's
ministry those who hold corrupt opinions. But, as we have said,
before the aforesaid few had made their defence in regard to those
faults of which they were accused, they gathered themselves
together, and they took the most religious Bishop John of Antioch as
a partner in their madness, (and he himself we have learned from
some who whisper it, feared that he should have to endure corrections for his delay); and without any Church order, [and] without
[any] canons, against the Ecclesiastical and Holy Synod, and
against the head of the most holy Archbishops (123) who have been
commanded [to assemble here], we mean the most holy Archbishop
Cyril, and furthermore against the most dear to God Bishop
Memnon, they put forth an injurious utterance, as they supposed,
which contained the insult and outrage of a deposition, though they
had neither received an accusation from any one, nor did they wait
for an accuser, nor moreover did they summon any one to judgment; but before trial or investigation they vomited forth that
insult and outrage in writing, and have dared to report things
so irrational to your Mightiness as though your Piety were
ignorant of the fact that there is only one Synod of the inhabited world! (124), and as though thy Piety did not know that the
gathering of a few who have fallen under accusation, and who have

---

NOTE 122.—Hardouin, Conc. tom. i, col. 1502, margin, states : "*Below in another Repor
of the Synod, thirty-seven, more or less, are said to have been lacking* [*to it*]."

NOTE 123.—Sophocles in his *Lexicon of Later and Byzantine Greek* under ἀρχιεπίσκοπος,
tells us that in the fourth century the title *Archbishop* " was given to the Bishops of
Alexandria, Rome, Antioch, and Constantinople; in the sixth century, also to the Bishop
of Jerusalem; and in the seventh, to that of Cyprus." See to the same effect in his *Glossary of Later and Byzantine Greek*, under the same word, where examples are given from
Ephesus.

NOTE 124.—Coleti Conc., tom. 3, col. 1185: ὡς τῆς ὑμῶν εὐσεβείας ἀγνοούσης ὅτι μία
σύνοδος ἡ τῆς οἰκουμένης ἐστί. This is a pertinent condemnation of the theory that a
part of the Church, Rome for instance and her prelates, can by itself constitute the
Ecumenical Synod of the *whole* Christian World.

Report of the Synod to the Emperors on the Orientals. 165

rent themselves off from the Holy Synod through fear of censure, should not be spoken of as a Synod. For they did not first prove them guilty of fault and then commit that outrage and insult, but probably knowing that they had no defence in regard to the crimes of which they themselves were accused, and seeing that they themselves were only a few, and fearing that after the proofs against themselves were brought forward they should have to suffer the penalty, they tried to get a start by acting with insolent audacity. And they thought that they could inflict that thing which they expected to endure after their conviction (125). But that thing, as unreasonable, seemed to us deserving of contempt. But since they dared to report their most irrational madness even to your Mightiness, and dared to make known to your Piety what had been done by them against laws and Canons, and all Ecclesiastical order, we did not longer overlook that unreasonable and violent assault; but following again the type of the Canons, we summoned the most religious Bishop John who dared in connection with others to do such gross outrages against the aforesaid [Bishops] (126). For those who were only a few and at the same time under accusation would not have ventured to advance to such a great madness unless they had grown audacious by the audacity of the most religious Bishop John of the Church of the Antiochians. We therefore having been assembled, statements (127) were first given in to us by the most holy and most dear to God Archbishop Cyril and the most dear to God Fellow-Bishop Memnon, and we summoned the aforesaid most dear to God Bishop John to tell now indeed the motive which had led him to rush headlong to that degree of outrage and insult against the first [prelates] (128) of the Holy Synod. And though he had been summoned once, and a second time, and a third time to plead his cause, he could not bear to come into the Holy Synod, because he had

---

NOTE 125.—That is, they thought that they could inflict deposition on Cyril and Memnon, and so save themselves from being convicted for their faults, and from suffering the same penalty.

NOTE 126.—Cyril of Alexandria and Memnon of Ephesus.

NOTE 127.—Or "booklets." The Greek is λιβέλλων.

NOTE 128.—κατὰ τῶν πρώτων τῆς ἁγίας συνόδου. Some such word as "*prelates*," or "*men*," is understood, with the plural "*first.*"

no reasonable apology to utter for those crimes which he had dared to commit; but having fenced his house about with soldiers and arms, he refused to receive the most holy Bishops who had been sent to him by the Holy Synod, and he did not deem the assembled Holy Synod worthy of the necessary (129) answer. Wherefore having ascertained that he has not the confidence to plead the justice of his own cause, for some things have been talked nonsensically and rashly and vainly by them, and written [by them] contrary to all the order of the canons, both against the most holy Archbishop Cyril and against the most religious Memnon our Fellow-Bishop; we have [therefore] justly decreed them to be both utterly invalid and vain. For a judgment that has nothing canonical nor just in it has nothing but abuse. Therefore we have judged it right that both he and those who with him acted so uncanonically and so disorderly, and outside of all ecclesiastical order and sequence, shall be deprived of communion until they shall bar out their absurd disorderliness, and come, and make their defence to the Holy Synod concerning those matters in which they acted with headlong audacity.

Therefore we necessarily report to your Piety those things which have been done, and beg that the gathering of those who are under accusation be not adjudged to be a Synod, for on a former occasion, when the Holy and Great Synod of the Three Hundred and Eighteen was gathered at Nicaea, some separated (130) from that Great Synod, because they feared punishment from it; and yet those [separatists] were not deemed a Synod by the great and among the saints Emperor Constantine, but were ordered to endure [due] punishments because they separated themselves and rejected the concord of those holy Bishops; for, just like the Nestorian conventicle now (131), those [Arians] also followed an evil conscience. For it is an absurd thing for thirty persons alone, some of whom have

---

NOTE 129.—Or, "*of the answer fitting:*" ἀποκρίσεως τῆς δεούσης.

NOTE 130—ἀποστῆναι.

NOTE 131.—Coleti Conc., tom.3, col. 1188, Καὶ μήτε κριθῆναι σύνοδον τούτους ὑπὸ τοῦ μεγάλου καὶ ἐν ἁγίοις Βασιλέως Κωνσταντίνου, ἀλλὰ καὶ κελευθῆναι δίκας ὑποσχεῖν, ὑπὲρ ὧν ἀποσχίσαντες τὴν τῶν ἁγίων ἐκείνων ἐπισκόπων συμφωνίαν ἠρνήσαντο, πονηρᾷ, καθάπερ οὗτοι, καὶ αὐτοὶ συνειδήσει κεχρημένοι.

been long since deposed, and others of whom are of the wicked opinions of Celestius, and still others of whom have been anathematized as holding the opinions of Nestorius, for those thirty to fight against a Synod of Two Hundred and Ten Bishops, with whom all the multitude of the holy Bishops of the West have co-voted in agreement and through them all the rest of the inhabited world (132); but we beg you to command that those things which have been formulated by the Ecumenical and Holy Synod for the approval and support of piety against Nestorius and his impious dogma, shall have their own proper force, and be strengthened by the consent and approval of your Piety.

I, Juvenal, Bishop of Jerusalem, have reported (133).

We, Arcadius and Projectus, Bishops, and Philip a Presbyter, ambassadors of the Apostolic See, have reported (134).

And all the rest of the Bishops also subscribed.

NOTE 132.—τῆς οἰκουμένης, that is all the rest of the Western World. Their sentiments could be in some sort gathered, though the extreme Western Christian lands were at this time very much tried by the irruptions of the barbarians, for the Vandals were in Spain and Africa; and parts of Gaul were ravaged; and the Britons, like the Gauls and the Spaniards degenerated by superstition, were harassed by their northern neighbors from Caledonia and were about to lose their own land to the heathen Saxons whom they had summoned to their assistance.

NOTE 133.—It will be remembered that Cyril and Memnon, at the beginning of Act IV. and in Act V., had, so to speak, stepped down from their positions of leadership in the council, and had presented themselves at its bar as complainants against John of Antioch and his Conventicle for having insulted and outraged them by a mock deposition, and the Ecumenical Synod by a mock excommunication. Then their right hand man, Juvenal with others of the Orthodox, take the lead temporarily, and probably he and the occupants of the chief sees drew up the above Report to the Emperors, as the representatives of the chief sees at Chalcedon drew up its Definition. As Cyril was one of the interested parties and as his name occurs so prominently in the Report, he seems during this period to have modestly and seemingly entrusted the leadership to Juvenal. As it does not appear from the Acts above that Celestine's legates to the Synod could write Greek, it seems most likely that the composition of the Greek of the above Report was wholly or almost wholly the work of Juvenal, with, of course, the approval of the rest of the Synod. And the gist of the statements as to the West, and probably more or less of the other matter might have come from Leo's legates, and possibly others of the prelates. For as being, with Besula the Deacon of Carthage, the only representatives of the Occident, and as legates of the first see, they naturally occupied a prominent and influential place. And they stood by Cyril against Nestorius.

NOTE 134.—Probably in connection with Juvenal, the chief Oriental after Cyril, or perhaps we may rather say after Cyril and Memnon, the Western legates had agreed to the gist of the Report before it was written by Juvenal and went to the rest of the Synod for signature.

A Report to the most holy and most God-revering Fellow-Minister Celestine (135).

The Holy Synod gathered by God's Grace (136) *in the metropolis of the Ephesians wisheth joy in the Lord to Bishop Celestine* (137).

The zeal of thy Holiness for piety, and thy solicitude for the right faith are both dear and pleasing to God the Saviour of us all. For it is the wont of you who are so great to be well approved in all things, and as a prop of the Churches to make their zealous labors your own. And because it was behoving that all that has passed should be reported to the knowledge of your Holiness (138), we necessarily write (139) that in accordance with the will of Christ, the Saviour of us all (140), and in accordance with the decree of the most religious and Christ-loving Emperors we were gathered in the metropolis of the Ephesians, from many and different provinces, being more than two hundred Bishops in number (141). Then, forasmuch as the pious

---

NOTE 135.—In the margin of Hardouin here we find the Greek for the following lection:
"*Or, Copy of an Epistle written by the Holy Synod to the Archbishop of Rome, Celestine, showing all things done in the Holy and Great Synod itself.*"

NOTE 136.—κατὰ Θεοῦ χάριν' Literally "*God's favor.*"

NOTE 137.—Hardouin in his margin here adds: "Or '*To the most Holy and most devout Fellow-Minister Celestine, the Holy Synod gathered by God's favor in the metropolis of the Ephesians, a Synod Holy and Great, wisheth joy in the Lord.*'" The facts stated in this document are largely a summary of Act. I. of *Ephesus* which is translated in Vol. I. of Chrystal's *Ephesus*.

NOTE 138.—More anti Scriptural, Byzantine, flattering titles, which mar so much of the documents of this Synod.

NOTE 139.—It was necessary to tell Celestine as the *first Bishop among his equals* in the whole Church, and as the first Bishop of the West. For the East alone could not constitute an Ecumenical Synod, nor can the West alone. The West as well as the Orient must know and approve all; and so must it be in a true Seventh Ecumenical Synod of the future, which will come to pass when it shall please God and when the Church is purged of the creature service and idolatry which still curse so large a part of it. But Rome's so called Church will be no part of it, for it is heretical, idolatrous and creature serving· and wafer worshipping, and therefore its so-called Bishop with all his clergy are deposed and all his laics are now anathematized by the decisions of the Third Fcumenical Council as his predecessor Honorius was deposed with all Bishops and clerics who held to his heresy of One-Willism, and anathematized as all Monothelite laics were. See in proof the Definition of the Sixth Ecumenical Synod, and see Rome's irreversible doom of utler destruction in Revelations XVIII.

NOTE 140.—Literally, "*of the Anointed Saviour of us all.*" τοῦ πάντων ἡμῶν σωτῆρος Χριστοῦ, Coleti Conc. tom. III., col. 1188, 1189. But Migne in his *Patrologia Latina* tom. 50, col. 514, gives τῶν instead of the τοῦ above. The *Collectio Regia* has τοῦ.

NOTE 141.—Chrystal's translation of *Ephesus*, Vol. I., pages 19-32, 486-504.

decrees of the Christ-loving Emperors by which we were summoned decreed the day of the Holy Pentecost as the time for the meeting of the Holy Synod, and all had run together, [and] especially because it says in the Letter of the Emperors, *If any one does not come* [to the session] *on the day decreed and fore-appointed, he is not absent with a good conscience, and is without apology before God and men* (142); [we would therefore state] that the most religious John, the Bishop of the Church of the Antiochians, was lacking, not from a mere want of knowledge [as to the proper time of meeting], nor moreover, was he absent by reason of the length of the journey ; but because he was concealing a mental design and aim which are not in harmony with God : he showed what they were not long after he came into the city of the Ephesians. We therefore delayed the meeting of the Synod in session till after the decreed day of the Holy Pentecost, sixteen days in all; although many bishops and clerics were pressed hard by sickness, and were distressed in the matter of their expenses and some had even departed from life; and, as thy Holiness sees, what had been done was, moreover, an outrage on the Holy Synod. For he made use of so long a delay perversely, and that too when those from longer distances arrived before him (143, 144). However, after the sixteenth day, some of the Bishops with him, [that is] two Metropolitans, Alexander of Apamea, and another Alexander of Hierapolis, arrived ahead of him. Then when we accused the delay of the most religious Bishop John in arriving, they said not once but very often, *He commanded us to tell your God-reveringness that if it come to pass that he delays still longer, not to put off the Synod but rather to do those things which ought to be done.* As this was told us, and as it was plain from his delay, and from those things which were signified by him, that he was begging off from the Synod, either because he was indulging his friendship for Nestorius, or also because Nestorius (145) had been a cleric of the church under

NOTE 142.—That document is in Chrystal's *Ephesus*, Vol. I., pages 32-41.
NOTE 143.—This fact and the sixteen days' delay speak volumes in favor of Cyril and the Orthodox and their action, and against the course of the Man-Worshipping heretical faction, and so do the other facts in the text just below.
NOTE 144.—Literally "*ran ahead*" of him: προέδραμον.
NOTE 145.—Literally "he," that is Nestorius.

him (146), or also because he had yielded to the entreaties of certain persons for him ; [therefore] the Holy Synod began their sessions in the great Church of Ephesus which is called Mary.

2. And because when all had readily run together, Nestorius alone was absent from the assembly, the Holy Synod warned him canonically, through Bishops, by a first and a second and likewise by a third summons. But he, having fenced his dwelling around with soldiers, acted as though without mind, against the canons of the Church, (147) and would not endure to make himself manifest, (148) nor, furthermore, to apologize for his unholy blasphemies. Therefore the letter written to him by Cyril, the most holy and most dear to God Bishop of the Church of the Alexandrians, was read (149),

NOTE 146.—Under John of Antioch, Some good men like Ignatius and Theophilus, both Bishops of that See in the second century, had done it honor by their faithfulness to the truth that God alone may be worshipped, but Diodore of Tarsus and Theodore of Mopsuestia of that school had corrupted its faith, by denying the inflesh of God the Word, and so making Christ a mere man, and then by worshipping that man, so bringing in the old Pagan sin of *worshipping a human being* (ἀνθρωπολατρεία), as Cyril, of Alexandria justly terms it, and what Cyril calls *Cannibalism* (ἀνθρωποφαγία) on the Eucharist.

These facts regarding Diodore and Theodore are clear even from the fragments of their works preserved for us in Vol. III. of *Cyrilli in Ioannis Evangelium*, P. E. Pusey's edition, Oxford, 1872. See also under those heresies and under *Diodore* and *Theodore* in the Indexes to Vol. I. of Chrystal's translation of *Ephesus*.

NOTE 147.—The reference may be to the so-called Apostolic Canon LXXIV, or to local canons, of which there were probably many, some in each province, which have now perished. Compare also canon XL, of the local Council of Laodicea, and canon IX of Chalcedon made later than Ephesus, but neither mentions three summonses.

NOTE 148.—Or "*to show himself*," καὶ οὐκ ἠνέσχετο ἑαυτὸν ἐμφανῆ καταστῆσαι. This means that he would not show himself to those who bore the summons of the Ecumenical Synod.

NOTE 149.—Migne's *Patrologia Latina*, tom. 50, col. 516—Λοιπὸν ἀνεγνώσθη τὰ γράμματα τὰ γραφέντα πρὸς αὐτὸν παρὰ τοῦ ἁγιωτάτου καὶ θεοφιλεστάτου ἐπισκόπου τῆς Ἀλεξανδρέων Ἐκκλησίας Κυρίλλου, ἃ καὶ ἐδοκίμασεν ἡ ἁγία σύνοδος ὀρθῶς καὶ ἀλήπτως ἔχειν, καὶ κατὰ μηδένα τρόπον ἀσύμφωνα εἶναι ἢ ταῖς θεοπνεύστοις γραφαῖς, ἤγουν τῇ παραδοθείσῃ πίστει, καὶ ἐκτεθείσῃ ἐν τῇ μεγάλῃ συνόδῳ παρὰ τῶν ἁγίων πατέρων τῶν ἐν Νικαίᾳ συνελθόντων κατὰ καιρούς, καθὰ καὶ ἡ σὴ ὁσιότης ὀρθῶς τοῦτο δοκιμάσασα ἐμαρτύρησεν.

The Greek expression above, τὰ γράμματα, includes his celebrated Shorter Letter to Nestorius which was voted on at Ephesus. The Greek in the *Collectio Regia* and that in Coleti has not the ἢ before ταῖς θεοπνεύστοις Γραφαῖς above. So that with that reading, which may be the true one, we should translate: "*as in nowise out of harmony with the God-inspired*

which the Holy Synod approved as being right and blameless, (150) and as in nowise out of harmony [either] with the God-inspired Scriptures or with the faith transmitted, and put forth in the great Synod by the holy Fathers who came together in becoming season in Nicaea (151), as thy Holiness also in approving that thing has testified (152). And the Epistle of Nestorius written to the aforesaid our most holy and most God-revering brother and Fellow-Minister Cyril himself, having been read, the Holy Synod justly decided that the dogmas in it are completely alien to the Apostolic and Gospel faith, and that it is diseased as much as possible with foreign blasphemy (153). And his most impious Expositions being likewise read (154), and besides the Epistle written to him, by thy Holiness, by which he was with good reason condemned as having written blasphemies and as having put unholy expressions into his own Ex-

---

Scriptures, that is with the faith transmitted and put forth in the Great Synod," etc., as above The account of the summonses sent to Nestorius are in vol. I. of Chrystal's *Ephesus*, pages 30-32, 44-50, and 359-418.

NOTE 150.—The reference is to Cyril's *Shorter Letter to Nestorius*. It is in Chrystal's *Ephesus*, vol I., pages 52-129. The voting on it is found there on pages 129-154, where it i unanimously approved, all in Act I. of *Ephesus*. Bishops in approving it often base that approval on its agreement with Scripture and with the Nicene Creed which had been read just before in the same Act, that is on pages 49-52 of vol. I. of Ephesus.

NOTE 151.—In A. D. 325, against Arius, the denier of the perfect Divinity of God the Word's Nature and Eternal Substance, and the worshipper, on his own confession, of him whom he made a creature. He was therefore a *creature worshipper* on his own theory contrary to Christ's own law in Matthew IV, 10. See also the note last but one above.

NOTE 152.—The reference is to the altered language of *Celestine's Epistle to Nestorius*, which, as in his Latin, he originally meant to apply to the short fifth century form of the Roman local creed, which he called the Apostles', for he evidently in his ignorance believed the yarn first found in Rufinus' *Commentary on the Apostolic Creed* that the Apostles had made it. As the East had never used that Creed, but that of the Synod of Nicaea at some time in 325 or after, they changed the words as they had a perfect right to, before approving Celestine's Letter, and made them refer to the Nicene Symbol in which sense alone they approved them, as the above language shows. See, moreover, what is said in vol. I. of Chrystal's *Ephesus*, page 185, note 414, on that whole matter.

NOTE 153.—See that Epistle in Act I. above. It denies the Incarnation, hints at his cannibal doctrine of the Eucharist, and at his creature-service, that is his service to the Man put on by God the Word. It is found translated in Chrystal's *Ephesus*, Vol. I., pages 155-178, and is there voted on by the Bishops in Act I. of *Ephesus* and condemned.

NOTE 154.—See the note last above. Those *Expositions*, or rather most important Extracts from them, are comprised in the *Twenty Blasphemies* of Nestorius, which were read and condemned in Act 1, of Ephesus. On the basis of them he was there deposed. Chrystal's *Ephesus*, Vol. I., pages 449-480, 486-504. They are analyzed on pages 529-551, in Note F. Their Blasphemy on *Man-Worship* (ἀνθρωπολατρεία) is told in detail in note 183, pages 79-123, and in note 664, pages 323, 324, and in note 679, pages 332-362; that

positions (154), a just vote of deposition was passed against him 155); especially because he had withheld himself so far from changing his mind or coming to a better knowledge as to those matters on which he had put forth blasphemies while he still had the Church of the Constantinopolitans, as even in the metropolis of the Ephesians itself to dispute with some of the holy Metropolitan Bishops, (who were men not insignificant but learned and most God-revering), and to dare to say : "*I do not acknowledge the two months old and the three months God* (156)'; and he said other and harder things besides.

3. So, therefore, as we have already told and said (157), we have put down an unholy and most foul heresy, which overturns our most pure religion (158) and takes away the whole Economy of the mystery from its foundations (159.) But it was not to be, as it seems, that those who have genuine love for Christ (160), and who are jealous for the Lord (161), should not be tried by many things. For we had expected the most religious John, Bishop of the Church

---

for their *relative worship* in note 940, pages 461-463, and note 456, pages 61-69. Their Blasphemy *against God the Word as the Sole Mediator by His Divinity and His humanity* is told in note 683, pages 363-406 ; and their Cannibalism and other Blasphemies on the Eucharist, in note 606, pages 240-313 ; in note 599, pages 229-238 ; in note F, pages 517-528 ; Note 692, page 407, and note 693, pages 407, 408. Their other Blasphemies may be found in the Note F, and under proper heads in the three indexes attached to that volume of *Ephesus.*

NOTE 155.—The XX *Blasphemies* are in Chrystal's *Ephesus*, Vol I., pages 449-480, the deposition of Nestorius on pages 486-504.

NOTE 156.—This plainly denies the Incarnation ; as the Ecumenical Synod understood it. And it must be remembered that it occurred in controversy with the Orthodox, and was an answer to their claim that God the Word was in the human babe, and was intended to ridicule that claim.

NOTE 157.—Both the *Collectio Regia* and *Coleti* omit "*told and*" for they have not φράσαντες like Migne, but φθάσαντες, which would give the above rendering, omitting "*told and*."

NOTE 158.—Both the *Collectio Regia* and Coleti have here, not τὴν εὐαγεστάτην [ἡμῶν] θρασκείαν as in Migne, but τὴν εὐσεβεστάτην [ἡμῶν] θρασκείαν, that is *our most pious religion*," which may be the true reading though it is not sure.

NOTE 159.—This is done by Nestorius denying the Incarnation, his making Christ a mere man, and then falling into the paganism and apostasy of worshipping him, a mere creature, contrary to Matthew IV., 10, which of course is *creature worship*, and *the worship of a human being* (ἀνθρωπολατρεία), and in the Eucharist into an assertion of the real substance presence of Christ's humanity there; into the paganism of worshipping it, and into the cannibalism of eating it, (ἀνθρωποφαγία).

NOTE 160.—Literally, "*for Anointed*," εἰς Χριστόν.

NOTE 161.—Compare the solemn utterance of God as to his jealousy against service to any

of the Antiochians, to approve the exactitude (162) of the Synod and piety, and perhaps even to complain of the slowness with which we had done the deposition. But the matters of our expectation have turned out to be wholly contrary. For he has been found to be a hater and an enemy both of the Holy Synod and of the right faith of the churches itself, as the circumstances themselves show. For as soon as he came into the city of the Ephesians, before he had washed off the dust of his journey, before he had put off his outer mantle (163), he collected some of those who had coapostatized (164) with Nestorius, and who were uttering blasphemies against their own heads, and were all but making a mock of Christ's glory; and so he made a sort of a gathering for himself of men about thirty in number, who had [only] the name of Bishops, of whom some were without cities, and others were idle, and had no churches, and others had been deposed many years before for terrible crimes by their own Metropolitans (165). And with them were also Pelagians and Celestians, (166) and some of those who had been cast

person or thing besides Himself, in Exodus xx, 5, and often: and the noble utterance of Elijah, the glorious opponent of serving any but God, in I Kings xix, 10, 14, whose example Cyril of Alexandria and the Third Ecumenical Synod did not forget.

NOTE 162.—Greek, τὴν τε ἀκρίβειαν τοῦ συνόδου καὶ τὴν εὐσέβειαν. The "*Piety*" here meant may be the piety of the Ecumenical Synod, or it may be used for Orthodox Piety itself, in brief for its Orthodoxy against denial of the Inman of God the Word, against the worship of a human being, and against Cannibalism and Host worship in the Eucharist.

NOTE 163.—Τὸ ἱμάτιον.

NOTE 164.—"*Coapostatized*," that is by favoring his apostasy from the fundametal doctrines of the Incarnation, that God alone is to be worshipped, and from what is in effect the symbolic view on the Lord's Supper.

NOTE 165.—By canons IV and V of the First Ecumenical Synod, the deposition of a Bishop would require the assent of the Metropolitan, without whom nothing could be done, but the vote of the Synod of the Province, to which the Bishop and the Metropolitan belonged would be also necessary.

NOTE 166.—The expressions *Celestians* and *Pelagians* were used to designate the same class of heretics, but the former was more used in the East than in the West. Those errors stated by the contemporary and opponent of Pelagius and Celestius, Marius Mercator, in his preface to his *Subnotations on the Words of Julian*, are as follows :

"1. Adam was made mortal, and must have died, whether he had sinned or not sinned.

2. The sin of Adam injured himself alone, and not the human race.

3. Infants who are born are in that state in which Adam was before his transgression.

4. The whole human race does not die by the death of Adam, because the whole human race does not rise again by Christ's resurrection.

5. Infants, even if they be not baptized, have eternal life.

These five heads breed one most impious and abominable opinion."

The learned Dr. Wall in his *History of Infant Baptism* has shown that the common

out from Thessaly (167); and so he dared to do an unholy thing, which no one before him had ever done. For he draws up, alone, a paper, and actually [uses] the name of deposition, and rubs an insult and injury upon the most holy and most God-revering Cyril, Bishop of the Church of the Alexandrians, and upon our most God-Revering brother and Fellow-Minister Memnon, the Bishop of the Church of the Ephesians, though none of us knew, and indeed none of those insulted and outraged knew what was done; nor for what sort of a reason they had dared to do that (168). Moreover just as though God were not angry at those things, just as though there were no ecclesiastical canons, or as though they were not going to run a risk for their impudence in those matters, they insult and outrage all the Synod also with the name of excommunication (169). And actually they even publicly put those things on a paper and put them forth to be read by those who wish, and affixed them to the walls of the theatre, in order that they might make a theatrical spectacle of their own impiety. And their impudent deeds did not stop even at those things, but they even took courage as though they had done some canonical thing, and reported matters such as those to the ears of the most pious and Christ-loving Emperors (170).

4. Those things being so done, Cyril, the most holy and most dear to God, Bishop of the Church of the Alexandrians, and, besides, Memnon the most dear to God Bishop of the city of the Ephesians, composed statements and brought accusation against both the most religious Bishop John himself and those who with

---

opinion of the first four centuries of the church was that infants unbaptized cannot enter heaven. They were not thought, however, to go to hell.

NOTE 167.—Mansi here remarks in a note: "*We should read* 'Out of Italy,' *as Garnier remarks in his notes to the Commonitory of Marius Mercator*." I am not sure on that point. The names of the 43 are given in the English translation of *Hefele's History of the Councils of the Church, Vol. 3, page 58.*

NOTE 168.—See on that, documents XI.-XVII., inclusive, in this volume on pages 46-56.

NOTE 169. See on that, documents XI., XII, on pages 46, 56, id.

NOTE 170.—All the above facts show the high-handed, rash, and unfair and uncanonical character of that party whose partizans in modern times represent them as meek and injured lambs, and accuse the Ecumenical Synod of wrong in condemning them. Their letter to the Emperors is mentioned on page 42, and another on page 56 of this volume. See also the Report to the Empress on page 61. Other emanations of the *Apostatic* Conventicle are referred to on other parts of pages 40-66.

him had done that thing, and offered them, adjuring our Holy Synod to send canonically for both John himself and those with him to apologize for their impudent actions, and, if they had any accusation to make, to tell it and to prove it if they could. For in the deposing paper, or rather in the insulting and outraging paper, written by them, they put forward the following pretence: *They are Apollinarians and Arians and Eunomians, and for that reason they have been deposed by us* (171). We therefore who have suffered the insult and outrage from them, are present, and again necessarily sitting together in the great Church, being above two hundred Bishops, have summoned by a first and a second and a third summons (172), in two days, both John himself and those with him to the Synod to convict those whom they have insulted and outraged, and to make their defence, and to tell the causes for which they had composed the paper of deposition; and they did not have the courage to come. But it was behooving him, if he was really able to convict the aforesaid holy men as being heretics, to meet with us and to show that that thing was really true (173) which he had taken as a strong and indubitable accusation and on the basis of which he had passed that headlong vote against them. But under the influence of a rotten conscience he did not come. And that was the prepared plan; for he supposed that when that absurd and unlawful insult and outrage of theirs is annulled, the just vote of the Synod which was put forth against the heretic Nestorius will also be overturned. We were therefore with good reason indignant, and we determined to put forth lawfully a vote and sentence against him and the rest, similar to that which he himself had unlawfully put forth against those who were in no respect guilty. But we have reserved for the judgment of thy God-Reveringness the matter as to

---

NOTE 171.—See page 53 in this volume. The slanderous and lying character of John and his partizans may be at once seen from the statement above. They villainously misrepresent Cyril and the Orthodox that they may cover the errors of the Man-server Nestorius and of themselves.

NOTE 172. Celestine of Rome in his Epistle to Nestorius writes as though the three summonses were the two Epistles of Cyril to him and his own; see Chrystal's Ephesus, Vol. I, pages 188, 189. The Council however did not deem them final, but give him three summonses of their own. For by Christ's law a Synod of the Whole Church is above any part of it: see Matt. xviii, 15-19, and I Tim. iii., 15.

NOTE 173.—Coleti and the Collectio Regia give here $ἀληθές$, but Migne has $ἀληθέν$. But I think that the ν (Nu) of the last Greek word is a mistake for σ, (Sigma).

overcoming his headlong rashness by long suffering (174), though he might most certainly have justly and lawfully suffered for it. Meanwhile we have deprived them of the communion and have stripped them of all priestly authority, so that they may not be able to injure any one by their own sentences. For as to those who are accustomed to proceed so savagely and harshly and uncanonically to such terrible and all-hard things in the way of actions, why was it not necessary, even though we were unwilling, to take from them the power and authority to do harm?

5. We are all therefore in communion with our brethren and Fellow-Ministers Cyril the Bishop and Memnon, who have endured insult and outrage from them, and since their headlong action (175) we have co-ministered and do co-minister with them, all of us in common going through the services with them (176); and we have cancelled and invalidated in writing their ridiculous actions, and have declared them utterly without force and ineffective (177). For they were an insult and outrage and nothing else. For what sort of an appearance of a Synod have men who are [only about] thirty in number, and some of them spotted with the stain of heresy and others without cities and cast forth? Or *what sort of force can they possess against a Synod gathered from the whole world under heaven?* For there co-sat with us those also who had been sent by thy Holiness, [that is] the most God-Revering Bishops, Arcadius and Projectus, and with them the most pious Presbyter Philip, who by their own persons favor us with thy presence, and fill the place of

NOTE 174.—Compare Rom. xii, 21, and II. Tim. iv. 2.

NOTE 175.—That is the headlong action of John and his partizans against Cyril and Memnon.

NOTE 176.—The action of the Ecumenical Synod in standing by their leaders Cyril and Memnon, even at the risk of deposition and excommunication, is deserving of all praise and shows their sincerity and self-sacrifice for God's truth against Nestorius' errors. And their peril was the greater because the Emperor was on Nestorius' side as is clear from a letter to Cyril mentioned in note 107, page 42, and in note 144, page 58, Vol. I, of *Ephesus* in this set.

NOTE 177.—This shows how we should regard all depositions and excommunications put forth against other God alone worshippers, by other *worshippers of a human being* and Real Presence Substanceities and Cannibalizers on the Eucharist. All such utterances of Roman, Greek, Nestorian, and Monophysite Bishops against the Reformers of the sixteenth century and since are, of course, null and void, for, as the Ecumenical Synod say, they are "*invalidated*" by the decisions of the whole Church at Ephesus and are—*ridiculous*," and "*utterly without force and ineffective;*" whereas the depositions and excom

the Apostolic See(178). Let therefore thy Holiness be suitably indignant at those things which have been done (179). For if license is given to those who wish to insult and outrage even the greater thrones, and put forth votes so lawless and uncanonical, aye insults rather against those over whom they have no authority (180), and against those who have undergone such great contests for piety, (by means of which contests even now piety shines forth through the prayers of thy Holiness), (181), the affairs of the Church will go to extreme disorder. But when those who have dared to do such things are punished in a becoming manner every tumult will be ineffective, and due respect will be preserved by all for the Canons.

6. Moreover, the minutes of the actions on the depositions (182) of the unholy Pelagians and Celestians, Celestius, Pelagius, Julian, Presidius, Florus, Marcellinus, Orentius, and those who hold the same opinions with them, were read in the Holy Synod, and we also have deemed it right that those things which have been decreed against them by thy God-revenringness

---

munications put forth by God alone worshipping Presbyters even, against such creature worshipping and Eucharist corrupting bishops are effective, because antecedently approved by the whole Church at Ephesus in A. D. 431.

NOTE 178.—They mean that the Synod was made one of *"the whole world"* by the presence of representatives of the West and East. We may add that this utterance condemns the merely local Vatican Synod of A. D. 1869-1870, for trying to undo the decision of the Sixth Ecumenical Synod against Pope Honorius, and the action of the Iconodulic local Council of Nicaea A. D. 787 and all other local Synods which opposed the decisions of the Ecumenical Synod of Ephesus against creature-worship and errors on the Eucharist.

NOTE 179.—That is by John of Antioch and his friends against Cyril and Memnon.

NOTE 180.—The Synod of the Apostasy was made up mainly of Bishops from one Patriarchate, that of Antioch. But by Canon VI. of Nicaea, as understood from the first, the Bishop of Antioch had no jurisdiction in the Patriarchate of Alexandria, in that of Rome, or elsewhere outside of his own Patriarchate of the East. But here he was trying with a handful to override the whole Church in Ecumenical Synod assembled, and that for the purpose of supporting a Man-Server, a denier of the Incarnation, and a corrupter of the doctrine of the Eucharist, by which he did vast harm. Surely all this was criminal and mad enough.

NOTE 181.—A Byzantine compliment, still in use among the later Greeks, but not to be imitated by us, nor indeed by any one, for it leads, when commonly used, to insincerity spiritual flattery, and lying. There is too much of such stuff, so different from the simple New Testament compliments, in the records of *Ephesus*.

NOTE 182.—A note here in Mansi says: "The above cited Garnier remarks that we should read *"condemnation"* [for *"deposition"* above], because laics, to whose number Pelagius belonged, are not deposed but condemned." But Julian was a Bishop as were thers of the above mentioned heretics. And the Greek word here used, καθαιρέσει,

shall remain strong and firm (183). And we are all voters on the

is used also in the general sense of *"putting down,"* which may be its meaning here In that case it would mean *condemnation* for laics and deposition for clerics. But perhaps the Council supposed Pelagius to be a Bishop or cleric. And the Synod in its Conciliar Epistle to the whole Church certainly deposed all Pelagian Bishops and clergy; see that Letter and its Canons I. and IV. The Synod probably knew Pelagius to be a laic and condemned him as such.

NOTE 183.—What particular *"Minutes"* and *"Actions"* are here meant is a question. When the things *"decreed against"* the Pelagians and Celestians by Bishop Celestine were first put forth by him is also a matter of some doubt. On those points Note "j," col. 521 of tome 50 of Migne's *Patrologia Latina* states (I translate it from Latin):

"What those Actions regarding the Pelagians are which were recited in the Synod and are here said to have been confirmed by it is a matter of question. Henry Noris, Book II. of his *Hist. Pelag.*, Chapter 7, infers from the above that some Actions were published by Celestine which have perished by the injury wrought by time. But Celestine nowhere makes mention of Actions or decrees of that kind, even when it seemed necessary for him to make mention of them. For though asked once and again and *often* what should be thought of the Pelagians, and when answering his [Nestorius'] repeated requests, he replies in the following way alone in II., 8:

"*As to those heretics also in regard to whom thou as being ignorant hast wished to consult us, a righteous condemnation has expelled them from their sees for saying unrighteous things*, where, as in what follows, he mentions nothing new as having been done or decreed against the Pelagians by himself, but deems it enough to recall to mind old Actions which Nestorius could not be ignorant of, as to which his own predecessor, Sisiunius, did not need to ask, to which even before that Atticus had assented, and sent to Rome the Actions in which the Pelagians were condemned by himself. Therefore no actions done against the Pelagians seem with any reason to have been read in the Synod of Ephesus, other than those which Celestine mentions in Epistle 13, just referred to. The following passage of Prosper (*Contra Collat.* c. 21, n. 58) pertains to the same matter.

"'*By that man* [Celestine] *the Oriental Churches also were purged of a double pest, because he aided with the apostolic sword Cyril, Bishop of the City of Alexandria, a most glorious defender of the Catholic faith, to cut off the Nestorian impiety, by which sword the Pelagians were also laid prostrate, for they were allied in kindred errors.*' For the Epistle to Cyril, in which the errors of Nestorius are condemned, and the Epistle to that heresiarch, in which the condemnation of the Pelagians is confirmed were written by Celestine at the same time. [The latter Epistle is translated on pages 178-203, Vol. I. of Chrystal's *Ephesus.*]

"Tillemont. tom. xiii., page 752, thinks that no other Actions were recited at Ephesus but those of that Roman Synod in which Zosimus presided, and in which Pelagius and Celestius were again condemned, and with them Julian and his fellows were also condemned and driven away from their sees."

Question. Who were the Pelagians mentioned in the Report of the Third Ecumenical Synod to Celestine, Bishop of Rome?

Answer. Celestius and Pelagius were the notorious leaders of the heresy. Julian was the Bishop of Eclanum in Italy. See on him in Smith and Wace's *Dictionary of Christian Biography.* He is there *"Julianus* (15)."

On two of the rest we find something in note "*h*," col. 521 of tome 50 of Migne's *Patrologia Latina* as follows:

"Our manuscripts have Lawrence [instead of *Orentius*]. In other books which imitate the Greek text we find *Orentius.* But it should undoubtedly be read *Orontius*, in regard to whom Nestorius above wrote in Epistle 6, n. 1, as follows:

"'*Julian, indeed, and Florus, and Orontius and Fabius, saying that they are Bishops of Western parts:*' And in Epistle 7 [Nestorius writes], '*I have often written to thy Blessedness on account of Julian, Orontius, and the rest.*' To that Orontius is inscribed an Epistle which Anianus, a noted follower of Pelagius, prefixed to the Homilies of John Chrysostom on Matthew."

On looking back to Nestorius' Epistle (Epistle 6 above mentioned) I find that Nestorius mentioned Julian, Florus, Orontius and Fabius as having appealed to him and the Emperor for help, as Bishops who had suffered persecution in the West. They, of course claimed to be Orthodox, though they were really Pelagians. Epistle 7 (a letter of Nestorious to Pope Celestine) mentions Julian and Orontius and *"the rest,"* how many is not specified, who claimed to be Bishops and to be Orthodox and to have been deposed unjustly in the West, and appealed to Nestorius and the Eastern Emperor for help. Perhaps *'the rest"* includes Presidius and Marcellinus, the others mentioned in the Synod's Report to Pope Celestine after its Fifth Act, but we can not say for certain.

With regard to the Acts mentioned in the Report matters are not so clear as we could wish.

The depositions of some at least, perhaps of all of those heretics had occurred long before A. D. 422, the beginning of Celestine's episcopate. Julian's, for instance, and his exile occurred about A. D. 418 (see Smith and Wace's *Dictionary of Christian Biography*, article *"Julianus* (15)"). Consequently *"the minutes of the things done on the deposition"* of those men does not refer to any deposition of some of them, perhaps of none of them, by Celestine himself. But *the minutes* seem to have been transcripts of the original depositions, some of which had been wrought in Italy, and others in North Africa.

The errors of Pelagius were Ecumenically condemned as they are in the above passage, and in Canons I., IV. and VI. of the Third Synod.

I have examined all the letters of Celestine before the Third Ecumenical Synod and find no clear allusion to Celestine's having sent any Actions to it, but he must have done so, for the Synod's Report after the Fifth Act shows that he did. I presume his place-holders took them to the Second Session with them, or they might have been received afterwards.

Canon Bright in his article *Coelestinus I.* in Smith and Wace's *Dictionary of Christian Biography,* shows that Celestine was zealous against Pelagianism,.but does not tell what the *Minutes* above mentioned were.

One of the great founders of Nestorianism, Theodore of Mopsuestia, had at first been favorable to Coelestius the heresiarch, but had afterwards turned against him. Davids in his article, *Julianus of Eclana,* in Smith and Wace's *Dictionary of Christian Biography,* gives the authorities on that matter as follows:

"When he was driven from the West, Julian and some of his fellow-exiles went into Cilicia, and remained for a time with Theodorus, Bishop of Mopsuestia in that province (*Mar. Merc. Theod. Mops,* praef. §2). who is charged by Mercator with having been one of the originators of Pelagianism (*Subnot.* praef. I., *Symb. Theod. Mops.* praef. §2), and who also wrote against Augustine (Phot. *Bibl. Cod.* 177; *Mar. Merc. Garnier, Ad Partem. Prim.* dissert. VI.)." Afterwards Julianus left Cilicia, and farther on we read, id, that he was also condemned, in his absence, by a Council in Cilicia, Theodorus concurring in the censure (*Mar. Merc. Symbol. Theod. Mops.* praef. §3; Garnier, *Ad Primam Part.* dissert. II., Migne, 359." Davids here uses *Theodorus* for our common form of the name *Theodore,* and *Julianus* for *Julian.*

Davids then goes on in the same article to show how Julian then went to Constantinople and was condemned by its Patriarch Atticus and his successor Sisinnius in A. D., 426, how on Nestorius' accession to that see in A. D., 428, he appealed to him and the Emperor Theodosius II., "both of whom, at first, gave him some encouragement," and that the Emperor made no mention of the Pelagians in the edict which he "issued against heresies at the instance of Nestorius," that Nestorius wrote to Celestine of Rome regarding Julian and his friends which favor towards them involved him in some trouble in Constantinople, so that he defended himself in a public discourse on the matter, how Marius Mercator then, in A. D. 429, exposed Julian and his errors and their condemnations, and how the Emperor then drove them from Constantinople. Davids adds:

"Whither he" [Julian of Eclana]" went after his expulsion from Constantinople does not appear, but he with other Pelagians seem to have accompanied Nestorius to the Convent of Ephesus, A. D., 431, and took part in the ' *Conciliabulum,* which was held by Joannes [John, in English]" of Antioch (*Relat. ad Coel,* in Mansi, IV., 1334). The reading of '*Thessalia*' is a clerical error for '*Italia*' (Noris, Opp. I., 361, 363). Baronius (s. a.,

431, LXXIX.) infers from a passage in one of the letters of Gregory the Great (Lib. IX., ind. ii., ep. 49 in *Pat. Lat.* XV., LXVII., 981), that the '*Conciliabulum*' absolved Julian and his friends, but Cardinal Noris (Opp. I., 362) has exposed his error. The Council in their Synodical letter to Celestine declare their approval of all that had previously been done in the case of the Pelagians, and repeat their condemnation, expressly mentioning Julianus by name (*Relat.* u. s.; *Mar. Merc. Nestor. Tract.* praef. 22)."

Julian tried to get back his position from Celestine's successor, Sixtus III., who when a presbyter had favored Pelagianism, and from Pope Leo I., his successor, for his see was suffragan to Rome as being in South Italy, but he failed, and died in Sicily about A. D., 454. See Davids, id.

Such an appeal as that of Julian from Rome to Constantinople and to the whole Church, distributed in sees, till an Ecumenical Council spoke was always allowed, just as it was allowed to make the same appeal to Rome, and to all other sees from Constantinople. Every Bishop condemned by his own local church had the same right to appeal to the whole Church, distributed in sees, so long as the Church was sound and one. Unlearned or partisan Romanists, when they read of an appeal from some Eastern to Rome, are prone to cite it as an appeal to Rome alone or to Rome as the sole judge in the matter. That stuff of making the Bishop of Rome absolute monarch over all the Church, East and West, is recognized by no Ecumenical Canon, but is, in effect, forbidden by those of the four first Synods. The only thing that was final was the decision of an Ecumenical Synod. For example, we find the leaders of the Pelagian party, Pelagius, Coelestius, and Julian of Eclana, appealing to the great sees of the Christian world, Rome, Carthage, Constantinople, and other Eastern sees; aye when Rome and Carthage had spoken, they tried to win the head see of the East, Constantinople, and to keep up the fight still, by showing that there was no Ecumenical decision against them. And the matter was not considered as wholly settled till the whole Church decided it in the Third Ecumenical Synod. Sometimes, however, *the Appeal to the whole Church, distributed in Sees, secured a practically unanimous answer*, and so rendered an Ecumenical Council unnecessary, as, for instance, in the matter of the heresy of Paul of Samosata in the third Century. That Appeal might be made by Orthodox or heretic.

Some times, even in the days of unity, the appeal to the whole Church, distributed in Sees, was impossible, as, for example:

1. When Constantius, the Arian, had become sole Emperor of the East and West, and had thrust out all sound men from their sees, and had put Arians into their places, when, as Jerome writes, "*The whole world groaned and wondered that itself was Arian,*" Jerome *adv. Lucif.*, quoted in note 3, on page 307 of Edgar's *Variations of Popery*, N. Y. edition of 1848. As any one can see at a glance, the Appeal to the whole Episcopate then would be an Appeal to a lot of heretics anathematized by the Creed of Nicaea, who were continually putting forth Creeds against that of Nicaea.

So the Appeal to the whole Episcopate to-day, even if they were all united, would be a farce, and treason to Christ, to the first Six, the only Ecumenical Synods, and to our own best interests in time and in eternity, for the great bulk of them are image and cross and relic worshippers, creature invokers, and therefore creature worshippers, contrary to Christ's law in Matthew, iv., 10, enemies of the VI. Synods, and of Christ and his saving truth, and servants of the devil, and sure to be eternally damned if they die as they are. And they would degrade us to their own level if they had the power over us, and so bring God's curses on us.

But such an appeal is now impossible, for the Greeks and the Latins have been separated for a thousand years, and the Greeks will not co-sit with the Latins, nor the Latins with them, but differ in doctrine, discipline and rite, irreconcilably.

2. Some times, owing to the fact that no appeal was allowed in one of the two Roman Empires, that of the East, or that of the West, *the Appeal to the whole Episcopate Distributed in Sees*, was impossible. In such a case, however, the Appeal was made so far as it could be. For example, Chrysostom's friends, when he was exiled by the Emperor of the East from his see of Constantinople, the chief see of the East, appealed to different sees of the West. Venables in his article, "*Chrysostom, John*," in Smith and Wace's

Dictionary of Christian Biography, tells the tale on that matter, and gives his authority as follows:

"All other help failing, the persecuted part of the Church of Constantinople" [Chrysostom's friends are meant] "appealed to the Western Church as represented by its chief Bishops. Letters were sent addressed to Innocent, Bishop of Rome, Venerius of Milan, and Chromatius of Aquileia, by Chrysostom himself, by the forty friendly Bishops, and by the clergy of Constantinople, (*Pallad.* p. 10).)" When such appeals are made to the Bishops of Rome, Romish controversialists are prone to try and make out that they were to him not as to one of the universal Episcopate, though, on political grounds alone, *the first among his equals*, but to him alone as the infallible ruler and monarch of a lot of unequals and inferiors. It is their old trick, which has bamboozled and deceived so many who are ignorant of the Ecumenical canons and decisions, and has led so many into the pitfalls of Rome's soul-damning and Ecumenically anathematized saint worship, Host worship, relic worship, and her other forms of creature service. Surely in view of the harm done by Rome to that class in the Anglican Communion and elsewhere it is full time for the sound part of Christendom to appoint a valid sound succession to the see of Rome in place of the present man, Leo XIII. whom the Greeks call unbaptized and unordained, and whom the Protestants deem an idolater. The Six Councils, in effect, teach that as a duty, for they always deposed all creature worshippers, as, for instance, the Arians, Macedonians, Nestorians, and Monophysites.

3. Sometimes a person convicted in a local synod of one Patriarchate, not in the whole of an empire, would appeal to other local councils, as, for instance, Eutyches, when condemned in a local Synod at Constantinople, in A. D., 448, appeals "*to a Roman, Egyptian, and Jerusalemite Council*" (Hefele, *History of the Church Councils*, Vol. III., page 218.)

4. It has been useless and foolish to make *the Appeal to the whole Church, distributed in sees*, that is, *not assembled in Ecumenical Council*, since the corruptions and what are practically the rebellions in the way of worship of saints by invocation, the worship of images, and of worship of the Host, against the doctrine, discipline and rite of the Six World Councils acquired full supremacy over them and were imposed on all Bishops by the civil powers, or by the tyranny of the uneducated and superstitious and idolatrous mob of women and men. In A. D., 754, the Iconoclastic Council of Constantinople forced men to accept the worship of saints by invocation. In A. D., 787, the image worshippers at Nicaea sanctioned the same sin, and the error of a substance presence in the Eucharist, but condemned the Iconoclasts for not worshipping images, etc. All three tenets are forbidden by the VI. Synods, but yet were enforced by the secular powers. Rome enforced the decisions of the latter Council in the West, where she had the power, and in the Fourth Lateran Council of A. D., 1215, she forbade the Real Substances Absence of the Third Ecumenical Council, and established for her Communion the error of Real Substances Presence by Transubstantiation, and the Greeks established the same error for theirs, though in a way to contradict Rome's, in her Council of Jerusalem of A. D., 1672, and in that of Constantinople of the same year. And for long centuries, contrary to the Third Ecumenical Council, both Communions have committed the idolatry of worshipping even both natures of Christ in the Eucharist. And Rome, at her Vatican Council of A. D., 1870, in effect contradicted and rejected the decision of the Sixth Ecumenical Synod that Pope Honorius was a heretic, and defined, on the contrary, the heresy of Papal Infallibility.

5. It has been utterly useless and foolish to make *the Appeal to the whole Church, distributed in Sees*, that is, to *the whole Episcopate distributed in Sees*, since the split in the Church consequent on its idolatries, which occurred in the ninth century. For the East and West differed on doctrine, discipline, and rite then, and they differ still more now. For the Greeks of the Patriarchates reject even the baptism and the orders of the Latins, and, so, deny that they are any part of the Church at all; whereas the Latins regards them as schismatics. And Pitzipios in his *L'Eglise Orientale* (Rome, Imprimerie de la Propagande, 1855), Part I., pages 37-106, states that there are ten differences between them, not to speak of others which he endeavors to minimize. Since Pitzipios published his work, Rome has added a new difference by contradicting, as has just been said,

same side with thee, and hold them deposed, (184). And for exact and good understanding of all that has been done, we have sent both the minutes and the subscriptions of the Synod. We pray that thou mayest be strong and make mention of us to the Lord, beloved and most desired (185). [And all the Bishops subscribed in succession by name (186), (187), (188).]

the decision of the Sixth Ecumenical Council, A. D., 680, against Pope Honorius as a heretic, and has put forth the doctrine of Papal Infallibility. That occurred in the Romish Council of the Vatican in A. D., 1870. The man who talks of an Appeal to these two Communions contradicting and opposing and excommunicating and anathematizing each other, and both contradicting and anathematizing expressly or impliedly more or fewer of the doctrines and canons of the Six Ecumenical Councils will be branded by wise men, either as an ignoramus, a fool, or a madman. Moreover, Revelations xviii., compared with Revelations xvii., 18, shows that Rome is irreformable and doomed to destruction, and that *God's people* must come out of it or *partake of its sins, and receive of its plagues*, and, in brief, be lost.

NOTE 184.—The Synod, composed almost wholly of Oriental Bishops, add their condemnation of the Pelagian heresy to the condemnation of it by the West, so making the sentence Ecumenical.

Garnier, as Mansi here notes, would read *"condemned"* instead of *"deposed,"* for the reason given in the last note above.

NOTE 185.—Here we have a specimen of the courteous and loving language used by Bishops to each other in that age. Similar expressions are found in documents from Latin Africa of a little before which resist Rome's claim to jurisdiction there.

In the Codex Seg. we find the following additional, in Greek, in Coleti's margin, at the end of this Report of the Ecumenical Synod to Pope Celestine: *"We have sent the Minutes and the Subscriptions of the Synod. We pray that thou mayst be strong and mindful of us."* But this looks like a mistake and repetition by the copyist.

NOTE 186.—This last sentence in brackets is not in the Greek, but is given in the Latin, in Migne, not in Coleti, nor in Hardouin, nor in Mansi.

NOTE 187.—I have translated most of the above epistle from columns 511-522 of tome 50 of Migne's *Patrologia Latina*, but have carefully compared Coleti with it throughout, and sometimes followed Coleti the *Collectio Regia* where I deemed their reading better.

NOTE 188.—As this Report is not mentioned in the Minutes of Act V., I presume that it was drawn up by Cyril and the chief prelates between Acts V. and VI. Was it signed by all the Bishops? To this question I would reply, that in the Greek nothing is said on that point further than the heading which marks it, as the utterance of the Third Ecumenical Synod, which it could not be unless it expressed their sentiments. That implies, therefore, the subscription or assent in some way of all or at least the bulk of the Bishops. The Latin translation, made from the Greek, says definitely that *"all the Bishops signed it by name."*

I have translated all Act V. and the Epistle to Celestine from Coleti, but have compared the remarks and notes in Hardouin and Mansi, and have in places compared the Collectio Regia.

A Homily of Cyril Against John of Antioch.

MATTER IN COLETI'S and MANSI'S EDITIONS OF THE COUNCILS BETWEEN ACTS V. AND VI. OF THE THIRD ECUMENICAL SYNOD. IT IS NOT IN HARDOUIN'S, WHO HAS NOTHING BETWEEN THOSE ACTS. I epitomize from Coleti.

This document consists of what bears the title.

"[A Homily] *of Cyril, Archbishop of Alexandria, against John of Antioch, who separated* [from the Synod.]" The Latin adds, "*delivered at Ephesus.*"

This is a plea against the conduct of John of Antioch for his course against the Synod. Cyril begins by speaking of the necessity of following Christ if we love him, and of being willing to suffer for him, and aptly quotes John XII; 26, "*Let him that loveth me follow me. And where I am, there also let my minister* [[or "*servant*" διάκονος] *be.*" Cyril then says that Nestorius as "*a terrible and all-hard serpent*" or "*dragon*" who had "*not merely one but many heads on one body,*" had appeared in the Church of the Saviour, and that it had became necessary to free it from the mischief wrought by such poison-throwing creatures; that accordingly God's Spirit had gathered His servants in the Synod to resist the dragon, and the Lord had given a command on the matter which was: "*Where I am, there also let my minister be,*" (John XII. 26). Then he chides John for being untrue to Christ and his ministry because he did not maintain sound doctrine with the Ecumenical Synod—"*As thou seest,*" he adds, "*the many headed serpent* [or "*dragon*"] *has raised his unholy and profane head and spits forth the poison of his own unholiness against the children of the Church.*" The "*many headed*" feature of Nestorius' errors referred to by Cyril here and in a passage above in the same epistle seems to mean the multifarious character of his errors, which included not only a denial of the Incarnation but also the error of serving a creature, of relative service, and of cannibalizing and, I may add, of idolatrizing the Eucharist, and others, (189).

Cyril proceeds, "*I have unsheathed the sword of the Spirit, and* have come against him" [Nestorius, the many headed serpent]. "I fight for Christ against the wild beast. Why dost thou not co-labor with one who wishes to do well? Why dost thou thyself not assist us? Let him be cast out by the hand of all." Then Cyril says that he and his brethren as true ministers of the Saviour, as stewards of his mysteries, had deemed those who spoke folly against His glory to be most hostile, and asks him why he had not so regarded them. "For," adds, he, "that thou didst not come forward nobly, the facts themselves testify against thee. Thou seest us covered as it were with the dust of battle. Thou seest us yet dripping with the sweat of the fight, and needing good spiritual courage and consolation; aye, rather thou seest us now victors. But

---

NOTE 189.—They are told in detail in Vol. 1 of Chrystal's *Ephesus*, on pages 449-480, in his *Twenty Blasphemies*, for which he was condemned and deposed, on pages 486-504, in Note F. pages 529-551, and in the *General Index*, under *Nestorius and His Heresies* and *Man Worship* and *Eucharist*, and other fit terms.

thou who art in the ranks of the brethren, thou who hast enrolled thyself under the Master, Christ, thou who oughtest to bear arms with us, wieldest thy weapons against the dogmas of the truth. O unlooked for thing! Thou hast not taken part in the fight. Thou hast not been fellow contestant by the side of us who have contested. Thou didst flee the time of war by the slowness of thy coming Thou stoodest afar off, viewing those who were acting manfully. Thou sawest the enemy fallen and the blasphemous tongue relaxed and punished. Then thou wast grieved. Tell me for what sort of a reason? Was it because Christ had conquered, that he had overcome those who had stood up against Him, that, the mouth that had spoken great things had become silent, that disease had ceased to fall upon the children of the Church? But it was better to act like a man with us and to say with David, [Psalm, cxxxix, 21, 22, Psalm, cxxxviii, Septuagint Greek version.] *"Did I not hate those, O Lord, who hated Thee? And was I not wasting away because of thine enemies? I was hating them with a perfect hatred. I regarded them as having become my enemies,"* and so on. But no such expression at all was in use with thee. But, on the contrary, thou dost shoot thine arrows at us after we have conquered, and thou dost attempt to wound us with the arrows of thy malice, when thou shouldest rather admire us." Then he tells John that in warring against the Synod and its work, he will not succeed, and that, though their weapons are only spiritual, yet they are powerful, and that at the worst they can suffer for Christ as well as believe in him (noble words!) and then concludes: "For to Him befitteth glory, might honor, and worship (literally bowing, προσκύνησις,) now and forever, Amen." And with that the document ends.

ACT SIXTH.

[REMARK.—The Greek of the part before the heading to the Creed of Nicaea in this Act is lost; and so is the Greek for the words, "*But because some pretend,*" to the 21 passages of Fathers below. There is a Latin translation of much of this Act VI. of Ephesus in Act I. of Chalcedon, most of the Greek of that Act VI. being lost. It was quoted in Act I. of Chalcedon. There is a Latin rendering ascribed to Marius Mercator in *Coleti's Concilia, tom. IV., col.* 121, and after. The Latin translation in Act. I. of Chalcedon is fuller than is given in Act. VI. of Ephesus in Coleti. The renderings in the two Latin Versions in Act VI. of Ephesus in Coleti are evidently abbreviated by omitting the list of the names of the Bishops of the Synod at the beginning of Act VI., and the twenty-one passages from the Fathers, and also Nestorius' XX. Blasphemies in that Act. Indeed, that is said in effect. I prefer to refer the reader to them as already translated by me above, not from the Latin, but from the Greek original in Act I. of Ephesus. See them on pages 418-480 of volume I. of Chrystal's *Ephesus,* for there is, however, but very little noteworthy difference. The Latin translation of those twenty-one passages in Act. I. of Chalcedon corresponds quite closely generally to the original Greek in Act I. of Ephesus, except that the three passages from Atticus, passages 17, 18 and 19 in Act I. in the Greek of Ephesus are separated in the Latin translation of Act I. of Chalcedon, the first two from the third, and are given in the following order there, namely, 17, 18 and 21. Otherwise they are almost word for word the same in sense. There are just twenty-one passages in each. There is no dogmatic difference between the twenty-one passages in Act I. and Act VI. of Ephesus and in Act I. of Chalcedon. They support Cyril and Orthodoxy, wherever found. But, as will be seen, the Bishops at Ephesus in their Act VI. quoted only those parts of Act I. of Ephesus which were most needed. They omit the rest. I will first, however, give the abbreviated Latin renderings of the first part of Act VI. of *Ephesus,* as given in columns 1199, 1200 of tome III. of *Coleti's Concilia.* By first part I mean the whole part before the Creed of Nicaea.]

The English of the Latin translation of the first part of Act VI. of Ephesus.	*The English of Marius Mercator's Latin Version of the first part of Act VI. of Ephesus.*
(190) In the Consulship of our Masters, Flavius Theodosius, Consul for the thirteenth time, and Flavius Valentinian, Consul for the third time, the ever Augustones, on the eleventh day before the Kalends of August (191), which day, according	[192] In the Consulship of our Masters, Flavius Theodosius, Consul for the thirteenth time, and Flavius Valentinian, Consul for the third time, ever Augustones, on the eleventh day before the Kalends of August, which day, according to the

NOTE 190.—"*See another Latin translation of this Act VI. in Act I. of the Council of Chalcedon, where this Act Sixth is much longer;*" note in *Coleti's Concilia,* tom. III., col. 1199, 1200.

NOTE 191.—This was July 22, 431, as we now reckon time.

NOTE 192.—"*This is the beginning of the Ancient Version of which Marius Mercator was the translator;*" note in *Coleti's Concilia,* tom. III., col. 1199, 1200. But from Stephen Baluze's Preface to the *Ancient Version,* in tome IV. of *Coleti's Concilia,* col. 1 and 2, it seems that there are variations in the extant copies of that ancient translation which are attributed to the desire to correct obscurities in it.

to the Egyptians, is the twenty-eighth of [the month] Epiphi, the Synod was gathered in the metropolis of the Ephesians in accordance with the decree of our most God-loving Princes, and the most religious Bishops sat down in the Episcopal residence of Memnon; namely, Cyril of Alexandria, who held the place of Celestine also, the most holy Archbishop of the Roman Church; and Arcadius, Bishop and Legate; and Philip, a Presbyter, [literally an Elder,] and Legate; and the rest who are reckoned above in the session before, and *Peter, a Presbyter*, [literally an Elder] *of Alexandria, and chief of the Secretaries*, said,

Your Holy and Great Synod, having all foresight for the right and apostolic faith, and for the truth of the dogmas, and having regard also to the discipline and order of the churches, put forth a Definition, which we have before our hands, and will read if it please your Holiness.

The Holy Synod said, Let the Definition put forth by this Holy and Universal Synod be read and

Egyptians, is the twenth-eighth of Epiphi, by the command of the most August and most pious Princes, the Synod was congregated in the metropolis of the Ephesians, and all the most holy and most dear to God Bishops sat down in the Episcopal residence of the most reverend and most religious Bishop Memnon; namely, Cyril of Alexandria, who managed the place of Celestine also, the most holy and most religious Prelate of the holy Roman Church; Juvenal of Jerusalem, Memnon of the Ephesians, and Flavian of Philippi, who managed the place of Rufus also, the most holy Bishop of Thessalonica, and all [the rest] together with Philip, a Presbyter, [literally *"an Elder"*] of the Apostolic See and a Legate of the Roman See. And when they had sat down together, *Peter, a Presbyter* [literally *"an Elder"*] of Alexandria, and *a* [Dionysius (193)] chief of the Secretaries, said,

Your Holy and Great Synod, exercising all foresight for the right and apostolic faith and for the dogmas of truth, and

---

NOTE 193.—As this name does not appear in the parallel place here, nor in this place as given in the Latin of this Act VI. as quoted in Act I. of Chalcedon, it is probably an unwarranted addition.

inserted in the Minutes of the Acts.

consulting for the peace and state of the churches, put forth a Definition which we have before our hands, and if it shall seem good to your Holiness, we will read it.

The Holy Synod said, Let the Definition put forth by the Holy and Great Synod be read throughout, and inserted in the present Actions.

[Then at once follows the Nicene Creed in the abbreviated form of this Act VI. of Ephesus. But for the sake of fuller and more accurate information we here give]

ACT. VI. OF THE THIRD ECUMENICAL SYNOD IN ITS FULLER FORM, AS QUOTED IN ACT I. OF THE FOURTH ECUMENICAL SYNOD, IN A. D., 451.

In the days of the consulship of our Masters, the Flaviuses (194), Theodosius, Consul for the thirteenth time and Valenturian for the third time, the Ever August Ones, on the eleventh day before the Calends of August, which, according to the Egyptians, is the twenty-eighth of the [the month Epiphi (195), when Nestorius had been deposed, as it is contained in the Action following (196), the Synod was congregated in the Ephesian metropolis by the decree of our most religious and Christ-loving Emperors; and there sat down in the Episcopal residence of the most dear to God [197] Bishop Memnon, the [following] most God-loving [198] and most religious Bishops [namely]:

Cyril of Alexandria, who also managed the place of Celestine, the most holy and most blessed Bishop of the Roman Church.

Juvenal of Jerusalem.

NOTE 194.—Each of the Emperors was named Flavius.

NOTE 195.—This was July 22, 431.

NOTE 196.—We have the Greek up to this. What follows to the Creed of Nicaea is in a Latin translation.

NOTE 197.—Or, *"most friendly to God,"* perhaps the Greek said.

NOTE 198.—Or, *"most dear to God,"* perhaps the Greek said.

Memnon of Ephesus.
Flavian of Philippi, who also managed the place of Rufus, the most reverend Bishop of Thessalonica.
Theodotus of Ancyra in the First Galatia.
Firmus of Caesarea in the First Cappadocia.
Acacius of Melitene in Armenia.
Iconius of Gortyna in Crete.
Peregrinus of Corinth in Hellas.
Cyrus of Aphrodisias in the province of Caria.
Valerian of Iconium.
Palladius of Amasia (199) in Hellespontus.
Hesychius of Parium.
Hellanicus of Rhodes.
Dinatus of Nicopolis in Old Epirus.
Eucharius of Dyrrachium in New Epirus.
Perrebius of Pharmalus.
Eudoxius of Choma in Lycia.
Silvanus of Chaeretapa in Phrygia.
Berinianus of Perga in the province of Pamphylia.
Amphilochius of Side.
Epiphanius of Cratia in the province of Honorias.
Gregory of Cerasus in Pontus Polemoniacus.
Senecion of Scodra (200).
Dalmatius of Cyzicus.
Docimasius of Maronea in Thrace.
John of the island of Proeconnesus.
Daniel of Colonia in the Second Cappadocia.
Romanus of Raphia.
Paulinianus of Maiuma
Paul of Anthedon.
Fidus of Joppa.
John of Sycamazon.

NOTE 199.—Spelled also, perhaps generally, *Amasea*.

NOTE 200.—Below Senecion is mentioned as Bishop of the "*Codrinae civitatis*," which may be meant, for the "Scodrinae civitatis," that is, the "*City of Scodra.*" See col. 1222, tom III. of *Coleti's Concilia*. See *Scodra* in *Wiltsch's Geog. and Statistics of the Church*, Vol. I., Index.

Theodore of Gadara.
Letoius of Libyas.
Apelles of Eleusis (201).
Theodore of Aribdela.
Peter of Parembola.
John of Augustopolis.
Sais of Phaenus (202).
Rufinus of Tabae (203).
Anysius of Thebes.
Callicrates of Naupactus.
Domninus of Opus.
Nicias of Megara.
Agathocles of Colonia in Achaia.
Felix of Apollonia and Bellida.
Theodore of Torone.
Andrew of Chersonesus in Crete.
Prothymius of Comana.
Paul of Lampe.
Zenobius of Gnossus.
Lucian of Topiris (204) in Thrace.
Ennepius of Maximianopolis.
Secundianus of Lamia.
Dion of Thebes in Thessaly.
Theodore of Echinus.
Martyrius of Helistra.
Thomas of Derbe.
Athanasius of Parositha.
Themistius of Jassus.
Aphthonetus of Heraclea.
Philip of Amyzon.
Apelles of Cibyrrha.
Spudasius of Ceramus.

NOTE 201.—Or, "*Eleus.*"
NOTE 202.—Or, "*Phaenon.*"
NOTE 203.—Or, "*Tava.*"
NOTE 204.—Or, "*Toperus.*"

Archelaus of Myndus.
Phania of Harpasa.
Promachius of Alinda.
Philip of Pergamus in Asia.
Maximus of Assos.
Dorotheus of Myrrhina.
Maximus of Cyma.
Ephorus of Hypaepa.
Alexander of Arcadiopolis.
Eutychius of Theodosiopolis.
Rhodon of Palaeopolis.
Eutropius of Evasa (205).
Aphobius of Colonia.
Nestorius of Sion.
Heracleon of Tralles.
Theodotus of Nyssa.
Theodore of Alydda (206).
Timothy of Briula.
Theodosius of Mastaura.
Tychichus of Erythrae (207).
Eusebius of Clazomenae.
Eulalius of Colophon.
Modestus of Athens.
Theosebius of Priene.
Eusebius of Magnesia on Sipylus.
Sapricius of Paphos in the island of Cyprus.
Zeno of Curium.
Rheginus of Constantia.
Evagrius of Solona (208).
Caesarius, Country Bishop of Arcesena (209).
Tribonianus of Aspenda in Pamphylia.
Nunechius of Selge.

NOTE 205.—Or, "*Evaza*,"
NOTE 206.—Or, "*Anineta*."
NOTE 207.—Or, "*Erythrum.*"
NOTE 208.—Or, "*of Soli.*" ?
NOTE 209.—Or; "*of Arce.*" ?

Solon of Corydalla.
Acacius of Cottiana (210).
Pabiscus of Apollonia.
Anysius of Corybrassus.
Matidianus of Coracesium.
Eutropius of Etennia in Galatia.
Philumenus of Cinna (211).
Strategius of Athribis.
Eusebius of Heraclea in Honorias.
Paralius of Andrapa in Hellespontus.
Hermogenes of Rhinocurura (212).
Evoptius of Ptolemais in Pentapolis.
Eusebius of Pelusium.
Adelphius of Onuphis.
Paul of Phragonis.
Phoebammon of Coptus (213).
Macarius of Metelis.
Adelphius of Sais.
Macedonius of Xois.
Marinus of Heliopolis.
Eulogius of Terenuthis.
Macarius of Anteus (214).
Metrodorus of Leonto.
Peter of Oxyrinchus.
Athanasius of Paralius.
Silvanus of Coprithis.
John of Hephaestus.
Aristobulus of Tmuis (215).
Theon of Sethroetus (216).
Lampetius of Cassium.

NOTE 210.—Or, "*of Cotyaeum*," or "*Cotena*," or "*Cotana.*"
NOTE 211.—Or, "*of Cina.*"
NOTE 212.—Or, "*of Rhinócorura.*"
NOTE 213.—Or, "*of Coptos.*"
NOTE 214.—Or, "*Antaeus*," or "*Antaeopolis.*"
NOTE 215.—Or, "*Thmuis.*"
NOTE 216.—Or, "*Sethroeta.*"

Cyrus of Achaea (217).
Publius of Olbia.
Samuel of Dysthis.
Zenobius of Barca (218).
Zeno of Zentyra.
Sosipater of Septimiaca.
Daniel of Dardanus (219).
Eusebius of Juliopolis.
Heraclides of Heraclea.
Chrysaorius of Aphrodisias.
Andrew of the Greater Hermopolis.
Sabinus of Pan (220),
Abraham of Ostracine.
Hierax of Asania (221).
Alypius of Selinus.
Alexander of Cleopatris.
Theopemptus of Cabasa.
Isaac of Tabia (222).
Ammon of Butus.
Heraclius of Ptenethis (223).
Isaac of Elearchia (224).
Heraclitus of Tamiathis (225).
Theonas of Psynchus.

NOTE 217.—Or, "*Achae.*"
NOTE 218.—Or, "*Barce.*"
NOTE 219.—Or, "*Dardanis.*"
NOTE 220.—Or, "*Panis?*"
NOTE 221.—Or, "*of Aphnaeum?*"

NOTE 222.—Or, '*of Tava*"? or "*of Tabae,*" or "*of Taba*"? Some of these names are badly spelled, owing to the ignorance or carelessness of transcribers. The Indexes in both volumes of *Wiltsch's Geography and Statistics of the Church* afford some help, and so do the lists of Dioceses, or Patriarchates, Provinces, and Sees in Bingham's *Antiquities of the Christian Church*, Book IX., and just after that book; though in Vol. 3 of Bingham, by his descendant, R. Bingham, Jun., Oxford, A. D., 1855, the summary of all comes at the end.

NOTE 223.—Or, "*Ptenetha*," or "*Ptenethus*"? Some of these sees are now so little known, that when in a passage we have nothing but an adjective to designate them, we cannot say what the exact spelling of the noun was. For their idolatry God gave them to be wiped out by the Mohammedan curse.

NOTE 224.—Or, "*Elearchius*"?
NOTE 225.—Or, "*Tamiatha*"?

Ammonius of Panephysus.
Bessula, a Deacon of Carthage.
Arcadius and Projectus, Bishops and Legates.

Philip, the most religious Elder [Presbyter] of the Apostolic Roman See and Legate (226).

Peter, a Presbyter [that is, "*an Elder*"] *of Alexandria and chief of the Secretaries, said:*

"Your Holy and Great Synod in exercising all foresight for the right and apostolic faith, and the truth of the dogmas, and providing truly for the state and discipline of the holy Churches, has put forth a Definition, which we have before our hands, and will read, if your Holiness commands.

The Holy Synod said: Let the Definition put forth by this Holy and Universal Council be recited and inserted in the Acts (227).

NOTE 226.—Here the representatives of Rome who had arrived after the First Act are mentioned last. Cyril, on the contrary, as Rome's proxy and as Bishop of Alexandria, then the second See of the Eastern Church, and the third in the whole Church, is mentioned first; Nestorius of the first see of the East and the second in the whole Church being a heretic and not eligible to a seat in the Council. Here, noteworthily enough, Carthage's representative is mentioned just before Rome's, who are last, though Carthage was the second see of the West, and the head see of the Diocese of Africa. It is observable that the Bishops are not always mentioned in the order of rank of their sees. Nor, moreover, are these names given in the same order in different lists. Compare on this last point the list given in *Coleti's Concilia*, tom. IV., col. 1133, with that in his tom. III., col. 1121, and after.

NOTE 227.—The reference, as we see, is not here to any document put forth by the Third Ecumenical Synod, A. D., 431, but to the Creed set forth by the First Ecumenical Synod, A. D., 325, which next here follows. Why, we may ask, is it ascribed then to this Council, which was held about 106 years later?

We reply that the Ecumenical Synod, that is, that of the whole Christian World, is represented here as a permanent or continuous body, like any other continuous body, as, for example, we say that the Parliament of England enacted in, say 1750, so and so, though no member of that particular parliament is now living, but the Parliament is, and the work of 1750, if it be still unabolished, is ascribed to it. So we speak of an enactment of our Congress in A. D., 1797. But, alas! it is now impossible to gather a Synod of the whole Church, East and West and North and South on account of the prevalence of idolatry and creature worship, but probably the Easterns will soon reform, let us hope within a century, or sooner, and Rome will be utterly destroyed according to the prediction in Revelations xviii., compared with Revelations xvii., 18; and then there will be another Ecumenical Council. None has been held since A. D., 680, the Sixth. But before that the whole Church must know the six sole Synods of the whole Church, A. D., 325–680, leave all their idolatries and other errors opposed to them, and go back to them. In such a future Council it should not be, as at the Vatican, local Western of A. D., 1869, 1870, when one nation, Italy, indeed one see in that nation, Rome, ruled, and formulated everything, but the strong, anti-idolatrous, God alone worshipping nations of the North should have their full proportionate representation in Bishops, according to their sound population. And no Prelate not receiving the God alone worshipping Six

The Synod in Nicaea set forth the following Faith :

WE BELIEVE IN ONE GOD, THE FATHER ALMIGHTY, MAKER OF ALL VISIBLE AND OF ALL INVISIBLE THINGS:

AND IN ONE LORD, JESUS ANOINTED, THE SON OF GOD, BORN OUT OF THE FATHER, SOLE-BORN, THAT IS OUT OF THE SUBSTANCE OF THE FATHER, GOD OUT OF GOD, LIGHT OUT OF LIGHT, VERY GOD OUT OF VERY GOD, BORN, NOT MADE, OF THE SAME SUBSTANCE AS THE FATHER, THROUGH WHOM ALL THINGS WERE MADE, BOTH THOSE IN THE HEAVEN AND THOSE ON THE EARTH; WHO FOR US MEN, AND FOR OUR SALVATION CAME DOWN, AND TOOK ON FLESH, AND PUT ON A MAN: HE SUFFERED, AND ROSE UP ON THE THIRD DAY, AND WENT UP INTO THE HEAVENS; [AND SITTETH AT THE RIGHT HAND OF THE FATHER (228;)] AND COMETH [AGAIN (229)] TO JUDGE THE LIVING AND THE DEAD.

AND I BELIEVE IN THE HOLY SPIRIT.

MOREOVER, THE UNIVERSAL AND APOSTOLIC CHURCH [OF GOD (230)] ANATHEMATIZES THOSE WHO SAY THAT THERE WAS ONCE WHEN THE SON OF GOD WAS NOT, AND THAT BEFORE HE WAS BORN HE WAS NOT, AND THAT HE WAS MADE OUT OF THINGS NOT EXISTING; OR WHO SAY THAT HE IS OUT OF ANOTHER SUBSISTENCE OR SUBSTANCE [THAN THE FATHER] OR THAT HE IS CREATED, ALTERABLE INTO SOMETHING ELSE, OR MUTABLE (231).

Synods must be allowed to sit in it and corrupt the faith and discipline. That is fundamental.

NOTE 228.—*Mansi Conc.* tom. IV., col. 1343, 1344, states that the Latin words for *"and sitteth at the right hand of the Father, and"* are *wanting in the old* manuscript Codexes. The same remark is in *Harduin, Conc.* tom. I., col. 1511, margin, (Paris, A. D., 1715). Hahn's *Bibliothek der Symbole*, third edition, page 161, note 8, tells of places where the Creed of the 318 is quoted with that clause, but it is probably an addition made from the Creed of the Second Ecumenical Council, for it is not in the Nicene, as given by Athanasius and Eusebius of Caesarea, both of whom were present at the Synod, nor is it in the Greek of the Creed, as in Act I. of *Ephesus*, this very Council. See Chrystal's *Nicaea*, Vol. I., pages 305–308, and 312, and his *Ephesus*, Vol. I., pages 50, 51; and those presentations of the Greek original are most authoritative.

NOTE 229.—Not in Athanasius or Eusebius; so probably an addition.

NOTE 230.—Not in Athanasius or Eusebius; an addition.

NOTE 231.—The Greek for all the above of the Creed is found in St. Athanasius, *Epistle to the Emperor Jovian*, as in Migne's *Patrologia Graeca*, tome 26, column 817. Eusebius of Caesarea, in his *Epistle to the Caesareans*, as in *Patrologia Graeca*, tome 20, col. 1540, has the same sense, but with a slightly different order of words in one or two places, and he leaves out the words *"the Universal"* (ἡ καθολικὴ) in the anathema. Owing to the errors of copyists, we sometimes find *created* or some other word left out here or there. See the Greek and the English translations on pages 305–329, volume I. of *Nicaea*, in this set, where we shall find variants of the Greek text, and also those of the Latin translations of it.

To this holy Faith, indeed, it is fitting that all should consent. For it is pious and suffices for the profit of the whole world.

But because some pretend that they confess it, and consent to it, but misinterpret the sense as they please, and evade the truth, because they are sons of error and of perdition; it seemed necessary to compare testimonies out of the holy and Orthodox Fathers which will avail to satisfy us as to the way in which they understood it and had confidence to preach it, so that it may be evident that all, having the right and unspotted faith, so understand and so interpret and so preach it (232).

NOTE 232.—It is not enough for any Church to have good doctrine and discipline and New Testament sacraments and customs. There must be discipline and disciplinarians enough to enforce their maintenance and sole sway. Take, for example, the very Creed which is mentioned above. When it was made at Nicaea, Ensebius of Nicomedia and Eusebius of Caesarea opposed it and at first refused it, but finally, to avoid deposition and excommunication, accepted it but insincerely, and were unwisely allowed to remain in the episcopate. But, as soon as they dared, they began to plot against it and its chief champions, got Eustathius of Antioch deposed from his see and banished, and induced the deceived Emperor, Constantine, to order Alexander, Bishop of Constantinople, to receive Arius, the denier of Christ's Divinity, and professed creature worshipper to communion, though that aim was not realized, for the God who forbids us to serve any creature (Matthew iv., 10) smote Arius with death, as Athanasius our brother tells us. They won over the successor of Constantine, Constantius the Emperor, and persuaded him to attempt the task of abolishing even the Nicene Creed itself and the Scriptural Orthodoxy which it enshrines. And many, aye, the bulk of the Bishops gave way. Yet Athanasius and the other Orthodox Bishops got their own again, enforced the faith on all Bishops and clerics, and the Church was saved.

The same thing occurred again in the days of Nestorius, who so misinterpreted the Creed as to deny its plain teaching of the Incarnation. He also and his sense of it were rejected, and its true sense was required of all, God having raised up Cyril of Alexandria and the Third Synod to condemn the errors of the heresiarch, not only his denial of the Inflesh, but also his Cannibalism on the Eucharist, and his worship of Christ's mere humanity which he associated with that error, and to depose the heresiarch himself and all Bishops and clerics of his party and to anathematize all his laics.

Still another example is found a little later. Eutyches, in effect, denies the plain teachings of the same Creed that Christ is Man as well as God, and the Universal Church condemns him and his, deposes him and all Bishops and clerics who hold his errors and anathematizes all laics who do.

Against Nestorius' denial of the Inflesh the words of the Creed of Nicaea are certainly clear; for they say that He who *was born out of the Substance of the Father, very God out of very God, for us men and for our salvation came down, and took on flesh and put on a man, suffered, and rose up on the third day;* and it was the man who was liable to suffering, not God the Word.

And the same passages of the Creed testify against Eutyches' denial of Christ's humanity and his assertion that it has, in effect, been transubstantiated into God, and Christ in Matthew iv., 10, and Ephesus testify against what is *in fact* his worship of

Peter, an Elder, [that is *a Presbyter*], *of Alexandria and chief of the Secretaries, said:*

Inasmuch as we have before our hands manuscripts of the holy and most blessed Fathers and Bishops, and different Martyrs; we have selected a few passages out of them, which, if it be pleasing, we will read again (233).

Flavian, Bishop of the Philippians, said, Let them also be read and inserted in the Acts.

And sample passages were read as they are given in the proceedings on the condemnation of Nestorius (234).

---

that humanity as God, though he did not intend that, for that humanity remains human still, for the substance of the creature cannot be changed into the substance of the uncreated Jehovah.

Another example still. Honorius, Bishop of Rome, fell into the heresy of denying that Christ is a perfect man, by denying to him a human will, a necessary part of a perfect man; an error opposed to the full sense of the Creed, which says that God the Word *put on a man*, not a part of a man, and the Sixth Synod of the whole Church, held at Constantinople A. D., 680, therefore rightly anathematized him as a *heretic* and *an instrument of the Devil*, and with him all who shared that heresy.

And, moreover, because the Bishops in the Middle Ages did not maintain and enforce the decisions of the Six Councils of the undivided Church it became corrupt and idolatrous, and large parts of it were wiped out for such paganizings.

Furthermore, though the Anglican Church has an excellent body of doctrine against the idolatries of Rome, yet because the Bishops did not enforce them on all the clergy at the beginning of the Puseyite idolatrizings, but permitted the paganized clergy to remain in the clericate, they corrupted the Church, Romanized its doctrine and rite, anarchized its discipline, and drove many to Rome, and made it as it is to-day, a wreck.

Those destroyers have followed their own effeminate heresies and their Romanizing leaders, Newman, Pusey, and Keble, but not the New Testament as understood by the Ante-Nicene Church and the Six Ecumenical Synods.

The above statement is, in effect, another form of the rule that whenever a question as to the sense of Holy Writ or the meaning of either of the two Ecumenical Creeds comes up, we must appeal:

1. To the decisions of the whole Church in its Six Sole Synods, A. D., 325-680, but if there be nothing definite on it in any of them, then we must look:

2. To *the historic testimony* of Orthodox writers from the beginning, especially to those of the Ante-Nicene period, for nothing that begins after it can justly be said to have been held *always, everywhere, and by all.*

NOTE 233.—They had been read before in Act I. In Coleti in Act I. of *Ephesus*, tom. 3, col. 1201, the *"Inasmuch as"* of the above is omitted; *"most holy Fathers,"* is found instead of *"holy and most blessed Fathers,"* and *"and"* is found before *"we have selected."*

As we have said above, they are given at this point with the XX. *Blasphemies of Nestorius* in a Latin Version in Act I. of the Fourth Ecumenical Synod, col. 871-902, tom. VI. of Mansi's *Concilia*. The passages from the Fathers and the XX. *Blasphemies of Nestorius* are found in Latin, not in Greek, in *Mansi's Concilia*, tom. VI., col. 876-902, in Act 1 of Chalcedon.

NOTE 234.—With *"of Nestorius"* the Latin ends. What next follows is Greek, and on

"*The Beginning of the Action in regard to Charisius, when he came to the Holy Synod against the Fourteenthdayites*" (235), [the Latin adds here, "*Peter, a Presbyter of Alexandria and chief of the notaries, said*"]:

"When, in accordance with the decree of the most religious and Christ-loving Emperors, Theodosius and Valentinian, there was assembled in the metropolis of the Ephesians, this holy Synod, out, so to speak, of all the world, of the most God-reverencing Bishops of the Holy Churches everywhere, and when it was in session, and had decreed that the faith set forth aforetime with the aid of the Holy Spirit by the holy Fathers, three hundred and eighteen in number, assembled in the city of the Nicaeans should be of force and should remain firm; and when, furthermore, it had formulated in a fitting manner certain things on those matters; a certain man, Charisius by name, being an Elder (236), and Steward (237) of the

---

the matter of Charisius. I have not deemed it best to give a translation of a translation, that is, not an English translation of a Latin translation of the passages from the Fathers, and of the Twenty Blasphemies of Nestorius, but to refer the learned reader back to the English translation of the original Greek. See it on pages 418-480, Vol. I. of Chrystal's *Epnesus*.

NOTE 235.—Called also *Quartodecimans*. The keeping of Pask (Easter) is not in the New Testament, but sprang up as early as the second century at least, perhaps among the Jewish Christians to commemorate the truth that by Christ's atonement on the cross by his blood, and by his resurrection, the destroying angel has passed over the houses of all Christians forever. But some kept it on the Lord's Day, while others kept that Christian Passover on the fourteenth day of the Hebrew month, Nisan, when the unbelieving Jews kept the old abolished Passover. This last custom was forbidden by the First Synod of the whole Church East and West in A. D., 325, and it ordered it to be kept always on the Lord's Day. But some who had kept it on the 14th of Nisan continued still to do so, and hence fell off from the Universal Church and formed a separate sect called from that peculiarity *Fourteenthdayites*. See on that whole matter pages 281-303, Vol. I. of Chrystal's *Nicaea*. After Nicaea it was considered to be a sort of Judaizing to keep the Pask with the Jews. See *Quartodecimans* in Blunt's *Dictionary of Sects*.

NOTE 236.—That is, a Presbyter, which means in English an Elder.

NOTE 237.—According to the New Testament, in the normal state of the Church the Deacon, under the orders of the Apostolate, that is, Episcopate, was to attend to that part of the income of the Church which went to the poor (Acts iv., 34-37 inclusive, and Acts v., 1-11; Acts i., 20, 25; Acts vi., 1-7).

Under the same Episcopal control the Elders had a delegated and subordinate control over the rest of the property and income of the Church, a fact clear from I. Peter v., 1, 3, though it is blurred in our common English translation. It is literally: "The Elders who are among you, I the Fellow-Elder exhort. . . . Feed the flock of God which is among you, overseeing it not by constraint, but willingly, not for filthy lucre, but of a ready mind, and not as *lording it over the heritages*," [that is, *the possessions* of the Church,] "but being examples to the flock."

holy Church of the city of the Philadelphians, stated that some heretics who come from Lydia, wished to leave their error, and to turn to the light of the truth, and to be initiated into the correct and pious dogmas of the Universal Church; that then when they should have been taken by the hand and led to the truth, a very great deception was practiced upon them; and they fell as if from one pit into a worse pit. For he stated that Antony and Jacob, who have the name of Elders (238), came down from Constantinople having letters of commendation from a certain Anastasius and from Photius, who were then with the heretic Nestorius, and who also themselves had the name of Elders (239), and whereas it was a duty to offer to those turning from error to truth, and seeking to come from darkness to light, the evangelic and apostolic tradition [that is, *transmission* (240)] of the faith, which the Fathers assembled in

---

Following the New Testament pattern on that, the whole Church in Canons XXVI. and XXV. of its Fourth Synod, Chalcedon, A. D., 451, orders every Bishop to manage the property of his jurisdiction, that is, Parish, by a steward chosen out of his own clergy, who in case of his death or of a vacancy is to take charge of the property. See on things pertaining to his office canons II. and III. of Chalcedon, and Canons VII. and VIII. of the local Council of Gangra, and as to the Bishop's power over the temporalities of the Church see page 284 of Fulton's *Index Canonum*. It may be interesting to some to know that one of the non-Episcopal Protestant denominations of our own land, the Dutch Reformed, manage all their church property by their pastor, and the Elders who do not labor in word or doctrine (I. Timothy v., 17), and the Deacons, in that setting a good example to the rest of us, who manage them by mere laymen or even unbaptized men in Trusteeships, Vestries, etc. Oh! what abuses exist under such non-New Testament bodies! See further on that, as to what is needed among us, Chrystal's translation of *Nicaea*, Vol. I., page 118 (a).

NOTE 238.—Presbyters.

NOTE 239.—Presbyters.

NOTE 240.—Greek, τήν τε εὐαγγελικὴν καὶ ἀποστολικὴν παράδοσιν τῆς πίστεως. The word *transmission or tradition*, in Greek παράδοσιν, is here used for the Nicene Creed, as it is used elsewhere for the Scriptures, which of course are a *tradition*, that is, as *tradition* means in Greek *a transmission*. See on that whole matter under Παράδοσις in *Suicer's Thesaurus*. *Transmissions* in the Church are of the following kinds:

1. *The divine and inspired in the Bible. All of it written there.*

2. *The historic transmission* of a few customs, all mentioned in the Ante-Nicene period 33-325, such as standing in prayer on all Lord's Days and during the whole period from Pask till Pentecost, etc. They are mentioned by Tertullian in his work *on the Soldier's Chaplet*, Section 3. See on the whole topic Chrystal's Nicaea, Vol. I., page 466, under *Tradition*, and under the same word in his *Ephesus*, Vol. I., page 659. No tradition comes under this head unless it is found in the second century or the third, and has been held to *"always everywhere and by all."*

3. *Tradition* is used to designate the image worship and creature invocation of the

the city of the Nicaeans had set forth in good season, they"] on the contrary] "proffered a certain Forthset of impious dogmas, put together as if in the order of a Symbol (241), and got those wretched men to subscribe it, and by that act exceeded every form of impiety. But for the sake of exact clearness, in regard to the matters aforesaid, there is here inserted the statement given in by the said Elder Charisius, and the Forthset of that impious and bad belief on the Inman of the Sole-Born Son of God (242), with the subscription of those on whom the deception was practiced (243)."

The Documents given in by Charisius, an Elder (244): To the most Holy, and most dear to God, Ecumenical Synod, assembled in the metropolis of the Ephesians, from Charisius, *an Elder, and Steward* of Philadelphia.

All who think aright wish always to render honor and proper respect to all, and especially to spiritual fathers and teachers. But if, somehow, it happens that those who ought to instruct, teach their hearers such things on faith as hurt the ears and hearts of all, it is necessary that the order of things be reversed, and that those who prefer to teach evil be reproved by those who are their inferiors.

Roman Communion, which are condemned like the Pharisees' traditions in the New Testament, and are not found in the Church in the Ante-Nicene period, but are against its teachings, and are condemned by the whole Church in its Six Ecumenical Synods, A. D., 325-680.

NOTE 241.—That is, Creed.

NOTE 242.—*Coleti's Concilia*, tom. 3, (Venetiis, 1728, col. 1204), περὶ τῆς ἐνανθρωπήσεως τοῦ μονογενοῦς υἱοῦ τοῦ θεοῦ.

NOTE 243.—Greek, καὶ δέον τήν τε εὐαγγελικὴν καὶ ἀποστολικὴν παράδοσιν τῆς πίστεως, ἣν ἐξέθεντο κατὰ καιροὺς οἱ πατέρες οἱ ἐν τῇ Νικαέων συνελθόντες, παραθεῖναι τοῖς ἐκ πλάνης ἐπιστρέφουσιν εἰς ἀλήθειαν, καὶ ἀπὸ τοῦ σκότους εἰς τὸ φῶς ἔρχεσθαι ζητοῦσι, προσεκόμισαν ἔκθεσίν τινα δογμάτων ἀσεβῶν, ὡς ἐν τάξει συμβόλου συντεθειμένην, καὶ ταύτῃ καθυπογράφειν τοὺς ἀθλίους ἐκείνους παρεσκεύασαν, πάντα τρόπον ἀσεβείας νικῶντες ἐν τούτῳ· ὑπὲρ δὲ σαφηνείας ἀκριβοῦς τῶν εἰρημένων ἐντέτακται ὁ ἐπιδοθεὶς λίβελλος παρὰ τοῦ μνημονευθέντος πρεσβυτέρου Χαρισίου, καὶ ἡ τῆς ἀσεβοῦς ἐκείνης ἐκθέσει κακοδοξίας, ἡ περὶ τῆς ἐνανθρωπήσεως, τοῦ μονογενοῦς υἱοῦ τοῦ θεοῦ, μεθ' ὑπογραφῆς τῶν ἠπατημένων.

NOTE 244.—Οἱ ἐπιδοθέντες λίβελλοι παρὰ Χαρισίου πρεσβυτέρου, etc.

Since, then, one of those teachers of evil is Nestorius, who is reaping the fruits of his own evil opinions, and since he is most evilly disposed in regard to the faith in Christ (245) and has often taught things which were not befitting. and has thoroughly troubled at once every land under the sun, so that the Christ-loving Emperors also have been compelled to issue a decree for your Holiness (246) to assemble here, and to strengthen the dogmas of Orthodoxy; and forasmuch as the Master, God, because of his love for men, has granted this, and has gathered all you holy fathers here, with reference to the matter aforesaid; therefore I prostrate myself to your Holiness (247), and state that not only he (248) but also the partners of his impiety, Anastasius and Photius, the Presbyters (249), are getting ready to spread the same evil belief in the other cities, and have applauded and do still applaud a certain Jacob who holds opinions like theirs, and make him a sharer of their table and of their intimacy; and they have already, by a letter, recommended him as Orthodox to the most God-reverencing Bishops of the Lydians. But he has dared to do things of such a character, as, when your Holiness (250) learns of them, will move you to inflict canonical punishment upon him and upon those who applaud him. For he came to the city of Philadelphia in Lydia, and deceived some of the more simple, but who were clerics, and treated the Forthset of the Faith of the holy Fathers at Nicaea as of no account, and got them ready to subscribe a certain other Forthset of faith, or rather of no faith (251). And forasmuch as they were of the more simple sort, they did so subscribe, as follows: '*We stand*, say

---

NOTE 245.—Literally, "*in the Anointed One*," (εἰς Χριστὸν.)

NOTE 246.—Mansi *Concil.*, tom. ιv., col. 1345, Act VI. of the Third Ecumenical Synod: τὴν ὑμετέραν ἁγιωσύνην. The title is in the singular, and is collective, because applied to the whole Synod. The decisions of the Synod are good, but alas! for such Anti-New Testament and flattering language.

NOTE 247.—The Greek of the title is literally "to your *Holiness*," (τῇ ὑμετέρᾳ ὁσιότητι), the singular number being used in the collective sense for the whole Council, as seems to have been the custom nearly always.

NOTE 248.—That is, Nestorius.

NOTE 249.—That is, "Elders."

NOTE 250.—See last note but two above.

NOTE 251.—Surely a Man-Worshipping, that is a creature-worshipping Creed, like that of Theodore of Mopsuestia referred to, is of "*no faith*," as denying the fundamental truth

they, *to this Orthodox faith.'* This Forthset, full of heretical blasphemy, and having the subscriptions of those who were caught [in that way] by him, is preserved; and I ask that it be read before your Holiness (252) in order that you may have in mind his intention to overturn Orthodoxy; and not only that that be read, but also the letter of the aforesaid, where they testify to the Orthodoxy of the heretic Jacob indeed, who dared to do such things, but debar me as a heretic from the communion and from the ministry, though I hold such pious opinions as are here subjoined. For when these things are read, your God-belovedness (253) will surely learn what those things are which he has dared to commit against Orthodoxy; but which God by your Holiness (254) will at last render utterly ineffective.

both of the New Testament and of the Old, that every act of religious service is prerogative to God, (Matt. iv., 10; Colos. ii., 18; Rev. xix., 10, and Rev. xxii., 8, 9; Isaiah xlii., 8, etc.). And, under the ancient dispensation, the Israelite who fell into the sin of worshipping any but Him, is said to *forsake His covenant*, which forbade it, *and Him* with it (Deut. xxxi., 16-30, and often), and so the Christian who, like the Man-Worshipping Nestorian, worships by bowing, prayer, or in any other way any creature, even though it be Christ's humanity, forsakes the Christian covenant which commands us to serve God alone (Matt. iv., 10), for it forbids it under pain of eternal damnation (I. Cor. vi., 9, 10; Galat. v., 19-22; Rev. xxi., 8, etc.), and they forsake the Giver and Binder of that covenant on us with it. For in worshipping by bowing, prayer, or in any other way, the humanity of Christ, a mere creature, they worship that which is not God, and make it, in effect, an idol, and give it an act of religious service, which, by Christ's law in Matthew iv., 0, is prerogative to God. And this is still more true, if possible, against all worship of the Virgin Mary, other saints, angels, or anything but the substance of the Triune Jehovah.

And it does not excuse a whit such God forbidden and false worship to say, as Nestorius in effect did, that he worshipped Christ's humanity relatively only, that is, not for itself, a creature, but for the sake of God the Word, for the Church wisely and well rejected that attempted evasion and deposed him notwithstanding; see in proof Chrystal's *Ephesus*, Vol. I., page 461, text, and note 949 there; pages 449, 479, 480, 486-504. And see also there note 183, pages 79-128.

Furthermore the same relative worship of Jehovah through the golden calf in the wilderness, and through the calf at Dan and through that at Bethel, did not save the Ten Tribes from cursing in their own land and from captivity in far-off Assyria, nor Judah from similar curses and captivity in Babylon. And that all that false worship was merely relative to Jehovah is shown in Chrystal's work on *Creature-Worship*, which see at length on that whole topic.

NOTE 252.—Greek, ἐπὶ τῆς ὑμετέρας ὁσιότητος. Some may prefer "Sanctity" as a translation for ἁγιωσύνη, and "Holiness" for ὁσιότης.

NOTE 253.—Greek, ἡ ὑμετέρα θεοφιλία.

NOTE 254.—Greek, διὰ τῆς ὑμετέρας ἁγιωσύνης, a collective Byzantine title of the Synod. How different from Christian Simplicity!

CONFESSION OF FAITH OF CHARISIUS, AN ELDER: I believe in one God, the Father Almighty, Creator of all things, and Maker of all visible and of all invisible things, and in one Lord, Jesus Anointed, his Son, the Sole-Born (255), God out of God, Light out of Light, very God out of very God, of the same substance as the Father, Who for us men and for our salvation came down out of the heavens, put on flesh, was born out of the holy Virgin, put on a man (256), was crucified for us, died, rose up on the third day, ascended into the heavens, and cometh again to judge the living and the dead;

And I believe in the Spirit of Truth, the Comforter, of the same Substance with the Father and the Son;

And I believe in a holy, Universal Church;

In resurrection of the dead,

[And] in life everlasting.

I, Charisius, have given in the documents as aforesaid, and have subscribed with my own hand.

Copy of the Forthset of the Counterfeited [or "depraved"] Symbol (257):

Those who either now for the first time are taught the exactness of the Church dogmas, or who wish to leave some heretical error for the truth, ought to be instructed, and to confess that we believe

---

NOTE 255.—Greek, τὸν μονογενῆ, that is, the "*Sole-Born . . . out of the Father's Substance*," as the Nicene Creed has it.

NOTE 256.—Greek, σαρκωθέντα, γεννηθέντα ἐκ τῆς ἁγίας παρθένου, ἐνανθρωπήσαντα.

NOTE 257.—*Mansi's Concilia*, tom. IV., (Florentiae. A. D., 1760), col. 1347, note, following *Hardouin's Concilia*, tom I., col. 1515, gives the reading "*deformed*" "*depraved*" here, and adds in Latin, which I translate:

"'*Deformed*,' that is to say into a Nestorian Symbol [that is, "Creed"]. It exists in another Latin form in the Council of Chalcedon, Act I.; in another in the Fifth [Ecumenical] Council, Conference IV.; [and] again in [still] another in Marius Mercator. Marius Mercator and the Emperor Justinian assert that it is the Symbol [or "a Symbol"] of Theodore of Mopsuestia. Facundus, book 3, chapter 5, denies [it]." But whether Theodore of Mopsuestia wrote this "*depraved Symbol*" or not, the whole context of the above shows that the Third Ecumenical Council understood this Creed to teach *Nestorianism*, that is, *Man-Service*, and *Relative-Service* and so condemned it. And the Fifth Ecumenical Synod followed the same line of action against it. The Greek heading of it in Mansi is,' Ἴσον τῆς ἐκθέσεως τοῦ παραπλασθέντος συμβόλου.

I would add that Marius Mercator and the Emperor Justinian were as likely to be right as to Theodore's being the author of "*the depraved Symbol*," as the heretical Facundus, Bishop of Ermiana or Hermiana in the Province of Byzacena in North Africa, for Facundus was a violent and perverse and obstinate partisan of the heretical Three

in God the Father everlasting, who did not later begin to be, but is everlasting God from the beginning; nor did he later become a Father, forasmuch indeed as he was always both God and Father (258).

And we believe in one Son of God, Sole-Born (259), being out of the Father's Substance, really a Son, and being of the same Substance with Him of whom he is and is believed to be a Son.

And we believe in the Holy Spirit, who came out of the Substance of God, which Spirit is not a Son, but is God in His Substance, forasmuch as He is out of that Substance, of which the God and Father is, out of whom He is as to His Substance. "*For we*," says he, "*have received*, not *the spirit of the world*, but *the Spirit which came out of God* (260), [thus] separating Him indeed from all the creation,

---

Chapters which favor the errors of Nestorius, and were therefore condemned by the Fifth Ecumenical Synod in A. D., 553, in its Definition, in which also it mentions Theodore of Mopsuestia by name and his impious writings; see its Anathemas 4, 5, 6, 12, 13, and 14, aye it anathematizes him and them, and every monk and laic, and deposes every Bishop and every cleric who opposes its decisions, and so, of course, by necessary inclusion this same Facundus. And when he was deposed and thrust out of his see by the Emperor Justinian, and nevertheless, still persistently and bitterly kept up the fight, as a layman, against the anti-creature worshipping decisions of the Whole Church in its Fifth Council, he therefore came under its decree of Anathema and so died outside the Church and a mad champion for the three creature worshipping Nestorian Chapters. See the article *Facundus* in *Smith* and *Wace's Dictionary of Christian Biography*, and *Hammond's Canons of the Church*, the Fifth Ecumenical Council, where part of the Definition and the 14 Anathemas are found translated.

NOTE 258.—This certainly sets forth the doctrine of Eternal Birth, which is now that of the Church of Rome. But on it see the note just below.

NOTE 259.—Greek, μονογενῆ, which is generally translated, but not exactly, *only begotten* in the King James Version of the New Testament, and in the Creeds. But that expression might be taken to imply that God the Word was not before He was begotten. But the general Ante-Nicene belief was that He was from all eternity abiding in the Father as a consubstantial part of the Divinity, but was not born out of Him till just before the worlds were made and to make them. Hence while the Ante-Nicene Writers like Justin Martyr, Tatian in his Orthodox time, Theophilus of Antioch, Tertullian and others held to the full and complete Divinity of God the Word, including both his consubstantiality and his co-eternity with the Father, they did not hold to his Eternal Birth; and their doctrine is embodied in the Nicene Creed in the words, "And the Universal and Apostolic Church anathematizes those who say . . . that, *Before He was born he was not*." In Chrystal's Catechism he quotes the Ante-Nicene Writers on that. He hopes to publish it if means come in. The other Creed, that of the Second Synod of the Christian World, I. Constantinople, A. D., 381, agrees, in effect, with the Nicene, when it teaches that He was "*born out of the Father before all the worlds*," and does not assert the birth to be eternal.

NOTE 260.—I. Cor. ii., 12. The Greek here in *Coleti's Concilia*, tom. 3, is ἀλλὰ τὸ πνεῦμα τὸ ἐκ θεοῦ. *Mansi, Conc.*, tom. IV., col. 1348, has the same.

but conjoining Him with God; out of whom He is as to Substance, in a peculiar way, and so, different from all the creation, for we do not consider creation to be *out of* God, as to its substance, but, to be *of* God because of its being created by God; nor do we deem the Spirit a Son, nor do we think that He has received His existence through the Son; but we confess a Father perfect in Person (261), and a Son in like manner, and a Holy Spirit, in similar manner. And thus preserving the doctrine of piety, we deem the Father and Son, and Holy Spirit likewise, to be not some three different substances, but we recognize them as *one Substance* in the sameness [that is, the oneness] of the Divinity.

And, furthermore, with reference to the Economy which the Lord God accomplished for our salvation in the Dispensation of the Lord Anointed (262) it is necessary to know that the Lord God the Word took a perfect man, which man is of the seed of Abraham and of David, as the Scriptures of God declare (263), and that man is all that, as to his nature, which those were of whose seed he was, being a perfect man as to his nature, and constituted of an intellectual soul and of human flesh; which (264) man, being like us as to his nature, was formed by the power of the Holy Ghost in the womb of the Virgin, *was made of a woman* (265), and *made under the Law, that he might redeem from bondage to the Law us all, who*

Note 261.—Greek, πατέρα τέλειον προσώπῳ.

Note 262.—That is, "*Lord Christ.*" δεσπότην Χριστόν.

Note 263.—Matt. i., 1, 17; Luke iii., 23 to 38 inclusive; Rom. i., 3; Galat. iv., 4.

Note 264.—On this word, note 1, col. 1349, tom. IV. in Mansi's Concilia states (I translate the Latin):

"From this place he recites [or "*reads out*"] that Symbol, and Agobard" [Archbishop of Lyons, who was born A. D., 779, and died A. D., 840,] "(*Against the Dogma of Felix of Urgel*, chap. 7), attributes it to Nestorius." The Latin is, "I, Ab hoc recitat symbolum istud, ac Nestorio tribuit Agobardus *adversus dogma Felicis Urgell., cap.* 7. But this depraved symbol, as is implied in the note above cited from col. 1347. tom. IV, of *Mansi's Concilia*, really begins with the words above quoted, "*Those who either now for the first time are taught the exactness of the Church dogmas*," etc. This the whole context shows. And whether Nestorius wrote this "*depraved symbol*" or not, we have in this Council and in the Fifth Ecumenical the clear condemnation of the Nestorianism which it contains. And the context shows that this Third Synod understood its heresy to be Nestorian. Compare the margin of col. 1515 of tome I. of *Harduin. Concilia.*

Note 265.—Galat. iv., 3, 4, 5, possibly, in part, loosely quoted. The Greek in the text of *Mansi, Conc.*, tom. iv., col. 1349, is γενόμενον ὑπὸ γυναικὸς; but his margin has γεγονέναι ἐκ instead of γενόμενον ἱπὸ.

The Man-Worshipping Creed of Theodore of Mopsuestia. 205

have received that adoption to sonship which was long ago foreordained (266); and that man God the Word conjoined to Himself (267) in a manner unspeakable, prepared him to undergo the trial of death in accordance with the law of man's mortality, and then raised him from the dead, and led him up into heaven, and seated him at the right hand of God. Wherefore, now, far above all principality, and power, and dominion, and might, and every name that is named, not only in this world, but also in that which is to come (268), he [that is, the mere man] RECEIVES WORSHIP (269) FROM EVERY CREATURE (270), ON THE GROUND OF HIS HAVING THAT INSEPARABLE CONJUNCTION WITH THE DIVINE NATURE; every creature (271) RENDERING TO HIM [that is, to the mere man] WORSHIP (272) BY REFERENCE TO GOD, AND IN CONSIDERATION OF

NOTE 266.—Or *"the henceforth predestined adoption to sonship."*

NOTE 267.—Neither Theodore nor any real Nestorian after him held to a real Incarnation of God the Word in His humanity. He merely held to such a *Relative Conjunction*, and *Relative Indwelling*, as the Orthodox Cyril explains, as existed between God and a prophet or an apostle, in which God's substance was wholly outside the man. See under those expressions and under *Relative Participation* and *Relative Worship* on pages 651, 652 and 653 of Vol. I. of *Chrystal's Ephesus*, and especially note 156, pages 61-69, where the difference between that heresy of Nestorius and Cyril of Alexandria's *Substance Union* of Christ's two Natures is explained more fully. Nestorius' Relative Worship of Christ's mere humanity, all there was of his merely human Christ, is connected with his doctrine of a merely Relative Indwelling and Relative Conjunction, for as he knew, from Matt. iv., 10, etc., that being a creature, it was incapable of being worshipped for its own sake, he worshipped it for the sake of God the Word, whom he deemed external to it; see id., page 461, and note 449 there; note 159, page 70; notes 169 and 170, on page 74, and note 183, page 79.

NOTE 268.—Eph. i., 21. The reading differs slightly from our Common English Version, that is, in putting *"dominion"* before *"might."*

NOTE 269.—Greek, προσκύνησιν, which literally means *bowing*, but as bowing is the most common act of religious service, for we bow when we stand in prayer, when we kneel, when we pray, or perform any other act of service to God, it hence stands for them all, and is used for them all. Προσκύνησις does not occur in the New Testament, but the cognate terms προσκυνέω and προσκυνητής do; see under them in *The Englishman's Greek Concordance to the New Testament*, and under προσκύνησις and cognate terms in the Greek Lexicons, and in Chrystal's *Ephesus*, Vol. 1., pages 725-750, and his *Nicaea*, Vol. I., page 482, under προσκυνέω and προσκυνητός. Under those terms will be found instances of the use of προσκύνησις in the sense of *worship*, again and again, and so the other terms in the same sense.

NOTE 270.—Or, *"from all the creation."*

NOTE 271.—Or, *"from all the creation."*

NOTE 272.—Literally *"bowing;"* that is, *worship*. See note third above.

Act VI. of Ephesus.

GOD(273) (274) [the Word]. And [yet] we do not assert that there are two Sons, or two Lords; forasmuch as God the Word, the Son, the

NOTE 273.—Or, "*by reason of the relation and consideration of God*," that is the relation of God the Word to that mere man and by the consideration of that fact, which is in effect the heathenism of *relative worship*.

NOTE 274.—Greek, τὴν παρὰ πάσης τῆς κτίσεως δέχεται προσκύνησιν, ὡς ἀχώριστον πρὸς τὴν θείαν φύσιν ἔχων τὴν συνάφειαν, ἀναφορᾷ Θεοῦ, καὶ ἐννοίᾳ πάσης αὐτῷ τῆς κτίσεως τὴν προσκύνησιν ἀπονεμούσης. This is plainly *creature service* and *relative service*, and is therefore a return to pagan errors, for the heathen worship images, altars, and such things *relatively only*, *relatively*, that is, to the god or goddess to whom the image or the altar belongs. This sin of the relative worship of a creature is set forth again and again in several of the Twenty Blasphemies of Nestorius for which he was condemned by the whole Church in Act I. of *Ephesus*. See them in Chrystal's *Ephesus*, Vol. I., pages 449-480, and note F, pages 529-551; and for his condemnation for them in id., pages 486-488, and 503, 504. Especially clear for his relative worship of Christ's humanity is his *Blasphemy* 8, and other Blasphemies in which he applies the name *God*, an act of worship itself, to Christ's humanity, a mere creature. St. Cyril of Alexandria in his Ecumenically approved *Long Epistle to him* quotes them and speaks of them as follows:

"Furthermore, WE DECLINE TO SAY OF ANOINTED" [that is, Christ, as *Anointed* means] "*I worship him who is worn*" [the mere man put on by God the Word] "*for the sake of Him*" [God the Word] "*Who wears him. I bow to*" [that is, of course, ' worship'] "*him who is seen*" ['he mere man] "*on account of Him*" [God the Word] "*who is unseen;* and it is A HORRIBLE THING to say also in addition to that:

"*He who is taken*" [the mere man] is "*co-called God with Him*" [the Word] "*who has taken him*" [Chrystal's *Ephesus*, Vol. I., page 221]. Just below Cyril adds that the doctrine of the "*True Union*" of the Divinity and humanity of Christ teaches that "*No one is co-bowed to*" [that is, "*co-worshipped*"] "*as one with another, nor is any one co-called* GOD *as one with another; but Anointed Jesus, Son, Sole-Born is understood to be only one, and is honored with*" [but] "*one worship within His own flesh.*" Cyril approved by the Third Ecumenical Council uses *Person* for God the Word alone, as did the Fifth Council of the Christian World. See in proof under *Person*, page 649, Vol. I. of *Chrystal's Ephesus*. And in Anathema VIII. of his *Long Epistle to Nestorius*, which was approved by the Third Ecumenical Synod and the three after it (Chrystal's *Ephesus*, Vol. I., note 520, pp. 204-208), he and the whole Church say clearly and finally against any worship to Christ's humanity, and for the worship of His Divinity only (id., page 331):

"If any one dares to say that the Man taken on" [by God, the Word] "ought to be co-bowed to" [that is, "*to be co-worshipped*"] "with God the Word, and to be *co-glorified*, and *to be co-called* GOD" [with God the Word], "as one with another, for the term '*co*' always [thus] added, of necessity, means that; and does not rather honor the Emmanuel," [that is, as "*the Emmanuel*" means, "*the God with us,*" "with but *one bow*" that is,] "*with but one worship*," that is, with absolute worship to his Divinity alone, not at all with any *relative worship* to his humanity, such as Nestorius gave in his Blasphemy 8 above] "and send up" [but] "one glorifying to Him," [that is, to God the Word,] "on the ground that *the Word has been made flesh*," [that is, on the ground of worship to Him as God] "let him be anathema." *The Word has been made flesh* refers back to the proclamation of His Divinity in John i., 1, 2, 3, and Its incarnation in John i., 14. The *relative worship* of Christ's humanity has been condemned no less than thirteen times at least by that "*one, holy, universal, and apostolic Church*," which Christ commands us *to hear* (Matt. xviii., 15-19), and which we confess in the Creed; see in proof Chrystal's *Ephesus*, Vol. I., page 461, note 949. Se further against any worship to Christ's humanity

Sole-Born out of the Father is [but] One Son [or "God"] (275) as to his [divine] Substance; to whom [that is, the Word] this [mere man] having been conjoined, and SHARING HIS DIVINITY, HAS [therefore] IN COMMON [with the Word,] BOTH THE APPELLATION AND THE HONOR OF SON: And forasmuch as God the Word is the Lord as to [His divine] Substance, THAT MAN [JESUS] WHO IS CONJOINED TO HIM, SHARES THAT [divine] HONOR; and for that reason we do not say two Sons nor two Lords; inasmuch as that One who is both Lord and Son in his [divine] Substance, has that inseparable conjunction with him [that is, with the mere man Jesus] who was taken on [by the Word] for our salvation, HE [that is, the mere man Jesus] is [therefore] CO-EXALTED [with the Word] WITH THE NAME AND THE HONOR OF BOTH SON AND LORD; not that we assert that he [that is, the mere man Jesus] is Son by himself [that is, in his mere human nature] as, for instance, each one of us is, in which sense, according to the blessed Paul, we are therefore said to be many sons (276). [No! we do not say that the mere man Jesus is a son in that sense]; but [in the sense] that he alone having that distinguished rank by his conjunction with God the Word, and SHARING HIS SONSHIP and HIS LORDSHIP, [by those facts] excludes

Vol. I, Chrystal's Ephesus, note 183, pages 79-128, and notes 679, 680, pages 332-362. In the Fourth Session of the Fifth Ecumenical Synod, A. D., 553, Hefele tells us that when the above Creed of Theodore of Mopsuestia was read the Synod exclaimed: "*This Creed* (Theodore's) *Satan has made! Anathema* to him who made this Creed! The First Synod of Ephesus anathematized this Creed with its author!"—Hefele's *History of the Councils of the Church*, English translation, Vol. IV., page 306. And, as we see in a note just below, the canons of Ephesus depose all Bishops and clerics who do not accept its definitions against the worship of Christ's humanity, and anathematize all laics who do not; and yet in the eighth century those decisions of the Universal Church were forgotten or ignored, and the image worshipping and saint-invoking idolatrous conventicle of Nicaea, A. D., 787, approved even the relative worship of creatures, such as saints, and mere things such as images and relics, and Rome and the Greeks, alas! reject the decisions on that of the Third Synod and the Fifth, and accept that abominable conventicle pre-anathematized in Galatians i., 8, 9, and by the whole Church, which has destroyed the bulk of the Eastern Church in Asia, and which wrought so much harm in the Middle Ages and since to the East and the West, and is still a curse wherever received. And it rejected the decision of the whole Church on the Eucharist and accepted, in effect, that real substance presence of Christ's humanity in that rite, and that Cannibalism there which were condemned by Ephesus and by the three World Synods after it.

NOTE 275.—The Greek in Coleti here is $\Theta\epsilon\grave{o}s$, for which he gives $\upsilon\grave{\iota}\grave{o}s$ in his margin. But the Latin has *Filius*, which makes better sense than $\Theta\epsilon\grave{o}s$.

NOTE 276.—Heb. ii., 10.

any and all thought of a duad of Sons and of Lords, and enables us to have all the faith and the thought and the consideration regarding him" [that is, regarding Christ's mere humanity] "IN THE CONJUNCTION WITH GOD THE WORD(277); for which reasons, he" [that is, the mere man] "RECEIVES from every creature BOTH THE WORSHIP AND OFFERING WHICH BELONG TO GOD (278).

NOTE 277.—The faith, thought and contemplation, so far as they are directed to the man, are here alleged as the basis of *relative bowing*, that is, of relative worship, that is *service*, for bowing is the most common act of service, and so stands for them all.

NOTE 278.—Greek, on page 232, second edition of Hahn's *Bibliothek der Symbole:* παρέχει δὲ ἡμῖν ἐν τῇ πρὸς τὸν Θεὸν Λόγον συναφείᾳ πᾶσαν ἔχειν αὐτοῦ τὴν πίστιν καὶ ἔννοιαν, καὶ τὴν θεωρίαν ὑπὲρ ὧν δὴ καὶ τὴν προσκύνησιν, καὶ ἀναφορὰν Θεοῦ, τὴν παρὰ πάσης δέχεται τῆς κτίσεως. In the margin in Coleti we find ἴσως, κατὰ, for the last καὶ above. But as that means ' probably '*with relation to*' " or "*in relation to*," the same reference to *relative worship remains*. The Latin of the last part, as in the parallel column 93, in Coleti is as follows: Ac essentialiter quidem dominus est Deus Verbum, cui hic copulatus particeps est honoris; ideoque nec duos filios, nec duos dominos dicimus; quia cum manifeste sit per essentiam dominus et Filius, is qui propter salutem nostram assumptus est, ipsi inseparabiliter conjunctus, domini filiique nomine et honore cohonestatur, non ad eum modum, quo unusquisque nostrum per se filius existit; unde sane etiam juxta beatum Paulum, multi filii dicimur; sed solus eximium hoc habens propter societatem conjunctionemque cum Deo Verbo; ac filiationis et dominationis particeps, omnem quidem dualitatis filiorum atque dominorum cogitationem excludit; per illam vero cum Deo Verbo conjunctionem efficit, ut uos omnem fidem omnemque cogitationem et contemplationem de illo habeamus; quare etiam adorationem, ob eam quæ in Deum refertur habitudinem, ab universa creatura suscipit. This last clause is based evidently on an old Greek reading, ἀναφορὰν Θεοῦ; translated into English it is as follows:

"WHEREFORE HE RECEIVES ADORATION ALSO FROM EVERY CREATURE, ON ACCOUNT OF THAT RELATION WHICH HE BEARS TO GOD," (literally "ON ACCOUNT OF THAT RELATION" or "RELATIVENESS," that is, of the humanity of Christ), "WHICH REFERS TO GOD" or "IS REFERRED TO GOD.") The word in Coleti's Greek text is ἀναφορὰν, and it means "relation" and "relativeness. Or the word σχέσιν, *relation*, may have been that which the ancient Latin translator of the fifth century, Marius Mercator, (see Coleti, Conc., tom. 3, col 1199, note 3,) had before him, and *habitudo*, used in the sense of *relation*, as it certainly is, whether the original were ἀναφορὰν, or σχέσιν, would be etymologically a good rendering, for it is connected with the root *habeo*, *I have*, as σχέσιν is connected with ἔχω, *I have*, The Greeks still say, σχετικὴ προσκύνησις *relative bowing*, that is, *relative worship*, to designate what every right minded and Orthodox man must deem their idolatry. I would add that the ligature or abbreviation for κατὰ is so much like that for καὶ, that a copyist might easily mistake one for the other. And the old manuscripts are often written in such ligatures.

I would add that Marius Mercator, as in Gallandius' edition (*Biblioth. Vet. Patr.*). tom. 8, page 626, renders the last words above, sed is singulariter hoc habens in id quod Deo Verbo conjunctus est, dignitatis filii et dominationis particeps, aufert quidem omnino duorum dominorum et filiorum intelligentiam, praestat autem nobis in conjunctione Dei Verbi omnem habere fidem omnemque intellectum et contemplationem ob haec et venerationem ex Dei societate ab omni percipit creatura.

"We assert, therefore, that the Son and Lord Jesus Anointed through whom all things were made, is" [but] "one. And this we do by having in mind firstly and chiefly God, the Word, who, as to his Substance, is Son of God and Lord; and by having in mind together with Him that which was taken on" [by the Word], "that is, Jesus of Nazareth, whom God anointed with the Spirit and power, as sharing, by his conjunction with God the Word, both Sonship and Lordship. And he" [that is, the mere man] "is called, according to the blessed Paul, *the Second Adam* (279), as being of the same nature with the" [first] "Adam, and as having made known to us the future state: and, moreover, as having such a relation to him" [that is, to the first Adam] "as there is between him who furnishes the unspeakable benefits of the future state and him" [that is, the first Adam,] "who furnished the beginning of our present sorrowful circumstances. And, in like manner he is called the second man" [or the second Adam], "as having brought to light the future state, for inasmuch as Adam was the beginning of the first, that is, the mortal and suffering state, which is filled with many miseries, and we have received his likeness in it; [so, on the other hand,] "the Lord Anointed has made known to us the second state by his appearing from the heavens, with reference to the future life, to lead us all to share his own. 'For,' saith he, *'the first man is of the earth, earthy: the second man is the Lord from heaven'* (280), that is, he will appear thence to make all men like himself. Wherefore he adds, *'As is the earthy, such are they also that are earthy: and as is the heavenly, such are they also that are heavenly. And as we have borne the image of the earthy, we shall also bear the image of the heavenly* (281). By that man, then manifested and seen by all those who are to be judged, will the Divine Nature, being Unseen, accomplish the judgment. *For the times of our ignorance God winked at* (282) *but now commandeth all men everywhere to repent: because he hath appointed a day in which he will judge the world in righteousness in that man, by whom he hath decreed*" [so to do], "*whereof he*

NOTE 279.—I. Cor. xv., 47.
NOTE 280.—I. Cor. xv., 47.
NOTE 281.—I. Cor. xv., 48, 49.
NOTE 282.—Literally, "*overlooked.*"

hath given assurance unto all men, in that he hath raised him from the dead (283).

"This is the teaching of the Church dogmas; and let every man who holds opinions contrary to them be anathema! Let every man who does not admit saving repentance, be anathema! Let every man who does not keep the holy day of the Passover (284) in accordance with the settled decision of the holy and Universal Church be anathema!" (285)

NOTE 283.—Acts xvii., 31.

NOTE 284.—That is, the Christian Pask, wrongly called *Easter*, a pagan name, in English.

NOTE 285.—Mansi's Concilia, tom. IV., col. 1348-1352, Ἴσον τῆς Ἐκθέσεως τοῦ παραπλασθέντος Συμβόλου. Τοὺς ἢ νῦν πρῶτον παιδευομένους τῶν ἐκκλησιαστικῶν δογμάτων τὴν ἀκρίβειαν, ἢ ἔκ τινος αἱρετικῆς πλάνης μεθίστασθαι βουλομένους ἐπὶ τὴν ἀλήθειαν, διδάσκεσθαι ὀφείλει, (marginal readings, προσήκει, προσήκεν), καὶ ὁμολογεῖν ὅτι πιστεύομεν εἰς ἕνα Θεόν, πατέρα ἀίδιον, οὔθ' ὕστερον ἀρξάμενον τοῦ εἶναι, ἀλλ' ἄνωθεν ὄντα ἀίδιον Θεόν, οὔτε μὴν, ὕστερον γεγονότα πατέρα, ἐπειδήπερ, ἀεὶ Θεός τε ἦν καὶ πατήρ. Πιστεύομεν δὲ καὶ εἰς ἕνα Θεοῦ υἱὸν μονογενῆ, ἐκ τῆς οὐσίας ὄντα τῆς πατρῴας, ὄντως υἱὸν, καὶ τῆς αὐτῆς οὐσίας ὄντα, οὗπέρ ἐστι καὶ πιστεύεται υἱός. Καὶ εἰς τὸ πνεῦμα δὲ τὸ ἅγιον, ἐκ τῆς Θεοῦ τυγχάνων οὐσία, οὐχ υἱόν, Θεὸν δὲ ὄντα τῇ οὐσίᾳ, ὡς ἐκείνης, ὃν τῆς οὐσίας, ᾗσπέρ ἐστιν ὁ Θεὸς καὶ πατὴρ, ἐξ οὗπερ κατ' οὐσίαν ἐστίν. Ἡμεῖς (marginal reading ὑμεῖς,) γὰρ, φησὶν, οὐ τὸ Ηνεῦμα ἐλάβομεν (marginal reading, ἐλάβετε) τοῦ κόσμου, ἀλλὰ τὸ πνεῦμα τὸ ἐκ Θεοῦ· τῆς μὲν κτίσεως ἀποχωρίσας (marginal reading, αὐτὸν χωρίσας.) ἀπάσης, Θεῷ δὲ συνάψας, ἐξ οὗπερ κατ' οὐσίαν ἐστὶν ἰδιάζοντι λόγῳ πιρὰ πᾶσαν τὴν κτίσιν ἣν οὐ κατ' οὐσίαν, ἀλλ' αἰτίᾳ δημιουργίας ἐκ Θεοῦ νομίζομεν (marginal reading in Coleti's Conc. here, νομίζοντες, in Mansi, (an error?), νομίζοντος) εἶναι, καὶ οὔτε υἱὸν νομίζομεν (marginal reading, νομίζοντες), οὔτε διὰ υἱοῦ τὴν ὕπαρξιν εἰληφός· Ὁμολογοῦμεν δὲ πατέρα τέλειον προσώπῳ, καὶ υἱὸν ὁμοίως, καὶ πνεῦμα δὲ ἅγιον ὡσαύτως· σωζομένου τοῦ λόγου τῆς εὐσεβείας ἡμῖν, τῷ Coleti, Conc., τὸν) πατέρα, καὶ υἱόν, ὁμοίως καὶ πνεῦμα ἅγιον, μὴ τρεῖς τινας διαφόρους οὐσίας νομίζειν, ἀλλὰ μίαν τῇ ταυτότητι τῆς θεότητος γνωριζομένην.

This, as the reader sees, treats of the dogma of the Holy Trinity. Next follows without a single intervening word, what is quoted below in this note.

This first part above of this Depraved Creed, that is Symbol, uses in the main, not wholly the common language of Orthodoxy. The poison appears, as the Synod says further on in

The Creature-Worshipping Creed of Theodore.

Subscription of those who were deceived.

"I, Rudius," [the son] "of Iconicus," [or "of Junicus"] "a Philadelphian, a Fourteenthdayite (286), having found out the true faith

> its Seventh Canon, in what it contains, "On the Inman of the Sole Born Son of God, that is the Soul and perverted dogmas of Nestorius, which are even its basis." I therefore here quote the part on the Inman of the Word. It is found in Mansi's Concilia, tom. IV, col. 1349, and after, and is as follows: after explaining the Trinity in a manner not wholly sound, for it brings in the error of Eternal Birth, which is condemned in the Anathema at the end of the Nicene Creed, on which see note 259, above, it begins and goes on regarding the Inman as follows:
>
> Χρὴ δὲ καὶ περὶ τῆς οἰκονομίας, ἥν ὑπὲρ τῆς ἡμετέρας σωτηρίας ἐν τῇ κατὰ τὸν δεσπότην Χριστὸν οἰκονομίᾳ ὁ δεσπότης ἐξετέλεσε Θεὸς, εἰδέναι, ὅτι ὁ δεσπότης Θεὸς λόγος ἄνθρωπον εἴληφε τέλειον, ἐκ σπέρματος ὄντα Ἀβραάμ, καὶ Δαβίδ, κατὰ τὴν διαγόρευσιν τῶν θείων γραφῶν, τοῦτο ὄντα τὴν φύσιν, ὑπερ ᾖσαν ἐκεῖνοι, ὦν περ ἐκ σπέρματος ἦν, ἄνθρωπον τέλειον τὴν φύσιν, ἐκ ψυχῆς τε νοερᾶς, καὶ σαρκὸς συνεστῶτα ἀνθρωπίνης ὃν ἄνθρωπον ὄντα καθ᾿ ἡμᾶς τὴν φύσιν, πνεύματος ἁγίου δυνάμει ἐν τῇ τῆς παρθένου (marginal reading, παρθενίας) μήτρᾳ διαπλασθέντα, γενόμενον ὑπὸ (marginal reading, γεγονέναι ἐκ) γυναικὸς, καὶ γενόμενον ὑπὸ νόμον, ἵνα πάντας ἡμᾶς ἐξαγοράσῃ τῆς τοῦ νόμου δουλείας, τὴν πόρρωθεν προωρισμένην υἱοθεσίαν ἀπολαβόντας, ἀπορρήτως συνῆψεν ἑαυτῷ· θανάτου μὲν αὐτὸν κατὰ νόμον ἀνθρώπων πειρασθῆναι κατασκευάσας, (marginal reading, παρασκευάσας), ἐγείρας δὲ ἐκ νεκρῶν, καὶ ἀναγαγὼν εἰς οὐρανὸν, καὶ καθίσας ἐκ δεξιᾷ ὦν τοῦ Θεοῦ. Ὅθεν δὴ ὑπεράνω πάσης ὑπάρχων ἀρχῆς, καὶ ἐξουσίας, καὶ κυριότητος, καὶ δυνάμεως, καὶ παντὸς ὀνόματος ὀνομαζομένου οὐκ ἐν τῷ αἰῶνι τούτῳ μόνον, ἀλλὰ καὶ ἐν τῷ μέλλοντι, τὴν παρὰ πάσης τῆς κτίσεως δέχεται προσκύνησιν, ὡς ἀχώριστον πρὸς τὴν θείαν φύσιν ἔχων τὴν συνάφειαν, ἀναφορᾷ Θεοῦ, καὶ ἐννοίᾳ, πάσης αὐτῷ τῆς κτίσεως τὴν προσκύνησιν ἀπονεμούσης. Καὶ οὔτε δύο φαμὲν υἱούς, οὔτε δύο κυρίους ἐπειδὴ εἷς Θεὸς (marginal reading, υἱός,) κατ᾿ οὐσίαν ὁ Θεὸς λόγος, ὁ μονογενὴς υἱὸς τοῦ πατρὸς ᾧπερ οὗτος συνημμένος τε, καὶ μετέχων θεότητος κοινωνεῖ τῆς υἱοῦ προσηγορίας τε, καὶ τιμῆς· καὶ κύριος κατ᾿ οὐσίαν ὁ Θεὸς λόγος, ᾧ συνημμένος οὗτος κοινωνεῖ τῆς τιμῆς· καὶ διὰ τοῦτο οὔτε δύο φαμὲν υἱούς, οὔτε δύο κυρίους ἐπειδὴ (marginal reading, δῆλον) εἰς τοῦ κατ᾿ οὐσίαν ὄντος κυρίου τε καὶ υἱοῦ, ἀχωρίστον ἔχει (marginal reading, ἔχων.) πρὸς αὐτὸν τὴν συνάφειαν, ὁ ὑπὲρ τῆς ἡμετέρας ληφθεὶς σωτηρίας συναναφέρεται τῇ τε ὀνομασίᾳ, καὶ τῇ τιμῇ τοῦ τε υἱοῦ, καὶ τοῦ κυρίου, οὐχ ὥσπερ ἡμῶν ἕκαστος καθ᾿ ἑαυτὸν ὑπάρχων υἱός (ὅθεν δὴ καὶ πολλοὶ υἱοὶ κατὰ τὸν μακάριον λεγόμεθα Παῦλον) ἀλλὰ μόνος ἐξαίρετον ἔχων τοῦτο ἐν τῇ πρὸς τὸν Θεὸν λόγον συναφείᾳ τῆς τε υἱότητος, καὶ κυριότητος μετέχων, ἀναιρεῖ μὲν πᾶσαν ἔννοιαν δυάδος υἱῶν τε, καὶ κυρίων, παρέχει δὲ ἡμῖν ἐν τῇ πρὸς τὸν Θεὸν λόγον συναφείᾳ πᾶσαν ἔχειν αὐτοῦ τὴν πίστιν, καὶ τὴν ἔννοιαν, καὶ τὴν θεωρίαν, ὑπὲρ ὧν δὴ καὶ τὴν προσκύνησιν, καὶ (marginal reading, ἴσως, κατὰ) ἀναφορὰν Θεοῦ, παρὰ πάσης δέχεται τῆς κτίσεως.
> Ἕνα τοίνυν τὸν κύριον (marginal reading, ἴσως, υἱόν.) φαμεν, καὶ κύριον Ἰησοῦν Χριστὸν, δι᾿ οὗ τὰ πάντα ἐγένετο· πρωτοτύπως μὲν τὸν Θεὸν λόγον νοοῦντες, τὸν κατ᾿ οὐσίαν υἱὸν Θεοῦ καὶ κύριον, συνεπινοοῦντες δὲ τὸ ληφθέν, Ἰησοῦν τὸν ἀπὸ Ναζαρὲτ, ὃν ἔχρισεν ὁ

NOTE 286.—That is a *Quartodeciman* which means a *Fourteenthdayite*.

of Orthodoxy, and having made request to the most holy Bishop

Θεὸς πνεύματι καὶ δυνάμει, ὡς ἐν τῇ πρὸς τὸν Θεὸν λόγον συναφείᾳ υἱότητός τε μετέχοντα, καὶ κυριότητος ὃς καὶ δεύτερος ʼΑδὰμ κατὰ τὸν μακάριον καλεῖται Παῦλον, ὡσ τῆς αὐτῆς μὲν ρύσεως ὑπάρχων τῷ ʼΑδὰμ ἀναδείξας δὲ ἡμῖν τὴν μέλλουσαν κατάστασιν καὶ τοσαύτην ἔχων πρὸς ἐκεῖνον τὴν ἀναφορὰν. [The marginal reading here is a mere surmise, seemingly, and is as follows, though utterly without manuscript authority, ἴσως, διαφορὰν.] ὅσηπερ ἂν γένοιτο τοῦ τὰ ἀπόρρητα χορηγοῦντος ἐπὶ τῆς μελλούσης καταστάσεως ἀγαθὰ πρὸς τὸν τῶν παρόντων λυπηρῶν δεδωκότα τὴν ἀρχήν. Τὸν ὁμοῖον, δὲ τρόπον καὶ δεύτερος ʼΑδὰμ (marginal reading, ἄνθρωπος,) καλεῖται ὡς τὴν δευτέραν κατάστασιν ἐκφήνας· ἐπειδήπερ τῆς μὲν προτέρας ἀρχὴ γέγονεν ὁ ʼΑδὰμ, τῆς θνητῆς, καὶ παθητῆς, καὶ πολλῶν γεμούσης ὀδυνηρῶν, ἐν ᾧ δὴ καὶ τὴν πρὸς αὐτὸν εἰλήφαμεν ὁμοίωσιν τὴν δευτέραν δὲ ἀνέδειξεν ὁ δεσπότης Χριστὸς, ὃς ἐξ οὐρανῶν ἐπὶ τοῦ μέλλοντος φανείς, ἅπαντας ἡμᾶς εἰς τὴν κοινωνίαν ἄξων (marginal reading, ἄξει) τὴν οἰκείαν. Ὁ γὰρ πρῶτος, φησίν, ἄνθρωπος ἐκ γῆς χοϊκὸς, ὁ δεύτερος ἄνθρωπος, ὁ κύριος ἐξ οὐρανοῦ, τουτέστιν, ἐκεῖθεν ἀναφαίνεσθαι μέλλων ἐπὶ τῷ πάντας εἰς μίμησιν ἄγειν ἑαυτοῦ. Ὅθεν ἐπάγει οἷος ὁ χοϊκὸς, τοιοῦτοι καὶ οἱ χοϊκοὶ, καὶ οἷος ὁ ἐπουράνιος, τοιοῦτοι καὶ οἱ ἐπουράνιοι· καὶ, καθὼς ἐφορέσαμεν τὴν εἰκόνα τοῦ χοϊκοῦ, φορέσωμεν καὶ τὴν εἰκόνα τοῦ ἐπουρανίου. Ἐν τούτῳ δὴ φαινομένῳ τε καὶ παρὰ πάντων ὁρωμένῳ τῶν κρίνεσθαι μελλόντων, ἐν ἀφανεῖ τυγχάνουσα ποιήσεται τὴν κρίσιν ἡ θεία φύσις. Τοὺς γὰρ χρόνους τῆς ἀγνοίας ἡμῶν ὑπεριδὼν ὁ Θεὸς, τανῦν παραγγέλλει τοῖς ἀνθρώποις πᾶσι πανταχοῦ μετανοεῖν, καθότι ἔστησεν ἡμέραν, ἐν ᾗ μέλλει κρίνειν τὴν οἰκουμένην ἐν δικαιοσύνῃ, ἐν ἀνδρὶ, ᾧ ὥρισε, πίστιν παρασχὼν, ἀναστήσας αὐτὸν ἐκ νεκρῶν. Αὕτη τῶν ἐκκλησιαστικῶν δογμάτων ἡ διδασκαλία, καὶ πᾶς ὁ ἐναντία τούτοις φρονῶν ἀνάθεμα ἔστω. The remainder of this depraved symbol condemns Novatianism and Fourteenth-day-ism, as follows: Πᾶς ὁ μὴ δεχόμενος τὴν σωτήριον μετάνοιαν, ἀνάθεμα ἔστω. Πᾶς ὁ μὴ ποιῶν τὴν ἁγίαν ἡμέραν τοῦ πάσχα κατὰ τὸν τῆς ἁγίας καὶ καθολικῆς ἐκκλησίας θεσμὸν, ἀνάθεμα ἔστω.

And so this depraved Nestorian Symbol, all of which I have given above, ends. It may be divided into two parts: 1. The part on the Holy Trinity which is faulty. 2. The part *"on the Inman of the Sole Born Son of God, that is to say the foul and perverted dogmas of Nestorius which are even its basis,"* which sanctions *relative service to Christ's mere humanity, which, of course, is not only relative service but also service to a creature,* and is therefore what the canons of the Third Ecumenical Synod justly call ἡ ἀποστασία, "THE APOSTASY;" so they term it in their canons I. and II. And in canon II. they speak of the counter Nestorian Synod of John of Antioch and *his fellow heretics,* because *creature servers and relative servers,* as *"the Council of* THE APOSTASY," [τὸ τῆς ἀποστασίας συνέδριον], and in canons I, 3 and 4, they speak of such *relative servers of Christ's humanity, and of such creature servers therefore,* as having *apostatized* [ἀποστατήσας in canon 1, τοῖς ἀποστατήσασιν in canon III, and ἀποστατήσαιεν in canon IV.] And for this sin of relative service, and of creature service the Universal Church inflicts the severest penalties on all clerics and laics guilty of them. See all the first seven canons. Next comes in this Depraved Symbol, part 3, the part against the savageness and unforgivingness of the Novatians, who refused to admit *"the saving repentance"* of the brother or sister who had fallen, which is of course perfectly sound, in conformity with the New Testament and with the canons of the first Ecumenical Synod and the Second. 4, comes the part against the Quartodecimans, such as were the heretics to whom the Nestorians gave this Depraved Symbol. This part is of course sound, because it is in consonance with the decision of the First Ecumenical Council on that matter.

Theophanes have [so] come to the most holy and Universal Church. And I anathematize every heresy, and especially that of the Fourteenthdayites (287), in which I formerly erred, and I assent to the above written Forthset of the Orthodox faith. And I anathematize those who do not keep the holy day of the Passover (288), as the holy, universal, and apostolic Church keeps it (289)," [and furthermore] "I swear" [to all this] "by the holy and same Substance Trinity, and by the piety and victoriousness (290) of the Lords of the World, Flavius Theodosius, and Flavius Valentinian, the ever August ones. And if I violate any of these things at any time I hereby subject myself to the severity of the laws. And, forasmuch as I do not know letters, I subscribe by Hesychius Flavius, a Senator, (291) to the Forthset, just read to me.

"I, Hesychius Flavius" [the Son?] "of Cerdanepius, a Senator, (292) a Fourteenthdayite, having ascertained the true faith of Orthodoxy, and having asked, have come to the most Holy and Universal Church. I anathematize every heresy, and especially that of the Fourteenthdayites; and I assent to the above written Exposition of the Orthodox faith, and anathematize those who do not keep the holy day of the Passover as the holy and Apostolic Church keeps it, and I swear" [to all this] "by the Holy Trinity, and the piety and victory (293) of the Christ-loving Emperors, Flavius Theodosius, and Flavius Valentinian, the ever August ones. And if I repudiate any of these professions at any time, I hereby subject myself to the severity of the laws; and I have subscribed with my own hand.

"I, Rufinus, a Philadelphian, a Fourteenthdayite, having ascertained the true faith of Orthodoxy, have made request, prostrating myself to the most Holy Universal Church; and I anathematize every heresy, and especially that of the Fourteenthdayites. And I assent, with all my house, to the above written Forthset of the Orthodox

---

NOTE 287.—See the last note above.
NOTE 288.—*Pask*, commonly called *Easter*.
NOTE 289.—The decision of the First Synod on that with matter on it, is found in Chrystal's *Nicaea*, vol. I, pages 281-303.
NOTE 290.—Or "*victory*," more pagan language derived from heathen Roman usage.
NOTE 291.—Or " *a councillor.*"
NOTE 292.—Or " *a councillor.*"
NOTE 293,—Or " *the* victoriousness."

faith, and I anathematize those who do not keep the holy day of the Passover as the Holy and Universal Church keeps it; and, furthermore I swear to all this by the holy and same Substance Trinity, and by the piety and victory of the Christ-loving Emperors, Flavius Theodosius, and Flavius Valentinian, the ever August ones; and if I shall violate any of these things at any time, I hereby subject myself, with all my house, to the severity of the laws. And the Forthset having been read to me, and having pleased me, I have subscribed with my own hand, and of my own judgment and choice.

"I, Eugene, a Philadelphian, and a Fourteenthdayite, having ascertained, with all my house, the true faith of Orthodoxy, and having made request to the most holy Bishop Theophanes, have come to the most holy Universal Church, and I anathematize every heresy, and especially that of the Fourteenthdayites, and those who do not keep the day of the Passover as the holy and Universal Church keeps it. And I assent, with all my house, to the forewritten Forthset of the Orthodox faith, and swear" [to all this my statement] "by the holy and same Substance Trinity, and by the piety and victory of the Christ-loving Emperors, Flavius Theodosius, and Flavius Valentinian, the ever August ones. And if I disturb any of these things at any time, I hereby subject myself, with all my house, to the severity of the laws. And the Forthset having been read to me, and having pleased me, I have subscribed with my own hand.

"I, Faustin, a layman, a Philadelphian, and a Fourteenthdayite, having ascertained the true faith of Orthodoxy, and having made request to the most holy Bishop Theophanes, have come to the Universal Church; and I anathematize every heresy, and especially that of the Fourteenthdayites, in which I formerly erred. And I assent to the above Forthset of the Orthodox faith. And I anathematize those who do not keep the holy day of the Passover as the holy and Apostolic Church keeps it; and I swear [to all this] by the holy and same Substance Trinity, and by the piety and victory of the Masters of the World, Flavius Theodosius, and Flavius Valentinian, the ever August ones. And if I shall repudiate any of these professions, I hereby subject myself to the severity of the laws. And the Forthset having been read to me, I have come forward with all my house, and have subscribed with my own hand, that pious faith.

"We, Dalmatius and Alexander, using the hand of Eutropius, a son of the most reverent Deacon Theodore, do hereby state that having learned what Orthodoxy is, and having made request to the most reverent Bishop Theophanes, we have come to the Universal Church, and anathematize every heresy, and especially that of the Fourteenthdayites, in which we erred; and those who do not keep the day of the Passover as the Orthodox keep it; and the Forthset having been read to us, we have sworn by the awe-inspiring oath of the Holy Trinity, and by the victory and safety of the Masters of the World, Flavius Theodosius and Flavius Valentinian, the ever August ones, not to repudiate any of the things above written; and thus believing, with our houses, we have subscribed.

"I, Flavius Nymphidianus, a Philadelphian, a scholar (294), hereby renounce all those dogmas and those customs of the heresy of the Fourteenthdayites, which are not received from the Orthodox faith; and I promise to make common cause with the Orthodox faith in all things, and to receive it.

" I, Polychronius Flavius,"[the Son?] "of Tatian, a Philadelphian, and a Senator (295) using the hand (296) of Flavius Hesychius" [or

---

NOTE 294.—Or, "*an advocate.*"
NOTE 295.—Or, "*a councillor.*"
NOTE 296.—That is "*using his hand as an amanuensis.*" We must remember that the day of common schools for all had not yet come, and did not till the Reformation. Then the Reformers, of blessed memory, in their desire to enable the people to read God's Word and to withdraw them from the Roman soul-damning idolatries contrary to it, fostered it, and finally, following out the same aim, it has become common in all Protestant lands, and thence has spread even to Romish or Greek Church lands. The spread of education enables men to read God's Word and to know what His religion of the New and better Testament is, and so promotes its spread: See on the value of the Christian grace of knowledge, II Peter I, 5, 8; II Peter, III 18; Luke 1, 77; Rom. X, 2; I Cor. I. 5; I Cor. XII, 8 II Cor. II, 14; II Cor. IV, 6; II Cor. VI, 6; II Cor. VIII, 7; Eph. I, 17; Eph. IV, 13; Philip I, 9; Philip III, 8; Col. III, 10; I Tim. II, 4; II Tim. III, 7; Christians are required to "*take the sword of the Spirit, which is the Word of God,*" as a part of *the whole armor of God that they may be able to stand against the wiles of the devil,* (Eph. VI, 13, 17). Christ used it in his conflict with Satan, and with success (Matt. IV, 1—11, and Luke IV, 1—13.) and all of us who know it and follow Him have been cheered in our fights against the temptations of the Devil by the joy of its promises and deterred from evil by the fears inspired by its threats and warnings. It is a means of grace as we see from the above, and a means of sanctification, that is of being

"Esychius"] [the Son?] "of Cerdanepius, because I write" [but] "slowly,"[hereby] "state that I, having ascertained what Orthodoxy is, and having made request to the most reverent Bishop Theophanes, have come to the Universal Church, and anathematize every heresy, and especially that of the Fourteenthdayites, in which I formerly erred, and also those who do not keep the holy day of the Passover as the Orthodox keep it.   And the Forthset having been read to me, I have furthermore sworn the awful oath of the Holy Trinity, and by the victory and the safety of the Masters of the World, Flavius Theodosius and Flavius Valentinian, the ever August Ones, not to repudiate any of the things above written (297). And" [so] "believing, with all my house, I assent to all things above written.

"I, Eustathius, a Philadelphian, a goldsmith, a Fourteenthdayite, and a son of Marcellus, having ascertained what Orthodoxy is, and having made request to the most holy Bishop Theophanes, have so come, of my own judgment and choice, to the holy Universal Church of God, and I anathematize every heresy, and especially that of the Fourteenthdayites, and those who do not keep the holy day of the Passover as the Orthodox keep it. And furthermore, I have sworn by the Holy Trinity, and by the piety of the Christ-loving Emperors, Flavius Theodosius, and Flavius Valentinian, the ever August ones, that if I repudiate any of the forewritten things, I will subject myself

---

made holy, for it teaches us what real, Christ-accepted holiness is, John XVII, 17, and keeps us from mistaking for it the creature worship of Arius, Nestorius, of Rome, of the Greeks, or of the middle ages or the infidelities of our day termed Unitarianism, Universalism, Mormonism and all other trash. But what could be expected from a clergy and a laity, so ignorant even often of the power to read God's holy and light giving word, as those Fourteenthdayites, but error and folly? How could they take the sword of the Spirit and wield it against error and Satan when they could not read it? Chrysostom in one place in answering the plea of a layman that being no cleric nor monk he was excused from reading it, tells him that that excuse came from the devil, and as being opposed to God's Word it certainly does—compare also John v, 39, Acts xvii, 11, 12 and ii Timothy iii 15, 16, 17; Psalm cxix, 130, etc.

NOTE 297.—This oath was of course, an oath to damn his own soul by the sin of creature worship, and was regarded as utterly null and void by the Church. It is one of those oaths which, like Herod's oath to Herodias, it is wrong to take, and when it leads to murder, as in that case (Matt. xiv, 1, 2, 6-12; Mark vi, 14-16, 21-27) or to any other sin, it is wrong to keep. We see a similar oath to day imposed on Perverts to Rome to accept and maintain all the soul-damning idolatries and heresies of that Harlot (Rev. xvii, 1—18), as they are set forth in the Creed of Pope Pius IV. which of course is therefore not binding, nor may it be kept under pain of eternal damnation.

to the severity of the laws. And I have subscribed with my own hand.

"I, Eutychius, having found out Orthodoxy by Philadelphus, and having made request to the most holy Bishop Theophanes, have" [so] "come, of my own judgment and choice, to the holy and Universal Church of God. And I anathematize every heresy, and especially that of the Fourteenthdayites, and those who do not keep the holy day of the Passover as the Orthodox keep it. And furthermore, I have sworn by the Holy Trinity and by the piety of the Christ-loving Emperors, Flavius Theodosius and Flavius Valentinian, the ever August ones, that if I violate any of the professions above written, I will subject myself to the severity of the laws. And I have subscribed with my own hand.

"I, Padicius, a Philadelphian, having discovered Orthodoxy, and having made request to the Orthodox and most holy Bishop Theophanes, have come to the Holy, Universal, and Apostolic Church of God. And I anathematize every heresy, and especially that of the Fourteenthdayites. And furthermore, I swear by the awful oath" [of the Holy Trinity?] "and by the piety of the Christ-loving Emperors, that if I violate any of the professions above written, I will subject myself to the severity of the laws. And I have subscribed with pleasure, by Martyrius, a Reader (298).

"I, Eutychius, of the hamlet of Aulax, a leader in the heresy of the Fourteenthdayites, having discovered the true faith of Orthodoxy, and having made request to the most holy Bishop Theophanes, and the most reverent Bishop James, and the most reverent Elder (299) and Steward (300) Charisius, have come to the most holy Universal Church of God. And I anathematize every heresy, and especially that of the Fourteenthdayites, in which I formerly erred. And I

NOTE 298.—The Reader was one of the lower clergy, whose duty it was to read God's Word to the people in their own tongue, for the Universal Church knew from God's Word the profit of knowing it and therefore early had a body of men to read it to them for as yet few of the masses could read. See more fully under *Reader* in the *Index* to *Bingham's Antiquities of the Christian Church.*

NOTE 299.—That is *Presbyter.*

NOTE 300.—On this officer see note 298 above, and *Bingham's Antiquities*, book II, chapter iv, section 6, and book v, chapter vi, sections 1-7.

assent to the forewritten Forthset of the Orthodox faith; and I anathematize those who do not keep the holy day of the Passover, as the holy, Universal and Apostolic Church keeps it. And, furthermore, I swear by the holy and same Substance Trinity, and by the piety and victory of the Masters of the World, Flavius Theodosius, and Flavius Valentinian, the ever August ones; that if I violate any of these things, I will subject myself to the severity of the laws.

I, Patrick, second Elder (301) of the village of Paradioxylsus, forasmuch as I do not know letters, hereby use the hand of Maximus, my fellow-Elder, and state that I having found out the true faith of Orthodoxy, and having made request to the most dear to God Bishop Theophanes, and having asked the most reverent Elder and Steward Charisius, have come to commune with the holy Church of God, that is the Church of the faith of the Orthodox. And I anathematize every heresy, and especially that of the Fourteenthdayites, and those who do not keep the holy day of the Passover, as the Universal and Apostolic Church of God keeps it; and I have sworn [to all this] by the holy and quickening Trinity, and by the piety and victory of the Masters of the World, Flavius Theodosius, and Flavius Valentinian, the ever August ones. And if I repudiate any of these professions, I will subject myself to the severity of the laws.

I, Stratonicus Flavius (302) the son of Ammonius, a Philadelphian and Fourteenthdayite, having discovered Orthodoxy, and having made request to the most holy Bishop Theophanes (303) have come to God's holy Universal Church of the Orthodox. And I anathematize every heresy, and especially that of the Fourteenthdayites, and those who do not keep the holy day of the Passover, as the Orthodox keep it. And I have sworn by the holy Trinity, and by the piety of the Christ-loving Emperors, Flavius Theodosius, and Flavius Valentinian, the ever August ones, that if I violate any of the forewritten professions, I will subject myself to the severity of the laws. And

---

NOTE 301.—That is, "*Second Presbyter.*"

NOTE 302.—The Greek reads, "I, Stratonicus Flavius, [the son] of Ammonius, a Fourteenthdayite, having discovered," etc., as above. The Latin omits "Flavius."

NOTE 303 —The Greek has "Epiphanicus."

forasmuch as I do not know letters, I have subscribed by the lawyer (304) Alexander.

We, Theodoret, and Alexander and Philadelphus, subscribe by one of us, that is Alexander, and state that we having discovered Orthodoxy (305) and having made request to the most holy Bishop Theophanes (306), have come to God's holy Universal and Apostolic Church of the Orthodox; and we anathematize every heresy, and especially that of those who are called the *Pure Ones* (307), and those who do not keep the holy day of the Passover, as the Orthodox keep it. And furthermore, we have sworn by the holy Trinity, and by the piety and victory of the Masters of the World, Flavius Theodosius and Flavius Valentinian, the ever August Ones, that if we violate any of the professions above written, we will subject ourselves to the severity of the laws, and that Forthset having been read to us, we have subscribed it.

I, Marinus [the son] of Evethius (308), making use of the hand of Neotarius, (309) a Reader among the Orthodox, hereby state that I having discovered Orthodoxy, and having made request to the most holy Bishop Theophanes (310), have come to the holy Universal and Apostolic Church of God. And I anathematize every heresy, and those who do not keep the day of the Passover, as the Orthodox keep it. And, furthermore, I have sworn the awe-inspiring oath of the holy Trinity, that if I violate any of the professions above written, I will subject myself to the severity of the laws, and so I have subscribed.

I, Cyriacus, a Philadelphian, of the heresy of the Novatians,

---

NOTE 304.—The Latin translation here reads "by his nephew Alexander."

NOTE 305.—Greek, τὴν ὀρθοδοξίαν, literally "*the right doctrine*," and so often in Greek, though we often omit the article in English.

NOTE 306.—"Theophanius" is in the Greek, instead of the "Theophanes" of the Latin.

NOTE 307.—That is that of the *Catharists*. This was the heresy of the Novatians, who denied the New Testament and Christ-given power of receiving to Church Communion again some who had fallen into image service or into creature service or other sins, and had sincerely repented.

NOTE 308.—The Greek here has "Marinus, [the son] of Synthius."

NOTE 309.—Latin, "Nestorius."

NOTE 310.—Greek, "Theophanius."

having discovered Orthodoxy, and having made request to the most holy Bishop Theophanes, have come to God's holy and Universal Church of the Orthodox. And I anathematize every heresy, and especially that of the Pure Ones (311). And furthermore, I have sworn the awe inspiring oath of the holy Trinity, that if I shall violate any of the forewritten professions, I will subject myself to the severity of the laws. And that Forthset of faith having been read to me, I have subscribed it by Eusebius Syrus Calliopius.

I, Euxenius (312), a Philadelphian and a Novatian, having discovered Orthodoxy, and having made request to the most holy Bishop Theophanes (313), have come to God's holy Universal Church of the Orthodox (314). And I anathematize every heresy, and especially that of the Novatians, and I assent with all my house to the above written Forthset of the Universal faith. And,

---

Note 311.—That is, that of the Catharists, that is that of the Novatians. They seem to have called themselves *the Pure Ones*, in contradistinction to the Universal Church, which they deemed too lax in receiving penitents.

Note 312.—The Latin has "Auxonius" instead of "Euxenius."

Note 313.—The Greek has "Theophanius" instead of "Theophanes."

Note 314.—Here notice that while the Church is called Universal, $καθολικὴ$, individuals are not, but *Orthodox*, that is, *right in faith*. This is the Greek custom, and has always been. But the Latins frequently render the Greek word "Orthodox," ($ὀρθόδοξος$) by the Greek transferred, not translated, term *Catholic* (Catholicus, which is the Latin form of the Greek, $καθολικός$), even where in the Greek it means individuals. This use of *Catholic* is as old as century IV. or V. among the Latins. Whereas among the Greeks the expression *Universal* is and always from of yore has been applied to the Church and to the faith, but generally *not to individuals, for no individual is Universal*. Common sense must ever prevent the peculiarly Latin custom of calling individuals *Catholics*, that is, *Universals*, from spreading among the Greeks so long as they retain the knowledge of their tongue. It is much to be desired that for the sake of greater accuracy we should use *Universal*, the translated and clearer word, always in the Creeds and elsewhere instead of the merely transferred form, *Catholic*, which the unlearned frequently do not understand, and which multitudes of them take to mean the Romish Communion. Scholars should always consider in their translations their brethren of the common people, whose guardians and enlighteners in a certain sense they are.

Instead of *Catholic as applied to individuals*, we might use *Universalist*, if that had not come into general use in these United States for those heretics who believe in universal salvation, and who are infidels on the doctrine of *"everlasting punishment"* (Matt. xxv., 46). I would therefore suggest instead *Universaler* for a believer in the Universal Church, as a term for *occasional* use, but not to the discarding of the ancient and excellent word *Orthodox*. Moreover, *Universal*, not *Universaller*, renders *Catholic*.

furthermore, I have sworn the awe-inspiring oath by the holy and Same-Substance Trinity, and by the piety and victory of the Masters and Emperors Flavius Theodosius and Flavius Valentinian, the ever August Ones; and if. I shall violate any of the professions above written, I will subject myself with all my house to the severity of the laws. And the Forthset having been read to me, and having pleased me, I have subscribed with my own hand (315).

I, Diomed, dwelling in the village of Caccaba, having discovered the Orthodox faith, and having made request to the most holy Bishop Theophanes (316), have come by my own unconstrained judgment and voluntary choice to the holy Universal and Apostolic Church; and I anathematize every heresy, and especially that of the Fourteenthdayites, in which I formerly erred; and I swear by the holy and Same-Substance Trinity, and by the victory and piety of the Masters of the World, that I will abide by the forewritten professions, and not violate any of them, but keep them in all things, and remain in the Orthodox faith; and that if I shall be found at any time to have violated any of the forewritten professions, I will subject myself to the severity of the laws. And, having heard the Forthset, I have subscribed with my own hand.

I, Julian, a Philadelphian, and a Fourteenthdayite, having become acquainted with Orthodoxy, have come to God's holy Church of the Orthodox; and I anathematize every heresy, and especially that of the Fourteenthdayites. And I swear the awe-inspiring oath by the holy Trinity, and by the piety of the Christ-loving Emperors, that if I violate any of the forewritten professions, I will subject myself to the severity of the laws, and I have subscribed with pleasure, by Martyrius a Reader.

I, Zeno, of the hamlet of Sagarou Pythe, a country Bishop (317) of the heresy of the Fourteenthdayites, having become acquainted

---

NOTE 315.—The Greek, as given in *Coleti's Concilia*, gives the above statement of Euxenius in much shorter form, entirely omitting much that I have translated above from the Latin. The Latin seems to be a rendering of a fuller Greek copy.

NOTE 316.—The Latin has "Theophanes"; the Greek "Theophanius."

NOTE 317.—The Latin here adds simply, "Zeno, a country Bishop of the heresy of the Fourteenthdayites," etc., as above. The Greek reads: "Zeno of the hamlet of Sagarou Pythe, of the heresy of the Fourteenthdayites," and has not "*a Country Bishop.*"

with the true faith of Orthodoxy, and having made request to the most holy Bishop Theophanes (318), and the most reverent Country Bishop James, and the most reverent Presbyter (319) and Steward Charisius, have come to the most holy Universal Church; and I anathematize every heresy, and especially that of the Fourteenth-dayites, in which I formerly erred; and I assent to the forewritten Forthset of the Confession of Orthodoxy (320).

And I anathematize those who do not keep the holy day of the Passover, as the holy Universal Church keeps it; and I swear to all this by the holy and Same-Substance Trinity, and by the piety and victory of the Masters of the World, Flavius Theodosius and Flavius Valentinian, the ever August Ones; and, further, that if at any time I violate any of these [my professions], I will subject myself to the severity of the laws.

And I, Flavius Palladius, have used my hand to write for him [that is, for Zeno just mentioned], because he himself is present and says that he does not know letters.

Decision of the Synod on the Faith, in which it also decided in regard to those matters which the aforesaid Charisius reported: it is as follows:"

[REMARK.—This decision is what is now called CANON VII. of the Third Ecumenical Synod, though in *Coleti* it has only the above heading, which it then follows without any break, thus:]

"These things, therefore, having been read, the Holy Synod has decreed that no one shall be allowed to offer or to write or to compose another faith (321) contrary to that decreed by the Holy Fathers gathered in the city of the Nicaeans with the Holy

---

NOTE 318.—The Latin here has "Theophanes," the Greek "Theophanius."

NOTE 319.—That is, *Elder*.

NOTE 320.—Another reading of the Greek has, (I translate), "*the Forewritten Forthset*" without "*of Orthodoxy.*" The Greek copies being taken by different notaries or reporters at the Synod, probably varied considerably; hence the different Latin translations being made from differing Greek manuscripts, vary as they did.

NOTE 321.—Greek, πίστιν, *faith*, not σύμβολον, that is, *Creed*.

Ghost (322). But those who dare either to compose or to bring for-

NOTE 322.—Greek, ἑτέραν πίστιν . . . παρὰ τὴν ὁρισθεῖσαν παρὰ τῶν ἁγίων Πατέρων, τῶν ἐν τῇ Νικαέων συναχθέντων πόλει, σὺν Ἁγίῳ Πνεύματι. Παρά means "*besides*," and also "*contrary to.*" If we take it in the sense of *besides* here, and at the same time take πίστιν in the sense of *Creed*, it will forbid any Creed except that of the 318 of Nicaea to be used as a baptismal or reception Symbol, and so will abolish that of the Second Ecumenical Council, the Constantinopolitan, which is now the only one used on those occasions in the Greek Church, and has been the only one for long centuries. Indeed it is the only Creed in use in their public services, for they never used the so-called Apostles'. See on that Chrystal's *Nicaea*, volume I., pages 21-42. The Constantinopolitan indeed was for a time in the middle ages the baptismal Creed of part of the West, as Assemani has shown in his *Codex Liturgicus*, and as Professor Swainson shows in his article *Creed*, section 17 on page 492, Vol. I. of Smith and Cheetham's *Dictionary of Christian Antiquities*, where he corrects an interpolation of Assemani; and it is the only Eucharistic Creed in the Roman Communion, and in the Church of England to-day. It was not obligatory to use it in the Eucharist in its American branch, till within a few years past, and yet the spurious Apostles' may, during the whole year, even there, be used for it except on a few occasions specified in the office. Among many of the Protestants the Apostles' and the Constantinopolitan are used, one or both.

In other words, if we take παρά here in the sense of *besides*, and πίστιν in the sense of *Creed*, we shall condemn the present custom of nearly the whole world calling itself Christian, and not only that, but must hold also that every cleric who uses any other Creed than that of the 318 in baptizing or receiving into the Church, must be deposed, and every laic doing anything of a like character must be anathematized, and that by the Universal Church in this Canon. In other words, it would depose all the undeposed ministry of the Christian world, and anathematize all unanathematized laics.

On the other hand, if we take παρά in the sense of "*contrary to*," all is clear, and those logical sequences from the other position just mentioned are avoided.

Then we can take πίστιν in its ordinary sense of *faith* and all is well. In that sense Canon VII. of *Ephesus* agrees with the historic facts and the historic interpretation of its sense in them.

For the Universal Church in its Ecumenical Synod did not regard it as forbidding any other Creed in consonance with the Nicene, even if it is fuller in some things and less full in others, is clear from the following truths:

1. The Third Ecumenical Synod itself put forth decisions on topics not mentioned in the Nicene Creed, that is, against Nestorius' three great heresies of denial of the Incarnation, worship of Christ's humanity, and his assertion of one nature Consubstantiation, that is of the real substance presence of his humanity in the Eucharist, and the cannibalism of eating and drinking it there.

And in its Canons it enforced the reception of those, its decisions on doctrine, by deposition in the case of opposing Bishops and clerics, and of anathema in the case of laics.

2. The Constantinopolitan Creed is recited in the Fourth Ecumenical Synod after the Nicene, and is regarded as authoritative and binding.

3. So it is in its Definition, where also the work of the Second Synod of the Christian world who made it, and of which it forms part, is approved.

4. In their address to the Emperor Marcian, they contend that while they may not oppose anything in the Nicene faith, they may defend it against the innovations of heretics, and so add new documents or definitions, as the Council of Ephesus did against Nestorius. See on that *Hefele's History of the Church Councils*, English translation, volume II., pages 351, 352.

5. As a matter of fact they did define against the Eutychian heresy, and did set

ward or to offer another faith (323) to those wishing to turn to the acknowledgment of the truth, either from heathenism or from Judaism, or from any heresy whatsoever; these, if they are Bishops or clerics, are to be aliens, the Bishops from the episcopate and the clerics from the clericate; but if they are laymen they are to be anathematized. In the same manner, if any are detected, whether they be Bishops or clerics or laics (324), either holding or teaching

forth the true doctrine of the Two Natures of Christ, and did approve two Epistles of Cyril of Alexandria to Nestorius and one of Leo I. of Rome to Flavian of Constantinople, and did define that any pre-eminence of Rome in the Church Universal was based not on its being a see of Peter, much less of its deriving any Primacy through him, but on its rank in the civil notitia as the old capital of the Roman Empire, and it did make Constantinople its equal, and guarded the rights of Provinces and Dioceses, outside of the jurisdiction of Constantinople. And it defined additionally on other matters besides.

6. The Fifth Ecumenical Synod, II. Constantinople, A. D., 553, approves all the work of the Third World Synod and the Fourth, and, of course, all the foregoing additional decisions. Besides it received all the definitions of the preceding Ecumenical Councils respecting the one faith, and they "*account all who do not receive those things as aliens from the Universal Church.*" and they condemn and anathematize all condemned and anathematized by the said Four Synods.

Furthermore, they condemn the Three Chapters, and in their XIV. Anathemas put forth an excellent additional body of doctrine, on the Trinity, the Two Natures of Christ, the Substance Union, against even the relative worship of Christ's humanity (Anathemas 9 and 12), and condemn certain heretics by name and their impious writings, and they define much more, all of which is outside of the Creed of the 318 and additional to it.

8. The Sixth and last Synod of the Christian World III. Constantinople, A. D., 680, received all the decisions of the five Ecumenical Synods before it, condemned the heresy of Monothelism, recited and approved the Creed of the 318 and that of the 150, and antecedently settled the question of Papal Infallibility by condemning Honorius, Bishop of Rome, as a Monothelite heretic, and it enforced all its own decisions and those of the five Synods aforesaid by pronouncing the following penalties on all its opposers and on all theirs, namely deposition for all Bishops and Clerics and anathema for all laics.

So, therefore, it is abundantly clear that the Third Synod and the three after it have authoritatively explained the sense of its Canon VII., by teaching that it does not forbid any faith (πίστιν) which accords with the Symbol of Nicaea, nor any additions in the way of Definitions, Ecumenically approved Epistles, and Canons, provided they agree with it, but only such as are *contrary to it.*

9. But that Canon VII., in forbidding any faith contrary to Nicaea, and, in effect, to *Ephesus* itself, does forbid all the Creature Worship of the creature invoking Council of Constantinople, A. D., 754, and all the image worship, invocation of creatures, real substance presence of Christ's humanity in the Eucharist, and all its adjuncts, of the idolatrous conventicle at Nicaea, A. D., 787, and all the so-called Ecumenical Councils of the Latins and of the Greeks since the Sixth, for all since that are contrary on fundamental doctrines necessary to salvation, even as regards idolatry, to the first Six.

NOTE 323.—Greek, πίστιν, *faith:* not σύμβολον, *Creed.*

NOTE 324.—The Greek here in col. 1364 of Mansi's Concilia, tome IV., (Florentiae, A. D., 1760,) omits *laics,* but it is found in the Latin of the parallel column in the same tome, as well as in the Greek given in Ralle and Potle's Σύνταγμα τῶν . . . Κανόνων, tome 2, Athens, 1852, from which I have translated.

The Creature-Worshipping Creed of Theodore. 225

those things which are in the Forthset, brought forward by Charisius the Elder (325), in regard to the Inman of the Sole-Born Son of God, that is to say, the foul and perverse dogmas of Nestorius, which are even its basis, let them lie under the sentence of this Holy and Ecumenical Synod, that is to say, the Bishop shall be alienated from the episcopate and shall be deposed; and the cleric in like manner shall fall out of the clericate; but, if any one be a laic, even he shall be anathematized, as has been said before (326)."

"And all subscribed [as follows:]

I, Cyril, Bishop of Alexandria, have subscribed, **pronouncing with the Holy Synod**.

I, Arcadius, a Bishop, and a Legate of the Apostolic See, have subscribed, pronouncing with the Holy Synod.

I, Juvenal, Bishop of Jerusalem, have subscribed, pronouncing with the Holy Synod.

NOTE 325.—That is, Presbyter.

NOTE 326.—Ralle and Potle's Σύνταγμα τῶν . . . Κανόνων, tom. 2, page 200; Canon VII. of the Third Ecumenical Synod:

Τούτων ἀναγνωσθέντων, ὥρισεν ἡ ἁγία σύνοδος, ἑτέραν πίστιν μηδενὶ ἐξεῖναι προφέρειν, ἤγουν συγγράφειν, ἢ συντιθέναι, παρὰ τὴν ὁρισθεῖσαν παρὰ τῶν ἁγίων πατέρων, τῶν ἐν τῇ Νικαέων συναχθέντων πόλει, σὺν ἁγίῳ πνεύματι. Τοὺς δὲ τολμῶντας ἢ συντιθέναι πίστιν ἑτέραν, ἤγουν προκομίζειν, ἢ προφέρειν τοῖς θέλουσιν, ἐπιστρέφειν εἰς ἐπίγνωσιν τῆς ἀληθείας, ἢ ἐξ Ἑλληνισμοῦ, ἢ ἐξ Ἰουδαϊσμοῦ, ἤγουν ἐξ αἱρέσεως οἱασδηποτοῦν· τούτους, εἰ μὲν εἶεν ἐπίσκοποι, ἢ κληρικοὶ, ἀλλοτρίους εἶναι τοὺς ἐπισκόπους τῆς ἐπισκοπῆς, καὶ τοὺς κληρικοὺς τοῦ κλήρου· εἰ δὲ λαϊκοὶ εἶεν, ἀναθεματίζεσθαι. Κατὰ τὸν ἴσον δὲ τρόπον, εἰ φωραθεῖέν τινες, εἴτε ἐπίσκοποι, εἴτε κληρικοὶ, εἴτε λαϊκοὶ, ἢ φρονοῦντες, ἢ διδάσκοντες τὰ ἐν τῇ προκομισθείσῃ ἐκθέσει παρὰ Χαρισίου τοῦ πρεσβυτέρου, περὶ τῆς ἐνανθρωπήσεως τοῦ μονογενοῦς Υἱοῦ τοῦ Θεοῦ ἤγουν τὰ μιαρὰ καὶ διεστραμμένα τοῦ Νεστορίου δόγματα, ἃ καὶ ὑποτέτακται, ὑποκείσθωσαν τῇ ἀποφάσει τῆς ἁγίας ταύτης καὶ οἰκουμενικῆς συνόδου· ὥστε δηλονότι, τὸν μὲν ἐπίσκοπον, ἀπαλλοτριοῦσθαι τῆς ἐπισκοπῆς, καὶ εἶναι καθῃρημένον· τὸν δὲ κληρικὸν, ὁμοίως ἐκπίπτειν τοῦ κλήρου· εἰ δὲ λαϊκός τις εἴη, καὶ οὗτος ἀναθεματιζέσθω, καθὰ προείρηται.

I, Projectus, a Bishop, and a Legate of the Apostolic See, have subscribed, pronouncing with the Holy Synod.

I, Flavian, Bishop of the Philippians, have subscribed, pronouncing together with the Holy Synod.

I, Philip, a Presbyter of the Apostolic See, and a Legate, have subscribed, pronouncing together with the Holy Synod.

I, Firmus, Bishop of Caesarea, have subscribed, pronouncing together with the Holy Synod.

I, Memnon, Bishop of Ephesus, have subscribed, pronouncing together with the Holy Synod.

I, Acacius, by the mercy of God, Bishop of the Melitenians, agree with the Holy Synod in the aforesaid decision (327), and have subscribed.

I, Theodotus, Bishop of Ancyra, agree with the Holy Synod, and have subscribed.

I, Palladius, by Christ's favor, Bishop of the Amaseans, agree with the Holy Synod in the aforesaid decision, and have subscribed.

I, Amphilochius, Bishop of Side, have subscribed, pronouncing together with the Holy Synod.

I, Iconius, Bishop of Gortyna in Crete, have subscribed, pronouncing together with the Holy Synod.

I, Daniel of Colonia, have subscribed, together with the Holy Synod.

I, Perigenes, Bishop of Corinth, have subscribed, pronouncing together with the Holy Synod.

I, Berinianus, Bishop of Perga, the metropolis, have subscribed by Timothy, a presbyter.

I, Severus, Bishop of Synnada, have subscribed.

I, Rheginus, Bishop of Constantia, in Cyprus, have subscribed.

I, Herennianus, Bishop of Myra (328), have subscribed.

I, Valerian, Bishop of Iconium, have subscribed.

I, Pius, Bishop of the metropolis of the Pisinuntians, have subscribed.

NOTE 327.—That is the decision in what we now call Canon VII. of Ephesus above.
NOTE 328.—Or, *"of the Myrans."*

I, Cyrus, the least, Bishop of Aphrodisias, have subscribed.

I, Maeonius, Bishop of the Church which is in Sardis in Lydia, have subscribed.

I, Hellanicus, Bishop of Rhodes, have subscribed.

I. Dalmatius, Bishop of Cyzicus, have subscribed.

I, Aristonicus, Bishop of Laodicea, have subscribed.

I, Paralius, Bishop of Andrapa, have subscribed.

I, Olympius, Bishop of Claudiopolis, have subscribed *by Bishop Epiphanius and Theosebius*.

I, Dinatus (329), *Bishop of Nicopolis in Epirus*, have subscribed.

I, Domninus, Bishop of the city of Cotia, have subscribed.

I, Eustathius, Bishop of the city of Docimium, have subscribed.

I, Epiphanius, Bishop of the city of Cratia, have subscribed.

I, Gregory, Bishop of the city of Cerasus, have subscribed.

I, Helladius, Bishop of Adramyttium, have subscribed.

I, Anysius, Bishop of the city of Thebes in Greece, have subscribed.

I, Domninus, Bishop of the city of Opus, have subscribed.

I, Callicrates, Bishop of the city Naupactus, have subscribed.

I, Nicias, Bishop of the city of the Megarans, have subscribed.

I, Callinicus, Bishop of Apamea, have subscribed.

I, Peter, the least, Bishop of the city of Prusis (330), have subscribed.

I, Eutrepius, Bishop of Vize, have subscribed.

I, Dion, Bishop of the city of Thebes, have subscribed.

I, Perrebius, Bishop of the Thessalonian Forests (331), have subscribed.

I, Paul, Bishop of the city of Anthedon, have subscribed.

I, Theodore, Bishop of the city of the Aninysians, have subscribed.

I, Eusebius, Bishop of Heraclea, have subscribed.

I, John, Bishop of Lesboscla (332), have subscribed.

I, Senecion, Bishop of the city of Codrina (333), have subscribed.

NOTE 329.—Or, "*Donatus.*"
NOTE 330.—Or, "*Prusa*," or, "*Prusias.*"
NOTE 331.—Or, "*Thessalonian Defiles.*"
NOTE 332.—Or, "*Lesbos.*"
NOTE 333.—It is called Scodra above, at the beginning of Act VI.

I, Tribonianus, Bishop of the Church which is at Primopolis, have subscribed.

I, Martyrius, Bishop of the city of Helystra, have subscribed.

I, Nesius, Bishop of Corybrassus, have subscribed.

I, Acacius, Bishop of Cotena, have subscribed.

I, Ablavius, Bishop of the city of Amorium, have subscribed.

I, Heradeon, who am also Theophanius, Bishop of the Trallians, have subscribed.

I, Philip, Bishop of Pergamus, have subscribed.

I, Daphnus, Bishop of the city of Magnesia on the Maeander, have subscribed.

I, Eusebius, Bishop of the city of Magnesia on Sipylus, have subscribed.

I, Anderius, the least, Bishop of Chersonesus, have subscribed.

I, Paul, the least, Bishop of the city of Lampe, have subscribed.

I, Eutropius, the least, Bishop of the city of Evasa, have subscribed.

I, Severus, the least, Bishop of the city of Sozopolis in the province of Pisidia, have subscribed.

I, Silvanus, Bishop of the city of Chaeretapa, have subscribed.

I, Commodus, the least, Bishop of Tripolis, have subscribed.

I, Constantius, Bishop of the city of Diocletiana, have subscribed.

I, Nestorius, Bishop of Sion, have subscribed.

I. Aphobius, the least, Bishop of Coluis, have subscribed.

I, Phoscus, Bishop of the city of Thyatira, have subscribed.

I, Paul, Bishop of Dardana, have subscribed.

I, Limenius, Bishop of the city of the Settenians (334), have subscribed,

I, Dorotheus, Bishop of the city of Myrina, have subscribed.

I, Theodore, Bishop of Attalia, have subscribed.

I, Aphthonetus, the least, Bishop of the Heracleans of the city of Lampis, have subscribed.

I, Philetus, the leas', Bishop of Amyzon, have subscribed.

I, Spudasius, the least, Bishop of Cerama, have subscribed.

I, Docimasius, Bishop of the City of Maronia, have subscribed.

NOTE 334.—Or, "*of Settae.*"

I, Ennepius, Bishop of Maximianopolis, have subscribed.
I, Euthalius, Bishop of the city of Colophon, have subscribed.
I, Lucian, Bishop of the city Toperus, have subscribed.
I, Rufinus, Bishop of the city of Gabae (335), have subscribed.
I, Romanus, Bishop of the city of Raphia, have subscribed.
I, Fidus, Bishop of Joppa, have subscribed.
I, Hesychius, Bishop of the city of Parium, have subscribed.
I, Timothy, of the city of Termessus and of Eudocias, have subscribed.
I, Eucharius, Bishop of the city of Dyrrachium, have subscribed.
I, Evagrius, Bishop of the city of Soli in Cyprus, have subscribed.
I, I Nectarius, Bishop of the city of Casa, have subscribed.
I, Agathocles, Bishop of the city of Coronia, have subscribed.
I, John, Bishop of Sycamazon, have subscribed.
I, Aedesius, Bishop of Syda, have subscribed.
I, Secundianus, Bishop of the city of Lamia, have subscribed.
I, Nunechius, Bishop of the city of Selge, have subscribed.
I, Matidianus, Bishop of Coracesium, have subscribed.
I, Cyril, Bishop of Cilina, have subscribed *by the hand of Selenespondius, a Presbyter*.
I, Sapricius, Bishop of Paphos in Cyprus, have subscribed.
I, Themistius, the least, Bishop of the city of Jassus, have subscribed.
I, Chromatius, the least, Bishop of the city of Alinda, have subscribed.
I, Eudoxius, Bishop of the city of Choma, have subscribed.
I, Libanius, Bishop of Palaeopolis, have subscribed.
I, Tarianus, Bishop of the city of Lyrba, have subscribed.
I, Alexander, Bishop of Arcadiopolis, have subscribed.
I, Theodore, Bishop of Nissa, have subscribed.
I, Rhodon, Bishop of Palaeopolis in Asia, have subscribed.
I, Tychicus, the least, Bishop of the city of Erythra, have subscribed.
I, Eugene, Bishop of the city of Apollonias, have subscribed.

NOTE 335.—"*Tabae*," above. One is a misspelling for the other.

I, Aetius, Bishop of the city of Paeonia in Hellespontus, have subscribed.

I, Timothy, Bishop of the city of Termana in Hellespontus, have subscribed.

I, Archelaus, Bishop of Myndus, have subscribed.

I, Apellas, the least, Bishop of Cibyrrha, have subscribed.

I, Philadelphus, the least, Bishop of Gratianopolis, have subscribed.

I, Eutherius, the least, Bishop of the Stratonicians in Lydia, have subscribed.

I, John, the least, Bishop of Aurelianopolis, have subscribed,

I, Maximus, the least, Bishop of Cuma, have subscribed.

I, Theodosius, the least, Bishop of the city of Mastaura, have subscribed.

I, Modestus, Bishop of the city of Aneatae (336), have subscribed.

I, Thomas, Bishop of Valentinianopolis, have subscribed.

I, Eusebius, Bishop of Clazomenae, have subscribed.

I, Eusebius, Bishop of Aspona, have subscribed.

I, Euporus, Bishop of the city of Hypaepa, have subscribed.

I, Saidas (337), Bishop of Phaenis, have subscribed.

I, Domnus, Bishop of Orcistus, have subscribed.

I, John, Bishop of Augustopolis, have subscribed.

I, Peter, Bishop of Parembola, have subscribed.

I, Netoras, Bishop of Gaza, have subscribed.

I, Zeno, Bishop of Curium in Cyprus, have subscribed.

I, Euoptius, Bishop of Ptolemais in Pentapolis, have subscribed.

I, Macarius, Bishop of Metelis, have subscribed.

I, Eusebius, Bishop of Pelusium, have subscribed.

I, Hermogenes, Bishop of Rhinocurora, have subscribed.

I, Marinus, Bishop of Heliopolis, have subscribed.

I, John, Bishop of Hephaestus, have subscribed.

I, Heraclius, Bishop of Tamiatha, have subscribed.

NOTE 336.—Or, "*of the Aenusites.*"

NOTE 337.—This is "Sais," at the beginning of Act VI., above.

I, Theon, Bishop of Sethroetus (338), have subscribed.
I, Solon, Bishop of the city of Parallia (339), have subscribed.
I, Alypius, Bishop of the city of Selenus, have subscribed.
I, Macedonius, Bishop of Xois, have subscribed.
I, Peter, Bishop of Oxyrinchus, have subscribed.
I, Metrodorus, Bishop of Leonta, have subscribed.
I, Paul, Bishop of Flavona, have subscribed.
I, Ammonius, Bishop of Panephysus, have subscribed.
I, Publius, Bishop of Olvia (340), have subscribed.
I, Hieraces, Bishop of Aphnaitis (341), have subscribed.
I, Samuel, Bishop of Dysthis, have subscribed.
I, Sosipater, Bishop of Septimiaca in Libya, have subscribed (342).

NOTE 338.—The spelling of this and other names of places varies, 1, because of the mistakes of copyists as to the right name.
2. Because there may have been different right ways of spelling the name of the same place; or it may have had two names; as Jerusalem, for instance, has in Greek.
Wiltsch's Geography and Statistics of the Church, Vol. I., English translation, gives *Sethroeta* for the above. See under that word in its Index.

NOTE 339.—*Caralia* in *Wiltsch's Geography and Statistics of the Church*. See its Vol. I. Index.

NOTE 340.—Or *Olbia*, for in Greek the Beta has now the sound of our V, and had in the time of Ephesus, probably. A copyist, writing by the ear, would naturally make this mistake in rendering into a Latin form such names.

NOTE 341.—Or, possibly, "*Aphnacum*," but I am not sure.

NOTE 342.—Alas! when we read names of so many sees wiped out by the Mohammedan curse for our idolatry and creature invoking in other days! Libya, so far as I know, has not now one Christian Church within its borders, nor has there been one for more than seven centuries, though it had Christianity soon after the Apostles, if not in their time. The fate of the Nubian Church is told by Wiltsch in his *Geography and Statistics of the Church*, Vol. II., page 159, as follows:

"The Bishopric in Nubia had reached its end before the close of the twelfth century, when Chemseddoula, brother of Saladin, the Sultan of Egypt, in his expedition to Nubia, destroyed the churches of that country, and brought thence 70,000 captives to Egypt, with the Bishop or Metropolitan, in the year 1173." God has removed her candlestick out of its place. So it has been with most of the churches of Egypt, and with the great bulk of the North African Latin Churches. Speaking of these last Wiltsch tells in the same work, Vol. I., page 432:

"No Christian country suffered so incalculably from the destroying fanaticism of the Mahometans as the northwest of Africa subsequently to the year 647. Out of more than 550 Christian foundations there were merely left the Archbishoprick of Carthage and a couple of Bishopricks." Further on he states, Vol. 2, page 118:

"From want of documents, the year in which the Archbishoprick of Carthage ceased to exist cannot be ascertained." In the days of Gregory VII. of Rome, A. D., 1073-1085, it still lived, and had two Bishopricks under it. "There is no further mention of an

I, Isaac, Bishop of Elcarchia, have subscribed.
I, Isaac, Bishop of Tava, have subscribed.
I, Heraclius, Bishop of Thynis, have subscribed.
I, Theonas, Bishop of Psynchus, have subscribed.
I, Cyrus, Bishop of Achaea, have subscribed.
I, Eulogius, Bishop of Terenuthis, have subscribed.
I, Alexander, Bishop of Cleopatris, have subscribed.
I, Silvanus, Bishop of Coprithis, have subscribed. But *I, Heraclius, a Bishop*, have subscribed [for him], because he was sick.

Archbishoprick of Carthage; probably the metropolis died out." But a Bishop of Bona is found again in A. D., 1179.

In the same volume, page 311, Wiltsch adds on the period A. D., 1216-1521:
"As there is no Archbishop of Carthage mentioned after the time of Gregory VII. we may assume with confidence that that Archbishoprick had been long extinct. Indeed, besides the bishoprick of Bona (Hippo Regius) there remained perhaps no other Christian institution at the beginning of the sixteenth century, and the mention of a Bishop of Hippo Regius in the Acts of" the Lateran Council "in 1512, together with the reference to him in Raynaldus in 1516 and 1517, furnish the sole evidence that Christianity had not entirely disappeared from Northwestern Africa." Alas! alas! for the once sound but afterwards idolatrous Church of Latin Africa; sound in Cyprian's day but fallen already in Augustine's, less than 200 years later; for in his work *On the Morals of the Catholic Church*, book I., chapter 34, he writes as follows:

"Do not, I pray you, collect professors of the Christian name, but who neither know nor show forth the power of their profession. Do not inveigh against crowds of ignorant men, who even in the true religion itself are superstitious, or are so given up to lusts as to forget what they have promised to God. *I have known many to be* ADORERS OF TOMBS *and* PICTURES. I have known many who drink most luxuriously over the dead, and, laying a banquet before the corpses, bury themselves over those who are buried, and put down their surfeiting and drunkenness to the score of religion," translation on page 199 of Tyler's excellent work *on Image Worship*. No wonder that, seeing idolatry come from the *use* of pictures, he should elsewhere express the opinion that *it is wrong to put an image into a temple of God;* though he himself was not without a share in the errors of his time, for in his work *on the City of God* he favors the invocation of martyrs, and elsewhere uses language which looks like the Nestorian heresy of worshipping Christ's humanity in the Eucharist, all of which, with his invocation of creatures, is condemned by Ephesus, A. D., 431. And no wonder that, as the result of all these sins, he saw his country devastated far and wide by the Vandals, and that he died in sorrow in his see City Hippo when it was besieged by them, and that it was taken by them soon after his death. And such paganizings, alas! caused the wiping out of hundreds, perhaps, we may say of thousands of episcopates in Asia Minor, Syria, Palestine and Pontus; and, alas! where in those lands and in Latin Africa and in Egypt there were perhaps 40,000 000 of Christians in the fifth century, there are now hardly more than 5,000,000, if that.

Well, therefore, does the English Church in its Homilies warn its people against even the use of images in Churches as sure to bring in their worship and against all relic worship and all invocation of saints. But alas! alas! in our degeneracy we refuse to heed such saving teachings. The idolatrizing and creature worshipping and Romanizing Oxford Movement of Pusey, Newman and Keble has corrupted large parts of the Anglican Church, and to some extent other Protestants also.

I, Adelphius, Bishop of Onuphis, have subscribed.
I, Abraam, Bishop of the city of Ostracine, have subscribed.
I, Athanasius, Bishop of Paralius, have subscribed.
I, Adelphius, Bishop of Sais, have subscribed.
I, Lampetius, Bishop of Cassus, have subscribed.
I, Chrysaorius, Bishop of Aphrodis (343), have subscribed.
I, Ammon, Bishop of Butus, have subscribed.
I, Eutychius, Bishop of Theodosiopolis, have subscribed.
I, Venantius, Bishop of Hierapolis, have subscribed *by my Secretary, Theodotus.*
I, Zeno, Bishop of the city of Teuchira, have subscribed.
I, Zenobius, Bishop of the city of Barca, have subscribed.
I, Eusebius, Bishop of Nilopolis, have subscribed.
I, Heraclides, Bishop of the farther Heraclea, have subscribed.
I, Macarius, Bishop of Anteus, have subscribed.
I, Sabinus, Bishop of Panis (344), have subscribed.
I, Athanasius, Bishop of the city of the Scepsians (345), have subscribed.
I, Philumenus, Bishop of Cinna, have subscribed.
I, Felix, Bishop of the city of Apollonia, have subscribed.
I, Timothy, Bishop of the city of Tomi in the province of Scythia, have subscribed.
I, Zenbinus, Bishop of the city of Gnossus, have subscribed.
I, Paulianus (346), *Bishop of Majuma,* have subscribed.
I, Phoebammon, Bishop of Coptus, have subscribed.
I, Pabiscus, Bishop of Apollo (347), have subscribed.
I, Andrew, Bishop of Hermopolis, have subscribed.

NOTE 343.—There was an *Aphrodisias* in Caria, another in Thrace, and an *Aphroditopolis* in Egypt. As the names about that of Chrysaorius' seem to be Egyptian, perhaps the last is meant. This seems to be the more probable because Chrysaorius signs in the list of Prelates at the beginning of the Council as of *Aphrodita* or *Aphroditae*, and at its end as "*Bishop of the Aphroditans.*" Cyrus was Bishop of the Aphrodisias in Caria; Chrystal's *Ephesus*, Vol. I., pages 23, 131, 490.

NOTE 344. —In Volume I. of Chrystal's *Ephesus*, page 561, he is called *Sabinus of Pan;* so he is on page 28, id., on page 499, *Sabinus, Bishop of Pan*, and on page 149, *Sabinus, Bishop of Pan in the Province of Thebais.*

NOTE 345.—Or, "of *Scepsis.*"

NOTE 346.—Above, at the beginning of the Act, this name is spelled "*Paulinianus.*"

NOTE 347.—Or "*Apollonia.*" There was a city of Apollo in the First Thebais.

I, Phanias, the least, Bishop of the city of Arpasa (348), have subscribed.

I, Theosebius, Bishop of the city of Priene, have subscribed.

I, Maximus, Bishop of Assus in Asia, have subscribed

I, Theoctistus, Bishop of Phocaea, have subscribed.

I, Hermolaus, the least, Bishop of the Attydans (349), have subscribed.

I, Theodore, Bishop of Gadara, have subscribed *by the hand of Aetherius, an Archdeacon.*

I, Athanasius, Bishop of the island of Paros, have subscribed.

I, Paul, Bishop of Orymna, have subscribed.

I, Timothy, Bishop of Briula, have subscribed.

I, Daniel, Bishop of Colonia, in Cappadocia, have subscribed.

I, Asclepiades, Bishop of the Trapezopolitans, have subscribed.

I, Theodore, Bishop of the city of Echinaeus, have subscribed.

I, Caesarius, Bishop of the city of Sarta, have subscribed.

I, Stephen, Bishop of Gajopolis, in Asia, have subscribed.

I, Theodulus, Bishop of Helusa (350), have subscribed.

I, Theodore, Bishop of Aribdila, have subscribed.

I, Letojus, Bishop of Libyas, have subscribed.

I, Aristocrates, Bishop of Olympus, have subscribed.

I, Bessula, a Deacon of the Church of Carthage (351), have subscribed (352).

NOTE 348. Or, "*Harpasa.*"

NOTE 349.—Or, "of *Attudaea*," or of "*Attyda.*"

NOTE 350.—Or "*Elusa.*"

NOTE 351.—See on him in Volume I. of Chrystal's *Ephesus*, page 29, text and note 57, and pages 481 to 486, and on the woful state of Carthage and its Civil Diocese of Africa because of idolatry in the Church, the letter of Capreolus on pages 481-486, and the notes there, particularly note 1033. Compare on Carthage and its jurisdiction, note 1023, page 479.

NOTE 352.—Here the Minutes of the Sixth Act of the Third Ecumenical Synod end; I have translated the above Act VI. from Coleti, compared to some extent with the *Conc. Collectio Regia*, and with Mansi and Hardouin.

MATTER IN COLETI OR IN SOME OTHER, AFTER ACT VI. OF THE THIRD ECUMENICAL SYNOD, BUT NOT INCLUDED IN ITS MINUTES; AND BEFORE ACT VII.

INDEX OF THIS MATTER.

As this Matter is indexed in the *Table of Contents* at the beginning of this Work, the reader is referred to it there.

ORTHODOX DOCUMENT I.:

A Homily of Cyril of Alexandria put between Acts VI. and VII. of the Third Ecumenical Synod.

The following Document is in Coleti, in the *Collectio Regia*, and in Mansi, but not in Hardouin here. In Coleti it comes in immediately after the Subscriptions to Act VI. (*Coleti's Concilia*, tom. III., col. 1225-1229), and just before the Matter on the Synod of the Apostasy put between Acts VI. and VII. of the Third Ecumenical Synod. It is not put with the other Orthodox Documents between Acts VI. and VII; because, I presume, it forms no part of the Orthodox matter which is intended to refute the falsehoods and misrepresentations of the Nestorian Documents which here follow.

The sense of this important document is so clear *against serving the humanity of Christ and for the worship of God alone,* that I here translate it in full.

"A HOMILY OF CYRIL, BISHOP OF ALEXANDRIA, DELIVERED IN EPHESUS BEFORE HE WAS ARRESTED BY THE COUNT, AND COMMITTED TO SOLDIERS TO BE KEPT UNDER THEIR GUARD.

"The blessed prophet David shows that those who put their trust in God were most courageous, when he says, '*Act like men, and let your hearts be strong, all ye who hope in the Lord*' (353). For those plants which are in pleasure gardens both increase, and bloom, and are raised to a great height, by abundant flowings of waters. And a man's soul, by the comforts and encouragements of the Holy Spirit, becomes manly in piety, is made firm in faith, and gets that unbreakable patience which the blessed Paul admired more than all other virtues, and so says, '*And not only so, but we glory in tribulations, knowing that tribulation worketh patience, and patience approval, and ap-*

NOTE 353.—Psalm xxxi:24; Septuagint rendering.

proval hope, and hope maketh not ashamed' (354). Patience is therefore the supplier and winner of all good to us, a way to approval and esteem, a curse of the hope which is unto the life to come. But in what way shall we correct ourselves and improve as it regards patience? The Scripture of God teaches by saying *'Child, if thou come to serve the Lord, prepare thy soul for trial. Keep straight thy heart, and be steadfast and endure'* (355).

"But, perhaps, some one will say, But was there no other way for man to acquire approval and esteem? Could he not have set himself straight as it regards good, without toil?

"'In no wise,' says he.

"And for what sort of a reason?

[I answer], "because those who plot against the saints are very many, and the war about them is terrible, and for that reason the Saviour Himself was saying, *Ye* [shall] *have tribulation in the world, but be courageous—I have overcome the world* (356). Therefore, precisely because there is much war from every side against the saints, it is necessary for them to bear up manfully and stoutly against the assaults of temptations and trials, and to keep in memory the following saying of a disciple, *'Blessed is the man who endureth tribulation and temptation, for when he is tried and approved he shall receive the crown of life which God hath promised to those who love him'* (357). But I wish to adduce some thing in the way of more ancient things (358), that ye may learn the result of good spiritual manliness. The tyrants of the Babylonians and those who had the administration of kingly thrones among them, were somehow always very prone to cruelty and arrogance. And overpassing the bounds of humanity they wished to usurp to themselves that honor (359) which belongs to the God over all alone. And therefore the accursed Nebuchadnezzar raised a golden image (360) while sweet-toned instruments sounded subservient to it, and he command.d the people subject to him TO BOW [to it] (361). AND THESE WHO HAD BEEN ACCUSTOMED TO SERVE THE CREATURE CONTRARY TO GOD THE CREATOR (362), WENT MOST READILY TO THAT THING, AND CHANGED THE GLORY OF THE UNCORRUPTIBLE GOD INTO THE LIKENESS OF AN IMAGE OF A CORRUPTIBLE MAN (363). But when the Babylonians led into the midst the

---

NOTE 354.—Rom. v: 3, 4, 5.
NOTE 355.—Ecclesiasticus II: 1.
NOTE 356.—John xvi: 33.
NOTE 357.—James i: 12.
NOTE 358.—Or, "*more ancient examples.*"
NOTE 359.—ἀξίωμα.
NOTE 360.—εἰκόνα χρυσῆν.
NOTE 361.—Daniel iii. Compare the Apocryphal *Song of the Three Holy Children.*
NOTE 362.—Rom. i: 25.
NOTE 363.—Rom. i: 23, 25.

Hebrew boys (they were Ananias and Azarias and Misael), they began to command them TO BOW TO THE GOLDEN IMAGE, and to force the most noble and God-loving race to slip down into THE SAME SIN WITH THEMSELVES, and TO BOW TO THE GOLDEN IMAGE (364); but they did not at all succeed. And so, BEING FOILED BY THE LOVE OF THOSE BOYS FOR GOD, they inflicted on them the punishment of fire. And the accusation against those thus overreached and maltreated was firmness in faith, fixedness in piety, [and] REFUSAL TO WORSHIP A MAN (365), AND THEIR NOT BEING WILLING TO HOLD THOSE OPINIONS WHICH INSULT AND OUTRAGE THE DIVINE NATURE (366). But when they were cast into the furnace of fire then, then indeed, occurred that great manifestation of the power unspeakable. For the power of the elements was changed into that which is against its nature, and the fire obeyed the wishes and decrees of the Creator (367) and the flame was transformed into a dewy whistling wind. And the young men (368) perceiving that the succor was from above, began to sing in the furnace of fire, and made the fire a mild thing by their singing of hymns to God. That furnace was a figure of the Church, which has, as holy choristers (369), not only men, but angels also. Thou hast admired THE VIRTUE of those men. Thou hast praised their patience, and THE GREATNESS OF THEIR LOVE FOR GOD. Let us see in what state matters are WITH US. For they indeed were under barbarian tyrants: but we are under pious sceptres, for we have most pious [men as] rulers of all things. How (370) [then] shall we give in to our enemies? For even though plotters kindle a furnace, and though they wake the flames of perversity(371), BY BRINGING IN TO US SERVICE TO A MAN (372), NEVERTHELESS

NOTE 364.—καὶ προσκυνεῖν τῇ εἰκόνι τῇ χρυσῇ.
NOTE 365.—ἀνθρωπολατρείας παραίτησις.
NOTE 366.—That is, opinions in favor of serving creatures for that sin is an insult to that God who calls himself Jealous (Exodus xx: 5, and Exod. xxxiv: 14, and often), and who says: "*My glory will I not give to another, neither my praise to graven images*," (Isaiah xlii: 8; Exod. xx: 1-8).
NOTE 367.—Greek, καὶ τοῖς τοῦ κτίσαντος νεύμασι παρεχώρει τὸ πῦρ.
NOTE 368.—Greek, οἱ νεανίαι.
NOTE 369.—Greek, χορευτάς.
NOTE 370.—Or, "*why*," (πῶς.)
NOTE 371.—Or, "*They wake the flames in perversity*": εἰ καὶ φλόγας ἐγείρουσι δυστροπίᾳ. The margin of Mansi has δυστροπίας, and the Latin given by him in the parallel column, means *of perversity* (perversitatis). I quote the whole of the Greek here: Πῶς ἐνδώσομεν τοῖς ἐχθροῖς; Εἰ γὰρ καὶ κάμινον ἀνάπτουσιν ἐπίβουλοι, εἰ καὶ φλόγας ἐγείρουσι δυστροπίᾳ, ἀνθρωπολατρείαν ἡμῖν εἰσφέροντες, ἀλλ' ἡμεῖς ἔχομεν Θεὸν ἐν οὐρανῷ, αὐτῷ προσκυνήσομεν. Θεὸς γὰρ ὢν φύσει, γέγονε καθ' ἡμᾶς, οὐκ ἀποβεβληκὼς τὸ εἶναι Θεὸς, τιμήσας δὲ τὴν τῶν ἀνθρώπων φύσιν· δυνατὸς ἐστιν ἐξελέσθαι ἡμᾶς.
NOTE 372.—That is *service*, that is *worship* to *a human being*, which is the meaning of the Greek term (ἀνθρωπολατρεία) here used and elsewhere by Cyril. On it and the cognate ἀνθρωπολάτρης, *a worshipper of a man*, see pages 695, 696, vol. I of Chrystal's *Ephesus;* and

WE HAVE A GOD IN HEAVEN—WE WILL BOW TO HIM. For being GOD BY NATURE, He became like us (373), not casting away his being God, but honoring the nature of men [by taking it on Him]. He is able to deliver us. For following the faith of the most religious Emperors, and knowing the greatness of the gentleness that is in them, WE WILL NOT ENDURE THE BUNGLING AND EVIL [doctrine] OF OUR OPPONENTS, but we will confess that the Immanuel (374) is God by Nature: and saying that, and so continuing we shall gain that recompense which is the greatest possible. And what is that? He Himself will teach by saying, *Whosoever shall confess me* (375) *before men, him will I also confess before my Father who is in the heavens. But whosoever shall deny me before men, him will I also deny before my Father who is in the heavens* (376). But he who says that He is very God and rebukes those who disbelieve [it], confesses Him. And on the other hand, he who says not that He is very God, but contends against those who do acknowledge him [to be so,] he denies Him. Therefore the Saviour of all will deny them, but will confess us: the Saviour of all, through whom and with whom be the glory and the might to the God and Father forever. Amen (377).

---

pages 725-751, on other Greek terms signifying worship, and pages 637-644, Nestorius' *Heresy* 1, 2, 5, and 6, and under *Man Worship* on pages 631-635, under *Creature Worship* on page 585, and on Cyril's Anathema VIII, and Nestorius' Counter Anathema VIII on pages 590-592.

NOTE 373.—That is, *He took flesh, and put on a man*, as we say in both the Ecumenical Creeds, that of Nicaea, and that of 1. Constantinople.

NOTE 374.—That is "*The God with us*," as Immanuel means.

NOTE 375.—Or "*shall make confession in me*": πᾶς οὖν ὅστις ὁμολογήσει ἐν ἐμοὶ ἔμπροσθεν τῶν ἀνθρώπων, etc.

NOTE 376.—Matt. x: 32, 33.

NOTE 377.—In the above document the reader will notice:

1. That Cyril likens the relative MAN-SERVICE of the Nestorians offered, by bowing, to the humanity put on by God the Word, for the sake of God the Word, to the relative worship of the image set up by Nebuchadnezzar. And that Nestorius' worship of Christ's humanity was *relative* only, that is given to it not for its own sake, but for the sake of God the Word, to Whom, he held, it had about such an external conjoinment as an inspired apostle or prophet had, is clear from several of his XX blasphemies for which he was deposed by the whole church at its Third Synod. Especially clear on that is his blasphemy 8. It reads as follows:

"*I worship him* [that is the man, that is Christ's humanity] *who is worn, for the sake of Him* [God the Word] *who wears. I bow to him who is seen* [the man] *for the sake of Him* [God the Word] *who is hidden—God is unseparated from him* [the man] *who appears*. For that reason *I do not separate the honor of the unseparated one*. I separate the Natures, BUT I UNITE THE BOWING" [that is, "THE WORSHIP"].

And the Fifth Ecumenical Synod (the Second of the three World Synods at Constantinople) A. D. 553, condemned the relative worship of Christ's humanity and anathematized every one who is guilty of it, as follows:

"*Anathema XII. of the Fifth Ecumenical Council:*

"If any one defends Theodore the Impious of Mopsuestia, who said that God the Word is One, and that the Anointed One (τὸν Χριστόν) is another who was troubled by the passions of the soul and the lusts of the flesh, and that little by little he separated himself from the more evil things, and so was rendered better by progress in works, and was made spotless in conduct, and *as a mere Man* was baptized in the name of the Father and of the Son and of the Holy Ghost, and that through the baptism [literally "*through the dipping*"] he received the grace of the Holy Spirit, and was deemed worthy of adoption, and IS TO BE BOWED TO [προσκυνεῖσθαι, that is "IS TO BE WORSHIPPED] FOR THE SAKE OF GOD THE WORD'S PERSON IN THE SAME WAY THAT AN EMPEROR'S IMAGE IS FOR THE SAKE OF THE EMPEROR'S PERSON, and that after his resurrection, he was made blameless in his thoughts and entirely sinless. . . . .

"If any one therefore defends the aforesaid most impious Theodore, and his impious writings, in which he poured forth the above mentioned and numberless other blasphemies against our great God and Saviour Jesus Christ and does not anathemathize him and his impious writings, and all who accept or defend him or who say that he was an Orthodox expounder, and those who have written in his favor and in favor of his impious writings, and those who hold like sentiments, or who at any time have held such sentiments and continued in such heresy till the last, let such a one be anathema."

Speaking of the Ecclesiastical authority of those utterances of the whole Church, we must remember furthermore that Ephesus in its canon VI. deposes every bishop and cleric and excommunicates every laic who disturbs its decisions, and the Fifth World Council inflicts the same penalties of deposition on all bishops and clerics, and anathema on all laics and monks who oppose its Anathema XII. above or any other of its enactments.

And as is shown in note 949, pages 461-463 of Volume I. of Chrystal's *Ephesus*, the Universal Church in its Ecumenical Councils, has no less than thirteen times condemned all relative service to Christ's humanity, and by necessary implication all relative service to any creature less than it, and as all admit all creatures are less than Christ's humanity, be it the Virgin Mary, any saint, archangel, angel, or any other. And much more is all relative service forbidden by necessary implication, to mere inanimate things like images pictured or graven, to altars, crosses, communion tables, relics, the Gospels, or any other part of the Bible, or to any thing else, whether it be by bowing, Exod. xx., 4, 5, 6; Josh. xxiii, 7; Matt. iv., 10; Rev. xix., 10 and xxii., 8, 9; kissing, Hosea xiii , 2, 3, 4; 1 Kings xix., 18; kneeling, 1 Kings xix. 18; prayer, or in any other way.

In short Nestorius' worship of Christ's humanity was based on the old heathen principle of *relative worship*, by which Arnobius, a Christian writer who flourished about A. D. 297, tells us they tried to defend and excuse themselves and their image worship: "Ye say," writes he, "*we worship the gods through the images.*" See in proof his work *Against the Gentiles*, book VI., chapter 9.

It was the same sin as the worship of the golden calf by the Israelites in the wilderness, and of the calf at Bethel and of that at Dan, in the time of the wicked king Ahab, for all these were intended by the deluded to represent Jehovah, the true God, to whom the worship rendered to the calves was intended by them to go. See in proof Chrystal's work *On Creature Worship*.

But Nestorius was too ignorant of God's Word, and of the fundamental principles of Christian worship to know these plain facts.

2. Cyril commends, as do the Scriptures, the noble refusal of the three Hebrew youths to take part in what he expressly calls that "SIN" of worshipping an *Icon*, (εἰκόνι), that is an image, that is an idol. He denominates their "REFUSAL TO WORSHIP A MAN [by the act of religious bowing just mentioned] AND THEIR NOT BEING WILLING TO HOLD THOSE OPINIONS WHICH INSULT AND OUTRAGE THE DIVINE NATURE," ["that is creature serving opinions"] as in accord with the qualities of "FIRMNESS IN FAITH, FIXEDNESS IN PIETY."

Then, 3, he comes to compare the circumstances of the Orthodox in his time with that of the three Hebrew youths, both parties being tempted to the same sin of "*serving a creature.*" He states that the Hebrews were under barbarous tyrants, whereas the Orthodox were under pious Christian Emperors, for either from wise policy or from some other cause, he takes the most forbearing and charitable view of their conduct, though Theodosius II at least, had been very unfair towards him; and so implies that Christians in his time should take courage as having fewer difficulties to contend against than Shadrach and his two companions.

"How" [then], he continues, "shall we give in to our enemies" [that is to the Man-Serving Nestorians, the worshippers of a creature]? "For *even though* PLOTTERS *kindle a furnace, and though they wake the flames of* PERVERSITY, BY BRINGING IN TO US SERVICE TO A MAN" [that is, as the context shows, service to the Man, the perfect and sinless creature put on by God the Word], *"nevertheless we have a God in Heaven; we will bow to HIM.* For, being God by Nature, He became like us, not casting away His BEING GOD," etc.

That is, we will worship His Divinity, not his humanity, and that, as Cyril elsewhere remarks again and again, in consonance with God's own command in Matthew IV, 10, and Isaiah XLII: 8. On that whole topic see under those texts in the *Scripture* Index, page 472, vol. 1. of Chrystal's *Nicaea*, and that in vol 1. of his *Ephesus*. Compare also those Indexes under Rev. XIX: 10, and XXII: 8, 9, and in the latter under Colos. II: 18, and Psalm LXXX: 9, Septuagint, Psalm LXXXI: 9 of our English Version, and Luke IV: 8. Arius' creature worship is found on pages 163-216, vol. 1. of Chrystal's *Nicaea*. Very valuable also against his creature worship are passages from Athanasius' Epiphanius, and others on pages 217-255, vol. 1. of Chrystal's *Nicaea*.

4. He speaks of the Nestorian Man-Worship as *"Bungling"* or *"Evil"* (σκαιότητος). For certainly it lacks logical coherence, for while professing to hold to the command of Christ to *bow to the Lord our God, and to serve Him alone*, the Nestorians served a creature, that is a Man also; for they worshipped both God the Word and the Man in whom He now dwells in Heaven; as they believed it right to worship the Man while he was on earth because of his external *"conjunction"* or *"conjoinment,"* as they termed it, to God the Word, that is, they worshipped His humanity relatively to Him, as the heathen worshipped their images, altars, etc., on the same plea of relative worship.

Moreover, by adding the worship of Christ's humanity to that of the Consubstantial and Coeternal Trinity, God the Father, God the Word, and God the Holy Ghost, they altered, as St. Cyril of Alexandria expressly teaches, the worship of a divine Trinity into the worship of a Quaternity, that is, a Tetrad, a Four, that is, they made our Christian God alone worship (Matt. iv: 10) to be a worship of the uncreated God and a creature together, and so gave God's glory to another, contrary to Isaiah xlii: 8. See in proof under *Tetradism*, page 656, Vol. 1. of *Chrystal's Ephesus*. Compare, for the Decisious of the Third Synod of the Universal Church and of the three after it, on that whole matter, the same volume, note matter on pages 108-112.

Below, 5, he teaches in effect that to maintain that Christ is God is to get *"the greatest possible . . . recompense,"* that is, eternal life; but to deny that doctrine is to cause Christ to deny us before His Father; and as we can not be saved unless he confess us, that means that if we do not believe Him to be God and worship him as such we must be eternally damned. This, of course, is connected with the doctrine of his worship; so that the Orthodox, believing that God the Word was in the Man Christ in the womb and ever afterwards, worshipped Him and not the Man put on by Him; whereas the Nestorians did not believe that the divine Substance of God the Word dwelt in the Man taken on by Him, but inhabited Him by His Spirit only as He did the prophets, and so worshipped that man *relatively* only; that is, for the sake of God the Word. For even their leader, Nestorius himself, admitted that no creature can be worshipped for his own sake, that is, not absolutely; see, for example, his Blasphemy 8, page 461, text, and note 949 there, and his Blasphemy 5, pages 458, 459, and note 935 there, his Blasphemy 14, pages 465, 467, and note 966 there. In Blasphemies 6, 7, 9, 10, and 15, he argues that Christ's humanity can be called *God*, which itself is an act of religious service, *and can be worshipped* also by bowing, the most common act of service and standing for all other such acts, because of its *conjoinment* with God, as he terms it, that is *relatively*, for which he is anathematized by Cyril in his Anathema VIII., and by the whole Church in its approval of it in the Third Synod and in the three after it. See in proof Chrystal's *Ephesus*, vol. 1., the following passages from *Cyril of Alexandria's Long Epistle to Nestorius*, approved by the whole Church, in its last four Ecumenical Synods, A. D. 431-680, namely, pages 331, 332, text, and notes 676, 677, 678 and 679 there; pages 217 to 223 inclusive;

The Synodicon of Monte Casino.   241

MATTER ON THE APOSTATIC SANHEDRIM IN COLETI BETWEEN ACTS VI.
AND VII. OF THE THIRD ECUMENICAL SYNOD: AND ADDITIONAL MATTER ON
THE APOSTATIC SANHEDRIM, FROM THE WORK, WHICH BECAUSE IT WAS FOUND
IN THE LIBRARY OF MONTE CASSINO HAS BEEN CALLED THE SYNODICON OF
MONTE CASINO, (SYNODICON CASINENSE), WHICH IS A MODIFIED FORM OF THE
NESTORIAN COUNT IRENAEUS' WORK ENTITLED TRAGEDY.

INDEX OF THIS MATTER.

See it in the *Table of Contents* at the beginning of this work.

[Most of the following Documents, though not at all a part of the Acts of the Third Ecumenical Synod are put next in Coleti because, I presume, of their historic value in explaining things in the Acts of the Ecumenical Synod.]

In Mansi they are found under the Greek title:

"THE ACTS OF THE APOSTATIC SANHEDRIM (378). The rest are from the Synodicon of Irenaeus the Nestorian. Not one of the whole is any part of the Acts of the Third Ecumenical Synod, but they are put here for the information which they contain bearing on the Council of the Orthodox, and on the opposition to it.

THE SYNODICON OF MONTE CASINO.

(THE SYNODICON CASINENSE).

Certain documents from the above named work are inserted in Hardouin's Concilia among the Documents on the Apostatic Sanhedrim which are not inserted there in Coleti or in Mansi, or in the Collectio Regia. The value of that Synodicon becomes therefore a matter of importance for us to decide.

Stephen Baluze in a Preface to his *Nova Collectio* as quoted col. 235-238 of tom. IV. of Coleti's Concilia gives the following account of it.

He states that in A. D. 1677 there came into his hands two old copies of an ancient Latin translation of the Council at Ephesus; that in one of them, or in the Contian edition, he found a Commonitory given by Pope Celestine to his Legates who were present at the Synod of Ephesus, that he himself wrote to Cardinal Jerome Casanata asking him to order searches to be made in the old Codexes in the Vatican library for that Commonitory; and that the Cardinal kindly granted his request, and sent him a copy of it from a codex in the Vatican, and that, besides, the Cardinal wrote to Venice, Florence and Milan, and gave an order to find out whether any thing of the kind could be found in the library of the monastery of Monte Cassino. As the result of the quest in

---

and 238-240, inclusive; and as to the Ecumenical approval and authority of that document, see the note on pages 205-208, there, and pages 79-82 of his *Shorter Epistle to Nestorius* which was approved by vote in Act I. of the Third Ecumenical Council.

NOTE 378—Or, "*The Acts of the Apostatic small council.*" Τὰ πρακτικὰ τοῦ Ἀποστατικοῦ Συνεδρίου. It was Apostatic, as Cyril, quoted in this work, shows again and again, because of its denial of the Incarnation, its Man-Service, Cannibalism on the Eucharist, etc., and for supporting those guilty of maintaining those iniquities, contrary to the Universal Church represented in its Third Synod.

the last mentioned place he shows that the *Synodicon Casinense,* that is the *Synodicon of Monte Cassino,* as it is termed, was brought to light. I translate the rest of Baluze's Preface here because it bears on this *Synodicon.* It is as follows :

"Two most ancient codexes were found, in which were contained very many Records pertaining to the Council of Ephesus and to that of Chalcedon. The same most eminent Cardinal made use of the service of a man of much reading, Christian Lupus, an Augustinian, who then happened to be at Rome, to go over them and to examine them. But he at once determined to publish them all, and prevailed on the Cardinal not to permit any one to copy them, nor to publish them, unless he was willing. Then not so [very] long after, Lupus published them, but so carelessly that he did not even tell what title that collection has in the Monte Cassino books, what order is preserved in it, what is omitted, [and] what is changed by himself. For learned readers sufficiently understand that very many things were omitted and changed by him. I left nothing untried by which I might become a possessor of the things which are contained in those Monte Cassino Codexes, but so great and so pertinacious was the obstinacy of the monks of that monastery that I could not get it from them by any art or by any prayers. If I had not suffered a repulse I could have written many notes on things which have been passed by by Lupus, and by my remarks on them very much utility might have redounded to the public. And so I have determined to give that collection as it was published by Lupus. But before I come to it, I will say a few things by way of preface regarding that work and its author.

It is certainly the work of a man writing after Justinian; who, besides, was a defender of the Three Chapters, and, (unless the conjecture is deceptive), it was the work of an African. That is inferred from chapter 193, where we read as follows :

"'Did they not, through the Emperor Justinian, with all the power of the whole world conspiring with them, try during a period of almost thirty years to procure a most bitter condemnation of the writings of Theodore and of Ibas, and of Theodoret?'* Surely he everywhere shows himself to be a friend of Cyril of Alexandria, of Theodoret, and of Ibas, and an adversary of Nestorius and of his followers. Furthermore, he entitled his collection *Synodicon,* as is evident from the end of Chapter 205. But he has written against the books which Irenaeus, the friend of Nestorius, called *Tragedy,* that is, perhaps a *Prophecy of an urgent Decree,* as Anastasius says in his Ecclesiastical History, page 51, out of Theophanes, regarding a similar book. For that reason, inasmuch as we do not know what title this Collection has in the Codex of Monte Cassino, we have called it a *Synodicon against the Tragedy of Irenaeus.* But it was copied from a Codex of the Monasterium Acoemetensis [*"the Monastery of the Sleepless,"* at Constantinople? CHRYSTAL], as is inferred from the end of the first chapter, and from chapter 22 and 221."

Sevestre, in his *Dictionnaire de Patrologie*, (Migne, Paris, 1854), under "Irénée, Comte de l'empire du temps de Théodose le Jeune," after stating that Count Irenaeus represented the Emperor Theodosius the Younger at the Third Ecumenical Synod, and that he opposed the Orthodox party, tells us further that on account of his opposition to the Council he was banished by the Emperor to Petra and that his goods were confiscated; and that there, while he was still a laic, he composed his work which is entitled *Tragedy*.

"That work," he adds, "is divided into many books from which are drawn almost all the pieces which compose the Synodical Collection published at first by Father Lupus and afterwards by Baluze and Garnier in the *Appendix to the Councils* (379). The aim of Count Irenaeus there is to justify Nestorius and those who had remained attached to his party to the end, among others Alexander of Hierapolis, of whom he always speaks with praise. A part of that work is employed to report what passed at Alexandria in the negotiation for the peace which was concluded in 433. The author defends himself in it with a certain energy and condemns not only Saint Cyril and the Egyptians, but furthermore, John of Antioch and all the Bishops of the Orient who had embraced the peace [between Cyril and John], and praises with a surprising obstinacy those who continued to remain separated from the Church. He did not publish it until after the troubles which arose in regard to Theodore of Mopsuestia in 437 or 438. But having obtained his liberty and his recall, on entering into the communion of the Church, Irenaeus was made Bishop of Tyre by Domnus of Antioch."

Although I have not time here to go into details, my own impression is that this work is the *Tragedy* of Irenaeus with later additions by some friend of the Three Chapters, and perhaps alterations also by him. Baluze wrote of it before certain facts were well known. This work seems to have suffered the fate of many another, in being altered to make it more saleable, as we have seen elsewhere, vol. I, p. 101, note, that Philip of Side's large work did. We have seen Philip's name dropped from his own work, and Cyril of Alexandria's name put in its place, and how that work was altered to make it more marketable. I infer that this has been the case with this work of Irenaeus. His name, as being that of one who was a heretic when he wrote it, and who afterwards, when he had become reconciled to the Church and had become Bishop of Tyre, was removed from it for being a digamist, though his fellow heretic Theodoret of Cyrus who had favored his ordination would like to have had him remain; his name, I say, would not help the sale of a work. And so the unprincipled fellow, Jew or Christian, who owned it, and had probably paid his money for

NOTE 379.—Sevestre *Dictionnaire de Patrologie*, article "*Irenée*, Comte." Ce fut là apparemment qu'il composa son ouvrage intitulé *Tragedie* . . . Cet ouvrage est divisé en plusieurs livres d'où sont tirées presque toutes les pièces qui composent le recueil Synodique, publié d'abord par le P. Lupus et ensuite par Baluze et Garnier dans *l'Appendice des Conciles.*

it, and did not wish to lose, would naturally omit Irenaeus' name or forge another, and perhaps alter it to help its sale. In this case the work seems to have fallen into the hands of some friend of the Three Chapters, and finding it to favor his ideas, he would naturally take it up, add to it matter pertaining to Chalcedon, etc., and do what he could to circulate it, with his own ideas attached to it here and there, for greater fulness. Perhaps then his copy had not Irenaeus' name. This would make him more unsuspecting. Even if it had, he might not have known enough of his history to tell whether he was Orthodox or not.

If, it be true, as Baluze above asserts, that the work as now published, is friendly to Cyril of Alexandria, to Theodoret and to Ibas, and is opposed to Nestorius, that would be precisely the position of the illogical party who were opposed to the condemnation of the Three Chapters. Yet after all changes and remarks by him, the great bulk of the work seems to be derived from Irenaeus' *Tragedy*. The remarks of the erring translator or copyist are but a small part of the whole.

Since writing the above I have found on page 106 of Volume III. of Hefele's *History of the Church Councils*, a reference to the above work, which is confirmatory of the judgment expressed, for he speaks of it as *"the Synodicon of Irenaeus."* Moreover, in the same p'ace, referring to a document below mentioned, that is the *"memorial"* sent to the Emperor Theodosius by the delegates of John of Antioch's Apostatic Synod from Chalcedon, he adds, "of which we no longer possess the Greek original, but of which we have two ancient Latin translations, diverging considerably from each other, *and in many places evidently* CORRUPT. On the whole, that text which is given by the *Synodicon* of Irenaeus (in Mansi, t. v., p. 802, sqq.) is less corrupt than the other (in Mansi, t. IV., p. 1401; and Hardouin, t. I., p. 1563), so that for the most part we adhere to the former."

There is, then, much that is corrupted in this altered work of Irenaeus, though such corruption is by no means confined to it. Indeed, Hefele in the case of the document above mentioned preferred the rendering in this work of Irenaeus to the other. So we give the Documents in Coleti between Acts VI. and VII. of the Third Ecumenical Council and those from Irenaeus' Work together, arranging them as nearly as I know how, in the order of time. But where a Document is from the *Synodicon* of Irenaeus, I will endeavor to inform the reader.

Another and a very important inquiry at this point is as to its *truthfulness*. I did at first look upon all its statements on critical points as doubtful unless they are verified from Orthodox sources, as now I think most of them are, though I deemed that some or most of the Documents might be unaltered and genuine. But I deemed it corrupted in places. And as it is the work of a heretic, and a pleader for creature-worshipping Nestorians, I must receive it with caution and reserve unless verified from Orthodox sources.

Baluze, above quoted, admits that he did not even know the title of the work in the Monte Cassino manuscript, and states that Lupus had so *"carelessly"* edited it *"that he did not even tell what title that collection has in the Monte Casino books, what order is preserved in it, what is* OMITTED [and] *what is* CHANGED BY HIMSELF. *For learned readers sufficiently understand that* VERY MANY *things were* CHANGED AND OMITTED BY HIM."

If Lupus changed it, I cannot surmise what motive could have induced him to so alter it, or the Monte Cassino monks to be so chary of letting Baluze see it, unless they deemed it an heretical production and therefore unfit to be published because of the harm which it might do. Whether any persons were desirous of selling it, and were fearful that it would bring much less, if its true heretical character were known, I know not.

But I deem that the bulk of it is Irenaeus', for Sevestre expressly says that:

"ALMOST ALL *the pieces which compose the* SYNODICAL COLLECTION, *published at first by Father Lupus and afterwards by Baluze and Garnier in the Appendix to the Councils,*" are drawn from Irenaeus' *Tragedy*. In other words, it is confessed that most of that *Synodicon* is Irenaeus' production.

In addition we have the additions and, possibly, though I am not sure, changes wrought in it by some partisan of the heretical *Three Chapters;* and lastly, we have the fact testified to by Baluze above, that "*learned readers sufficiently understand that* VERY MANY *things were omitted and changed by*" Lupus himself. After all these changes we can not be sure that we are reading what the heretic Irenaeus wrote, or the alteration, or entire production of a later hand.

Yet as it seems though corrupted to belong with some other utterances of the Nestorian party here in Coleti, I shall therefore put all the Documents which I epitomize from that somewhat interpolated and heretical work of Irenaeus, with the said other Nestorian documents.

Indeed, since writing the above and on further comparing in certain of these writings, the same heretical document in the *Synodicon* with it in tome III. of Coleti, I often find the renderings in the Synodicon more in agreement with the facts of that time; so that it is often preferable, perhaps generally, though not always to it. Indeed, I do not know that either translation was made by an Orthodox man.

This Synodicon of Irenaeus contains much of value to Ecclesiastical History where its utterances are verified.

I would add that as given by Lupus, the different documents are not all arranged in chronological order. For instance, Chapter XXXIX. precedes in the order of time Chapter XVII., and Chapter XVIII. precedes in the same order Chapter XVII. I have epitomized those documents below. I will arrange them in their order of time to each other and to other documents.

Furthermore as *to the name* of this work. Baluze, as above, shows that its name is not given by Lupus, but he infers, from the end of Chapter CCV. of it, that it was termed *Synodicon*. On turning to that I find that the advocate of the Three Chapters and opponent of the Fifth Ecumenical Synod who wrote the comments there on the Epistle of Cyril of Alexandria which forms the bulk of that Chapter, writes as follows at the end of his remarks:

"We beseech you, by Christ, all ye who read, study to remember what we have said, and that, for that very reason, we have translated other similar writings also into Latin in this *Synodicon*" [or "*Synodical Work*"]. The expression in Latin, "*in hoc Synodico*," may mean that the work was called "*Synodicon*," or only that it was "*a Synodical work*," whose title we know not. It is *Synodical* because it treats of the Ecumenical Synod of Ephesus, and that of Chalcedon, and was probably written at some time between A. D. 553, the date of the Fifth Ecumenical Synod, which it opposes, and A. D. 680, the date of the Sixth, after which opposition to the Fifth and its condemnation of the Three Chapters died out in the West, to which the translator seems to have belonged.

As to the *manuscript from which this translation was made*. Baluze infers that it was made from one in the *Acoemitensian Monastery*, that is *the Monastery of the Sleepless*. The expression here used for *sleepless* is Greek, and seems possibly to refer to that monastery of the *Sleepless*, which was in the vicinity of Constantinople, where prayer was going on day and night always. Hence the monks of it, as Sophocles in his Greek *Lexicon of the Roman and Byzantine Periods*, shows, were called οἱ Ἀκοίμητοι, that is, "*the Sleepless*." See under ἀκοίμητος in that work. On that matter I find at the end of chapter 1., the expression, "*It is XCI. in the* [manuscript, or in the library] *of the Sleepless*." Or, "*It is in the ninety-first Chapter*," [or "*in the ninety-first work*"] *in* [the library of the monastery] "*of the Sleepless*" (380). But whether that note was written by the original translator or by a scholiast or by some other I know not.

I have looked in Photius' *Myriobiblon* to see whether he mentions Irenaeus' "*Tragedy*," but he says not a word of it there. In chapter XVI., however, of that work, he speaks of the book called *The Acts of the Third Synod* (πρακτικὸν τῆς Τρίτης Συνόδου), but from the description he gives of it, I do not think he means the *Tragedy* of Irenaeus.

Since writing the above I have found the "Praemonitio" of Mansi on this *Synodicon*, in col. 551, 552 of tome 84 of *Migne's Patrologia Graeca*. He mentions additional facts of much importance.

The chief ones are as follows:

1. The Monte Casino Codex of this work has no title, so that he states that Baluze had no cause for faulting Lupus for publishing it without any. Mansi, however, for convenience sake retains the title put upon it by Baluze, that is because the learned had then become accustomed to it. It is "*Synodicon against the Tragedy of Irenaeus*."

2. Mansi divides the work into chapters, though he states that "*The*

NOTE 330.—Coleti *Conc.*, tom. IV., col. 252. "*In Acoemitensium jacet XCI.*'

documents are numbered only in the Codex of Monte Casino." He adds further in the same place, *"But be on your guard against believing that those documents succeed each other in order in that Codex. Lupus selected from here and there"* [in it] *"the unpublished ones which he stumbled upon."* I have not seen the work of Lupus in his own edition, but the number of chapters in the "Index of Chapters," in Coleti, 225, is exactly the same as in tome 84 of Migne's *Patrologia Graeca*. I do not understand them, however, to be the *whole* work as in the Codex of Monte Casino, though I do not feel certain as to this. But in tome 84 of Migne some things are given more fully in this Synodicon than they are in Coleti, and it seems to have some document or documents which are not in Coleti, as, for instance, a commonitory of Pope Celestine at the end, which is not in Coleti there. In Migne I find cap. "ccxxv.," the heading of the last chapter in Coleti, and the last but one in Migne, followed by the figures "314" in brackets. But what the "314" means I know not. Does it mean that document 225 in the published form is document 314 in the manuscript of Monte Casino?

In Hardouin the following documents of John of Antioch's *"Apostatic Conventicle"* are headed in Latin:

"HERE BEGIN THE SECOND SET OF LIES OF THE SYNOD WHICH CONVENED WITH JOHN, BISHOP OF ANTIOCH IN EPHESUS" (*Harduin. Conc., tom I., col.* 1531). It is chapter XII. in *Irenaeus' Synodicon*.

By the *second set of lies* is meant the emanations of the Conventicle addressed to the Emperor, &c., in its second session and after.

Mansi (*Conc. tom.* IV., *col.* 1735), note, writes on the above:

" Hardouin here brings in a '*Second Set of Lies of the Synod which convened with John, Bishop of Antioch, in Ephesus,*' and '*An Epistle of the Synod of the Orientals,*' from the *Synodicon Casinense*. We will bring it in below with the entire Synodicon out of Baluze."

[I give it here with Hardouin. JAMES CHRYSTAL.]

DOCUMENT I. FROM JOHN OF ANTIOCH'S "APOSTATIC CONVENTICLE."
(It is given in Hardouin here in Latin alone.)

THIS IS AN ACCOUNT OF A FORMAL CONVERSATION BETWEEN JOHN, BISHOP OF ANTIOCH, ANd COUNT CANDIDIAN IN THE PRESENCE OF JOHN'S SYNOD.

That Synod also takes part in it. Its impudence reaches the sublime. John tells the Count that the Orthodox Synod (which, as we have seen was about 200 in number and had acted in strict accordance with the canons in its controversy with the handful of the Nestorian Conventicle), had done all things unjustly and forbiddenly, and were guilty of rashness and pertinacity, because, that is, seemingly, they had not submitted to the ideas of the handful of creature servers led by Nestorius and John, that therefore he, John, and his Synod, or John alone, had in writing asked the Count to go to the Orthodox Synod, and to protest against their meeting, on the ground that *"some of them had been justly deposed, and others of them deprived of communion on account of their heretical madness,"* etc., by the Apostatic Handful of the Conventicle. John then asks the Count whether he had told the Orthodox Council. The Count replied that after he had received John's petition aforesaid, he did not give any warning, because there was no reason to do so. He adds that he had gone to see *"the most reverent,* the Bishops, Cyril and Memnon, and the rest" of the Orthodox, and that he had found the most [or "very many" *plurimos*] assembled *"there with them"*; that he had asked them, 1, not to celebrate the Eucharist by themselves; and 2, to wait for the reply from the Emperors as to what they (the Orthodox Synod) had already done. Candidian adds "I wish neither party to celebrate a meeting, lest perchance some schism be generated in the holy and Orthodox Church."

Candidian's language implies that he still regarded Cyril of Alexandria and Memnon as Bishops, and that therefore he did not recognize the deposition pronounced by John and his Synod, and that he was not now so decided against the Orthodox Synod as John of Antioch and his party were.

JOHN'S SYNOD next ask the Count whether Cyril and Memnon and the Orthodox had learned of the deposition of Cyril and Memnon and the excommunication of the rest of them by their Conventicle; and they further state that they had set it forth throughout the whole city in order that it might become known to the Bishops of Cyril's party, that is the Orthodox.

COUNT CANDIDIAN in reply states that being so widely published it must be known to Cyril and Memnon; that the whole city were co-murmuring in regard to it, and that a great multitude had taken copies of it. He adds that when he asked the Orthodox Synod not to celebrate the Eucharist on the Lord's Day, Memnon Bishop of Ephesus "said before them all: I have ascertained as much as that the most holy Bishop John and the Synod which is with him have deposed even us. I will not say that he has been able to prevail in any thing whatsoever against this Synod. Believe that he could not have prevailed even against me alone, without a Synod" [at my back]. The Count subjoins that inasmuch as that language implied that he knew of his deposition by John and his Synod, it was superfluous to ask him whether he knew of it.

John's Synod next ask the Count whether Cyril and the Orthodox Council had obeyed his counsels and warning not to meet together at all. This question seems to betray a fear on their part of consequences to themselves, which indeed came to them in the form of their own deposition or suspension from communion by the Orthodox Synod.

Count Candidian replied:

"On the Sabbath itself [Saturday in our time] at evening I made the request, and on the following day at the very dawn I went to the most reverent Cyril, that is on the Lord's Day, and did not cease to ask and to entreat that he would yield to my demand" [or, "to my request"]. "But they would not acquiesce, but went out and made an assembly. I was not able to contend against them further" A weaker man than Cyril would have given way. But he knew he was right, and so went ahead to do God's work. And the time demanded it.

John's small Synod then brand the lawful action of the great bulk of the Ecumenical Council as audacious and forbidden, and state that they will report it to the Emperors, who, by the way, were their great hope, and not the Orthodoxy of the Universal Church. And so this document 1. ends.

DOCUMENT II. OF THE APOSTATIC CONVENTICLE.

THIS IS AN EPISTLE OF JOHN'S SYNOD TO THE CLERGY AND PEOPLE IN HIERAPOLIS IN EUPHRATESIA, WHICH WAS IN JOHN'S PATRIARCHATE.

It is in Latin alone in Hardouin here. It is chapter XIII. in the *Synodicon* of Irenaeus. From it we learn that the Ecumenical Synod had written or were likely to write letters to the Churches, and this seems perhaps to be a circular designed to frustrate them. It slanders the Ecumenical Synod by charging them with attempting to destroy the right faith, speaks of them as doing evil in despair of their own salvation, and states that they, (the Nestorian Conventicle), had deposed some of the Ecumenical Synod and excommunicated others, because of their signing what it calls "*Cyril's heretical Sentence,*" or "*opinions,*" and claims that the Apostatic Synod was standing up for the faith of Nicaea, and exhorts the Hierapolitans to side with them. Strangely enough, the Second Ecumenical Synod is not as yet even mentioned in the Minutes of the Third Ecumenical Synod or in those of the Apostatic Conventicle.

This Second Document is signed by fifty-three bishops, two of whom, Bosphorus, Metropolitan Bishop of Gangra, and Flaccus, Bishop of Laodicea;. marginal notes in Hardouin here tell us, were among the subscribers to Act I. of the Orthodox Synod. The example of those weak and too-easily frightened brethren did not affect many, for about four-fifths of the whole number of those who had assembled stood firm for God against serving any creature, and for the Incarnation, and against Nestorian views on the Eucharist, and against relative worship. Throughout these Documents, the Apostatic Council,

1. Continually speaks of its own little fragment and minority as the Synod, and the Ecumenical Synod as no part of it practically.

2. It mentions the noble stand of the Synod for sound doctrine as a stand for heresy, and as a wanton troubling of the Church. Such is the logic of all such sinners from the beginning, which is couched in the words of the creature-serving King Ahab to Elijah, "*Is it thou, thou troubler of Israel?*" (I. Kings xviii: 17). And as God's faithful and uncompromising prophet answers: "*I have not troubled Israel; but thou, and thy father's house, in that ye have forsaken the commandments of Jehovah, and thou hast followed the Baalim*" (I. Kings xviii: 18, Canterbury Revision); so Cyril might have answered, *I have not troubled the Church, but thou, John of Antioch and Nestorius, and Theodoret, of Cyrus, and Theodore of Mopsuestia, and Diodore of*

Tarsus, in that ye have forsaken the truth that every act of religious service is prerogative to God, and have brought in the innovation of giving relative religious worship to a CREATURE, that is to the perfect man, put on by God the Word, and by denying the doctrine of the Incarnation, and by corrupting the doctrine of the Eucharist by bringing in the absurdity of the Real Presence of the substance of God the Word's humanity in that rite, and the cannibalism of eating it there.

But there are many instances to-day when, if you oppose the innovations of creature worshippers, they will lay all the blame upon you for standing up for God, and charge upon you all the trouble which they make because they refuse to be reformed. Compare Psalm l: 16, 17, Prayer Book Version.

Throughout these Documents they seem to take it for granted that they are writing to a very gullible lot, and act on the principle, "*Lie stoutly, and some of it will stick.*" What else could have prompted the Herculean lie to the Hierapolitans mentioned above, where they say that Cyril and the Ecumenical Council were troubling the churches because they were in despair of their own salvation ! ! ! Some of their lies were detected by those whom they would have duped. Others, alas! were not, but are believed by the Nestorians or others to this day.

DOCUMENT III. OF THE APOSTATIC SYNOD.—*Document I. in Mansi and Coleti here.*

This is headed "*A Report of the Orientals*" [that is, the Bishops of the Patriarchate of the Orient, which was John of Antioch's] "*to the Emperor: to which they had prefixed the Symbol of the holy Fathers in Nicaea. These Orientals Report what had been defined by the Holy and Ecumenical Synod as to the statements* (381) *presented to it by the most holy Cyril and Memnon. This Report was sent to Count Irenaeus, and through him was transmitted to the Emperor.*" This seems to be chapter XIV. of the *Synodicon*.

This Report is a marvellous instance of the "*We, the people of England,*' of the three tailors of Tooley Street, London. It is at most the voice of about one-fifth of the whole Synod, trying and deposing or excommunicating the other four-fifths.

It lyingly accuses the Orthodox Synod of making a mock of the great and secret mysteries of the Church as though on a stage and a theatre, "*For,*" it adds, "*Cyril and Memnon, who had been deposed by us on account of their many infractions of law and because of their holding the impious opinion of Apolinarius* (382), *which opinion we have found in the Chapters* (383) *sent*

NOTE 381.—Greek, τοῖς λιβέλλοις.

NOTE 382.—The notorious heretic. The Nestorians in their ignorance or malice were prone to call Cyril and the Orthodox *Apollinarians*.

NOTE 383.—Cyril's XII chapters at the end of his long Epistle to Nestorius.

forth by him, gave in statements (384) *as we have now learned, to the rest of those who had done those unrighteous acts and had subscribed those heretical Chapters* (385). The reference here is to the statements presented to the Third Ecumenical Synod by Cyril and Memnon in its fourth Act, against the Action of the heretical Conventicle in deposing them and in suspending the rest of the Orthodox Synod from Communion, in response to which it had declared the whole farcical proceeding of the minority invalid, and had suspended John of Antioch himself and all his partisans of the Apostatic Council from Communion, till they should repent. And all the Orthodox had afterwards communed in the Eucharist together, as the custom then was on every Lord's Day. This was, according to the impudence of John and his partisans, to make a mock of the mysteries, that is, of the Sacraments. Then this Nestorian Council go on, humorously and childishly enough, to complain that the about four-fifths of the Synod whom the Nestorian about one-fifth had suspended from the Communion, had not recognized the right of the one-fifth to depose Cyril and Memnon and to suspend the about four-fifths of the Synod, who stood by them, from the Communion; but had actually called the small minority to account for usurping the name and authority of the whole Ecumenical Council. Then remembering, seemingly, that when summoned they did not dare to face the music and have their minority weakness and wind-bag pretensions exposed, and had begun to hedge, they tell the Emperor piteously enough that at that point they told the Orthodox Synod that they ought to wait for the Emperor's decree on the matter, as though the Emperor had a right to usurp the functions of Bishops and practically override the decisions on faith of an Ecumenical Synod! Though John and most of his small faction were Bishops, yet in that remark they voluntarily degraded themselves, in their hatred of sound doctrine, under the boot taps of a weak secular ruler to induce him to do the outrageous thing of enabling an heretical creature serving one-fifth of the Ecumenical Synod to override the Orthodox four-fifths. *"Then,"* say they, when summoned by the Orthodox Synod, the great majority of all, *"we answered fitly that we ought to await the decrees of your Piety, and this we said twice or thrice" ! ! !* Then they complain that the Ecumenical Synod had not recognized the action of the handful of heretics in usurping the functions and prerogative of the Ecumenical Synod and in deposing Cyril and Memnon and in excommunicating the other about four-fifths. This course they call *"violation of law."* Then they ask the Emperor to recognize the action of the Nestorian one-fifth of the Synod as that of the whole and to support them with his authority! They do not, however, mention the smallness of their proportion, but try to give the idea that they are the Synod.

"But if this suggestion is not approved by your Serenity, we beg that we

---

NOTE 384.—Greek, λιβέλλους.

NOTE 385.—*Mansi Conc.*, tom. iv., col. 1372.

may be summoned to Nicomedia, in order that we may more easily make known to your Mightiness what is being done, and may receive the commands of your Piety."

The baseness of this proposal is beneath contempt. They were willing, seemingly, to degrade themselves into the very dirt to induce a weak, not to say a superstitious secular ruler to override the voice of the Universal Church legitimately and canonically expressed by the great Orthodox majority of an Ecumenical Synod lawfully assembled. They were willing to get near that mere layman and accept his commands or decrees (386), his usurpation of the Christ-given duties and prerogative functions of the Episcopate. They probably felt sure, from the tone of this Emperor's letter of censure to Cyril of Alexandria before the Council, that he was their man, and that he would become their accomplice in stifling the voice of the Ecumenical Synod, or rather the Voice of the promised Holy Spirit, the Comforter, speaking through the Orthodox Synod: that Spirit who was to be with the Apostolate forever to guide them into all truth (387). And their base trickery would have succeeded unless God's power had intervened to help His servants, and had stirred up help for them among pastors and people throughout the Christian world.

Next they make the crafty proposal that the Emperor order that no more than two Bishops and the Metropolitan shall be summoned from each province, to sit in the new Council at Nicomedia, "*For*," they add with deep design, '*a multitude is superfluous in the investigation of dogma, and they know only to work up tumults.*" Then they speak of the Orthodox majority as relying on their number but not on truth and on correctness of dogma, and as having a design to obtain their ends by their multitude and by the multitude of their subscriptions also. Then flatteringly they tell the Emperor of their devotion on the other hand, to his decrees; and tell him that considering that a few would be sufficient to make an examination of the dogmas involved, they had come only three from each province.

The guile of all this lies here. Under Antioch were about ten or twelve provinces, which would give thirty to thirty-six votes; under Alexandria only about three to nine or ten, which would give from nine to thirty votes.

This would at once banish from the Council many or most of the fifty Orthodox Egyptians who had come with Cyril, and give Man-serving Antioch as compared with God alone serving Alexandria a clear majority.

And with the Emperor's aid and with the management of the Council given up into his hands, they could hope to worry out the Bishops of Asia Minor and of Pontus, and the more easily and swiftly if the weak Emperor should accede to their request to regard Cyril and Memnon as deposed and the rest of the Orthodox Ecumenical Synod as suspended from communion and as incapable

---

NOTE 386, -τοὺς τῆς ὑμετέρας εὐσεβείας . . . τύπους.

NOTE 387.—John xiv: 16, 17. Compare Matt. xviii: 15-19, and xxviii: 19, 20, and I. Tim. iii: 15.

Lies of the Apostatic Conventicle against the Third Synod. 253

of sitting (as the Nestorian party assert in this document), till that suspension by the heretical one-fifth should be removed. Till that was done the one-fifth would be the Ecumenical Synod, and would exclude the 200 so long as would suit their own ends.

Then the Nestorian Conventicle ask the Emperor "*to command all to subscribe to the Faith* (τῇ . . . πίστει) *of Nicaea, which*, say they, *we have prefixed to this our letter, and to add nothing foreign to it, and not to assert that our Lord Jesus Christ is a ψere man, for he is perfect God and perfect man; and not to introduce a passible Divinity of Christ* (τοῦ Χριστοῦ), *for either of those assertions is equally rash.*" And with that ends their epistle. The object of this last fling seems to have been to give the Emperor the idea by innuendo that the Ecumenical Synod did not hold to the Symbol of the First Ecumenical Synod, though they had approved it and had it read in their first Act; and to imply that their real Incarnation, anti-Man-serving sense of it, was something "*foreign*," to it, and an *addition* to it, while their Nestorian anti-real Incarnation, Man-serving sense, was in accordance with it, and to convey the false notion that the Ecumenical Synod were Monophysites, that is believers in Christ's Divine nature only, hence that they denied the reality of Christ's human nature, and so they introduced *a passible Divinity of Christ*, though Cyril and the Council show by their language that they were perfectly Orthodox on all those points.

Two things the Nestorian Separatists from the Synod suppress,

1. The fact that they were only a small minority, about one fifth of those assembled.

2. The fact that they had all been suspended from communion by the Ecumenical Synod, and that very justly.

These facts might be very unpleasant things for the Emperor to know, for they might militate against them.

DOCUMENT IV. OF THE APOSTATIC COUNCIL.—*Document II. in Mansi and Coleti here.*

(It is Chapter XXII. in the *Synodicon*.)

This bears the heading "*On the Schismatics*," and has the following title:
"THE HOLY SYNOD, BOTH THAT OF THE ORIENTAL DIOCESE (388) AND THOSE ASSEMBLED WITH THEM OUT OF DIFFERENT DIOCESES, AND PROVINCES [that is] BITHYNIA, PISIDIA, AND THE SECOND CAPPADOCIA, PAPHLAGONIA, EUROPA, [that is the Province Europa in Thrace] MYSIA, RHODOPE, [and] THESSALY, have discoursed what here follows": (389.)

NOTE 388.—Greek, διοικήσεως.

NOTE 389.—Greek, ἐκ διαφόρων διοικήσεων καὶ ἐπαρχιῶν. According to Bingham's *Antiquities of the Christian Church*, book IX., chapter I., there were about a hundred and twenty Provinces included in thirteen civil *dioceses*, or *governments* in the Roman Empire; and the Church in Canon VI. of the Second Ecumenical Synod, I. Constantinople,

This document, like others which emanate from the Apostatic Synod, is

A. D., 381, followed that division, and made the Bishop of the chief city of every such Diocese a Patriarch, as Socrates in explaining that canon states in chapter 8 of book V. of his *Ecclesiastical History*. Sometimes they were, practically, national Churches, as was the case with Latin Africa under Carthage; Egypt and some adjoining territories under Alexandria; the Syriac Diocese of the East under Antioch, etc. So Britain, Gaul and Spain were Dioceses, though as yet their Diocesan Churches were not so prominent as those just mentioned. Indeed, they were then corrupting and therefore scourged by the barbarians. Rome itself seems to have had as its jurisdiction not all of Italy, but as Bingham in his *Antiquities*, book IX., chapter I., sections 9, 10, 11 and 12 shows, only the seven Provinces of South Italy and the three islands, Sicily, Sardinia and Corsica. North Italy was under Milan. Rome had no canonical or rightful jurisdiction outside of Italy, aye, none outside of the seven Provinces and the three Islands just specified. All her claim to jurisdiction in Britain, Gaul, Spain, or elsewhere outside of Italy, even when she was sound in faith was wholly without foundation, and was never admitted in the Eastern Patriarchates. And now that she is idolatrous and heretical, and has trodden under foot the decisions of the VI. Ecumenical Synods, she has no jurisdiction anywhere, but all her Bishops and clergy are deposed and all her people are anathematized by them. In brief, she is the Harlot of the Revelations, as John in effect clearly explains: "And the woman whom thou sawest is that great city which reigneth over the Kings of the earth." Rev. xvii: 18. And that description fitted Rome alone in John's day, as the early Christian writers saw, and therefore God bids His faithful ones to come out of her under dread penalties implying eternal damnation: "And I heard another voice from heaven, saying: Come out of her, my people, in order that ye be not partakers of her sins, and in order that ye may not receive of her plagues." Rev. xviii: 4.

How blessed those nations were and are who obeyed that call from Heaven and came out of her at the Reformation, let England, Scotland, Protestant Germany, the Scandinavian countries, Holland, and ourselves, their descendants, testify. How cursed they were and are who disobeyed that call, partook of the sins of her spiritual whoredom, that is, image worship and saint worship, and cross worship and altar worship and wafer worship and relic worship, let Spain, once mighty, but now stripped of her colonies and wealth, and Austria, France, with revolution upon revolution, and losses of territory to the Protestant powers, and Italy and Ireland, who have received of her plagues, witness.

Another thing, therefore, we must remember from that action of the Second Council of the whole Church in establishing Patriarchates, and it is that they based whatever privileges Rome and Constantinople had in the Church in that day on their rank in the civil notitia, that is, as secular capitals, not at all on any alleged claim of divine right, and, in that they were followed by the Fourth Ecumenical Council, A. D., 451, in its Canon XXVIII.

Besides, the Second Synod, in their Canon VI., forbade Bishops to invade the territory of other sound Bishops, which much more forbids the invasion of the God alone worshipping Diocese of Britain or any other Protestant land, by the idolatrous so-called Bishop of Rome. See that canon.

Socrates here writes of the action of the Second Synod:

"And they confirmed again the faith of Nicaea, and they appointed Patriarchs and distributed the Provinces" [under each], "so that the Bishop over a Diocese should not invade the churches beyond its boundaries, for that had been done formerly without any distinction on account of the persecutions."

See further under *Diocese*, page 602, vol. I. of Chrystal's *Ephesus*, under *Appeal*, on page 573, and *Church Government*, on page 582; and in vol. I. of Chrystal's *Nicaea*, page 433, under *Appellate Jurisdiction;* on page 463, under *Rome, Church of*, and *Rome, Bishop of;* and on page 432, under *Anglican Communion*.

false in some of its statements, and in its general purport is calculated to give an utterly wrong idea of the facts, though its authors make great pretensions to piety and zeal for the truth.

They begin by stating that they had met at Ephesus by order of the Emperors, of whom they speak complimentarily, probably from motives of policy and because they knew, through Nestorius, of Theodosius the Second's partiality for them and his hostility to Cyril of Alexandria, and they keep silent as to Nestorius having been canonically summoned thrice to make his defence before the Ecumenical Synod, accuse the Orthodox of wasting time, say nothing of the just deposition of Nestorius and their implied condemnation with him, and repeat the stale stories of Cyril and Memnon having excited tumults, forgetting their own irregular and anti-canonical attempt to pass off their own about a fifth of the Synod at most, (including those with them who were deposed or without Sees), as the whole four-fifths, and they speak as though the Orthodox were not satisfied with the Creed of the First Ecumenical Synod, and then falsely speaking as though they were the great majority of the Ecumenical Synod, they refer as follows to the famous Twelve Chapters of Orthodoxy written by Cyril and approved in different Ecumenical Synods since then, as well as in the Third Council itself:

"*We tried to persuade the Bishops who held the opinions of the Egyptian Cyril and who had subscribed the heretical Chapters put forth by him, to do them away as plainly and outrageously hostile to the Orthodox faith; and to be content with the Exposition made in Nicaea, in accordance with the command of our Christ loving Emperors.*" Then they say that as they could not persuade them they, [the Nestorian Split off, that is,], were compelled to state their own confession, and to strengthen it with their signatures. They give the Creed of the 318 of Nicaea, not that of the 150 of I. Constantinople, which they do not even mention. They speak of the Creed of Nicaea as "*sufficient to teach the exactness of piety and to show the beaten path of the truth, and to confute the error of heretical misbelief,*" meaning in all such high talk that they will not accept the Orthodox Incarnation, God alone worshipping sense of it put forth by the Ecumenical Synod, but only that, relying on the favor of the Emperors, they are going to fight against the Orthodox sense of it contained in Cyril's crucial and much misunderstood and much belied Twelve Chapters. Then they add of that Creed,

"*This is the faith which the Fathers put forth, at first indeed against Arius who blasphemed, and said that the Son of God is a creature, and against every heresy, both that of Sabellius, and that of Photinus, and that of Paul of Samosata, and that of Manichaeus, and that of Valentinus, and that of Marcion, and against every heresy, which has raised itself against the Universal Church: whom also the 318 Bishops assembled in the city of the Nicaeans condemned. And in that Exposition*" [or "*Forthset*"] "*of the Faith we all profess to abide,"* [*that is*] *"both we who have come together in Ephesus, and the most God-revering Bishops in our provinces."*

The plain English of all this, when it is boiled down, is that the one-fifth of the Synod hold to their own heretical sense of the meaning of the Creed of the 318 which had been condemned in Nestorius' letter to Cyril, and reject the sense of it set forth in the two letters of Cyril to Nestorius, the longer of which contains the Twelve Chapters of Cyril. The Third Ecumenical Synod in its First Act had condemned the said letter of Nestorius to Cyril and approved the said two letters of Cyril to Nestorius.

The reader will notice the remark that the Synod of the 318 had condemned the heresy of Paul of Samosata and himself. We must consider whether this makes for the genuineness of a Creed of theirs used, some may think, in receiving Paul's followers when they came to the Church. It is the document which approves the worship of the divine nature in Christ but condemns worship of his humanity because it is a creature. But more of that hereafter.

Then the Apostatic Conventicle proceed again to attack the Twelve Chapters because really, when we come to their bottom motives, they condemn their false sense of the Creed, as follows:

"But as to the heretical Chapters lately set forth by Cyril of Alexandria, with which he has joined superfluous and vain anathematizations also, and which he has tried to make valid both by a vote and subscription of Bishops, the Holy Synod gathered in Ephesus rejects them and proclaims them to be alien to the Orthodox faith."

"I, John, Bishop of Antioch of the East," [that is, he means, of the Diocese of the East which contained many provinces] *"have consented to the forewritten holy Faith. And the rest of their Bishops subscribed in like manner, and by their Epistle below they asked Bishop Rufus also to aid them."* An Epistle to Bishop Rufus is found in column 1411 and after, in tom. IV. of *Mansi's Concilia*.

The unscrupulous character of the Apostatic Conventicle is evidenced by their lying statement in the last sentence above before the subscription that *"the Holy Synod gathered in Ephesus* rejects and proclaims to be alien to the Orthodox faith" Cyril's Twelve Chapters; whereas they had approved them as did the three Ecumenical Synods following. But these favorers of heresy have no scruple in representing their heretical one fifth of the Ecumenical Council as all of it. Such is the wonted perversity of idolaters and creature invokers and other errorists. And so this wicked document ends.

DOCUMENT V. AMONG THE PAPERS OF THE APOSTATIC CONVENTICLE.—
Document III. in Coleti and Mansi.

THIS HAS THE FOLLOWING BEFORE THE HEADING—"COPY OF THE IMPERIAL LETTER, SENT INTO EPHESUS TO THE HOLY SYNOD THROUGH PALLADIUS OF MAGISTERIAL RANK AS AGENT, TO ANNUL WHAT HAD BEEN DONE BY THEM, AS THOUGH THE INVESTIGATION SHOULD BE BEGUN ANEW."

This is a letter to the Ecumenical Synod from the Emperors in which they say, or Theodosius II., Emperor of the East, writing in the name of both says, that he has learned from Count Candidian (whom we have already seen to be a partizan of Nestorius and a hinderer and opponent of the Ecumenical Synod), that all the Synod did not meet, that there were disorders, that they did not wait for John of Antioch, and that the Emperor's order as to the mode of procedure by examination and discussion first, and decision afterwards, was not obeyed, and he therefore annuls all that they have done and commands the discussion to be commenced anew.

Count Candidian, who was wholly in sympathy with the Nestorian party, had seemingly suppressed the fact that the Synod had waited quite a number of days after the time set by the Emperor to open its first session, that John of Antioch had delayed inexcusably, seemingly to defeat the holding of the Synod at all, or to wear out those Bishops who were infirm, or aged, that some of them were sick, others were dead, and that others still had by remaining fifteen or sixteen or even more days before the opening of the Synod exhausted their slender means and so were oppressed by poverty and in straits; that the material power, the power of force in the shape of the military arm, had from the first been on the side of Nestorius and his small faction, and that it had used it to perpetuate the plain injustice of preventing the regular Canonical Summonses being served on Nestorius, and that the proceedings of the Orthodox Council throughout had been canonical and regular; that the heresiarch had been thrice summoned, by about four-fifths of the Synod then present, to appear and to make his defence; that the very Count Candidian who had slandered the Ecumenical Synod had used his soldiers to hinder the citations being served; that his soldiers had even threatened the Bishops who were messengers of the Council, though they were on a legitimate and canonical errand, and had conducted themselves very well on it; that first the Creed of the 318, the meaning of which was in dispute, had been read; that passages of the Fathers, as well as passages from Nestorius' own heretical writings, and a letter from each of the then chief Western Churches, Rome and Carthage, each of them the head of what would now be called a Patriarchate; that one letter of Nestorius had been examined and condemned, and two of Cyril to him had been examined and approved as norms of interpretation of the sense of the Creed of Nicaea, and of doctrine, and that all these had been read before the Decision against Nestorius and his Deposition were reached, and that every thing was regular, clear and convincing.

Yet deceived by the misrepresentations of Candidian, the Emperor annuls the action of the Ecumenical Synod, and commands them to commence anew. The Emperor therefore interfered with the prerogative functions of the episcopate, then, as their decisions against all creature worship show, sound and deserving of all respect.

And he threatens the Bishops if they refuse to obey him, or if they act as freely and Orthodoxically as their duty to God and to the souls committed to them demanded. Certainly therefore they were in evil case. And Cyril and the leaders and foremost champions of Orthodoxy might well fear that the weaker brethren in their ranks might give way when they found the civil and military force arrayed with the Man-Serving faction to crush them. They had been true to Christ and had held the first Session, and done a noble work in the first act of the Synod right against all the hindrances and trouble made for them by this very Candidian, the representative of Theodosius II., the imperial friend of Nestorius, and, so to speak, his chief parishioner. But would they stand firm if further persecution came? In the time of Athanasius, Cyril's predecessor, when the whole civil and military forces of the Empire had been used against him to maintain another kind of professed Creature Service, that is the Arian Service to a God the Word whom they called a creature, many Bishops had given way. Would it be so now?

Besides some of the Orthodox might fault Cyril, if not for helping to bring on a Synod after the unjust and threatening letter written him by Theodosius II. before the Council, at least for attending it, as though it were wise or possible for him not to attend. They might say that he should have known from that letter that the Emperor would crush the truth and its defenders, and that he should not have imperilled their vast interests by trusting such a man.

Besides, by this time the small faction of the Apostatic Conventicle had gone through the farce of attempting a deposition of Cyril and Memnon, and of suspending the rest of the Ecumenical Synod from the Communion. The Emperor and Candidian might recognize this as valid, at least so far as Cyril and Memnon were concerned, and God's anti-creature-serving truth would suffer.

Furthermore, in this very document, the Emperor tells the Ecumenical Synod as follows as to their future course;

"Our Piety will not suffer designed acts of presumption" [so he speaks of the acts of the Ecumenical Synod in daring to decide on purely Ecclesiastical questions in a purely canonical manner—*Chrystal*], "and it is so angry at the things which have been done, that it" [the Emperor's Piety, that is himself] "commands, that no one of the assembled Bishops shall depart from the city of the Ephesians, nor, moreover, come to our divine court, or return to his own country, till the dogmas of piety have been examined by all the Synod;"

[that very thing had been done—*Chrystal*] "and till some one shall be sent from our divine palace, to take cognizance, together with the most magnificent Count Candidian, of the things done contrary to our command, and to stop those things which do not follow our order. Therefore this letter suffices to inform (390) your God-Reveringness that that" [sort of conduct] " will not be allowed in any one, and that no one shall proceed " [with the Synod, or in that direction] "without cause to fear ; and that your God-Reveringness will not be allowed to add anything else to what has been done, contrary to our command. And let your Holiness know that an order has been sent to the most illustrious rulers of the provinces, to permit no one at all who returns to his own country and city to be received without our command " (391).

Furthermore, we see that in this very document the Emperor tells the Ecumenical Council that one from his palace is to be present to represent the imperial power, which would naturally imply, whatever else might be pretended, that he should bully the Ecumenical Synod into favoring Man-Worship, and the Real Presence of the substance of Christ's humanity in the Eucharist, and Cannibalism in that rite. No one as yet held to the Substance presence of His Divinity there. Whatever may be the wording of the milder parts of the document, it meant war on the freedom of the Universal Synod to do their God-given Work, and was also against the worship of God alone.

All this was the meaning of this tyrannical edict of the erring Theodosius II. This letter is dated the third day before the Calends of July, or according to the marginal emendation in *Mansi*, tom. IV., col. 1379, the thirteenth. This would be June 29, or June 19, A. D. 431 (392). But as the First Act of Ephesus did not take place till June 22 of that year, June 19 must be wrong. In the seven days following tidings in some form of what had been done in that Act reached the Emperor and called forth from him this Document. A sentence in it is so indefinite that we cannot positively say that he had at this time heard of the deposition of Nestorius, but it may possibly be reasonably inferred that he had. It is where at the end he says that he had put forth that, " Not," he adds, "as though our Divinity were now exercising care for men, nor furthermore for the most holy and most God-Revering Bishop Nestorius, or of any other, but on behalf of the dogma itself and the truth itself" (393).

From the fact that the result of the first session of the Ecumenical Synod was known in Ephesus on the night of June 22, and that the multitude gave

---

Note 390.—Or, " Therefore let this letter suffice to inform," etc.
Note 391.—*Mansi Conc.*, tom. III.. col. 1236.
Note 392.—In a note in Mansi's *Concilia*, tome IV., col. 1379, 1380, we read as to the date of the above mentioned decree, "*In Latin Manuscripts and in the edition of Contius*," [we read] "Given on the Calends of July."
Note 393.—Coleti Conc., tom. III., col. 1237. He calls Nestorius there, τοῦ ἁγιωτάτου καὶ θεοσεβεστάτου ἐπισκόπου Νεστορίου, that is, "*the most holy and most God-Revering Bishop Nestorius*," as above.

the Orthodox Bishops a torch-light procession over the result, to their lodgings, I think that it can hardly be doubted that Candidian and Nestorius, to whom it was so vital a theme, knew it then, and that the former at once sent swift tidings of it to his Master, the Emperor. And indeed the Emperor would probably not have annulled that Act of the Council if he had not learned the gist of its doings. And he does take upon him, practically, to annul it here, and to speak of Nestorius as still a " Bishop," notwithstanding his deposition in that Act. As yet Nestorius' hold on him was unbroken. The employment of his friend Candidian as an intermediary helped Nestorius to retain his grip on the weak and probably unorthodox secular ruler, who used without shame such a God-angering title as "*our Divinity*" of himself, a poor erring creature, needing the compassion and help of the only Being who has a right to that title. By Anathema VIII. of Cyril's XII., we may not give that title even to Christ's humanity, much less to any other creature, under pain of Anathema. See vol. I. of Chrystal's *Ephesus*, pages 331, 332, text and notes.

As the Second Session of the Synod did not occur till July 10, there was ample time for this edict to reach Ephesus and be made known to the Ecumenical Synod before it: and it tells well for their faithfulness to Christ and to their obligations as teachers of His truth that with the banded might of absolute, secular, imperial power against them they met notwithstanding, affirmed the validity of all their Action, and went forward further in the same path. The prospect was chains and exile. But they were loyal to the truth that all acts of religious service are prerogative to Divinity, and that the Substance of God the Word was incarnate in the womb of the Virgin Mary, and that Christianity abhors cannibal views on the Eucharist.

DOCUMENT VI. AMONG THE PAPERS OF THE APOSTATIC CONVENTICLE.—*Document IV. in Coleti and Mansi here.*

This bears the heading:

"A REPORT OF JOHN, ARCHBISHOP OF ANTIOCH, (394) AND OF THOSE WITH HIM, TO THE EMPEROR, *which they wrote in reply through Palladius of Magisterial rank.*"

This document in its misrepresentations of the Orthodox Synod and of Cyril of Alexandria is simply vile.

It begins by praising the Emperor for annulling the work of the Third Ecumenical Synod, and falsely asserts that it had already been annulled by the canons. It commends him also for ordering a new investigation to be made by the Synod. Then, after some further words of praise or flattery for so acceding to their wishes, the heretical Conventicle proceed to state that they have condemned Cyril of Alexandria and those who acted with him, that is to put it in

NOTE 394.—As Sophocles shows in his *Greek Lexicon of the Roman and Byzantine Periods*, and in his *Glossary* under ἀρχιεπίσκοπος, the title *Archbishop* was not in the fourth century given to all Metropolitans, but only to those who were of the greatest sees. Afterwards it was given to them all.

plain English, they modestly claim to condemn four fifths of all that did assemble at Ephesus, that is all who canonically met in the Ecumenical Synod, of whom they say as follows:

"It is necessary for us to give an account to your Mightiness of the reasons which drove us, when we came into the city of the Ephesians, to pass a Vote and a Sentence against those who from the beginning trod under foot your decrees because they were pressed by their own consciences, and wished to confirm and to renew (395) the dogmas of Apollinaris and of Arius (396) against piety, among whom Cyril, lately the Bishop of Alexandria sent to the imperial city (397) certain Chapters with anathematisms with all will-worship (398), [and] before they touched the investigation of the divine dogmas, they indulged their hostility and enmity, by which things they dared, contrary to your pious decrees, to pass such an unjust vote against so great a throne as that of Constantinople, the Empress of cities." Then after contending that their doctrine had come down from the first, as is the manner of such creature servers ever, and after accusing the Orthodox of being the innovators

---

NOTE 395.—Or "to revive," ἀνανεῶσαι

NOTE 396.—The Latin translation reads here, "*the dogmas of Arius, of Eunomius, and of Apollinarius,*" but col. 1379, tome IV. in *Mansi's Concilia* states that Eunomius' name is lacking in the Greek. It is however found in Latin in the parallel column there.

NOTE 397.—Constantinople.

NOTE 398.—Greek, μετὰ πάσης ἐθελοθρησκείας. The last Greek word is found in Colossians ii: 23, where the Apostle Paul warns against "the commandments and doctrines of men, which things have indeed a show of wisdom *in will worship and humility*, and in unsparingness towards the body, not in any honor to the satisfying of the flesh." Robinson in his *Greek and English Lexicon of the New Testament*, under ἐθελοθρησκεια, *will worship*, thinks that the expression "*will worship and humility*" refers to the words used just before in verse 18, "*Let no man beguile you of your reward in an affected humility and in a worshipping of angels*," that is, an affected or man made humility which would move you to say, *I am not good enough to go to God directly, or through the one, sole Mediator Jesus Christ* (I Tim. ii: 5), *but I must go to him through angels*, to whom we are forbidden to give any act of religious service, be it bowing, prayer, kneeling, prostration, or any other, under pain of losing our eternal reward, see Matt, iv: 10; Colos. ii: 18; Rev. xix: 10, and Rev. xxii: 8, 9, and John xiv: 6, for he who gives any of those acts of service to a creature is of course a creature server, and if he prays to any creature, he practically makes that creature a god as Bishop Fell says (Tyler's *Primitive Christian Worship*, page 166), by ascribing to him the infinite attributes of God, omnipresence and omniscience. And blessed be God, we need no other than the "*one Mediator*" appointed by the Father, for "*He is able also to save them to the uttermost that come unto God by Him seeing He ever liveth to make intercession for them.*" As God he hears our prayers, as man He intercedes for us. The High Priest alone, our great High Priest's fore-type, could enter the most holy place to intercede for Israel (Levit. xvi: 2, 15, 16, 17, 29-34), and our great High Priest has entered the most holy place above, and He alone can intercede in Heaven for the Israel of the New and Better Testament, (Heb. ix: 3, 7-18; Rom. viii: 34; Heb. ix: 23, 24; John xiv: 6; John x: 9; Heb. vi: 19, 20). The only intercession that we read of in Heaven since Christ became the Mediator except His own is a cry, not for mercy but for vengeance, on persecutors, Rev. vi: 10, 11. But we are especially invited to go to the Father, through Him and also to Him as our High Priest and Intercessor, John vi: 37; John xiv: 13, 14; John xv: 7, 16; John xvi: 23, 24; Rom. viii: 34; Heb. iv: 14, 15, 16; Eph. ii: 18; Heb. vi: 19, 20; Heb. vii: 15-28; Heb. viii: 1-6 inclusive; Heb. ix: 11, 12, 24; Heb. x: 19-24; I John ii: 1, 2.

and corrupters of the faith, and cunningly professing a great desire to have the imperial decree as to a new examination carried out, which they deemed favorable to their own ends and their aim to get rid of the Orthodox majority, they make the crafty proposal that the Council shall consist of the Metropolitans and two Bishops with each of the Metropolitans, and that the rest of the Prelates shall be refused permission to sit in the Synod. The outcome of this request, if granted, would have been as follows:

In Century IV. Alexandria, Cyril's see, according to Wiltsch's Geog. and Statistics of the Church, vol. I. p. 191, was the only Metropolitical see in Egypt, Libya and Pentapolis. If there were a Metropolitan in Abyssinia, that would make two. According to Wiltsch's Geog. and Statistics of the Church, vol. I. page 192, *"Several metropolitan seats arose at the beginning of the fifth century* in the Patriarchate of Alexandria. He mentions one, Ptolemais, created by Cyril's predecessor, Theophilus, and states further that, *"In the imperial proclamation, at the Second Synod of Ephesus, in 449, Dioscurus received the command to appear with ten metropolitans."* That, of course, was about eighteen years later than the Third Ecumenical Synod, of which we are speaking. Wiltsch adds, *"As the Metropolitans in the Alexandrian diocese never subscribed themselves as such at the Councils, it is not certain what cities were their seats,"* (Ibid).

While no doubt there were at this time (A. D. 431) civil provinces in Egypt it is doubtful whether Alexandria was not practically the sole Metropolitical see, as Wiltsch shows, on the preceding page, that it was in the preceding century, and whether the relation of the so called Metropolitans was not practically that of suffragans to the Bishop of Alexandria as their Metropolitan, and whether it was not so regarded by John of Antioch and his party. So that it is not certain that Cyril's jurisdiction would have been represented at all in a new session of the Council, if John and his friends had got their request. For the Bishop of Abyssinia does not appear to have been present, and I am not sure whether at this time there was a Metropolitan there. And Cyril, according to John and his friends, was deposed. And as the two Bishops to go with each Metropolitan had not a Metropolitan to go with from Egypt, it is not clear that any Egyptian or Abyssinian Bishop would have sat in the Council. Indeed John held that all of them in the Synod were suspended. So that by that sharp trick the Egyptian Orthodox vote there would have been disfranchised.

As Memnon of Ephesus had been deposed by the little Conventicle, that of course, according to them, would throw him out and the two Bishops who might have sat with him.

But there were present in the about forty who composed that little Conventicle of John no less than thirteen who sign themselves as Metropolitans; and, besides, there were John of Antioch, and Nestorius of Constantinople, who, being of course Metropolitans as well as Patriarchs, would have a right to sit in the new Synod, and with two Bishops to each Metropolitan, (and by the terms of this heretical document they might doubtless be suffragans,) the heretical assembly could muster forty-five members against none from the Patriarchate of Alexandria, and none from Ephesus. Their sentence of deposition against Cyril and Memnon, passed in their first Act, has forty-three names appended to it. And Nestorius' is not among them. The new arrangement would therefore just admit all they had, and one suffragan more.

Besides, as in that Act they had excommunicated all the rest of the Bishops of the Orthodox Synod till they should forsake Orthodoxy and go over to their heretical views; if they could get the weak Emperor to go one step further and approve their action in deposing Cyril and Memnon and in excommunicating four fifths of the Council, including Juvenal of Jerusalem and his prelates, and all of other civil Dioceses, that is Patriarchates, the game would have been wholly in their own hands. And even if he would not go so far as to admit their action in deposing Cyril and Memnon and in excommunicating the rest of the Orthodox Bishops; but would only consent to their cunning proposal to admit to the Synod only the Metropolitans, and two suffragans with each, it would throw out most of the Egyptians and others of the Orthodox, and enable the Nestorians to meet the majority with more of hope. But even then they could not have prevailed. And this they knew so well that they talk against having many present, and accuse the Orthodox Egyptians and the Asiatics, that is Cyril's and Memnon's Bishops, of being inferior to their own party in learning, which was not true, if sound Orthodox learning be meant, for the immortal Cyril alone was worth more than all the Oriental Nestorians together, for most if not all the ablest men of their own party, like Theodoret for instance, were heretical and Man Worshipping. He especially was. They say further that unless their proposition to admit to the Council only two Bishops with each Metropolitan be granted there would be confusion again, by which they mean that the Orthodox majority could not be overcome and won over to heresy or made to submit to it: For they write:

"For if this be not done, there will necessarily be confusion again, for there are fifty Egyptians, and forty of the Asiatics under Memnon, the leader of the tyranny, and twelve of the heretics called Messalians from Pamphylia: and, besides those who are with that same Metropolitan, there are also others deposed and excommunicated in different places by Synods or by Bishops who are" [all] "nothing but a multitude of men who know nothing that is exact and accurate on divine dogmas, but are full of troubling and uproar" (399).

Of the two hundred Orthodox Bishops it will be seen that they at the start condemn about half at once, namely,

50 Egyptians;
40 Asiatics, (that is Bishops of the diocese of Asia Minor, under Memnon);
12 whom they call Messalians, which, as we shall soon see, was a plain lie.

NOTE 899.—*Coleti Concil*, tom. III., col. 1240.

Besides those whom they mention as adhering to the same Metropolitan Memnon, they denounce others whom they slanderously accuse of having been deposed and excommunicated in different places, a downright lie, aye, a charge justly brought by the Ecumenical Synod against some of their own party ; and indeed all of their party were suspended justly from Communion by the Ecumenical Synod.

Then they complain that when they went to the chapel of the Apostle John to render thanks for the Emperor's letter which favored them, they were shut out of it, and, after praying outside, were troubled by a mob of house servants, and they ascribe it to Memnon, whom they say they have deposed, and they beg the Emperor to banish him from the city or they say they can not have peace or fulfil the Emperor's wish, they mean in condemning the truth of God and in putting their Man-Service and other errors in place of it. And so they end (400). As to the struggle in the Church of St. John and out of it, see this Document IV. of Coleti above and below, and Memnon below.

From the wish expressed in an epistle of John of Antioch and his Apostatic Handful to the Senate in Constantinople, above epitomized, to clasp or embrace all the relic-containing chests of the Martyrs, there is only too much reason to suppose that if they had come near St. John's relics, they would have committed the Man-Service of worshipping them *relatively*, and so would have angered God. They had no right to enter Memnon's Churches without his permission, even if they had been Orthodox, and that on canonical principles ; much less had they as persons under discipline. Indeed they had no right to enter any Christian Church without the Bishop's permission to whom those Churches were subject, much less had they any right to go there and officiate as clerics and as Bishops, nor to hold a session of their Apostatic Handfull there in another Bishop's jurisdiction, and represent it as the whole Ecumenical Synod, and there is no proof from what we know they actually did in the way of sheer impudence and outrage and misrepresentation, that they would not have done that if they had been allowed to do as they would. They give their own side of the story, which is that when the Orthodox saw them, they at once closed the temple, so that John and his fellow heretics were compelled to do outside their thanking God that the Emperor had undone the work of the Ecumenical Synod. They add that after they had prayed outside, and had said nothing to any one, they started on their return, but that a crowd of certain house servants, as is said above, came out and took hold of some of them or hindered them, took away the beasts of others, wounded others, and pursued them a long distance with sticks and stones, so that they were compelled to flee with much haste. The other side of the story should be heard before we accept this heretic's one sided statement, and condemn the Orthodox Memnon. There is no

---

NOTE 400.—I have epitomized the above document from columns 1237-1241 in tom. III, of *Coleti's Conc.*, and have compared to some extent the *Collectio Regia*, tom. V., Paris, 1644, pages 687-691 ; *Mansi Conc.*, tom. IV., col. 1379-1381 ; and *Harduin. Conc.*, tom. I, col. 1539, 1544.

proof that Memnon had anything to do with their being troubled by that crowd of servants, though it is clear from Memnon's account that their outrageous attempt to pass themselves off as the Ecumenical Synod, when they were only about a fifth of it, and their attempt to take from the Ephesians their well beloved and sound Bishop and to put a heretic in his place had roused some domestics to oppose outrage with some force, though the account, like the other emanations of John and his Apostatic Synod, is highly colored and exaggerated. If Memnon had permitted them in their state of heresy to enter one of his Churches and use it against God's truth, he would have justly been liable to censure as an accomplice, through his supineness, with their heresy. And happily we have among the Orthodox documents below a letter of Memnon himself on this very matter, from which it appears that John entered the Church or Apostle's Memorial (401) and indicated that he deemed himself under obligation to ordain a successor to Memnon, and that the Orthodox people, who had been warned beforehand of his attempted outrage by a notice posted in a part of the city, simply drove them out of their Church. Whatsoever was beyond that, if anything was, is to be ascribed to the over-zeal of some, not to all. But John and his fellow heretics suppress these all-important facts which show that he was the aggressor. See Memnon's letter translated below, from which it will be seen that John and his fellow Man-Worshippers, pursuing his outrageous usurpation of authority in another Bishop's jurisdiction, had gone up to the Church with disorderly persons who were armed, the better to overcome legitimate resistance to his heretical villainy, and then had indicated his belief that he was under obligation to ordain some one in the place of the Orthodox and uncondemned Memnon! It was that conduct and his persistance and action then, contrary to the faith and canons of the whole Church, which precipitated the struggle. And so Memnon lays the blame of the affair on him, by saying that he made a sedition and trouble there and half killed some of the beggars there. Surely when a man defends his house and his rights against a robber who comes to wrong him, the fault is the robber's and not the honest man's.

But John was emboldened to attempt outrages by the favor shown to his

---

NOTE 401.—In the following Nestorian Documents between Acts VI. and VII. of Ephesus in Coleti, we find them complaining of their treatment when they went up to ordain a successor to Memnon in the basilica of John the Apostle; that is in Document IV. as above, and in Document VI., which is the Letter of John of Antioch and the Synod of "*the Apostasy*" *to the Praepositus, even to* "*Scholasticus*," (or "to the Scholasticus"); or according to the margin, "to the Praepositus who was Scholasticus." See also Document VIII., in Coleti here, which is a Report of John and his Apostasy to the Emperor through Count Irenaeus, their fellow heretic, and fellow persecutor, as Memnon's letter among the Orthodox Documents between Acts VI. and VII. shows him to have been. In this Document John and his Synod refer to that Irenaeus to testify in their favor. I find no other allusions to the difficulty in any of the other Documents of the Nestorians or their friends in Coleti between Acts VI. and VII. of *Ephesus:* at least none so clear as those above.

Man-Serving party by the Emperor and his representative, Count Candidian. And hence he makes bold to take with him armed men and to attempt an uncanonical ordination when supported by their violence. And from the fact hat, as Memnon relates, he half killed by their means some of the beggars there, who probably as being wont to beg on the outside of the Church, may have been the first to resist his tyranny against their Bishop and Church, or the first to meet his assault, his disorderly and armed assistants were not slow to use their weapons and to attempt to force their way into the Church and to use it for John's own iniquitous purpose. They failed, only because they were well and courageously met by the people inside, who simply contended for their own against wicked usurpation and heretical work. Their aim, as Memnon shows, was to keep John from ordaining in their Church, and it was well that they succeeded. For there are times when wickedness and usurpation must be resisted by force, as all the world admits, and this was one of them. It is simply one of many similar cases, such, for instance, as the armed resistance of the Reformed in Germany, Holland, England and elsewhere in the sixteenth century and after against those who would bring them under the creature serving usurpation and tyranny of Rome. Clear as was their right in the long war waged to maintain truth among them, this case is, if possible, even more clear against the creature-serving John of Antioch and his mob.

The injustice of accusing members of this Synod of any sympathy with the Messalian heretics is rendered more clear by the fact that they condemned them and their heresy, regarding which see this work elsewhere, and Hammond on the Canons, pages 78, 79 of the New York edition of 1850 (Stanford & Swords, publishers).

DOCUMENT VII. AMONG THE PAPERS OF THE APOSTATIC CONVENTICLE.—*Document V. in Coleti and Mansi here.*

This bears the heading:
"AN EPISTLE OF THE SAME PERSONS" [that is John and his little Conventicle] *"to the Prefect and the Master"* [of the Imperial Household].

This is a stilted and false account by malefactors who had attempted to pass themselves off for the whole Synod, though they were but a handful, and so were guilty of swindling those who believed them, of their fears of injury in Ephesus, and a request that they be called to Constantinople to testify against the Orthodox Cyril of Alexandria and Memnon of Ephesus, and what it calls *"their heretical misbelief,"* and that of the Synod. They were appealing from a legitimate Council and its perfectly canonical action to a weak and warped Emperor, and to another layman to override and to annul decisions given, as the Church has ever held, with the promised aid of the Holy Spirit. They tell the usual falsehood that the Council had acted uncanonically, and, humorously enough, fault the Bishops of the Ecumenical Synod as trampling the canons under their feet because they did not obey the action of the Apostatic Handful in deposing Cyril and Memnon and in excommunicating the rest of them.

They profess to be in great fear, say that their houses had been marked twice for attack, and in brief write in an extravagant strain, evidently with the design of getting the Council removed from Ephesus to some place where the populace would be more heretical and more under their influence, and more in sympathy with themselves. They beg to be helped in their evil career and conjure to that end the person written to *"by children, by those dearest,* [and] *by the judgment of God,"* but I do not know what children are meant, whether those of any married Bishops or those of the prefect, but suppose the latter. And with such requests they close. (402.)

DOCUMENT VIII. AMONG THE PAPERS OF THE APOSTATIC CONVENTICLE.—*Document VI. in Coleti and Mansi here.*

This bears the heading:

"AN EPISTLE LIKEWISE OF THE SAME PERSONS" [that is John of Antioch, and his Apostatic Conventicle] *"to the Praepositus* (403) *and the Scholasticus"* [or better perhaps, *to the Praepositus, even Scholasticus (or Scholasticius)*]. (404.)

This is much like the last Document above in its deceptive portraiture of itself as the true Synod, and Four-fifths of the Ecumenical Synod as despising the Church laws, trampling under foot the edicts of the Emperor, (this last, as usual, to soft-soap him and win him more firmly to their side) and it complains that John and his party were shut out of the churches, which was perfectly right and canonical, because they had involved themselves in Nestorius' cause and to some extent in his heresy, and had subjected themselves to the penalties pronounced for such conduct by the Canons. And, in refusing them admission to the Churches, Memnon exercised his own prerogative of controlling the temporalities of his charge in accordance with the law of obedience to the

---

NOTE 402.—I have epitomized the above Document from the Greek of it in column 1241 of tome III. of Coleti's Concilia, and have compared it as on pages 691, 692 of tome V. of the *Collectio Regia*; *Mansi Conc., tom.* IV., *col.* 1383-1386, and *Harduin. Conc., tom.* I., *col.* 1543-1544.

NOTE 403.—This officer is called by Gibbon the *"prefect of the sacred bedchamber."* See his account of his duties and his great influence in *Gibbon's Decline and Fall of the Roman Empire,* chapter XVII., (page 223 of vol. 2 of Bohn's edition, London, 1854). Professor Stokes in his article "Scholasticus (1)" in *Smith and Wace's Dictionary of Christian Biography,* tells us that he was the "principal Eunuch of Theodosius the Emperor," and refers to "Hefele, *Councils,* tom. III., pp. 81, 112, Clark's English trans." and to Mansi, t. V., p. 777.

NOTE 404.—So the above may be rendered, *"Epistle of the Same* [John of Antioch and his Conventicle] *"to the Praepositus, even Scholasticus."* If for *"Scholasticus,"* we read as in document XI., (see below) *"Scholasticius,"* the reference may be to the Chamberlain of the imperial bed chamber there mentioned, which I suspect to be the true meaning. He is there termed Cubicularius, if the same person be meant. And *Cubicularius* means *chamberlain.* Indeed Hefele and Stokes as quoted or referred to on Document VIII. above, so understand the allusion, and his name may have been *Scholasticus,* not *Scholasticius,*

Ecumenical Synod. Indeed if he had permitted maintainers of a deposed heretic and of some or all of his heresies, maintainers who were themselves heretics, and that on most vital points of creature service, to gather in the Churches under his control, he himself would have been justly liable, by all canons, to ecclesiastical discipline, aye even to deposition; compare Matt. xviii: 17; Titus iii: 10.

They use flattering or complimentary terms to the person or persons addressed, and beg him or them to read their letters to the Emperor, to the end that the enactments of the Ecumenical Synod might be annulled, and that the Synod might be managed after their ideas, and, in effect, that each party meet in debate, so that after deposing farcically Cyril and Memnon, and brazen-facedly setting their one fifth of the Synod up for the whole four fifths, they might change the Council into a debating society in which heretics might with impunity endlessly assail the truth of God, rather than a defining Council of the whole church. And with that in effect, they conclude. (405.)

Their conduct was the more inexcusable, because, from the first until they wholly separated from the Ecumenical Synod and took ground against its leaders and against itself and against its action as to Nestorius and his heresies, they were always free to attend the Ecumenical Council, which indeed, had three times summoned him as it had summoned Nestorius to appear, before it took any action against him, and after John of Antioch had attacked them, it had thrice summoned him to meet with it, and it had never refused permission, till it was itself assaulted and wronged by the lawless acts of the Conventicle, to any Bishop canonically such, to meet with it.

DOCUMENT IX. AMONG THE PAPERS OF THE APOSTATIC CONVENTICLE.—*Document VII. in Mansi and in Coleti here.*

This is headed:

"A REPORT OF THE ORIENTAL SYNOD *to the gloriously triumphant Emperor, showing again also that Cyril and Memnon had been deposed.*"

This, like the other documents put forth by the Apostatic Conventicle, is designed, as the request at the end of it shows, to smother the sentiments of the Orthodox majority of the Ecumenical Synod, and to procure the imperial approval of their ridiculous and uncanonical deposition of the leaders of the Ecumenical Synod, Cyril of Alexandria and Memnon of Ephesus, and to get the Synod transferred to some place nearer to Constantinople, where they evidently hoped their ally, the weak Emperor, Theodosius II., would be their pliant tool in forcing the necks of the Orthodox majority under an heretical yoke. The document throughout is highly complimentary, or, rather, flattering to the Emperor, and most outrageously unjust to Cyril, to Memnon and to

---

NOTE 405.—I have epitomized the above document from columns 1241-1244 of tome III. fo *Coleti's Concilia;* and have compared to some extent, pages 602, 603 of tome v. of the *Collectio Regia, Mansi Conc.* tom. IV., col, 1385-1386, and *Harduin.* tom. I., col. 1543, 1544.

the Orthodox. But if the expression, "*Report of the Eastern Synod,*" in the heading, is theirs, it would serve to show that they did not pretend in this document to be now the whole Ecumenical Synod, but only a part of it, though they seem to have lost all idea of what a true Ecumenical Council may do, or of its authority against the action of heretical parts of the Church.

They begin with the old and crafty repetition about the Emperor's having assembled the Synod to produce profit and peace to the Church, and charge the Orthodox Synod with having produced confusion and disorder instead, as though it were not true then, as at Nicaea in A. D. 325, and at Constantinople in A. D. 381, that the conflict of truth against error had always produced war, and always will; and as though those advocates of Creature-Service, the Arian minority at Nicaea, and the Macedonian minority at I. Constantinople, could not or did not say the same things against the Anti-Creature Serving majority in those Synods, for condemning them as John of Antioch and his Man-Serving faction said at Ephesus in A. D. 431, against that Anti-Man Serving Synod for condemning them; and as though Christ with reference to the irreconcilable conflict between God and the Devil, between truth and error, between right and wrong, had not said that he *came not to send peace but a sword on the earth* (Matt. x: 34 to 42 inclusive; Luke xii: 51 to 54), and as though the way to gain by the Church had not always been in sticking to the truth, and in defending it, and not in compromising with falsehood, which is the work of Satan. They then come to particularize more on the dogmatic question, and attack those celebrated Twelve Chapters which so pointedly condemn their denial of the Incarnation and their Man-Service; and their language against them is plain and precise notwithstanding Cyril's explanations and defenses of them, against Theodoret, against the Orientals, and at Ephesus itself. So in his *Five Book Contradiction of the Blasphemies of Nestorius* he is so clear against the Nestorian heresies as to leave their patrons without due explanation and without defense. For they assert of Cyril and his *Twelve Chapters* as follows:

"Cyril accused in regard to the dogmas of Apollinaris, aye, rather, himself convicting himself by those things which he lately sent with his own signature with anathematisms to the imperial City" [Constantinople] "by which things he is convicted of holding the opinions of the impious and heretical Apollinaris."

And then after saying that Cyril was opposed to exact examination and trial on faith with unanimity and peace, and that he acted as though he lived in times when there were no Emperors, (another sop to imperial vanity on this matter), as though they could regulate the faith of the Universal Church, they assert that Cyril's canonical action against Nestorius and his heresy and its maintainers was a proceeding onwards "*to all lawlessness.*" Further on this document speaks of Cyril's Orthodox views which the Synod had approved, as "*his corrupt opinion concerning our Lord Jesus Christ,*" for which "*he must*" [or "*should*"] "*be called to give account.*" Below it states that "The holy Synod," [that is the Apostatic Handfull], "would not admit" *his* [Cyril's] *pestiferous inventions on the Faith,*" and that they had deposed him "*for all the things aforesaid,*" that is for his Orthodox views against Nestorian errors, and for his maintenance of them by energetic and forceful and obligatory action against perverse and obstinate heretics. Again, further on, they call Cyril's Orthodox views "*his heretical misbelief*"; and they state, moreover, of their farcical cutting off of Cyril and Memnon from the Church, that "*To cut them off, is nothing other than to establish Orthodoxy,*" that is, to cut off Cyril and Memnon for their Orthodox views on the Incarnation, against Man-Service and against Cannibalism in the Eucharist, and against the Real Presence of the substances of Christ's humanity there, and for the truth that Christ as God is Mediator, etc., is to establish that sort of infidelity and of Man-Service, and of corruption which makes against them.

And then, with reference still to the celebrated Twelve Chapters which, and their maintenance, by Cyril and Memnon form the staple of their denunciations and misrepresentations up to this point, they subjoin the following outrageously false and horrible language regarding Cyril and his Orthodox doctrine approved by the whole Church in the Third Ecumenical Synod:

"And Your Mightiness can ascertain his impious mind from his Chapters themselves. For he is convicted by them of, so to speak, arousing from Hades the impious Apollinaris, who died in his heresy, and of making war upon the Churches and upon the Orthodox faith, and of anathematizing in what he has set forth, the Evangelists and Apostles at the same time, and also our progenitors in the Church after them, who, impelled by the Holy Ghost, but not by their own private opinions, preached the pious faith, and told on that Gospel which is contrary to those things which he" [Cyril] "both holds and teaches; and he wishes that his own impiety, on the strength of his own command, shall prevail every where in the world." Again, further on, speaking of "*opposers of the Apostolic dogmas,*" they add, "*of whom is the aforesaid Cyril,*" and assert that, with Memnon of Ephesus, he had been "*justly deposed.*" Then they profess to have obeyed the Emperor, and then proceed to show clearly their hostility to Orthodoxy and their desire to get the Council removed to some place nearer Constantinople, where they might gratify their heresy. And those who had outraged Cyril and Memnon and Orthodoxy by an uncanonical deposition, passed by one-fifth of the Council, against the leaders of the other four-fifths, and by suspending from Communion or excommunicating the rest of the four-fifths, now commence to talk as though in fear, though protected and supported by all the troops in Ephesus and the Empire, while the Orthodox had no military protection, for the Conventicle writes:

"And we are now a useless sacrifice to tyranny unless your Piety come to our assistance and decree that we shall assemble elsewhere, some where near" [to Constantinople], "where we shall be able, c'early to convict by the Scriptures and by the books written by the Fathers, both Cyril and these who have been led on by him; whom we have subjected to excommunication but with a disposition to spare them, for we give them a glimpse of hopes of salvation if they repent!!!" Impudence and heresy could hardly go further than this language of the Apostatic Handful against the Ecumenical Council. Then follows seemingly an utterly unsupported charge that some of the Bishops of the Orthodox Synod had long been deposed and notwithstanding were received by Cyril, that others had been suspended from communion by their own Bishops, and notwithstanding had been received to commuuion by Cyril, and that he had honored others who had become transfixed on many accusations. And then comes the slanderous charge, which however shows their own heresy and Cyril's Orthodoxy and strength before the Church, namely:

"And he was doing those things by way of trying to give validity to his *heretical* way of thinking, not considering that in religion not numbers are to be sought for, but correctness of dogmas, and the truth of the apostolic dogmas." But Cyril had both on his side, as the whole church in Ecumenical Council testified. They then beseech the Emperor to use the secular power to crush the work of the Bishops of the Third Ecumenical Synod, which they vilify as *"their madness and tyranny, which like a hurricane, sweeps away"* [even] *"the more courageous to heretical misbelief."* These and the other expressions above do certainly show that even John of Antioch and his friends looked upon the matters in dispute as involving heresy, and not as personal merely in regard to Nestorius whom they do not even name in this document. Then with a further appeal to bear down the Orthodox Synod and its decisions they end. (406).

DOCUMENT X. AMONG THE PAPERS PERTAINING TO THE APOSTATIC CONVENTICLE.—*This is Document VIII. in Mansi and Coleti here.*

This bears the heading:

"*Report of the Orientals*" [that is the Bishops of John of Antioch's Diocese of the Orient], "*to the most religious Emperor, which they gave to the most magnificent Count Irenaeus with the forewritten Report.*"

This is sent through Count Irenaeus to the Emperor, Theodosius II.

They open in a way shows as usual their reliance on the secular power and the fear which it might inspire, not on the strength of their cause, in the Bishops of the Ecumenical Synod. For they say:

"*When we received the letter of your Piety*" [seemingly the one which assumed to annul the decisions of the Third Ecumenical Synod] "*we hoped*

NOTE 406.—I have translated part of the above document and epitomized the rest from *Coleti's Concilia*, tom. III., col. 1243-1246 and have to some extent compared pages 693-696 of tom. V., of the *Collectio Regia; Mansi's Conc.* tom. IV., col. 1385 to 1390, and *Harduin., Concilia*, tom. I., col. 1345-1348.

that it would be a deliverance from the Egyptian deluge which has assaulted the holy Churches of God, but we were deceived in our hope, for the men have become bolder in their madness."

"*The men,*" referred to are Cyril of Alexandria, Memnon of Ephesus, and the Bishops of the Third Ecumenical Council; and they call them "*men,*" and omit their titles as *Bishops*, probably because they had deposed Cyril and Memnon, and excommunicated the rest. It will be seen that here as elsewhere again and again, they speak with a certain measure of subdued contempt or hatred of Egypt, Cyril's home, and seem in an underhand manner to stir up the jealousy of Constantinople and its Emperor against the city which it had displaced as head of the East, because, before Constantinople became the seat of Empire, Alexandria had been its largest city. Then they go on in the old and by this time threadbare way, to fault the Synod for not regarding as valid, the deposition of Cyril and Memnon and the excommunication of themselves, by this Apostatic small minority of the Council, and speak of them as treading under foot the Emperor's laws, and the canons of the Holy Fathers, the last of which charges is of course an impudent falsehood, and they had violated no righteous imperial law; then they call "*some of them deposed and others excommunicated,*" which is another lie in substance because it was a thing utterly unknown to the canons that one fifth of a Synod had power to depose or to excommunicate all the other four fifths; and they fault them as doing an uncanonical thing by holding festival and meetings in houses of prayer, that is because those things were done by them right against the Apostatic Handfull's farcical deposition and excommunication of the Ecumenical Synod. Then they go one step further and accuse the Orthodox of having mobbed them when they were returning from outside the Church of the Apostle John, where they had been to render thanks for the Emperor's letter which had presumed to annul the God-guided decisions of the Ecumenical Council. On that they speak much as in the last document above, only that in this there is no mention of its being done by house servants, but the language is so indefinite that one might get the idea that it was actually done by all the Third Ecumenical Synod!!! The truth on this matter is told by us from Memnon in the fourth of the Documents from Coleti above. Then the Apostatic Handfull go on to fault, humorously enough, four fifths of the Ecumenical Synod (who had already thrice summoned this same John, and on his refusal to appear had excommunicated him and his aiders and abetters of his little Synod), because they would not go and meet with the heretical one fifth, and investigate anew the questions which had been already decided, and because, "*They did not endure to defend the [Twelve] Heretical Chapters of Cyril, because they lose heart at the plain proofs of his impiety in them.*" This expression shows their heresy, as well as their lying.

Then they say that seeing the Orthodox party so confident, they had determined to send Count Irenaeus to the Emperor to tell him the whole business, and they add an expression which shows that they had confided to him some unnamed ways of defeating the Orthodox, for they add:

"And he" [Irenaeus] "has learned from us many ways of cure, by which ways freedom from trouble may be given to the holy Churches of God." Wherefore] "we supplicate your Clemency to learn from him forbearingly, and to command quickly that to be done which seems good to your Piety, in order that we may not spend time" [or "be consumed"] "here in doing nothing, contrary to what is due and necessary." And so this document ends (407).

This was a crafty trick to crush God's truth, but they do not give the details—they were reserved for the Emperor's ears, that the intriguing might not be exposed to the light of day and of refutation and of warning.

DOCUMENT XI. AMONG THE PAPERS PERTAINING TO THE APOSTATIC MINORITY OF THE ECUMENICAL SYNOD.—*Document IX. in Mansi and Coleti here.*

This is headed:

"EPISTLE *written by the* COUNT IRENAEUS *to the Easterns concerning the Actions on the Business after his entrance into Constantinople, and the*" [or "*his*"] "*delivery of the Reports.*" (408).

In this letter Irenaeus states that he arrived in Constantinople two days after the Egyptians, the delegates of Cyril and of the Council, and found that they had turned most of the men in high station in civil and military service against John and his little minority of the Council, and that the men in high station deemed the decision of the Orthodox Ecumenical Synod to be deserving of admiration: or to put it in his own words:

"They were persuaded that inasmuch as an orderly examination had been made, and that a decision had followed it, and all the most dear to God Bishops together had set forth but one and the same vote against the person condemned by them [Nestorius] in default [of his appearing], that therefore that deposition was admirable. Moreover they had confessedly persuaded the most magnificent and Christ-loving Chamberlain of the Emperor's bed-chamber, Scholasticius (409), that he [Nestorius] would not bear at all to hear the

---

NOTE 407.—I have epitomized the above document from the Greek of column 1248, tome III of *Coleti's Concilia*, and from it as on pages 697, 698 of tom, v. of the *Collectio Regia*. and have to some extent compared it in *Mansi's Conc. tom.* IV., col. 1389, 1390, and *Harduin. Conc.* tom. I., col. 1547, 1548.

NOTE 408.—In Coleti here is a note which I translate: "In the *Synodicon Casinense*, this document has the following title: *Epistle of Count Irenaeus, which he wrote back to all the Bishops who had sent him, before the arrival of John, Count of the Largesses* [or "*Count of the Imperial Treasury*," from which the largesses were given]. The Latin of the note is found in col. 1247, 1248 of tome III. of *Coleti's Concilia*.

NOTE 409.—On this person, see notes 403, 404, page 267, above. The name is elsewhere spelled *Scholasticus*.

expression *Bringer Forth of God* [θεοτόκον] at Ephesus." He certainly had opposed the expression from the first. And there is no proof that he had at this time changed or admitted really the Incarnation, or given up his Man-Worship.

Irenaeus states that, notwithstanding the perils in which he stood, he succeeded in stating his own [heretical] side of the story to the men of high rank in the state, and that they were forced to tell it to the Emperor. And Irenaeus speaks of the faults of the Orthodox *"about the Egyptian"* against himself, as though their refusal to let him usurp the rights of an Ecumenical Synod of sound bishops were a crime. I suspect also from the constant tone of the Nestorian party, to which he belonged, that he represented the maintenance by the Bishops of their God-given prerogatives against himself, as an insult to the Emperor. Finally he says that after much disputing between their own party and those who held Cyril's opinions, and after much had been said and done, it seemed good that both he and the Egyptians should go to the Emperor and that the Egyptians should defend themselves and their business itself, and hear the Emperor's decision, though he adds craftily that he [Irenaeus] often protested that he had not come for that purpose, nor had he received any commands from John and the Bishops of his party on that matter, but only as the bearer of their letter. *"But"* adds Irenaeus, *"I came within a little of being torn in pieces on account of those words!"* After all the ways mentioned in the last letter above of the Apostatic Conventicle to the Emperor of managing the affair in their own interests, and crushing the Orthodox majority, their craft was seen through, and Irenaeus was discovered to be the misrepresenter of the truth and the facts that he was. Nevertheless, Irenaeus continues, he won the victory with the Emperor so that as the result, he writes:

"Those of the opposite party" [the Orthodox] *"are condemned, for it behooves me to come briefly to the result, as they were in no way able to defend either the Minutes of the deposition"* [of Nestorius, whether the Emperor faulted the sound doctrine of the Synod, or only its canonical procedure is not said here]; *"or those things which they have falsely said here: but it was even conspicuously shown in all the circumstances that the Egyptian did not call the Synod in a fit manner* (410)," [He certainly did, as the minutes show], *"and that he could not be a Judge inasmuch as he was one of those who were to be judged,"* [He did not judge till the Synod had approved his doctrine and condemned his opponent's errors]; *"and that he could not touch the business at all contrary to the judgment of the most magnificent Count Candidian."* [This is a strange position and a very absurd one to take, as though a layman like an Emperor or his lay representative, could rob Bishops of their freedom to conduct the business of God's church, and to preserve its sound faith, and to condemn error, which is their solemn and inexorable duty. For Cyril had

---

NOTE 410.—ἀκολυίθως.

not been condemned, and from the start the great majority of the Council looked upon him as their rightful and Orthodox leader. And *that majority of the Bishops at Ephesus were, under God, the voice of the Universal Church, and neither Candidian nor the Emperor was.* We are told to *render unto Cæsar the things which are Cæsar's and unto God the things which are God's* (411). So we must remember to give the civil government due respect in its sphere, the secular; and the sound ministry due respect in the sacred and churchly things. These two powers should always support each other, each in its own sphere and way, and never interfere with each other's due Scriptural prerogatives. But Irenaeus would have the Emperor or Count Candidian interfere with the Christ given prerogatives of the sound Bishops in Ecumenical Council assembled; and to admit his Erastian theory would be to enslave the Church, and so to insult Christ by violating his laws in the New Testament. For he told the apostles and their successors, not Emperors and Counts, to define on doctrine. Irenaeus goes on to try to show in his own erring way that Cyril could not touch the business of the Council. [For he adds] *"And all the commands* (412) *of the same most Magnificent Count Candidian, and the sacred* (413) *letter written through him to the Synod, and the other such things were used at once in the examination, at the Emperor's command, and in accordance with your wishes* 414), *there is nothing which is omitted of those things which show the audacious things lawlessly done there"* [at Ephesus], *"so that, as a rational consequence, the enemies of the truth got condemnation from all; and the judgment of your God-Reveringness was accepted and confirmed, and the deposition of the Egyptian"* (415) [Cyril of Alexandria] *"was sent off straightway by the most religious Emperor throughout the holy Church of God, as if* (416) *those of Cyril's party have done all things tyranically and against established rules, and that they should receive other punishment for the errors into which they have fallen. At this point, therefore, the matters of the affair had ended, and this was the conclusion of the hearing* (417). *But when John the Physician and*

NOTE 411.—Matt. xxii: 21; Mark xii: 17; and Luke xx: 25.

NOTE 412.—Or, *"warnings."*

NOTE 413.—Literally the '*sacred*" letter, σάκρα, that is the Latin *sacra:* a term applied in that servile age and time to what was *imperial*, and sometimes far from sacred. The term was a relic of the pagan worship of the Roman Emperors on which see Chrystal's EPHESUS, volume I., page 19, note 20, and pages 505-512, note B.

NOTE 414.—That is, the wishes of the Apostatic Conventicle; or it may perhaps better be rendered, *"through your prayers,"* a common compliment to the assumed efficacy of Bishop's, etc., pleadings with God. The Greek is διὰ τάς ὑμετέρας εὐχὰς.

NOTE 415.—Notice the hatred and contempt implied in this. He uses it again and again instead of giving Cyril his usual title of Bishop. He would regard him as deposed, but God foiled him and his Man-serving party.

NOTE 416.—ὡσανεί, which may be rendered here, *"on the ground,"* or *"which implies,"* or *"which leaves us to infer that those of Cyril's party,"* etc.

NOTE 417.—That is *the hearing* before the Emperor, in which Count Irenaeus alone, or chiefly, represented the apostatic Handfull.

cell-mate (418) *of Cyril came, and came as you know, we see the most of the ruling men become changed, and will not endure even to hear therefore from us those things which were decided in their presence"* [by the Emperor against Cyril and the Ecumenical Synod] *" or even by them."* [This looks very much as though they had learned how Irenaeus had deceived them]; *"for some of them now say that the things done by each of the two parties should remain valid, and that the depositions not only of the two persons"* [Cyril and Memnon], *"should be confirmed, as seemed good"* [to the Nestorian party], *"but also of the three"* [that is of Cyril, Memnon and Nestorius], *"others say that it is a fit thing to annul the depositions of all equally, and that frank and open ones of the most dear to God Bishops should be summoned here, so that investigation may be made with all the facts, both in regard to the doctrines concerning the faith, and in regard to what was unlawfully done at Ephesus. And there are some who are doing every thing and putting forth every sort of effort to get permission to go from the most pious Emperor with clear orders to the city of the Ephesians, and to take a comprehensive view, and to settle the whole business, in whatever way* (419) *they may be able to; but that is just the thing which those who love you pray may not be done, for they know accurately the purpose of those who are eager for it, and whence they have been guided to that plan. But let those things proceed as the Lord will: yet, I entreat, let your Holiness* (420) *deign to pray earnestly for me, who endure such dangers, and who live now not without danger, because of the multitude of those who plot against me daily. For God is witness, that when I was summoned to the examination before the Emperor, I hoped for nothing else than to be cast into the flow of the sea; but* 'the Lord, as it is written, stood by me, and I was delivered out of the mouth of the lion,' [2 Tim. iv: 17,], *"aye, rather out of the mouths of ten thousand lion's whelps* (421)." And so this Document ends.

This whole account shows how the deceived secular magnates turned against this able but evil instrument of the Apostatic faction against Cyril and the Orthodox Synod. The Emperor however, to whose vanity, Irenaeus had appealed by representing Cyril as disobedient to him, and John of Antioch and his fellow errorists as obedient, seems to have remained deceived longer. And the reader will notice that Irenaeus won his temporary victory over the Orthodox in his and their audience before the Emperor, not on *doctrinal* or *theologi-*

NOTE 418.—Or "*Syncellus,*" which often became a mere title, as perhaps in this case.

NOTE 419.—In the *Collectio Regia* and in *Coleti* here I find ἡ, but should prefer to write ᾗ, "*how,*" "*in what way,*" "*in whatever way.*"

NOTE 420.—A collective title of the Conventicle, a reprehensible title of slavish Byzantine flattery.

NOTE 421.—I have translated part of the above document, and epitomized the rest from the Greek as in columns 1248-1252 of tome III. of *Coleti's Concilia;* and have, to some extent, compared it as on pages 698-702, of tome V. of the *Collectio Regia,* and in col. 1547-1552 of tome I. of *Harduin. Conc.*, and in col. 1391-1394 of tome IV. of *Mansi's Conc.*

cal grounds at all, but on the assumption that John of Antioch and the Apostatic Synod had been *more Erastian* than Cyril, and had followed the Emperor's commands at the expense of God's truth. The anger excited against him when his wicked course became known shows how much the Orthodox deemed that they had been cheated by him. From his own account nearly all seemed to have turned against him, though as many of them seem to have been mere worldings, or poorly instructed in the vital doctrines involved, with the proverbial lack of wisdom of such men they endeavor to compromise the truth of God with the devil's lie, but they are to fail, as we shall soon see. We can not mix oil and water.

But God had raised up a man to be the leader of the militant hosts of His elect, at a time when the enemies were many, and weak men's hearts were failing them for fear; and that man was Cyril. And He had given him an able lieutenant in Memnon; and two hundred sound Bishops, most of whom never swerved, were at his back in support.

DOCUMENT XII. A DOCUMENT AMONG THE PAPERS ON THE APOSTATIC CONVENTICLE.—*From chapter XV. of the Synodicon Casinense. It is not put here in Mansi, but is placed here by Hardouin.*

This claims to be an Epistle of NESTORIUS *written about this time to Scholasticus, the Eunuch, that is the Chamberlain of the Emperor Theodosius II.* In it, Nestorius, evidently frightened at the storm which he had raised, begins to hedge and to retreat from the position which he had originally taken that the expression "*Bringer Forth of God*" (Θεοτόκος) should not be used of the Virgin Mary. Indeed, as appears from his own assertion here, and from his language quoted by Cyril at the end of book I. of his *Five Book Contradiction of his Blasphemies* (422) and from his third letter to Celestine ascribed

---

NOTE 422.—Nestorius there says in his "*Homilies*" (as the work is termed by Cyril of Alexandria, in section 9, in book I. of his Five Book *Contradiction of the Blasphemies of Nestorius*, page 4 of the Oxford translation) [Cyril's Greek there as in col. 13, tom. 76 of *Migne's Patrol. Graeca*, speaks of the work as a *collection of many Homilies*," ὁμιλιῶν]:

"But I have already very often said that if any simpler one either among you or even among any others rejoices in the expression *Bringer Forth of God*, (Θεοτόκος), I have no grudge against the word: only let him not make the Virgin a goddess," (*Migne's Patrologia Graeca*, tom. 76, col. 57).

To this insult from that relic server and server of the Man, that is the creature put on by God the Word, the anti-creature serving Cyril quickly and justly retorts:

"Again dost thou rail upon, and put on a mouth so bitter? and reproachest *the congregation of the Lord*" [with being creature servers, Cyril means. Chrystal], "*as it is written?*" [Num. xxvii: 17; I. Peter ii: 5, 9; John x: 16; Rom. ix: 8; Rom. xi: 19-24, and elsewhere.

"But WE, Oh sir, who call her *Bringer Forth of God* (θεοτόκον), have never yet deified any one of those that are numbered among creatures, but we are accustomed to know as God the One who is God both by NATURE and in truth; and we know that the blessed

by an annotator in *Migne's Patrologia Latina*, to the end of November, A. D. 430 (423) Nestorius had admitted the expression *Bringer Forth of God* at least half a year before the Third Ecumenical Synod met, perhaps even before it was summoned by the Emperors. Whatever importance therefore may be attached to his hostility to the expression at the first as the spark which set the whole set of controversies under the head of Nestorianism in motion, nevertheless it must be remembered that while still holding to his heresies he had gotten so far as dishonestly to accept the term which condemned his anti-Incarnation error at least.

Furthermore, the party of John of Antioch at Ephesus, as is shown in an Orthodox document given or quoted below, were not united in rejecting the expression, and those who favored it would not continue their support to Nestorius, if he did not consent to use it, and make a common fight with them mainly or wholly against Cyril's Twelve Chapters on which all could be united against that champion of the truth. And from the outset, after John of Antioch's arrival at Ephesus, that was he policy of all his heretical party, for they pass by the term *Bringer Forth of God* in silence, and force the fighting on those celebrated Twelve Chapters of Cyril instead. Nestorius alone refers to that expression, because, presumably, so much had been said on it before, at the beginning of the struggle in Constantinople, and it was therefore necessary for him to speak that he might disarm the opposition of some and curry favor for himself and his party.

This Epistle is headed:

"*Epistle of Nestorius to Scholasticus, the Eunuch of the Emperor Theodosius.*"

He begins his letter by saying that he "*wonders*" how Scholasticus "*could* approve the fables of the unclean who say of us that we have abjured the expression by which the *Bringer Forth of God* (424) is designated, which" [expression] "as thou knowest, we have often uttered. But we have so uttered it, lest any one should suspect the Lord Jesus Christ to be a mere man or bare

---

Virgin was a human being, as we are. But thyself wilt be caught, and that at no long interval, representing to us Emmanuel as a" [mere] "inspired Man, and putting upon another" [that is the Orthodox Cyril, CHRYSTAL] "the condemnation due"[for the sin of serving a creature. CHRYSTAL] "to your own essays" [in that direction. CHRYSTAL]. (*Migne's Patrologia Graeca*, tom. 76, col. 57).

Though Nestorius gave up opposing *the expression Bringer Forth of God* [Θεοτόκος], Cyril, in the context, shows that when he wrote that *Five Book Contradiction*, Nestorius did not hold the *doctrine* which that expression was meant to guard, namely that the substance of God the Word took flesh and a man in the womb of the blessed Virgin, and came forth out of that womb into the world by a human birth, and so could ever be worshipped in the Man put on by Him.

NOTE 423. Nestorius' third Epistle to Celestine is in col. 499-501 of tome 50 of Migne's *Patrologia Latina*. The annotation referred to is note "d," col. 499, id.

NOTE 424.—*Coleti Conc.* tom. IV, col. 272, Dei genetrix.

God in humanity." This language does not in express terms assert that the substance of God the Word dwelt in the man put on by Him, but seems to be skilfully evasive, as Cyril, in his commonitory to Posidonius, accuses him of being. (425.)

Below he says that he is willing "to name the Holy Virgin 'particen of God and Man,' ("*Dei particen et hominis*"),'' so as to preserve what he looks upon as the true doctrine on Christ. But what is meant by "particen?" I have looked in the Paris edition of Stephanus' *Thesaurus Graecae Linguae*, (A. D. 1842-1847), and in other Greek Lexicons and do not find that term, nor do I in Facciolati's Latin Lexicon nor in other Latin Lexicons. Nor does Hardouin in his text where the expression occurs (*Conc.*, tom I., col. 1552), nor Mansi in his (*Conc.* tom. v., col. 777), give us the Greek for "particen." I suppose however from the context (426) that the original Greek expression may have been Θεοτόκον, the common old Latin for which however, was *Deipara* "Bringer Forth of God" an exact rendering of the Greek.

But the text is so corrupt here that we must desire the original (427).

Below, in the same document, he says of Cyril of Alexandria's Twelve *Chapters* that "*They are heretical, without contradiction,*" and accuses Cyril of shunning a disputation with him, a deposed Bishop! As though we are not commanded to avoid such (Titus iii: 10). Further on he writes, "We believe that the expression by which the *Bringer Forth of God* (428) is designated is a most genuine mark of piety, if with that expression be put another, that is *Bringer forth of a man*." (429). Below he speaks of using both those expressions as "*Significative of both natures, that is, of the divinity and the humanity*" "that no man," he adds, "may fail to see that we can not run into the error of Manicheus nor into that of Paul." By "Paul," I presume he means Paul of Samosota. He subjoins "For he who says that what is consubstantial with us was born full of inseparable divinity of the Virgin, does in reality frankly proclaim the whole mystery of the Lord's Dispensation. But a denial of either one of these is doing away of the whole Dispensation, which whosoever abjures, it is

---

NOTE 425.—Col. 455 of tome 50 of *Migne's Patrologia Latina*.

NOTE 426.—The whole of the Latin where "particen" occurs is as follows: Scito tamen, quia hoc a nobis saepius ad ipsos dictum est, et bene se habere, et ipsis et a nobis est creditum, Dei particen, et hominis, sanctam Virginem nominare Dei particen non ita quasi ex ipsa Deus Verbum sumpserit exsistendi principium. Quomodo enim hoc esset, dum Virginis ipse Creator sit? Sed ne purum quis hominem fuisse illum qui est genitus suspicetur, hominis vero particen; ne dispensationem, nostras primitias, cum Manichaeis pariter abjuremus (Haec enim ab ipsorum velut in praeexercitatione sunt episcopis dicta, et mutue adinvicem saepius et bene se habere frequenter utraque pars dixit, ita ut hinc plaudentes quoque recederent.) Cyrillus tamen colloqui nobis et ante omnino fugit, et hactenus fugit. Capitulorum quae scripsit convictionem, eo quod absque contradictione sint haeretica, per hoc evadere putans.

NOTE 427.—See the note last above for the Latin.

NOTE 428.—Dei genetrix.

NOTE 429.—Hominis genetrix.

visited on their heads and will soon be more fully visited on them." If Nestorius really meant sincerely to receive now the doctrine of the Incarnation he had certainly changed from his former denial of it. (430.)

Then he goes on to fault Cyril of Alexandria in the strongest and most violent language for attributing to God the Word death and the other human things of the Man united to God the Word, forgetting or ignoring the explanation so often given by Cyril himself, that he attributes such human things to the Word *Economically* only, in order to preserve the due preeminence of God the Uncreated and Eternal Word, even when joined to a creature and incarnate in that creature, and to avoid serving that creature, or any but God, as Athanasius and Cyril explain. (431.)

Next Nestorius brings the unsupported accusation against the Orthodox that they quoted the heretical Basil of Ancyra as the Orthodox Basil of Caesarea in Cappadocia, and other heretics as Orthodox writers of the same given name, in order to deceive the simple. He again calls the Orthodox *"most unclean,"* and contends foolishly and slanderously that if they triumph, the churches would embrace the doctrines of Arius, Eunomius, and Apollinarius.

Then he exhorts him to stand by the Nestorian opinions, or Orthodoxy as understood and held to by Nestorius, and calls Cyril's faith *"heresy,"* and professes his willingness to hand in his resignation of the episcopate and retire to his former monastic life, provided his own ideas prevail, and provided that Scholasticus the Chamberlain should ask it of him; conditions which, so far as his errors prevailing, never occurred but for a brief season; and so far as Scholasticus' asking it of him were absurd, for no mere chamberlain of the Emperor, nor indeed the Emperor himself, had any right to ask it of him if he were Orthodox. And it is not likely that the Emperor would have brooked any such assumption in the matter on the part of Scholasticus. And if his own heresy were pronounced Orthodox no request for his resignation would be heeded, for he would be in great glory. Then he adds the request that the reports sent by the Orthodox against him and the Oriental Bishops should be discussed before the Emperor, "either" he adds, "*I also being present there,*" [in Constantinople] "or before some persons sent hither, so that by them ye may be moved to exile [or ' to exterminate '] those who have disturbed all things by their false utterances. For nothing at all of all that they have reported is true." And so this document ends (432). From the allusions to the Reports of

NOTE 430.—For proof of his former denial see under Nestorius' *Heresy* I., pages 637-639, vol. I. of Chrystal's *Ephesus*. See also pages 156, 157, 161, there, where his denial of the birth of God the Word in flesh is thrice proclaimed.

NOTE 431.—See in proof Passage 13 of St. Athanasius approved by St. Cyril, pages 237-240, volume I. of Chrystal's translation of *Nicaea*. Compare other Orthodox passages against all worship of creatures from Athanasius, Epiphanius, Lucifer of Cagliari, and Faustin the Presbyter, of Rome, pages 217-255, there.

NOTE 432.—The above epitome is made from *Coleti Conc.*, tom. IV., col. 973 and context, and I have to some extent compared the same document in *Harduin. Conc.*, tom. 1, col. 1552-1554, and *Mansi Conc.*, tom. V., col. 777-779.

the Orthodox which were not made till after they had deposed him, we see that this document was written after that event.

And, indeed, he alludes in it to his leaving his see as a possibility, or a probability, a thing new to him. He had heard of his deposition.

I would put it therefore either just before or not long after he had read the edict of the Emperor which confirms his deposition and that of Cyril and Memnon. Perhaps it may have gone up with the Delegates of the Apostasy to Constantinople, or perhaps later. See in Document XVI., below, as to the date of the Edicts of the Emperor to the Synod.

On it I would remark as follows:

1. It contains some downright falsehood, such as its last sentence above which accuses all the two hundred Bishops of the Orthodox Council of lying in their Reports.

2. As has been said above, Nestorius now takes the back track and gives up all further resistance to the expression "*Bringer Forth of God*," though he had so strenuously opposed it at first as to persuade the people that he denied the Incarnation in the sense of a dwelling of the Substance of God the Word in the Man put on in Mary's womb by Him, and with John of Antioch and his party he changes his tactics, and says nothing definitely of the differences between Cyril and himself on the right of worshipping the Man put on, or on the Eucharist, but confines himself to attacking Cyril and the Orthodox on the Twelve Chapters of Cyril generally, and particularly against their teachings on Economic Appropriation which he outrageously slanders, because he deemed them the most vulnerable points. And he perverts Cyril's sense and meaning in them inexcusably; for Cyril had already explained it. I give a sample from this very document. Nestorius writes:

"But what is altogether worse, and most of all now provokes the Lord Christ's great indignation, and is worthy of a thousand lightnings and thunderbolts is the assertion that the Divinity of the Sole-Born, and the Word of God died and needed solace in the sepulchre, and merited resurrection with [His] flesh, all which things are alien to Church Orthodoxy and will never be received by us. For, far be it from us, that I should at any time suppose that the Divinity which is the Quickener of our First-Fruits (433), was itself deprived of life, or needed a greater Quickener [than Itself]. For inasmuch as not even His flesh saw corruption (434) why will not anyone who says that His Divinity was corrupted with His flesh, be worthy to share the lot of the demon"? (435).

Now all there is of truth in this representation is that Cyril taught in the aforesaid Twelve Chapters that all the *human things* of the Man put on should *Economically only* be attributed to God the Word, for the sake of teaching men, as he elsewhere writes, to worship, not that *creature*, but *God the Word* in him

NOTE 433.—I. Cor., xv: 20, 23.
NOTE 434.—Acts ii: 27, 31; Psalm xvi: 10; Acts xiii: 34-38.
NOTE 435.—*Coleti Conc.*, tom. IV., col. 273.

(436), for as he teaches again and again, all religious service is prerogative to God alone (Math. iv., 10) (437). And he furthermore teaches that God the Word did not die, and that He did not suffer, and did not need solace nor quickening, and that His Divinity is not liable to corruption. Hence the above language of Nestorius is downright misrepresentation and sin. But such misrepresentations constitute from this point onward the stock-in-trade of his party.

3. A noteworthy fact is that neither Nestorius, nor John of Antioch and his party, nor Cyril of Alexandria and the Orthodox Synod, in any of these Reports and Letters, mention the topic of the Worship of the Virgin Mary, except at the end of Cyril's First Book of his *Five Book Contradiction of the Blasphemies* of Nestorius, where both parties condemn and reject it, as we shall soon see, but they do mention again and again the difference, between the Orthodox and the Nestorians as to worshipping Christ's humanity, on the Eucharist, and on the doctrine of the Incarnation as involved in the use of the expression, *Bringer Forth of God* (438). The doctrine of the Incarnation was the thing involved in that expression from the start, as the writers of that time certify, and Man-Worship and Eucharistic errors, were lugged in by the Nestorians as by them connected with their denial of the Inflesh, and as resulting from it. The notion that there was any advocacy of the worship of the Virgin Mary by the Orthodox is an invention of later times, when the meaning of the whole controversy had been lost in a night of image worship and other idolatry and creature invocation and apostacy from the fundamental truth that God alone is to be invoked and served, and when men, while admitting the Incarnation, had nevertheless gone even further in worshipping creatures than even Nestorius himself, for while he *relatively* bowed to, that is relatively worshipped the humanity, as his own testimony shows, and probably, like his co-patriarchan, Theodoret of Cyrus, *relatively* bowed to, that is *worshipped relatively* the bread and wine in the Eucharist because of their relation to God the Word or to His humanity, there is no clear proof that he ever invoked any saint or angel or archangel, or bowed to any image painted or graven, for that sin had not yet entered the Church. Hence he was not so degraded a creature-server as the men of the middle ages who forsook the faith of Cyril and of the Third Ecumenical Synod, which forbids us to serve any thing but the Triune Divinity Itself.

But to quote the passage just mentioned, at the end of the *First of his Five*

NOTE 436.—See his approval of a passage of Athanasius to that effect, pages 237-240, vol. I. of Chrystal's *Nicaea*, and in Chrystal's *Ephesus*, vol. I., notes 183, 664, 669, 949, and 156.

NOTE 437.—See vol. I. of Chrystal's *Ephesus*, under Nestorius' *Heresy* 2, pages 639-641; pages 641,642, under his *Heresy* 3; pages 631-635 under *Man Worship*, and on pages 662-666 under *Word* and *Worship*; on pages 694-696 under ἀνθρωπολατρεια and ἀνθρωπολάτρης, and on page 720 under οἰκειώσασθαι and οἰκονομικήν οἰκείωσιν.

NOTE 438.—Greek, θεοτόκος.

Books of Contradiction of the Blasphemies of Nestorius, where Cyril justly shows how false the accusation is that the Orthodox worshipped the Virgin Mary or any other human being, and referring to the fact that Nestorius was a worshipper of a merely human being on his own profession, for that was all there was of the Nestorian Christ, he in effect retorts on him and justly the change of anthropolatry, that is a charge of being ⁱ *worshipper of a human being*. I translate and quote.

"But what has persuaded thee to so let loose thy uncontrolled and unbridled tongue against those who have been zealous to hold correct beliefs, and to pour forth a terrible and all hard accusation against every worshipper of God? for thou saidst furthermore before the Church:

"'*And I have already very often said that if there be any one of the simpler sort among us, and if there be such a person among any others, who rejoices in the expression Bringer Forth of God* (439) *I have no grudge against that expression ; only let him not make the Virgin a goddess.*'"

[Cyril answers]. "Wilt thou again furiously rail at us and inflict so bitter a mouth upon us, and as it is written (440) dost thou reproach *the congregation of the Lord?* But WE, at least, O Sir, who say that she was the *Bringer Forth of God* (441), HAVE NEVER YET DEIFIED ANY OF THOSE RECKONED AMONG CREATURES, BUT WE HAVE BEEN WONT TO ACKNOWLEDGE THE ONE GOD WHO IS SUCH BOTH BY NATURE AND TRULY. *And we know that the blessed Virgin is a human being like us.* And, moreover, thou thyself wilt be caught before long representing to us the Emmanuel," [that is as Emmanuel means, *the God with us*] "as a" [mere] "inspired man (442) and putting upon another the accusation due to thy own undertakings" (443) [in the way of

---

NOTE 439.—Θεοτόκον.
NOTE 440.—Compare Numbers xxvii: 17.
NOTE 441.—Greek, Θεοτόκον.
NOTE 442.—The proof that Nestorius worshipped the humanity of Christ is abundant, from his own confession, the testimony of Cyril, his opponent, and the decisions of the Third Ecumenical Council, deposing him for that among his other errors. See, for example, in the Oxford English translation of *St. Cyril of Alexandria on the Incarnation against Nestorius*, his *Five Book Contradiction of the Blasphemies of Nestorius*, book II., section 8, pages 67-80 there, and more in the same book but beware of P. E. Pusey's mis translations of θεοτόκος, by *Mother of God*, etc. Always compare the Greek in doubtful points. Compare also Nestorius' confession of his worship of Christ's humanity in his Counter Anathema VIII., against Cyril's Anathema VIII., Chrystal's *Ephesus*, volume I., pages 68, 69, note matter, and all of note 156 of which the note matter there forms part, and especially also, note 183, pages 79-128; note 664, pages 323, 324; note 679, pages 332-362; and on *relative worship* page 461, note 949. See also under *Man-Worship*, pages 631-635, under *Nestorius' Heresy* 2, his *Man-Worship* on pages 639-641; and on pages 694, 695 under ἀνθρωπολατρεία, and ἀνθρωπολάτρης, and pages 449-504 for his xx. Blasphemies, some of which favor Man Worship, and his deposition for them.

NOTE 443.—Cyril of Alexandria's *Five Book Contradiction of the Blasphemies of Nestorius*, book I., chapters 9 and 10: Greek as on pages 90, 91 of vol. vi. of Cyril's works by P. E. Pusey, Oxford 1875, Parker: τί δέ σε τὸ πεπεικὸς, ἀκρατῆ καὶ ἀπύλωτον οὕτω χαλάσαι τὴν

worshipping a human being; that is Cyril means, thou accusest us of the sin of worshipping a human being, that is the Virgin Mary, which is false, but thou thyself wilt soon be proven to be guilty of worshipping a human being, Christ's humanity, and then Cyril goes on to prove that he was such a man-worshipper.

4. Nestorius goes so far, perhaps under the influence of the opposition to him, and of some of his former companions of the Patriarchate of Antioch, as to use language which looks somewhat Orthodox at first glance, though he

γλῶτταν κατὰ τῶν ὀρθὰ φρονεῖν διεσπουδακότων, καὶ παντὸς τοῦ σεβομένου Θεὸν ἔγκλημα καταχέαι δεινὸν καὶ παγχάλεπον; ἔφης γὰρ πάλιν ἐπ' ἐκκλησίας.

"Εἶπον δὲ ἤδη πλειστάκις, ὅτι εἴ τις ἢ ἐν ἡμῖν ἀφελέστερος, εἴ τε ἐν ἄλλοις τισὶ, χαίρει τῇ τοῦ θεοτόκος φωνῇ, ἐμοὶ πρὸς τὴν φωνὴν φθόνος οὐκ ἔστι· μόνον μὴ ποιείτω τὴν παρθένον θεάν."

Πάλιν ἡμῖν διαλοιδορῇ καὶ πικρὸν οὕτως ἐπιθήσῃ στόμα; ὀνειδίζεις δὲ τὴν συναγωγὴν Κυρίου, κατὰ τὸ γεγραμμένον· ἀλλ' ἡμεῖς γε, ὦ τᾶν, οἱ θεοτόκον λέγοντες αὐτήν· τεθεοποιήκαμεν δὲ οὐδένα πώποτε τῶν τελούντων ἐν κτίσμασι· κατειθίσμεθα δὲ Θεὸν εἰδέναι τὸν ἕνα καὶ φύσει καὶ ἀληθῶς· ἴσμεν δὲ ἄνθρωπον οὖσαν καθ' ἡμᾶς τὴν μακαρίαν παρθένον. ἄνθρωπον ἡμῖν θεοφόρον ἀποφαίνων αὐτὸς τὸν Ἐμμανουήλ, καὶ τῶν σῶν ἐπιχειρημάτων τὴν κατάρρησιν ἐπιτιθεὶς ἑτέρῳ.

It should be added here by way of warning and for the sake of accuracy that the Oxford translation is very faulty and inexact in rendering θεοτόκος *Mother of God*, and θεοφόρον ἄνθρωπον, "*a God bearing Man*," whereas the former word means literally *Bringer Forth of God*, and the last expression *a God-borne man*; that is a mere *God-inspired man*, as Sophocles well shows under θεοφόρος, in his *Lexicon of Later and Byzantine Greek*. Liddell and Scott's Greek Lexicon defines the cognate terms θεοφόρεω, "mostly Pass" [ive] "*to be possessed or inspired by a God*," θεοφόρησις, *inspiration* and θεοφόρητος *inspired, possessed*. Liddell and Scott give the same word with the acute accent on the antepenult, θεόφορος, as meaning in ecclesiastical usage, *borne, possessed by a god, inspired*," but we find the same sense in the paroxytone θεοφόρον in Sophocles' Lexicon, so that the accenting of the word in that sense differed. But the context in Cyril above shows that *an inspired man* is meant, for that was all that Nestorius made Christ to be. Sophocles in his *Glossary of Later and Byzantine Greek*, under θεοφόρος, gives both meanings, or "*God bearing, inspired*," and gives examples from Ignatius, Cyril of Alexandria, Theodoret of Cyrus, his contemporary, and John of Damascus. That from Theodoret certainly means *inspired*: it is τῶν τριακοσίων δεκαοκτὼ ἁγίων θεοφόρων πατέρων, "*the 318 holy God-inspired Fathers*." With the similar sense of *inspired by God* he defines the cognate term θεοφορέομαι, "*to be under the immediate influence of God, to be inspired*."

In modern Greek we find the sense *inspired* yet in use. For example, in Contopoulos' *Greek English Lexicon*, under θεοφόρος, we find the expression οἱ Θεοφόροι πατέρες, "*the inspired Fathers* of the Church," and the cognate expression θεοφόρητος is defined, the only sense there given, "*divinely inspired*;" and the *Greek French Lexicon* of Byzantios, which omits θεοφόρος, word and accents, agrees with Contopoulos' as to θεοφόρητος, for the only sense there given is "*inspiré de Dieu*." None of these Lexicons, except Liddell and Scott, give the proparoxytone θεόφορος at all. In other words, Sophocles' Lexicon, his Glossary, Contopoulos and Byzantios give θεοφόρος alone.

probably did not mean it in the sense of a complete acceptance of the dogma of the Incarnation, and we doubt his sincere reception of it, the more especially as he is guilty of lying and slander in this same document in charging all the well attested Reports of the Orthodox Synod with falsehood, to speak of nothing else. And some of his language is so ambiguous as to admit a double sense; as, for instance, his confession above that Christ's humanity "*was born full of inseparable divinity*, of the Virgin, in which to the simpler of the Orthodox who did not know his obstinate rejection of Cyril's explanations before the Synod met at Ephesus, there, and afterwards, he might seem to acknowledge the dwelling of *the Substance* of God the Word in the Man united to him, but which Nestorius might explain in his own heretical sense by asserting that Christ's humanity was full of divinity, merely in the sense that a prophet was, that is in the sense of being inspired by the Holy Ghost, not in the sense of any real indwelling of *the Substance* of God the Word Himself in that Man.

Moreover, 5, we must remember that this letter of Nestorius is the utterance of a man already deposed by four-fifths of the whole Synod, including all who had met with it, of a man, therefore, who was, as we say, "*on his last legs*" theologically, who could no longer hope for help in the Church, but must seek imperial favor to undo its work, and reinstate him in his former dignity and honors. And hence we find him eating, to some extent, his own words, and giving up and abandoning the position he held in the controversy till Cyril of Alexandria had gone to the assistance of the Orthodox of Constantinople whom he had persecuted. It is therefore no longer a struggle as against his original opponents. It is a struggle now, primarily at least, against Cyril of Alexandria and his celebrated Twelve Chapters *and against their condemnation of creature service*. And, in order to make his own desperate cause more plausible, he resorts to misrepresentation of their teaching, of Cyril, and of the Orthodox. But the change of front and of tactics came too late. And from one of these Nestorian Documents above, Count Irenaeus' letter to the Orientals (Document XI.) we see that not even Scholasticius, or Scholasticus, to whom this epistle was addressed, was deceived on that point, for as there stated, he did not believe that Nestorius had accepted, even at Ephesus, the expression, "*Bringer forth of God*" (θεοτόκος).

DOCUMENT XIII. AMONG THE PAPERS ON THE APOSTATIC COUNCIL.—
Document X. in Coleti and Mansi here.

AN EDICT OF THE EMPERORS ADDRESSED TO THE THIRD ECUMENICAL SYNOD.

This approves the deposition of Nestorius, Cyril of Alexandria, and Memnon, and the whole tenor of it shows a most lamentable ignorance on the part of the Emperor as to the great doctrines involved in the discussion. I give it entire, for if in any future Ecumenical Synod any such thing should appear, it will not be without its use, and that the Bishops may not be swayed or governed by it, even as Cyril and the Third Ecumenical Synod were not governed by this which here follows:

"*A copy of the Sacred*" [that is *imperial*] (444) "*letter, sent through John the Count of the sacred*" [*imperial*] "*affairs* (445) *by the most religious Emperors to the Holy and Great Synod.*"

To Celestine, Rufus, Augustine (446), Alexander, Acacius, Tranquillinus, Valentinus, Iconius, John, Acacius, Ursus, Firmus, Himerius, Dexianus, Berinianus, Palladius, Asterius, Juvenal, Flavian, Helladius, Rabbulus, another Alexander, Maximus, Phritilas, Perigenes, Cyrus, another John, Eutherius, Hellanicus, Bosporius, another Cyrus, Vinatius, Peter, Dynatus, Dorotheus, Antiochus, Dalmatius, Eusebius, Seleucus, Eleusius, Eulogius, Sappius, Timotheus, Pius, Troïlus, Herennianus (447), Monimus, Olympius, Theophilus, Julian, Basil, and the rest of the most religious Bishops.

How much zeal we continue to have for piety and for the ancestral faith, we deem has been plainly shown by many things past, and we have believed that it has been made clear to all throughout the whole world, and not least by the calling of your present Synod. For when some controversy arose we did not suffer it even for a brief space, but sent to your Holiness (448) to assemble in haste in order that a settlement of it should the more swiftly and closely follow it, and, though we did not think that labor on behalf of piety would be burdensome to your God-Reveringness, nevertheless, by our imperial foresight we lightened (449) the difficulty of this affair by supplying a fit time and place. For we appointed the city of the Ephesians which is easy of access to those who travel by land and to those who travel by sea, and it affords abundantly to sojourners in it, everything necessary in the way of native and foreign produce, so that the pious aim of our Serenity and of your

---

NOTE 444.—The Greek is σάκρας, literally "*sacred*" from the Latin *Sacer*.

NOTE 445.—'Ιωάννου τοῦ κόμητος τῶν σακρῶν; literally, "*John, the Count of the Sacred things.*" The article on him in Smith and Wace's *Dict. of Christian Biography* terms him, 'Count of the sacred bounties." See "Joannes (560)" in that work. On the use of such relics of the worship of the pagan Roman Emperors see Chrystal's *Ephesus*, vol. I., page 19, note 20, and note B. pages 505-512.

NOTE 446.—According to the note in col. 1251, 1252 of tome III. of *Coleti's Concilia*, "Baluze and others think that Augustine's name has been inserted here by an error of the imperial Secretary." A summons had been sent to him to sit in it, but he died before it. Compare *Hefele's History of the Church Councils*, English translation, vol. III., page 41. See under "*Augustine*," in Chrystal's *Nicaea*, vol. I., General Index, and in the General Index to vol. 1. of his *Ephesus*.

NOTE 447.—Or "*Irenianus*," or "*Ireniacus*," but I find no such name in the lists of Bishops present in Act I. of Ephesus, but I do find *Berinianus of Perga in Pamphylia*; page 556, vol. I., Chrystal's translation of *Ephesus*. And at the end of Act VI., among the signatures I find the same Berinianus and also Hereunianus, Bishop of Myra, who seems to be the one meant; see page 226, vol. 2 of Chrystal's *Ephesus*.

NOTE 448.—A Byzantine non-New Testament title for the whole Synod.

NOTE 449.—That is, "*relieved*," ἐπεκουφίσαμεν.

most holy Synod may easily concur, and be realized. Wherefore we now also, accept the deposition of Nestorius, and of Cyril, and of Memnon made known to us by your Piety. And as to the rest of what has been done by you, we acknowledge and guard that faith and correctness in Christianity which we have received from [our] fathers and ancestors, which the most holy Synod, held in the time of Constantine of the divine lot (450), harmoniously confirmed. Let each one therefore of your most holy Assembly take care to settle every controversy, and to cut off the scandals, and so to return to your own homes in peace and harmony. And that your Holiness may be turned not only by the letter of our Piety towards unanimity, and have regard to peace on all pious doctrine, we have, after reading it, sent you the letter of Acacius also, the Bishop of the Berrhoeans, who advises the same course, though on account of his advanced age (451), he can not be present at your most holy Assembly; nevertheless he suggests by what he has written those things which befit his God-Reveringness and conduce to the Orthodox religion. The reading of the same letter will show of what sort they are. Let your Holiness therefore know that we have sent to you, the most magnificent and most glorious Count of the sacred [imperial] things (452), to the end that he knowing the aim of our Divinity (453) concerning the faith, may accomplish that which he shall see to be useful and profitable."

DOCUMENT XIV. AMONG THE PAPERS ON THE APOSTATIC SYNOD.—
Document XI. in Coleti and Mansi here.

This is given in Coleti in Latin only. It is headed " *Copy of* AN EPISTLE

NOTE 450.—That is, in blessedness in the other world: τοῦ τῆς θείας λήξεως Κωνσταντίνου. The meaning seems to be that he is in heaven.

NOTE 451.—Acacius was at this time about 100 years old. The Berrhoea of which he was Bishop is Aleppo in Syria. At first he was against the XII. Chapters, but became sounder toward the last, according to Lightfoot's article on him in Smith and Wace's *Dictionary of Christian Biography.*

NOTE 452.—Greek, Κόμητα τῶν σακρῶν. In a note in cols. 1253, 1254 of tome III. of Coleti this Count John is called "*Comes Largitionum Joannes,*" that is, "*John, Count of the Largesses,*" and so of the Treasury. He was a sort of High Almoner of the Emperor. As one skilled in Greek and Latin may readily see, the Greek σάκρα is from the Latin *sacer, sacred,* a relic of the deifying of the pagan Roman Emperors. I have heard the statement, I think, that in Russia a relic of that Byzantinism yet exists in the form of worshipping the picture of the Emperor. But I am not sure that it is true.

NOTE 453.—Greek, τῆς ἡμετέρας θειότητος; literally, "*our divinity,*" but this term *divinity* came to be used of and by Christian Emperors but not indeed in its full sense of *divinity*. But it was a grievous fault to keep up that old pagan Roman use of terms. It was probably used first by those who flattered the pagan Emperors that they were *gods,* and should have died with them. Some would see in the curse of defeat, and being compelled to pay tribute to Attila the Hun, and in the manner of Theodosius the Second's death and in the deaths of some others who used it, a rebuke and judgment for their blasphemy in doing so. See Chrystal's *Ephesus,* vol. I., page 19, note 20, and page 505, note B; and on

of JOHN COUNT OF THE SACRED THINGS [IMPERIAL TREASURER] (454), *written from the city of Ephesus to the Emperors"* (455). It is found in another Latin translation in chapter XVI. of Irenaeus' *Synodicon*, col. 605, 606, and 607, in tome 84, of Migne's *Patrologia Graeca*.

This, the production of a favorer of Nestorius, and of John of Antioch, and of one, who, as its whole tenor shows, could not appreciate the vital questions involved, makes manifest even in his prejudiced account, the firmness of the Orthodox Bishops for the decisions of the Synod, and for Cyril and Memnon their leaders. John probably exaggerates when he speaks of there being fighting.

In the margin of col. 1253, tome III. of Coleti's *Concilia*, we read on this document as follows:

" What follows is not found in Greek, but it was published in the last Cologne edition of the Councils, from a most ancient manuscript book, as is asserted in the same work ; and Peltanus also took it thence." As this document is given in Coleti in Latin only, from that therefore I translate. I have not seen the Greek. I give the whole document.

" Forasmuch as I know that it will conduce to piety, if all things which I have done in acting a man's part, in accordance with a mind of purest loftiness (456), be committed to the imperial records, you will learn from this letter what has been done. On the day before this letter should be (457) given to the

---

Theodosius the Second's defeat and his becoming a tributary of the Huns, *Gibbon's Decline and Fall of the Roman Empire*, chapter XXXIV., pages 549, 565-580, vol. III. of Bohn's VII. vol. Edition, London, 1854.

NOTE 454.—John is called "*Comitis sacrensis*" in the title above; but in the Latin of the title in the Synodicon Casinense, quoted in the next note below, he is called *Comes Largitionum*" Both those expressions are reconciled and to some extent explained by what is said under "largitio" in *Harper's Latin Dictionary*, where "largitiones" is defined to be "*the imperial treasury, public chest, or imperial fund* for presents and distributions, Eutr. 8, 13; Cod. Just. 7, 62, 21; both sacrae (for public or state purposes) and privatae (for personal outlay,) id. 10, 23, 2; Cod. Th. 12, 6, 13."

On the duties of that officer see further in *Gibbon's Decline and Fall of the Roman Empire*, chapter XVII., page 236, of vol. II. in Bohn's seven volume edition.

NOTE 455.—Note 2, cols. 1253, 1254 of tome III. of Coleti's Concilia, adds here on this letter:

" This Epistle is also read in another Latin form among the various Epistles in the *Synodicon Casinense*, with the following title: '*After these things, John, Count of the Largesses was sent with an imperial letter on the deposition of Nestorius and of the blessed Cyril and Memnon, which we have placed in a part of the former Codex; The report of that Count is this:*' " that is to say what [there] follows. The *imperial letter* which is here [above] mentioned is that very one which next precedes this epistle; "the imperial letter" here meant is Edict Second to the Synod during its session. In Coleti it precedes the Epistle of John above. The Imperial letter is translated above, just before this letter of John, and is Document XIII. there, and Document XI. in Coleti and Mansi.

NOTE 456.—Coleti Conc. tom. III. col. 1253 Omnia, quae juxta purissimae Celsitudinis mentem pro virili feci. I am not sure whether John means by purissimae Celsitudinis mentem, the Emperor's mind, or his own mind, or, "*a most most pure and lofty mind*," absolutely, but suppose that he means the Emperor's.

NOTE 457.—Or "*on the day before this letter was given?*" Pridie quam hae literae darentur is the Latin.

messenger, I came through with great labor and with wonderful hastening into the city of the Ephesians. But I would have come more quickly, were it not that I was impeded by very great matters, which I will recount to your Majesty, when God being propitious, I come into your presence. And straightway I reverently saluted the most holy Bishops" [of both parties] "who had come together here or there. But on account of the discord which existed between them, it was a suitable thing to summon the" [two] "parties" [to meet]. "But as all were disturbed, and Cyril and Memnon were walling themselves about, I, by my own person, warned those who had convened, and informed those who were absent, that they should all on the following day, without any delay, come into my stopping place. Furthermore, lest there might arise some sort of a conflict, in case they came mixed up together (for even that event was to be feared on account of the fierceness, which had happened to them, I know not whence), I arranged the order of their entrance. But when Nestorius was present almost with the dawn itself, and the most pious Bishop John (458); Cyril came also with all the most pious bishops, except Memnon alone, who was absent;" [and] "there began to arise a great confusion, and uproar; for those who had come with Cyril said that not even the sight of Nestorius, who had been deposed by them, was to be endured; but nevertheless they were willing to come together and that the reading of the divine" [imperial] (459) "letter

NOTE 458.—The Latin translation in the Synodicon Casinense, as given in col. 274, tome IV., of *Coleti's Concilia*, gives a little different sense here. Translated it reads:

"But Nestorius came at once with the dawn, and not much after the most religious Bishop John with the most holy Bishops who are of like mind" [with him], "and Cyril came with all the most dear to God Bishops, except Memnon alone."

NOTE 459.—The Latin is "divinarum scripturarum lectionem." Here we have again the old pagan Roman way of speaking of what pertained to their Emperors as *divine*. Surely the Emperors and their courtiers and others should have remembered what occurred to Herod Agrippa when after his oration to them the people shouted in flattery and called his voice that of a god. I give it as in Acts xii: 22, 23:

"And upon a set day Herod arrayed in royal apparel, sat upon his throne, and made an oration unto them. And the people gave a shout, saying, It is the voice of a god, and not of a man. And immediately an angel of the Lord smote him, because he gave not God the glory, and he was eaten of worms and gave up the ghost." That lesson was lost on Theodosius II. and on some of his officers as here. And in another of these documents, Document V. above, pages 258, 259, he twice speaks of himself as *our Divinity*, and of his "*divine court;*" and his "*divine palace.*" See in proof the Greek. And under θεῖος, divine and θειότης, *Divinity, Sophocles* in his *Glossary of Later and Byzantine Greek*, and in his *Greek Lexicon of the Roman and Byzantine Periods*, shows example after example of the use of those terms for the Roman Emperor, and for things pertaining to him. The whole influence of such lying flattery is degrading for it leads to insincerity and deception. And the use of the Emperor's images and the worship of them, led to the worship of images of Christ, of angels and of saints. Daniel strongly condemned the worship of Nebuchadnezzar's, and Jerome on Daniel III., (the place is purposely omitted in one or more late Romish editions of his works) says that the sin is the same if men worship the images of the Roman Emperors.

But forasmuch as the Universal Church at Ephesus approved Cyril's Anathema VIII.,

should be gone through with. But those who were favoring Cyril kept affirming that the reading of the divine" [imperial] (460) "and terrible letter ought not to be gone through with without Cyril, and that Nestorius must not be present, nor those most holy bishops who had come from the East (461), and on that account a great dissension was made, yea a battle and a fight. And the most holy Bishops who stood on the most pious Bishop John's side, contended for the same points also, by saying that Cyril ought not to be present at the reading of the divine" [imperial] (462) "letter, inasmuch as he also with Memnon had been deposed by themselves. A contention was therefore made on that matter. But as the greatest part of the day was already past, I thought it worth while to make known the imperial decisions to all but Cyril and Memnon, since indeed the letter was not written by the Masters of the World (463) to the" [two] "aforesaid (464). But the most religious Bishops who had come with Cyril refused that course also, and were unwilling to lend their ears" [to the reading] "if those who had come with John were" [to be] "present; because, they said, they (465) had unlawfully deposed Cyril and Memnon. I was scarcely able therefore by persuasion and force (since indeed the truth ought to be spoken), to induce the whole Synod to listen to the imperial rescript, after I had removed Nestorius and Cyril. So all being congregated, I went through the reading of the imperial letter, in which Cyril, and Nestorius, and Memnon, are deposed (466). But when those who had come with the most which proclaims a curse on every one who gives the name *God* to Christ's humanity even, the hightest of all creatures, and inasmuch as it condemned Nestorius' even merely relative worship of that humanity in his Blasphemy 8, and deposed him for such errors, it is certainly guiltless in that matter, no matter how later Synods, that is, the Second of Nicaea, A. D., 787, and others, approved such idolatry; see in proof Chrystal's *Ephesus*, vol. I., pages 331, 332 text and notes there, and 461, and note 949 there, and pages 221-223 inclusive; pages 231-240; and note 183, pages 79-126, and especially pages 106-112, as to the verdict of Ephesus and the whole Church afterwards against the worship of Christ's humanity; and for Nestorius' deposition for that and all his xx. Blasphemies, pages 479, 480, 486-504.

NOTE 460.—Coleti Conc., tom. III., col. 1254, "lectionem divinarum et terribilium scripturarum."

NOTE 461.—This is, John of Antioch and his party, who had been ecumenically condemned as heretics in Act I. of the Synod, and the direction of an inspired Apostle in Titus iii: 10, applies to all such: "*A man that is a heretic after the first and second admonition reject*," or *avoid*, as Robinson in his *Greek and English Lexicon of the New Testament* here renders it. The Greek word is παραιτοῦ, literally, *excuse yourself from*; that is, *have nothing to do with him*.

NOTE 462.—*Coleti Concil.*, tom. III., col. 1255, "divinarum literarum lectioni."

NOTE 463.—That is, the Emperors.

NOTE 464.—That is, Cyril and Memnon.

NOTE 465.—That is, John of Antioch and his little party.

NOTE 466.—Literally, "*royal rescript*," "*regium rescriptum*," but the Greek was probably not "*royal*," but "*imperial*" or "*divine*," for "*royal*" means *what relates to a King*, but the Romans would look upon that term as not sufficiently high for their Emperor. The translation "*decreta imperialia*," in the other Latin translation of this document, seems much nearer the original Greek. See it in col. 275, A, tom. IV. of *Coleti's Concilia*.

NOTE 467.—It is noteworthy that in this same place in the *Synodicon* of Irenaeus

Epistle of Count John from Ephesus to the Emperors. 291

pious John acknowledged and approved in a friendly way the reading, they heard from an aggrieved auditory (468) that the deposition of Cyril and Memnon had been unlawfully made (469). But lest the dissension should become greater, Count Candidian, of the noble body guards (470), who took part in all my plans and operations took Nestorius, into his own keeping; but Cyril himself I delivered to Jacob, a circumspect Count and Prefect of the fourth school" (471)[of the imperial palace guards],"to be kept also by him. Memnon, however, as I said before, was absent—Wherefore, I sent a steward, and a lictor, and the first deacon of the most holy church of the Ephesians, and informed him that he had been deposed. But the said Memnon, with the aforesaid persons (472) pledged their good faith to them that they themselves will keep at their own peril, with all security, the church monies. When those things had been done in that way, since it was behooving me also to give myself to prayers, I descended into the most holy Church. But having learned that Memnon was acting in the Bishop's house" [as Bishop] "I sent, of my attendants, the chief of the noble chamberlains to himself, to come to me, in order that I might learn whether he utterly refused to come to me. But he himself came without delay, and when he was rebuked by me, for not having come in the morning, he said that he had been seized by sickness and therefore was not present. But lest he should hear my other admonitions or counsels, he

Nestorius as well as Cyril and Memnon are mentioned as deposed. See it in chapter XVI., of that work in Mansi (v., col. 780), and in col. 606 of tome 84 of Migue's *Patrologia Graeca*.

NOTE 468.—*Coleti Conc.*, tom. III., col. 1255. "audierunt a gravi auditorio depositionem Cyrilli et Memnonis illegitime factam."

In the *Synodicon* the latter part of the above is fuller, and I presume more accurate, for instead of the words "they heard from an aggrieved auditory that the deposition of Cyril and Memnon had been unlawfully made," it reads:

"Those who had congregated with the most reverend Flavian" [Metropolitan of Philippi, who seems, now that the Emperor had taken away their leaders, to have succeeded to the leadership of the Ecumenical Synod. CHRYSTAL] "heard the reading with grief, because the condemnation of Cyril and Memnon had not been made canonically" (canonice). It had certainly been an anti-canonical and farcical proceeding; for it was done by about one-fifth of the Synod without the ordinary three citations of the accused to come and defend himself.

NOTE 469.—In the *Synodicon Casinense* is added in this place, "*So therefore the reading was celebrated as the day was declining towards evening;* note, col. 1255, vol. 3 of Coleti.

NOTE 470.—Ibid. Comes nobilium domesticorum. Sophocles in his "Greek Lexicon of the Roman and Byzantine Periods," under δομέστικος, defines it as "the Latin domesticus—οἰκεῖος, *one of the imperial body-guard.*" They were what the English call "Household Troops;" for *domesticus* means *belonging to the household, or relating to the house hold*

NOTE 471.—The school here referred to was one of the divisions of the imperial palace-guard. See under σχολή and σχολάριος in *Sophocles' Greek Lexicon*, and *Schola* and *Scholaris* in Harper's Latin Dictionary.

NOTE 472.—This document is quite different here in chapter XVI. of Irenaeus' Synodicon, col. 606 of tome 84 of *Migne's Patrologia Graeca*, for it reads:

"But since Memnon, as has been said before, 'was absent, I called the steward and the defensor' [that is 'the defender'] "and the first deacon also of the most holy city or

anticipated my words, and rushed (473) into my house. He himself, therefore, was delivered to Jacob the circumspect Count, to be kept by the noble shield bearers and by the most reverend chamberlains. Those things were done by me on the first day. But inasmuch as it was behooving to discourse to the most pious Bishops in regard to peace also, lest heresies and schisms be made in the Orthodox religion, therefore I have applied myself to that task with all the power that I possess, and henceforth will labor to that end, provided it please those who are better (474) and be consonant to piety, and provided there be a right mind towards the Masters of the world (475). But if I shall see that the most pious Bishops are unappeased and not reconcilable (I know not whence (476) they have come into that rage and asperity), and if any thing more is done. I will at once signify it to your Amplitude " (477).

DOCUMENT XV. A.—ON THE APOSTATIC CONVENTICLE.

This and the next Document are from the *Synodicon of Monte Casino* (*Synodicon Casinense*), and are given in Coleti in a Latin translation alone. Mansi omits them here. Another Document is given in Hardouin before this. It is there mentioned as chapter XVII., and is an Epistle of John of Antioch to the Emperor Theodosius, but as, according to Liberatus, quoted in note "b," col. 276 of tome IV. of *Coleti's Concilia*, it was held at Antioch, and, as it seems, after the Synod, it does not belong here. It is chapter XVII. in the *Synodicon Casinense*. Mansi omits it. It will be mentioned in its proper place. It belongs to the period of reconciliation and submission of the Orientals to the Third Synod. We therefore put next the Epistle of the Apostatic Synod of the Orientals in Ephesus to the clergy and people of Antioch.

---

church of Ephesus, and made those very things clear to the same persons, that the same Meiunon was condemned with the persons aforesaid " [Cyril and Nestorius] "and I warned them to keep their church monies with all security and at their own peril." I prefer this reading as likely to be more accurate than the other.

NOTE 473.—Or "*burst into,*" In the other translation of this document, col. 275, tome IV. of *Coleti's Concilia*, the sense is as follows in this place: "And so that he might not have to endure a second admonition, and the offering of my counsel to himself, but would anticipate my words and come to my house" [so] "yielding to the divine and imperial precepts." There is no *rushing in* here.

NOTE 474.—*Melioribus* is here used. Whether it is a compliment for the Bishops, or not is a question. The other translation. in col. 275, tome IV. of *Coleti's Concilia* is quite different, for it does not have "*better*" [melioribus] at all, but simply reads, "the Lord helping, and piety and right intentions, ye Masters of the World."

NOTE 475.—The Emperors.

NOTE 476.—Or "*how.*"

NOTE 477.—I have translated the above from the Latin translation of it in col. 1253-1256 of tom. III. of *Coleti's Concilia*. Compare another Latin translation of it in col. 274, 275, of tom. IV. of *Coleti Conc.* The Greek, as seems to be implied above, seems not to be extant. See at the beginning of the translation of it above.

DOCUMENT XV. B.—ON THE APOSTATIC COUNCIL, FROM THE SYNODICON CASINENSE.

This is chapter XVIII. of the *Synodicon Casinense*, and is a letter addressed by the Bishops of the Apostasy, JOHN OF ANTIOCH AND TWELVE OTHERS, "to the *Presbyters, and Deacons, and the rest of the clerics, and the monks, and the Christ-loving laity, who are in Antioch of the Orient,*" John's own city. They say further that on account of the haste of the bearer, some of the Bishops of their party could not subscribe. It was written, judging from its contents, shortly after the reception of the decree of the Emperors, which announced their determination to annul the Decisions of the Ecumenical Synod, and speaks the language of triumph and confidence against it and its leaders. It calls itself "*the Holy Synod of the Orientals and of other regions and provinces, which by God's grace is congregated in Ephesus.*" This often repeated representing themselves as the Synod is rather *cheeky*, to say the least.

They speak of themselves as defenders of ancestral faith and Apostolic doctrine, when the fact is, their doctrine began in the preceding century with Diodore of Tarsus and was continued by Theodore of Mopsuestia and Nestorius. Then they speak of the Orthodox as follows:

"We confidently despise the multitude who have turned aside to heretical madness; and we have made Cyril of Alexandria, the author of the impiety, an alien from the episcopate, and in the same decree we have condemned Memnon of Ephesus, who coöperated with him in everything, and we have made excommunicate their subjects who have even presumed to confirm impiety by their own subscriptions. And we have made these things known to the most pious and most dear to God Emperors. And when they received the records of what was done by us, they wrote back signifying that they accepted the condemnation of the aforesaid Fathers. And they have commanded that we shall all subscribe the faith set forth in Nicaea by the holy and blessed Fathers, and that the rising scandals be cut away and rejected from the correctness of faith. And indeed John, the most magnificent and most glorious Count of all Largesses, has been sent to bring these things to pass. He holds Cyril and Memnon in most strongly guarded custody, having thrust each away separately by himself, and has put a multitude of soldiers about their houses."

The Apostatic Conventicle, in confessing "*the multitude of the Orthodox*" imply their own fewness, and evidently put their trust in princes for success in their heresy. But they were doomed to disappointment. For they confess in what follows in this document the agitation which filled the city, and which we know to have been caused by their outrageous injustice and that of the Emperor Theodosius the Younger against Cyril and Memnon and against four-fifths of all the Bishops who came and who constituted the Ecumenical Council, and they grieve because the Council disregarded their little bull against the moon, that is, their deposition of Cyril and Memnon and their excommunication of the Ecumenical Council, and that they all continued to officiate and commune with each other. Then they speak lyingly of the Orthodox Synod as acting in despair of any hope of restoration, and so as confounding and disturbing the churches and filling them with seditions! As though to maintain their own rights and the lawful decrees and decisions of the Ecumenical Synod against a few Man-Worshipping, Incarnation denying and Cannibalizing men under discipline, were seditious! Surely the impudence of John and his fellows was simply astounding. They speak perhaps contemptuously of the Bishops with Cyril and Memnon as "*their subjects.*" They mean "*their suffragans,*" or, in hate, all of the Third Synod led by them.

Then they call upon the Antiochians to feel secure as to them, and to praise God in canticles for their success, and to pray for the Third Synod that it may be delivered from what they blasphemously call its "*most fell disease,*" which included zeal for the worship of God alone, and hatred of all creature worship, and to ask the teachers of the Church to preach continually in the congregations against "*that impious dogma,*" as they call God's truth, and to lead the people of God in the footsteps of the holy Fathers, by which they really mean in the errors of Diodore of Tarsus and of Theodore of Mopsuestia, "*that all,*" they add "*may know what sort of impiety we are fighting against.*" They then direct that if any person whosoever be sent by the Third Ecumenical Synod to their "*most great city, which is the mother of piety,*" as they call Antioch, they should arrest him "*and deliver him to the judges, that those who try to excite sedition may learn how good a thing discipline is, and how big a dish of evils a pertinacious and tyrannical will*" [produces]. Then follows the subscription of John of Antioch, and those of twelve other Bishops.

DOCUMENT XVI. ON THE THIRD ECUMENICAL COUNCIL.—*It is from Chapter XXIX. of the Nestorian Synodicon of Monte Casino. It is omitted by Mansi here.*

This production is found only in Latin. At first I did deem it doubtful or spurious for the following reasons:

1. The first part of it seems to be much like the imperial letter sent through John the Count of the Imperial Bounties, to the Ecumenical Synod, translated in this work elsewhere, and approves the deposition of Nestorius, Cyril, and Memnon, which is found in Greek and is genuine. This document seemed to follow its ideas in some places, but in others to modify them in the interests of Nestorianism. Furthermore, it reads much like the letter of the Emperors found in Greek and translated and given elsewhere in this work, in which they permit the Bishops of the Third Ecumenical Synod to return to their own cities because they cannot agree; but there is one very important difference introduced in this document; it consists in altering the sense of the last part of the other document, where the Emperors permit Cyril to go back to Alexandria and Memnon to remain at Ephesus, but says not a word of re_

garding them as deposed, whereas this document speaks of them as deposed, I suspected to favor the Nestorians and hurt the Orthodox. Furthermore I suspected that the meaning of allowing them in this document to act with the Bishops of their own province, was to convey the impression that the heretical prelates who had been suspended from communion by the Ecumenical Council were still Bishops and could act with their own comprovincial prelates and so still oppose, in their local Synods, the Ecumenical Synod. Those words do not occur in the other document which is found in Greek in column 1320 of tome. III. of *Coleti's Concilia*. It seems not likely, I thought, that both that and this document in the *Synodicon Casinense* could be genuine, and that the one who wrote this document in the *Synodicon Casinense* must have seen the other document which relates to the same matter and must have altered it in the interest of his own party, for the Emperor in finally dismissing the Synod accepts Cyril and Memnon as still Bishops, and that fact, I thought, seemed to agree with the other document and to oppose the alleged facts of this document in the *Synodicon Casinense*. Yet, on reconsidering the full facts and the documents, and the well known hostility of the Emperor to Cyril at the start, I now fully accept this document as genuine, at least till more is known against it; and I hold that there were four Edicts to the Synod after its Act I., not to mention those before it. Those after Act I. are then as follows:

1. The edict of June 29, 431, which nullifies, so far as Theodosius II. could do it, Act I. of the Ecumenical Synod, and speaks of Nestorius, notwithstanding his deposition by them, as still a "*Bishop.*" This is document V., page 257, above. It is in col. 1236, 1237 of tome III. of *Coleti's Concilia*.

2. That which accepts the deposition of Nestorius, Cyril, and Memnon, nullifies all the first work of the Synod against Nestorius and for Cyril, and commands it to proceed with the whole matter as though the action of the Ecumenical Synod against the Nestorian prelates should go for nothing, and the whole affair be begun anew. This is in *Coleti's Concilia*, tome III, col. 1252, 1253. It is document XIII., page 285, above.

3. That which dismisses the Bishops of the Ecumenical Synod to their homes, but regards Cyril of Alexandria and Memnon of Ephesus as alone deposed from the episcopate. This is the document which we are considering. I confess that I was not wholly free from doubt regarding its genuineness, but accept it because no clear case nor solid objection has been made out against it, and because all the facts of the time and especially the allusion in the Synod of Anazarbus, not very long after the Ecumenical Synod, seems to prove its genuineness.

This is the in *Synodicon* of Monte Casino, (tome IV. of *Coleti's Concilia* col. 291, 292; and in *Migne's Patrologia Graeca*, tome 84. col. 625, 626).

4. This is the final edict, which dismisses the bishops to their homes, and permits Cyril to return to Alexandria and Memnon to remain at Ephesus, (evidently from the context and the facts afterwards), as Bishops.

This is found in the Greek in col. 1320 of tome III. of *Coleti's Concilia*, and in col. 631, 632 of tome 84 of *Migne's Patrologia Graeca*.

Some marks of time and sequence as to imperial edicts second and third here, (Documents XIII. and XVI. respectively), are as follows:

The Nestorian Count Irenaeus in his Epistle to the Easterns after his entrance into Constantinople, as narrated in that Document above, p.273 (Document XI.), tells them that he had turned the tide as to the Emperor Theodosius II. and others against the Ecumenical Synod and the Orthodox Cyril and Memnon. For he says that then he condemned the Orthodox, but, after the arrival of John, Cyril's physician, there was at least a partial turn in the tide in favor of the Orthodox again. But he testifies that there were varying opinions current there, some wishing to recognize the deposition of Nestorius, Cyril, and Memnon, and others wishing some one to be sent by the Emperor to heal the divisions at Ephesus. And Document XIII. above, (Edict 2nd,) follows both those courses, for it recognizes the degradation of the three above mentioned prelates, and mentions the sending of Count John. Its priority to Document XVI is shown by the fact that it does not send the Bishops to their homes but exhorts them to a then hoped for union.

Further, Document XIII. makes no mention of the arrival of any delegates from the two Synods at Ephesus, from which it seems to have been yet future: whereas Document XVI. does mention it, and the failure of Count John's mission at Ephesus to unite the two Councils; and confesses that all attempts at union had failed, and sends the Bishops home. Document XVI. is therefore the latest of the two and seems to have been not long before the Council separated; though there seems to have been some little interval between it and the last edict which differs from it in acknowledging Cyril and Memnon as still Bishops. Inasmuch as the Synod of Anazarbus, of A. D. 431 according to Sevestre, makes no mention of edict 4th it may perhaps be doubted whethe it was put forth before the Nestorian party left Ephesus in that year.

The Emperor, Theodosius II., in the edict to the Synod in which he speaks of Cyril and Memnon as, being deposed, (Document XVI. here), but is silent as to Nestorius, writes that he had written to them of the deposition of Cyril and Memnon before. The only edict which mentions that before is the one above (Document XIII.). Edict I., (Document V.) says nothing on that subject. This edict (Document XVI.) seems therefore to be the third to the Synod *after it met*.

Its precise date seems clear from the Report of Count John after his arrival at Ephesus to the Emperor Theodosius II. (Document XIV. here). There referring, according to Sevestre, (*Dict. des Conciles, art. "Ephese* . . . 431"), to a time after Act V. or Act VI. of the Ecumenical Council, for he did not get there till as late, at the earliest, as after Act V., perhaps after Act VI., he says that he "*congregated*" the Bishops of both Synods, the Orthodox and the heretical, and then "*went through the reading*" [to them] "*of the Imperial Letter, in which Cyril and Nestorius and Memnon are deposed."* This is the reading in tome III. of Coleti, col. 1255. And it points clearly to decree II. as then read there. Decree III. seems to have been after that.

But we have further indications of time in a Report of the Delegates of the Apostasy at Chalcedon, who say that after they arrived there, they heard a report that, seven days before they appeared, Nestorius had been sent away from Ephesus to go whither it might please him. See Document XXII. below. But in Document XXX. written by the same Delegates from Chalcedon at a later period of their stay there, they state that the Council had been finally dismissed by the Emperor, and that Cyril and Memnon were to remain in their own places, but that an innocent man, by whom they evidently mean Nestorius, was to be sent to his own monastery.

It seems then that after the Emperor had sent his Edict 2nd above to the Synod (Document XIII.) in which he accepted the deposition of Nestorius, Cyril and Memnon, he never swerved from his resolve in the case of Nestorius. The testimony of the Nestorian Delegates at Constantinople is that he refused to hear any plea for him or any mention of his name, and that he held that the Decision of the Ecumenical Synod had settled that question finally. Aye, he went further and even while the Nestorian Delegation were forbidden to enter Constantinople, he had allowed the Orthodox Delegation to enter it and to ordain a successor in the room of the deposed Nestorius.

If in Document XVI. he does not mention him therefore as deposed with Cyril and Memnon there was no need of it, for he had before that accepted the Decision of the Third Ecumenical Synod in removing him from the Episcopate as settling that matter. Some later writers seem to have got the idea from the non-mention of his name in it that he admitted him to be a Bishop still. But this is a mistake. Even the Nestorian delegates do not claim any such thing, much as they wished it.

Yet in that Document XVI., the first in which the Emperor Theodosius II. dismisses the Synod to their homes, he had not yet laid aside his hostility to Cyril and Memnon, for he speaks of them in it as deposed. But yet as we see by Document XXX., the Nestorian Delegates tell us before they leave Chalcedon, that he had dismissed the Bishops in such a sense as to admit the return of Cyril and Memnon to their own sees as valid Bishops. The illogical character of his third Edict in admitting the action of the Ecumenical Synod on Nestorius, and nevertheless condemning its leaders, Cyril and Memnon, had probably been impressed on him by its numerous and powerful friends and he finally does justice to them so far as to withdraw his denial of their episcopate and to admit it.

According to *Peltier's Sevestre's Dict. des Conciles* art. *Ephèse*, col. 875, Count John arrived at Ephesus at the beginning of the month of August, and according to Hefele's *History of the Church Councils*, vol. III., page 110 of the English translation, Cyril reached Alexandria on his return on Oct. 30, 431, nearly three months afterwards. There was time for the two last edicts (Edicts 3 and 4) in that interval. And I infer that Theodosius II. never released Cyril from his confinement and admitted his right to his episcopate till he found it useless to oppose the Orthodox world in his favor. He had written him a hostile letter before the Synod met. In his first edict to the Synod after its assembling he had censured him and the Orthodox Synod for their action against Nestorius; in his second he had proclaimed him deposed, while admitting the deposition made by the rest of the Orthodox as well as by Cyril against Nestorius; in the third he had proclaimed him still deposed, and not till the fourth and last when he had no longer the semblance even of a backing among the Orthodox did he admit his episcopate; and in all those he and the Orthodox are censured by the Emperor for their uncompromising stand for the truth, and his representatives Candidian and John at Ephesus, favored Nestorius, and further, Cyril and his trusty lieutenant Memnon were deprived of freedom and given into custody by that same autocrat till murmurs became loud. All these facts and the assertions of Nestorius himself and his partisans that the Emperor held with them show how great were the obstacles in the way of the work of the Ecumenical Synod and Cyril in their duty of formulating against heresy and crushing it. That they did it against such formidable odds, when their property, their honors, their liberties, and even their lives, were at the mercy of a creature serving absolute ruler on the heretical side, bears eternal witness to their self-sacrifice, their courage, and their loyalty to God and to His truth and to His Church. And the day will come when this will be seen by all Orthodox Christians.

Or, to go more into details :

It is to the immortal honor of Cyril and Memnon and the other Orthodox Bishops of the Ecumenical Synod with them that they vindicated the truth that God alone should be served (Matt. iv., 10), and the correlated doctrines of the Incarnation and the Spiritual and Anti-Cannibalistic view of the Lord's Supper, against autocratic power, backed by jails, magistrates, armies, and the aid of the Man-Serving party in the church, at the head of which stood two men of the then four greatest sees, Nestorius and John of Antioch, and scholars like Theodoret of Cyrus, though the Orthodox had neither armies nor secular power. God chose the weak things that time to confound the mighty. His Spirit raised help for them from among the Christian clergy and people, which even a heresy-favoring Emperor deemed it unwise to resist. May all God's faithful clergy and people come up to the help of the Lord against the mighty by supporting a future reforming and uniting Seventh Ecumenical Synod, of all Orthodox Christendom, which shall complete the blessed Reformation of the sixteenth century by restoring all New Testament doctrine, discipline, rite, and custom, all in the VI. Synods which agrees with it, and the entire Christian System, including the worship of the Triune God alone, as Jeshua the high priest, Zerubbabel, Ezra and Nehemiah, restored the full system and worship of the Mosaic Economy at Jerusalem after the Reformation in Babylon.

I proceed then with this *Document XVI. on the Third Ecumenical Synod, from the Synodicon Casinense.*

This is given as Document XII. on the Apostatic Council, not in Coleti, Mansi, or in the *Collectio Regia*, but in Hardouin from the *Synodicon Casinense.* It belongs after the Council as the purport of it shows. Its contents prove it to have been sent to the whole Council. It is as follows, as in the Latin translation, the Greek not being found:

THE EMPERORS, CAESARS, THEODOSIUS, AND VALENTINIAN, *Victors, Triumphers, Greatest, ever August, to the Holy Synod which has convened in the City of Ephesus* (478).

Even if we should not write now, ye would know our aim indeed, from many other things; and what a great zeal we have for the right faith, and for the union of the Churches, for we have been thoroughly taught it by [our] fathers and by [our] ancestors; and continually hitherto we have put nothing before the sound faith, on account of which [faith] also, we hastened a short time ago, to congregate your Holiness in Ephesus. And after you were assembled, we wrote all things of that kind by which the true faith might properly continue without contention, and that what had been formerly held might remain unshaken, ye being united in friendship. But since by reason of impious intention and often, certain contentions have been made among you, and some things have been undoubtedly done as the result of dissensions, we wishing to terminate discord among you all, have sent the most magnificent and most reverent John, the Master of the imperial offices, that the contentions which have arisen among you may be done away. Forasmuch indeed as it seemed necessary that some of you should come hither in order that our Piety [as if] present may hear among those who are present, so that the union which we strive for might come forth from a pious assent, we accomplished that also, for we were thoroughly eager that all things might be settled and arranged pleasantly. But, because the dissension which was excited still continues, we, reckoning that your Religiousness is enduring labor from the very necessity of the Council, have conceded that all shall return from Ephesus to their own and obtain their own churches again, that each one may act with the Bishops who have come from his province. Only we do not reckon as of your number Cyril, who was formerly Bishop of Alexandria, and Memnon who was Bishop of Ephesus, and we have recognized the fact that they are aliens to the episcopate, as was formerly written by us to your Holiness. Returning [therefore] to your own churches, look out for the quiet of the cities and embrace that mildness which is in all respects worthy of the priesthood. And if indeed it is becoming that there shall be any satisfaction

---

NOTE 478.—Literally "in the Ephesian city," [in Ephesina Civitate].

in regard to those things which ye have here done in any way whatsoever, it will be given by those things which are to follow hereafter, but only if ye shall have preserved ecclesiastical decorum with public propriety" (479).

Hefele (480) perhaps furnishes us with some data towards determining the precise epoch of the last edict of the Emperor (edict 4th): for he states that an addition to it in the Synodicon informs us that "*Cyril, even* BEFORE *the arrival of that" decree, had been released from his imprisonment, and had set out on his return to Alexandria,* and that he got there Oct. 30, 431. But "after Cyril and Memnon had been set at liberty," and the fourth imperial edict had appeared, which dissolved the Synod and permitted Cyril and Memnon to retain their secs, the Delegates of the Apostasy still remained at Constantinople, and thence inform their Conventicle of the fact of Cyril's and Memnon's being still acknowledged as Bishops by the Emperor.

Furthermore, we see that in Document XXVI. below the Delegates of the Apostacy at Chalcedon write to their little Council at Ephesus of having gained a victory over the Orthodox before the Emperor; and in Document XXVIII. below the Synod of the Apostasy answer them in words of hope at the tidings. And in Document XXIX. below the Apostasy of Ephesus themselves write to the Emperor as though there were still hope for Nestorius and against Cyril.

But in Document XXX., below, the Delegates of the Apostasy change their tune, and speak of the Emperor as not only admitting the deposition of Nestorius but also that Cyril and Memnon are still Bishops. About the time when Document XXVI. was sent I deem it not unlikely that we should place the date of edict III. of the Emperor to the Synod, the more particularly as some things in Document XXVIII., which is a reply to Document XXVI., seem to refer to the incousistent provisions of that edict, as for instance, where in Document XXVIII. the Bishops of the Apostasy at Ephesus speak of its inconsistency in condemning the Twelve Chapters and their authors Cyril and Memnon, and the Third Ecumenical Council, and yet approving their condemnation of Nestorius for differing from their doctrine, and from that of the Third Ecumenical Council. In the same document they write as though their views had triumphed with the Emperor, and indeed an expression of Theodosius II. in Edict III. to them favors their view. And all along he seems to treat them as being of chief account as compared with the Orthodox Synod.

Furthermore, we see from the statement of the local Synod of Anazarbus referred to in *Peltier's Sevestre's Dict. des Conciles* to A. D. 431, and mentioned elsewhere in this work, that Maximinus, its Nestorian metropolitan, speaks as though the last edict of the Emperor to the Bishops at Ephesus was the Third, which dismisses the Synod and still deems Cyril and Memnon deposed. Either

---

NOTE 479.—I have translated the above document from col. 291, 292 of tome IV. of *Coleti's Concilia.*

NOTE 480.—Pages 110, 111 of vol. III. of the English translation of his *History of the Church Councils.*

the Nestorian Conventicle at Ephesus went home after it, and did not learn of the fourth at all, or he is guilty of suppression of the truth. Things at least have such a look as to permit the notion that the Bishops of the Apostatic Conventicle had gone home leaving Cyril still held at Ephesus. In that case we must put this Fourth Edict to the Council after its close and the dispersion of its members. By the terms of the Third Edict, which acknowledges the excommunicated Apostasy to be a part of the Ecumenical Synod, and which, so far, slights and contradicts the latter, the Bishops of the Apostasy and indeed those of the Ecumenical Synod might have gone home. Yet if Hefele be correct, the Delegates at Chalcedon of the Apostasy write to their Synod after the Fourth Edict as though they were still there. Yet they may have thought their Epistle would reach them before they broke up.

We learn some more facts from some utterances of John of Antioch and other Nestorians in chapters XVII., XIX. and XXXIV. of *Irenaeus' Synodicon.* The last mentions three Edicts of the Emperor ; the first sent through Count Candidian, the reading of which went for nothing with the Orthodox.

The Second, in which the Emperor attempted to nullify the proceedings of the Ecumenical Synod, and, so far as appears, those of the Apostatic Conventicle, and commands both parties to meet together and to begin the Synod anew. This had been sent through Palladius of Magisterial rank. This the Orthodox, according to this chapter XXXIV., treated with their "*accustomed contempt.*" It was sent from Constantinople after the Council's Act I. This is Document II. above in our enumeration, though it is really the fifth from the beginning. But our three or four are those sent from Constantinople, one before and three after Act I. of Ephesus.

The Third was brought to the Synod at Ephesus and to the Apostatic Separation from it by Count John. It is the one which approves the deposition of the three, namely, Nestorius, Cyril of Alexandria, and Memnon of Ephesus. It is Document Third of our four. The description given in that chapter XXXIV. enables us to identify them.

I would at any rate, in view of all the facts, place the Fourth Edict after the close of the Ecumenical Synod, and some little time after the Third Edict.

Since writing the above I find a more definite mark of the late date of edict 4th, and last in col. 631, 632 of tome 84 of Migne's *Patrologia Graeca*, where that 4th edict is preceded by the following preface :

"After the protest of John and of the other Bishops who were retained in Chalcedon when the Emperor entered Constantinople with the opposing party" [the Orthodox, that is. CHRYSTAL] "the following imperial edict (481) was sent to Ephesus to the Bishops who had convened with the Bishop of Alexandria," [that is, to the Ecumenical Synod, CHRYSTAL] "the text of which

NOTE 481.—Literally "*sacred edict,*" or "*sacred letter.*" the term "*sacred*" [*sacra*] as here being continually used in Byzantine Greek for *imperial.*

after the Preface is as follows." Then the 4th edict is given. At its close is added:

"This imperial edict is the last of all. It was sent when the blessed Cyril, Patriarch of Alexandria, had already returned into his own city" (482).

This shows very plainly the Emperor's bitter enmity to Cyril, the leader of Orthodoxy. And Cyril's self sacrificing labors to bulwark God's anti-creature serving faith and his putting himself in peril of deposition and exile for it, are a sufficient answer to his slanderers who accuse him of selfish motives in the matter. And in fact he never got wealth or power by his course even at the best. But his vilifiers will not do him justice.

DOCUMENT XVII. ON THE APOSTATIC SYNOD.—It is *from the Synodicon of Monte Casino.*

This according to note 2, col. 1256, of tome III. of *Coleti's Concilia* appears next in Hardouin, but not in Coleti nor Mansi. It is addressed by THE ORIENTAL BISHOPS IN EPHESUS OF JOHN OF ANTIOCH'S PARTY TO ACACIUS OF BERRHOEA. From its contents it seems to have been written at the same time as one last mentioned above, and like it celebrates the decision of the weak and unsound Emperor Theodosius the Younger to annul the Decrees of the Third Ecumenical Synod, and part of the language is much the same as that in that Epistle. It belongs here chronologically. It is chapter XIX. in the *Synodicon*. It dwells on the Twelve Chapters of Cyril of Alexandria, and denounces them as Apollinarian and heretical, according to the common tenor of all these documents which emanate from John and his party. It glories in the deposition of Cyril and Memnon by themselves and the approval of it by the Emperor, and exults in the temporary success of the Anti-Incarnation, Creature Serving party as a providence of God. It calls upon Acacius to hymn God on account of their victory. The tenor of this Epistle shows also that the Orthodox were stoutly maintaining the Twelve Chapters, and that justly, for the great Ecumenical condemnation of the Nestorians' denial of the Incarnation, and against their creature service is in them especially, as well as in Cyril's two Epistles to Nestorius approved in Act I. of the Third Ecumenical Synod, and in its deposition of Nestorius for those and cognate errors in his xx. Blasphemies. I would add that most of those xx. *Blasphemies* are quoted in *Cyril's Five Book Contradiction of the Blasphemies of Nestorius*, where Cyril refutes them at length. That is shown in Note F, pages 529-551 inclusive in volume I. of Chrystal's *Ephesus*. After the Ecumenical Synod, as is shown in the letter of John, Bishop of Antioch, which he wrote to the Prefect from Ancyra, the Orientals John of Antioch and his fellow Bishops state of the Orthodox prelates, Firmus, Bishop of Cæsarea in Cappadocia, and Theodotus, Bishop of Ancyra

NOTE 482.—*Migne's Patrologia Graeca*, tome 84, col. 631, 632.

"*They thems'lves have been deposed by us because they subscribed Cyril's heretical Chapters, and presumed to strengthen their impiety*" (483).

I quote part of this *Epistle of the Apostatic Synod* to *Acacius*.

They tell him that they had shown before with "*how great zeal*" they had acted "*in order*," they add, "*that we may lop off at the roots from Church dogmas the insanity of Apollinarius revived by the doctrines of Cyril of Alexandria.*"

Below, in the same document they show that the Orthodox Bishops. nothwithstanding the imprisonment of their leaders, were still holding fast to Cyril's Anti-creature-serving Twelve Chapters. For, after stating that they had received the Emperor's letter in which he had admitted the deposition of Cyril and Memnon, and *had commanded them to hold the Nicaean faith, and to forswear those scandals* which had arisen, by which they understand him to mean that he commanded them to do away Cyril's Twelve Chapters, they add what shows that the Orthodox Bishops were acting still rightly against the ridiculous claim of John and his small Fragment of creature-servers, to depose Cyril and Memnon, and to excommunicate the Ecumenical Synod, and that now that the doctrine of the Twelve Chapters was made the chief accusation by the heretics, the Anti-Creature-Serving Synod was coming up nobly to their support. In the First Act of the Council they had been read without a single dissenting voice. And from that time to this the Universal Church has ever championed them (484). For these heretics add to Acacius:

"But now we announce to thy Holiness that even though that letter" [of the Emperor against the Orthodox, and admitting the deposition of Cyril and Memnon] "is delivered" [to all], "they themselves," [the Bishops of the Third Ecumenical Council], "notwithstanding, whom the preoccupation of error (485) now once for all has held fast, contend for that very heretical madness; that is those who have presumed to subscribe the aforesaid Chapters (486), and they are not willing to cast them away from the Orthodox faith, as

---

NOTE 483.—*Coleti Concilia, tom.* IV., col. 305, cap. XXXVIII. of the *Synodicon Casinense. Epistola sancti Joannis Antiocheni episcopi, quam Praefecto scripsit ab Ancyra.* Firmus atque Theodotus . . . prius ipsi a nobis excommunicati sunt, eo quod haereticis subscripserint Cyrilli Capitulis, eorumque impietatem roborare praesumperint, dumque excommunicationis conculcaverunt terminum, et comministraut condemnatis [Cyril and Memnon], etc. The last words show the just contempt felt by Firmus and Theodotus for the ex communication put forth against them by creature-servers like John and his fellow paganizers, who were themselves under discipline and censure from the Third Ecumenical Synod.

NOTE 484.—That is shown in Chrystal's *Ephesus*, volume I., pages 204-208, note 520.

NOTE 485.—The error here meant is the belief in the Twelve Chapters against denial of the Incarnation and against Creature Service, etc.

NOTE 486.—This expression, taken in connection with what follows, seems to imply that all the Bishops of the Third Ecumenical Synod had by this time subscribed the Twelve Chapters of Cyril of Alexandria. We can see therefore, why it should be said that the Third Ecumenical Synod approved the Twelve Chapters of Cyril. See the English translation of

the decrees of our Christ-loving Emperors have commanded. And, moreover, when challenged to a discussion by us, they do not agree to answer our objections (487) (for we have refutations prepared of the aforesaid heretical Chapters both from the Scriptures divinely inspired and from the writings of

---

Hefele's History of the Councils, vol. III., page 48, note 2, where the original authorities for that statement are given. Referring to Cyril's *Long Epistle* to Nestorius, at the end of which we find the XII. Chapters, Hefele writes:

"This is the Synodal Letter to which the twelve anathematisms were appended. We were formerly of opinion that these anathematisms were read at Ephesus, but not expressly confirmed, as there is hardly anything on the subject in the Acts. But in the Fifth Ecumenical Council (Collatio VI.) it is said "Chalcedonensis sancta Synodus Cyrillum sanctae memoriae doctorem, sibi adscribit et suscipit synodicas ejus epistolas quarum uni 12 capitula supposita sunt, (Mansi, t. IX., p. 341; Hardouin, t. III., p. 167)." I translate this Latin: "The holy Synod of Chalcedon took Cyril of holy memory as its teacher, and accepted his Synodical Epistles, to one of which the 12 Chapters are appended," [Chrystal.] "If, however, the anathematisms of Cyril were expressly confirmed at Chalcedon, there was even more reason for doing so at Ephesus. And Ibas, in his well-known letter to Maris, says expressly that the Synod of Ephesus confirmed the anathematisms of Cyril, and the same was asserted even by the Bishops of Antioch at Ephesus in a letter to the Emperor, of which mention will hereafter be made in sec. 145. (Hardouin, t. II., p. 530)."

In note 520, pages 204-208, vol. I. of Chrystal's *Ephesus*, it is further shown that the said XII. Chapters were approved by the Fifth Synod of the whole Church and by the Sixth also; so that their Ecumenicity is beyond dispute.

NOTE 487.—The Ecumenical Synod having decided and approved the Twelve Chapters, by the aid of the Holy Ghost, it was according to the Gospel after that to avoid heretics who had been admonished more than the once or twice, the rule laid down by the Holy Spirit through the Apostle Paul: See Titus III; 10, and compare Matt. xviii; 15-19, and John xx: 23.

NOTE 488.—That is the Scriptures as understood by their own private opinions contrary to their plain sense, which is that defined by the Universal Church; and the so-called Fathers here are the notorious heretics Diodore of Tarsus and Theodore of Mopsuestia whom these heretics had been wont to follow in their Man Worship, Cannibalism on the Eucharist, and denial of the Inflesh, etc. As both those writers were Syrians by abode at least, John and his fellow Syrians were for that reason more inclined to follow them because they were their countrymen, and they felt proud of them as such, and because of the good service which they had done against Arianism and some other errors. And, finally, nearly all who adhered to Nestorius were Syrians or Assyrians of John's Patriarchate.

So the Monophysite revolt in Egypt followed certain national lines. So many an Italian clings to the heresies of Rome because it is Italian. So many a Greek and many a Russian clings to the present idolatries of the Eastern Church because he wrongly deems them national. And so some English speaking people approve not only the good but the evil, the creature-serving and Romanizing and traitorous in Pusey and Keble, because those notorious heretics were English.

But all this is a snare and a leading into eternal damnation. For the history of all heresy proves incontestibly that if there is a seductive fault against which every nation should be on its guard, it is the fault of being led into some heresy or soul-damning creature-service such as invocation of saints and angels and martyrs, and worship of images, and worship of a wafer, or of bread and wine as God, *because some man of ability of our own race or of our own speech has favored it*. We must follow in all things the inspired New Testament, the supreme rule by which everything is to be tested and judged, and after that, the VI. sole sound Synods of the Universal Church, East and West, against errors opposed to the New Testament, for it is the Christ-authorized interpreter of the new Tes-

The Conventicle of Antioch to Acacius of Berrhoea.

the holy Fathers (488) which they composed with many labors), but they confuse and disturb all things, and fill cities and provinces with dissensions (489) sending out unjust and illicit letters against us, which are of no validity at all. For what power can those possess who have been removed from every office of the priesthood? (490). Nevertheless they are able to disturb the simple. But let your Religiousness well understand that they have been already excommunicated by us, because they co-operated with the insanity of

tament, and, on disputed points, or on points on which the Universal Church has not spoken, that faith and practice of the Church which is found in the first three centuries, which did not begin in them, but has come down *from the beginning*. This was the principle on which the Six Ecumenical Councils acted and decreed. And so, though Arius, and Macedonius, and Nestorius, and Eutyches, and Theodore of Mopsuestia, were Greek speaking, we find Greek Bishops, putting the Bible and its faith so understood, first, and identity in speech or in race last, and anathematizing them as heretics and misleaders; and the Latins did the same with the heretic Pope Honorius, when he was condemned by the Sixth Synod, though he spoke Latin and was of the Latin Church. And we must reject the idolatry of the Synod held at Nicaea in A. D. 787, because it rejects God's Word, the vi. Synods and the witness of the early Church.

We must not make gods even of our Reformers, and of such eminent men as Bull and Beveridge, and Wall, and Waterland, by deeming them infallible, practically, but must follow them only so far as they followed the doctrine, discipline, and rite of the New Testament, and that in the Church, which has been held, "*always, everywhere, and by all.*" There can be no union of entire Christendom on the basis of the Six Synods, which defined in accord with the New Testament, until such dogmas as oppose them be forsaken by all Christian nations, no matter if any of their eminent men have opposed them, or any one of them; as in fact has been the case more or less everywhere, from ignorance, or malice. For corruptions began to be favored by individual writers as early as the last half of the fourth century, though not approved by any of the vi. Synods. But in urging that we follow the vi. Synods we do not put them on an equality with Holy Writ, but only insist that on the disputed points where they have spoken they are best, because they are Christ-authorized explainers of Holy Writ, and that, because they agree with and strictly follow the New Testament in their decisions, we should hear them, Matt. xviii: 17, 18; I. Tim. iii: 15. To reject them is to laud in endless divisions on doctrine, discipline, rite and customs; in brief, in anarchy.

Yet every man, woman and child should read the Scriptures. They are a part of every Christian's armor (Eph. vi: 17); with them Christ vanquished the Devil (Matt iv.1-12). So must we; and they are means of sanctifying them by teaching them what true holiness is (John vii: 17), and we are encouraged to read and to heed and to hear, even their most difficult part, prophecy (II. Peter I: 19, 20, 21; Rev. I: 2; Rev. xxII; 7). And we must remember that "he worst abusers of them are Romanists and all others who while keeping them from the people, nevertheless so blasphemously abuse them as to teach men that they approve the worship of images, crosses, altars, and relics, the invocation of creatures, and other forms of idolatry and creature worship; and that, moreover, Rome, which claims to put what she calls the sense of the Church on them is the worst perverter and denier of that sense of the "*one, holy, universal and apostolic Church*," which, in its vi Synods, has most clearly condemned all the aforesaid errors, and her claim to supremacy and even to be of the Universal Church at all, under pain of deposition for Bishops and clerics and excommunication for all laics. The man who opposes their use by the people does the work of ruining souls. No man is fully developed even intellectually till he has read and profited by them. Their abuse is warned against in Holy Writ (II. Peter III: 16, 17, 18), but it commends their use by all as above and often elsewhere. The abuse does not abolish their necessary and profitable use.

NOTE 489.—Or "*Seditions*." Here as was the case with the creature-serving King Ahab against the anti-creature-serving prophet of God Elijah, the creature-serving John and his Synod throw the whole blame of the evils caused by their creature service on God's faithful servants, Cyril of Alexandria and the Third Ecumenical Synod, who as in duty bound, had, in God's name opposed it. It is ever so with creature servers and other heretics in their fights against God's truth.

NOTE 490 —Here John and his little fragment of the Synod again brazen-facedly represent themselves as having that power which belonged to the whole Ecumenical Synod, and

the heretic Cyril (491), and with those things which have been illicitly and unjustly done, and they have presumed to officiate and to commune with those who have been condemned. But your Religiousness knows what canons bear on such persons, and that they leave them no place for pardon (492). And they commit those things though they see that the most injurious Cyril and Memnon have been thrust away, and are guarded by a multitude of soldiers. For they have thrust each of them away by himself and keep them in custody day and night."

But God was with Cyril and His own truth, and was soon to vindicate both for ever.

DOCUMENT XVIII. ON THE APOSTATIC CONVENTICLE.—*Document* XII. *in Coleti and Mansi here.*

It is chapter XXIII. in Irenaeus' *Synodicon.*

This is addressed by that Conventicle to John of Antioch and their other representatives whom they sent to Constantinople to dispute against the Orthodox, and forms a sort of letter of Instruction to them. It is given in Greek in Coleti (493), and is headed "COPY OF A MANDATE."

"THE HOLY SYNOD ASSEMBLED IN EPHESUS TO THE MOST DEAR TO GOD AND MOST DEVOUT JOHN, ARCHBISHOP OF THE GREAT CITY OF THE ANTIOCHIANS, *and to John, Bishop of the metropolis of the Damascans; and to*

which, far more than a majority of it, that is about four-fifths of all who assembled, had already used it to condemn John's and Nestorius' heresies and those of his fellows, against the Twelve Chapters.

NOTE 491.—Surely such abuse and railing at a servant of God, whose great crimes according to Nestorius and his faction, had been his advocacy of the Incarnation and his noble Elijah-like stand for the Worship of the Consubstantial and Triune Jehovah alone (Matt. iv: 10, and Isaiah xlii: 8) is simply anti-Scriptural and utterly vile. It, in effect, brands most blasphemously those sound doctrines of Holy Writ as *insanity.* What a horrible, shocking insult to the living God! Surely after all that, no man should defend these men or their infidelities and paganizings.

NOTE 492.—The reference here is perhaps canon IV. of the local council of Antioch which was then not made Ecumenical, which decrees that if any cleric who had been deposed, dared to perform sacred offices, he should have no hope of restoration or defense in another synod, and all who communicate with such deposed parties were to be cast out of the church. But that canon did not apply to the Orthodox Cyril and Memnon, because they had not been deposed by the Ecumenical Synod, but were approved by it, and John and his fellows had been condemned by it. But as the canon had not then been made Ecumenical, it could not be quoted against Cyril, nor indeed has it ever been thoroughly adopted *in practice* in the West, whatever may be the meaning of Canon I. of the Fourth Ecumenical Synod. I will speak of that in its proper place, God willing. But if it had been applicable to crush either of the parties in the dispute it would have smitten John and the Nestorians alone, not Cyril and his at all.

But John and his little Apostatic Conventicle were adepts at misrepresenting and giving false impressions, and they keep at that trick here, thinking to hoodwink the Bishop Acacius as they did the weak Emperor, who, there is too much reason to fear, was at first at any rate opposed to Cyril's Twelve Chapters.

NOTE 493.—In *Coleti Concilia,* tom. III., col. 1256, 1257.

Himerius, Bishop of the metropolis of the Nicomedians (494); and to *Paul*, Bishop of the Emesans, who speaks also for the most holy Bishop Acacius of Berrhoea; and to *Macarius*, Bishop of the city of the Laodiceans, who speaks also for the most holy Cyrus, Bishop of the City of the Tyrians; and to *Apringius*, Bishop of the Chalcidians, who speaks also for Alexander, Bishop of Apamea; and to *Theodoret*, Bishop of the Cyrestans, who speaks also for Alexander, Bishop of the metropolis of the Hierapolitans; and to Helladius of Ptolemais; we, in their presence, enjoin what follows":

The Apostatic Conventicle and Fragment of the Synod first state that some of them had been summoned by the decree of the Emperors to Constantinople, but not all; yet it was desirable that their deputies above should represent them all, and therefore they give them power to do so, and expressing confidence in their ability, charges them to do so in discussion before the Emperor, the Emperor's Cabinet, the Senate, or a Synod of Bishops there, and they approve all their acts ahead. Then they turn to the question of a reconciliation with the Orthodox Bishops, and here alone put in a salvo and a limit on the actions of their representatives, for they show that they would not assent to a peace unless Cyril's Twelve Chapters were to be condemned. Not a solitary word is said on the expression *Bringer Forth of God* (Θεοτόκος) which had given rise to the controversy, but here as elsewhere, the great point which the Apostate and Creature Serving Conventicle make is against the Twelve Chapters. I quote this part. It is as follows:

"And if in any way" [any] "necessity arise either for a reconciliation, or for an ecclesiastical peace, or for any other thing demanding subscription from us all, in regard to that very matter also we pray your Holiness (495) not to hesitate to do what shall be advantageous for the general good and for the glory of the Master Christ (496). And if it seem good" [to you] "to send a Synodical letter demanding (497) subscription from us here, we promise that we will all subscribe it in common, and each one of us separately, with all readiness of mind, and that we will send it to the pious Court (498), this one proviso being clearly

NOTE 494.—Himerius, Bishop of the metropolis Nicomedia, as he is termed in the Mandate of the Apostasy to their Delegates (chap. XXIII in the Synodicou) had not reached Chalcedon when the rest of the Delegates of the Apostasy wrote a letter to announce their arrival there to the *Conventicle* which sent them. That letter is Chapter XXVI. in the Synodicon. They say that they suppose that he is detained by sickness or by infirmity. His name appears however in the last Document of those Delegates from Chalcedon (Document XXIV. in Coleti), from which it seems that he finally got there.

NOTE 495.—Greek, τὴν ὑμετέραν ἁγιωσύνην, a collective title of the Deputies, more flattering titleism against New Testament simplicity.

NOTE 496.—Greek, Χριστοῦ, literally "*of the Master Anointed.*"

NOTE 497.—Or, *asking*, ἀπαιτούντων, which seemingly is a mistake of the copyist or printer, for ἀπαιτῶν.

NOTE 498.—The imperial Court at Constantinople, to which seemingly the Bishops of the creature-serving Apostasy would leave the settlement of purely dogmatic questions right against the sound decisions, already rendered, of the Third Ecumenical Synod, in order that

understood, that the heretical Chapters added to the faith of the Fathers of Nicaea by Cyril the Alexandrian, with their anathematisms, must, by all means be cast away, as" [being] "alien to the Universal and Apostolic Church.

Alexander, Bishop of the metropolis [*Hierapolis*], said: If you do anything in accordance with the faith set forth by the holy Fathers in Nicaea, nothing being added to the faith of the holy Fathers, and the heretical Chapters of Cyril of Alexandria being cast out, I approve it. For I also have already subscribed with our own holy Synod that Forthset of the faith.

I, Theodore, Bishop of Marcianopolis in the Second Mysia, have written in like manner, commanding as above. And all the rest also subscribed."

The Greek here adds:

"And the Mandate being given, a document was also added, the contents of which are as follows:"

But in the Latin versions of this same document this last sentence is lacking. The first of them is in *Coleti Conc.*, tome IV., col. 169, which adds directly after the subscription of Theodore of Marcianopolis the words "*And all the rest subscribed,*" and with that expression it ends. The second is in *Coleti Conc.*, tome IV., col. 285, 286; it omits the words of Alexander of Hierapolis, and of Theodore of Marcianopolis, and ends as follows: "as" [being] "alien to the Universal and Apostolic Church.

And all the Oriental Bishops subscribed that Mandate."

From both those endings it seems most probable that all the rest of the Bishops of the little Conventicle subscribed in full, but that the first copyist omitted all but the first two, and added the words, "*And all the rest subscribed,*" but the second copyist omitted all the subscriptions and added the note last above to his work.

A third Latin version, that of the "Editio Basil.," in col. 170, of *Coleti Conc.*, tome IV., ends with the subscription of Alexander of Hierapolis and with that of Theodore of Marcianopolis, immediately fol'owed by the note "*But all the rest also subscribed,*" which does not differ much from the first version nor from the Greek. The first and third translations are in the Ancient Latin Version of the Council of Ephesus; the second is in the *Synodicon Casinense*.

But in none of those translations do I find anything in the way of a rendering of the words in Greek for,

"And the Mandate being given, a document was also added, the contents of which are as follows:"

What document is meant in this last sentence?

To this I answer that in the Ancient Version of the Council of Ephesus,

---

they might overturn and crush God's truth and its champions. They did not remember the adage, "Put not your trust in princes," who, it should be added, as mere laics had no right to usurp to themselves the decision of doctrinal questions, which according to the Scriptures and the practice of the Universal Church at the beginning and for long centuries after was deemed prerogative to the sound (not the unsound) apostolate, that is episcopate alone. Compare Acts 1: 20 with 25.

there next comes, that is immediately after the above document, an Epistle of the Orthodox Council signed by Cyril of Alexandria to the Emperors, which of course cannot be meant.

In the *Synodicon Casinense* the Mandate of the Orientals above is immediately followed by an Epistle of the Prefects relegating Nestorius to his monastery whence he had been called to the Episcopate, which can not be meant for it is later. I confess therefore that I do not know what document is meant, nor whether it is extant or not.

In all these documents emanating from the Apostatic and Creature-Serving Conventicle, it is a remarkable fact that

1. As yet we find not a word against the expression *Bringer Forth of God* (Θεοτόκος), nor any allusion to it good or bad.

And that, 2, they base all their opposition to Cyril and the Third Ecumenical Synod on their approval of the anti-creature-serving Twelve Chapters.

I infer from the sudden change of front on the part of Nestorius in withdrawing all opposition to it in his letter to Scholasticus or Scholasticius mentioned among the documents from the *Synodicon of Monte Casino* in this work (Document XII., page 277 above), and in opposing Cyril's Twelve Chapters alone that the Bishops of the Apostacy had persuaded him to that course in order to get rid of dead weight, which some of them, as appears from an Orthodox writing below given were not disposed to carry, for some of them admitted the expression *Bringer Forth of God* (Θεοτόκος). They could then throw their united weight against Cyril's anti-creature-serving Twelve Chapters, blinking the question as to the use of the term *Bringer Forth of God*, to avoid dissensions and a division in their small clique, whose implied claim to represent the Universal Church against the Third Ecumenical Synod would be made more ridiculous by such a separation of their coterie.

DOCUMENT XIX., RELATING TO THE APOSTATIC CONVENTICLE.—*It is Document* XIII. *in Coleti and Mansi here.*

This document is CHAPTER XXXII. in the *Synodicon Casinense*, col. 295 in tome IV. of Coleti's Concilia. It is found in a Latin translation alone. It is given also among the Documents on the Nestorian Conventicle of John of Antioch in tom. III. of *Coleti's Concilia*, col. 1357 [correctly, col. 1257] and after, whence I translate it. In this last place in Coleti it bears the heading, "FIRST PETITION OF THE SCHISMATICS WHICH WAS SENT FROM CHALCEDON TO THE EMPEROR."

A note in Coleti here (*Conc, tom.* III., 1357, rightly col. 1257) reads as follows on this document:

"The Old Version from the Basel edition of Robert Winter. The Greek is not extant. The entire title in Hardouin is as follows: "*The First Petition of*

310   *Matter Between Acts VI. and VII. of Ephesus,*

the Seven Oriental Bishops sent to the Kings" [It should be *"Emperors"* CHRYSTAL], *"because they were not permitted to enter Constantinople.* This Epistle is in another Latin translation in the *Synodicon Casinense* with the following title: *'The First Testimony'"* [or *'Petition'*] *"' of John, Patriarch of the Antiochian See, and of the six others, whom they sent to the Emperor Theodosius from Chalcedon, when they were left there, and he entered Constantinople with those* [others] *who had been sent and were in the delegation from the blessed Cyril and from the Synod which likewise convened in Ephesus* (499).' "

"The Synod which likewise convened in Ephesus" is the Ecumenical Synod, thus spoken of I presume by the writer of that part of that Synodicon.

The Seven Bishops of the Apostasy begin by invoking the Emperor's help against Cyril of Alexandria and the Third Ecumenical Synod, and charge him and them impliedly with *adulterating "the doctrine of piety by absurd expositions,"* and slander the Bishops of the Third Synod by accusing them of supporting Cyril from a desire to preside over other Bishops and from ambition and because of certain *"vain promises"* given them and with despising *"all Christian mandates,"* to serve *'a man,'* of whom they further add, *"We mean Cyril the Alexandrian, who, from a trifling disposition alone, has introduced heretical dogmas into the holy Churches of God, and has the confidence to believe that he will prove them by arguments, and has hoped that he will escape correction for his sins, by the sole help* 500) *of Memnon and of the aforesaid conspiracy of Bishops."* It is thus that they speak of Cyril's Christian teachings and those of the Third Synod, and represent the Ecumenical Council as a conspiracy of Bishops, because they approved of the Twelve Chapters, and so forbid all service to creatures and guard necessarily and well the prerogative of Divinity to all religious bowing and all other acts of religious service. The reference to ambition for precedence seems as we shall see below, to be directed against Juvenal of Jerusalem, and perhaps the Metropolitan of Cyprus.

Below they beg the Emperors to crush those twelve Orthodox Chapters and their maintainers, as follows:

"Therefore for the sake of God who sees all things, and by our Lord Jesus Christ, who will judge all men in righteousness, and by the Holy Ghost, by

---

NOTE 499.—In Coleti Conc., tom iv., col. 295, 296, we find the following note on this document:

'Theodoret makes mention of this and the two following testimonies, in [his] epistle CXII. to Domnus of Antioch [as follows]: *'Having been summoned to Constantinople we had five investigations, the Emperor himself being present, and after them we sent three Protestations to the same'* [Emperor]. They are extant from another version in the Basel edition of Robert Winter, and in the third tome of the Councils, page 1258, where the title of the Basel edition is omitted which reads as follows: *"First petition of the seven Oriental Bishops which was sent to the Kings from Chalcedon, because they were not permitted to enter Constantinople.'* "

NOTE 500.—Or *"ministry alone," "solo ministerio."*

whose grace ye govern the Empire, and by the elect angels who keep you, and whom you will see standing at the terrible throne, and always offering to God that awful sanctification [or *"that awe inspiring holy worship "*] which certain persons now strive to adulterate; we have besought your Piety which is beset by the craftiness of certain persons, *who are really taking away that worship* (501) and establishing the heretical Chapters on the faith, which have been introduced, which are wholly alien to sound dogmas, and agree with the heretical opinions (502), we have besought your Piety," [we repeat]" that if any one either

NOTE 501.—The Latin here in col. 1259 of tome III. of Coleti is as follows: "et per electos angelos, qui vos custodiunt, quos assistentes videbitis terribili throno, et horrendam illam sanctificationem semper Deo offerentes, quam nunc quidam adulterare nituntur; pietatem vestram, quae vafritia quorumdam obsidetur, id re ipsa adimentium, et haeretica capita fidei introducta stabilientium, quae omnino a sanis dogmatibus aliena sunt, et cum haereticis opinionibus conveniunt; obsecravimus, ut vel si quis illic" [illis? CHRYSTAL.] "subscribat vel consentiat, et post promissam a vobis veniam contendere ultra nolit, pracipias illum in medium venire et ecclesiasticis poenis subjacere, quo pugnare proprietate melius possis." *In the Synodicon Casinense* the same passage in Latin reads as follows (*Coleti Conc.* tom IV., col. 206): "et electis angelis qui vos servant, quos et adstantes videbitis illi terribili throno et illas terribiles actiones, quas incessanter offerunt Deo, quas quidam nunc obliterare pertentant, quaesumus ut eam quae nunc expugnatur ulciscamini pietatem. et jubeatis ut haeretica illa capitula, quae super introducta sunt fidei, expellantur, quia sunt omnimodo a rectis dogmatibus aliena et haereticis vesaniis consona, aut certe si quis eorum qui consenserunt et subscripserunt eis et post veniam, quae a nobis promissa est, vult ultra contendere, hunc venire ad medium jubeatis, et manifeste illum sub ecclesiasticis increpationibus tuae pietatis judicio vindicate." I will remark on this passage at the end of this document.

NOTE 502.—Here we see how wide even in the opinion of John of Antioch and his fellow heretics the difference was between the Orthodox Third Council and Cyril on the one side and themselves on the other. For the Nestorians brand as heretical those Twelve Chapters which in effect condemn all worship to the Man put on by God the Word, and by necessary implication, all acts of worship to any other creature, and besides, in Chapter or Anathema x. they forbid all idea of mediatorial work in heaven separate from God the Word who prays by His humanity, but hears us as God. Hence Intercession and Mediation there is done by him alone who is God and Man, not at all by the Virgin Mary, Angels, Saints or any other creature; that is all *go-between* work there, as *mediatorial* means such as interceding for us etc., is prerogative to Him, and it is blasphemy to assert that it can be shared by any other. We pray for each other on earth. Christ as our High Priest and the one sole Mediator prays for us in heaven (1. Tim. ii: 5). Only through Him may we go to the Father (John xiv: 6). He alone is a fit and perfect Intercessor because being omnipresent and all-knowing as God, he knows not only what is best for us, and can hear us, but will ask for us as man; but only what as God He knows to be best for us, not always exactly what we ask, for we sometimes put up foolish or sinful petitions.

And, blessed be God! he is an all sufficient Intercessor above (Heb. vii: 25), and therefore we may well exclaim against all our enemies:

'Who shall lay any thing to the charge of God's elect? It is God that justifieth. Who is he that condemneth? It is Christ that died, yea rather that is risen again, who is even at the right hand of God, *who also maketh intercession for us*" (Rom. viii; 33 34). "If any man sin, we have an advocate with the Father, Jesus Christ the righteous, and he is the propitiation for our sins; and not for ours only, but also for the sins of the whole world." Indeed to mediate for us by intercession is part of his prerogative work as our High Priest. It is blasphemy to suppose therefore that a saint or angel can share it. His foretype, the Jewish

subscribes to them or consents to them (503), and is unwilling of his own accord to hasten to get the pardon promised by you [or, better, "*by us*"], that thou command him to come into the midst (504) and to be subjected to the ecclesiastical penalties, [for] in that way thou mayest be able to fight better for piety."

Then they further request that the Emperor cause the doctrinal questions or investigations before him to be put in writing, "For," they add, "so those who sin may be the more easily discovered, and bear the blame in all time hereafter." They hoped, I think, to force the Orthodox to contend on certain points of creature service, especially as to worshipping the man, the *creature* put on by God the Word, where Theodosius himself or some of the women of the imperial family would be against them and in favor of that sin. And probably there may have been others who had fallen into that error whom they hoped to win.

Then they express the wish that the Orthodox be not allowed, to reject the appeal to "the *Doctors*" (that is "*Teachers*") of the Church, by which, I presume, they mean those whom they deemed their great Syrian lights, namely Diodore of Tarsus, Theodore of Mopsuestia, and perhaps other Syrians of like views.

Next John of Antioch and his fellow errorists make mention of the struggle between Antioch and Jerusalem to get the ecclesiastical jurisdiction and

High Priest, went in always alone into the holy of holies on the day of Atonement to intercede for Israel. Heb ix:7-28; and Levit. xvi: 17.

Anathema or Chapter VIII. of Cyril, as is shown in the note matter or page 109, vol. I. of Chrystal's *Ephesus*, where it is given in full, anathematizes every one who worships Christ's humanity with the Word; and so the great difference between the Nestorians on the one hand and Cyril and the Orthodox and the Universal Church on the other was as Cyril puts it, that they were guilty of what he terms ἀνθρωπολατρεία, that is *the worship of a human being*, that is Christ's humanity, which, of course, is *creature worship;* whereas we, following Scripture strictly, worship God the Word alone in him.

So we obey:

I. The inspired Scripture, Matt. iv: 10; and Isaiah xlii: 8, etc.

II. We give no act of worship to any angel, so obeying Holy Writ, Colossians ii: 18; Rev. xix: 10 and xxii: 8, 9, nor to any other creature, Matt iv: 10.

III. When we pray to Christ in accordance with Chapter or Anathema X. of Cyril approved by the whole Church at Ephesus, we address our prayers and other acts of worship to God the Word alone in strict accordance with Christ's own law in Matthew iv: 10, not in the humanity in which He ever dwells. See further note 183, pages 79-126, vol. I. of Chrystal's *Ephesus*.

Cyril and the Orthodox are just as far as John of Antioch from considering the matters involved in the discussion as a mere ogomachy, for he anathematized them in his Twelve Chapters, and the Third and the three Ecumenical Synods after it approved those Twelve Chapters and condemned those who opposed them.

NOTE 503.—The Latin here is *illic*, which means "*there*," that is, Constantinople. But I am inclined to think that it is a mistake for *illis*, that is "*to them*," meaning the Twelve Chapters. This surmise is made the more likely because the Synodicon Casinense has actually here, "*eis*," "to them."

NOTE 504.—The first Latin rendering given in *Coleti Conc.*, III., 1259, is "in medium venire;" that in col. 296 of tom. IV., id, has "ventre ad medium."

control of Palestine and Arabia. Above they slander Bishops of the Synod by charging their Orthodoxy as being the result of *"vain"* or *"foolish promises"* given to them. They seem in this to hint at the idea that Cyril of Alexandria and some other Bishops, had given Juvenal of Jerusalem a promise to help him to free himself from the yoke of Antioch, and to help him to autonomy in Palestine and in Phenice and in Arabia, a thing not at all verified in the result, for this Synod did not touch that matter at all by any formal enactment. Indeed even after this we find Cyril opposing the claims of Jerusalem. That was reserved for the Fourth Ecumenical Synod about twenty years afterwards to do (505). But, if any others had encouraged Juvenal with promises of help to get free from the yoke of Antioch, it does not follow that they were moved to do so by any unworthy motives. For though when Canon VI. of Nicaea, A. D. 325, was made it guaranteed its former privileges to Antioch, and though by that enactment all Palestine may have been included in her sway, and though by Canon VII. Jerusalem in its ruined state was certainly suffragan to its metropolis Caesarea, nevertheless it does not follow that it should ever remain so, for those Canons deal with a matter of discipline where changes deemed proper and necessary are allowed, not with unchangeable doctrine. For, as the years rolled on, the former capital of Palestine gradually grew, and Caesarea relatively declined, and so, about 106 years after Nicaea, a vast change had occurred, and it was seemly that Jerusalem should resume its old position again, and it desired it and got it. And we must remember that though, under pagan Roman domination, Palestine may have been included in the government of Syria (Luke ii: 2), as it may have been, some think, as late as A. D. 325 under Constantine the Great (Bingham, IX., I), nevertheless it was a Jewish and not a Syrian land, and therefore should naturally and reasonably be governed in civil things as well as in the Churchly by its own inhabitants. Indeed long before A. D. 431, the Bishop of Constantinople which, as Byzantium, had long been suffragan to the Bishop of Heraclea, became his metropolitan when Constantinople became the capital of the province of Europa in which both those cities are. And by Canon III. of I. Constantinople, A. D. 381, the Bishop of Constantinople became the Second Prelate of the then Christian world, and by Canon XXVIII. of the Fourth Ecumenical Synod notwithstanding the protest of the legates of Rome, he got the three great dioceses of Thrace, Asia, and Pontus. And it was that same Ecumenical Synod which raised Jerusalem to Patriarchal rank by giving it the three provinces of Palestine. And such changes in the mere precedences of sees have been quite common, in accordance with the Eastern principle made

NOTE 505—See on that and the whole question, the English translation of *Hefele's History of the Church Councils*, Vol. III., page 77, and notes 3 and 4 there, and page 107 and note there, and pages 355, 356, in section 195; the English translation of Wiltsch's *Geography and Statistics of the Church*, Vol. I., pages 214-226, section v., and Bingham's *Antiquities*, book IX., chapter 2, sections 7, 8 and 9, and book IX., chapter I., sections 1-9, and indeed all that chapter.

Ecumenical by the Second Synod of the Christian World and the Fourth that Ecclesiastical precedences should follow the rank of sees in the civil Notitia, the chief city of the civil diocese being a patriarchal see, and its jurisdiction all the provinces of its civil diocese (see Canons II. III. and VI. of the Second Synod, and Socrates' *Eccl. Hist. V.* 8 and *VII.* 31), the only exception being Constantinople which has three such Dioceses as told above; the chief city of each province being a metropolis, and its jurisdiction being the whole of its province, and every other city of the province being counted as suffragan to it.

The Eastern principle that the Ecclesiastical precedences should follow the civil has been made Ecumenical by those Canons and by Canon XVII. of Chalcedon

Rome, on the contrary, opposed those Ecumenical Canons because they condemn her claim to a divine right primacy as well as much more, her claim to a divine right supremacy over the whole Church, and because she saw that if the principle embodied in those enactments were to be followed she would lose all Churchly preeminence outside of Italy with the passing away of the Western Roman Empire, which died about A. D. 476. But her ambition is spurned by the East and by the Protestants of the West, and she will in time be totally destroyed (Rev· xvii: 18 and xviii), and then her ambitions will perish with her.

And one thing the Northern nations who have made the Reformation of the Sixteenth century and so saved us all from the Turk and slaughter and slavery should ever remember, and that is not to be swayed or influenced at all by the old Churches of the East which are idolatrous, nor by Rome of that ilk. If they do, all will be lost again and we shall suffer untold miseries as we did in the middle ages. We must preserve the leadership ourselves, and finish the work of the Reformation by a full Restoration of all New Testament doctrine, discipline, rite and custom, all in accordance with it in the VI. Synods, and all since developed in the Church which agrees with it. "As it was in the beginning, is now, and ever shall be world without end." We must do a full Ezra and Nehemiah work of restoring the whole Christian pure system and keep it so. The times are favorable for it. God's word demands it. Error will be banished. Idolatry will be destroyed. Men will cast their idols, that is *images* as *idols* means, *"to the moles and to the bats"* (Isaiah ii: 20), and true religion will everywhere prevail. We shall hold a Seventh Synod of the Christian world, do away all paganizings and infidelities and reunite all Christians in perfect truth.

And to do that we must remember that on the Ecumenically approved principle of those canons II., III. and VI. of the Second Synod, and canons XVII. and XXVIII. of the Fourth, that *the civil precedences should be followed by those that are ecclesiastical.* Rome and idolatrous Constantinople should be inferior to the chief cities of the great Northern nations, London in England, Paris [if it becomes Orthodox] in France, Berlin in Germany, and St. Petersburg in

First Petition of the Nestorian Delegates to the Emperor. 315

Russia, if it also reforms and restores, and New York or Washington in the United States. The Reformed must lead and guide under God. But to return to the Document which we are considering.

John and his fellow delegates thus refer to what they slanderously term the *"mutual conspiracy"* of the Bishops of the Orthodox Synod.

"For already through those who have been ordained it is manifest, that certain of them have been planning in favor of that impiety, in order that they may deserve well of certain persons in the matter of having dignities conceded to themselves, and they have been continuing [to procure them] by certain other means. And that fact will appear more clearly; and thy Piety will see that not far hence they will distribute the wages of their betrayal [of the faith] as though they were the spoils of the faith. But we have kept silent on the fact that certain of ours (506) were some time ago ordained by the most pious Juvenal, Bishop of the Jerusalemites; although we should contend in favor of

NOTE 506.—In *Coleti Conc.*, tome III., col. 1260, this reads: At *ex nobis quidam* a pientissimo Juvenali Hierosolymitanorum episcopo olim ordinati, siluimus; quamvis pro canonibus certandum esset, ne videremur nostrae gloriae causa dolere. Et nunc quoque illius studia et praestigia tales per Phoenicem secundam et Arabiam non ignoramus. Sane de illis nobis non vacat curam habere, qui civitatibus ipsis, quarum nobis ministerium contraditum, atque adeo vita nostra destitui maluimus, quam ista pro fide promptitudine. Verum adversus illorum conatus, Dei ac vestrae pietatis judicium opponemus. Nunc autem oramus, ut una ac primaria pietas curetur, etc.

In tom. IV., col. 296 of Coleti's *Concilia*, the same passage is translated somewhat differently, as follows: Nos vero olim quidem, dum quaedam praesumpta sint a reverentissimo quondam Hierosolymitanorum Juvenali, quievimus, dum certe quae debeamus bellare pro regulis videremus. Tunc quasdam festinationes et phantasias ejus hujusmodi contra utramque Phoeniciam et Arabiam minime ignoramus. Nec tamen de his interim contendere possumus, qui certe de ipsis quoque civitatibus, quarum nobis cura commissa est, et ab ipsa, si oportuerit, vita facilius abscedemus quam relinquamus devotionem pro fide bellundi. Sed contra horum quidem spes tam Dei judicium quam tuae pietatis opponimus. Nunc autem quaesumus ut de prima et sola fidei pietate sit cura, etc. In a note on this in the same place in Coleti, we read:

"Lupus thinks that the" [Latin] "Version of the *Codex Casinensis* is the better of the two. But although it may be difficult to pass judgment on that matter, for we lack the Greek text, nevertheless I think that the Basel edition agrees the best of the two with the history of Juvenal. See above, page 98." On looking there I find in note "*h*" that he deemed Juvenal ambitious and much given to increasing the dignity and authority of his own see, which he infers from Epistle 62 of Leo I., Bishop of Rome, and from the Acts of the Council of Chalcedon. He refers also to "Marca, lib. 2 de Concordia, cap. 3, et lib. 6, cap. 1." I translate the Version of the *Codex Casinensis* in this place:

"Some time ago, indeed, while certain things were done presumptuously by the most reverent former Bishop of Jerusalem, Juvenal" [John here regards him as under discipline by his Conventicle, a farcical idea], "we kept quiet, while we assuredly saw things as to which we are under obligation to wage war for the canons. Besides, we are not at all ignorant of certain speedings and apparitions of his of that sort against both Phoenicias and Arabia. But we cannot contend for the present in regard to those matters, for we will more easily" [or "more readily"] "retire from the very cities also, the care of which is committed to us, and from life itself, if it behoove so to do, than give up our devoted determination to wage war for the faith. But against their hopes, indeed, we oppose the judgment of God as well as the canons, lest we seem to feel grief on account" [of the loss] "of our own glory" [alone] (507). "And now also we are not ignorant of his plots and tricks in regard to such persons (508), throughout the second Phoenice and Arabia. But certainly we have no time to devote care to them, for we had rather be deprived of those cities, the ministry to which has been wholly transmitted (509) to us, and even of our lives than of that promptitude for the faith. Indeed against their attempts we will oppose the judgment of God and and of your Piety. But now we pray that the one and primary Piety be cared for, etc."

So they leave that subject and refer to the matter of the faith again and pray the Emperor to favor their heretical side against the Orthodox, and finally say that if he will not, then they ask that they may be permitted to return *"safely and happily"* to their own homes, and then they close with a remark which shows that some of their own people were taking sides with the Orthodox and were contending against heresy. For this is implied in their closing words which they write as a reason why they should go to their own homes:

"For we see the cities committed to us to be not a little injured on account of those who even in pious things, as it seems, seek contention, when no profit can come from it." (510)

---

that of thy piety. But now we ask that there may be care for the first and sole piety of the faith," etc.

In places this serves to make the former translation better understood, though as we have not the Greek original of Count Irenaeus' work, we can not tell which of the two is the more exact.

NOTE 507.—John means the *"glory"* of his patriarchate, for to subtract Palestine and Arabia from it would of course lessen its extent, and thereby his *"glory."*

NOTE 508.—The Latin in col. 1300 of tome III. of Coleti here is *tales*, "*such persons*"; bu the rendering in col. 296 of tome IV., that of the *Synodicon Casinense*, has *hujusmodi, of that sort*.

NOTE 509.—The rendering in the Codex Casinensis quoted in note 506 above is, "*is committed to us.*" The sway of Antioch over Jerusalem was probably gained in its period of ruin. It was now rising again.

NOTE 510.—The translation of this passage in col. 297 of tome III. of *Coleti's Concilia* is as follows: Nam videmus civitates nobis commissas ex tali mora non parum offendi; propter eos qui etiam in rebus piis, ut videtur contentionem quaerunt, nulla inde proveniente utilitate. The translation in col. 297, tome IV. of *Coleti's Concilia* is somewhat different for it reads, Commissas enim nobis urbes non parum noceri ex hac mora conspicimus, dum certe hic nihil haec ipsa proficiat propter eos qui et contra tuam, sicut claret, eligunt contendere pietatem.

Those who favored Juvenal were Orthodox. Those who favored John were Nestorians, Compare Document II. above, page 249, which shows John's and his party's anxiety as to their own. Either rendering above shows that there were some in Syria, Palestine or Phenice or Arabia even, corrupted by man-service and creature-service as Syria already was, who, because they sided with Juvenal, or from some other cause opposed those errors, and whose efforts to maintain the anti-Creature Serving faith of the Third Ecumenical Synod were beginning to make trouble for John of Antioch and his creature-serving Apostasy, and to disquiet them as to results; and they might well fear deposition and excommunication for what that Universal Council in its canons calls their *"Apostasy."* And indeed action

EXPLANATION OF IMPORTANT LANGUAGE.

WHAT DO THE SEVEN BISHOPS OF THE APOSTASY MEAN BY CHARGING ON PAGE 311 OF THE DOCUMENT LAST ABOVE, UPON CYRIL OF ALEXANDRIA AND THE THIRD ECUMENICAL SYNOD THE DESIGN "TO ADULTERATE" THE WORSHIP OFFERED BY THE ANGELS ABOVE TO GOD, (evidently to God the Son as that alone was involved in the discussion), AND BY ACCUSING THEM OF "REALLY TAKING AWAY THAT WORSHIP AND ESTABLISHING" CYRIL'S Twelve "CHAPTERS," THE EIGHTH OF WHICH, BY THE WAY, FORBIDS WORSHIP TO CHRIST'S HUMANITY, AND CONFINES IT TO HIS DIVINITY ALONE?

This brings in another question, as serving to throw light on this matter, namely: WHEN THE FATHER SAID (Heb. 1: 6) *"And let all the Angels of God worship Him"* (by bowing as the Greek shows) "DID HE MEAN WORSHIP BOTH NATURES IN CHRIST, THE UNCREATED AND ETERNAL WORD, AND THE MAN, THAT IS THE CREATURE PUT ON, SO SERVING WITH GOD A CREATURE CONTRARY TO THE PROHIBITION IN MATT. iv: 10, OR DID HE MEAN TO SERVE GOD THE WORD ALONE IN ACCORDANCE WITH MATT. iv: 10?

EXPLANATION OF PASSAGES ABOVE SPECIFIED, IN THE LAST DOCUMENT ABOVE.

The following came in on page 311 above as part of note 501 there, but on account of its length is put here as a separate explanation. The Latin is found there. To proceed.

At the beginning, I would remark that in the margin of this place in *Coleti's Concilia*, tome III., column 1259, occurs the following statement, *"All these expressions are obscure and mutilated."* No wonder he makes that remark, for being a server of Christ's humanity, he did not understand Cyril and the Fifth Ecumenical Synod.

One vastly important question occurs here, namely: What do John of Antioch and his fellow prelates of the Apostasy mean by *"that awful sanctification,"* which *"the elect angels . . . standing at"* God's *"terrible throne"* are *"always offering, to God, which sanctification certain persons now strive to adulterate"*? The translation in the *Synodicon Casinense* terms them *"those terrible"* [that is awe-inspiring] *"acts which they"* [*"the elect angels,"* just looking to that result was taken at last in those canons, and justly, for from the utterances of divers members of that Sanhedrim it is clear that they looked upon Nestorius as innocent, and the facts were so clear then that their course in so doing is explainable only on the ground of their believing that his creature-service and man-service was not error at all. And this is not wonderful, for they were all pupils of Diodore of Tarsus and Theodore of Mopsuestia. See, for instance, Theodoret's unmodified approval of the latter, in his *Ecclesiastical History*, book V., chapter 27, and of Diodore in id., book II., chapter 24; and book IV., chapter 25, and his thorough, and so far as creature-service is concerned unmodified praise of Nestorius against Cyril of Alexandria in his Epistle CLXXII., in col. 1485, 1486, of tome 83, of Migne's *Patrologia Graeca*, which is found in the Acts of the Fifth Ecumenical Synod as noted in Migne there; and his Epistles CLXXIII. and CLXXIV., and in other parts of his heretical writings.

mentioned] "*incessantly offer to God, which*" [acts] "*certain persons now try to abolish,*" literally·"*try to obliterate*" or "*thoroughly try to obliterate.*"

John and his party evidently agreed with Nestorius that the angels in heaven worship Christ's humanity as well as his Divinity. Hence we find John himself, when a delegate at Chalcedon as quoted elsewhere in this work (511), contending in a discourse that Christ's humanity is to be worshipped, and this with reference probably to Cyril's denial of it in the Eighth of his Twelve Chapters and in his *Five Book Contradiction of the Blasphemies of Nestorius*. Elsewhere in this work I have given a brief summary of the chief facts on this subject and the chief utterances in favor of serving Christ's humanity, by the Nestorian party, and of the utterances against that error by Cyril of Alexandria and the Third Ecumenical Synod. (512). John of Antioch's utterances in favor of Man-Service with those of other heretics will be found on the side of Nestorius: those of the Orthodox with Cyril and the Third Synod. I will limit myself here mainly to showing how both parties differed as to the meaning of Hebrews i: 6, as it affects the matter mentioned above by John in his Sermon, that is the question of *the right of the angels to worship Christ's humanity*, that is of *creature-service*, which Nestorius and John of Antioch and their party assert and which Cyril of Alexandria and the Third Synod and the Fifth decide against, forbid, and anathematize, and for which both those Ecumenical Synods depose every cleric who practices it and anathematize every laic so guilty.

For that sin of creature-service, the heretics and Man-Servers adduced the words in Hebrews i: 6, "*And, again, when He bringeth in the First Brought Forth*(513) *into the inhabited world He*" [the Father] "*saith. And let all God's angels worship Him,*" literally, "*bow to Him,*" (514) that is "*bow to Him*" as an act of *religious worship to Him*. That worship of bowing, the Nestorians ascribed to the humanity as well as to the Divinity of the Son, whereas Cyril of Alexandria and the Third Ecumenical Synod and the Fifth following it, ascribed it *to God the Word alone*, though they teach that the Word is in His tabernacle of humanity.

NOTE 511.—In document xxv. below.

NOTE 512.—The chief Nestorian utterances will be found in *Nestorius*' Ecumenically condemned *Epistle to Cyril of Alexandria*, pages 154-176 of volume I. of Chrystal's *Ephesus*, where the Bishops vote its condemnation; in his *Twenty Blasphemies* which were made the ground of his deposition, pages 449-480; and his condemnation and deposition for them are told on pages 486-504 in the same. Compare also Note " F," pages 529-552. More details in the way of Nestorian worship of Christ's humanity will be found in the note matter on pages 112-128, section III., where will be found quotations from or notices of Diodore of Tarsus, Theodore of Mopsuestia, Nestorius himself, Theodoret, Bishop of Cyrus, Andrew, Bishop of Samosata (see especially what he says of Cyril on page 117), and Eutherius, Bishop of Tyana, and see especially also above in this volume the Creed of Theodore and the notes on it on pages 202-210, and Nestorius' profession of Man-Worship on page 238, note 377, and page 283, note 442.

NOTE 513.—Greek, τὸν πρωτότοκον.

NOTE 514.—Greek, προσκυνησάτωσαν αὐτῷ.

The passages in Cyril on Hebrews i: 6, are too long to be all quoted here, but they are found in the English translation of *Cyril of Alexandria on the Incarnation Against Nestorius*, on the following pages and their contexts, from which any scholar who wishes may find the Greek.

1. Page 358, where Theodore of Mopsuestia, the instructor of Nestorius and of John of Antioch, advocates the service of Christ's humanity from Hebrews i: 6, and Cyril of Alexandria denies his interpretation and his Man Service and refutes both. Both these quotations are given there from Cyril's "*Second Book Against the Words of Theodore*"

2. Page 57 and after. This is section 4 and after of the Second Book of Cyril's *Five Book Contradiction of the Blasphemies of Nestorius*.

3. Pages 79 and 80. This is in Section 13 of the same Book II. of Cyril's *Five Book Contradiction*, and is a clear passage against Man-Service.

4. Page 118 and the context. This is found in Section 5 of book III. of the same work.

5. Page 229 and the context, especially page 230. This occurs in Section 36 of Cyril's *Scholia on the Incarnation of the Only Begotten*.

Page 212, Section 25 of the same *Scholia*, contains a noteworthy condemnation by Cyril, of worshipping Christ's humanity though it does not mention Hebrews i: 6. But he shows that it is against Christ's command in Matthew iv: 10, "*Thou shalt bow to the Lord thy God, and Him only shalt thou serve,*" as he does also in other places, as, for example, on page 310, id., which is plain against that error.

Other comments on the words, "*And let all the angels of God worship Him,*" (Heb. i: 6), are to be found in Cyril's other writings, but we search no further at present. Five testimonies ought to be sufficient to all fair men, particularly as those passages taken together are so full and clear, though the translator, Pusey, does not always give the *entire* force of Cyril against Man-Service, for he is not always exact, aye, sometimes mistranslates on this topic.

And how Cyril condemns and denounces the Nestorian worship of Christ's humanity is told by himself in volume I. of Chrystal's *Ephesus*, note 183, pages 79-128, in notes 677, 678 and especially 679, on pages 331-362, and how plainly the Universal Church has condemned the error see in the note matter on pages 108-112; see also the error as taught in *Nestorius' Twenty Blasphemies*, pages 449-480, and his condemnation and deposition for them by the Third Synod of the Undivided Church, on pages 486-504, and see its canons IV., VI. and VII. for the deposition of all Bishops and Clerics and the anathematizing of all laics who share it and oppose the Synod.

From the foregoing we see that Cyril's position, in which he was followed by the Third Synod and the Fifth, is well and often set forth by himself in the above and many other passages, to the following in effect: *In Christ we worship not His humanity at all, but only His Divinity, and that in strict conso-*

nance with his *three favorite texts*, Matthew iv: 10; Isaiah xlii: 8, and Psalm lxxxi: 9; lxxx: 9, in the Septuagint Greek version used by Cyril, which reads: "*There shall be no new god in thee; neither shalt thou worship a new god,*" which Cyril constantly quotes against worshipping Christ's humanity, which, inasmuch as all worship is prerogative to God, and to give it to any one is an indirect confession that he is God, really, in effect, makes that creature "*a new god.*" See in proof under that text in Chrystal's *Ephesus*, vol. I., page 677, both places where it occurs. The word used in that verse of the Psalm is the same as that translated *worship* in Matthew iv: 10.

And we see also that he was so understood by his Nestorian opponents cited on pages 112-128, volume I. of *Chrystal's Ephesus*. For example, one of the ablest of them all, Andrew of Samosata, writes that Cyril himself had said that God the Word, must be bowed to *with flesh*, that is, as Cyril means and in effect explains elsewhere, *within flesh*, but "*forbids the flesh to be co-bowed*" to [that is, "*to be co-worshipped*"] "*with his Divinity.*" (515.)

A Greek preposition μετά here used is understood by Andrew in the sense of *together with* as it often means, whereas Cyril using it, seemingly in the sense of a certain *Confession of Faith* of the Synod of *Nicaea* against Paul of Samosata, uses it not in that sense, but in the sense of *within*. But we will treat of that document further on, just before the Orthodox documents which follow these. It is found in the Greek on page 182 of the third edition of Hahn's *Bibliothek der Symbole* (Breslau 1897, Morgenstern).

Meanwhile we should warn all men against the mistranslations in some of the Oxford English versions, particularly those of Athanasius and of Cyril which make them contradictors of what they say above, Man-Worshippers, and therefore anathematized by the Third Synod, which Cyril himself led!!!

Let us add a few more passages out of many on Hebrews i: 6, "*And let all God's angels worship Him,*" and on the general topic, from our Elijah like and great Alexandrian, as they are quoted in Chrystal's *Ephesus*, vol. I.

Cyril's utterances againt the worship of Christ's humanity will be found in note 183, pages 79-112, where also, pages 98-101, he quotes Athanasius, his great teacher under God, against that error; and on pages 90-94, he shows that to understand Hebrews i: 6, "*And let all God's angels bow to*" [that is "*worship*"] "*Him,*" results in worshipping a Tetrad, that is the uncreated Trinity and a mere created man, instead of the divine Trinity alone, and in a return to the sin of the heathen, creature worship, and that to represent the angels as bowing to, that is as giving worship to Christ's humanity, is to represent them as having been "*deceived*" by being led astray into the sin of worshipping a creature, and as having "*given drunkards' insults to God*" if they had done that. The passage is remarkably strong. See it there.

NOTE 515.—See the place, with the context and the Greek quotations on pages 97 and 117, volume I. of Chrystal's *Ephesus*.

And Cyril indignantly asks Nestorius (Section 6, Book IV. of *St. Cyril's Five Book Contradiction of the Blasphemies of Nestorius*):

"*Since we have been ransomed from the ancient deceit*" [the sin of worshipping creatures, the sin of the heathen] "*and have refused as a* BLASPHEMOUS THING TO WORSHIP THE CREATURE, WHY DOST THOU WHELM US AGAIN IN THE ANCIENT SINS AND MAKE US WORSHIPPERS OF A MAN?" [that is of a mere human Christ, that is of his humanity.] As is evident from the utterances of Nestorius and his partisans in that note, they worshipped both natures of Christ together, *with*, as they claimed, but *one bow*, that is *with* [but] *one worship*, which they elsewhere contradict, for Nestorius teaches in his *Blasphemy* 8 and in other Blasphemies that he worshipped Christ's humanity not for its own sake, but in effect *relatively* to God the Word. So he writes in his counter Anathema VIII, page 238, note 377 above. See in Chrystal's *Ephesus*, vol. I., page 461, note 1., how often that heathen plea has been condemned by the Universal Church. Of course he worshipped God the Word absolutely.

See also notes 677 and 679, pages 331-362, of the same volume. On pages 338, 339 is a brief summary of Cyril's and the Universal Church's utterances against the worship of Christ's humanity, and a reference to prove that the Nestorians so understood him. See also, note matter on pages 108-112, for a detailed account of the utterances of the Universal Church against that sin of creature worship, and pages 112-128 to show that the Nestorians understood Cyril to condemn all worship of Christ's humanity both that with his Divinity, and also that given to his humanity as separate from His Divinity.

See further in the *General Index* under *Cyril*, *Nestorius*, the names aforesaid of his partisans, and under *Man Worship*.

Again Cyril in the following passage from his work entitled *Christ is One, against Theodore*, charges that to worship Christ's humanity with the Trinity is to make it a new god and to change a worshipped Trinity into a worshipped Tetrad. I quote:

"But there are, there are" [persons] "who deny their Redeemer and Lord, and assert that He who in the last times of the world endured for our sakes birth in flesh out of a woman, is not indeed the real Son of God the Father, but, on the contrary, that A RECENT AND LATE GOD HAS APPEARED TO THE WORLD, *and that he has the glory of a Sonship which has been acquired from without as ours also has, and that he glories in certain adulterous quasi honors, so that it is now* THE WORSHIP OF A MAN AND NOTHING ELSE *and* A CERTAIN MAN IS ADORED WITH THE HOLY TRINITY, *as well by us as by the holy angels*. (516.) Some persons who are very proud and wise in their great knowledge of the Scriptures of God (517), have inserted those heresies into their writings,

---

NOTE 516.—Hebrews 1:6.
NOTE 517.—Diodore, and Theodore of Mopsuestia, the inventors and propagators of the heresies of Man Worship, denial of the Inflesh, and Cannibalism on the Eucharist, who had a great and wonderful influence in the Patriarchate of Antioch and over the Syrian race. The language of Cyril is of course sarcastic.

and so, as the Lord of all says by one of the holy prophets, *They have set a trap to corrupt men.* (518). For what else than a snare and a stumbling block is a tongue which utters things which are perverse and abhorrent to the holy Scriptures, and which shamelessly oppose the tradition (519) of the holy Apostles and Evangelists? We must therefore repudiate those men who are guilty of such wicked crimes, whether they are among the living (520) or not (521); for it is necessary to withdraw from that which is injurious, and not to have regard to any one's person, but to what pleases God" (522).

Cyril in his work *Against Diodore of Tarsus*, one of the founders of Nestorianism and of its Man-Worship, writes as follows:

"Thou darest also to clothe in the Master's forms him, whom thou sayest to be a Man from Mary, and who at first was not at all different from us nor superior to us, but afterwards by much effort merited the name and the divine glory of the Son, that is after he had come out of the womb. Therefore, ACCORDING TO THY OPINION, THERE ARE TWO SONS, AND CHRIST IS A NEW GOD who was endowed with supernatural honor from God somewhat more than the rest of the creatures; so that He" [God the Word] "IS CO-ADORED WITH A MERE MAN, *even that Man who in the course of time*, and only towards the end" [of his earthly career] "got possession of glory, and WAS MADE A COMPLEMENT OF THE TRINITY AND IN NATURE EQUAL TO IT" (523).

So Cyril reasons in his *Address to Pulcheria and Eudocia*, page 313, Part I., vol. VII. of P. E. Pusey's Greek of Cyril's works; and again on page 359 in the same volume Cyril in his *Christ is One* condemns the worshipping of Christ's humanity, a creature, with His Divinity as resulting in a worshipped Tetrad instead of a worshipped Trinity.

Again on Hebrews i: 6, "*And when He bringeth in the First Brought Forth into the inhabited world, He saith, And let all God's Angels bow to*" [that is "*worship*"] "*Him,*" Cyril writes:

"The Word who has come out of God the Father has been named *Sole Born* with reference to His [Divine] Nature, because He alone has been born out of the Father. And He was called *First Brought Forth* also when having been made Man He came into the inhabited world and" [became] "a part of it. And besides He is bowed to by the holy angels, and that too when THE RIGHT TO BE BOWED TO BELONGS TO AND BEFITS GOD ALONE. *How then is Christ not God*, SEEING THAT HE IS BOWED TO" [that is, "WORSHIPPED"] "EVEN IN HEAVEN"? (524).

Again Cyril in his *Thesaurus*, in arguing for the Divinity of God the Word against the radical Arian Eunomius, writes what shows his belief in the teaching of Holy Writ that all worship is prerogative to God.

NOTE 518.—Jerem. v: 26.
NOTE 519.—That is the transmission of doctrine in the Epistles and Gospels.
NOTE 520.—Nestorius, John of Antioch and others were among the living, and so were the Bishops of their Conventicle and all their partisans.
NOTE 521.—Diodore of Tarsus and Theodore of Mopsuestia were among the dead.
NOTE 522.—See the above place with the context, on pages 92, 93, vol. I. of Chrystal's *Ephesus*, note matter.
NOTE 523.—See pages 93, 94, vol. I. of Chrystal's *Ephesus*, note, where additional matter is found.
NOTE 524.—See more fully on page 727, vol. I. of Chrystal's *Ephesus*.

"Forasmuch as the Scripture of God calls the *Son Lord*, thou wilt therefore grant that He is *Lord*, and that in accordance with the truth; or thou wilt refuse to Him that title also as thou dost to the rest. For if indeed thou wilt say that He is not Lord, thou wilt hold an opinion which is contrary to the Scriptures of God and to the Spirit which has said that He is. But if thou agreest and sayest that He is *Lord* thou wilt be convicted of IMPIETY by applying the title *Lord* to him whom thou deniest to be of the same substance as the God and Father, and by bowing to" [that is, "by worshipping"] "him" [that is, that mere creature according to thee,] "and" [so] "thou worshippest a creature contrary to Him who is God by Nature. For that which is a substance other than God, can not be God by Nature. And the Scripture of God is a witness to this, for it says, *The Lord our God is*" [*but*] "*one Lord*" [Mark xii: 29; Deut. vi: 4]; "for the Nature of Divinity is" [but] "One, *and* THAT WE MUST BOW TO" [that is "*worship*"] "THAT NATURE ALONE hear again" [the following words of Christ] "*Thou shalt bow to*" [that is "*worship*"] "*the Lord thy God, and Him only shalt thou serve.*" [Matt. iv: 10]. (525).

In condemning the worship of Christ's humanity Cyril simply follows in the steps of his very distinguished predecessor Athanasius. In the following places in Newman's English translation of "Select *Treatises of S. Athanasius, Archbishop of Alexandria, in Controversy with the Arians,*" where he is commenting on the words in Hebrews 1:6, "*And let all God's angels worship Him,*" he condemns service to Christ's humanity and so anticipatively condemns the later started Nestorian perversion of that text.

1. Page 149, section 49 of Athanasius' *Epistle concerning the Councils, held at Ariminum in Italy and at Seleucia in Isauria*, where is proving that the Son must be God from the fact that He is worshipped by the angels in that text. That, of course, implies that all religious service is prerogative to Divinity alone, as Christ teaches in Matthew iv. 10., and therefore when we find it given to Christ in Holy Writ, it proves that he must be God.

2. Pages 238 to 242, sections 40 to 44 of his *First Discourse against the Arians*, where he is proving the same thing from the same text, Hebrews i: 6. He brings in also Philippians ii: 5 to 12, which he interprets as teaching the worship of God the Word, but the Nestorians perverted it to the sense of Man Worship which Athanasius and Cyril of Alexandria deny, as can be seen by referring to that passage in the *Index on Scripture* in their writings. But, as that passage is not here under discussion, we do not here give each particular reference. See also the seventh of the twenty Blasphemies from Nestorius in Act 1. of Ephesus, on which he was condemned and deposed for teaching error, for it treats of part of the passage in Philippians ii: 5 to 12.

Compare Blasphemy XI. also of Nestorius' Twenty.

3. Pages 267, 268, section 61, of Athanasius' *First Discourse Against the*

NOTE 525.—See the above place more fully in *Chrystal's Ephesus*, vol. I, pages 747, 748 and the context.

Arians, where he is proving the Divinity of God the Word, from his being bowed to, that is *worshipped* by the angels in Hebrews i: 6.

4. Pages 313, 314, sections 23 and 24 of Athanasius' *Second Discourse against the Arians*, where he again proves, against them, that worship is prerogative to God, and since in Hebrews i: 6, He commands it to be given by the angels to the Son, therefore the Son must be God.

5. Page 372 and its context, section 64, in Athanasius' *Second Discourse against the Arians*, where speaking of the Arian cavil on the words *First Brought Forth of all creation*, he explains it Orthodoxically, and quotes Hebrews i: 6, to prove in effect that inasmuch as Christ receives worship therefore He must be God, and not a mere creature as the Arians contended.

We come now to the *Action of the Third Ecumenical Synod, in condemnation of Nestorian service to Christ's humanity*. The decision of *the Third Ecumenical Synod* being that of the *"one, holy, universal and Apostolic Church,"* which we confess in the Creed, and being in strict agreement with the New Testament, settles the question forever. And he who opposes it is a heretic.

That Man-Service is plainly taught in the following of the Twenty Blasphemies from his writings, for which he was condemned and deposed in Act 1. of the Third Synod.

In Passage, that is Blasphemy 8.—Expressly.

In Blasphemy 9.—Impliedly, because Nestorius makes the dignity of God the Word and the creature He put on *the same;* and so as *the right to be worshipped* is part of *His dignity as God*, Nestorius gives that to *the creature* put on also.

In Blasphemy 10.—Expressly.

In Blasphemy 14.—Expressly or impliedly, because it gives *worship*, all of which is *prerogative to God alone*, to the Man united to God the Word, and commits the creature-serving act of calling that creature *God*, and that also in the sense of being served as God by the act of bowing.

In Blasphemy 15.—Expressly or impliedly, because to the Man united to God the Word is given *cosession* with God the Word, evidently from comparison with the other Blasphemies, in the sense of cosession in *divine* dignity and for the sake, among other things, of being *worshipped* with Him; and *co-glorification* with Him in the *"same" dignity* of God. (See *passage* 9 above.)

In Blasphemy 20.—Impliedly, because it condemns all Orthodox teachers, because they do not agree with Nestorian heresies, among them that of worshipping by bowing, etc., the creature, that is the Man united to God the Word.

Though the words, *"Let all the Angels of God worship him,"* of Heb. 1: 6, occur in none of those twenty blasphemous Passages, nevertheless the Nestorian perversion of them to *Man Service*, that is to *Creature Service*, does, and is condemned; and that is the all-important point.

To the foregoing I would add another sample Orthodox passage on Hebrews i: 6, which I have since found and incorporated in note 582, page 225 of volume I of my translation of *Ephesus*, where the Greek also is found. It is in Cyril of Alexandria's *Address on the right Faith to Arcadia and Marina*, where he is arguing against the Nestorian assertion that Christ is a mere Man, and contending that *He is God, because religious bowing, being prerogative to Divinity alone, and being* given to the Son in the New Testament proves that He must be God. I quote the passage as I find it on page 193 of Part I, volume VII. of P. E. Pusey's edition of the Greek of Cyril of Alexandria's works. I translate:

"*From the Epistle to the Hebrews*" [Heb. i: 6].

"' And *when He bringeth in the First Brought Forth into the inhabited world, He saith, And let all God's angels bow to*'" [that is "*worship*"] "'*Him.*' "

"The Word who has come out of God the Father has been named *Sole Born* (526) with reference to His" [Divine] "Nature, because He alone has been born out of the sole" [Divine] "Father. (527) And He was called *First Brought Forth* (528) also when having been made Man He came into the inhabited world and" [became] "a part of it. And besides He is so bowed to" [that is "worshipped"] "by the holy angels, and that too when THE RIGHT TO BE BOWED TO" [that is, "*to be worshipped*"] BELONGS TO AND BEFITS GOD ALONE. How then is Christ not God, seeing that He is bowed to" [that is, "*worshipped*"] "even in heaven?"

See furthermore under Hebrews I: 6, page 688, vol. I of Chrystal's *Ephesus*, and under *Philippians* II: 5-12 on page 687, id.; and under the same texts, pages 474, 475, volume I of Chrystal's *Nicaea*, Athanasius, Epiphanius, and Faustin, a Presbyter of Rome, all champions of God in the fourth century against the professed creature worship of the Arians, all argue that religious bowing, that is bowing as an act of religions service, being prerogative to God, the fact that in Hebrews I: 6, it is ordered by the Father to be given to God the Word, just mentioned in the context of that passage, proves Him to be God. And that was a frequent argument of the ancient Christian Orthodox against creature-servers. And I would add and repeat that *bowing* and *bow*, are used both in the New Testament and in ancient Greek writers for *worship*, aye as the general term for it, and as in some sense including all other acts of religious service and as standing for them all, because it is a part of every other act of religious service, for we bow our heads when we stand in prayer, when we

---

NOTE 526.—Greek, Μονογενής.

NOTE 527.—That is, as the Nicene Creed well has it, "*born out of the Father, Sole Born, that is, out of the Substance of the Father.*" The term Μονογενής is generally though less accurately translated *only begotten* in our Common Version. It is so rendered in six out of the nine places where it occurs in the New Testament, and by *only* in the other three, and so γεννηθέντα is translated *begotten* in the Credal clause which should be rendered "*born not made,*" for He was eternally in the Father and Consubstantial with Him before He was *born* out of Him, and therefore was "*not made.*"

NOTE 528.—Greek, Πρωτότοκον.

kneel, when we prostrate ourselves, or perform any other act of worship to Almighty God, the only object of allowed religious service by any act, Matthew iv: 10, and Isaiah xlii: 8, Colos. i.: 18, Rev. xix: 10, and Rev. xxi: 8, 9.

In times of corruption, in the middle ages and since, the creature worshipping Communions have made but little use of the argument that Christ must be God because every act of religious service being prerogative to God, *bowing* as an act of religious service is given to Him in Holy Writ, for any logical mind can at once see that that argument for His Divinity utterly fails when an opposer of it can at once retort. But you bow in worship to angels and archangels and saints departed, aye and give them another act of worship, prayer, and yet you admit that they are not God. Aye more you give other acts of service, mentioned in Holy Writ, to mere inanimate things such as relics, images painted that is pictures, graven images, crosses painted, and graven, or otherwise made, altars, Communion tables, the book of the Gospels, the Bible, or any part of it, the wafer, or the leavened bread and wine of the Lord's Supper, which you worship as God (529).

Such acts to mere inanimate things are *bowing* in defiance of Christ's law in Matthew iv: 10, bending of the knee or genuflection, kneeling (1 Kings xix: 18), incense (Ezek. viii: 6-13) such as the idolaters gave to things and do still, and kissing, such as the idolatrous Israelites gave to the calves, (Hosea xiii: 1-4, and 1 Kings xix: 18). And for the sake of greater clearness on worship and against the excuses of creature worshippers for their sin, see the *General Index* to Chrystal on *Creature Worship* under "*Worship*," page 101.

And it will not do to say, We do not worship such things, or even animate creatures *absolutely*, for we admit, as Nestorius did, that by Christ's law in Matthew iv: 10, nothing but God, the Triune Jehovah, can be religiously bowed to, that is, worshipped for its own sake, but we worship it *relatively*, that is for the sake of Jehovah, as Nestorius worshipped, as he held, in consonance with Hebrews i: 6, the humanity of Christ, a view which is clearly that of his *Blasphemies* 5, 8, and 14, not to speak of others.

But to that we reply that the idolatrous Israelites worshipped the golden calf in the wilderness, and the calf at Bethel and that at Dan, *relatively only to*

NOTE 529.—The Romanist so worships the wafer, the Greek the leavened bread and wine, and the One Nature Consubstantiationist Theodoret worshipped the elements as being unchanged as to their "*substance*,' but as *types* of Christ's broken body and shed blood, and as being them also, somehow. See in proof his own words to that effect on pages 276-285, vol. 1 of Chrystal's *Ephesus*. The traitorous Puseyite idolater in the Anglican Communion is a Two Nature Consubstantiationist and worships both natures of Christ in the Eucharist after consecration, giving, like Theodoret as above quoted, the worship to the bread and wine or wafer and wine as "*types*" of Christ's body and blood, and besides as being the very substance of that body and blood, and besides as containing the very Substance of His Divinity; or to the substances of both His Natures, the Divinity and the humanity as *with*, *in* or *under* the leavened bread or the wafer, which is called *impanation* and *invination*. But some of the Puseyites are not so definite and clear on that last point in their soul-damning idolatry as the Romanists and the Greeks are in theirs, but are misty.

Jehovah, as is shown at length in Chrystal's little work on *Creature Worship*, pages 1 80. See also, for particulars, under *Worship* in the *General Index* to that work, and in the *Index of Holy Scripture Referred to*, under Exodus xxxii: 1, Kings, xii: 26; xiii: 34, and other parts of Holy Writ involved in the Controversy.

And we know what fearful curses from Jehovah fell on them for such God-forbidden sins, and what horrible woes in the form of slaughter by Arabs, Turks, and Tartars, confiscation of houses and lands, and long centuries of slavery, and other punishments have come upon Christendom for such and similar corruptions and disobediences to God condemned in His holy Word, and we know how the Third Ecumenical Synod condemned Nestorius and his worship of Christ's humanity, and his perversion of Hebrews 1: 6, and Philippians ii: 5 12 to defend it. See under those texts in the Indexes to Scripture in volume 1. of *Ephesus* and in volume 1. of *Nicaea*, Chrystal's translations.

But now to quote a few passages more fully out of many from Orthodox writers of the fourth century for the doctrine that all bowing as an act of religious service is prerogative to God, and against the Nestorian perversion above of the words of Hebrews i: 6, to make them favor the worship of a mere creature, Christ's humanity, with God the Word.

St. Athanasius in his *Second Oration* or *Discourse against* the *Arians*, sections 23 and 24.

"Moreover if as the" [Arian] "heretics hold, the Son were '*a creature or a work*, but not *as one of the* creatures,' (530) because of His excelling them in glory, it were needful that Scripture should describe and display Him by a comparison in His favor with the other works; for instance that it should say that He is greater than archangels, and more honorable than the thrones, and brighter than the sun and moon, and greater than the heavens. But it does not in fact so describe Him; but the Father shows him to be His Own and Sole Son, saying *Thou art my Son* (531), *and This is my beloved Son, in whom I am well pleased* (532). And therefore the angels ministered unto Him (533) as being one beyond themselves, AND HE IS BOWED TO" [that is, "WORSHIPPED"] "BY THEM (534), not merely as being greater in glory, but as being

NOTE 530.—That is, the Arians meant, While we assert that the Word is a made God and so a creature, we do not make him one of the common creatures, but one much superior to them.

NOTE 531.—Psalm ii: 7; Acts xiii: 33; Heb. i: 5, and Heb. v: 5.

NOTE 532.—Matt. iii: 17; Matt. xvii: 5; Mark i: 11; Luke ix 35; and II. Peter i: 17.

NOTE 533.—Matt. iv: 11; Mark 1: 13.

NOTE 534.—Heb. i: 6. The Son, God the Word, is worshipped in heaven under the name of *the Lamb*, of course in accordance with His own law in Matt. iv: 10, and therefore as God alone, within his body, Rev. v: 8-14 inclusive; Rev. vii: 9-12; and Heb. i: 8-13; where Paul, our brother, proves that Christ must be God because He is called *God* by the Father, and because the work of Creation is ascribed to him.

I would add that Cyril of Alexandria in his *Scholia on the Incarnation*, section 13, pages 200-203 shows that he understands all the divine names of the Son, like, for example, *Word*

a separate" [Person] "beyond and aside from all the creatures, and as beyond and aside from themselves, and as being the Father's Sole and Own Son, as it relates to His" [divine] "Substance. For if He was bowed to" [that is *"worshipped"*] [merely] "as excelling them in glory, each of the lower creatures ought to bow to" [that is *"to worship"*] "every other one who is above himself. But that is not the case, *for creature does not bow to*" [that is, "does not *"worship"*] "*creature, but the servant to the Master and the creature to God.* Therefore Peter the Apostle hinders Cornelius who wished to bow to him," [that is *"to worship"* him, by] "saying, *I also am a man* (535); and an angel in the Revelations hinders John when he wishes to bow to" [that is to *"worship"* him" [by] "saying, *See thou do it not; I am thy fellow-servant, and of thy brethren the prophets, and of those who keep the sayings of this book, bow to*" [that is *"worship"*] "*God* (536). *Therefore* IT BELONGS TO GOD ALONE TO BE BOWED TO" [that is "TO BE WORSHIPPED"] "and this the angels themselves know, for though they excel" [or *"are above"*] "others in their glories, nevertheless they are all creatures and *are not of those who are bowed to*" [that is *"are not of those who are worshipped"*] "but of those who bow to" [that is *"worship"*] "the Master. Therefore when Manoah, the father of Samson, wished to offer sacrifice to the angel, the angel forbade him" [or *"prevented him"*] "saying, *Offer not to me, but to God"* (537).

But, on the other hand, THE LORD IS BOWED TO" [that is, "IS WORSHIPPED"] "even by the angels; for it is written, '*And let all God's angels bow to Him*'" (538) [that is, *"worship* Him"]. "and" He is *"bowed to"* [that is *"worshipped"*] "by all the nations as Isaiah says, '*Egypt hath discovered thee and the merchandise of the Ethiopians, and the Sabeans, tall men, shall come through to thee and they shall be thy servants*' (539). Then thereafter it reads: '*And they shall bow to*'" [that is, *"worship"*] "' *thee*, and by'" [or "*in*"] '" *thee shall they pray, for God is in thee, and there is no God besides thee*' (540). And He accepts His disciples' worship, and certifies them who He is, saying, *Do ye not call Me the Lord and Teacher? And ye say well, for so I am.* (541).

God, etc., and all his divine acts, raising the dead, for instance, as belonging to His Divine Nature, and all the human names, like *Son of Man*, and *Man* for example and all his human acts, like sleeping, hungering, and suffering, for instance, as belonging to God the Word economically, as he and his great predecessor Athanasius explain elsewhere, to avoid invoking or otherwise worshipping a creature, His humanity. On this last point see Chrystal's *Nicaea*, vol. I., pages 237-240. No man can understand Cyril, and the decisions of the Third Council whose teacher under God he was, till he knows and recognizes these facts. In section 36 of the same *Scholia*, Oxford translation of *S. Cyril on the Incarnation against Nestorius*, pages 229-231, Cyril well shows that in Christ we worship only His Divinity.

NOTE 535.—Acts x: 25, 26.
NOTE 536.—Rev. xxii: 8, 9; compare Rev. xix: 10.
NOTE 537.—Judges xiii: 16.
NOTE 538.—Heb. 1: 6.
NOTE 539.—Isaiah xlv: 14.
NOTE 540.—Isaiah xlv, 14.
NOTE 541.—John xiii: 13.

And when Thomas says to Him, *My Lord and My God* (542), He allows him so to speak; aye more, He accepts Him" [b)] "not hindering him. For He Himself is, as the other Prophets say and as David sings, 'The Lord of Powers, the Lord of Sabaoth which is interpreted, *The Lord of Armies* and very and Almighty God,' even though the Arians burst themselves at this. BUT HE HAD NOT BEEN BOWED TO" [that is "*not worshipped*"], "NOR HAD THOSE THINGS BEEN SAID OF HIM, IF HE HAD BEEN A CREATURE AT ALL."

"But now, *because He is not a creature, but the own Offspring of the Substance of the God who is bowed to*" (543) [that is, "*is worshipped*"] "*and Son* by" [His Divine] "Nature, THEREFORE *He is bowed to*" [that is, is " *worshipped*"], "*and is believed to be God, and Lord of Armies and Ruler and Almighty as the Father is;* for He Himself has said, '*All things that the Father hath are Mine*' (544). For it belongs to the Son to have the things of the Father, and to be such that the Father is seen in Him, and *that 'through Him all things were made*' (545), and that in Him the salvation of all both comes to pass and stands fast." (546).

Of the 13 Passages quoted from Athanasius on pages 217-240, volume 1. of Chrystal's *Nicaea*, in Passage 3, he argues that the Angel whom the Patriarch Jacob invoked in Genesis xlviii: 15, 16, must be God because prayer, an act of worship, was given him by Jacob and that if the patriarch had invoked any creature *it would have been a rejecting of God.*

In Passage 6, he again argues that inasmuch as Abraham *bowed to* that is *worshipped* the Word even before He took flesh, under the Old Testament (Gen. xvii: 1-4 and after), He must be God.

So in effect he writes in Passage 7, and in effect in Passage 8, and so very plainly in Passage 9 just quoted above.

In Passage 10, he denies all worship to any creature including of course Christ's humanity, for in Section 3 of his *Epistle to Adelphius* he writes:

"*We do not bow to*" [that is, "*we do not worship*"] "*a creature. God forbid! That is the error of the heathen and the Arians.*"

In Passage 11, he in effect limits his worship of Christ to His Divinity, for at the end of Section 6 of his *Epistle to Adelphius*, he teaches:

"Let them" [the Arians] "know, that when we bow to" [that is "*worship*"] "the Lord in flesh, we are not bowing to" [that is, "*we are not worshipping*"]

NOTE 542.—John xx: 28.

NOTE 543.—In the Greek of John viii, 42, God the Son says, "*I came out of God*," and in John xvi: 28, He says, "*I came out of the Father*," and in Hebrews i: 3; not "*express-image of His Person*," but "*Character of His Substance*," as the ancient fourth century champions for God taught against the Arians.

NOTE 544.—John xvi: 15.

NOTE 545.—John i: 3. Greek, πάντα δι' αὐτοῦ ἐγένετο. Compare John i: 10, Psalm xxxiii: 6; Eph. iii: 9; Col. i: 16, 17; Heb. i: 2, and Rev. iv: 11.

NOTE 546.—See the whole of the above passage with additional matter in Chrystal's *Nicaea*, vol. 1., pages 233-235.

"*a creature, but the Creator who has put on the created body, as we have said before.*"

In Passage 13, Athanasius, like canon XXXV. of Laodicea, mentions, according to Coleti's Greek, the giving of invocation to a creature, aye to any but God, as an act of idolatry, which view is well guaranteed as sound by Christ's own words in Matthew iv: 10.

For the great and noble Alexandrian, one of the greatest two Bishops of the ancient Church, (Cyril, his successor, being the other), in explaining the doctrine of Economic Appropriation, writes in section 33 of his *Third Oration*, or *Discourse against the Arians*, as follows:

"It became the Lord in putting on human flesh, to put it on whole with its own sufferings, that as we say that the body was His own, so also it may be said that the sufferings of the body belonged to Him" [God the Word] "alone, even though they did not touch Him so far as His Divinity is concerned. If the body had been another's, the sufferings too would have been said to belong to that other. But since the flesh is the Word's (*for 'the Word was made flesh'*) (546) of necessity then the sufferings also of the flesh are to be ascribed to Him whose the flesh is. And to whom" [the Word] "the sufferings are ascribed, such especially as are the being condemned, the being scourged, the thirsting, and the cross, and the death, and the other infirmities of the body, to Him too belong the setting of things right and the grace. For this cause therefore, consistently and fittingly such sufferings are ascribed, not to another but to the Lord, that the grace may be from Him, and *that we may not become* IDOLATERS (547), BUT TRULY WORSHIPPERS OF GOD, BECAUSE WE INVOKE NO CREATURE, NOR ANY COMMON MAN, *but Him who has come out of God by Nature and is the very Son, even that very one become Man, but yet nothing less the Lord Himself and God and Saviour,*" that is, of course God the Word, not that humanity which He has put on. And all these Passages of Athanasius make strongly for the Orthodox and at Ephesus universally approved sense of Hebrews 1: 6, that the worship there meant was given to God the Word alone, not at all to his humanity.

Furthermore, to put it briefly, St. Athanasius' 13 utterances on pages 217-240, volume I. of *Chrystal's Nicaea*, contain many and strong testimonies against all the creature worship of the Arians; he teaches that it is from the devil (548), that the creature serving "*Arians are not Christians*" (549), that they are Polytheists because they serve a creature with the true God, the Father (550), that "*they wallow along with the pagans by serving a creature and different gods*" (551), that is two Gods, one, according to them, a created and

---

NOTE 546.—John i: 14.
NOTE 547.—Or according to another reading: "*that we may not become servers of another,*" which, with what follows above, makes equally against all service to Christ's humanity.
NOTE 548.—*Chrystal's Nicaea*, vol. 1., page 222.
NOTE 549.—Id., pages 222, 217, 236, 237.
NOTE 550.—Id., pages 225-229, 230, 232, 233.
NOTE 551.—Id., pages 229, 232, 233, 236, 237.

Explanation of Important Language on Man Worship. 331

so non eternal God, the Word, and another, an uncreated and eternal God, the Father, and that bowing and prayer and by necessary implication every other act of worship is prerogative to God alone (552).

St. Epiphanius, the friend of Athanasius, is very clear for bowing, that is for *worshipping* God alone. Passages from him to that effect and for the doctrine that wherever Scripture gives worship to any one, that one must be God, and hence for the Ecumenically approved sense of Hebrews i: 6, are found in Chrystal's translation of *Nicaea*, pages 240-247, passages 14 to 18 inclusive there. I quote only a part.

In passage 14, he quotes that verse in the Orthodox, Anti-Man-Serving sense, as follows: he is speaking in section 50 of his *Ancoratus* against the Arian creature worshippers of his day.

"And let them not vainly heap up blasphemies to themselves. *For if the Son is a creature He is not to be bowed to*" [that is *"not to be worshipped"*] "according to the doctrine of those" [texts of Scripture] (553). "For it is foolish to bow to" [that is, *"to worship"*] *"a creature* and to do away the first commandment; which saith, *Hear, O Israel, the Lord our God is*" [but] *"one Lord*(554). *Therefore the Holy Word is not a creature, because He is to be bowed to*" [that is, *"to be worshipped"*]. "*The disciples bowed to*" [that is, *"worshipped"*] "Him. The angels in heaven bow to Him," [for Scripture saith], "*And let all the angels of God bow to Him*" [that is *"worship Him"*] (555).

Here then we have an anticipative condemnation of the above heresy and slander of the Delegation of the Apostasy that Cyril of Alexandria and the Third Ecumenical Council in denying worship to a creature, Christ's humanity, in heaven, were *adulterating the worship offered by* the angels above to God, and that they were "*really taking away that worship*" by "*establishing*" *Cyril's Twelve Chapters, the Eighth of which forbids worship to Christ's humanity, and confines all worship to him to his divinity alone.*

Nestorius rejected the doctrine of Cyril against serving the humanity of Christ set forth in the shorter Epistle to him which was approved by the vote of the Third Ecumenical Synod in its first Act. See in proof Chrystal's *Ephesus*, vol. I., pages 79-82; and for the approval of the said Epistle pages 129-154.

He rejected also Cyril's longer Epistle which has the Twelve Chapters, that is the Twelve Anathemas at its end, which quotes Nestorius' words in favor of the relative worship of Christ's humanity and condemns them. That Epistle also was approved by the Third Ecumenical Council and by all the other three Ecumenical Synods after it. See in proof Nestorius' profession of belief in the relative worship of Christ's humanity, as quoted and condemned by Cyril in his *Long Epistle* to him, on pages 221, 222 and 223, volume I. of Chrystal's

NOTE 552.—Id., pages 222 240.
NOTE 553.—See Matt iv: 10; Isaiah xlii: 8; Psalm lxxxi: 9, etc.
NOTE 554 —Deut. vi: 4, 5; Mark xii: 29, 32; John xvii: 3; I. Cor. viii: 4, 5, 6.
NOTE 555.—Heb. I: 6.

Ephesus, and as to the approval of that letter in note 520, pages 204-208 of that same volume.

For the sake of fuller information I quote that whole passage:

"Furthermore, WE DECLINE TO SAY OF ANOINTED" [*Christ*, which means *Anointed*] "'*I worship him who is worn*'" [the mere Man put on by God the Word] "for *the sake of Him*" [God the Word] "· *Who wears him. I bow to him who is seen*'" [the mere man] "'*on account of Him*'" [God the Word] "'*Who is unseen*, and it is A HORRIBLE THING, to say also in addition to that : '"

"'*He who is taken*'" [the mere Man] '*is co-called* GOD *with Him*' [God the Word] '*Who has taken Him.*'"

"For he who says those things cuts" [the Son] " again into two Anointeds" [that is into two Christs] "and places the Man separately by himself and God" [separately by Himself] "in like manner. For, confessedly he denies the" [true] "Union *in accordance with the doctrine of which*" [Union] " NO ONE IS CO-BOWED TO AS ONE WITH ANOTHER, NOR IS ANY ONE CO-CALLED GOD, AS ONE WITH ANOTHER, but *Anointed Jesus, Son, Sole Born, is understood to be*" [only] "*one*, and is honored with" [but] "ONE *worship within His own flesh.*"

The first of those two places is *Blasphemy* 8 of Nestorius, on page 461, volume I. of Chrystal's *Ephesus*, and the second is in substance in Nestorius' *Blasphemies* 5, 6, 7, and 14. They are on pages 459, 460, and 467, of the same volume. Nestorius' worship of Christ's humanity is plainly expressed in his Blasphemies 8, 10, 14, also on pages 461, 464, and 466.

And we must remember that all those passages of Nestorius, were branded in the Council as "*blasphemies*" (556), as "HORRIBLE AND BLASPHEMOUS" (557), as "BLASPHEMY" (558), and as "*an* ACCUSATION *against him*" (559), and that on the basis of them and his other blasphemies he was deposed by the whole Church in its Third Synod. See in proof the same volume, pages 486-504.

The Third Ecumenical Synod in its Act VI. condemned the "*Depraved Creed*" ascribed by some to the heresiarch, Theodore of Mopsuestia, which contains and approves *relative* service to *the Man*, that is to *the creature* united to God the Eternal Word; and it deposes all clerics from the clericate, and anathematizes all laics, who hold or teach its Nestorian errors (560) one of which, of course, is that service to the created humanity of the Son (561).

NOTE 556.—Chrystal's *Ephesus*, vol. I., page 449.
NOTE 557.—Id., pages 479, 480.
NOTE 558.—The same.
NOTE 559.—The same.
NOTE 560.—See the *depraved Creed or Symbol* in this volume, pages 202 and after, and the decision of the Council on page 222 and after. Indeed the whole of the context on pages 197-234 ought to be read.
NOTE 561.—The plain profession of Man-Worship is made in it on pages 205, 207, 208 and 209, and the authority of the Church is claimed for it and other errors on page 210. The parts on worshipping a human being are in capitals.

That enactment is now numbered the Seventh Canon of the Third Ecumenical Synod.

When that Man-Worshipping Creed was read in Act IV. of the Fifth Ecumenical Synod, held at Constantinople, A. D. 553, the Bishops cried out:
"That we have already condemned, that we have already anathematized, anathema to Theodore and his writiugs . . . a Theodore, a Judas."

At the end of the whole reading they exclaimed:
"*That Creed*" (Theodore's), "SATAN HAS MADE! *Anathema to him who made that Creed! The First Synod of Ephesus*" [*the Third Ecumenical*] "*anathematized that Creed with its author*" (562).

The same Fifth Ecumenical Synod in its Definition, probably with reference to the Nestorian perversion of the words in Hebrews I. 6, "*And let all the angels of God worship Him*," speaks of that heresy as "*introducing the* CRIME *of* SERVING A MAN *into heaven and on earth*." And in the same context just before, it condemns those who are guilty of the Nestorian "HERESY or CALUMNY, *which they* made against the pious dogmas of the Church, by WORSHIPPING TWO SONS" [that is the man, the *creature*, to whom by Matt. IV. 10, service does not belong, with God the Word to Whom it does], "*and by dividing the Indivisible*" [that is, in the sense of ascribing what belongs to God the Word, to His *created* humanity], "*and by bringing* THE CRIME OF SERVING A MAN INTO HEAVEN AND EARTH. *For the holy multitude of the spirits above with us worship*" [but] "*one Lord Jesus Christ*" (563), that is God the Word, as he shows in the context of this passage, and in the eighth section of the Second Book of his *Five Book Contradiction of the Blasphemies of Nestorius*, where he makes worship prerogative to divinity "ALONE."

This allusion to "*bringing Man-service into heaven*," and to "*the angels above*" is so clear a reference to the Nestorian perversion of the words "*And let all the angels of God worship Him*," in Hebrews I. 6, to "MAN-SERVICE" and so clear a condemnation of it as a "CRIME," as to be evident to all fair men, without further remark.

The same Fifth Synod in its Fourth Anathema condemns the idea of a union of God the uncreated Word and the man whom He has put on, in an "EQUALITY OF HONOR" *or authority* . . . *or power* . . . *as Theodore in his madness says*;" as though the honor, which of course includes worship,

---

NOTE 562.—See the English translation of Hefele's *History of the Church Councils*, vol. iv., page 306.

NOTE 563.—The Greek here is lost, but we have the Latin translation, which reads as follows: (*Coleti Concilia*, tom. VI., col. 203). Consequens enim erat, uno semel pro suis tam profanis vaniloquiis condemnato, non contra unum tantum venire, sed (ut ita dicam) contra omnem eorum haeresim, sive calumniam quam fecerunt contra pia ecclesiae dogmata, duos colentes filios, et dividentes individuum, et anthropolatriae crimen inferentes coelo et terra. Adorat enim nobiscum supernorum spirituum sancta multitudo unum Dominum Jesum Christum.

of the worshippable God and the unworshippable creature could be the same! In the same Anathema below, it tells us that the Nestorians teach that the two natures of Christ constitute but one Person in the sense that they have but "*one honor and dignity and* WORSHIP!"

And in its Fifth Anathema it condemns the Nestorian Man-Worshipping heresy which holds that the two natures of Christ are "*one Person*" [only] "*as respects* DIGNITY *and* HONOR AND WORSHIP *as Theodore and Nestorius have madly written*," as though a creature could share *worship* with God the Word, or be of the same *dignity* and the same *honor!!*

And the same Council in its Twelfth Anathema condemns the relative worship of Christ's humanity by "*the impious Theodore of Mopsuestia*," which is found in full in the note matter on page III. volume I. of Chrystal's *Ephesus;* see also the other decisions of that Synod and of *Ephesus* against his worship of a human being, Christ's humanity, on pages 108-112 there in the note.

And not only does the Fifth Synod of the whole Christian Church, East and West, in its undivided time condemn, by necessary implication, all creature worship when it condemns all worship of the highest of all creatures, Christ's humanity, and when it expressly anathematizes Theodore of Mopsuestia the notorious teacher of worship to His humanity, but at the end of its Twelfth Anathema it condemns every man who defends "*his impious writings*," including of his course, his Creed aforesaid and its Man-worship. I quote:

"If any one therefore defends the aforesaid most impious Theodore, and his impious writings, in which he poured forth both the aforesaid and numberless other blasphemies against our great God and Saviour Jesus Christ; and moreover if he does not anathematize him and his impious writings, and all who admit or even try to avenge him, or say that he was an Orthodox expounder, and those who have written in his favor and in favor of his impious writings, and those who hold like errors, or who have at any time yet held like errors and have remained in such heresy till the end, let him be anathema."

Furthermore, the same Ecumenical Synod anathematizes every one who defends what Theodoret wrote against Cyril of Alexandria's XII. Chapters, the VIIIth of which anathematizes every one who co-worships Christ's humanity with his divinity, and much more of course every one who worships it alone and by itself. And it also anathematizes all who have written against those chapters, including of course the said VIIIth, "*and have died in such impiety*"

And Anathema XIV. condemns the defenders of Theodore and Nestorius (as does Anathema XIII. also), "*and their impious dogmas and writings*," and it condemns "*the impious epistle*" of Ibas for branding Cyril's XII chapters as "*impious and opposed to the right faith*," and it adds there more to the same effect against that Ecumenically condemned Letter.

We see then how the "*One Holy, Universal and Apostolic Church*" has repelled the slander of the aforesaid seven Bishops of the Apostasy, that Cyril and the Orthodox in refusing to worship Christ's humanity, a mere creature, had "*adulterated*" *the worship offered by the angels to God*, and that its action in establishing Cyril's XII. Chapters is "*really a taking away that worship;*" and how it deposes all clerics and anathematizes all laics who worship that humanity, and, by necessary implication, all who worship any lesser creature, and much more all who worship images, crosses, or any other mere things.

DOCUMENT XX., BUT XIV. IN COLETI AND MANSI HERE, RELATING TO THE APOSTATIC CONVENTICLE.

This bears the following title in column 1260, tome III, of *Coleti's Concilia*: "*Another Petition of the same*" [that is John of Antioch and the six other prelates who with him constituted the delegation of the Apostasy to the Emperor Theodosius II.] "*sent from Chalcedon to Theodosius the August*" [that is the Emperor].

In the *Synodicon* of Irenaeus, it is chapter XXXIV., and is called "The SECOND TESTIMONY" of the delegates of that fragment of the Synod (564). Like other documents emanating from that Apostatic Little Council and its representatives, it is full of lies and misrepresentations.

They begin by accusing the Orthodox of corrupting the doctrines of the correct faith, of rending the Church, and of treading under foot "*every ecclesiastical constitution and every imperial law*," the last evidently to anger the Emperor against them; and they add,

"*And they have thrown every thing into confusion together, in order that they may establish the heresy set forth by Cyril the Alexandrian*."

Below they subjoin of the Bishops of the Third Ecumenical Synod and of its Ecumenical action :

"For when we were convoked by your piety to Ephesus, to inquire into questions which had sprung up, and to establish the Evangelical and Apostolic faith set forth by the holy Fathers, before all the Bishops who had been called together were present, those who have held a part of a Council, strengthened by written Commentaries" [or, "by written expositions"], "those heretical Chapters which agree with the impiety of Arius and of Eunomius and of Apollinarius, and some they deceived, others they terrified, but others accused of heresy they received to" [their] "communion ; and to others who did not take part with them they gave a reward that they might take part ; finally others they inflamed with the hope of honor of which they were unworthy ; and so they congregated a multitude to themselves (565), as though they were ignorant that not multitude but truth makes manifest pious religion."

The "written Commentaries" (566) here referred to were, I suppose, Cyril's explanation of the Twelve Chapters delivered at Ephesus, and his other

---

NOTE 564.—See it col. 298, tome IV. of Coleti's Concilia.
NOTE 565.—Et ita sibi multitudinem congregarunt: *Coleti Conc.*, tom. III. col 1221.
NOTE 566.—Scriptis Commentariis roborarunt: *Coleti Conc.*, tom. III., col. 1261. The Greek of this document is not given, if indeed it is extant.

writings on the Twelve Chapters, including his two Epistles and the passages from the Fathers which were read in Act I. of the Third Ecumenical Synod. One of the Two Epistles read in Act I. of the Council contains those Twelve Chapters. And though the Twelve Chapters are not mentioned in Cyril's *Five Book Contradiction of the Blasphemies of Nestorius*, nevertheless their *doctrines* are; and that work was evidently largely the guide of the Council on them (567).

This gives them and it a great value and importance. And undoubtedly the Five Books which take up and refute *seriatim* the chief errors of Nestorius have that place, in view of what occurred in the Synod. For in them Cyril quotes Nestorius' chief heretical utterances, which, remarkably enough, are, for the most part, exactly what are condemned of Nestorius' in that Act. So that we can see the mind of the refuter of those utterances in the said *Five Book Contradiction of the Blasphemies of Nestorius* in the selection of those passages as chief errors to be condemned by the Ecumenical Synod, as they then were in that First Act. The selecter in all probability was Cyril of Alexandria himself, and they were presented to the Synod by his Presbyter Peter, Chief of the Secretaries, his factotum and medium, and at times spokesman (568).

Cyril's *Five Book Contradiction* had been circulated before the Synod met. Cyril was reticent as to Nestorius' name when he put them forth, for the fight was not yet certain. Peace might come. Yet he was plainly meant. The other statements of this delegation of the Apostasy are disproven by the facts. For the Bishops here slandered as bribe takers in effect, stuck by Cyril and God's truth against the whole might of the secular power when for a time it seemed very likely that they would be deprived of their sees; indeed the Emperor tried to nullify their action, as we have seen, and there is not a particle of evidence of any such reward being given or taken, nor of any deception or terror being used by Cyril. Those things, so far as that Act of the Council is concerned, were wholly on the other side, the creature-serving party using the deception, and the secular power using the terror for them.

These delegates however admit that the multitude at Ephesus were in or for the Orthodox Synod. For so they expressly call the Orthodox Bishops or theirs or both here. See above.

NOTE 567.—See on those books pages c. and ci. of the Preface to the Oxford translation of "*S. Cyril of Alexandria on the Incarnation against Nestorius,*" where we read of that work. "Nestorius is not named in it. Hence it has been inferred that it was written before the Council of Ephesus." In a note on this last statement, page ci., the writer refers for proof to "Tillemont, Art. S. Cyrille d'Alex. c., 156."

Professor William Bright dates them in 429 or 430: see page 767, vol. I. of *Smith and Wace's Dictionary of Christian Biography*. See Chrystal's *Ephesus* also, vol. I., Preface, pages xxxi., xxxv. They seem to have been written not far from the beginning of the controversy.

NOTE 568.—Chrystal's *Ephesus*, vol. I., page 449. An account of their contents and sources will be found in Chrystal's *Ephesus*, vol. I., Note F., pages 529-551.

Next they proceed quite adroitly to try and represent the action of the Third Ecumenical Synod in guarding its peculiar and God-given ecclesiastical rights against the assaults of the Emperor and his three representatives at Ephesus, Count Candidian, Palladius and Count John, and their disregard of the Emperor's own arbitrary act in assuming to nullify their purely ecclesiastical action, as an act of improper disobedience and rebellion against his just authority, so degrading their own office as Bishops by such Erastianism to procure assent to their heresies of Creature Service, denial of the Incarnation, Cannibalism on the Eucharist, and the rest.

Below they assert further that when the Emperor had nullified the decisions of the Third Synod, that Synod had treated his annulment with contempt, and had refused to sanction what they term the *"true doctrine,"* that is Nestorianism, that after that, when he recognized the depositions of three persons, that is that of Nestorius made by the Ecumenical Synod, and that of Cyril of Alexandria and that of Memnon of Ephesus made by the little Nestorian Conventicle of John and the rest of the Apostasy, and had ordered the Ecumenical Synod to do away with what gave offense, which evidently meant in the minds of these seven Nestorians to do away with the Twelve Chapters of Cyril and their teachings, and that all should confirm *"the sole faith set forth by the holy and blessed Fathers in Nicaea"* as though that was not the very thing the Ecumenical Council was doing and John and his fellow heretics opposing, that then the Third Synod was not obedient. For straightway and without any break they add:

"Those who make sport of everything transgressed that law also" [of the Emperor] "as they are wont. For in truth, even after its reading they did not cease from what they had begun, and they held communion with those who had been deposed, and make mention of them as though they were still Bishops, and do not permit those Chapters set forth to the damage and corruption of the pious faith to be hissed off the stage, though they have been invited by us to a colloquy. For we have refutations of the heretical Chapters in readiness (569). Of these things the most magnificent Master" [Count John, the Nestorian] "is witness, who after he had called together us and them a third time and a fourth time, and dared not force those matters forward because of their disobedience" [the Ecumenical Synod's], "deemed it worth while after that to call us hither. We, making no delay, came, and did not rest till we had arrived hither, making petition both before your Piety and before your illustrious cabinet, that they

---

NOTE 569.—*Coleti Conc.*, tom. III., col. 1261. Habebamus enim in promptu haereticorum Capitulorum argumenta. This Latin may mean that they would show from *the argument*, as we say, of the Chapters that they are heretical, or it may mean instead that they were prepared with proofs to prove them to be heretical.

The Latin translation in Count Irenaeus' Synodicon, in col. 299 of tome IV. of Coleti, best agrees with this last view, for it reads: *"For we have prepared refutations of the heretical Chapters."* (Paratas enim haereticorum Capitulorum convictiones habuimus).

themselves" [The Third Ecumenical Synod or its delegates then at Constantinople] "should undertake that struggle for the Chapters and come to a colloquy or hiss those chapters off the stage as alien to the right faith, and abide by the Exposition alone of the Faith of the blessed Fathers who came together in Nicaea. And they indeed were not willing to do any of those things; but abiding in heretical contention, they are permitted to frequent the Churches and to exercise the functions of the priesthood. But we have remained for so long a time deprived of a congregation, both in Ephesus and here." Then they go on to complain of their being in perils, and of having been stoned by slaves or servants in the dress of monks. They state further that afterwards it had seemed good to the Emperor that they and the Third Synod or its delegates should be called together, and that the disobedient should be compelled to make investigation as to dogmas, that is probably those of the Twelve Chapters, so often denounced by John's party. They add that while they were in expectancy of such a common meeting of the two parties, the Emperor had set out for the city of Constantinople, and had commanded both those who were accused of heresy, and others of them who had been deposed for it by John and his Synod of the Apostasy, and others still who had been excommunicated and thereafter subjected to canonical punishments, to go into the city of Constantinople and to perform the functions of the priesthood, (they mean those of the Episcopate), and ordain, that is, ordain a successor to the deposed Nestorius, their friend, for whom and his Man-Service they were making this obstinate fight. Then they represent themselves as contending for piety and right dogmas, by which they mean their Man-Service, etc., say that they are not permitted to enter Constantinople to act in the business of the imperilled faith and to be urgent for right dogmas, by which they mean those heresies which the Synod had condemned already once for all, and that the Emperor would not let them return to their homes, but kept them in Chalcedon while the Church was harassed by schism, of which through their perverse fight for creature-service, they should have added, they were the sole authors and maintainers. Then they begin as a last resource to threaten as follows:

"Therefore inasmuch as we get no answer, we have deemed it necessary to inform your Piety by the present letter, before God and Christ Himself, and the Holy Ghost, that if any one be ordained before a discussion be held as to what doctrines are right, by those who hold heretical opinions:" [the Third Ecumenical Synod, or its delegates, they mean], "it will necessarily come to pass that the whole Church will be divided, for both clergy and flocks will separate. For none of the pious" [the Man-Servers, they mean] "will endure that communion be given to those who cherish (570) heretical opinions, and their own salvation to be annihilated. But when these things shall:occur, then your Piety will be compelled to ACT

NOTE 570.—Or, "*cultivate,*" "haeretica colentibus." Coleti *Conc.*, tom III., col. 1262.

AGAINST HIS OWN MIND (571). For a Schism CONTRARY TO" [HIS] "SENTIMENT (572) will grow strong and will sadden those who contend for piety, who will not endure that their souls shall perish and agree with the contentious in regard to the impious dogmas of Cyril, which they wish to justify. But many who are eager for piety, and all of us who are of the Oriental Diocese, and your provinces of the Diocese of Pontus, and of" [the Diocese of] "Asia Minor, and of that of Thrace, and of that of Illyricum, and of the Italies (573) will not suffer the dogmas of Cyril to be admitted; who have also sent to your Piety, book of the most blessed Ambrose, in which he taught what is opposed to that superstition (574) when it first sprouted forth. Wherefore, that that may not be the outcome, and your Piety be more thoroughly disturbed, we supplicate, we pray, we beseech your Piety to decree by an edict, that the ordination be not performed till the Orthodox faith be set forth in a formula; on account of which Orthodox faith also your Christ loving Highness congregated us" (575). And that is the end of this one of the last desperate efforts of the Creature-Serving party to undo the Anti-Creature-Serving work of the Third Ecumenical Synod.

NOTE 571.—The Latin of the Synodicon here is *"against his own"* [present] *"intention."* See it quoted in a note below.

This implies that the delegation of the Apostasy believed Theodosius II. to be really on their side in sentiment, and that for policy alone he had given way to the Orthodox Council.

NOTE 572.—This is *"contrary* to" [his own] "wish" in the Latin version in the *Synodicon* of Monte Casino. See it in a note below.

NOTE 573.—This is *"Italy"* in the *Synodicon* (col. 300 of tome IV. of Coleti's *Concilia*).

NOTE 574.—That is, they mean, the fear of offending God by serving *a creature*, that is the Man put on, which is contrary to Matthew iv: 10, which these creature servers call a *superstitious*, that is an unwise fear.

NOTE 575.—*Coleti Conc.*, tom. III, col. 1262, Idcirco qui nullum responsum obtinemus, necessarium duximus, ut praesentibus literis doceremus vestram pietatem coram Deo, et Christo ipso, ac Sancto Spiritu; quod si quis ordinatus fuerit, antequam discutiantur recta dogmata, ab his qui haeretica sentiunt, necesse sit ut tota ecclesia scindatur, tam clero quam plebibus dissidentibus. Nullus enim piorum feret, haeretica coleutibus communionem dari, propriamque salutem annihilari. Ubi autem haec futura sunt, tunc vestra pietas praeter suam mentem agere cogetur. Nam et schisma praeter sententiam invalescet, et eos qui pro pietate certant, contristabit, non ferentes ut suae animae pereant, et consient contentiosis impia Cyrilli dogmata, quae justificare volunt. Multi antem qui pietati student, et omnes nos, qui ex Orientali diocesi, et vestrae provinciae ex diocesi Ponti, et Asiae, et Thraciae, et Illyrici, et Italiarum, Cyrilli dogmata admitti non sinent, qui et vestrae pietati librum beatissimi Ambrosii miserunt, adversa pullulanti huic superstitioni docentem. Quapropter ne hoc eveniat, et vestra pietas magis conturbetur, supplicamus, precamur, obsecramus, ut edicat, ne ordinatio antea fiat, donec orthodoxa fides formetur, propter quam et nos congregavit vestra, quae Christum amat celsitudo.

The same document in the Synodicon (col. 300 of tome IV. of Coleti's Concilia) reads somewhat differently. One part of the above quotation it renders as follows:

Dum vero id contigerit, vestra praeter intentionem propriam pietas agere compelletur. Schisma enim utique contra voluntatem confirmabitur, etc.

It will be noticed by the learned reader here, that

1. These delegates of the Apostasy represent the work of the Ecumenical Synod in deciding on dogma and in deposing Nestorius for his denial of the Incarnation and his Man-Service and his wrong views on the Eucharist, as still annulled by the Emperor's edict, except the deposition of Nestorius, which they do not at heart admit.

Hence they wish to turn the Synod into a debating society, and failing in that at Ephesus, after it had decided, they wish to regard the *decided* matters as still *undecided*, and wish the delegates of the Synod to do that also practically by making them the subject of a discussion before a layman who had no power to settle doctrine, as though the time for discussion had not now passed.

2. They represent their own farcical action, that of about one-fifth or one-sixth of the whole Synod, in deposing Cyril and Memnon, and in excommunicating the rest of the Orthodox Council as perfectly valid. But the folly and wrong and uncanonicity of that step must by this time have been made clear to the Emperor himself by the delegates and friends of the Synod.

3. It will be noticed also that there is not a single word above in the way of an allusion to the expression, *Bringer Forth of God* (θεοτόκος), but throughout this whole document its whole force and energy is spent against Cyril of Alexandria's Twelve Chapters, which these delegates of the Apostasy brand as *heretical* again and again. This was their course after the Third Ecumenical Synod met. Those chapters condemn not only the denial of the Incarnation of God the Word, but also serving the creature, the Man whom He put on, and relative service also, and cannibal views of the Eucharist, and hence smote not only Nestorius but themselves; themselves, that is, so far as all those errors, except denying the Incarnation are concerned, and on that also in the case of some or all of them.

Theodoret, one of those seven delegates of the Apostasy, as his own works show worshipped the humanity of Christ, and even the symbols of it, the bread and wine in the Eucharist (576). And probably that view was more or less common in Syria, as the views of Diodore of Tarsus and of Theodore of Mopsuestia had been for some time corrupting it on most or all the points involved. John of Antioch in another document quoted in this work advocates service to the creature put on by God the Word. See his words on pages 310-312, and 317 and after, above.

4. But what shall we say of the assertion of these creature servers against the Twelve Chapters that the Bishops of *"the Italies"* (the reference in the plural being possibly but not surely to the Ecclesiastical Jurisdictions then in Italy, Milan in the North and Rome in the South) (577), *"will not permit the*

NOTE 576.—See under his name on page 656, vol. I. of Chrystal's *Ephesus*, where proof is given that he held all the heresies aforesaid of Nestorius.

NOTE 577.—The translation in the altered or modified *Synodicon* of Count Irenaeus has "*Italy*" instead of "*the Italies.*" See it in col. 300 of tome IV. of Coleti's *Concilia*.

Second Petition of the Delegates of the Apostasy to the Emperor. 341

dogmas of Cyril to be admitted," and that the Bishops of the Apostasy had sent to the Emperor Theodosius *"a book of the most blessed Ambrose in which he had taught what is opposed to that superstition"* [in the Twelve Chapters of Cyril] *"when it sprouted forth"* (579).

To this we reply, that from what the heresiarch and Man-server and corrupter of the Eucharist, John Keble, adduces from him in favor of worshipping Christ's humanity, coupled with this assertion of the delegation of the Apostasy who assert that he oppose[d] the doctrine of the Twelve Chapters which they insultingly call *"that Superstition,"* there is only too much reason to believe that Ambrose on that point did not differ from Nestorius and these seven prelates of the Apostasy, and that he held views on the Eucharist similar to those expressed by Ambrose in what is quoted from him by Keble in his abominable and heretical work on *Eucharistical Adoration*, that is that he held to one Nature Consubstantiation as did Theodoret and that like him he worshipped Christ as really present in his human (not his divine) nature, and in other words that he held to both those Nestorian heresies (580). All the Orthodox held, like Cyril, and Cranmer, and the Third

NOTE 578.—See what Bingham says on that in his *Antiquities of the Christian Church*, book ix., chapter 1., sections 6, 9, 10 and 11, and compare the English translation of Wiltsch's *Geography and Statistics of the Church*, vol. 1., page 249, and after, 291 and after. Compare on Aquileia at first independent, also of Rome, id., pages 81 and after and 251, 253, 262 and 296.

NOTE 579.—This note is too long to be inserted here and so will be found at the end of this Document xx.

NOTE 580.—See Ambrose's Eucharistic and Man-worshipping errors, in the paganizer Keble's *Eucharistical Adoration*, fourth edition, Oxford and London, Parker & Co., pages 108-112, and Augustine's, on pages 112-114. Poor unlearned Keble gives those testimonies, which seemingly make not for Two Nature but for One Nature Consubstantiation, as though they favored and taught the former. And, on pages 118-120, he actually quotes the avowed one nature Consubstantiationist Theodoret, who expressly rejects the alleged real presence in the rite of the Lord's Supper of the Substance of God the Word as did his fellow heretic Nestorius. See in proof Theodoret's own words in Chrystal's *Ephesus*, volume I., pages 276-285, note matter, and as to Nestorius, his ecumenically condemned Blasphemy 18, pages 472-474 of the same volume.

And the wretched idolatrizer Keble was so ignorant of Cyril and the Third Ecumenical Council's action against Nestorius and Theodoret's Eucharistic and Man-Worshipping heresies that he says that the latter's *"public statements"* in their favor and in favor of his worship of one nature of Christ in the rite, his humanity, "remained uncensured and uncontradicted," whereas, though the Council does not quote all of every heretic's volumes, he was nevertheless deposed by the Council for such heresies, and that is the great point. And he writes further that *"the fact,"* (plainly, the lie,) that they were not censured nor contradicted "is an additional warrant for our believing that on the Eucharist, at any rate, he did but express the known mind and practice of the holy church throughout the world" !!! Can besotted ignorance of the verdicts of the whole, the undivided Church, East and West, go further and speak more evilly to the deception and ruin of hundreds, aye, thousands of the unlearned clergy, who have been led astray into idolatry on those themes, and have led astray tens of thousands or even hundreds of thousands of laics, especially simple sensuous, idolatrously inclined women! Kenrick, the Irish Romish Archbishop of Baltimore, in his utter ignorance of the decisions of Ephesus against Man-Worship and antici-

Synod, to the real absence of the substances of both His natures from the Eucharist, but to the real presence of what we need, His sanctifying and saving grace.

Nor need that surprise us, for Ambrose had been made a Bishop in direct contravention of the law of the Holy Spirit expressed in I. Timothy iii: 6, which decrees that no one *newly planted* (νεόφυτον) in the waters of baptism shall be ordained (compare the reference to that figure of planting in Romans vi: 1 to 6). Indeed, he had been chosen to it at the fancy of a child before he had been baptized at all, which was still worse; and that, too, when both choice and ordination to the episcopate in his case were in direct opposition to the prohibition of such persons being made Bishops contained in Canon II. of the First Ecumenical Synod, then well known and of force as now.

It must be confessed that Ambrose bore himself well on some points of the Arian controversy, but it is equally true that because he became a teacher before he became a pupil in the Church, he never was wholly separated from his creature-service; for while he forsook the creature-service of paganism, he erred by worshipping, contrary to Christ's own prohibition, in Matthew iv: 10, the Man, that is, the *creature* whom God the Word had put on. He did more, for he corrupted on that point his pupil, Augustine, and made a heretic of him by making him a Man-Server, and by himself writing on that theme what the Bishops of the Apostasy use against the action of the Universal Church in approving the Twelve Chapters at Ephesus and in the Three Ecumenical Synods following. Both, therefore, fall under the condemnation and anathema of the Third Ecumenical Synod (581), though, as in the case of millions of others, their names are not mentioned.

It is to be noted, as is told in the last note above, that the Bishops of the Apostasy give us exactly the title of Ambrose's book, to which they refer, and that, as there stated, it contains both Man-Service and Cross-Service, so that if it be uninterpolated, it favors the Nestorians as they claimed.

He and Augustine, while, like Diodore of Tarsus and Theodore of Mopsuestia, they opposed some heresy, nevertheless like them wrought much evil by corrupting the West on Man-Service and on the Eucharist (582), as Diodore and Theodore corrupted the East on the Incarnation and on Man-Service.

---

patively against his later Transubstantiation, quoted parts of some of the same passages of Ambrose and of Augustine for the Romish idolatry of worshipping the alleged real substances presence of Christ's Two Natures in the Eucharist, and for one of Rome's latest heresies, aye, one of the latest forms of *Man-Worship*, that is of Creature Worship, the Worship of the Sacred Heart of Jesus, contrary to Matthew iv:10, and to the decisions of the Holy Ghost led Third Ecumenical Synod and the Fifth; see on those points Chrystal's *Ephesus*, vol. 1., pages 337-343, note matter.

NOTE 581.—See its Canons VI. and VII.

NOTE 582.—See under *Ambrose* and *Augustine* in the *General Index* to vol. 1. of Chrystal's *Ephesus*; see especially also *Fathers* there and in the *General* Index to vol. 1. of *Nicaea*, and pages 8, 9 and 160 for some idea of the relative importance of Holy Writ, the definitions of the VI. Synods of the whole Church, and the utterances of those called Fathers.

The Ecumenical Synod would have disregarded the proof alleged from Ambrose against them if they had deemed it his, for it is opposed to the inspired Scriptures, and to the faith of the whole Church from the beginning, and began in the fourth century.

I ought, however, to add that the letter of the delegation of the Apostasy to Rufus of Thessalonica did not specify any opposition of Ambrose or of any other Father or writer quoted in it to any other doctrine of Cyril or the Third Synod, except *the attributing the sufferings of the Man united to God the Word*, that is, to his doctrine of *Economic Appropriation*, which is stated in his three Ecumenically approved Epistles (583), and which is therefore the doctrine of the whole Church East and West, however much it may have been departed from since in different Communions claiming to be Christian.

5. It is noteworthy that these seven Bishops of the Apostasy believed that Theodosius II., the Emperor, was still on their side, doctrinally, as was true, judging from the tone of one of his Epistles to Cyril, before the Synod, from his action in attempting to nullify the work of the Ecumenical Synod, and from his refusal to condemn John of Antioch afterwards. For they call the doctrines of Cyril's Twelve Chapters *"heretical,"* even after their approval by the Third Synod, and they would hardly have dared to use such language if they thought Theodosius believed them, and they tell him that if the doctrines of the Twelve Chapters become established they will make a schism, and that in crushing them, they mean, he "*will be compelled to act against his own mind,*" [or according to the translation in the *Synodicon* "*contrary to his own*" [then] "*intention.*"] And further, they tell the Emperor, "For a schism contrary to his decision," [or, according to the reading in the *Synodicon*, "*contrary to his wish*"] "*will grow strong, and will sadden*" John and his fellows of the Apostasy, that is, they will not stop it, but will sympathize with it, and regard the schismatics as "*pious.*"

And we must remember that in a public discourse delivered in Constantinople, before the Ecumenical Synod met, Nestorius boasted that the Emperor was on his side and against Cyril of Alexandria, and certainly that seems to have been the belief of the Bishops of the Apostasy all along. The action of Count Candidian, the Emperor's representative, who acted under his instructions in doing all he could to hinder the Ecumenical Synod from beginning its sessions, and his close connection with John of Antioch, afterwards at Ephesus; and the actions of the other representatives of the Emperor, were on the side of Nestorius and of John of Antioch and against Cyril. So that Nestorius' boast was probably true, as it regarded the sympathies of the Emperor.

The boast of those heretics of support from the Diocese of the Orient, from that of Pontus, and that of Asia [Minor], and that of Thrace, and that of

---

NOTE 583.—See *Economic Appropriation*, on page 602, vol. I. of Chrystal's *Ephesus*, and er *Appropriation*, on page 573.

Illyricum, and from Italy, was destined to be vastly less than they evilly hoped. The mass of the teachers of the Church would not reject the faith of God's Word, as set forth at Ephesus. At the last it was seen that Nestorianism had no hold worth speaking of outside a part of the Syriac race, to which, what little is left of it, is now chiefly or wholly confined.

REMARKS ON A STATEMENT OF THE SEVEN BISHOPS OF THE APOSTASY THAT AMBROSE, BISHOP OF MILAN, HAD OPPOSED THE ORTHODOX DOGMAS OF CYRIL, ONE OR MORE, WHICH HAD BEEN APPROVED BY THE THIRD ECUMENICAL COUNCIL (584).

The Seven Delegates of the Apostasy, in a letter to Rufus of Thessalonica, state as follows in regard to Cyril of Alexandria's Twelve Chapters:

"*And it is clear that the Italians also will not endure that innovation. For the most dear to God and most holy Martin, the Bishop of the Milaners, has both sent us a letter, and has sent to the most pious Emperor a book of the blessed Ambrose on the Inman of the Lord, which teaches things opposed to those heretical Chapters* (585).

On looking over the work of Ambrose *on the Mystery of the Lord's Incarnation*, chapter v. in col. 817 and after in tome 16 of Migne's *Patrologia Latina*, I find that he denounces in it the ascribing of the human things, that is, what pertains to the Man put on by God the Word, to God the Word, but in a sense which agrees *in substance* with the *meaning* of the Twelve Chapters, as explained in documents approved by the Third Ecumenical Synod and in the three Universal Synods after it. For the Church in those documents admits Cyril's explanation that such infirmities and weaknesses as are peculiar to the created Man put on can be asserted Economically only of God the Word to guard His due preëminence, and to avoid Man-Service. And *that* I have seen no proof that Ambrose would deny. But in opposing Apollinarianism or something like it in that work, he directs his remarks against those *One Natureites*, who held to a sort of transubstantiation of Christ's humanity into Divinity, or into a Third something (tertium quod), and so ascribed to Divinity, not Economically, but absolutely and really and in the full sense the infirmities, such as suffering, death, etc., which can not be asserted of God the Word, except Economically, in Cyril's sense, as above.

NOTE 584.—This is what is referred to in note 579, page 341, above.

NOTE 585 —*Coleti Conc.*, tom. III., col. 1273: Δῆλοι δέ εἰσι καὶ Ἰταλιῶται τῆς καινοτομίας ταύτης οὐκ ἀνεξόμενοι. Ὁ γὰρ θεοφιλέστατος καὶ ἁγιώτατος Μαρτῖνος ὁ τῆς Μεδιολάνων ἐπίσκοπος καὶ γράμματα πρὸς ἡμᾶς ἀπέστειλε, καὶ τῷ εὐσεβεστάτῳ βασιλεῖ βιβλίον ἐξέπεμψε τοῦ μακαρίου Ἀμβροσίου περὶ τῆς τοῦ Κυρίου ἐνανθωπήσεως, ὅπερ τὰ ἐναντία τοῖς αἱρετικοῖς τούτοις διδάσκει κεφαλαίοις.

Theodoret, one of the Delegation of these seven Bishops of the Apostasy to the Emperor, in his *Polymorphus*, quoted in col. 847 and after in the same tome of Migne's *Patrologia Latina*, quotes a fragment of a work of Ambrose entitled an "*Exposition of the Faith*" ('Εκθέσει πίστεως) in favor of the two Natures of Christ and against supposing that the Divinity of Christ could *really* suffer. But that appears to be from a different work from that "*on the Inman of the Lord.*" And the author of a note in the same volume 16 of Migne, columns 849, 850, deems that it is a fragment of some work of Ambrose which has been lost.

The same seven Bishops of the Delegation of the Man-Serving Apostasy to the Emperor in their letter to Rufus of Thessalonica, just quoted above, advocating the not ascribing to God the Word the hunger, thirst, and the other human things of the Man put on by Him, say that in that view they follow the dogmas of Eustathius of Antioch, Basil of Caesarea, Gregory, John, Athanasius, Theophilus, Damasus of Rome, and Ambrose of Milan; and, in fact, in that work entitled, "*Eranistes, or Polymorphus, Dialogue* II., *Unconfused*— (Dialogus II., Inconfusus), Theodoret does quote among others, against any *mixing* of the Natures in Christ, which he mistakenly supposed Cyril of Alexandria to favor, the following writers:

Eustathius of Antioch;
Basil of Caesarea;
Gregory of Nazianzus;
Gregory of Nyssa;
John, Bishop of Constantinople;
Athanasius of Alexandria;
Theophilus of Alexandria; and
Ambrose of Milan.

In the same work in Dialogue III., *The Unsuffering* (*Dialogus* III., *Impatibilis*), he quotes among others Damasus, Bishop of Rome, and Ambrose, Bishop of Milan, against the error that Christ's divinity is passible. But, so far as I have seen, he quotes none of those writers for his own heresy that the Man put on by God the Word may be worshipped, nor for his own erroneous views on the Eucharist. And that is of chief importance in our inquiry. Indeed, the subjects of his three Dialogues would not necessarily call for that, for the first is intended to show that God the Word is *immutable*, as is the humanity also which He put on; the Second Dialogue is intended to show that the two natures *cannot be mixed and confused*, though in his remarks on the Eucharist in it, he falls into the error of giving worship, all of which is peculiar and prerogative to God, to the creature put on by God the Word, instead of limiting it to Him, and so, while he does not mix the Two Natures, he does their *attributes*, by giving what is prerogative to Divinity to a creature put on by Divinity; and in the Third Dialogue, the last of all, he shows that **the** *Divinity of God the Word is not liable to suffering.*

He quotes some of those authors again and again in those Dialogues.

We find Cyril of Alexandria quoted in the second of them, against the heresy of mixing the Two Natures, but I suspect that to be the work of a later hand, for I do not think that Theodoret was ever so just to Cyril as thus to represent him in his true colors.

And instances of such interpolations in manuscripts occur again and again, for instance, in the Catechetical Lectures of Cyril of Jerusalem, which were on the local Creed of Jerusalem, we find that of Nicaea in some manuscripts now, as we are told in the Oxford translation of them, page 58, note "c."

But in his work *on the Inman of the Lord, as it is now extant in Migne's Patrologia Latina*, tome 16, col. 837, Ambrose certainly does teach that he worshipped flesh, and therefore he opposed, antecedently of course, the doctrine of the Eighth of Cyril's Twelve Chapters, and therefore he and his doctrine are anathematized in it, and in Anathema IX. of the Fifth Ecumenical Synod, for he implies it in his question there:

"*Do we divide Christ when we adore both his Divinity and his flesh?*" (586). Indeed, in the sentence next following, if it be genuine, he goes further and shows that he worshipped the cross, for he writes:

"*Do we divide Him when we worship in him the image of God* (587), *and*" [when we worship] "*the cross?*" (588).

If those passages be really Ambrose's, then we must deem him one of the earliest of cross-servers and of Man-Servers, and justly to be classed with Diodore of Tarsus, and Theodore of Mopsuestia. But I will not attempt here to investigate their genuineness, for it is not demanded by the scope of my work; but will leave that for others who can make it a specialty, and who are Orthodox themselves. I know that much interpolation has been done in ancient writers by errorists, that indeed, writings have been ascribed to noted and distinguished men to make them sell better, as, for instance, a work of Philip of Side to Cyril of Alexandria, and that changes have been made to make works more valuable *pecuniarly* by making them more erroneous, and it is perfectly possible that certain passages or writings alleged to be Ambrose's, and others alleged to be Augustine's may be really the work of heretics and others, but until that is proven they must be deemed unpurged of heresies on Creature-Service, which are anathematized in these Twelve Chapters of Cyril of Alexandria, which are approved by the Third Ecumenical Synod and by the three Universal Councils after it, and by the Definition of the Fifth Ecumenical Synod and its Anathema IX. Till then their authors should never

---

NOTE 586.—*Migne's Patrologia Latina*, tome 16, col. 837: Ambrosii *de Incarnationis Dominicae Sacramento*, cap. VII, sect. 75· sed vereudum est, inquis, ne si duos principales sensus aut geminam sapientiam Christo tribuimus, Christum dividamus. Numquid, cum et divinitatem ejus adoramus et carnem, Christum dividimus? Numquid cum in eo imaginem Dei crucemque veneramur, dividimus eum?

NOTE 587.—That is, in his humanity, Genesis 1: 26, 27.

NOTE 588.—For the Latin see note 586 above.

be mentioned as Orthodox on such themes lest the unlearned clergy and people be led into soul-destroying creature-service by relying on them as authoritative and sound interpreters, as millions have been led astray into Nestorianism and its creature-service by so regarding Diodore of Tarsus and Theodore of Mopsuestia. And as Cyril of Alexandria exposed and denounced those last two to save the souls of men from being led astray by them, even so we must now expose and denounce the creature-service of Ambrose and of Augustine for the same reason. If the task be difficult, on account of their reputation in the West, we reply that it can be no more difficult than was the task of doing the same in Syria in Cyril's time, where Diodore and Theodore were deemed eminent and Orthodox writers. And, indeed, they had both done good service in the East against some heresy, as did both Ambrose and Augustine in the West against some heresy. But as that fact did not blind Cyril to his duty to warn God's flock against the errors of Diodore and Theodore, so it should not blind us to our duty to warn God's flock against the ruinous errors of Ambrose and Augustine.

The Bishops of the Apostasy might also have learned something of Ambrose's utterances in favor of Man-Service and of Cannibalism in the Eucharist, if what Keble quotes from him be his, from the one or two Pelagian prelates from Italy who met with them at Ephesus. The name of *Theodore, a Bishop of Italy*, occurs in an Epistle of Bishops of Nestorius' party to Cyril of Alexandria and Juvenal, at Ephesus, just before the First Act of the Third Ecumenical Synod. And though the author of a note in columns 299, 300 of tome IV. of Coleti's *Concilia* (compare note "1", cols. 263, 264, id.) denies that it is correct, yet Hefele, a German Latin, in his *History of the Church Councils*, English translation, vol. III. pages 86, 98, shows from the words of the Third Ecumenical Synod itself that there were *"many"* Pelagian Bishops in Nestorius' gathering at Ephesus, and id. page 11, that before it he had received or favored a Pelagian leader, Julius or Julian, Bishop of Eclanum. So that it is perfectly possible that either he or some other may have called the attention of the Nestorian Conventicle to Ambrose's well-known utterances in favor of serving the creature put on. Indeed, if Ambrose is quoted correctly in *Hagenbach's History of Doctrines* (*Smith's Eng. trans.*, vol. I, p. 338, and p. 339, note 3), he has the evil preeminence of being one of the first or the first among the writers of the Church to fall into the heresy of serving angels by invoking them, and not only that, but recommending their invocation to others, as he does also the invocation of martyrs. The passage referred to where both those sins are recommended is in his *De Viduis*. cap. IX., Section 55. Theodoret, as Hagenbach shows on the same pages, disapproved the invocation of angels, and hence, with all his faults, was, so far, more orthodox than Ambrose.

If it be said, as it well may be, that among the passages adduced by the Orthodox in the First Act of the Third Ecumenical Council there are two from Ambrose's work "*On Faith,*" and that he is there mentioned as "*Ambrose, who was the most holy Bishop of Milan,"* that is true, but it does not vouch for him on other themes than what are there mentioned, nor, for his heretical utterances, which the Ecumenical Synod had never seen, or they would not have quoted him at all. And we must well remember that those two passages contain not a particle of Man-Service nor of any other creature-service. The first teaches the doctrine that God the Word took flesh, that is the doctrine of the real Incarnation of God the Word against Nestorius' denial of it, and the second passage sets forth the truth that in Christ are two natures, the divine and the human, and that while it is his humanity alone which endured the sufferings, they are nevertheless to be ascribed, in Cyril's sense, that is, to God the Word, that is Economically, though the term *"Economically"* is not used.

I ought, however, in justice to Ambrose, to say, 1. that in the Index to his utterances on *Christ*, in Tome 16 of Migne's *Patrologia Latina*, none of the references in favor of *Man-Service* is to the Five Books on Faith alleged to be his, and in looking over them cursorily I have found nothing in favor of that error in any of them, but on the contrary what makes against it, as for instance, the following passages.

Book I., chapter XI., section 69, and book I., chapter XVI., sections 103 and 104, where he, in effect, reasons against the Arians, in substance somewhat after the manner of Athanasius and Cyril of Alexandria, that no creature may be worshipped, because Holy Writ forbids it, and so that it is wrong to worship Christ if He be a creature, or any thing but the uncreated God. In book I., chap. II., sections 12 and 13, Ambrose pleads for Christ's worship on the ground that He is God, and one of the Trinity, as even the author of the *"Admonitio"* before those books in columns 523, 524 of tome 16 of Migne's *Patrologia Latina* shows. In book II., section 102 of the same work, he reasons that very God the Word co-sits with the Father, somewhat after the manner of Cyril.

2. The first passage from Ambrose *On Faith*, quoted with approval in Act I. of the Third Ecumenical Synod, is from the First Book, chapter XIV., section 94, in tome 16 of *Migne's Patrologia Latina*, in the context of which in chap. XVI. in the same book is found the argument of Ambrose just referred to against serving a creature.

The other quotation from Ambrose in the same Act is from his *Book Second on Faith*, chapter IX., sections 77 and 78.

But there is some reason for believing that those are the only books on Faith which Ambrose wrote, though five are ascribed to him. For in column 1415 of tome 16 of *Migne's Patrologia Latina* we read on that very point as follows:

"But it is to be observed that, in some manuscripts, only the first two of the five books on Faith are contained."

And the author of the *"In Libros De Fide Admonitio,"* that is the *"Warning as to the books on the Faith,"* in columns 523,

524 of tome 16 of Migne's *Patrologia Latina* gives there some matter which makes me doubt whether the last three books are any part of this work, though as yet I express no opinion. I do not feel sure that the last three books are not part of another work. The author of the "*Admonitio*" above informs us that they have been quoted by the Master of the Sentences, by Gratian and Thomas Aquinas under the title *De Trinitate, On the Trinity*, and he states, besides, that the first Two Books were written about one or two years before the last three, for he ascribes the first two to the end of A. D. 377 or the beginning of A. D. 378, the last three to A. D. 379. But the Master of the Sentences, Peter Lombard, was of the twelfth century, Gratian of the eleventh and twelfth, and Aquinas of the thirteenth, late and uncritical ages, when spurious works were quoted as genuine, and interpolated passages as the writer's own. See, for example, towards the end of the article *Gratian* in *McClintock and Strong's Cyclopædia*, especially Berard's work, which professes to *separate the apochryphal from the genuine canons* in Gratian and *to correct those which are corrupt*, and Le Plat's work "*On the Spurious Canons in Gratian.*" We must never receive unlearned mediæval Romish works without examination.

Works have been so much jumbled together by accident, carelessness, or design, that I prefer to hold the question of the last three books being any part of the work *on Faith* under advisement, till all the facts are brought to light.

We come now to say a few words as to the alleged works of Ambrose which advocate service to the creature, that is to the Man put on by God the Word and the alleged work of his which approves invocation of angels and martyrs and worship of the cross.

The former are I., Ambrose in his book "*on the Mystery of the Lord's Incarnation*," chapter VII., section 75, column 837 of tome 16 of *Migne's Patrologia Latina*, quoted in this note above, where Ambrose is represented as worshipping the humanity of Christ.

But this work does not bear Ambrose's name or any other in its text as its author. And happily we have no clear proof that it is his. It looks somewhat like a compilation by an unknown author, for in chapter I., it is addressed to his "*brethren*" (fratres), but in chapter VIII., section 80, he addresses the "*most clement Emperor*" (clementissime Imperator). In chapter VII., section 63, the author states that he had promised to end his answer on the Divinity of the Father and of the Son in the former books, "but," he adds, "*in this book a fuller digest has been made as was due, on the mystery of the Lord's Incarnation*," which looks very much as though it were the concluding book of some work on the Father and the Son, the more especially as he writes in chapter VIII., section 79, "I *had concluded the book, but*" (589), and then he goes on to add a few further remarks.

NOTE 589.—*Migne's Patrologia Latina*, tom. 16, col. 838: Concluseram librum ; sed religionis fuit ne praetervecti videremur, quod solvere nequiremus.

But cap. VIII., section 87, affords us the best clue to the faith of the writer, for speaking of Christ, he there subjoins:

"*For in our own very use*" [of terms] "*he is both the* ADOPTIVE SON *and the real Son. We do not say that the Adoptive Son is the Son by*" [divine] "*Nature*" [that is God the Eternal Word, he means] "*but we say that He who is the very Son*" [God the Word] "*is the Son by nature*" (590).

It is clear then that this work is a production of an Adoptionist heretic, and belongs to the eighth century or the ninth, and was addressed to an assembly of Bishops, the "brethren" (fratres) by whom he was tried, in the presence of an Emperor, probably Charlemagne, less likely his son, Lewis the Meek.

It is certainly not Ambrose's, nor was it written till about four hundred years after his death.

Yet Elipandus, the Adoptionist heretic, who was Archbishop of Toledo, in an Epistle to Albinus, one of his opponents (col. 872, tome 96 of *Migne's Patrologia Latina*), quotes an expression, not indeed the same exactly in words, yet similar to part of the above, as from Ambrose in his *Dogmas*, as follows:

"Blessed Ambrose in his *Dogmas* says, '*In our use Adoptive Son and real Son*'" (591). This, however, does not prove clearly that Felix of Urgel, or whatsoever Adoptionist spoke or wrote the address falsely ascribed to Ambrose, under the title of "*Book on the Mystery of the Lord's Incarnation*," had ever seen this alleged passage from Ambrose on Dogmas, which I judge to be of doubtful or spurious authenticity. In the context Elipandus quotes for his Adoptionist heresy, Jerome, Augustine, Pope Leo, and Isidore of Spain, but such passages should not be admitted without full proof of their genuineness.

But, however that may be, there can be no doubt, for the foregoing reasons, that the alleged book, now extant, under the title of *Ambrose on the Mystery of the Lord's Incarnation*, is a fragment of an address before a Council of Bishops and the Emperor Charlemagne by Felix of Urgel, or some other adoptionist heretic, and is a fragment of the discussion on his side of the question, to which something was afterwards added.

Felix disputed for his heresy of Adoptionism before Charles the Great and a Council of Bishops at Ratisbon, in A. D. 792, where he was condemned, and at Aix la Chapelle A. D. 799, where he retracted. Either place may have been where, in the above work, he addressed the Emperor and the Bishops.

NOTE 590.—Id. col. 840, Nam et in ipso usu nostro est adoptivus Filius, et verus Filius. Adoptivum Filium non dicimus Filium esse natura; sed eum dicimus natura esse, qui verus est Filius.

NOTE 591.—*Elipandi Epist. ad Albinum*, col. 872, tom. 96 of *Migne's Patrologia Latina*: Beatus Ambrosius in suis Dogmatibus dicit; Nostro usu adoptivus Filius, et verus Filius.

He made other retractions, but did not hold to them but to his heresy so that a Council at Rome in 799 calls him a *"thrice perjured heretic"* (592).

I would add that the same Elipandus (tome 96 of Migne's *Patrologia Latina*, col. 872, and after) quotes the Spanish Liturgy as sanctioning Adoptionism. But J. M. Neale, note 1., page 665 of vol. 2 of his *History of the Holy Eastern Church*, states that *"Elipandus depraved that Liturgy by 'reading adoptivi' for 'assumpti hominis'*, that is *'adoptive man'* for *'man taken on'* by the Word."

If he depraved that Liturgy why may he not have depraved such Fathers as Ambrose, Jerome, Augustine, and Leo, by making them teach that heresy? So that I doubt whether what he quotes for it from any of them is theirs. And, what is vastly important, we must remember that if any work of Felix of Urgel or Elipandus contains any worship of creatures that need not surprise us, for,

1. They both lived in the corrupt eighth century when that sin had spread every where, and

2. That they both held to the Nestorian denial of the Incarnation, applied the name *God* to Christ's humanity, and held to the worship of Christ's humanity, which errors were condemned by Ephesus. See on all that the article on *Felix*, and that on *Elipandus* in McClintock and Strong's *Cyclopædia* and in Smith and Wace's *Dictionary of Christian Biography*, and under *Adoptionists* in *Blunt's Dictionary of Sects*, etc.; though it should be said that the writers of some of those articles, not understanding or not knowing the decision of Ephesus against Man-Worship, do not emphasize the condemnation of the Adoptionists for that same sin.

I would add, what has been mentioned before, that the same Theodoret of Cyrus, who was a chief opponent of Cyril of Alexandria, in his *Polymorphus, Dialogue* II., quotes a passage about a column and a quarter in length from *"the holy Ambrose, Bishop of Milan,* in his *Exposition of the Faith,"* which one writer thinks has an especial affinity with this alleged work of Ambrose *on the "Mystery of the Incarnation,"* I mean the annotator in columns 849 and 850 of tome 16 of *Migne's Patrologia Latina*. He thinks it is from a lost work of Ambrose. I would say that it is not found in this Adoptionist work on the *Mystery of the Lord's Incarnation*.

The author begins this work *on the Mystery of the Lord's Incarnation* in a way to show that it was *spoken*, as does also the vocative, "O *most Clement Emperor,"* above cited. For he begins it as follows:

"*I wish, brethren,* to pay my debt, but I do not find my creditors of yesterday, perchance because they supposed that we were to be disturbed by an unexpected gathering; but the true faith is never disturbed. And so while perchance they are coming, let us turn to " so and so; and then he takes up a theme which he deems germane to his subject.

NOTE 592.—See David's article *Felix of Urgel*, pages 497, 498, volume 2 of *Smith and Wace's Dictionary of Christian Biography*.

This looks as though it was a part of a defence of this Adoptionist heretic, and that he had undertaken to meet his opponents on some points before the Bishops and the Emperor, and that certain of his friends, or favorers or others, had not yet arrived; and he seems to imply that they were in fear of some unexpected assembly of his foes. This implies that there had been a previous session, in the discussion, and agrees with the fact that at the Council of Aix la Chapelle in A. D. 799, the dispute lasted from Monday to Saturday. At Ratisbon there may have been several sessions also.

The expression "*I had concluded the book*," in chap. VIII., above quoted, seems to be a later addition, made either by the Adoptionist heretic who was the writer of the address, which has this fragment of the first part of the Adoptionist side of a dispute before an assembly, or by some forger who added it to round off the work, and make it bring a better price as Ambrose's.

Is this a work of the Adoptionist Felix of Urgel, who spread that heresy in Septimania or Languedoc, then under the domain of Charlemagne? Mosheim adds: "But in the view of the pontiff *Hadrian*, and of most of the Latin Bishops, this opinion seemed to revive the error attributed to *Nestorius*, or to divide Christ into *two persons*. Hence *Felix* was judged guilty of heresy, and required to change his opinion; first in the council of Narbonne, A. D. 788; then at Ratisbon, in Germany, A. D 792; also at Frankfort-on-the-Main, A. D. 794; and afterwards at Rome, A. D. 799; and lastly in the Council of Aix le Chapelle. And he revoked his opinion ostensibly, but not in reality; for he died in it at Lyons, where he was banished by *Charlemagne*. No law of thinking could be imposed on *Elipandus*" [the Adoptionist Archbishop of Toledo] "by the Christians, because he lived under the Saracens of Spain" (*Murdock's Mosheim's Eccl. Hist.*, vol. II., page 47). Was this Adoptionis Address delivered by Felix in one of those Councils?

Ambrose is quoted for the real presence of the substance of Christ's humanity in the Eucharist, for its worship there and elsewhere, and for the invocation of saints and martyrs. And Augustine of Hippo is quoted for the same errors. And I will not say that some of those quotations are not genuine; nor, on the other hand, will I assert that they are. But this I can say without successful contradiction, that to-day a mass of spurious stuff is quoted under the names of different Fathers which is not theirs, but is the utterance of others, some of whom were heretics. Take for instance the books of Philip of Side, or what of them are still extant, which pass under the name of Cyril of Alexandria, as is shown elsewhere by me in a work yet to be published if God will. A passage which favors clinic baptism, so-called, in an Epistle of Cyprian of Carthage to Magnus seems to one or more, from the evidence furnished in the Vindobona edition, to be spurious and an addition. And that edition shows, moreover, how his writings have been interpolated or tampered with.

And councils, and especially some that are local, have been altered, forged, or falsified in similar manner.

David Blondel exposed the spuriousness of the False Decretals; but the work of publishing *critical* editions of the Fathers and Councils has not yet been perfectly achieved. The Benedictines and others have done something in that direction; though the Benedictines have admitted readings in favor of Rome against the bulk of manuscript evidence, as in an Epistle of Augustine, for instance, in defence of the Canonical rights of Carthage and Latin Africa against the attempt of Rome to get Appellate Jurisdiction there, where the bulk of the manuscripts speak of appeal "to the *apostolic sees*" (apostolicas sedes), that is to the then whole Church East and West, being allowable. The Benedictines, to favor Rome, have admitted the exceptional lection, "*apostolic see*" (apostolicam sedem). See on this my articles in the Church Journal, of New York City, for 1870, *on the struggle between Carthage and Rome in Century V.*, etc.

The Vindobona editions of the Latins are much better. But as yet they include only a few volumes, I think, and these are all, I think, of early Writers. But the whole learned world has need to groan for the issue of *critical, thorough* editions which shall separate the chaff from the wheat, both as to genuine and spurious works and as to their true readings; so that we may be rendered certain that the work which we are reading and quoting as that of a Father is really his, and that the passage which we quote is uninterpolated.

I would like to examine the alleged passages from Ambrose, Augustine, and Leo, for the errors above specified. But space and time forbid. I must leave that for the able and erudite critics, who will, I hope, attend to it after I am dead. A society should be formed to support them at the work and to enable them to search and note all Manuscripts of Fathers and their varying readings, much as Tischendorf has done for those of the New Testament.

As aids to such a critic let me suggest the following cautions :

1. See what name or names the alleged work bears in the oldest manuscripts of it.

2. If it bears more than one name, consider which of them has the most evidence in its favor, and remember that if there are two names given as its author, one in one manuscript and another in another, that the claims of the less distinguished are not to be ignored, not even if he were a heretic. For there was always a temptation from the greater monetary value of the work with a distinguished man's name on it to forge it in place of the real author's in the title place. In this way, for instance, the name of Cyril of Alexandria has been put on the remnant of the work of the less known Philip of Side against Julian the Apostate.

3. On all points of difference prefer the readings of the oldest and best manuscripts, though they may not contain some forged or interpolated

passage which some desire as a proof text for some error or even truth. For while every genuine passage which favors true doctrine must be jealously retained, the truth is a thousand times too strong at every point to need any man's lie or forgery to sustain it.

4. Consider what historical proof there is in statements, allusions, and quotations that the alleged author ever wrote the work ascribed to him, and see whether those quotations agree with the text of it, and give those allusions, references, and quotations in full, and every thing else that bears on the *external* evidence. And in this connection consider how much of the alleged work is in the oldest manuscripts, for parts of works are genuine, as for instance, the first part of Cyprian's epistle to Magnus which is found in old manuscripts, while other parts are not genuine if they are found in later manuscripts only and are an addition, as for instance, some may think, the part on clinic baptism, in that same epistle of Cyprian to Magnus. So the authorship of the last three books of Ambrose's work *On Faith* does not seem to be his.

5. Next consider the *internal* evidence which is sometimes very important and decisive, for it may contain allusions to persons and things long after the age of its alleged author; in which case, of course, it could not be his.

Or it may be a hodge-podge of odds and ends like the alleged book of Ambrose *On the Mystery of the Lord's Incarnation;* and, like that, may contain heresy not known, like the Adoptionist of the eighth century form and name, till after his day, which is therefore a proof of its falsity. It was a recrudescence of Nestorianism.

6. Put all works well proven by quotations, allusions, and references to be genuine, under the head of *Genuine* with the evidence for that fact in full before the beginning of them. That will be class first.

Next put all works not clearly proven to be genuine, and yet not clearly proven to be spurious under the head of *Doubtful.* That will be class second.

Then finally put all clearly spurious works under the head of *Spurious.* That will be class third.

These things have been done to a limited and imperfect extent only; so that many things are put among the genuine which belong to the doubtful, or at least not fully proven, and others which are clearly spurious.

Such a critical work would simplify and render more accurate researches into historical dogma, discipline, and rite, and pave the way for more accurate statements.

Of course the setting forth of the full truth by impartial scholars would sweep away many a text book of error with the error that it bolsters, by proving its proof texts to be forgeries and lies; but God's truth and Church would be vastly the gainer by the result, and faithful champions for both would be less hindered in their holy work of enlightening and saving souls.

And remember one thing more, and that is in the matter of *authority*.

1. The chief and only infallible authority is Holy Scripture, which is inspired by the Holy Ghost (592).

2. Next comes in weight the decisions of the Six Ecumenical Synods, which being guided and ended, notwithstanding the human things in them, such as passions, etc., by the promised aid of the Holy Ghost (593), have reached right conclusions in strict accordance with the New Testament.

And 3, a vast distance behind them and lower than they *the utterances of local councils*, and lower still *the opinions* of mere individual Fathers, all of which are to be rejected where they contravene the New Testament or the VI. Synods.

But among the Fathers, *the historic testimony of* those of the first three centuries, or of the Ante-Nicene period is especially valuable, on Christian doctrine, discipline, rite and custom.

DOCUMENT XXI., (XV. IN COLETI AND MANSI.) RELATING TO THE APOSTATIC CONVENTICLE.

This bears the heading in Coleti, "THIRD REQUEST, OF THE SCHISMATICS *sent from the same city*" [Chalcedon] "*to the Emperors.*" "In Hardouin" says note 6, col. 1261, 1262 of tome III. of Coleti' "the title is, "*Third Testimony*" [or, "*Third Protest*"] "*which the same seven Bishops sent from Chalcedon to Theodosius the Emperor.*" This is chapter XXXV. in the *Synodicon* of Irenaeus.

In this document the desperate misrepresentation of John of Antioch, Theodoret, and their five fellows of the Deputation of the Man-Serving Apostasy becomes still more violent and unscrupulous as they see their cause failing, and victory turning to the Third Ecumenical Synod, whose leaders, Cyril and Memnon they had presumptuously dared to attempt to depose, and whose other members they had attempted to excommunicate. Even now they speak of their farcical and minority action against them as though it were valid, and wish the Emperor to recognize it as such, absurdly and unjustly enough.

They begin by pleading in Erastian style that they had done what the Emperor wished, but that, nevertheless, their side had not been successful, and "*now*" they add, "*we who up to this time have been detained in Chalcedon, are at last with difficulty sent to our several homes.*" Then they proceed to slander the Orthodox Council and its representatives, as follows:

"But those who have thrown all things into confusion, and have filled the world with disturbances, and are eager to tear the churches to pieces, and mani-

NOTE 592.—II. Tim. iii:15, 16, 17; II. Peter i:19, 20, 21; Rev. i:3; Rev. xxii:7, 18, 19; Luke xi:28; John v:39, and I. Cor. xiv:37.

NOTE 593.—Matt. xviii:15-19; John xiv:16, 17, 26; John xv:26; John xvi:7-15; John xx:21-24; Acts xv:28, and I. Tim. iii:15.

festly fight against piety, exercise the functions of the priesthood, make use of the churches, and obtain firm promises, as they suppose, of an unlawfully hoped for ordination" [of some one for Nestorius' place in the see of Constantinople], "excite seditions in the Church, and use up on their own soldiers what should be expended for the use of the poor."

Thus do those creature-servers lay on the Ecumenical Synod and on the Orthodox the fault of those struggles which were made necessary in resisting their own heresies. But one can see that what galled them most was the resolution to ordain a successor in the See of Constantinople to their deposed frien l Nestorius, with whose Creature-Service at least they fully sympathized, as their conduct and utterances show. In the Document next following this we shall see them sympathising with him, and condemning the Actions of the Third Synod, as *"done forbiddenly"* [or *"illegally"*] *"and without judgment."*

The charge that the Orthodox had used up on their own soldiers what should have been expended for the use of the poor, rests on their word alone, which we have found false so often as to be of no account against godly men. There is no proof that the Orthodox Synod at any time, or its Delegation, used any more means than prudence would dictate in protecting themselves. Indeed all along at first the government soldiers were used for the service of the Nestorian party, to repel the canonical and peaceful messengers of the Orthodox Council who had been sent to summon Nestorius and John of Antioch to answer for their sins and errors, and to give all the prestige and appearance of secular arms to the Man-Serving party.

But these heretics speak with very poor memory, seemingly, of the hard facts, and pervert and misrepresent to suit their own heretical aims.

Next they come to represent their own party as stronger than it proved to be among the Bishops, though their implied boast that many of the people held their Man-Service was only too true, for the Orthodox Cyril himself witnesses to the fact that some of them were already warped and sunken; and such might readily become Man-Servers. They write further against the Orthodox Synod and its Delegation:

"But thou art not only their Emperor but ours also. For the Orient" [that is, "the Oriental Diocese," that is, the jurisdiction of John of Antioch,] "in which the correct faith has always shone, is not a small portion of thy Empire, and with it are also other provinces and dioceses from which we are gathered. Wherefore let your Majesty not despise the faith which is adulterated, in which you also have been baptized, and your progenitors, on which the foundations of the Church have been established, etc." To represent Man-Service as the original faith is akin to the pleadings of heretics in all ages like image-servers, creature-invokers, and a multitude of those of ancient times and in our day, all of whom will have it that their errors have been from the beginning, when they really began at a time which we can fix like, for instance, Nestorianism and its Man-Service in the days of Diodore of Tarsus in the fourth century, and in those of Theodore of Mopsuestia just after him. But no such error can stand the test of examination by the touchstone of the historic transmission from the very beginning, the rule, of holding to what was held, "*Always, everywhere, and by all*" the Orthodox.

Then referring to the African war against the Vandals they promise the Emperor help from God if he will favor their heresies "*and*," they add, "*forbid the body of the Church to be burst to pieces. For it will be burst to pieces, if the opinion which Cyril has added to the faith and other heretics have confirmed prevails*" [or "*grows strong*"]. "*These things we have often indeed testified before God both in Ephesus and here, and have taught your Piety.*" Below they add:

"We deem it necessary again to teach your Majesty that those who are permitted to have Churches, teach in the Churches those things which Apollinarius and Arius and Eunomius have taught, exercise the functions of the priesthood illegitimately and against the canons, and destroy the souls of those who go to them, if any one is willing to hear even them. For by the grace of God, who cares for all men, and who wishes all men to be saved, *the greatest part of the people are sound, and are solicitous for the pious dogmas.*" Alas! creature worship had begun to come in in some places where such teachers were, aye, as early as the last part of the fourth century.

Then they ask the Emperor to take their side and to "*permit nothing to be added to the faith of the holy Fathers who were congregated in Nicaea,*" as though the Orthodox were corrupting the work of that Anti-Creature-Serving and therefore glorious Synod; as though indeed they were not strengthening it and acting on the same lines of opposing Creature-Service.

Then they tell him that if he will not do what they wish, that is, to put it in brief, override the decisions of the Ecumenical Synod, and crush it and the truth of God which it had set forth, they will shake off the dust of their feet against him. They were prostituting the functions of their episcopate, and deserved therefore to be deprived of them. For they were giving the poison of Creature Service instead of the saving bread of God's Anti-Creature Serving truth. And after some perversion of Holy Writ, and recounting their efforts in behalf of their heresies and against the Orthodox Synod, before the Emperor, the princes or chief men, the soldiers, and priests, and laics, they close.

The reader will notice their persecuting spirit against Cyril and Memnon and the Third Synod of the whole church, when they find fault because they "*are permitted to have churches,*" and their egregious lying in asserting that they "*teach in the Churches those things which Apollinarius and Arius and Eunomius have taught.*"

DOCUMENT XXII. (XVI. IN COLETI AND MANSI), RELATING TO THE APOSTATIC CONVENTICLE.

This is Chapter XXVI. in Irenaeus' *Synodicon*.

This bears in Coleti the heading:

"AN EPISTLE OF THE SAME" [Seven Bishops of the Apostasy it means] "*to their own in Ephesus.*"

Note 1., columns 1263, 1264 of tome III. of Coleti's *Concilia* states further on this Document:

"The title of this Epistle in Hardouin, from the old Basel version cited is, "*John*" [John], "*Paul, Macarius, Apringius, Theodoret,*" [Helladius], "*to the most holy and most wise Synod which is in Ephesus, wish salvation in the Lord.*"

This is a short letter but it reveals the sympathy of the Delegation of the Apostasy for Nestorius and their hatred to the Anti-Man-Serving Twelve Chapters in such a clear light that I here give it entire:

"After we came to Chalcedon, (for by reason of the seditions of the good monks (594) neither we nor our adversaries are permitted to enter Constantinople)(595), we heard a report that seven days before we appeared (see the boast" [or "the glory"] "of the most pious Emperor!)(596) the lord Nestorius was sent away from Ephesus to go whither it might please him. Wherefore we have been powerfully grieved because indeed those things which have *been done forbiddenly and without judgment now really seem to have force.* But let your Holiness know that we are ready to enter on a contest for the faith and are willing to contend even till death. But we expect to-day, that is the eleventh of the mouth Gorpiaeus" [our September] "that our most pious Emperor will pass over to Rufinianus" [a suburb of Chalcedon], "and will there hear the case. Let your Holiness therefore pray that the Lord Christ may aid us, in order that we may be able to strengthen the faith of the holy Fathers, and to tear up by the roots the *Chapters* which have risen up to the damage of the holy Church. We pray that your Holiness may also think and do the same, and continue in its alacrity for the Orthodox faith. Moreover, when the Epistle was written the Lord Himerius had not yet come to us, for perhaps he has been impeded in his journey. For we hope that the sad things will be extin-

---

NOTE 594.—This is *satirical*, or perhaps it has been changed from *bad* monks by some transcriber, as seems to have been done in the document next after this in Coleti.

NOTE 595.—The monks may have opposed the entrance of both parties together to dispute, for that would imply that the Ecumenical Synod had not already settled the questions at issue, which would be an insult to its authority. They could not have refused to admit the Delegates of the Synod if alone. As a fact they were admitted.

NOTE 596.—*Coleti Conc.*, tom. III., col. 1263 (En. gloriam pientissimi regis). The remark is parenthetical. The term *regis, King*, is evidently an ignorant man's blunder for Imperatoris, *Emperor*.

guished, and that the truth will shine forth, provided only your Piety strenuously help us" (597).

The expression, "*See the boast of the most pious Emperor,*" seems to imply that Theodosius II. had given Nestorius or his partizans a promise in his favor, which now he violated. And it looks very much as though the monarch was really at first in sympathy with Nestorius and his errors, but was now taking the back track under pressure from the Orthodox Synod and its friends.

Here, as in all these documents, the Creature-Serving Delegates do not oppose the expression *Bringer Forth of God* (θεοτόκος), but concentrate all their efforts, and fight their battles against Cyril's Anti-Creature-Serving Twelve Chapters, wholly or almost wholly.

This document seems to have been written before the Emperor's final decision in favor of the Orthodox Delegates and the Third Ecumenical Synod (598).

DOCUMENT XXIII. (XVII. IN COLETI AND MANSI) RELATING TO THE APOSTATIC CONVENTICLE.

This bears in Coleti the heading:

"AN EPISTLE OF THEODORET, BISHOP OF CYRUS, *written from Chalcedon to Alexander of Hierapolis.*"

The Delegation of the Apostasy begin this Document by stating that they had omitted nothing in the way of courtesy, nothing in the way of sharpness with the Emperor and his Cabinet against the Twelve Chapters of Cyril. I quote it all. Their bitter though sincere hostility to those Incarnation asserting and Anti-Man-Serving Anathemas is a not uncommon feature of the course of errorists and heretics. They write:

"We have omitted nothing in the way of courtesy, nothing in the way of sharpness, nothing in the way of exhortation, nothing in the way of declamation, which we could use before the most pious Emperor and his illustrious cabinet, testifying before God who sees all things, and before our Lord Jesus Christ, who will judge the world in righteousness, and before the Holy Ghost, and His elect angels, that the faith be not despised, which is adulterated by those who have received the heretical dogmas, and have dared to subscribe to them; and that a command be given that the faith be set forth only as it was in Nicaea, and that the heresy which has been added to it to the damage and ruin of piety be cast away" [they mean the decisions of the Third Ecumenical Synod.—CHRYSTAL.] (599) "and [yet] up to this day we have not been able to effect any thing, for our hearers have turned themselves now hither and now

---

NOTE 597.—I have translated the above from col. 1263, 1264, tome III. of Coleti's *Concilia*.

NOTE 598.—Compare as to historical events connected with the Council the prefatory matter in volume I. of *Ephesus*.

NOTE 599—The plain English of that is that these Nestorians wished to reject that authoritative and needed explanation of the Nicene Creed which, in accordance with Christ's law in Matthew xviii: 15-19, the Universal Church in its Third Synod had put forth. They

thither. But nevertheless none of those things has been able to persuade us to desist from pressing our affair and purpose, but we have followed up the case by God's grace. For we have endeavored to persuade our most pious Emperor by an oath, that it is impossible for Cyril and Memnon to be made friends with us, and that it can not be brought to pass that we shall communicate with those who have not yet rejected the heretical Chapters. And so we, for our part, have that mind; but the study of those who seek their own interests, but not those of Jesus Christ, is that they may be reconciled to them, even against our mind." [This abuse of those at Constantinople who were now inclining to the truth is similar to the lying abuse and misrepresentation of the aims and conduct of the Third Ecumenical Synod and its Delegation at Constantinople. It is the old yarn, so characteristic of these Creature-Servers.— CHRYSTAL.] "But our care is not for that. For God demands our purposes, and searches our virtue, and does not impose punishment" [on us] "on account of those things which are done contrary to our mind" [by them] (600).

wished still to make it teach denial of the Inman of the Word, and the worship of a mere man put on by Him, the first error contrary to John i: 1, 2, 3, 14, and the second contrary to Christ's own words in Matthew iv: 10.

Moreover, they seem to have overlooked or blinked the fact that the teaching and defining power of the Universal Church, given and enjoined on her by Christ himself, did not end with *Nicaea* in 325, but continued all through the period of the VI. Synods, A. D. 325-680, while it was one, and that even since the division every sound part has the same right in its own sphere and way to witness against all idolatrous and all infidelizing errors till the end of time. But in time those local protests and definitions will be ratified, so far as they are in consonance with the inspired Scriptures, and with the preceding definitions of the VI. Synods, by a Seventh Synod of the whole Church. For the errors of the so-called seventh Ecumenical Synod, the Conventicle at Nicaea in A. D. 787, all its idolatry, worship of creatures by invocation, and all its Eucharistic errors are most plainly and clearly, and by necessary implication, condemned antecedently by the VI. Ecumenical Councils, as we see from all that has here preceeded on Ephesus, and as we shall see from what is to come; and condemned, moreover, under penalty of deposition in the case of Bishops and clerics, and of anathema in the case of laics. And we must remember that the aforesaid idolatrous Conventicle of A. D. 787 is the only Synod deemed Ecumenical besides the first Six by the creature worshiping Greeks and Latins, though the Latins now reject its condemnation of Pope Honorius as a Monothelite heretic, as they do the Sixth Synod's strong condemnation of him also for that same heresy; and both Greeks and Latins in accepting as Ecumenical or even as local or in any other way the said so-called Seventh Synod of A. D. 787, by necessary implication reject the Third Ecumenical Synod and the Fifth and are therefore, if Bishops or clerics, deposed, and therefore may not be heard nor officiate, and their laics are anathema and have no right to communion.

Furthermore these inconsistent Judaizers and Creature Servers were trying to do that for which they were censuring the Orthodox and Universal Church; that is, to fix a sense on the Creed, which they would require of all by compelling men to condemn the opposite and sound sense in the Twelve Chapters. The great difference was that their sense is against the New Testament and against the Universal Church and unauthorized, whereas the sense of the Orthodox is in strict agreement with the New Testament, and is the doctrine of the Universal Church, defined in its Third Synod, and is therefore authoritative in the highest sense. But such was the logic of these corrupters of the faith.

NOTE 600.—In the Nestorian Count Irenaeus' *Synodicon*, or *Tragedy*, this reads some-

[Next, and without any break Theodoret takes up the case of Nestorius, and shows that both himself and his party had not a word of censure for him but heartily agreed with him in dogma, (except that some of them may have admitted the Incarnation, though that is not sure, although for policy's sake they were compelled, now that he was deposed as a heretic, to observe caution and craft in his defence. For he writes]:

"But let thy Holiness know in relation to our friend" [Nestorius is meant.— CHRYSTAL], "that whenever we made mention of him either before the most pious Emperor, or before his illustrious Cabinet, we were branded as guilty of defection (601). So great is the hostility of those who are within" [the higher circles, or the court circles] "against him (602). And that is most annoying. The most pious Emperor, before all others, turns away from his name, openly saying: *'Let no one speak to me regarding that man; for he himself once for all, has furnished proof'*" [against himself: or, "*He himself, once for all, has*

what differently, as follows. I translate from the Latin of it in col. 293, tome IV. of *Coleti's Concilia*, as I have translated the above from the Latin in columns 1264, 1265 of tome III. of that work:

"We have told, with an oath, the most pious Emperor, that it is a thing impossible that we should restore Cyril and Memnon to the office of Bishops, and that it can not be brought to pass that we should communicate with the rest, unless before it, they remove the HERETICAL CHAPTERS. We therefore hold to that resolution. But those who seek their own interests, not those of Jesus Christ, are in a hurry to restore them even without our wish. And none of those purposes are ours. For God demands our purpose and persevering virtue, and will not inflict vengeance on us for what is done contrary to our will" [by others].

"In regard to that true friend" [Nestorius is meant. CHRYSTAL] "let your Holiness understand that as often as we have made mention of him, either before the most pious Prince or before the Cabinet of the Prince, we have been judged as having done an injury. So great is the opposition against him of those who are within" [the Court circle], "and, what is worst of all, is that even the most pious Emperor himself is more averse to his name than the rest" [are], "for he says openly to us, *'Let no one say anything openly to me regarding that man. For those matters which pertain to him have already, once for all, received a formal decision.'*" [This seems a reference to the action of the Third Ecumenical Synod in deposing him for his various heresies; and may include the Emperor's approval of at least his deposition, either on the grounds enacted by the Council, or for policy's sake only on the Emperor's part. CHRYSTAL]. "But, nevertheless," [while] "we are here, we will not cease to care with all our power for that part also" [of our business], "knowing the iniquity which has been committed against him by those who are without God."

"But we are in a hurry to be liberated hence, and for your Religiousness to be delivered thence. For it is not possible to hope for anything pleasant hence; because all have been satisfied with gold; and the Judges themselves contend that there is" [only] "one nature" [composed] "of divinity and humanity. But the people, by God's favor, are all safe, and come out to us incessantly."

Undoubtedly a large part of the people there, happily not everywhere, had become creature-servers, though they might not, some of them at least, deny the Incarnation, while others might.

NOTE 601.—Rather a mild term for apostasy.

NOTE 602.—The more intelligent would more readily be persuaded by the Delegation of the Third Synod of the evil of that creature server's heresies.

given us a specimen of himself" (603)]. "But nevertheless, while we are here, we shall not cease to care with all our power for that Father, for we know that injustice has been done to him by the impious" (604).

[The injustice in the heretic Theodoret's esteem done to Nestorius was the deposing of him by the Third Ecumenical Synod for his denial of the Incarnation of the substance of God the Word in the Man put on, and for his creature service and cannibal views on the Eucharist, etc. And "*the impious*" are the defenders of God's truth, those vital truths which are essential to every man's salvation. Next without any break they take up the subject of their own doings and the circumstances about them and misrepresent the Synod and its Delegates and friends as usual. And they show that while many of the corrupting and degenerating laity were inoculated with their errors, the Orthodox justly looked upon them and their heresies with abhorrence. For they say]:

"We have a desire also to be liberated hence and that your Piety may be liberated. For no good is to be hoped for from this quarter because all the judges themselves trust in gold, and contend that there is but *one nature composed of deity and humanity*." [For this last charge of Apollinarian Monophysitism in the judges I have seen no proof. And the assertion of these heretics needs proof. That heresy is irreconcilable with the documents and utterances of the Third Synod, and there is no proof of the statement that any of the Orthodox Judges trusted in gold.—CHRYSTAL.] "But, by God's grace all the people are well disposed, and come out to us continually. Moreover, we began to discourse also to them, and we celebrated very large communions (605), and on Fourth Day" [that is on Wednesday.—CHRYSTAL.] "in accordance with the prayers of thy Piety we gave them detailed explanations on the Faith, and they heard with so much pleasure that they did not go away till the seventh hour" [or about twelve to one o'clock P. M.—CHRYSTAL], "but held out till the sun was hot. For the multitude was congregated in a very large court, which has four porches, and we addressed them from above, from a raised place which was nearly covered. But all the clergy, with the good monks were very hostile to us, so that there might have been a co-stone

NOTE 603.—See the last note but two above for the reading of this passage in Irenaeus' *Synodicon*, which is quite different, and I presume more accurate, as the *Synodicon* often is, as compared with the other translation in Coleti of these Nestorian Documents.

NOTE 604.—In the *Synodicon* the reading is "*by those who are without God*," instead of "*by the impious*."

NOTE 605.—These Delegates speak in this Document below as though they then had no communion in the sense of the Eucharist. Were the communions here meant Eucharists, or only communions in feeling, sentiment, belief, or assemblies only? Or, do the "*communions*" refer to what had occurred before the interview with the Emperor mentioned in this Document below and before the meeting on that day?

throwing" [or "a stone throwing together" (606)] "when we should return from Ruffinianum," [or "from Ruffinianis" (607)] "after the arrival of the most pious Emperor, and many of the laics and false monks who were with us might have been wounded" (608). [The *"false"* and *"good"* as applied to monks are here sarcastic, or altered by some stupid copyist.—CHRYSTAL.] "But the most pious Emperor had learned that a multitude had congregated against us, and meeting us when we were alone, said: "*I have ascertained that ye are assembled wickedly* (609). *But I said to him, 'Because thou hast given us liberty to speak, I have dared so to do with that permission. Is it a just thing that excommunicated heretics should officiate in the Churches; while we who contend for the faith, and for that reason have been made aliens from the communion by them, are not to enter a Church?*

And he answered, *And what can I do?*

I therefore replied to him" [Thou canst do] "*What a chief man* [610], *thy*

NOTE 606.—The Latin here is "collapidatio." We have not the Greek. This expression might naturally mean that the stone throwing would be done by both sides, the friends of the Third Synod against the Delegates of the Apostasy and their friends: and these last against the friends of the Third Synod.

NOTE 607.—The name of this suburb of Chalcedon or Constantinople is in the singular in this letter above: here it is plural.

NOTE 608.—But this Latin subjunctive may here be rendered as though it were the indicative, and judging from the Latin version of this document in the *Synodicon* of Irenaeus it should be I so translate then as follows:

"But all the clergy with the good monks were very hostile to us, so that there was a co-stone throwing, when we were returning from Ruffinanum" [or *from Ruffiniana"*] "after the arrival of the most pious Emperor, and many of the laics and false monks who were with us were wounded."

This reads in the same document in col. 293, tome IV. of Coleti's *Concilia*, in cap. xxx. of Irenaeus' *Synodicon* as follows:

"But all the clergy with all those good monks fight against us powerfully, so that on one occasion a fight took place when we were returning from Ruffiniana after the first conversation with the most pious Prince And many were wounded as well of the laics who were with us, as of the false monks also. But the most pious Emperor had ascertained that a multitude had gathered to us, and in a conversation with us alone, he says, *I have ascertained that ye make* extraordinary gatherings" [or *"gatherings outside* of order"].

Hefele would correct the above to: "*And many of those who were with us were wounded by laics and false monks.*" In another place it is, according to his reference: *"by servants clad in the garb of monks."* See *Hefele's History of the Church Councils*, vol. 3, page 105, note 1.

NOTE 609.—See the different reading here of the *Synodicon* of Irenaeus in note 608, last above.

NOTE 610.—*Magister* is the Latin here which I render, "chief man." It means "*Master*," and was applied to different sorts of "masters" or chief men. The *Synodicon* reads here: "what he did who is now Magister," [that is "Master"] "when he was thy Count of the Largesses," [that is, "thy Count of the Treasury"] "when he came to Ephesus. For on his finding that they" [the Orthodox] "made gatherings, but that we made none at all, he restrained them, saying, Unless peace is made between you, I will not permit one party to celebrate a meeting" [alone]. The Count here meant is John, whose Report to the Emperor is given above in Document 14th, on pages 287—292 above. Some think that no session of

Count of the Largesses did in Ephesus. For when he found that some were congregated, but that we were not congregated, he restrained them, saying, If ye are not at peace I will not concede to one party alone to assemble. And it was behooving thy Piety also to command the Bishop here" [that is of Chalcedon or whosoever was Bishop there.—CHRYSTAL], "*not to permit either them or us to assemble until we come together, that thy just decision may be made known to all.*" [Here this noted enemy of Orthodoxy and of its exponent the Third Ecumenical Synod, still persists in regarding his handful of Bishops of the Apostasy, all of whom were under discipline by the enactment of that Council of the whole Church, as the equals of the Ecumenical Synod, and deserving of as much consideration! And he speaks with approval of the unwarranted act of a layman in attempting to degrade the representatives of the whole Church to their level. The slightest common sense should have taught that Man-Server better.—CHRYSTAL].

"To that he said, *I, surely, can not command a Bishop.*

And so I replied to him, *Therefore do not command us either, and we will take a Church, and will assemble; and thy Piety will ascertain that there are many more with us than with them.*

We said to him furthermore, *Our assembly was having neither the reading of the Sacred Scriptures, nor the oblation* (611); *but only prayers for the faith and for your Majesty* (612) *and colloquies for religion.*

Therefore he approved and did not further forbid that to be done. Therefore the meetings of a multitude coming to us and hearing [our] teachings with pleasure, are increased (613). Let your Piety therefore pray that our cause may have an outcome which shall be pleasing to God. For we are in danger daily, both suspecting plots on the part of monks and clerics, and seeing their power and recklessness" (614).

And so this document ends. Theodoret's boast of the size of his party was destined to be falsified for some time in the Christian world, as it had been before the Ecumenical Synod of Ephesus.

---

the Ecumenical Synod was held after his arrival at Ephesus. If that be true we must put the visit of the Delegates of both Synods to the Emperor Theodosius at Constantinople or Chalcedon after the Ecumenical Synod, and this Document belongs there too. The members of the two Synods were at liberty to go after Edict 8d by its terms. See it on page 299 above.

NOTE 611.—The Eucharist seemingly, though the term which means *offering* is applied also to other things, as for instance the collection or *offertory* as it is still called in the Anglican Church for the poor, etc.

NOTE 612.—This reads a little different in the Latin translation of the same document in the *Synodicon* of Irenaeus, as follows: "but we have only made litanies [or "supplications"] for the faith and for your Empire; and sermons for pious religion."

NOTE 613.—The Latin of the *Synodicon* of Irenaeus as given in col. 294, tome IV. of Coleti here reads, "since then therefore our meetings increase, a multitude of the people sailing over to us, and hearing our teaching with all good will." The "sailing over" I presume was from Constantinople which was directly opposite Chalcedon, and quite near.

NOTE 614.—The Greek of the above Document seems to be lost. Two different Latin translations of it are found, one on col. 1264, 1265 of tome III. of Coleti's *Concilia*, from which the rendering in the text above is mainly made; and the other in col. 292, 293, 294 of tome IV. of that work. The last forms chap. xxx. of Irenaeus' *Synodicon* as there given.

DOCUMENT XXIV. (XVIII. FROM MANSI AND COLETI), RELATING TO THE APOSTATIC SYNOD.

This is found in columns 1265, 1266 and 1277 of tome III. of *Coleti's Concilia*, and also in the *Synodicon of Monte Cassino* in columns 302, 303 and 304 of tome IV. of *Coleti's Concilia*. The Greek appears to be lost. It is found in both places above in Latin only, though the translations differ somewhat. It is found also in columns 56, 57 and 58 of tome 84 of *Migne's Patrologia Graeca*, and is there followed in columns 58 and 59 by Garnier's notes on it; and in column 60 by the Latin version of part of it found in the Acts of the *Fifth Ecumenical Synod*, Session, or Conference V. I translate it from the Latin in Migne as above, modifying his text by the other readings, and sometimes following that of Irenaeus' *Synodicon*.

As to its *authorship* Garnier, (note in column 58 of tome 84 of Migne's *Patrologia Graeca*,) states:

"There is no room to doubt that this is Theodoret's. For it is mentioned both in the second part of the Council of Ephesus among the Acts of the assembly of the Orientals, and in the Fifth Synod in Act V., where a judgment is instituted regarding the writings of Theodoret. It is contained almost entire in the former place, in a mutilated form in the latter, in neither in Greek. But three things of great moment, as it regards Church History, are thence clear; first with how great closeness of friendship Theodoret was conjoined with Nestorius; secondly, how hostile his mind was towards the Fathers of the Ecumenical Synod of Ephesus; lastly, how surely he clung to the heresy of Nestorius and taught it before a congregation."

I ought here to append a caution as to the expression of Garnier that this Document is "*in the second part of the Council of Ephesus among the Acts of the Assembly of the Orientals.*" We must not understand by this that it is in the Acts of the Third Synod proper, but only among outside Documents sometimes bound up with it for fuller information. It never came before the Third Ecumenical Synod. The title of this Document varies. In the old Basel version it is (according to *Coleti*, III., col. 1265):

"PART OF THE HOMILY OF THEODORET, BISHOP OF CYRUS, *delivered at Chalcedon to the Delegates of the Schismatics, and favorers of Nestorius.*"

In Hardouin it reads, "*Part of a Homily of Theodoret, Bishop of Cyrus, delivered in Chalcedon, when they were about to depart.*"

In the *Synodicon of Monte Cassino*, chapter XXXVII., the title is as follows: "*Part of a Sermon which, they say, Theodoret, Bishop of the Church of Cyrus used in Chalcedon.*"

In column 56, tome 84 of Migne's *Patrologia Graeca*, it bears the heading: "*Homily delivered in Chalcedon by Theodoret Bishop of Cyrus.*"

This Document may be divided into three parts as follows:

In Part I. Theodoret faults his opponents, that is the Third Ecumenical Synod and its friends the Orthodox, as though they were untrue to Christ; and speaks of himself and the other Delegates of the Man-Serving Apostasy as impugned for their faithfulness to Him and excluded from Constantinople for His sake, though he contends that they will not be shut out of heaven. He does not define how the Ecumenical Synod had sinned against Christ, but, I presume, he means by its condemning the worship of His Humanity, the creature put on, and by its economically ascribing the sufferings of that creature to God the Word, as it in effect did by approving documents which so taught, notably Cyril's two Epistles approved by the Synod.

Then he comes to Part II. of this *Homily* in which he identifies himself with the cause and errors of Nestorius against the Third Synod. His language is full of vile misrepresentation of the Third Synod's stand for God and against Nestorius' errors; and yet is so important as showing the animus of the Apostatic Synod and their Delegation by the voice of the ablest scholar of their party, that I here quote all this part of it. Theodoret says to his auditors, the friends of Nestorius who had crossed over from Constantinople: "Let Christ be our leader and guide in this Sermon." . . . . "It is Christ by whom ye have dared to cross the terrible waves of the Propontis (615), to hear our voice, which ye consider to be an image of the voice of your shepherd" [He means Nestorius.—CHRYSTAL].

"For ye desire to hear the pleasant piping (616) of your shepherd; (617) a shepherd, whom his fellow shepherds (618) have slain with their

---

NOTE 615.—The water between Constantinople and Chalcedon.

NOTE 616.—The comparison of the pleasing influence produced by the shepherd's pipe on his flock to the preaching of the Gospel on true Christians, was not applicable to the influence of Nestorius' heresies against the Incarnation and in favor of creature-service; for such errors are doctrinal discords, not harmonies.

NOTE 617.—"Of *your shepherd.*" On this Garnier, (note in col. 59 of tome 84 of Migne's *Patrologia Graeca*) writes:

"He" [Theodoret] "seemed to his hearers another Nestorius, and he was not very much unlike him. For he had the same master, Theodore; he had been instructed in discipline in the same monastery [with him], the Mandra of St. Euprepius: he had proposed to himself to imitate the same Chrysostom; he was wont to write and speak in the same style. I omit their bond of intimacy, their communion in a common cause, etc.

NOTE 618 — "*His fellow-shepherds.*" On this Garnier, (note in col. 59, tome 84 of *Migne's Patrologia Graeca*), remarks: "From this it is clear how hostile and unjust a mind he" [Theodoret] "had against the holy defenders of Christ, against whom he sacrilegiously quotes passages from the prophets, and calls them murderers of their '*fellow-shepherd,*' corrupters of the vineyard entrusted to themselves, defilers of the Lord's portion, desolators of the Lord's part, a tongue speaking injustice," [and] "a mouth exercised in iniquity. Where" [now] "are those who defend a man who belches forth such things? He was erring, say they, because he thought that Nestorius held correct opinions and that the Ecumenical Synod followed the party of Apollinarius. But after all this what defence can be made for a man whom thou wishest to be deemed the most learned man of the Oriental Church?"

This is a just judgment from a man who was not himself sound. On the same page

pens (619), as they suppose; to them God cries by the prophet: '*Many shepherds have destroyed* (620) *my vineyard; they have defiled my portion; they have turned my desirable part into an impassible solitude,*' (621). And let Him speak to them by another prophet a'so. '*According to their multitude, so have they sinned against me: therefore will I change their glory into shame* (622).' And let Him speak again through another prophet, '*Woe to ye, apostate sons; ye have made a plan, and not by me; and compacts, and not by my Spirit; that ye may add sin upon sin* (623). Ye who consult on a deep and unjust design, have been changed (624).' Let Isaiah also speak to them, '*For your hands are polluted with blood and your fingers with sins: your tongue hath spoken injustice, and your mouth hath practiced* (625) *iniquity. None speaketh just things, for they conceive labor and bring forth iniquity; they hatch the spider's eggs and they weave the spider's web*' (626). Behold an accusation of malice, and a proof of

in Migne in the *Variae Lectiones* some one attempts to make a weak defence of Theodoret by claiming in effect that he abandoned his heresies after the Fourth Ecumenical Synod. But of this there is no sufficient proof. For certain matter found now in his writings which looks that way is suspected of being interpolated; and the suspicion seems the more just when we remember that it is clear as is evident by the Acts of the Fifth Ecumenical Synod which condemned his writings against Cyril of Alexandria's "Twelve Chapters, that after *Ephesus* he was as much a heretic as ever before. And there is no sufficient reason to make us believe that he did not live and die in his heresy. I have seen a suspicion cast, by one of his defenders, on the genuineness of the passages cited from him in the Fifth Ecumenical Synod but have found no cause for deeming it well founded. His utterance of exultation at Cyril's death, and his stigmatizing the signing of Orthodox documents of Cyril and the Third Synod as *blaspheming* is one of the most heretical and brutal things in Christian history. The Universal Church therefore has done well in not enrolling him among her saints. She came near anathematizing him in the Fourth Ecumenical Synod when at first he refused to anathematize Nestorius; and only desisted in her purpose when he reluctantly did so, and then only because he was forced to, to save his honors, etc. I have heard an infidel, a bitter enemy of Christianity, quote with exultation his bitter language of joy at the Orthodox Cyril's death. That utterance, as found in the Acts of the Fifth Synod, is given in column 62 of tome 84 of Migne's *Patrologia Graeca*.

NOTE 619.—In Irenaeus' *Synodicon* this reads *'whom his fellow-shepherds have slain, as they suppose, by the subscriptions of their pens,*" that is by their subscriptions to his deposition in the first Act of the Third Ecumenical Synod for his denial of the Incarnation, and of the truth that God alone may be worshipped, and for his cannibal views on the Eucharist. And they supposed aright.

NOTE 620.—Or "corrupted" [corruperunt].

NOTE 621.—Jerem. xii: 10. From the words: "Let Christ be our leader" to "impassible solitude" inclusive, as given above are quoted in another version in the Acts of the Fifth Ecumenical Synod, in its Fifth Conference, as we are told in col. 60, tome 84 of Migne's *Patrologia Graeca*, where they are given.

NOTE 622.—Hosea iv: 7.
NOTE 623.—Isaiah xxx: 1.
NOTE 624.—Or, "Change ye," according to another reading.
NOTE 625.—Or, '*meditated*.''
NOTE 626.—Isaiah lix: 3, 5.

the rottenness of iniquity (627) in *the viper's eggs* and in *the spider's web*. For that which is brought forth means malice, and the plot (628) is a proof of weakness. The viper's eggs are the evidence of malice, and the spider's web is the proof of weakness. '*And he who eateth one of their eggs shall find a monster when he breaks it*' (629). Ye have seen malice growing weak. Ye have seen one" [Cyril of Alexandria is meant.—CHRYSTAL] "committing an offence against one who has committed no offence (630)" [Nestorius is meant.—CHRYSTAL]. "Ye have seen him crowned (631) who is fought against (632). Because, saith he, '*he who eateth of an egg of theirs shall find a monster when he breaketh it*' (633). But what is *a monster* except something which cannot generate? As if he would say, that malice can not come to completion (634).

"Proclaim therefore to us, Isaiah, the hope of malice." [He replies], "*And in it will be a basilisk* (635). But it is wonderful that there should be in it both a basilisk and a monster. But *a basilisk* signifies *a monster*. For because that animal is the most bitter of all reptiles he has compared to it that which has been brought forth by malice. But, again, he has called the same thing a monster on account of the weakness of malice (636). For malice is weak.

NOTE 627.—The *Synodicon* has "*fragility of iniquity.*"

NOTE 628 —Theodoret seems here slanderously and sacrilegiously to apply this to the just design of Cyril and the Bishops of the Third Ecumenical Synod to do their duty in crushing the anti-Incarnation, Man-Serving heresies of Nestorius.

NOTE 629.—Or, according to another reading, "he shall find a wind egg" [that is, "a shell only"]"when he breaketh it."

NOTE 630.—This sentence, as to committing an offence is not found in the Synodicon, col. 303, tom. IV. of Coleti, but whether its omission is a slip of the copyist or by the design of the editor, I know not. It is found in the other Latin translation of the same Document in col. 1206 of tome III., id.

NOTE 631.—This and the two sentences preceding beginning with "*Ye have seen malice growing,*" etc., are made interrogative in some or all of the editions; but I have preferred the non-interrogative form, and understand Theodoret's allusion to be to the temporary victory of the Nestorian party before the Emperor and the chiefs when Count Irenaeus misrepresented matters and suppressed the full facts, as he tells in his Epistle to the Orientals-written from Constantinople. See it above. Theodoret seems to mean that Nestorius' deposition crowned him as a martyr.

NOTE 632.—Irenaeus' *Synodicon* has "*who is overcome,*" (Coleti *Conc.*, IV., col. 303).

NOTE 633.—Isaiah lix: 5.

NOTE 634.—Or, "*to perfection.*"

NOTE 635.—Isaiah lix: 5,

NOTE 636.—In col. 1206 of tome III. of *Coleti* and in col. 57 of tome 84 of Migne *Patrologia Graeca* this reads somewhat differently. I translate it as in the Latin version of both those places:

"'*And he who eateth of an egg of theirs shall find a wind-egg*'" [that is, a mere shell. CHRYSTAL] "*when he breaketh it.*' But a wind-egg means any thing unfruitful, that is, imperfect. Isaiah tells us also what the evidence of malice is." [He replies], "'*And in it a basilisk.*' But it is a wonderful thing, that there should be in it a basilisk and a wind-egg, that is, unfruitfulness. But a *basilisk* signifies malice. Because that little animal is the most fierce of all reptiles, he compares its offspring to malice. Moreover, that very offspring is a wind-egg, because of the weakness of malice: For malice is weak."

Finally comes in sequence the following sentence: '*Their web shall not become a garment, neither shall they cover themselves with the works of their own hands*' (637). Why? '*Because their works are works of iniquity*' (638). Tell us a proof of their unrighteousness." [He answers]. "'*Their feet run to evil* (639). To do what?'" [He answers] "'*and they are swift to shed blood*' (640). What then does he add to that?" [He replies] "'*Grinding and unhappiness are in their ways. For their paths which they walk* (641) *are perverse* (642) *and the way of peace they have not known*' (643). These things are truly deserving of lamentations, that priests can say such things against priests. But we say them not so much to accuse them, as to exercise foresight (644) for you" (645).

One can here see the adroitness of the cunning pleader and scholar against God's sound ministers and against the Incarnation, Anti-Creature-Serving truth which they maintained. In the craft displayed by this heretic we are reminded of the skill and craft with which Shakspear in his Julius Cæsar makes Antony pour his lamentations over the body of that dead Chieftain and sway the unlettered multitude.

Next comes what we may term the Third Part of this Homily: the burden of it is to charge the Third Ecumenical Synod with making God the Word liable to suffering; and with laying down the law that such a passible God must be adored, and so with being worse than the heathen, because according to Theodoret here, they did not worship a passible heaven and a passible sun, but termed them impassible, and either because of that alleged fault of Cyril and the Synod, or because by approving certain documents of Cyril's, notably one or both of his letters to Nestorius and the eighth of his Twelve Anathemas, they had forbidden worship to Christ's *humanity, a creature*, Theodoret charges them with having forsaken God, misapplying to them the words in Jeremiah ii: 13, "*They have forsaken Me, the Fountain of living water, and hewed them out cisterns, broken cisterns that can hold no water.*"

But to all this lying and misrepresentation the answer is very easy:

NOTE 637.—Isaiah lix: 6.
NOTE 638.—Ibid.
NOTE 639.—Isaiah lix: 7.
NOTE 640.—Ibid.
NOTE 641.—Or, "which they travel."
NOTE 642.—Gr, "crooked."
NOTE 643.—Isaiah lix: 7, 8.
NOTE 644.—The Latin, as in col. 1266 of tome III. of Coleti, and col. 57 of tome 84 of Migne's *Patrologia Graeca* reads, in the last clause above, "as to exercise care for you."
NOTE 645.—I have spoken above of following columns 56, 57, and 58 of tome 84 of *Migne's Patrologia Graeca*, modified in the above English rendering, but I should say that I have followed both translations mentioned above wherever they agree, and one or the other wherever I deemed it wisest to follow it in preference to the other. The translation in col. 1265, 1266, and 1267 of tome III. of *Coleti* is in the main or wholly that in col. 56 and after of tome 84 of Migne's *Patrologia Graeca*; and that in the *Synodicon*, col. 302-304 of tome IV. of Coleti, is in the main, or wholly, that in col. 637 and after in tome 84 of Migne's *Patrologia Graeca*.

For, 1., The Third Ecumenical Synod not only did not make God the Word liable to suffering, and did not command men to worship a God liable to suffering, but they did the very opposite; for in accepting and in approving Cyril's two letters to Nestorius, one of which contains the Twelve Chapters, they forbade anything but the *unsuffering* Divinity to be worshipped; and, further, by adopting Anathema VIII. of Cyril's XII., they anathematized all who worship the *creature*, the *passible humanity* of Christ, and, by necessary implication, all who worship any lesser creature, be it the Virgin Mary, archangels, angels, martyrs, or other departed or living saints, or any but *God*, the Father, His Coeternal Word, and his Coeternal Spirit, the Consubstantial Trinity.

2. The passage quoted by the Man-Server, Theodoret, from Jeremiah 11: 13, is applicable to him and to his fellow-Nestorian, and not at all to the Third Synod of the whole Church, for in it God is rebuking, by his prophet Jeremiah, his apostate people for the sin of *serving creatures, of having forsaken him in that sense*, not that they had forgotten Him absolutely, but had mingled the service of creatures with the service of Him, the uncreated and eternal God. So that had any of his hearers been sound in faith, they could very easily have turned the rebuke of the passage upon himself. It has been rarely the case that a heretic of such learning has ever quoted a passage which may be so easily turned against himself.

And so this document ends.

DOCUMENT XXV., (XIX. FROM COLETI AND MANSI.) RELATING TO THE APOSTATIC SYNOD.

This is found in a Latin translation in chapter XXXVII. of the *Synodicon of Monte Casino*, in column 304 of tome IV. of *Coleti's Concilia*, and in column 639, 640 of tome 84 of *Migne's Patrologia Graeca*. Its heading in both those places is, "*A Sermon of John of Antioch, which he delivered in Chalcedon after the Sermon of the presbyter Aphthonius and of*" [that of] "*the Bishop Theodoret.*" In both it is given in full.

The first part of it only is given in column 1267 of tome III. of Coleti's *Concilia*, and bears there the title of "*A Homily of John Bishop of Antioch, delivered in Chalcedon after the Homily of Theodoret, to animate their own* [partisans]." The translation there is different somewhat from that mentioned first above. But it is given in full in this second translation in col. 60 of tome 84 of Migne's *Patrologia Graeca*, with the last mentioned heading.

The Greek seems to be lost.

Seemingly, John delivered this just after that of Theodoret above, and so at the same time and place.

The CONTENTS of this brief Document are in short as follows. John begins by complimenting them for their piety, and zeal on his own heretical side, says that he has risen up among them to salute them and at the same time to bid

A Homily of John, Bishop of Antioch, delivered in Chalcedon. 371

them farewell. And referring to their presence as Deputies of the Apostasy he tells them that he and his fellows were with them, and were hastening to return to their brethren, that is to the Conventicle of the friends of Nestorius at Ephesus, he means. Then he urges them to contend strongly for his and their own errors, and then indirectly charges the Orthodox Synod of Ephesus and its partisans of holding to a mixing of the Two Natures in Christ, and proclaims as his own the doctrine that the *creature*, that is the Man united to God the Word *is to be relatively worshipped with Him*. And after promising them God's peace if they maintained those things, and ascribing glory to God, he ends this Document with the word "*Amen*."

Theodoret had only hinted at the difference between the Nestorian party and the Orthodox as to the matter of worshipping Christ's *created* humanity (646). But John dwells specially on that theme, and as chief of the partizans of Nestorius makes it a chief thing. And the thing most important and to be remembered in regard to this sermon is that John of Antioch in a sermon delivered in Chalcedon during his visit to that place, while the Third Ecumenical Synod was sitting, openly advocated the worship of Christ's humanity seemingly in opposition to the Eighth of Cyril's Twelve Anathemas or Chapters which treats on that subject. He spoke after a sermon by Aphthonius a presbyter and after Bishop Theodoret, his fellow heretic who worshipped, as he himself shows, not only Christ's humanity but also the elements in the Eucharist relatively to that humanity (647). The language of the following passage is found in that sermon as quoted in chapter XXXVII. of the *Synodicon Casinense*. I give it. John there says:

"Let us one persuade you that Divinity is liable to suffering, nor that there is" [but] "one nature of the Divinity and the body" [of Christ]. "For that divine Substance is always self-existent, but It has taken on that" [human nature]. "Wherefore we preach a conjunction, but not a mingling" [of the Two Natures], "a uniting, but not in the sense of a mixture of certain things.

"*That thing*" [is] "*God, because of That*" [other] "*Thing: this thing*" [is] "*the Son, because of That*" [other], "*Thing*". This *thing*" [is] "*every thing, because* of That" [other] "Thing. It" [the human nature] "*is* ADORED *with Him*" [that is with God the Word]; "*it is* GLORIFIED *with Him*. And hence it being conjoined inseparably" [to God the Word] "is itself named *the first fruits* (648) of our nature" (649).

NOTE 646.—That difference is told in note 183, pages 79-128, vol. I. of Chrystal's *Ephesus*, notes 677, 678 and 679, pages 461-463, of the same work.

NOTE 647.—That is, as consubstantiated with it; see on that whole theme Chrystal's *Ephesus*, vol. I., pages 240-313, note 606; and Theodoret's worship of the consecrated but unchanged elements, stated in his own words in the note matter on pages 276-286. How widely he differed from the Orthodox doctrine of Cyril and the Third Synod is told in what follows there, and in the rest of that note.

NOTE 648—I. Cor. xv: 20, 23. On the figure see Romans xi: 16.

NOTE 649.—*Coleti's Concilia*, tom. IV., col. 304: Caput xxxvii; *Sermo Joannis Antiocheni*,

Here plainly and beyond a doubt, John sets forth his Man-Service, in the expression, "*It is* ADORED *with Him*," that is the humanity of Christ is adored with God the Word.

And though we have not the Greek, and the Latin is not so clear as we might desire, nevertheless, remembering the views so often expressed by Nestorius and his party in favor of creature service, with which it is clear that John and Theodoret and most or all of his party in substance agreed, as we see by their own writings, we can understand a passage above as follows.

"*That thing*" [Christ's humanity] [is] "*God, because of That*" [other] *Thing*" [God the Word, who inhabits that humanity *relatively only* by his Spirit, according to Nestorius; not by His own *divine Substance*, according to him and John's party]; "*this thing*" [Christ's humanity] [is] "the *Son*" [that is, is God the Word] "*because of That*" [other] "*Thing*" [that is, he means, because of God the Word who dwells relatively by His Spirit, not by His divine Substance *in* that Man]. "*This thing*" [Christ's humanity] [is] "*every thing*, because of That" [other] "Thing" [that is because of God the Word]. "And hence it itself" [that is, Christ's humanity] "*being conjoined*" [with God the Word] "*inseparably*, is named '*the first fruits*' of our nature." All that is condemned in Cyril's Anathema VIII., which is approved by the Third Ecumenical Synod·

That is, what we find quoted in Cyril's *Five Book Contradiction of the Blasphemies of Nestorius*, from Nestorius is here meant: that is Nestorius' doctrine condemned in Cyril's Twelve Chapters and in the Fourteen Anathemas of the Fifth Ecumenical Synod, that the creature put on by God the Word may be so-called *God* with Him, and may be co-worshipped with Him, *relatively*, that is because God the Word dwells in him by His Spirit, not by his substance. This doctrine was derived from Diodore of Tarsus or from Theodore of Mopsuestia, or from both, and appears at this time to have been held to by all or nearly all the prominent Syrians, so wide had been its corrupting and creature serving influence. For it was really a return to the old pagan principle of *relative worship* and to the sin of the idolatrous Israelites in relatively worshipping Jehovah through the calf in the wilderness and through the calves of Jeroboam the Son of Nebat whose sad work is denoted by the often repeated expression "*who made Israel to sin*." Expressions setting forth that *relative worship* are found in the *Twenty Blasphemies* of Nestorius, for (650) which he was condemned and deposed in the First Act of the Third Synod of the Christian World.

---

quem dixit in Chalcedone post sermonem Aphthonii presbyteri et episcopi Theodoreti . . . Nemo vobis deitatem persuadeat esse passibilem, neque unam naturam diviuitatis et corporis. Nam illa quidem semper est per se divina substantia, illam, vero suscepit. Unde conjunctionem praedicamus, non vero confusionem: unitionem, non tamquam aliquorum misturam. Deus istud propter illud, omnia hoc propter illud. Adoratur cum illo, glorificatur cum illo. Et hinc conjunctum inseparabiliter, ipsum naturae nostrae primitiae nominatur. Haec custodite, et Deus pacis erit vobiscum, defendens vos quo ipse novit modo. Ipsi honor et gloria in saccela. Amen.

NOTE 650.—See them in Chrystal's *Ephesus*, vol. I., pages 449-480, and note "F." See also on them in pages 529-551; and his deposition for them on pages 486-504.

The Delegates of the Apostasy to their Conventicle at Ephesus. 373

DOCUMENT XXVI. ON THE APOSTATIC CONVENTICLE (XX. *from Mansi and Coleti*).

It is chapter XXVII. in Irenaeus' *Synodicon*.

At this point comes in Coleti III. 1268, and Mansi IV. 1414, a Document headed:

"ANOTHER EPISTLE OF THE SCHISMATICS *to the same persons*" [that is to their own friends at Ephesus] "*in which they boast too soon of their victory.*" It is chapter XXVII. in the *Synodicon Casinense*, where it has in col. 621, in tome 84 of *Migne's Patrologia Graeca*, a different title, and where the Latin rendering is different. The title there is, "ALSO, ANOTHER EPISTLE OF THE SAME BISHOPS ABOVE TO THE SAME BISHOPS ABOVE." I translate from both versions, following each where I deem it best. It is as follows:

"By the prayers of your Sanctity (651) we have been granted access to our most pious Emperor, and he has held a conference with us, and by God's grace we have overcome in the contest those who hold opinions contrary" [to ours], "so that all our utterances were accepted by the Christ-loving Emperor, but what was said by them seemed unacceptable and inconsequent (652). For though they were making mention of Cyril up and down (653), and were praying that he might be summoned so that he himself may give account for himself, they have as yet not been at all able to obtain their wish, but have heard that there behoves to be discussions (654) on piety, that is on the system (655) of the faith, and that the faith of the blessed Fathers should be strengthened. And in truth we confuted Acacius (656), who, during the

NOTE 651.—A collective title to the Synod of the Apostasy.

NOTE 652.—The other Latin version (col. 1268, tome III. of *Coleti's Concilia*) has here a different sense. For it reads (translated into English) as follows:

"But we rejected what was read" [or "said" "and offered by them, and what seemed unworthy of being received, and had no relation" [or "was of no consequence"].

NOTE 653.—That is, "*every where*," or, "*hither and thither.*"

NOTE 654.—"Sermonem" is one reading here, "sermones," another.

NOTE 655.—*Coleti* III.., 1268, id est, de ratione fidei.

NOTE 656.—"This was Acacius, Bishop of Melitine; in the Second Armenia, one of the Orthodox Bishops who had been sent to Constantinople. It is best, and only fair to him, not to receive this heretical account till his own side can be heard. Certainly, if he held to any such heresy, he differed from Cyril's explanations and the Third Synod's on that matter. If he had made any such wicked slip we may be sure that he at once corrected himself, or was at once corrected by the rest of the Orthodox Delegation, there present, I presume. There is an account of him under "Acacius (6)" in Smith and Wace's *Dict, of Christ. Biogr.* See also the index to vol. III. of *Hefele's History of the Church Councils*, under *Acacius, Bishop of Militine*," and the pages there specified. From those places Hefele speaks of him in the index there as "*of Monophysite tendencies, and opposed to Cyril.*" As yet, however, he had not become known as opposed to Cyril; and the above is the first accusation of his uttering any thing that favored Monophysitism and that comes from a Nestorian source. Afterwards, however, he is reported to have gone further in that direction (Hefele, *Hist. of the Church Councils*, pages 140, 183, English trans.) If he did so, he is simply an instance of men like Entyches, for instance, who in their zeal against one heresy have finally become involved in another.

conference (657) confessed that the Divinity is liable to suffering, and our most pious Emperor was so moved at those words that he shook off (658) the purple mantle which he was wearing, and drew backward at the magnitude of the blasphemy. Aye, we saw that the whole Senate also who were at the session strongly approved us because we were in reality sweating very much in labors for the true faith. Therefore it was pleasing to our most pious Emperor, that each one (659), should set forth his own faith, and offer it to his piety. But we answered that it is impossible for us to make any other Forthset (660) of Faith, except what was made in Nicaea by the most blessed Fathers (661). And that also was pleasing to his Imperialness. It remains, therefore, to offer to his Piety that Exposition in which your Sanctity has subscribed (662). Moreover, all the people of the city of Constantinople sail over to us (663), without cessation, asking that we shall valiantly contend for the faith, and we labor very much to keep them valiant, and at the same time quiet, and that we may not seem to give occasion (664) to our adversaries. Furthermore we have sent to your Religiousness a copy of the Exposition (665), that ye may deign to transcribe two authentic copies and subscribe them both" (666).

NOTE 657.—In *Coleti Conc.*, tom. III., col. 1268, this reads, "*in commentaries*," while in the *Synodicon* [col. 621, tome 84 of Migne's *Patrologia Graeca*, it is "inter gesta." The former may mean "*in the comments*," or "*remarks*," and hence may not be different in sense from the other version. Perhaps the *comments* or *remarks* were on the Twelve Chapters; as to which an annotation in column 1358 of tome III. of *Coleti's Concilia* remarks, with reference to a denunciation of them in the Mandate of the Apostatic Conventicle at Ephesus to their Delegates at Chalcedon above, as follows:

"Wonderful is the rage" [of the Apostasy] "about Cyril's Chapters, for no writing of the Schismatics is extant, in which there is not some mention of them, (Mira circa Cyrilli Capita rabies; nec enim ullum schismaticum extat scriptum, in quo illorum non fiat mentio).

NOTE 658.—Or, "shook out," excuteret.

NOTE 659. Unusquisque: this would seem to mean "*each one*" of the Delegates of the Apostasy. The Delegates of the Ecumenical Synod seem to have handed in the Acts or such part of them as had already been done, and they answered for its faith.

NOTE 660.—Expositionem; that is, the Nicaean Creed.

NOTE 661.—This showy way of speaking meant, after all, not that they were willing to accept the Orthodox sense of the Nicaean Creed as expounded by the Third Ecumenical Synod, which expressed the voice of that Universal Church which Christ commands us to hear (Matt. xviii: 17), but only their own creature-serving self will and wicked misinterpretation of that Creed.

NOTE 662.—Document XXVIII. below (Document XXII. from Coleti and Mansi) is an answer to this; and mentions the Exposition or Forthset above referred to. It alludes to Nestorius' case also, which is mentioned in Document XXX. below (Document, XXIV. from Mansi and Coleti),

NOTE 663.—The distance between Constantinople and Chalcedon, where the Delegates of the Apostasy were, is short, and can in ordinary weather be traversed by a rowboat or caique.

NOTE 664.—"Occasionem"; which in this case may be rendered "*advantage*" also, perhaps.

NOTE 665.—Latin, Expositionis.

NOTE 666.—I have translated the above Document from chap. XXVII. of the *Synodicon* in tome 84 col. 621 of *Migne's Patrologia Graeca*. It is also in tome IV. of Coleti and tome V. of Mansi. I have compared it with the other Latin version in tome III., col. 1268 of Coleti and tome IV., col. 1414 of Mansi.

On this document I would remark:

1. The last missive of the Synod of the Apostasy at Ephesus below, (Document XXII. from Coleti,) mentions the copies of the Exposition referred to in the last part of the above document, and states that it had subscribed them.

2. The sympathy of the erring Emperor for those creature servers appears thoughout this whole document, as does that of the Senate also. And it is clear that their heresies had many friends in Constantinople, though their boast that *"all the people"* of it were in their favor is doubtless untrue. God alone could enable the Ecumenical Synod to triumph against such odds in an absolute government, or, for that matter, in a democracy or in any other form of civil rule.

DOCUMENT XXVII. (XXI. FROM COLETI AND MANSI), RELATING TO THE APOSTATIC CONVENTICLE.

This Document is found in Greek in columns 1268-1274 of tome III. of Coleti's *Concilia*, and bears the heading there:

"AN EPISTLE OF CERTAIN ORIENTALS *who had been sent to Constantinople, to Rufus a Bishop.*"

It begins, *"John, Himerius, Theodoret, and the rest"* ["of the Bishops"] *"in order, wish joy in the Lord to the most dear to God and most holy fellow-minister Rufus."*

This therefore is an emanation of John of Antioch and the rest of the Delegation of the Apostasy at Chalcedon, to Rufus, who is thought to be Rufus, Bishop of Thessalonica.

Its aim is to enlist his aid, and the large Ecclesiastical jurisdiction of which he was the head against the Twelve Chapters of Cyril and the Third Ecumenical Synod. It says not a word on the expression, *Bringer Forth of God* (θεοτόκος).

It begins by complimenting Rufus, and regretting that he was not present at the Synod, and says that he would have been on their heretical side against what they are pleased to call, *"the confusions and daring disorders"* of the Ecumenical Synod and of the Orthodox, and charges it with *"adding heresies to the Orthodox faith and to the Evangelic and Apostolic teaching."* For, they tell Rufus that they knew his mind from the scope of his letter to Julian, Bishop of Sardica, because it held that the faith of Nicaea should be maintained and that nothing contrary to its expressions should be brought in, for, *"They suffice to show the truth and to convict the falsehood."* And they add, in effect, that Julian had followed that counsel by siding with them against Cyril and the Third Synod. And then directly follows an instance of their hatred of the Twelve Chapters. It reads thus:

"But many of those who came to the Synod, '*have gone out of the way,*' as the prophet writes, '*and have become unprofitable*,' (667) by forsaking that faith which they had received from the holy Fathers, and by subscribing the Twelve Chapters of Cyril of Alexandria, which are full of the wicked opinions of Apollinarius and agree both with the impiety of Arius and with that of Eunomius, and anathematize every man who does not receive that naked impiety. We have exceedingly opposed that outrage (668) on the faith, that is both those of us who have come together out of the Eastern Diocese (669) and the rest of us out of different Dioceses, in order that the faith set forth by the blessed Fathers in Nicaea may be strengthened. For, as thy Holiness knows, it lacks nothing" [useful] "for the teaching of the Evangelical dogmas, and for the refutation of all heresy (670). For that reason we continue to contend

NOTE 667.—Rom. iii: 12, quoted from Psalm xiv: 3, and Psalm liii: 3.

NOTE 668.—Or, "*That defilement* (λυμη) *of the faith*," or "*that ruin of the faith*."

NOTE 669.—That is the jurisdiction of the Patriarch of Antioch, which included all that part of the Roman Empire which is called the Diocese, or Government, of the Orient. That Diocese, as being the home of Diodore of Tarsus, and Theodore of Mopsuestia had become especially infected with their heresies on the Incarnation, Man-Service, etc. For the Oriental Diocese was proud of them, and so followed them especially as its teachers, as the Nestorians. I think, still do.

NOTE 670.—The Faith of Nicaea, that is, its Creed, Canons, etc., on faith, would have sufficed to meet heresies before it; but the rise of heresies after it rendered new Definitions necessary, as the rise of Arianism made the Definitions of Nicaea necessary. And those new heresies were the Nestorian opinions against the Incarnation, for Man-Service, and for Cannibalism in the Eucharist. I should add, however, that often a local Synod was sufficient to crush out a new heresy, or it smouldered along for years without becoming widely known, in which case no Ecumenical Synod decided on it. But if then, or afterwards, the heresy which had been crushed by a local council, or had only smouldered unnoticed by most, rose again, or burst forth, and became more general, it was met and crushed by a Universal Council. And so what are called Nestorian errors which arose in the fourth century in Syria, were not met by an Ecumenical Synod till they had spread much and endangered the purity and Orthodoxy of the whole Church. Then they became a common danger to all, and were condemned by all in the Third Universal Synod. The smouldering fire had burst forth and kindled a conflagration, and it was necessary to quench it. But this plea of the sufficiency of the Nicaean faith was intended to hide the heresies of those who made it. For, as we have said, again and again, above, they wished to be able to take those definitions in *their own heretical sense*, as the Arians wished to take the Scriptures in their own heretical sense. And when we hear a certain class of men in our day, who pervert the Scriptures to make them teach infidelity as to Christ's Divinity, declaiming against the Creed of Nicaea, and professing great respect for the principle, "*The Bible, the Bible alone the religion of Protestants*," we know that their concern and anxiety is not for the Bible, which they do not really believe in its entirety, but to be enabled to fix their own heretical and anti-literal interpretation on it. It was so with the profession of this Delegation of the Apostasy for the faith of Nicaea, and with their opposition to the faith of Ephesus. They wished to get rid of the latter that they might get free without penalty to pervert the sense of Nicaea to the ruin of souls by denying the Incarnation, and the Christ inculcated truth that God alone is to be served, (Matt. iv: 10). That is an old trick of heretics. In the struggle against the errors of Arius, which Diodore of Tarsus had opposed, and in the conflict against those of Apollinarius which Theodore of Mopsuestia had opposed, the great mass of the Syrian Church, in admiration of their work, had not noticed the grave blem-

for it, all of us together despising both the delightful and the sorrowful things of life, to guard and keep unharmed that paternal inheritance. For that reason we have degraded by deposition both Cyril and Memnon, the former as a heresiarch, the latter as having become his fellow-worker, and as his ally in all things to make firm and settled those Chapters which have been set forth to the corruption of the Churches. And we have excommunicated (671) those who dared to subscribe and to ally themselves with those dogmas which are hostile to piety, till they anathematize them, and return to the faith of those who assembled in Nicaea, but our long-suffering has in no respect profited those men, for till the present day they fight for those corrupt dogmas," (672)

Then they, humorously enough, tell Rufus that the Ecumenical Synod had done wrong, because they had not regarded those uncanonical and presumptuous and invalid inflictions of penalties enacted by about one-fifth of its members who were heretics and who had withdrawn from it. And further they accuse them of violating a canon (Canon IV.) of a local council of their own Antioch, which forbids a deposed Bishop to officiate till a Synod releases him, and orders all who communicate with such an officiator to be expelled from the Church. As though one-fifth of a Synod could depose or excommunicate four-fifths of it! Then they accuse them of making light of the power of binding and loosing left by Christ to the Church, because they would not regard such an outrageous and silly perversion of it by a mere heretical minority against an Orthodox majority!! And then they confess the failure of their outrageous perversion of the binding and loosing power, call the faith of Cyril and the Synod in those chapters "IMPIOUS HERESY," and again attack the Twelve Chapters and most inexcusably lie about them. The passage is so important as giving the Nestorian view of these Anathemas, that I here quote it in full:

"These things we at once determined to make known to Thy Holiness. And we have waited till the present in the expectation that there would be some change from these grievous circumstances, but have been deceived in that hope. For they have continued to fight for that impious heresy, and do not respect the counsels of the most religious Emperor either. For he, having met with them and us five times already, commanded them either to reject the Chapters of Cyril as contrary to the faith, or to undertake the contest for them" [by discussion], "and to show that they agree with the confession of the blessed Fathers (673). For we have ready the proofs, by which we have shown

---

ishes, the poisonous errors in those men's works. But insensibly, so far as the great mass of the Church was concerned, they had spread, especially in Syria, and God raised up the Third Synod to stay them. And, guided by his infallible Spirit, it did that work for all time. For all must finally come back to it.

NOTE 671.—Greek, ἀκοινωνήτους πεποιήκαμεν; literally, "We have made them excommunicate," or "we have put them out of the Communion."

NOTE 672.—*Coleti Conc.*, tom. III., col. 1269.

NOTE 673.—The Creed of Nicaea, not that of I. Constantinople. Another Credal state-

that those Chapters fight against the teachers of Orthodoxy (674), and very much agree with the teaching of the heretics. For he who composed those evil productions, teaches by those very Chapters that the Divinity of the Sole-Born (675) Son of God suffered, and not the humanity which he took (676) for our salvation: that is to say," [he teaches] "that the Divinity indwelling" [that humanity] "appropriates to Itself those sufferings as" [being those] "of His own body, though His Divinity did not suffer any thing in Its own Nature (677)

"And in addition to all that, he teaches that there has become but one nature from that Divinity and humanity. For he has so interpreted the expression, *The Word became flesh* (678) as" [to imply] "that His (679) Divinity underwent some sort of a change, and was turned into flesh.

"In addition to all that, he anathematizes those who separate (680) the expressions in the Gospels and in the writings of the Apostles concerning the Master Anointed (681), and understand those which are lowly, of the humanity, and those which are God-befitting of the Divinity of the Anointed One (682).

ment, said by some to be of Nicaea, condemns the Man-Service of the Nestorian party, for it forbids *bowing*, that is, *service* to Christ's humanity. See it elsewhere in this work. These heretics do not notice that.

NOTE 674.—No, not against the teachers of Orthodoxy, but against Diodore of Tarsus, and Theodore of Mopsuestia, both of whom and their writings, the first impliedly and the latter expressly, are now condemned in the Fifth Synod. Indeed, their heresies maintained by Nestorius were by necessary inclusion condemned with him by the Third Synod.

NOTE 675.—Greek, ἡ θεότης τοῦ μονογενοῦς Υἱοῦ Θεοῦ ἔπαθε, etc.

NOTE 676.—Greek, ἀνείληφε.

NOTE 677.—Greek, in *Coleti Conc.*, tom. III., col. 1272; τῆς ἐνοικούσης δηλονότι θεότητος οἰκουμένης μὲν τὰ πάθη ὡς ἰδίου σώματος, οὐδὲν δὲ πασχούσης εἰς τὴν ἰδίαν φύσιν. The Latin in the parallel column is: Enimvero homo perversorum germinum auctor per haec ipsa docet, divinitatemque unigeniti filii Dei passam esse, non autem humanitatem, quam pro salute nostra suscepit; cum divinitas inhabitans passiones corporis quasi proprii sibi attribuerit, et tamen in propria natura nihil ipsa pateretur. If the words above from "*That is to say*" to "*Its own Nature*," inclusive, are not an interpolation of some Anti-Nestorian copier they would serve to show that the Delegation of the Apostasy understood Cyril's view and explanation expressed in them. But the difficulty in deeming them a part of this document is that they seem to conflict with their other representations of Cyril where they accuse him of teaching that the Divinity of God the Word Himself suffered. Cyril had certainly made his meaning clear in the very Epistle which contains the Twelve Chapters, and in the other Epistle approved by the Synod as well as in his *Five Book Contradiction of the Blasphemies of Nestorius;* so that the Apostasy were inexcusable if they did not know them; and if they did, their conduct in accusing him of making the Divinity of the Word liable to suffering was still more inexcusable.

NOTE 678.—John i: 14.

NOTE 679.—Literally, "*the Divinity*" (τῆς θεότητος); that is, Christ's Divinity.

NOTE 680.—Or, "*divide*," Greek, τοὺς διαιροῦντας.

NOTE 681.—Greek, τοῦ δεσπότου Χριστου.

NOTE 682.—Greek, τὴν θεότητα τοῦ Χριστοῦ. These Man Servers do not tell the all important reason why Cyril attributed everything of both Natures of the Son to His Divinity. It was to secure, as he himself teaches, His due prerogative of service, etc., to God the Word, and that men might be taught not to worship the *Creature* whom God the Word had put on, which then as now, was a great and constant danger in the minds of the unlearned and unstable.

That is the very error which the Arians and the Eunomians hold to, and they, referring the lowly expressions on the Economy to the Divinity, have been busy to assert that God the Word is both a creature and a work, and of another substance than the Father and unlike Him" [in His Substance, etc]. (683)

"But from thence what may result, even of a blasphemous character, it is easy to see. For a mixing together of the Natures is brought in, and the expression, '*My God, my God, for what purpose hast thou left me*' (684) is ttributed to God the Word. And so is '*Father, if it be possible, let this cup pass from me*' (685), and the hunger and the thirst and the being strengt ened by an angel, and the saying, *Now is my soul troubled*' (686), and the expression, '*My soul is deeply grieved, even unto death*' (687), and all such things which happened to the humanity only of the Lord. And those assertions plainly agree with the impiety of Arius and of Eunomius, as any one can easily see. For those" [heretics] "not being able to make out with their *difference of substance*" [doctrine] (688) "ascribed, as has been said before, the sufferings

NOTE 683.—Here is another instance of the inexcusable misrepresentation and falsifying done by the Apostasy and its Delegates against Cyril of Alexandria and the Third Synod. The facts are as follows:

1. *Cyril opposed all service to creatures*; but the Arians and the Eunomians served a *created Word*, and the Apollinarians, I will add here, served a *Man*, or rather a part of a Man according to their ideas, that is the Man united to God the Word, whom the radical wing of them believed to have been destitute of a rational mind, and to have been transubstantiated into Divinity, or something else than common humanity, and whom all parties of them worshipped, and were therefore, in reality, according to the view of the Church, whatever their intentions may have been, *Servers of a Creature*. For the Church Universal in that Third Synod held that the Man put on was still *a creature*. And the Nestorian party, as two of these delegates, John of Antioch and Theodoret, in their yet extant writings show, worshipped that *Creature*, along with the Word, and were hence, on their own showing, *Creature-Servers*. See under their names in the *General Index* to this volume.

If the Arians and the Eunomians referred absolutely, and not economically only, the lowly expressions on Christ, that is the expressions which especially belong to his humanity to His Divinity, they did it that they might degrade his uncreated Divinity to the rank of a mere creature, and lead men to worship Him as a creature, whereas Cyril, *Economically* only, attributed them to God the Word, that he might teach men to look away from the creature, the Man put on, to God the Word for help, and to worship neither that Man, nor any other *creature* but God *alone*, according to Christ's command in Matthew iv: 10.

This Delegation of the Apostasy were therefore classing the Third Synod, which approved Cyril's Twelve Anathemas, and Cyril himself, with *creature servers*, when they were opposing *creature-service*; and when the "*Apostasy*," as the Ecumenical Synod term it, of John of Antioch and his party, had really become an "*Apostasy*" by going over to that error, which is fundamentally hostile to Christianity.

NOTE 684.—Psalm xxii: 1, quoted in Matt. xxvii: 46 and Mark xv: 34. I have made the English more literal by the translation above.

NOTE 685.—Matt. xxvi: 39; Mark xiv: 35.

NOTE 686.—John xii: 27.

NOTE 687.—Matt. xxvi: 38; Mark xiv: 34.

NOTE 688.—Greek, ἑτεροούσιον.

and the lowly expressions (689) to the Divinity of the Anointed One (690). And let thy God-Reveringness know that the teachers of the Arians now teach nothing other in their Churches (691), than that the teachers of the *same substance* (692) now hold hold to the doctrines of Arius, and that after a long time the truth" [Arianism] "has reappeared (693). But we abide in the doctrines of the blessed Fathers who assembled in Nicaea and of those who after them were eminent in the teaching" [that is] "Eustathius of Antioch, Basil of Caesarea, and Gregory (694), and John (695), and Athanasius, and Theophilus (696), and Damasus of Rome, and Ambrose of Milan (697) and those

NOTE 689.—That is the expressions in the Scriptures which speak of Christ as born in flesh as hungering, thirsting, suffering, dying, and all those which refer to his humanity.

NOTE 690.—Greek, τῇ θεότητι τοῦ Χριστοῦ.

NOTE 691.—Greek, ἐν ταῖς ἐκκλησίαις αὐτῶν. Perhaps we should translate by *assemblies* here, for St. Athanasius well teaches that, *"being Arians, they are not Christians."* See page 222, vol. I. of Chrystal's *Nicaea*.

NOTE 692.—Greek, Οἱ τὸ ὁμοούσιον διδάσκοντες. The Arians and the Eunomians both held that God the Word is of a different substance from the Father, and a creature.

NOTE 693.—As though, they mean, the Orthodox teachers now admitted that the creature-serving Arians were right all along! This misrepresentation of Cyril and the Third Synod is simply infamous; for the fact is that the Apostasy held with the Arians to the principle of *creature service;* for while they did not, like them, worship God the Word *as a creature,* they did worship the *created humanity* which He had put on, and so they were *Apostates,* as Ephesus calls them, to the Faith of Nicaea, because they forsook its fundamental principle that *God alone is to be worshipped* (Matt. iv: 10); a principle which Athanasius, its great champion, sets forth, again and again against the Arians as of the very essence of the difference between the Orthodox and them. See in proof Chrystal's *Nicaea*, vol. I., pages 217 240.

Furthermore, Cyril's ascribing of the human things of the Man put on to God the Word in his Twelve Chapters and other writings was intended, as He Himself states, to guard that truth, by giving its due pre-eminence to the uncreated Word over the creature put on, and to teach men to worship in Christ God the Word alone. See in proof Chrystal's *Nicaea*, volume I., pages 237-240; compare all the passages of Athanasius, on pages 217-240, and Epiphanius, Lucifer of Cagliari and Faustin on pages 240-252, id., and Chrystal's *Ephesus*, vol. I., preface, page ii.

NOTE 694.—Does this mean Gregory of Nyssa, or Gregory of Nazianzus? I have epitomized some of their utterances as to worshipping Christ's humanity, and on some things else elsewhere in this work: see also Tyler *on Image Worship, on Primitive Christian Worship* and on *Worship of the Blessed Virgin,* all three published by the London *Society for Promoting Christian Knowledge.* And see also in the General Index to Chrystal's *Ephesus,* vol. I, under *Fathers, Ambrose,* and the other patristic names above, and in that to this volume, and in that to vol. I. of Nicaea.

NOTE 695.—The reference is to John, Bishop of Constantinople, called Chrysostom, whose Orthodoxy is very much questioned, and, I am inclined to think, justly. The opposition of Theophilus of Alexandria and Cyril of Alexandria to that child of corrupted and creature-serving Antioch, was not without good reason, for it would have been a wonder, if, brought up as he was among the teachings and influence of Diodore of Tarsus and Theodore of Mopsuestia, he was wholly free from their heresies.

NOTE 696.—Theophilus of Alexandria, who did not hold the errors of the Apostasy.

NOTE 697.—This allegation of Ambrose's being on the side of not ascribing the lowly things of Christ's humanity to God the Word, (and nothing else is specified here by these

who taught the same as they did, and we follow their pious footsteps. And following the Gospel and Apostolic and Prophetic utterances (698), all of us who dwell in the East (699) study to keep unbent and unshaken the exact rule of Orthodoxy which they left us, and so also in like manner do the Bithynians, and the Paphlagonians, and the Second Cappadocia, and Pisidia, and Thessaly, and Mysia, and Rhodope, and very many others (700) from different provinces. And it is clear that there are also Italians who will not endure that innovation (701). For the most dear to God and most holy Bishop of the Church of Milan (702) has sent a letter to us and has sent forth to the most religious Emperor, a little book of the blessed Ambrose *On the Inman of the Lord* (703), which teaches things opposed to those heretical Chapters (704). And let thy Holiness (705) understand that it has not sufficed Cyril and Memnon to outrage and injure the Orthodox faith, but they have also trodden all the canons under their feet. For those who had been excommunicated from (706) different provinces and

delegates of the Apostasy), is not true, if it be meant that on that theme he wholly opposed the teaching of Cyril's Twelve Chapters and the Economical attributing to God the Word of the sufferings of the Man put on; unless certain documents alleged to be his, but which it seems to me may be spurious or interpolated, are really his. If he was, however, on the side of the heretics, so much the worse for him. If he was, he did not hurt the Ecumenical Synod, but is himself a heretic condemned justly by its decisions. The Synod approve only the work which they quote of his. They do not pronounce on all his writings or on the genuineness of those of them which are now suspected and doubted.

NOTE 698.—The Gospel utterances are those in the four Gospels, the Apostolic are those in the rest of the New Testament, and the Prophetic are those of, "the Prophets of the Old Testament, and the Revelations, the Prophetic book of the New, though there are prophecies in the Gospels and Epistles also.

NOTE 699.—That is in the Patriarchate of Antioch which included all the civil Diocese of the East.

NOTE 700.—As the issue proved, the above boast of numbers outside of the Patriarchate of Antioch, was for the most part, vain talk.

NOTE 701.—Greek, τῆς καινοτομίας ταύτης; they mean Cyril's doctrine approved at Ephesus.

NOTE 702.—Or, "*of the Milaners*," (τῆς Μεδιολάνων.);

NOTE 703.—Greek, βιβλίον . . . τοῦ μακαρίου 'Αμβροσίου περὶ τῆς τοῦ Κυρίου 'Ενανθρωπήσεως, (*Coleti Conc.* III, 1273).

NOTE 704.—Of Cyril, he means, which were approved by the Third and the other Ecumenical Councils after it. The Third deposed every Bishop and cleric who opposed their doctrine, and anathematized every laic; and the Fifth Synod anathematizes all who defend what the very Theodoret above named and what-others have written against them. See its Anathemas 13 and 14. These decisions are of force forever. Indeed they anathematize all who do not anathematize all those who wrote against "the *holy Cyril and his Twelve Chapters and continued in their impiety unto their death.*" See both those Anathemas for full statements. All that condemns all who write against the doctrine of the Incarnation or in favor of the Nestorian worship of Christ's humanity or against any tenet of the said Twelve Chapters, and all who do not anathematize them.

NOTE 705.—Greek, σοῦ ἡ ἁγιότης.

NOTE 706.—Greek, τοὺς γὰρ ἀπὸ διαφόρων ἐπαρχιῶν καὶ διοικήσεων γενομένους ἀκοινωνήτους εὐθὺς εἰς κοινωνίαν ἀνεδέξατο. This reception of excommunicated persons, provided the parties referred to had been justly excommunicated, would have been a violation of the

dioceses (707), they received at once to communion, and in addition to those, others also, who were accused of heresies, and of holding the same opinions as Celestius and Pelagius (708). For they are Euchites (709), that is Enthusiasts (710). And, therefore, they were excommunicated both by the Diocesan Bishop (711) and by the Metropolitan (712). Nevertheless they" [Cyril and Memnon] "despising the good discipline of the Church (713), received them into communion, and collected their multitude from every side and hastened to set

Canons; for as a Christian, cleric or laic, held communion with Christ and with his body, the Universal Church, through the sound Bishops of his own province and civil diocese alone, therefore if they cut him off from communion, the law had ever been to consider and to treat him as cut off by all. And they bring it as a grave charge against Cyril and the Third Synod that they had received such persons suspended from communion or utterly excommunicated, as the case may have been. It is enough to say in reply to this that there is not a particle of proof to show that either Cyril or the Ecumenical Synod at any time received any such person, who had been thrust out of communion by Orthodox Bishops. And we must well remember that no others, such as the creature-serving prelates of the Apostasy, had any authority to depose or excommunicate. For the Church never suffered any of her people so to regard heretical clerics of any order. On the contrary all the canons of the first four Ecumenical Synods forbid their authority to be regarded. Indeed they were regarded as having no authority at all. This is the teaching of the canons of Ephesus against those very Man Servers.

NOTE 707.—See the last note. By "Dioceses" here is meant the extent of a civil Diocese comprising two or more provinces. The Ecclesiastical Dioceses generally followed the civil forms, that is they were conterminous with the civil—see on that whole topic *Bingham's Antiquities*, book IX, chapters I. and II.

NOTE 708.—Here we see the Delegates of the Apostasy even, forsaking the Pelagians whom the Ecumenical Synod condemns in its canon IV.

NOTE 709.—These heretics took their name from εὐχή, *prayer*; and according to Sophocles were the same as the Massalians, "who maintained that men ought to pray always. . . . Theodoret intimates that the Massaliani exemplified their doctrine by *sleeping incessantly*." See Sophocles' *Greek Lexicon of the Roman and Byzantine Periods* under εὔχεται and Μασσαλιανοί. But they must have been bad enough to be too bad in their folly for the stomach of Theodoret, for in one of his works, his *Philotheus*, he exalts and praises the most warped and perverted types of monastic life, who came nearer being madmen or fools than Christians. See what Ruffner, in his *Fathers of the Desert*, vol. II, Chapter XXIII., has quoted or taken from him. The excesses of such unwise ascetics as Theodoret glorifies help Ruffner to reason, as he does in his vol. I, chapter X, against the Scriptural single life in wisdom.

NOTE 710.—They seem like many since to have had a zeal not according to knowledge and to have substituted rant and folly for sound Christian religion. They were therefore justly condemned by all Orthodox and sensible Christians.

NOTE 711.—The Bishop of the Civil Diocese, that is of the chief city of it is here meant—I purpose, God willing, to speak of that more at length when I come to write on canons II. and VI. of the Second Ecumenerical Synod, where this power of Patriarchs is authorized.

NOTE 712.—The Metropolitan was below the Diocesan, for he was Bishop of the metropolis of a province, whereas, the Diocesan was Bishop of the chief city of a Diocese. And as that chief city was the metropolis of a province also, it hence follows that the Diocesan was a Metropolitan also, but only in *his own province;* outside of it in the Diocese he was the Diocesan Bishop. He is termed a *Patriarch* by Socrates in chapter 8, book v. of his *Ecclesiastical History*, and an *Exarch* in Canons IX. and XVII. of Chalcedon.

NOTE 713.—Greek, τῆς ἐκκλησιαστικῆς εὐταξίας.

forth dogma tyrannically rather than piously. For inasmuch as they had stripped themselves of piety, they, as a matter of necessity, contrived another so: t of power for themselves" [that is] "walls of men," [for] "they thought that by streams of money they could overcome the faith of the Fathers, but none of those things will advantage them if thy Holiness puts forth strength, and defends piety with its shield as is its wont. Be exhorted therefore, most holy Lord (714), to be on thy guard against the communion of those who have dared to do those things and have brought in that heresy, and to make known to all, far and near, that those Chapters" [of Cyril] "are the heads and points of doctrine for which the thrice blessed Damasus (715) deposed (716) Apollinarius

NOTE 714.—Greek, δέσποτα ἁγιώτατε. More slavish, flattering, and disgusting Byzantinism, contrary to God's inspired Word.

NOTE 715.—This is an instance of the common enthusiastic and extravagant language of the East, an instance of which may be seen on pages 79 and 80 above, where Celestine is called a "*new Paul.*" That expression much better befits Cyril, to whom it is also applied there.

NOTE 716.—Damasus of Rome is meant. He was Bishop of that see from A. D. 367 to 384. Apollinarius was not of his jurisdiction, but by ancient custom, confirmed by canon VI. of Nicaea, was under the Patriarch of Antioch. What, then, do those seven Bishops of the Apostasy mean by the statement that Damasus had deposed him? I answer that the Canons of Nicaea, which were the only Ecumenical Canons when Apollinarius was condemned in Councils at Rome under Damasus in 377 and 378, gave Rome no right in the jurisdiction of Antioch, but, on the contrary, guard the rights of Antioch there. Nor does any of the canons of the first Four Ecumenical Synods (the only Ecumenical Synods that made Canons) allow of any appellate jurisdiction of Rome in any part of the Oriental Church. They allow, 1, an Appeal to the Synod of the Bishops of the Province, as, for instance, in Canon V. of Nicaea, Canon VI. of I. Constantinople, and Canon XIX. of Chalcedon.

2. An appeal above that to the Synod of the Bishops of the Diocese; as, for instance, in Canon VI. of I. Constantinople.

And, 3, Canon IX. of Chalcedon seems to allow a further appeal to the Patriarch of Constantinople; but that appeal to him has never been tolerated in any part of the Western Church. And, indeed, that is very unpalatable to some of the Eastern Communion and is not admitted in Bulgaria, anciently a part of the Thrace of Canon XXVIII. of Chalcedon, and though the Greeks have deposed or excommunicated the Bulgarians for their stand, nevertheless Russia does not accept that act.

Moreover, no appeal to Rome from outside of Italy is known to the Canons or tolerated in them. North Africa rejected it and forbade it under severe penalties in the fifth century. That is shown in Chrystal's *Articles* on that in *the Church Journal* (N. Y.) for 1870. That action was approved by the whole Eastern Church in the Trullan Synod of A. D. 691. I am inclined to think that the attempts of Rome to secure appellate jurisdiction over Carthage and Latin Africa under it, just before Chalcedon, induced the Orientals in that Ecumenical Synod to interpose that Canon IX. of theirs against all such tyrannous efforts. For in making the final appeal to Constantinople they most effectually forbade it to Rome, both impliedly and from the very fact that Constantinople, as the head of the Eastern half of the Church, was most interested from Church and State reasons to repel all dependence on that then great Western see, and to centre in the Eastern capital all the ecclesiastical forces of the Orient as its secular force was centered there; so unifying both, and making them mutually helpful. And that was the result.

What then do these Orientals mean by saying that Damasus deposed Apollinarius?

I answer that in cases of doctrinal controversy each Bishop, by regarding as valid a anonical deposition pronounced by the proper local authorities, that is to say, the pro-

and Vitalian, and Timothy, the heretics (717), and that no heed should be given in simplicity to the letter sent forth by him (718), for he has hid his heretical meaning in it and has" [merely] "colored it with the dogma of piety. For in those Chapters he has made very plain his impiety, and there has dared to anathematize those who do not so think. And in the Epistle he has attempted by every means (719) to injure the more simple sort. Let not thy Holiness therefore, despise this business, lest hereafter when it (720) sees that heresy strengthened, it be grieved and distressed in vain, because it can no longer succor piety. Moreover, we have also sent a copy of the document (721)

vincial or diocesan Synod, was said to depose that man. And Antioch before that had deposed Apollinarius, who was of its Patriarchate. So, if he recognized a canonical excommunication of another's jurisdiction he was said to excommunicate him, as indeed he did from his own jurisdiction. And when all the great sees had so spoken in confirmation, the decision was practically universal and rendered an Ecumenical Synod unnecessary. But in case some recognized the ocal sentence of the proper Synod to which the offender was subject, and others did not, an Ecumenical Synod became necessary, and its decision was final and settled the thing forever. Pelagius is a case in point: his excommunication by Rome did not settle his case, but it was settled by the Third Synod. And Apollinarius was finally condemned by the Second Ecumenical Synod in its canons I. and VII.

Or to put the same thing in other words; there was an appeal to the episcopate, the sole supremely governing power of the church, as individuals; like this appeal to the episcopate of the whole world on the case of Apollinarius. And their general agreement often settled the matter without an Ecumenical Synod. This was *the appeal to the church distributive.*

And there was an *appeal to it collected in Ecumenical Synod*, and this matter of Apollinarius came, after Rome and some Eastern Sees had decided, but it was finally settled forever by that supreme and final tribunal. In both these ways every Bishop had a hand in settling every controversy everywhere in the whole Church. Compare what the learned Bingham says on this theme in chapter V., book II., of his *Antiquities*. Another thing should be noted here. The Metropolitan of Thessalonica, though it was a Greek see, was at this time, owing to the former civil division of the Empire, under the Bishop of Rome to a certain extent; see Wiltsch's *Geography and Statistics of the Church*, English translation volume I., pages 17, 27, 30, 46, 130, and especially 463 and after. So that the Delegates of the Apostasy could in effect say to Rufus of Thessalonica, You should decide for us against Cyril because he is an Apollinarian, (a Nestorian lie, of course,) and the Roman see to which you belong has already decided against him in assenting to the deposition of his master Apollinarius. Macedonia had formerly belonged to the Western Empire, yet for some time after that its Church and its Metropolitan see, Thessalonica, were still deemed to be under Rome, but later were reunited to the more congenial race from which they had sprung, and to the Eastern Empire. See on that, Wiltsch as above, and Gibbon's *Decline and Fall*, under "*Empire, Roman,*" and "*Macedonia.*" Besides, as the Delegation of the Apostasy probably did not understand Latin, and did Greek, they may have supposed that they could make a Greek, Rufus, connected with Rome, an intermediary to the Latin speaking Churches to win them to their heresies.

NOTE 717.—These were all Apollinarian leaders, on whom see under "*Apollinaris,*" page 134, vol. I. of Smith and Wace's *Dictionary of Christian Biography*, "Timotheus (3)," page 1028, vol. IV., id. and *Vitalius*, (the *Vitalian* above,) on page 1164 of the same volume. The last two had visited Rome and tried to prove their Orthodoxy, but finally failed and its Bishop at last agreed with the prior judgment of their own East on them.

NOTE 718.—The letter here meant is not specified.

NOTE 719.—Or "*villainously*" or "*craftily,*" πανούργως.

NOTE 720.—That is, Rufus' Holiness, that is, himself.

NOTE 721.—Greek, τοῦ τόμου.

An Epistle of the Delegates of the Apostasy to Rufus.   385

which we have given in to our most pious and Christ-loving (722) Emperor, which contains the faith of the holy Fathers" [who met] "in Nicaea. In it we have rejected the heretical Chapters recently brought in as an addition" [to it] "by Cyril, because we have judged them to be alien to the Orthodox faith. But inasmuch as only eight of us have come to the city of Constantine (723), (the most religious Emperor having so commanded), we have subjoined also a copy of the mandate given to us by the Holy Synod to give information of the provinces represented in it (724): what they are, thy Holiness can ascertain from the subscriptions of the (725) Metropolitans (726). We greet all the brotherhood together with thee" (727).

And so this Epistle of the eight Delegates of the Apostasy to Rufus ends.

It failed of its errand. It was to stir up opposition to the Third Council in Europe, but it fell flat and stale. Rufus himself was absent on account of sickness but had given his proxy to Flavian of Philippi in the same Macedonia, who vouches for his Orthodoxy and signs third among those whose names are subscribed to the deposition of Nestorius (728), pages 23, 489, vol. I. of *Ephesus*.

The reader will notice again that throughout this whole Document, the strength of the Apostasy was directed against Cyril's Twelve Chapters, that is Anathemas. They are the only doctrinal difference mentioned. Not a word is said by them specifically in it on the expression *"Bringer Forth of God"* (θεοτόκος), which is authorized and approved in Anathema or Chapter I. But they oppose again and again the doctrine of Cyril's Chapter VIII, which condemns the co-worship of Christ's humanity with God the Word, and anathematizes every one who is guilty of it.

And one other thing should be well remembered, and that is that though John and his friends of the Apostasy constantly in the foregoing Documents accuse Cyril and the Third Synod of being Apollinarians, nevertheless they themselves agreed with those heretics in worshipping the humanity of Christ, the only difference between them on that point being that the Nestorians worshipped all of it, body, soul and mind, whereas the Apollinarians, not believing that it had any human mind, worshipped only his body and soul.

NOTE 722.—Literally. "Anointed-One-loving Emperor," that is, "our Emperor who loves the Anointed One:" (φιλοχρίστῳ βασιλεῖ ἡμῶν.)

NOTE 723.—That is, Constantinople.

NOTE 724.—Literally, *"lying in it:"* τῶν ἐγκειμένων αὐτῷ ἐπαρχιῶν, hence perhaps also *"devoted to it."*

NOTE 725.—Or, *"their Metropolitans."*

NOTE 726.—John's Apostasy had in it a large proportion of Metropolitans to suffragans, and the Diocese of the Orient, John's jurisdiction, was especially rich in Metropolitical sees. And the design of mentioning them seems to have been to give a false impression of the number of Bishops at the Apostasy or represented in it, so as to make a big showing and so win Rufus. See page 32, note 73, and pages 32-38, vol. I., *Ephesus*.

NOTE 727.—I have translated the above from *Coleti's Concilia*, tome III., col. 1268-1273.

NOTE 728.—See these facts told by Flavian in col. 1009 and 1077, in tome III. of *Coleti's Concilia*.

On that I find the following matter quoted in note 30, page 311, volume I. of *Smith's Gieseler's Church History*, from Apollinarius in Gregory of Nyssa's *Contradiction of the Dogmas of Apollinarius*, chapter 44.

"*The flesh of the Lord is to be worshipped, forasmuch as it is one Person and one living being with him. Nothing made is to be worshipped with the Lord, as His flesh is*" (729).

Again in chapter 23 of the same work Apollinarius says what shows that his man was only a part of a man:

"*He is not a man, but like a man*" [Philippians ii: 7], "*because he is not of the same substance with man as respects the chief thing;*" [the mind?] (730).

The assertion that he is not of the same substance as man contradicts Holy Writ, as for example Heb. ii, 14.18; Galat. iv: 5, etc., and I. Cor. ii: 16; and it contradicts also the Definition of the Fourth Ecumenical Synod, Chalcedon, A. D., 451, and that of the Sixth, III. Constantinople, A. D., 680, both of which assert that God the Word is Consubstantial with the Father as respects His Divinity and Consubstantial with us as respects his humanity, and that he is a complete, a perfect man, and not two-thirds only of a man as Apollinarius held.

Apollinarius held furthermore that while the Word is in place of a human mind, lacking in Christ's manhood according to his heresy, the other two parts of it, the body and soul, are mixed with Divinity, for as in Maii *Script. Vett. Nova. Coll.*, VII, 1, 16, he writes:

"*We call the Lord a man with a mingled nature, even one nature of flesh and Divinity mingled together.*" (731)

Hence he was a creature worshipper like Nestorius, but worshipped only two parts of Christ's humanity and those mingled with his Divinity, as has just been said. But in the main error they were alike, contrary, as Cyril often writes, to Christ's own law in Matthew iv; 10, "*Thou shalt worship the Lord thy God, and Him only shalt thou serve,*" and contrary also to another favorite text of Cyril, Isaiah XLII: 8.

NOTE 729.—Greek, Ἡ σὰρξ τοῦ Κυρίου προσκυνεῖται, καθὸ ἐν ἐστι πρόσωπον καὶ ἐν ζῶον μετ' αὐτοῦ. Μηδὲν ποίημα προσκυνητὸν μετὰ τοῦ κυρίου, ὡς ἡ σὰρξ αὐτοῦ.

NOTE 730.—Greek, Οὐκ ἄνθρωπος, ἀλλ' ὡς ἄνθρωπος διότι οὐχ ὁμοούσιος τῷ ἀνθρώπῳ κατὰ τὸ κυριώτατον.

NOTE 731.—Greek, Μιᾷ δὲ συγκράτῳ τῇ φύσει ἄνθρωπον τὸν Κύριον λέγομεν, μιᾷ δὲ συγκράτῳ τῇ φύσει σαρκικῇ τε καὶ θεϊκῇ.

Another of Apollinarius' followers, Polemius. differed from him and went still further from God's Word of the New Testament by asserting that "*the body of the Lord came down from the heavens, and that the body of Christ is of the same substance as the Divinity*" ! ! !

DOCUMENT XXVIII. (XXII. FROM COLETI AND MANSI) RELATING TO THE APOSTATIC CONVENTICLE.

This is found also in the Basel edition of Robert Winter, where it bears the title:

"*Copies*" [of a letter] "*of* THE ORIENTALS (732) *to their brethren who are at Constantinople*" (733).

There is another Latin translation in the *Synodicon of Monte Casino*, which a note in col. 1275, 1276 of tome III. of Coleti pronounces to be "*less approved.*" That however is disputable, though both are imperfect. It is in chapter XXVIII there, and according to note "c," col. 289, 290 of tome IV. of *Coleti's Concilia*, it has no title there. Coleti gives it in his tome III. from Winter's edition, as he tells us in col. 1275, note 1, in that tome.

In tome III. col. 1275, 1276 of tome III. of *Coleti's Concilia*, the heading is as follows: I translate availing myself of the different or varying readings there and in the *Synodicon of Monte Casino*. The Greek seems not to be extant.

"Copies of a Letter to the Brethren who in the common name of all, were acting as a Delegation at Constantinople.

"To the in all respects most pious and most holy and most religious Fellow-Bishops, John," [another] "John, Himerius, Paul, Macarius, Apringius, Theodoret, Helladius, Bishops; the Synod which is congregated at Ephesus (734), wisheth salvation in the Lord.

"Since we have learned of the struggles (735) which by God's grace ye have maintained for the piety of the faith before our Christ-loving and most pious Emperor, we have perceived by experience that the Lord Jesus Christ has not forsaken his Churches; and so that He has shown such favor to us as is deserved by those who are Orthodox, and has put our enemies to much shame and confusion, and has made (736) our most pious Emperor to favor (737) the right faith of the most holy Church. And we trust that if ye, able priests of Christ, contend with the liberty and confidence which befits ye, and if the Lord preserves the most pious life of our Emperor, the present affair will have a pacific termination and that the heresies will be branded with infamy, but that the Orthodox faith of the holy Fathers will again shine forth throughout

---

NOTE 732.—That is the Bishops of John of Antioch's Patriarchate of the Orient who formed the bulk of the Apostatic Conventicle. It seems to be used here for the whole Synod of the Apostasy.

NOTE 733.—That is the Delegation of the Apostasy who, however, whatever may have been the expectations of that Conventicle, were not allowed to enter Constantinople, but were halted at Chalcedon, opposite it.

NOTE 734.—The Apostasy, not the Ecumenical Synod.

NOTE 735.—The Basel edition (in col. 1275. tome III. of *Coleti's Concilia*) has "*your labors*", instead of "*the struggles.*"

NOTE 736.—The *Synodicon* has "*prepared*" instead of "*made.*"

NOTE 737.—The Basel edition has '*to approach*" instead of "*to favor.*"

all the Churches of the whole world. But our enemies do not yet cease to use their wonted tyranny, because they have experienced no punishment (738). For sending everywhere throughout our Churches their unlawful condemnations, they disturb both clerics and laics.

"Moreover, we have subscribed in the two uniform Epistles which have been sent to us by your Sanctity, in respect to which we pray that ye oppose even unto blood that impiety which has lately risen, and so war for the truth, knowing that we, remaining in accord with your Sanctity, are prepared to give up life sooner than to to receive any one of the heretical Chapters of Cyril of Alexandria (739).

"Verily when we learned of those things which have been done against the person" [Nestorius] "who has suffered injustice, we were shocked into the silence that comes of utter amazement (740). For those who have deposed him, have in their heretical Acts themselves, joined the heretical Chapters, as ye know, to the faith of the Fathers (741), and by that fact they have branded themselves as heretics and as aliens from the Orthodox faith. How therefore, I ask, (742), can those two things which are contrary to each other agree, that is the approving of the deposition" (of Nestorius] (743), "and the disapproval of the Chap-

NOTE 738.—The *Synodicon* has "*no vengeance*," that is, "*no punishment*;" the Basel edition (col. 1275, tome III. of Coleti) has "*no indignation*." The *Synodicon* reading is in col. 289, tome IV. of *Coleti*.

NOTE 739.—Hence not the Eighth of them which condemns and anathematizes the Nestorian worship of Christ's humanity, and by necessary inference the worship of any other creature, be it saint or angel, or any other of the XII. Chapters, be it that which teaches the Incarnation, the doctrine of Economic Appropriation or any other. This reveals to their own who shared it the depth of their heretical unbelieving and creature worshipping degradation.

NOTE 740.—The Emperor had failed them.

NOTE 741.—This certainly implies that even the Apostasy knew that Cyril's Twelve Chapters had been received by the Bishops of the Third Ecumenical Synod as an authoritative explanation of the Creed of Nicaea. That they have been approved by Ecumenical Synods is shown in Chrystal's *Ephesus*, vol. I., pages 204-208, note 520.

NOTE 742.—As the singular is here used in both Latin versions, (in one *Quaeso;* in the other *oro*,) it looks very much as though this document was the work of one man; and as, farther on, he states "*we have with us several Bishops who have remained alone*" [or "*desolate*"] "*in their own places of abode*," it seems that some of them were really forsaken by their own clergy and people. See pages 247, 248 above. The language of the Orthodox in one or more of these documents states that some of the Bishops of the Apostatic Conventicle were really not Bishops, but were under censure. This language agrees so far with that. But their names are given to make a show on the Apostatic side; perhaps there had been an agreement that they should help the Apostasy and the Apostasy should help them to regain their sees. At any rate the Apostasy try to help them now, while confessing, however, that they had been forsaken so thoroughly in their own provinces as to be "*alone*." See n. 750 below.

NOTE 743.—Nestorius' name is not mentioned by the Apostasy here on account probably of the odium attached to identifying themselves with him, but the whole tenor of this epistle shows that they were heartily in sympathy with him and his heresies, with the possible exception, in the case of some of them, of his denial of the Incarnation. And even that is not so certain. The bulk of them, surely never at this time, none of them so far as appears, had formally and definitely approved that fundamental and necessary doctrine.

The Conventicle of the Apostasy to their Delegates. 389

ters? For if those men (744) deserve to be trusted" [and followed] "in their condemnation" [of Nestorius], "those same persons are not to be held as undeserving of trust" [and of being followed] "in those heretical Chapters which they have set forth (745). But if the Chapters prove them to be heretics, the deposition also has been made by heretics. We have said these things even to our most pious Prince and have sent a copy of them to your Sanctity, that ye may do what shall seem good to you (746). For we are agitated, in regard to what we say in sadness for the truth, lest if the degradation" [of Nestorius] "which has been made by the heretics, and the heretical Chapters obtain any strength and validity, so also may the other things which have been done by them against many priests (747). And inasmuch as your Sanctity knows them all, we trust that it will do that in regard to them which shall result in the annulling of all those things which have been done against all by the heretics,

---

NOTE 744.—The Bishops of the Third Ecumenical Synod are meant.

NOTE 745.—The Bishops of the Third Ecumenical Synod had embodied in their Acts the Epistle of Cyril of Alexandria, which contains his Twelve Chapters, and had sent it forth to the Emperor and to the world with their approval. Indeed, above we find the Nestorian statement again and again that the Bishops of the Third Synod approved, aye, even subscribed them; see for example on that whole topic, pages 250, 251, 255, 256, 261, 269, 270, 279-285, 302-312.

NOTE 746.—The reasoning above is designed evidently for the Emperor, and those who with him at first rejected the Twelve Chapters of Cyril, while they later admitted as just Nestorius' deposition by the Ecumenical Synod, inflicted for opposing the doctrines in them. They had felt sure of the Emperor being doctrinally on their side. Nestorius himself had boasted of it in a sermon at Constantinople before the Council met. And it seems most likely that he was in part so still, though he was in the drift to change. But he and all like him were inconsistent so long as they admitted Nestorius to have been righteously deposed, and yet sympathized with the heresies for which he had been righteously degraded from the episcopate. But at this time the Emperor had become so thoroughly disgusted with him, that, as one of those heretical documents attests, he refused to listen to any thing further in his favor. See above, pages 358, 359, 361, 362.

But from the tenor of this document and from that of their Delegates to them, just above (Document xxvi. here, page 373 and after), it seems likely that they were written about the time of the Emperor Theodosius' the Second's Third Edict, when he recognized as valid the deposition of Cyril and Memnon by the Apostasy, and so gave them joy; while, on the other hand, he saddened them by recognizing also as valid the deposition of their friend and fellow heretic, Nestorius.

NOTE 747.—"*Priests*" is here as often used for "*priests*" in the highest sense; that is, Bishops: in this case all the Bishops of the Apostasy who, by their maintenance of the cause and heresies of Nestorius had brought themselves under the censures of the Ecumenical Synod, and were justly liable to deposition and excommunication. But in a true sense every Christian laic is a *priest* "*to offer up spiritual sacrifices acceptable to God by Jesus Christ*," I. Peter ii:5, 9; compare Rev. i:5, 6. He is also one of "*a chosen race*," as the Greek of I. Peter ii: 9, γένος έκλεκτόν, literally means, not "*chosen generation.*" And his sacrifices, being "*spiritual,*" are for that very reason higher than the *carnal*, that is, *fleshly ordinances imposed on the priesthood of the Jewish people* (Exod. xix:6, etc.), only *till the time of Reformation* in Christ (Heb. ix:10). Christians are now the only people of God and His only priests (I. Peter ii:5, 9), the Jews being rejected (Mark xvi: 16: John iii: 5; Rom. xi:7-36; Rev. iii: 9), etc.

that is either by deposition (748), or by excommunication, by Synodical letters and by imperial decrees (749). For your Religiousness is not ignorant that we have with us several Bishops who have remained alone in their own places of abode (750).

"Finally, we have sent to your Sanctity that Explanation which has lately been made by the Alexandrian Cyril of his heretical Chapters. Even in that very Explanation he shows still more clearly (751) his impiety. (752).

"Moreover, as we have prayed your Sanctity, deign to have a care that we may be dismissed" [homewards] "straightway (753), especially because the winter time is at hand.

"I, Tranquillinus, Bishop of the Antioch, which is the Metropolis of Pisidia (754), beseech that ye may be safe and sound and pray for me to God.

NOTE 748.—The Basel edition (in Coleti *Conc.*, tom III., col. 1275) has "*deposition*" but "*condemnation*" is the reading of the *Synodicon of Monte Casino*, which in this document seems to be more correct than the other translation, generally, though not perhaps in this case.

NOTE 749.—Nestorius had been deposed, and John of Antioch and his little Synod of the Apostasy were practically and indeed canonically excommunicated; and so they now fear for themselves, though whoever subscribed this heretical document still showed his virus against God's Anti-Creature Serving truth. See what is said in the above quoted words a few notes below this.

NOTE 750.—The Latin translation in the Basel edition (in col. 1275, 1276 of tome III. of Coleti) here reads, "*For thy Piety is not ignorant that we have with us certain Bishops left alone*" [or "*desolate*"] "*in their own provinces.*" But the readings are reconcilable; for their places of abode were, of course, in their own provinces. See note 742, page 388, above.

NOTE 751.—The Basel edition here (col. 1276 of tome III. of Coleti) has "evidentius," the *Synodicon of Monte Casino* has "subtilius." But *subtilius*, like *evidentius*, has sometimes the sense of '*more clearly*.' So that there is no contradiction in the two renderings.

NOTE 752.—In the translation in col. 1276 of tome III. of Coleti this reads, Demum misimus vestrae Sanctitati recens factam Expositionem ab Alexandrino haereticorum capitulorum, evidentius etiam per illam ostendente suam impietatem.

In the *Synodicon*, chap. xxvii. (col. 623 of tome 84 of Migne's *Patrologia Graeca*) this place is rendered:

Direximus autem Sanctitati vestrae et eam quae nuper facta est, interpretationem haereticorum Capitulorum ab Alexandrino Cyrillo, impietatem suam etiam per ipsam subtilius ostendente.

I understand the reference here to be to Cyril's explanation of the *XII. Chapters*, which was delivered at Ephesus.

Three works of Cyril of Alexandria on his *Twelve Chapters* are extant: 1, his *Apology for the Twelve Chapters against the Orientals*, his opponent in that case being Andrew, Bishop of Samosata, writing as a representative of his Patriarchate of the Orient. 2, his *Apology*, or *defence of the same Chapters against Theodoret*. And, 3, his *Explanation of the Twelve Chapters delivered at Ephesus*. The first two, according to Garnier, in col. 313-316 of tome 76 of Migne's *Patrologia Graeca*, were written before the Ecumenical Synod of Ephesus, the last during its continuance. Andrew remained a bitter and irreconcilable opponent of the *Chapters*, but owing to ill health was not at the Ecumenical Synod. He and Theodoret were considered two of the ablest men of the Patriarchate of Antioch, but were heretics whose errors are condemned by the Third Synod.

NOTE 753.—The *Synodicon* has "*quickly*," "celerius;" the Basel edition, "*straightway*," "statim.'

NOTE 754.—The Apostolic sees sometimes, as here, went far astray.

An Epistle of the Conventicle of the Apostasy to their Delegates. 391

"And the rest subscribed likewise," [namely]
"Helladius, Bishop of Tarsus
"Alexander, Bishop of Apamea,
"Julian, Bishop of Sardica.
"Bossorus" [better, "Bosphorus"], "Bishop of Gangra.
"Peter, Bishop of Trajanopolis.
"Cyrus, Bishop of Tyre.
"Rabbulus, Bishop of Edessa.
"Alexander, Bishop of Hierapolis.
"Maximinus, Bishop of Anazarbus.
"Dorotheus, Bishop of Marcianopolis.
"Asterius, Bishop of Amida.
"Pausinus, Bishop of Hypata.
"Dexianus, Bishop of Seleucia.
"Basil, Bishop of Larissa in Thessaly.
"Eutherius, Bishop of Tyana.
"Gerontius, Bishop of Claudiopolis.
"Musaeus, Bishop of Aradus.
"Placeus, Bishop of Laodicea.
"Martianus, Bishop of Abrytus.
"Cyril, Bishop of Adana.
"Fritilas, Bishop of Heraclea.
"Cyriacus, Bishop of Diocletianopolis.
"Antiochus, Bishop of Bostra.
"Daniel, Bishop of Faustinianopolis.
"Marcellinus, Bishop of Arca.
"Salustius, Bishop of Coria" [or according to Hardouin, of "Cotyeium"].
"Jacob, Bishop of Dorostolus.
"Theophanius, Bishop of Philadelphia.
"Meletius, Bishop of Neocaesarea.
"Diogenes, Bishop of Ninopolis" [or according to Hardouin, "of Jonopolis,"] "or 'Lonopolis,' according to the data given by Coleti in a note here.
"Polychronius, Bishop of Epiphania.
"Hesychius, Bishop of Castabala.
"Irajan," [or "Tarianus," according to Coleti,] "Bishop of Augusta.
"Cyrus, Bishop of Marcopolis.
"Polychronius, Bishop of Heraclea.
"Helliades, Bishop of Zeugma.
"Anastasius, Bishop of Tenedos.
"Valentinian, Bishop of Mallus.
"Julian, Bishop of Larissa.
"Diogenes, Bishop of Seleucobelus.
"Theotistus." [Theoctistus?] "Bishop of Caesarea."

This makes forty-two names, who with their eight delegates, make fifty, all told.

They were only about a fifth of all the Bishops who met at Ephesus. The other four-fifths were in the Ecumenical Synod. If those Bishops who were *"left alone in their own provinces"* be omitted, there is, of course, less than that aggregate.

In the above document, which, on account of its own importance as a matter of history, I have given in full, the reader will notice that not a word is said on the expression *Bringer Forth of God*, (θεοτόκος) but everything is made to turn on *Cyril's Twelve Chapters*.

One can see also that these heretics fully sympathized with their fellow heretic Nestorius. In not one of the foregoing documents of this Conventicle, or of its delegation at Constantinople is there a single syllable of condemnation of him; while on the other hand they do speak in his favor on the ground, according to them, that he was guiltless. This speaks volumes as to their own guilt.

DOCUMENT XXIX. (XXIII FROM MANSI AND FROM COLETI) RELATING TO THE APOSTATIC SYNOD.

This document is found only in Latin, but in two different versions: one in col. 1276 of tome III, of Coleti, and the other in col. 291 of tome IV. of Coleti, from the *Synodicon*. I use both for the following English rendering, but the latter from the *Synodicon* is sometimes the clearer.

Report of the Orientals who were sojourning at Ephesus, (755) *to Theodosius and Valentinian, the Emperors.*

To the most pious and Christ-loving Emperors, Theodosius and Valentinian, the August Ones, THE HOLY SYNOD WHICH IS CONGREGATED IN EPHESUS"(756).

This is a last effort, or one of the last efforts, of the Apostasy with the Emperor before they left Ephesus. They begin by thanking Theodosius II., because they had learned from their delegation at Chalcedon, whom they speak of as representing *"the whole Synod,"* that they had a benign access to him, *"and because,"* they add, *"your Majesty has much zeal for the Orthodox faith:"* they mean, of course, their own kind of orthodoxy, that is, Nestorianism and its errors. "For," they subjoin, *"we have learned how unacceptable to your just judgment were those things which have been done by our adversaries,"* that is, by the Orthodox Synod they mean, and they add that they had learned also on the other hand that their own understanding of the faith had merited a reception on his part. And then they say in effect, though in other words, that they believe that God had established him to maintain their own views; and that therefore they give God thanks. Then they make a last effort in behalf of Nestorius and against Cyril and the Twelve Chapters, and of course against

---

NOTE 755.—The Bishops of John of Antioch's Patriarchate of the Orient.

NOTE 756.—This full heading is found in the Latin in tome III. of Coleti, col. 1276. It is in a briefer form in the *Synodicon* in col. 291, tome IV., id.

A Report of the Conventicle of the Apostasy to the Emperors. 393

the Third Ecumenical Synod. And their language shows that they regarded Nestorius as right and Cyril and the Synod as heretical. And they imply, what was probably true at the first, that the Emperor had been on their side. For they add.

"But since priests have great liberty and confidence under your reign (757,) we trust also that your Majesty has learned of those things which affect us with sadness and with solicitude, and that it (758) seeks a remedy" [for them]. "Wherefore we entreat" [you] "and prostrate ourselves at your feet that you receive (759) with patience us who humble ourselves to your Piety, and justly make petition in regard to the person who has been injured by those (760) who have received the heretical Chapters of Cyril the Alexandrian (761) and have acted impiously against God Himself. For those who have introduced (762) the heretical Chapters have disturbed, in the very minutes of their acts, (763) so far as they could, the faith of the holy Fathers, and have made an unlawful deposition" [of Nestorius]. "And we believe that to your unbending" (764) [or "incorrupt"] "judgment it will by no means seem just that the condemnation made by them shall stand, for they themselves should certainly be condemned seeing that they are proven to be heretics. Moreover, your Majesty has already learned in detail, from many, those things which have been done by them both against ecclesiastical laws, and your most pious letters (765), while he" [Nestorius], "on the other hand, who has suffered injustice from them, has not gone against your edicts in any way, and has preached the Church faith Orthodoxically. For although he himself" [Nestorius] "is a man of the kind who would a thousand times rather flee from tumults and disturbances and avoid them, and would prefer to act in a private and quiet manner, nevertheless there is need for public action for we must fear lest some damage happen to the faith because that unlawful deposition has been wrought by those who have brought in, as an addition, the heretical Chapters. And the subscriptions" [follow]. And so ends this last effort of the Apostasy at Ephesus, for an Apostate from the truth that God alone should be served. The ancients well spoke of him as an $ἀνθρωπολάτρης$, that is 'a *Man-Server*,' and the Fifth Ecumenical Synod afterwards righteously

---

NOTE 757.—The *Synodicon* (Coleti IV., col. 291) has "*before your Imperialness.*"

NOTE 758.—"*Your Majesty,*" that is.

NOTE 759.—Or, "*lift up.*" The *Synodicon* here reads after "reign" instead of the words "we trust," etc., above: "We presume also to mention to it" [that is, "to thy majesty"] "those things which have greatly and closely agitated us, and we ask thee to care also for them."

NOTE 760.—The *Synodicon* reads, "*that person against whom a prejudgment has been made by those,*" etc., as above.

NOTE 761.—Here we see again further proof that the Orthodox Third Synod had received Cyril's XII. Chapters, and the condemnation of Man-Worship in the VIIIth. of them.

NOTE 762.—The *Synodicon* has "*subintroduced.*"

NOTE 763.—The *Synodicon* has "*in their very Acts.*"

NOTE 764.—The translation in col. 1476 of tome III. of Coleti has "*incorrupt*" instead of "*unbending.*"

NOTE 765.—His letters and commands to the Third Council.

warned the Universal Church against him and them as bringing in the sin of ανθρωπολατρεια, that is '*Man-Service*' (766), that is '*the worship of a human being.*'"

DOCUMENT XXX. (XXIV. FROM COLETI AND MANSI) RELATING TO THE APOSTATIC SYNOD.

It is the last document of the Apostasy here in Mansi and in Coleti.

This Document is found only in Latin renderings, one of them being in col. 1277, 1278 of tome III. of Coleti, and the other being in col. 294, 295 of tome IV., id., and more fully in col. 628, 629 of tome 84 of Migne's *Patrologia Graeca*. The latter constitutes chapter XXXI. of the *Synodicon* in the last mentioned places. I make a translation comparing both, and following each where I think it best.

In the translation in tome III. the heading is:

"AN EPISTLE *of* THE LEGATES OF THE SCHISMATICS *to their own in Ephesus.*"

In the *Synodicon* it reads:

"AN EPISTLE *of* THE LEGATES" [that is "*the Delegates*"] "OF THE ORIENTALS *from Constantinople to their own in Ephesus.*"

The reader will notice in it the usual hostility of these Man-Servers, that is worshippers of a human being, to Cyril of Alexandria's Twelve Chapters, and to the Third Synod which approved them, for so doing, and their entire sympathy with Nestorius and his errors, and the usual slanders on the Synod and on Cyril.

He will notice again also that neither in this, nor in any preceding Document here, did the Apostasy or their Delegation to the Emperor refer to the question of the expression "*Bringer forth of God*," (θεοτόκος), at all.

The Document begins:

"To the most honored (767) and most dear to God Bishops who sojourn in Ephesus, John," [another] "John, Himerius, Paul, Macarius, Apringius, Theodoret, the Bishops, wish health in the Lord.

"We have already gone in before the Emperor five times, and have contended much on the heretical Chapters. And we have more than often sworn to the most pious Emperor, that it is not possible for us to hold communion with those who hold contrary opinions, unless those Chapters be renounced; and that even if Cyril should cast away his Chapters, he will not be received by us because he has become the heresiarch" [or "the leader"] (768) "of that late

NOTE 766.—See on those two Greek words in Sophocles' Greek Lexicon, and on the last in the Definition of the Fifth Ecumenical Synod, and in the Greek Index to Chrystal's *Ephesus vol.* and vol. II., and in that in his *Nicaea*, vol. I., under the same and ανθρωπολατρεω.

NOTE 767.—Or, "*to the most honorable.*"

NOTE 768.—Or, according to the reading, in the Basel edition, "*chief*," (princeps).

An Epistle of the Legates of the Apostasy to the Conventicle. 395

heresy (769), but up to this time we have not been able to obtain any thing, because our adversaries (770) press on strongly, and those who hear do not chide them when they impudently resist, and do not compel them to come to an investigation (771) and a colloquy. For they flee in every way from a discussion on the Chapters, and do not permit any dispute at all on them (772). But we, through your prayers (773), are prepared to persist even to death, in not admitting Cyril nor the Chapters which have been set forth by him, and in not holding communion with those men, until those things which have been evilly added to the faith are banished. We therefore beg your Sanctity also, *as ye hold the same opinions with us*, to show the same perseverance (774) also. We have a contest for" [that] "piety (775) in which is our sole hope, and on account of which we hope to enjoy the kindness (776) of our Saviour in the future world (777)."

Here we see this little fragment who were under discipline speak with the tone of Masters and Lords of the Ecumenical Synod, which had rightly judged them. Can any thing be more impudent than their modest demands:

1. That the Bishops of the Ecumenical Synod, representing the Universal Church, regard themselves as excommunicate, and their leaders, Cyril and Memnon, as deposed, till they shall renounce their opposition to Nestorius and to the Apostasy's struggle against the true Doctrine of the Incarnation and for their heresy of Man-Service, that is creature service.

2. Even then they will not receive Cyril, whom they mention as a *heresiarch*, because he maintained the truth of God against their Apostasy to Man-Service. Of course, as the Bishops of the Ecumenical Synod followed the heresiarch, they were meekly to regard themselves as heretics, because this handful of heretics, with loud pretensions, called them so.

And then, without any break, and this time with a distinct and open mention of his name, they come to the case of Nestorius, and impliedly at least, identify themselves with his person and his heresies, and separate

---

NOTE 769.—In the Basel edition we find "*of the so impious heresy*," instead "*of that late heresy.*" Diodore of Tarsus, the founder of their own heresy, seemed ancient to them, only because they had been corrupted by his innovations of the preceding century. But the witness of the whole Church at Ephesus was that Cyril's faith was the ancient, and had been from the beginning.

NOTE 770.—Or, "*the adversaries,*" that is, the friends of the Third Ecumenical Synod, and their Delegates at Constantinople.

NOTE 771.—The *Synodicon* has "*debate*" instead of "*investigation.*"

NOTE 772.—The Basel edition has *from an examination of*" instead of "*from a discussion on,*" and the Synodicon has, "*and of themselves are not content to speak at all,*" instead of "*and do not permit any discussion at all on them.*"

NOTE 773 —A courteous expression to Bishops, still used sometimes in the East.

NOTE 774 —The Basel edition has "*labor*" instead of *perseverance.*"

NOTE 775 — Basel edition, "*for religion,*" instead of the *Synodicon* reading, "*for piety.*"

NOTE 776.—Or, "*benignity.*"

NOTE 777.—*Synodicon,* "*future life,*" instead of "*future world.*"

themselves from Cyril, and the Third Synod, from their persons and their Orthodoxy. For they continue immediately.

"But in regard to the most dear to God (778) and most holy Bishop Nestorius, your Religiousness knows that we were eager to mingle" [in our matters] "speech concerning him; but as yet we have not been able because all our adversaries are hostilely disposed even at the very mention of his name. Nevertheless though those things are so now, we will hasten, if we can find time, and placable hearers, to do that also without hesitation, if God will" [only] "stand forth as co worker with our intention. But as your Sanctity is not ignorant of that thing, know ye that we seeing that the Cyrillians (779) have turned, as we may say, (780) almost all upside down (781) by tyranny, and leading astray, and adulation, and gifts, we" [we repeat] "have frequently besought the most pious Emperor, and the most magnificent Judge (782) to permit us to go to the Orient (783) and your Religiousness to your own homes, for we deem that we are delaying here in vain, inasmuch as we make no progress in the present cause, because Cyril in every way flees from having a conflict with us, for he knows that the blasphemies which he has put forth in his Twelve Chapters will be clearly proven (784). Nevertheless after our many prayers it has pleased the most pious Emperor that each one of us shall return to his own home, so that the Egyptian and Memnon of Ephesus also shall remain in their own places. For the same Egyptian has been able so to blind all by his own gifts (785), that he himself indeed, after he has perpetrated many thousands (786) of evil things, shall return to his own see, but that an innocent man (787) shall be sent to his own monastery.

NOTE 778.—Or, "*most God-loving.*"
NOTE 779.—Notice the spite in this appellation. It reminds us of the spite of Arians in calling the Orthodox *Athanasians.*
But the faith was not from Cyril or Athanasius, as its source, but from the Scriptures, even from the Holy Spirit, although the Holy Spirit used them as instruments.
NOTE 780.—"As I may say," Basel edition.
NOTE 781.—Basel edition, "*deceived,*" for "*turned upside down.*"
NOTE 782.—The Basel edition has "*most magnificent princes,*" or "*most magnificent chief men,*" instead of "*most magnificent judge.*"
NOTE 783.—That is to John of Antioch's Diocese of the Orient, from which this Apostatic Delegation came, all or nearly all of them.
NOTE 784.—The true reason was that they were irreformable convicted heretics; and such persons, the Church, following the language of the Holy Ghost by Paul in Titus iii: 10, had ever avoided till they repented. Another motive might have been to avoid casting holy things before dogs, that is creature-servers, who might have turned upon and rent them then, but who could not later when the faith against Man-Service became established. And it is very doubtful whether the Emperor Theodosius II., and some others were sound on that point, especially the Empresses and perhaps others in high secular places.
NOTE 785.—There is no proof of course that Cyril bribed any one, or that any of the Orthodox did.
NOTE 786.—The Basel edition has instead of the reading above, *has "done numberless"* [or "*unnumbered*"] "*evils.*"
NOTE 787.—No! a heretic convicted on plain evidence of holding to the errors of denial of the Incarnation, worship of Christ's humanity, and Cannibalism on the Eucharist, not to speak of the others enumerated in note "F," pages 529-551, vol. I. of Chrystal's *Ephesus.*

"Both we and those who are with us, wish all the Brotherhood who are with you very good health.

"I, John, Bishop of Antioch, in the" [Diocese of the] "Orient, pray that ye may be strong in Christ, Lords most pious and most holy.

"Moreover, all the others also subscribed in like manner."

Here Cyril is a heresiarch, the Third Synod is the body of heretics whom he leads, Nestorius is innocent of heresy, and the Apostasy to creature-service who champion his cause are the defenders of Orthodoxy; and all those who had learned how the Universal Church had spoken by the Ecumenical Synod at Ephesus, and followed its Incarnation, Anti-creature Serving Decisions, according to Christ's command in Matt. xviii. 17, to *"hear the Church,"* are moved by the *"tyranny of the Cyrillians,"* as the Apostasy spitefully call them, that is of those who received the Third Synod and the Twelve Chapters read in its Act 1; though the tyranny of the civil power had at that time been wholly on the side of the Nestorians, and had been worked by them for all that it was worth to hinder the Ecumenical Synod from beginning its sessions, and after that from reaching Nestorius personally and face to face with their three citations to appear; and through it had imprisoned its leaders, Cyril and Memnon, because of their stand for God's imperilled Anti-Creature-Serving truth. Then follows the stale slander, strange enough on the lips of these Man-servers, that the Orthodox had been led astray; that they had been successful by adulation, when the fact is that these creature-servers had carried their Erastian adulation of the secular rulers so far as to give them the power to defeat the voice of the Universal Church, and were glad and exulted when they had deceived it into using it in attempting to stifle the Church's voice and to nullify its Decisions in that authoritative Council. They add the infamous and unproved assertion that the Orthodox had succeeded by gifts; a lie of a piece with their other slanders, if it means that the Orthodox had won by such means, in the great matter of all, the decisions of the whole Church at Ephesus against the Nestorians' denial of the Inflesh(788), and against their assertion of *the worship of a human being*(789), their real substance presence of Christ's humanity in the Eucharist, their worship of it there, and their Cannibalism of eating it there (790), and their other errors.

NOTE 788.—See vol. I., of Chrystal's translation of *Ephesus*, page 637, *Nestorius' Heresy* 1, and Nestorius' *Twenty Blasphemies* on pages 449-480, and note "F," pages 529-551, id.

NOTE 789.—'Ανθρωπολατρεια St. Cyril calls it. See under that word, page 694, vol. I. of Chrystal's *Ephesus*, and under 'ανθρωπολάτρης on page 693, id., and under *Man-Worship*, page 631, id., and Nestorius' Heresy 2, page 639, id., and under the connected heresies of denying the doctrine of *Economic Appropriation*, and of making a mere Man, a creature, our High Priest and Mediator, and not God the Word, on page 641, Nestorius' Heresy 3, and page 643, his Heresy 6, etc., and Nestorius' *Twenty Blasphemies*, pages 449-480, id., and note "F," pages 529-551, id.

NOTE 790.—See id., page 696, under ανθρωπυραγια, and page 642, Nestorius' *Heresy* 4, and his Heresy 5. See also under *Ephesus*, pages 604-611 id., and under *Keble*, *Kenrick*, and *King* and *Kneeling* on pages 629-630 id., and Nestorius' Blasphemy 18, pages 472-474, id., and for

But if it means that, after a custom then prevailing in the East, Cyril strove by gifts to propitiate certain powerful laics of doubtful Orthodoxy at Constantinople, and to win them not to hinder the decision of the Third Ecumenical Council from being received and enforced to the salvation of the faith and of souls, the assertion may be true, and that such gifts had some influence on them may or may not have been true. At any rate the Universal Church as represented in the Third Synod had nothing to do with Cyril's conduct in that matter, and was not responsible for it. Whatever responsibility there was, was wholly Cyril's and personal to him. And the laics referred to had no part in deciding at Ephesus against the heresies of Nestorius (791).

---

his deposition for that and his 10 other "*Blasphemies*" and his blasphemies at Ephesus pages 479, 480, 486-504, id.

NOTE 791.—On the gifts referred to see Hefele's *History of the Church Councils*, vol. 3, pages 81, 108, note 3; 112-114, and 134. So far as appears, the statement that Cyril sent gifts to Scholasticus, the influential Eunuch and Chamberlain, to win his favor, comes from Nestorian sources only, and is not absolutely certain.

WRITINGS OF THE ORTHODOX, BY WHICH THE PRECEDING CRAFTY FABRICATIONS OF THE SCHISMATICS (792) ARE REFUTED. (793)

INDEX OF THIS MATTER.

IT IS GIVEN AT THE BEGINNING OF THIS WORK IN THE TABLE OF CONTENTS.

ORTHODOX DOCUMENT I.:

"*Copy* (794) *of a* REPORT OF THE HOLY COUNCIL *sent off through Palladius the Magistrian* (795) *on the Calends of July, the seventh day of the month Epiphi* (796) on the xvth Indiction" [that is, July 1, 431, in modern time. CHRYSTAL.].

"TO THE MOST RELIGIOUS AND MOST DEAR TO GOD THEODOSIUS AND VALENTINIAN, VICTORS, TROPHY BEARERS, EVER AUGUST, THE HOLY SYNOD GATHERED IN THE METROPOLIS OF THE EPHESIANS BY GOD'S FAVOR, AND BY THE COMMAND (797) OF YOUR MIGHTINESS" [sends greeting].

"Your Mightiness wishing to make piety firm, enjoined the Holy Synod to make an exact (798) investigation regarding the dogmas" [of the Faith],

---

NOTE 792.—Literally, *Off-splitters*, τῶν ἀποσχιστῶν It may also be rendered *Seceders*

NOTE 793.—In Hardouin, Coleti, and Mansi, there are just sixteen of these documents of the Orthodox, which follow above. The *Collectio Regia* has only the first fifteen. Some of them, like the letter of Alypius for instance, are mere individual productions, while others, like the Reports of the Third Ecumenical Synod, speak the mind and decision of the whole Church.

NOTE 794.—The marginal reading in Hardouin, here, tom. I., col. 1581, 1582, is as follows: "otherwise, '*A Report of the Synod, written in reply to the imperial letter, and showing that the things reported by Candidian are false.*'" Hardouin (ibid), adds in explanation:

"But that imperial letter is put above, page 1538, and its beginning is: '*The most magnificent Candidian.*' It is the imperial letter to the Third Ecumenical Synod, which bears the date; '*the third day before the Calends of July,*'" that is, June 29, 431. It is among the Nestorian Documents between Acts VI. and VII. of the Third Ecumenical Council; and is the fifth of them in Hardouin, and the third in Mansi. It is Document V., page 257, above.

NOTE 795.—That is "*of Magisterial rank.*"

NOTE 796.—This is an Alexandrian and Egyptian month. It seems to imply that this Document was drawn up by an Alexandrian. On the relation of the Egyptian months to the Roman, see page xiii. of the Introduction to the Oxford translation of *S. Athanasius' Festal Epistles*. Both the date and the contents show that this Report was written between Acts I. and II. of the Ecumenical Synod. Its second session did not occur till July 10.

NOTE 797.—Greek, νεύματι.

NOTE 798.—Or, "*earnest*," σπουδαιοτέραν.

"which we have done, and we have obeyed (799) the ancient" [written] "transmission of the Fathers, and moreover of the holy Apostles and Evangelists and of the Three Hundred and Eighteen who were gathered at Nicaea, and we explaining it with" [but] "one voice and one mind, have made it clear to your Piety in the very Minutes which have been made" [of what was done]. "And in those proceedings, inasmuch as we found Nestorius to plainly hold opinions contrary" [to that written transmission of the Faith] "we deposed him. For, that there might be no lack of other proofs against him, he did not conceal even in the metropolis of the Ephesians (800) his own way of thinking, but kept crying out every day, and preaching to many his dogmas foreign to the Faith. And in the Minutes of the proceedings we have made plain to your Piety each thing part by part, (801). But since the most magnificent Count Candidian, preferring the friendship of Nestorius to Piety, has hastened to snatch away the hearing of your Piety, before your Mightiness exactly and thoroughly learned what has been done and before your Mightiness has received the Minutes," [and] "before your Mightiness has examined the things which have been done," [since] "that Candidian himself has hastened to report to your Piety those things which are dear to himself and which favor and please Nestorius, before your Mightiness ascertained the truth by reading the Minutes of what has been done; in which Minutes we show that we exercised no enmity against Nestorius, but set forth the very dogmas of piety, in which proceedings, comparing the things uttered by Nestorius, which furnish the proof of his guilt, and which were taken out of Nestorius' writings, both from his letters and from his discourses delivered in public, we passed the vote (802) with the Holy Gospel lying in the midst and showing us Christ (803) the Master of the Universe present to us" (804), [since, we repeat, those are the facts], "we beg therefore your Mightiness, that none of those who prefer men's friend-

---

Note 799.—Or, "*followed*," πειθόμενοι.

Note 800.—That is Ephesus. On this see the testimony adduced against Nestorius' utterances there in Act I. of the Third Ecumenical Synod, pages 377-418 text, and note 716 on page 416.

Note 801.—Or, "*separately and in detail*," ἕκαστα κατὰ μέρος.

Note 802.—Greek, τὴν ψῆφον ἐξηνέγκαμεν. Nestorius and his heretical letter to Cyril of Alexandria were both condemned by vote, and subscription, which in such a case is practically a vote. See in proof Chrystal's *Ephesus*, vol. I., pages 154-178, 449-480, and 486-504.

Note 803.—That is "*the Anointed One.*"

Note 804.—Greek in Coleti *Conc.*, III., col. 1280; τοῦ ἁγίου Εὐαγγελίου ἐν μέσω κειμένου, καὶ δεικνύντος ἡμῖν παρόντα τὸν Δεσπότην τῶν ὅλων Χριστόν. As Cyril's own writings show, he condemned the Nestorian one nature consubstantiation, that is, the error of a literal presence of the substances of Christ's flesh and blood in the Eucharist, and their manducation there. It is enunciated by Theodoret, one of that party. Both Cyril and Nestorius also condemn the error that the Substance of God the Word is in the Eucharist, and, of course, the blasphemy that it is eaten there. See his *Five Book Contradiction of the Blasphemies of Nestorius* in the places noted elsewhere in this work on that topic and other passages of his writings, there also noted. His view was the *symbolic spiritual energy* one, from

ship to piety be deemed worthy of acceptance (805). For we have perceived that the most dear to God Bishop John of Antioch also is of such a disposition as to wish to indulge his friendship (806) rather than to look to the advantage of the faith. We so infer from the fact that he, neither fearing the threat of your Piety (807), nor being moved by zeal for the dear to God faith which has been handed down from the beginning, delayed the Holy Synod for twenty-one days after the day granted and foreappointed by your Mightiness, and all of us, the Orthodox of the Holy Synod, who love the faith alone, were compelled to make an examination of the matters concerning piety" [without them]: "for we suspected that the most dear to God Bishop John was suffering from that

which no one of the Third Ecumenical Synod dissents. On the contrary, as Cyril's Five Books above mentioned were circulated before that Council, and as the quotations from Nestorius, on which, as a criterion, he was condemned in Act I. of it, emphasize the errors which Cyril especially condemns and denounces in that work, among them those on the Eucharist, the Third Ecumenical Council in condemning him for them, condemned his error of the Real Substance Presence of Christ's humanity in the Eucharist, which seems to have been that of his party. It is set forth by chief men of them, like their ablest scholar for instance, Theodoret. See in proof the note matter on pages 276-313, vol. I. of Chrystal's *Ephesus*. So that we must say that the Third Ecumenical Council condemned all Real Substance Presence views, both of the one nature kind, and the two nature kind, and approved the ancient symbolic spiritual energy doctrine. Cyril rejects in strong language the charge that he held to the real presence of the Substance of Christ's Divinity in the Eucharist and the eating of it there, and blames Nestorius' heresy of one nature Consubstantiation as resulting in *Cannibalism*. See vol. I. of Chrystal's *Ephesus*, under *Cannibalism, Eucharist*, and pages 472-474.

If the Synod had held to the Real Presence of the *substance* of one or both natures of Christ in the Lord's Supper, they would naturally have placed the consecrated Eucharist in the midst of the Council for it was then sometimes reserved, whether in the Church or in the Bishop's or Presbyter's home I know not, to send to the absent, to the sick and for the nst baptized, adults and infants, to whom it was then always given in the East (and *Ephesus* is in the East) at once after their baptism, and if they had held the Romish heresy that the Substance of Christ's Divinity and that of His humanity were there, they would, of course, have worshipped them as the idolater of our day does.

But the Orthodox Synod does nothing of the kind, but places the book of the Gospels there as His representative. And yet, what is noteworthy, they do not give even it relative worship as idolaters now do, by kissing, incense, etc. They reserve all acts of relgious worship for Divinity Itself, to whom, Father, coeternal Word, and coeternal Spirit, the alone God, they are prerogative (Matt. iv: 10), and to whom they are to be given directly and absolutely, not relatively through any material thing nor through any creature, which is soul-damning paganism.

See on the whole topic of the Eucharist and the decision of the Universal Church on it in the Third Synod, and the heresies of Nestorius on it and his worship of it, in vol. I. of Chrystal's *Ephesus*, notes 606, pages 240-313; 599, pages 229-238, and note E, pages 517-528; note 692, page 407, and note 693, pages 407, 408.

NOTE 805.—Or, "*of a reception*," παραδοχῆς.

NOTE 806.—For Nestorius, the meaning is.

NOTE 807.—The reference is to the Emperor's letter to all the Metropolitans in which he threatens them if they do not get to Ephesus by Pentecost, (Whitsunday, as it is faultily called among us, the day appointed for the Ecumenical Synod to begin its work. Pentecost on that year fell on June 7. See the Emperor's edict above, pages 33-42, and note 90 there.

same disease" [of preferring Nestorius to piety] "from which it is clear the Most Magnificent Count Candidian was suffering, for it is not characteristic of all to prefer friendship for men to piety (808). And our suspicion in regard to the most dear to God Bishop John, as the issue proved, was not rash nor vain. For when he came he made it plain to the Holy Synod, that he holds to the opinions of Nestorius, either to indulge his friendship for him, or because he is really a sharer of the error of the doctrine of that man.

"But since, as we have said, we are hindered from making clearly known to your Mightiness the things which have been done (for the most magnificent Count Candidian hinders us, on the one hand, from making known the things which have been done in accordance with the pious Word (809), and on the other, distributes all his zeal and efforts to favor Nestorius); we" [therefore] "pray your Mightiness that the godly efforts of the Holy Synod may be made known,(810) and the most Magnificent Candidian, be sent for" [by you] "and five of the Holy Synod to state and to defend before your Piety the things done. For those who hold opinions contrary to the right faith are skillful in hiding their error, so that some of the most holy Bishops even were deceived, because Nestorius concealed his error, and" [so] "they joined themselves to him, and subscribed to the things which were done under him. But since they questioned him clearly, and found him disclosing his own blasphemies, they have forsaken him and have come to the Holy Synod, and made clear his very blasphemy (811), and with us have voted the condemnation of the said Nestorius; so that only a little more than thirty-seven are left with Nestorius and with the most religious Bishop John of Antioch, of whom the most being under accusations, and fearing the vote of the Holy Synod (812), have joined themselves to Nestorius, as we have said, whose names we have sent off to your

---

NOTE 808.—The Synod mean that though John of Antioch and Candidian were actuated by mere human friendship as their controlling motive, the Orthodox were not but by regard for the faith alone which was imperiled.

NOTE 809.—Greek, τὰ κατὰ τὸν εὐσεβῆ λόγον πεπραγμένα; Coleti III., col. 1280. This may be rendered "done in accordance with pious reason," or, "in accordance with God's" inspired "Word," for the Greek admits both translations.

NOTE 810.—Or, "we pray your Mightiness that the godly efforts of the Holy Synod may be made known, and to send," etc.

NOTE 811.—Or, "have exposed his very blasphemy."

NOTE 812.—Although the primary intention of calling the Third Ecumenical Synod was to deal with the matters respecting Nestorius' error, yet, like Nicaea and I. Constantinople, it dealt with other matters, and had supreme jurisdiction on all Church matters, because of its being Ecumenical.

Hence it decided on the case of Eustathius, on the Massalians, on the rights of Cyprus, and by implication, it not by name, against the claim of Rome to jurisdiction in North Africa and antecedently against Rome's claim to sway in Great Britain and Ireland and here, and anywhere outside of Italy, and against any validity in Roman orders, etc., since she has become idolatrous. For, by the canons and other decisions of *Ephesus* all her Bishops, including the Bishops of Rome, and all her clerics, are deposed, and all her laics are anathematized.

A Report of the Orthodox Synod to the Emperors. 403

Mightiness. Some were accused for perversion in regard to dogmas, as being both Pelagians and holding opinions contrary to piety; while others were deposed many years ago, and others still being under other charges of evil, after their conviction, are to receive the" [due] "penalty from the Synod (813). And the Synod has all the most holy Bishops of the inhabited world holding one and the same doctrine" [with itself], "for both the Bishop of the great Rome (814) is present with the Synod and the Bishops of Africa through the most God-revering Archbishop (815) Cyril (816); to whom also they have joined their own judgment, and are separated from us in place only, and have assented to the vote both of him (817) and of us all. For not one of the most dear to God Bishops would have met with Nestorius and with the most religious Bishop John, if he himself had not been skillful in covering up his impiety under the appearance of" [good] "reasonings, and if those who are now with him had not feared the penalty (818) which was about to be decreed against them by the Holy Synod. But we are under durance and have not been able to write" [even] "a little of the breadth of those things which we have suffered, even from the Most Magnificent Count Irenaeus, who has thoroughly troubled all the Holy Synod, and has infused into the most holy Bishops the fear of overhanging dangers, by means of certain tumults, and of assault from the outside, so that even the majority of us were in peril of our lives from him. But we will tell the details (819) to your Mightiness, if indeed what we have asked be granted to us by your Piety. And" [so] "let five of the Holy Synod go and tell your Mightiness, in detail, those things which have been decreed

---

NOTE 813.—The Greek here shows that the Synod referred to is the Third Ecumenical. The penalty here meant is the action of the Third Synod in their cases in the future. But at this time only Act I. of the Ecumenical Council had been held. The canons, made later, depose all Bishops who oppose the decisions of the Ecumenical Council.

NOTE 814.—Constantinople was the lesser Rome as being the newer capital, the rights of secular seniority, at this time and till the fall of the Western Empire, a few decades later, being reserved by Canon III. of the Second Synod and by Canon XXVIII. of the Fourth, to the elder chief city, Rome. Rome, being now heretical, according to the decisions of Ephesus, in holding to the worship of Christ's humanity, to the real substance presence of Christ's two natures in the Eucharist and to the Cannibalism of eating the real substance of his flesh there, and drinking the real substance of his blood' there, and contrary to Canon VIII. of Ephesus usurping Appellate Jurisdiction outside of Italy, her Bishops and clerics, as has just been said, are deposed and now excommunicate, and all her laics are also excommunicated, by the whole Universal Church in its Third Synod.

NOTE 815.—Or, "*chief Bishop.*" He was the chief of the Bishops personally present in the Ecumenical Council.

NOTE 816.—Cyril is here said to represent Carthage as well as Rome. Probably Besula, the deacon of Carthage, who came, bore a request from Capreolus, Patriarch of Carthage, to Cyril, to act as his place holder, as Celestine of Rome had asked him to be his place holder.

NOTE 817.—Cyril.

NOTE 818.—Greek, τὸ . . . ἐπιτίμιον.

NOTE 819.—Or, "*part by part,*" κατὰ μέρος.

(820). And, moreover, we who sat together (821) and enacted and set forth a canonical vote of deposition against the heretic Nestorius are more than two hundred" [in number], "and we have been collected from all the inhabited world; and all the West voted' [it] "with us (822). But only a few of us have subscribed this Report (though all are present and assenting together), because the most devoted Magistrian (823) Palladius is very much pressed for time, and can not wait for the delay of the subscription of all.

"The God who is over all, guard your reign through many periods of years, most religious, Victors, Ever August.

"I, Flavian, Bishop of Philippi, have subscribed.

"And the names of the Schismatics are as follows:

"John, Bishop of Antioch in Syria:
"Macarius,
"Helladius,
"Julian,
"Tranquillinus,
"Alexander,
"Maximinus,
"Diogenes,
"Helladius,
"Apringius,
"Dexianus,
"Placon,
"Gerontius,
"Alexander,
"Asterius,
"Theodoret,
"Antiochus,
"Dorotheus,
"Melitius,
"John,
"Zebinus,
"Paul,
"Peter,
"Musaeus,
"Fritilas,
"Jacob,

NOTE 820.—Greek, τὰ καθ' ἕκαστον τετυπωμένα.

NOTE 821.—Greek, συνεδρεύσαντες, that is, in the Ecumenical Synod.

NOTE 822.—That is by Cyril, the representative by delegation of its then two greatest sees, that is Rome and Carthage. The rest of the Christian West was either weak or dependent on Rome, so far as secular power was concerned and not so fully civilized as Rome, but most of the Occident was still pagan. The future Seventh Synod, fast approaching to unite the Church again in the worship of God alone, will see a vastly increased set of episcopates of the National Churches of the West, such as the English, American etc., and also of the newer Churches of the East, such as Russia, etc.

NOTE 823.—Greek, τὸν . . . μαγιστριανόν.

"Zebinus,
"Marcellinus,
"Himerius,
"Theosebius,
"Eutherius,
"Anastasius.
"Basil,
"Iliades, and
"Maximus.

"Those, the only sharers of the impious dogmas of Nestorius, go about the city, set in motion tumults and seditions, and promise ordinations against all the Orthodox who are in the city (824); and they, fearing and suspecting in regard to that, hinder them from their absurd attempt" (825).

ORTHODOX DOCUMENT II.

AN ANSWER OF THE BISHOPS FOUND IN CONSTANTINOPLE TO THE MEMORIAL (826) FROM THE SYNOD.

"THE HOLY SYNOD GATHERED IN EPHESUS in accordance with the decree of our most pious and Christ-loving Emperors, having found the enemy of the Christ (827), persisting in his same errors, and preaching his impieties, has deposed him, that, for the future, causes of stumbling may be cut off from the whole inhabited world. And when that was noised about in Constantinople,

---

NOTE 824.—Greek, χειροτονίας ἐπαγγελόμενοι, which may be rendered "*announce ordinations.*" As the small fragment of the Council under John of Antioch had been so audacious as to pass a sentence of deposition on Cyril and Memnon, and a sentence of excommunication on four fifths of the whole Synod, they were capable of any other brazen-faced absurdity, and might proceed, though out of John's patriarchate, to uncanonically order an election for a Bishop in Memnon's place and ordain him themselves, and they might attempt to do the same thing in the other two hundred sees represented in the Ecumenical Synod. And there was no telling how much trouble such iniquity would make among the ignorant, especially if backed by an Emperor of the East, who, originally at least, was on Nestorius' side. Hence the desire of Memnon's flock to avoid that evil by keeping those creature-serving heretics out of any place where they might effect their ends; especially out of any Church building or other Ecclesiastical property of Memnon's jurisdiction, for, of course, they had no right there except what he might grant them. Least of all had they any right to attempt so to enforce practically their own sentence against him in buildings over which, as an Orthodox Bishop, he had sole control.

NOTE 825.—I have translated the above Document from the original Greek in Coleti's *Concilia*, tom. III., col. 1277-1284; but have discovered one or more typographical or other errors in it by comparing the "*Collectio Regia*" with it, and in that case have followed the latter edition. I have looked over this document as in Hardouin and Mansi to some extent.

NOTE 826.—This seems to be an answer to the Document sent in a reed to them through a beggar. It is mentioned below.

NOTE 827.—Greek, τὸν ἐχθρὸν τοῦ Χριστοῦ. Nestorius is meant.

all those who are zealous for his opinions, kept circumventing that fact; we mean that they watched the ships" [and] "the roads and would not permit any one from the Holy Synod to enter Constantinople, nor any one to go thither (828): but only what favored the enemy of the Christ was reported here (829) and carried from here (830). And, nevertheless, since no one can do any thing against God, (for what is man?), by God's ordering there arrived an Epistle written from Ephesus to the holy Bishops and monks, which had been sent through a certain beggar, who had bound it up, within a reed: and so begging and leaning on the reed, he brought the letter. And all the monasteries together with their archimandrites arose and went out to the Palace, chanting antiphons (831). And one of the archimandrites was the holy Dalmatius, who for forty-eight years had not gone out of his monastery, but had shut himself up within it. Moreover, our most pious Emperor was wont to go away to him and pay heed to him (832): and so when earthquakes occurred at Constantinople as they often did, and the Emperor besought him to go out and make supplications (833), he" [Dalmatius] "was never persuaded to go out and make supplications. But when he" [Dalmatius] "was praying on this matter (834), a voice came down out of heaven to him saying that he should go out (835). For

NOTE 828.—That is, to the Ecumenical Synod.
NOTE 829.—Constantinople.
NOTE 830.—Constantinople.
NOTE 831.—Greek, ψάλλοντες ἀντίφωνα. May it mean also "*chanting antiphonally*"?
NOTE 832.—Greek, καὶ ἔβλεπεν αὐτόν.
NOTE 833.—Greek, καὶ λιτανεῦσαι.
NOTE 834.—On the memorial or letter sent in a reed, through a beggar, from the Third Ecumenical Synod to the Bishops who might be found at Constantinople. According to the Seg. manuscript Cyril of Alexandria seems to have written it in their behalf. See it, col. 1089-1093 of tom. 3 of Coleti.
NOTE 835.—The virginal and monastic state is from Christ (Matt. xix: 11, 12). Nevertheless as to the wisdom of a man shutting himself up in a monastery without going out of it for forty-eight years, there can be but one opinion in most cases. And that is against it. For Christ prays his Father, not that He would take His disciples out of the world, but that he would keep them from the evil of the world (John xvii; 15).
Indeed the world is the field in which the Christian must fight his battle and win heaven. Nevertheless monks and nuns should each have their monasteries or convents and should confine themselves mainly to their own sex to avoid unnecessary temptations, and should be kept under close watch and discipline as to faith, morals, and every thing else, and kept at godly work in the way best suited to each, that idleness may not be a means of temptation to them as it has been to so many. Some of them can do a good work for God in teaching; others in hospitals, orphanages, homes for the aged; others in missionary work among the heathen; while others with no talent for such labor can do the work of the monastic household, the monastic farm, the monastic handicraft, etc. And this has ever been the view of the wisest of the monks themselves. They should be clean, subject to their Bishops according to the canons, and live in such a way by themselves, and work two by two, as to help and watch over each other and give the enemy no occasion to blaspheme. Of course in such mere *obiter dicta*, such were *incidental allusions* as the above on topics not under discussion in the particular Synod referred to, we must remember that the Ecumenical Synod is not to

God was not willing for His flock to finally perish. And many of the Orthodox people were together with them. So then they came to the palace, and the archimandrites, being invited by the Emperor went in, and the multitude of the monks and the laics remained outside chanting antiphons (836). Then they" [the archimandrites] "came out, having gotten a righteous answer. All shout, The Mandates of the Emperor.

"Then they" [the archimandrites] "reply" [to this demand for the Mandates of the Emperor] "Let us go away to the Martyry of the holy Mocius (837), and we will read the letter; and ye shall learn the answer of the Emperor.

"Therefore all departed, both the monks and the laics (for the distance was

be understood as approving them. Indeed this very Third Synod did condemn certain silly asceticism. See on that matter elsewhere in this work under *Monks* in the *General Index* to vol. I. of *Nicaea* and in that to vol. I. of *Ephesus*, and the Decision of the Third Council on the Massalians below. An account of Dalmatius is given in *Smith and Wace's Dictionary of Christian Biography*.

As to the story of a voice from heaven to Dalmatius ordering him to go out and take part in the struggle I see nothing at all improbable in it. There was need of *miraculous* help, for Man Service and denial of the Incarnation had been set forth by Nestorius the first Patriarch of the East, and he was powerfully seconded by John of Antioch, another of the first four prelates of the Orient, and by a powerful party, prominent among whom was the able paganizer Theodoret. The Emperor was their friend and co-worker, and had undertaken to nullity and cancel the dogmatic definitions and the rest of the work of the First Act of the Third Ecumenical Synod.

Besides, the leaders of the Orthodox, Cyril of Alexandria and Memnon of Ephesus, had been or were soon to be deprived of their liberty by him and treated as deposed heretics and to be in durance, and the Synod was hindered even then, more or less.

But one man stood high in influence with the Emperor and the people. That man was Dalmatius. It was no wonder then that God spoke to him when the truth seemed about to expire under the blows of His enemies. He took part in the struggle, and the wearied champions of the truth at Ephesus were succoured and delivered.

In saying this I do not mean that because God has spoken to a man, or given him some miraculous manifestation, that therefore God is to be understood as having guaranteed him as infallible; for that is contradicted by the fact that Peter, who was favored with inspiration like other Apostles that he might write his Epistles which all believe to be inspired as being a part of Scripture; Peter, who had a vision from God at Joppa; that same Peter denied the faith, swore with an oath that he was not a follower of Christ, and began to curse and swear after that when accused of being such. And Caiaphas who was endowed for God's own purpose with the gift of prophecy, (John xi; 51) never acknowledged Christ, and, so far as we know, died in his sin of opposition to Him.

NOTE 836.—Greek, ψάλλοντες ἀντίφωνα. See note on that expression above.

NOTE 837.—On this saint I find nothing in *Smith and Wace's Dictionary of Christian Biography*. But in the work entitled "*Constantiniade, ou Description de Constantinople Ancienne, et Moderne; Composée par un Philologue et Archéologue; traduite du Graec, par M. R. Constantinople, . . . Coromila et P. Paspélli, Galata, . . . 1846*, pages 44 and 109, a Church of St. Mocius or Mucius is mentioned, (for the name is spelled both ways, though in the Errata on page 219 *Mucius* is corrected to *Mocius*.

Smith and Cheetham in their *Dictionary of Christian Antiquities*, under *Mocius* and *Mucius* speak of three martyrs of that name. One of them had a church dedicated to him and St. Menas at Constantinople." That Mocius is put down there as a "Presbyter, native of Byzantium, martyred under Diocletian at Heraclea." Another, whose name is spelled "Mucius," was a "Martyr at Constantinople." See there. I know not which Mocius is here meant.

one head (838); and while they were singing the very last psalm in the last place (839), of the city, the people met them; and the monks were-singing with wax candles, and when they saw the multitudes, they cried out against the enemy (840). They go into the Martyry of the holy Mocius, and the Epistle is read to them."

[In the margin here in Coleti, col. 1285, tome III. we read: "In the Seg. manuscript the Epistle of the Synod is subjoined which, after the deposition of Nestorius, was sent to Constantinople and begins προσεδοκῶμεν. See it above, page 1090." I give it here.   CHRYSTAL].

"*Epistle of Cyril to certain of the Clergy in Constantinople.*

"Cyril, Archbishop of Alexandria, wishes the most joy possible to Comarius and to Potamon, Bishops, and to the archimandrite of the Monasteries Master Dalmatius, (841) and to Timothy and Eulogius, presbyters, beloved and most desired, and to the sanctified (842) in Christ.

NOTE 838.—Coleti's *Concilia*, tom. III., col. 1285: ἦν γὰρ ἡ ὁδὸς κεφαλὴ μία. The Latin rendering of this in the parallel column there is: "(erat enim via, qua incedebant, ex capitalibus una)." The question difficult to decide here is as to the meaning of κεφαλή. It literally means "*head*." But does it mean here a definite or indefinite space, a section of the Psalms, or some thing else? Or should κεφαλή be in the genitive, as the Latin translator seems to have taken it, and then should it be rendered "*For the street*" (that is, where Mocius' martyry was) "*was the first from*" (that is, "*outside of*") "*the capital*"? I confess I am puzzled to decide.

NOTE 839.—Or, "*the last part of the city.*"

NOTE 840.—That is, Nestorius.

NOTE 841.—"*The Master*" or "*Mr. Dalmatius,*" τῷ Κυρίῳ Δαλματίῳ, seems a better rendering, than "*the Lord Dalmatius;*" Δεσπότης means *Lord*.

NOTE 842.—Greek, ἡγιασμένοις. This is a frequent expression in the New Testament. Every Christian is "*sanctified*" in a covenant sense; that is they are of the "*holy nation,*" the "*chosen race,*" as the Greek reads, (1 Peter ii:9); this is one sense of the term. Other Christians are personally sanctified in the sense of "*made holy*" as "sanctified" means, in their thoughts, words, and deeds. *Sanctified* is used in both senses in the New Testament as well as in the Old. And in both covenants many have belonged to the first class who have not to the second. Under the Old Testament all of Israel's descendants are called *a holy nation* (Exod. xix:6), though many of them were personally unholy and even idolaters and died in their sins. In the New all the baptized are called "*holy,*" "*a holy nation*" or "*saints*" and "*sanctified*" though the very epistles in which those terms occur show that some of them were personally unholy. For example Romans i: 7; "To all that be in Rome, beloved of God, called "*saints*": the "*to be*" of our English Version before "*saints*" is not in the Greek and should not be in the English. And the same applies to passages below.

I. Corinthians, i: 2, "Unto the Church of God which is at Corinth, *sanctified* in Christ Jesus, called, "*saints.*"

II. Corinthians i: 1, "Paul an Apostle of Jesus Christ by the will of God, and Timothy our brother, unto the Church of God which is at Corinth, with all the *saints*, who are in all Achaia."

And Christians and their children, as the New Testament teaches, and as the whole Church has ever held, are now the only "*chosen race*" of God, put in the place of the rejected unbelieving Jews and are now the only "*holy people,*" *sanctified* in the sense of being members of a holy covenant, even the new and better covenant of Christ. And in I. Corinthians vi:, 11, Paul in addressing a whole Church, tells them, "*But ye have been washed,*" [that is, *baptized*,

"We were expecting that the honorable Nestorius would come, and repent

(Hebrews x. 22), by which rite they were inducted into the number of the *saints*], "but ye *have been sanctified*," (so the Greek is). And in accordance with I. Peter ii: 9, "*ye are a chosen race*," Paul in II. Corinthians vi:, 14, 15, 16, forbids Christians to marry any unbeliever, and in I. Corinthians vii, 39, tells a Christian widow that, if she marries again, it must be "*only in the Lord*."

Yet, of course, it would often happen, that only one of the two partners was converted. In that case what should be done? Would their offspring be of the *chosen race*?

Paul replies that they might then live together, "*for*" he adds, (I. Cor. vii, 14), "*the unbelieving husband is sanctified by the wife, and the unbelieving wife is sanctified by the husband, else were your children unclean, but now are they holy*," that is, "*saints*," for the word here rendered *holy* is the very same Greek word that is rendered *saints* at the beginning of several Epistles, and elsewhere, as, for example, in Romans i: 7; I Cor. i: 2, and II. Cor. i: 1.

The case of such children is like that of Rehoboam under the Old Testament. His father, Solomon, was of the former *chosen race* the *holy nation*, Amos iii: 2; (Exodus xix: 6; I. Chron. xvi: 13; Psalm xxxiii: 12; Deut. vii: 6; etc.), but his mother was Naamah, an Ammonitess, (I. Kings xiv: 21-31, and II. Chron. xii: 13), yet he was numbered with the then chosen people because one of his parents was of them, and so he inherited the crown and throne of Israel.

And as the promise of God is to the children equally with their parents (Acts ii: 39), and as whole households were baptized (Acts xvi: 15; Acts xvi: 33, and I. Cor. i: 16), and as Christ has told us to baptize not part of a nation, but "*all the nations*" (Matt. xxviii: 19), and has made, in ordinary circumstances, that rite necessary for all of every age (John iii: 5), we therefore find *children* among the *saints* as we see by comparing Ephesians i: 1, with Ephesians vi: 1, and Colossians i: 2, with Colossians iii: 20. And all Christians, parents and children, are addressed as "elect *of God*," that is "*chosen of God*," for example in Colos. iii. 12.

And yet we do not find that all who are called *sanctified* and *saints* in the New Testament were *personally holy*, (and *holy* and *saint* mean the same thing, *holy* being from the Anglo-Saxon, and *saint* from the Latin). For some of those members of the Church of Corinth who are addressed in I. Corinthians i: 2, as "*sanctified in Christ Jesus*," and "*saints*" were actually "*drunk*" at the Lord's Supper (I. Cor. xi: 20, 21, 22), so ignorant and unspiritual were they! And some were cursed with sickness and others with *death* for so profaning the Holy Supper, and are rebuked and taught better by the Apostle (I. Cor. xi: 17-34). Some of the "*saints*" of the Ephesian Church, (Eph. i: 1), are blamed for being *thieves* in Eph. iv: 28, where the words, literally rendered, are "*Let him that stealeth steal no more*," Greek, ὁ κλέπτων μηκέτι κλεπτέτω. And James (iii: 1-12) warns his Christian Hebrew brethren against profane language, and his words imply that some of them were guilty of it. For he writes: "The tongue can no man tame; it is an unruly evil, full of deadly poison. Therewith bless we the God and Father; and therewith curse we men who are made after the similitude of God. Out of *the same mouth* proceedeth blessing and cursing; *my brethren*, these things ought not so to be." And directly after he shows that the profane cursing and the blessing proceed as he has just said, "*out of the same mouth*." For he goes on: "Doth a fountain send forth out of the same hole sweet water and bitter? Can the fig tree, my brethren, bear olive berries? Or the vine figs? So can no fountain yield both salt water and fresh." That is the literal rendering.

And we find Christians, who were *slaves* as the Greek of Titus ii: 10 is, warned against "*purloining*," and again the *saints* of the Ephesian Church (Ephesians i: 1) in Ephesians iv: 25, are warned to "*put away lying*," and the "*sanctified in Christ Jesus*" and "*saints*" of I. Cor. i: 2 are warned against *fornication* (I. Cor. v: 1, and vi: 13-20; and I. Thess. iv: 3-9.

Now if we ask whether such Christians, who are addressed as *saints* and "*sanctified in Christ Jesus*," and "*elect*," that is, "*chosen*," and of the "*chosen race*," "*a holy nation*," "*the people of God*," and that in the New Testament itself, were not at once excommunicated from

of the blasphemies which he has uttered since his ordination, and ask pardon

---

the Church, the answer is No. For there are only three instances of *binding* (Matt. xviii: 15-19 and John xx: 21-24), that is, of excommunication, in the whole New Testament, all of them inflicted by one not of the original Twelve but of the newer Apostles, Paul. They are, one for persistent continuance in gross and flagrant immorality, even incest, in the Church of Corinth, the man who had his father's wife and would not part from her, (I. Cor. v: 1-13 inclusive), and two for errors in faith, that is, denial of a literal resurrection of the body, (I. Tim. i: 25, and II. Tim. ii: 16-19), the result of which is to take the fear of its future punishment out of the minds of men, and to leave them to be more easily led astray into immorality; and probably the preaching of Judaizing heresies in the case of Alexander the coppersmith, if, as is thought, he be the Alexander who was put forward by the Jews to oppose Paul at Ephesus (Acts xix: 33-35).

There is only one case of *loosing*, that is, of releasing a man from the bond of excommunication, in the whole New Testament, that is that of the incestuous person in the Church of Corinth on his repentance (II. Corinthians ii: 1-12).

But why should binding and loosing, powers instituted by Christ Himself (Matt. xviii: 15-19, and John xx: 21-24), be so seldom used when there was so much sin among the *saints*, and ever will be as long as man is sinful by nature?

I answer, Because to excommunicate a person from the Church is a sort of ecclesiastical capital punishment, for Paul speaks of it as an act "*to deliver such a one unto Satan for the destruction of the flesh*" (I. Cor. v: 5), and he writes of Hymenaeus and Alexander, "*whom I have delivered unto Satan, that they may be taught not to blaspheme*" (I. Tim. i: 18, 19, 20: compare I. Tim. iv: 14-19).

Hence we find the Apostle not expelling the abusers of the Lord's Supper in the Church of Corinth, but instructing them as to the rite and the meaning of its symbols, the leavened bread and the wine, and, so instructed, he tells them: "*But let a man examine himself, and so let him eat of that leavened bread, and drink of that cup*," (I Cor. xi. 28).

And considering the state of society in the Apostolic age and indeed even much later, it is no wonder that we find such imperfect "*saints*" and such members of the Church who were "*sanctified in Christ Jesus*" in such an imperfect, aye, largely in a mere covenant sense, that is in the sense of being among God's elect, that is as elect means God's *chosen* New Testament race and people by baptism and the Lord's Supper. For all Christians are so called in the New Testament again and again; for example, I. Cor. i: 27-28; Eph. i: 4, to Eph. ii: 22; Mark xiii, 27; Col. iii: 12; Titus i: 1, Rev. xvii; 14, etc. Gibbon in chapter ii: of his *Decline and Fall of the Roman Empire* computes that in the reign of Claudius, A. D. 41-54, there were about 120,000,000 persons in the Roman Empire, of whom about half, that is 60,000,000, were slaves, while Robertson holds that two-thirds, say about 80,000,000, nearly all white, were bondmen. And these poor people with no earthly hope turned pleadingly and willingly to the kindly religion of Christ with its teaching of blessings here and vastly increased blessings in the world to come, where there is no slavery nor misery. And yet, like the slaves in our southern states, they were full of inconsistencies, such as *lying* and *stealing*, and millions of the freemen of the Empire were little better. For few in that age had any education. But the Church took them in by baptism on their faith and their children with them, trained them spiritually and morally, made men, and women of them, and finally freed them; and in the brotherhood of the Church, they had always been Christ's freemen before.

And if we find evils in the Church to-day we must never deny that all in it, parents, children, and all, are of the *saints* and *sanctified* as the New Testament teaches, but we must try to make them not only *saints and sanctified* in name, as members of the covenant of the saved, but in very fact and word and deed.

To sum up, 1, God has always had a holy people; at first Adam and all his posterity, then Noah and all his, then Abraham and all his initiated by the rite of circumcision, or, if females, so by birth, and then Moses and those under the Sinai Covenant and the Law, and

from the holy Synod; even though it would have been a most perilous thing so

now all who believe in Christ and are baptized, for all previous covenants are *"abolished"* (II. Cor. iii; Heb. viii; 1-13; and Heb. ix: 1-28, and Heb. x.)

2. Christians alone and their children are therefore the only *"chosen race,"* I. Peter ii. 9; not the plain mistranslation *"chosen generation"* of our *version* in I. Peter ii; 9, for γένος ἐκλεκτόν means *"chosen race,"* that is, *"elect race,"* and nothing else.

3. They are *"kings and priests unto God to offer up spiritual* sacrifices the highest of all sacrifices, *"acceptable to God by Jesus Christ"* (Heb. ix: 10, and Heb. x, 1-26, I. Peter ii: 5 9, and Rev. i: 5, 6), who as kings and priests, are to *reign on the earth* (Rev. v: 8, 9, 10; Rev. xx: 1-7). And they come *"out of every kindred, and tongue, and people, and nation,"* Rev. v:8, 9, 10.

4. The church is *the ministration of the spirit which giveth life* as opposed to the *ministration of the letter,* the Mosaic Dispensation, which *killeth* (II. Cor. iii); and is *"done away"* and *"abolished"* (II. Cor. iii: 11-12; and Heb. viii: 6-13 inclusive); for it was born amidst the outpourings of the Spirit on the day of Pentecost (Acts ii), and Christians have vastly greater spiritual helps than any dispensation before ours.

But to deny that all the baptized are of his flock and to refuse to admit them to the Lord's supper, is to result in the mournful state of things which we find in our land to-day, where out of some 65,000,000 of Protestants, 45,000,000 are counted to be not Christians at all, but outsiders, and perhaps 10,000,000 of them are without anything that even claims to be baptism. The Antipaedobaptist heresy alone in all its sects claims about 6,000,000 members, and utterly rejects the baptism and the Eucharistizing of Infants, and for that matter millions of its children who do believe in Christ; and that too when it is one of the clearest facts of Church history that for about 200 years after Christ all Christians used the trine immersion as the common mode of baptism and gave it, confirmation, and the Lord's supper to infants as Bingham shows in his *Antiquities of the Christian Church,* (book xi., chap. xi., sec. 6, 7; book xii., chap. i., sec. 2-6, and book xv., chap. iv., sec. 7: see also Chrystal's *His tory of the Modes of Christian Baptism* and Zorn's *Historia Eucharistiæ Infantium*), and as is done still in the Eastern Church.

And there never was any sect for the first 800 years which used baptism at all, which did not give all those three rites to infants.

But too many of us are to a greater or less extent affected by that Antipaedobaptist heresy, and the denial of the plain New Testament teaching, that there is no promise in the New Testament to any unbaptized person adult or infant, that Christ's words in John iii: 5, are in ordinary circumstances, a forbidding of such a notion, the words, I mean as the Greek is, *"If any one be not born out of water and the spirit he cannot enter into the kingdom of God."* That is the ordinary law, but we do not assert it of those who in response to God's call in Revelations xviii: 4, came out of Rome (Revelations xvii: 18) in the sixteenth century, for their position to-day is like that of the Jews in Babylon; they had thrown away their image worship and creature worship, but had not yet gone up to Jerusalem to make a full restoration. They did that later in the days of Ezra and Nehemiah. So we came out of Rome and had our Reformation in the sixteenth century, which consisted in getting rid of our image worship and creature worship, and idolatry, and cannibalism heresies on the Eucharist; and now that the facts regarding God's Word, the utterances of the Universal Church in the VI. Synods, and the testimony of the Ante-Nicene Church, are known, we must make a full Restoration and unite the Church again on the basis of the New Testament as understood by the first three centuries and the VI. Synods. But we must restore to full membership among the *saints* and the *holy people,* the infant, by baptism confirmation and the Eucharist, and avoid all Novatian and Donatist unforgivingness toward the penitent believer, all Antipaedobaptist denial of the New Testament truth that the infant is of the chosen race, and is not to be 'eft outside of the Christian covenant by denying him baptism, and so by Christ's law leaving him to perish (John iii: 5). The result of that in our own land is that such children marry by the hundred Jews, Romanists, and others, and apostatize from the sound Christian faith or, with the longing for God and his help which is natural to the human heart in its feebleness, they give in to every new fangled heresy which comes along, and become Mormons, so-called

to grant him pardon; for it was not possible (843) to grant it to a man who has preached such things. For he has perverted all the inhabited world, and has done away the worshipping faith (844) of the Churches. For if he who dared to put forth even one abusive expression against our most pious and Christ-loving Emperors is justly subject to the ireful penalties of the laws; ought not the utterly impious man to be so punished still more, the utterly impious man who overturns our holy mystery and abolishes the Economy which the holy and man-loving Sole-Born Son of God the Father fulfilled for us when he deigned to become man, to save us all and to deliver the whole world under heaven from sin and death? But we wondered at the hardness of the man's heart. For he did not change his mind, nor did he weep over those things which he had dared to say against the glory of Christ, the Saviour of us all. For even after he came into Ephesus, he made use of the same expressions as he had before, and again showed that he held

---

Christian Scienceites, Theosophists, and devotees of any other humbug which is vented. See on the practical denial of salvation to infants by the Antipaedobaptist themselves, pages 262, 263 of Chrystal's *History of the Modes of Christian Baptism*. See also for the doctrine that Christians ministers and people, are the only true priesthood and people of God now, on page 650, vol. I. of Chrystal's *Ephesus* under *Priest* and *Priesthood, the doctrine of the Christian*, and under John iii: 5, vol. III. of Tertullian in the *Ante-Nicene Christian Library*. Tertullian's work *on Baptism* chapters xii and xiii, and chapter xxxix of his work *On the Soul*, which are on pages 245, 248, vol. I., and vol. 2 of that author, page 503. See also the Latin of both works.

NOTE 843.—Greek, ἐνεδέχετο.

NOTE 844.—Greek, Οὐ γὰρ ἐνεδέχετο ἀνδρὶ τοιαῦτα κηρύξαντι (πᾶσαν γὰρ διέστρεψε τὴν οἰκουμένην καὶ τὴν θρησκευομένην τῶν Ἐκκλησιῶν παρέλυσε πιοτιν) χαρίσασθαι συγγνώμην. Nestorius "*paralyzed*" or "*did away*," so far as he could, "*the worshipping faith*" of the Church, that is the faith of the Church as it regarded *God, the sole object of its worship*, by doing away with the Incarnation of God the Word and denying that the substance of the Divinity of God the Word was in the Man Jesus and denying furthermore that God the Word was in that man in any other than a *relatve* sense, as he was in the inspired prophets and apostles, that is by His Spirit Which is *related* to Him as being His Spirit; and so he *worshipped* Christ's *mere humanity*, that is, *a creature* and so by bringing in such creature service he *paralyzed or did away the worshipping faith of the Churches*;" that is, the faith of the Churches as to *the object of worship* which had ever been God alone and that, too, from the beginning. And so he had corrupted the faith of the Church on the Eucharist by teaching men that in the Supper we eat real human flesh and drink real human blood, as his *18th Blasphemy* shows (pages 472-474, vol. I. of Chrystal's *Ephesus*). Well might Cyril use of that disgusting Cannibalism the strong language of denial and denunciation that he does in his Ecumenically approved *Long Epistle to Nestorius*, pages 238-240, id., and pages 250-294 note matter, and indeed all of note 606, pages 240-313, and note 599, pages 220-238 of the same vol. I. of *Ephesus* And his chief champion, Theodoret, Bishop of Cyrus, teaches the worship of the consecrated bread and wine of the Lord's Supper, not indeed as the substance of Christ's Divinity but as the substance of His real humanity, which form of creature-worship, contrary to Matthew iv: 10, Nestorius seems to have held, for in that respect there is no proof that he ever differed from Theodoret or any others of his heretical party. And he certainly held to creature worship, for he maintained, as we see by his Blasphemy 8th, page 461, vol. I. of Chrystal's *Ephesus*, and note 949 there, the relative worship of Christ's humanity. See others of the xx. Blasphemies there to the same effect.

the same perverted opinions. So that, moreover, when the distinguished Metropolitans and the most God-revering Bishops justly disputed against him and then shut him up by the God-inspired Scripture, and taught that He who was born in flesh out of the holy Virgin is God; he made use of nefarious language and said, *I do not call a two months' old and a three months' old God*, and he uttered other wicked expressions besides," [so] "abolishing the Inman of the Sole-Born (845).

"The holy Pentecost (846) therefore was the day fore-appointed and granted for the Holy Synod by our most dear to God Emperors. For the first letter by which we were called" [to the Ecumenical Synod] "so decrees (847). And so we came to the city of the Ephesians before the day appointed. For it was not a fit thing to despise the Imperial Masters' decrees (848). But inasmuch as we heard that the most religious and most dear to God Bishop of the Antiochians, John, was coming, we waited sixteen days (849), although all the Synod kept shouting out and saying, *He does not wish to co-sit*" [with us], "*for he fears that forsooth*" [or "*perhaps*"] "*the most honored Nestorius who has been taken out of the Church under him*" [John], "*may have to endure deposition; and likely he*" [John] "*is ashamed in regard to that thing*" which also, experience afterwards showed to be a true suspicion. For he" [John] "delayed his coming. For certain of the most religious Bishops from the East (850) who are with him" (851) [John], "said: *Master John, the Bishop, commanded us to say to your God-Revereingness, 'If I delay, do what ye have to do.'* The Holy Synod, therefore, being assembled on the twenty-eighth day of the month Pauni, according to the Alexandrians (852), in the great Church which is called Saint Mary (853), summoned him, by sending most religious

NOTE 845.—Migne's *Patrologia Graeca*, tom. 77, col. 133. This was a denial of the Incarnation of God the Word. And we must remember that the Orthodox Metropolitans and Bishops and the Patriarch Cyril himself have in mind here not merely the expression of Nestorius above, but its context in his utterances. So that there can be no reasonable doubt of his heresy on the Inman of God the Word, and of his worship of the man Christ being mere creature service, as Cyril asserts elsewhere. See *Man Worship*, p. 631, vol. 1. of *Ephesus*, and under ἀνθρωπολατρεία and ἀνθρωπολάτρης, pp. 694, 695, id.

NOTE 846.—Whitsunday, in our paganized nomenclature. Pentecost is better.

NOTE 847.—Literally, "*has that decree.*"

NOTE 848.—That is the Emperor's decrees. See vol. 1 of Ephesus, pages 20, 21, 33-41.

NOTE 849.—Fifteen days, according to our way of reckoning, for the Greeks and Romans in computing the interval between two days counted in the one from which they started as well as the day on which they stopped, whereas we omit the former.

NOTE 850.—John of Antioch's Patriarchate.

NOTE 851.—That is in John's company. They seem most or all of them to have been from his Patriarchate. and his fellows in error.

NOTE 852.—On the Alexandrian method of reckoning time see the Oxford English translation of S. Athanasius' *Festal Epistles*. Introduction, page XIII. and before.

NOTE 853.—Greek, ἐν τῇ μεγάλῃ ἐκκλησίᾳ τῇ καλουμένῃ ἁγίᾳ Μαρίᾳ. This is one of the first instances in the world of the name of the Virgin being applied to a Church. The Synod did not decide as to the propriety of the innovation, and it would be wrong to infer their approval of it from their silence. Indeed Cyril does not name it himself, St. Mary's Church,

Bishops for him to come and to stand for himself and to make his defence (854) in regard to those things which he had taught and written. And he made his first answer by saying; '*I will consider and will see*' (855). He was summoned by a second citation to be read to him, from the Holy Synod, most religious Bishops being again sent to him. But he did a thing out of place (856) by taking soldiers from the most magnificent Count Candidian, and standing them before his house with clubs, and so he hindered anyone from going in to him. And when the most holy Bishops who had been sent stayed there and said: '*We have not come to say or hear anything harsh*, but the Holy Synod summons him;' then he made use of different pretexts, for he did not wish to come: for his conscience was smiting him. Then we made use of a third summons also" [to him] "to be read" [to him], "and again Bishops were sent to him from different provinces, but he again made use of the violence of the soldiers and was unwilling to come. The Holy Synod, therefore, began its session, and having followed the canons (857) of the Church, and having read his Epistles and his Expositions, and having found them full of blasphemies; and, furthermore, distinguished and most pious Metropolitan Bishops having testified, that in the very city of the Ephesians, he (858) even in his discussions against us, clearly said that *Jesus is not God;* it (859) has deposed him, and passed a righteous and lawful vote against him.

"But inasmuch as it was necessary that your God-Reveringness should learn of those very things and inform those whom it behooves especially to learn of them, in order that neither" [Nestorius] "himself nor his partisans may snatch any away with themselves, I have therefore as a matter of necessity declared them" [to you.] "And, moreover, we have a letter of the most God-revering and most dear to God Bishop John written to him" [Nestorius], "by which he very much censures him for bringing new and impious dogmas into the Churches, and doing away the preaching which has been traditioned," [that is,

---

but speaks of it as the Church "*which is called St. Mary.*" No Church should be named after any creature. A future Ecumenical Synod should prohibit that evil custom. It has resulted in much evil. In after times Romanists spoke of Churches being dedicated under the invocation of St. Mary, St. Peter, St. Swithin, St. this and that instead of God; and so the soul-damning sin of creature-service has been taught and spread. All churches should be named after the Triune Jehovah alone, never after any creature. That Church was called *the Mary Church*, according to some because the Virgin was buried there.

NOTE 854.—Greek, ἀπολογήσασθαι.

NOTE 855.—Literally, "*I consider and see*," but of course with reference to the future, according to the Greek idiom. The Latin translation in the parallel column in Migne's *Patrologia Graeca*, tom. 77, is in the future, well, and we put it in English in the same tense.

NOTE 856.—Greek, πρᾶγμα . . . ἄτοπον.

NOTE 857.—Greek, τοῖς τῆς Ἐκκλησίας θεσμοῖς, the established rules of the Church, that is, the Canons.

NOTE 858.—Nestorius.

NOTE 859.—The Third Ecumenical Synod.

An Answer of the Bishops found in Constantinople to the Synod.

transmitted as *traditioned* means,] (860) "to the churches out of the holy Evangelists (861) and Apostles. But since he" [Nestorius] "could say nothing for his blasphemies, he said by way of pretext, *I asked for a delay of four days, till the Bishop of the Antiochians should come, and they did not grant it;* although" [we reply,] "the said most holy Bishop John had declined to come (862). For if he had wished to be present, why did he declare through the Bishops under his hand (863), '*If I delay, do what ye have to do.*' For as I have said, he did not wish to be present, for he knew that the Holy Synod would certainly pass a vote

---

NOTE 860.—"*Traditioned,*" that is, "*transmitted.*" The Christians of the first three centuries included every thing that had come down in the Scriptures and also what is not in Scripture, but had been transmitted in *doctrine, discipline, rite* and by *universal custom* in the whole Church and attested as such by Church writers from the beginning. All of it came under the name of the historic *tradition*, that is, the historic transmission; and that is a perfectly correct use of the term and of the words for which it stands in Greek and Latin, for they and it mean only *transmission*. The Council of Nicaea, in its Canon VI, proclaims, "*Let the ancient customs prevail.*" Among them was the non-use of images painted, the non-use of images graven, the non-use of the material wooden or painted cross or any other material cross, though some made the non-material sign over their foreheads; the non-use of invocations to any creature, or to any but the uncreated Jehovah; Father, coeternal Word, and co-eternal Spirit. *Primitive tradition*, that is transmission in the written Word and in *universal* faith, and practice and custom *from the beginning, attested by early Christian writers* is of obligation forever. So the Universal Church in the Six Ecumenical Synods has ever decided in express terms and by necessary implication. If we once leave it, we are at sea, with a heavy press of sail; with neither rudder, anchor, nor ballast, nor pilot, and the end will be wretched. Our land has perhaps one or two hundred sects to-day and England about the same number, because in our horror of the legendary and late traditions of Rome which contradict the earlier tradition, that is, transmission in the New Testament and the faith and practice of the first 300 years, we have forsaken in our ignorance and blindness and folly that *written* and therefore *historic* witness as to Christian doctrine, discipline, rite, and custom, all of which has come down from the beginning, and all of which is either in the Scriptures or in the writings of the early Christians and none of which is either unwritten or legendary or false. Cyril does not mean here, however, to vouch for John's *entire* Orthodoxy. If he had so done he would have been wofully deceived. For John's utterances after this at Chalcedon, show that he worshipped Christ's humanity. See them in this volume, pages 370-372 above. John therefore agreed with Nestorius against the Universal Primitive Christian tradition in Scripture and in the Third Synod, by serving the created humanity of Christ; but did he differ from him originally on the Incarnation? though Nestorius had by this time satisfied John by admitting the expression *Bringer forth of God*, which guards the doctrine of the Incarnation, though it is not sure that any of John's conventicle received the doctrine embodied in it. See more fully on this topic under *Tradition* on page 466, vol. I. of Chrystal's *Nicaea*, and under the same term, on page 659, volume I. of Chrystal's *Ephesus*. Compare also παράδοσις in Suicer's *Thesaurus*.

NOTE 861.—Or, according to another reading, "*Fathers.*"

NOTE 862.—He had failed to put in an appearance on the day set, he had kept the Synod waiting for fifteen days longer, and at expense to those who had been punctual, and finally had failed to come, as he might, with his own suffragans who were at Ephesus in time for the opening of the Council, and had sent word by them for it to proceed with its business. Cyril and the Egyptians had come from a more remote land and were on time, because they honestly meant business. John did not, and therefore delayed the Council, seemingly with the intention of preventing its being held.

NOTE 863.—That is his suffragans, metropolitans and parecian, that is Parish Bishops.

of condemnation and of deposition against Nestorius, for uttering impious and blasphemous things against Christ (864), the Saviour of us all. Since therefore, as I have learned, Reports have been borne up" [to Constantinople] "from (865) the most magnificent Count Candidian, take care to state that the Records of what has been done regarding his (866) deposition, are not yet completed on paper. Wherefore we have not been able to send the Report which ought to have been sent to our pious and victor Emperors: but take care to say that, with God's help, the Report shall be received with the Records, if we are only permitted to send one who can bear them. If therefore the arrival of the Records, and of the Report delay, know ye that we are not permitted to send them. Farewell;" (867) (868).

"The people in Constantinople, all with one voice said, *Anathema to Nestorius!*

"*Answer*" [or, "Statement" (869)] "*of Dalmatius*:

"The holy Dalmatius went up above (870) and said, If ye wish to hear, keep quiet and learn, and do not wish to interfere with and hinder what is to be said; but be long suffering (871) in order that ye may hear accurately. The most reverent Emperor has read the Epistle which has just been read to your Piety, and he has been persuaded. For I had said to the Emperor, when it" [or "*he*"] (872) came to me, that he ought to write to the Holy Synod, in regard to what had been said to him, and not written" [to him], (873). "And he sent to me, and it was read (874). And in order that I might not grieve him, I had sent forward

NOTE 864.—Greek, Χριστοῦ, literally "*the Anointed One.*"
NOTE 865.—Greek, παρὰ . . . Κανδιδιανοῦ: "*from*" (or "*by*") "Candidian."
NOTE 866.—Nestorius.
NOTE 867.—Or, "*Be strong,*" (Ἔρρωσθε.)
NOTE 868.—I have translated the above document from the Greek original, as in columns 132-137 of tome 77 of Migne's *Patrologia Graeca*. It is also in Coleti, tom. III., col. 1069-1093. At this point the Epistle ends in Migne, and therefore, for what follows, I return to Coleti *Conc.*, tom. III., col. 1285.
NOTE 869.—Greek, ἀπολογία.
NOTE 870.—Greek, ἐφ' ὑψηλοῦ: in a pulpit or an ambon, or perhaps from the steps of what we would call the chancel of the church, which, however, the Greeks call "*the holy place.*"
NOTE 871.—Or, '*be patient,*" μακροθυμήσατε.
NOTE 872.—Or, "*when it came to me,*" that is, the letter from Cyril for the Holy Synod in a reed which a beggar had brought to Constantinople. The Greek has simply ὅτε ἦλθε πρὸς μέ; and so we are not sure as to what nominative we should supply, whether *he* or *it*.
NOTE 873.—The letter in a reed from Cyril was not addressed to the Emperor, but to the Bishops Comarius and Potamon, to the Archimandrite Dalmatius, and to the Presbyters Timothy and Eulogius. Cyril might well be dubious as to what greeting such an Epistle would receive from an Emperor who had censured him before the Synod met, and had used the secular power to undo its work in its Act I, and who seemed completely under the control of the Nestoran heretics as Nestorius had in effect boasted before the Council met.
NOTE 874.—Seemingly to the Emperor's messengers, who seem to have been Nestorians from the substitution which they made for the Document from Cyril to the Emperor, as told below.

An Answer of the Bishops found in Constantinople to the Synod. 417

the narration in its order (875), which however those who bore it away did not show" [to him], "but underhandedly showed him another letter instead of it. Therefore I told him what was fitting and the narration in its due order, which things it is not now permitted to tell before your Piety. For do not suppose that I am some lifted up or boasting person: For God will shatter the bones of the hypocrites. For the" [imperial] "Master (876) heard all that has been done (877) in its due order, and rejoiced with thanksgiving to God, and agreed with the words of the narration of the Holy Synod, as befits his Imperialness; not following my words, but the faith of his grandfathers and fathers. Moreover, as was fitting, he took' [it], "and read" ['it], "and was persuaded, and said as follows: *If things are so, permit the Bishops who are to be present to come.* And I said to him, *No one permits them to come.* And he said, *No one hinders.* But I said, *They have been held fast and hindered from coming.* And I said, moreover, *Many of that*" [Nestorius'] "*party come and go unhindered, but no one permits the things done by the Holy Synod to be reported to your Piety.* And, for the other party, that is for the party of Cyril, I said to the Emperor himself before all: *Dost thou wish to hear some one of the Bishops, six thousand in number, or one impious man? The six thousand,* I said (878), *who are under the authority of the holy Metropolitan Bishops?* (879), I did all that therefore, in order that an order might be sent, and that those who are to come may come, and make what has been done to stand out clear; I mean the most holy Bishops, who are now to come from the holy Synod. And I (880) said, *Thou hast sought*" [for information] "*well.* And furthermore he added one word and said, *Pray for me.* And I know that the Emperor has followed God and the Holy Synod in preference (881), and perverted men no longer. Pray therefore, for the Emperor and for us (882).

"The people (883) in Constantinople, all with one shout, said, *Anathema to Nestorius* (884)."

NOTE 875.—The letter which came in a reed, given just above.

NOTE 876.—Greek, ὁ δεσπότης.

NOTE 877.—In the First Act of the Ecumenical Synod at Ephesus, the only act which had been gone through when the letter in a reed was written. So at least I infer from the fact that it mentions only what was done in that session.

NOTE 878.—The marginal reading is, "he said."

NOTE 879.—Or, "*who are under the authority of the Metropolitans of the holy Bishops,*" οἱ τινές εἰσιν ὑπὸ τὴν ἐξουσίαν τῶν μητροπολιτῶν τῶν ἁγίων ἐπισκόπων. Owing to the smallness of the territory under each Bishop, the number of prelates was then greater than it is now. It was the best system because it gave closer oversight and care to the clergy and people. The Bishops then had entire control over temporalities and spiritualities, like the apostles whom they succeeded; see Bingham's *Antiquities of the Christian Church*, book II., chapter IV., section 6, and book V., chapter VI.

NOTE 880.—"Perhaps, *He* said," marginal note in Coleti, III., col. 1285.

NOTE 881.—Or "*rather*," (μᾶλλον.)

NOTE 882.—Here ends Dalmatius' statement to the people in the martyry of Saint Mocius. What next follows is their response.

NOTE 883.—Greek, ὁ λαός, that is the Christian people, that is the laity.

NOTE 884.—I have translated all of the "*Answer of the Bishops found in Constantinople to the Memorial from the Synod*," that is Document II. above, page 405, (except that Memorial itself, that is Cyril's letter to the Bishops Comarius and Potamon, the Archimandrite Dalmatius, and the Presbyters Timothy and Eulogius), from the Greek in columns 1284, 1285 of

ORTHODOX DOCUMENT III.

COPY OF AN EPISTLE WRITTEN BY THE CLERGY OF CONSTANTINOPLE TO THE HOLY SYNOD:

"*To our most God-Revering and most devout Fathers, who are assembled in accordance with the command of the most religious Emperors, from the whole world* (885) *in the Metropolis of the Ephesians,*" [that is] "*to Cyril, Juvenal, Memnon, Flavian, Firmus, Theodotus, Acacius, Amphilochius, Eleusius, Palladius, Irenaeus, Iconius, and all the rest of the Holy Synod, from* DALMATIUS, TIGRIUS, SAMPSONIUS, MAXIMIANUS, JOHN, EVANDER, MODESTIANUS, ADELPHIUS, PHILOTHEUS, EULOGIUS, BASILISCUS, FLORENTIUS, AND ALL THE CLERGY IN CONSTANTINOPLE.

"We, ever priding ourselves from our childhood (886) on the Orthodox, doctrine, zealously endeavour to guard the transmission of the Holy Fathers. And just now again being reminded of it (887) by your Holiness (888), through what the most God-revering and most holy Bishop Cyril (889) has deigned to write to us, we make grateful acknowledgment to God our Saviour, that now therefore the many and great settings-right (890) on behalf of the same correct faith have been made plain to us. Wherefore, most devout!" [prelates], "having learned that your God-Reveringness had deposed our former Bishop (891) Nestorius for adulterating the apostolic and pure and pious doctrines, we took the sheets of the letter mentioned to us, from our most religious and Christloving Emperors, Theodosius and Valentinian, as written and sent by you

---

tome III. of Coleti's *Concilia*, and have to some extent compared the *Collectio Regia*. That memorial I have translated from columns 132-137 of tome 77 of Migne's *Patrologia Graeca*. I have compared somewhat Hardouin and Mansi in places.

NOTE 885.—Literally, "*from the earth under the Sun,*" (τῆς ὑφ' ἡλίῳ.)
NOTE 886.—Greek, ἐκ νέας ἡλικίας.
NOTE 887.—That is, of "*the Tradition*" [that is, as "*Tradition*" means "*Transmission*"] "*of the holy Fathers;*" that is, all that had been handed down from the beginning, from Holy Writ as attested by the faith and practice of the Universal Church: "*As it was in the beginning,*" not in the middle ages first, "*is now and ever shall be* world without end" as the church ever sings, and witnesses.
NOTE 888.—A collective title of the Holy Synod, as often, but against God's Word.
NOTE 889.—This language shows that though Cyril wrote the letter sent in a reed, it was nevertheless considered the work of the Holy Synod.
NOTE 890.—Or, "*and great corrections,*"(κατορθώματα . . . καὶ μεγάλα.)
NOTE 891.—Greek, τοῦ πάλαι προεδρεύσαντος ἡμῶν Νεστορίου: literally "our former fore-sitter Nestorius." The Bishop in the East and generally in the West then sat and now sits on a throne *before* the people often in the choir outside what we would call the chancel, sometimes within it.

Report of the Holy Synod in response to the Imperial Letter. 419

(892) and caused them to be read at once before all the assembled people of the holy Church of God. Let your Holiness know therefore, that the people have come into harmony with us, and have uttered many praises both for your holy and Ecumenical Synod, and for the trophy-possessing Emperors for bestowing care on your dear to God Assembly. And we write this present answer with pleasure, and, further, beseech your famous God-Revereingness to pray for us, and to take care for what is lacking in the settling of God's holy Church among us. For your great foresight for the Orthodox doctrine perceives at once that that alone is wanting, so that all things may be brought to such a termination as shall be pleasing to the Master Christ (893) and all our betterments will be ascribed to no one other than your Holiness, and to the most religious and Christ-loving Emperors.

"I, Dalmatius, (894) a presbyter (895) and archimandrite, Father of the monasteries, beseech your Holiness, (896) O godly and sacred assembly to pray for me" (897).

ORTHODOX DOCUMENT IV.

COPY OF A REPORT OF THE HOLY SYNOD IN RESPONSE TO THAT IMPERIAL LETTER (898) WHICH WAS READ BY JOHN, THE MOST MAGNIFICENT COUNT OF THE IMPERIAL (899) LARGESSES.

"To the most religious and Christ-loving Theodosius and Valentinian, Victors, Trophy-possessors, ever-August ones, THE

NOTE 892.—The letter, judging from the matter foregoing, seems to have been delivered to some one of the Bishops, Archimandrites, or Presbyters to whom it was addressed; but the Emperor's connection with it is mentioned here to strengthen the hands of the Orthodox and to weaken those of the Creature-Servers. For hitherto the secular power had been wholly in the hands of the Nestorians.

NOTE 893.—Literally, *"to the Master Anointed,"* ($τῷ\ Δεσπότῃ\ .\ .\ .\ Χριστῷ$.)

NOTE 894.—In Mansi's margin here, col. 1432 of his tome IV., is found a remark on this signature which I translate. *"This is altogether spurious, and is not found in the"* [or "a"] *"manuscript."*

NOTE 895.—That is *"Elder,"* ($πρεσβύτερος$) as it is rendered in our common version of the Scriptures.

NOTE 896.—Greek, $τὴν ὑμετέραν ἁγιωσύνην$; more wretched Byzantine flattering titles common then in the East among all parties.

NOTE 897.—I have translated the above Document from column 1288 of tome III. of Coleti's *Concilia*, and have compared on doubtful points pages 743, 744 of tome V. of the *Collectio Regia* (Paris, 1644) and, to some extent, have looked over Hardouin and Mansi.

NOTE 898.—Greek, $τὴν σάκραν$, literally *the sacred letter*, for things merely *imperial* were so called at this time; see under $σάκρος$, in Sophocles' *Lexicon of Later and Byzantine Greek*, and in his *Glossary* of it. It was a relic of the pagan Roman deification and worship of their Emperors. Compare $Σάκρα$ in Suicer's *Thesaurus*.

NOTE 899.—Greek, $τῶν σακρῶν$, literally *"of the sacred"* largesses. See the last note above.

HOLY AND ECUMENICAL SYNOD GATHERED BY GOD'S FAVOR (900) AND THE ORDER (901) OF YOUR MIGHTINESS IN THE METROPOLIS OF THE EPHESIANS"[sendeth greeting]:

"Your Christ-loving Imperialness, most religious Emperors, has shown zeal for the faith and the canons (902) from your childhood. And moved by that motive your Imperialness, by a pious decree ordered the Bishops of the whole world to come to Ephesus. (903). But the letter of your Serenity, just read to us by the most magnificent and most glorious Count John, has made not a little trouble for us, for it shows that some deceit and lying has troubled your not lying ears. For your Mightiness has made it clear by your letter that your Mightiness has received a Report purporting to be from us (904) which contains a deposing of the most holy and most devout Cyril and of the most devout and most dear to God our Fellow Bishop Memnon. Wherefore, praying and eager that that lie may have no power at all in the minds of your Christ-loving Imperialness, we make bold (905) to report to your Serenity that the Ecumenical Synod, which has co-sitting in it all the West with your great Rome (906) and the Apostolic See (907), and all Africa, and all Illyricum (908), has

---

NOTE 900.—Or, "*by God's grace*," χάριτι θεοῦ.
NOTE 901.—Greek, νεύματι, literally, "*nod*."
NOTE 902.—The ancients and others, so long as the Church was one in the period of the Six Ecumenical Synods, professed attachment to "THE FAITH AND THE CANONS" of the Synods of the whole Church, which is here commended by this Universal Synod. The one way of godly union is to return to them both. The very moment we do so, the present heresies and anarchies disappear. See what I have written on the *Canons of the First Four Ecumenical Synods* in the *Church Review* for 1877-8, on the importance of those canons. The faith of the VI. Synods must ever remain, but there are certain things in a few of the canons relating to the relations of the Church to the now dead Roman Empire, and to the now apostate See of Rome, which have lapsed with it, but the good principles in them are to be preserved.
NOTE 903.—Literally, to come "*to the city*" [or "*to the metropolis*"] "*of the Ephesians*."
NOTE 904.—Or, "*as from us*."
NOTE 905.—Or, "made bold," ἐθαρσήσαμεν.
NOTE 906.—The reference is to the Rome on the Tiber, which was under Valentinian, Emperor of the West, who is one of the two Emperors addressed in the title of this Document. Constantinople, the capital of the Eastern Empire, was called New Rome.
NOTE 907.—That is, Rome, called so by courtesy in the West as being deemed by some the only Apostolic See there, and, used by courtesy in the Council which represented many apostolic sees of the Eastern Church, including Jerusalem, the mother Church itself.
NOTE 908.—Rome and Latin Africa were always of the Western Empire at first, but Illyricum was sometimes divided, and again at times under Rome, and at other times under the Greek Emperor at Constantinople. On the Church Sees of Illyricum see Bingham's *Antiquities of the Christian Church*, book IX., chapter I., section 5, and after. But Latin

Report of the Holy Synod in response to the Imperial Letter. 421

certainly not deposed the aforesaid most holy and most dear to God Bishops, nor has it so reported; but on the contrary, admiring those men for their zeal for Orthodoxy, it deems them worthy of many praises from men and of crowns from the Master Christ (909), but we report (910) to your Christ-loving Imperialness that we have deposed Nestorius alone the preacher of the wicked heresy of THE MAN-SERVERS (911). Moreover, another thing has distressed us not a little, which seems to have been wrought by joint deceit; and that is the inserting among our names" [the names of] "those who have apostatized (912) from the Ecumenical Synod, that is those who are with John of Antioch, and the deposed Celestians who are with him; and the sending of one imperial letter to us and them (913). In

---

Africa was then ravaged by the Vandals. Other parts of the West were then of not so much ecclesiastical or other importance as they are now. Indeed, many of them were not converted to the faith till later.

NOTE 909.—Literally, *"the Master Anointed,"* (τῷ Δεσπότῃ Χριστῷ). This implies, I think we may fairly say, of itself, an approval of Cyril's Twelve Chapters, which had been read before the Council, and were now the chief thing objected to by the Nestorian party, for they contained in a brief form the whole faith of Orthodoxy on the points involved in the controversy, and a condemnation of all the Nestorian heresies.

NOTE 910.—Or, *"We reported"* ἀνηνέγκαμεν. The reference may be to the Report of the Synod to the Emperors after its Act I. It is the first of these Orthodox Documents above, and was sent by Palladius.

NOTE 911.—Coleti's *Concilia*, tom. III., col. 1289; Greek, ἐθαρσήσαμεν ἀνενεγκεῖν τῇ ὑμετέρᾳ Γαληνότητι ὑπέρ ἡ οἰκουμενικὴ σύνοδος, ἡ πᾶσαν μὲν τὴν δύσιν μετὰ τῆς μεγάλης ὑμῶν Ῥώμης καὶ τοῦ Ἀποστολικοῦ Θρόνου συνεδρεύουσαν ἔχουσα, πᾶσαν δὲ τὴν Ἀφρικήν, καὶ πᾶν τὸ Ἰλλυρικὸν, οὐκ ἐποίησε καθαίρεσιν τῶν προειρημένων ἁγιωτάτων καὶ θεοφιλεστάτων ἐπισκόπων, οὔτε ἀνήνεγκαν ἀλλὰ μᾶλλον τους ἄνδρας ἐπὶ ζήλῳ Ὀρθοδοξίας θαυμάζουσα, πολλῶν ἡγεῖται καὶ παρὰ τοῖς ἀνθρώποις ἐπαίνων, καὶ παρὰ τῷ Δεσπότῃ Χριστῷ στεφάνων ἀξίους· μόνον δὲ τὸν τῆς ἀθεμίτου αἱρέσεως τῶν ἀνθρωπολατρῶν κήρυκα Νεστόριον καθελόντες, ἀνηνέγκαμεν τῷ φιλοχρίστῳ ὑμῶν βασιλείᾳ.

NOTE 912.—Or, *"who have stood off;"* Greek, ἀποστατήσαντας ἀπὸ τῆς Οἰκουμενικῆς Συνόδου. It comes to about the same thing, whichever of those two ways we translate, for those who stood off from the Ecumenical Synod are considered in its Documents as constituting an "APOSTASY," as the canons call them, from Orthodoxy to heresy, or, as it is here worded, to "WICKED HERESY."

NOTE 913.—That mingling of the names of the Orthodox with heretics in one and the same Document is found in the Edict of the Emperors sent to the Synod by Count John, in which the monarch approves the deposition of the three chief actors in the struggle, namely, Nestorius, Cyril of Alexandria, and Memnon of Ephesus. It is translated above, among the Nestorian matter, where it is Document XIII. pages 285-287. Though in the name of both Emperors it was really the work of but one, for Valentinian was at this time too young to be of any account in such a matter. On page 286 one may see how Theodosius II. has mixed up the names of the Orthodox Bishops with those of the Nestorian prelates who were Apostates, and how he addresses the latter as though they were members of the Orthodox Council.

regard to those matters we have already, even sometime ago, made clear to your Piety how they separated from us (914), and how they turned round and insulted and outraged our presidents (915), and

---

NOTE 914.—The *Collectio Regia* has here ἡμῶν; but Coleti by mistake. I presume has ἱμῶν.

NOTE 915.—Greek, τῶν ἡμετέρων προέδρων, Cyril and Memnon. Cyril's see was the first in order of all represented in Act I. by its own Bishop, who besides by delegation from Celestine was place-holder *in that Act* for the see of Rome And according to Bingham in his *Antiquities of the Christian Church*, book IX., chap. I. section 6 the diocese of Asia was originally under Ephesus, and by canon VI. of the second Ecumenical Synod its Bishop was a Patriarch. For the Patriarch and the Exarch originally seem to have been the same thing. The first canon which, at least *in express terms*, subjects Ephesus to Constantinople is canon XXVIII. of the Fourth Ecumenical Synod; though canon III. of the Second Ecumenical seems to squint perhaps at such a primacy or influence of Constantinople over the East as Rome had gotten over much of the West; the motive of the civil power in favoring it in the case of each of those capitals, being, so to speak, to influence the whole Church of its *respective* half of the empire from the capital as a centre as it influenced the state from the same capital. Perhaps the grasping spirit of Rome in seeking to get jurisdiction in the West, which had been partly successful by A. D. 451, induced the Orientals, Emperor and Bishops, to give in canon XXVIII. of Chalcedon, such a right of appellate jurisdiction to the see of Constantinople as should guard the Eastern Church and the Eastern Empire against the ambition, the encroachments and the tyranny of what was to them practically a *foreign* Church of an Empire of a foreign tongue, though in communion with them. For the Greeks were not willing to allow such an influence of the capital of an alien race and power in their own bounds. The same feeling which we find in Germany, England, the Scandinavian nations, and among other non-Italians in the sixteenth century against the influence of the Pope of Rome as a foreign prelate of another race and another speech had much to do with making canon XXVIII. of the Fourth Synod. There was danger to the Eastern Church not only from the ambition of the Bishop of Rome against it, if he should ever get jurisdiction over it, but also to the state, for the Roman Bishop being still a subject of the Western Emperor, and needing his approval to his election and continuance in office, and so to some extent his creature, might be forced to use his influence and power against the Eastern secular power from whom he was so far removed and on whom he was not dependent even if his local feeling did not make him do so voluntarily. The canon was therefore a wise one, on the whole, for the Easterns to make. The secular powers in England and in almost every other Western European country had a similar feeling of alarm now and then, and expressed it in enactments and action of different kinds. Augustine and the Latin Africans, though in the Western Empire, resisted the attempt of Rome to get appellate jurisdiction in Africa. And as the Eastern Church. after Chalcedon A. D. 451, converted new races to the faith, like the Bulgarians, Servians, Roumanians, and Russians, it found them as much disposed as the years rolled on and the spirit of nationality rose and and dominated in them. to resist any influence of Constantinople which they deemed inimical to their ecclesiastical and secular freedom and interests, as the Westerns were to resist similar encroachments of Rome. There is no truth better taught from experience than the necessity of respecting national and race feelings so long as they do not contravene the doctrine discipline and rites of the Universal Church as set forth in the Six Synods. This must he done in the enactments of a future Seventh Ecumenical Synod. And while the principles already laid down in the Ecumenical canons, respect nationalism, *so long as nationalism does not contravene the Ecumenical doctrine, discipline and rite*. nevertheless so many nations have been gathered into the fold of Christ, and so many nations have risen to power since the last Ecumenical Synod met, in A. D. 680. that there is much need of a further application of those principles to the needs and conveniences of their positions. That, in effect, will be to enforce Canons II. and IV. of the Second Ecumenical

dared to tread the canons under their feet, and made themselves excommunicate from all the Ecumenical Synod by their reckless and headlong conduct against us (916), and how when they were summoned for trial, they by no means suffered themselves to obey, and that, for that reason, they have been utterly deprived of communion and of all sacred functions by the Ecumenical Synod. And now we make known and declare these facts to your Christ-loving Imperialness, that by reason of such absurd and extraordinary conduct of theirs, and their struggles even until now on behalf of the deposed Nestorius (917), we have in no wise suffered ourselves to admit them to communion; and they do not allow themselves to subscribe to the deposition of Nestorius; and besides they plainly hold his opinions, and have fallen under the penalties of the canons both by their disorderly attempt against our presidents (918) and because

Synod. But in a national Church, large enough to contain several civil Dioceses, *of one race, of one language, and of one heart*, like, for example, the United States, and other such nations, an appeal may be allowed from the Bishop of the capital of each said Diocese, that is, from its Exarch, that is its Patriarch, to the chief Patriarch of the nation, that is to the Bishop of its national capital, and to a Synod of all the sound Bishops of that nation, for example in the United States to the Patriarch of Washington, in Russia to the Patriarch of St. Petersburg, from Russian, not Polish Slavs, nor from Finns, and so on in every *other large nation, of the same race, language and heart*, which will be a following all that is good, without what is evil, and has wrought evil, in the principle set forth in canons IX. and XVII. of the Fourth Ecumenical Council, and there applied to the National Church of the Eastern Empire. That principle worked well when applied to its Greeks, but not to the Armenians, Syrians, and Egyptians and Bulgarians and other non-Greeks. From the Patriarch and the Synod of his National Diocese there should not, therefore, be any appeal except to all the sound Bishops of the Christian World, and beyond that again to an Ecumenical Synod; but no decision shall be accepted if it be against the New Testament, the VI. Ecumenical Synods, and the first three Christian centuries. Such decisions, justly rejected, are those of the Robbers' council of Ephesus A. D. 449, and all synods putting forth wrong decisions since the Sixth Ecumenical Synod, A. D. 680, including the creature-invoking conventicle of A. D. 754, at Constantinople, the image worshipping and creature-invoking conventicle of Nicaea A. D. 787, wrongly called by its idolatrous favorers the Seventh Ecumenical, and all the Western Councils since, which, though merely local, are called *General* and *Ecumenical* by Rome, and all Eastern Councils since A. D. 680. And so it should be in the case of every nation, and so when national race, language and heart rights are respected will there be peace and content. But no heretical Exarch, Patriarch or Synod may be respected, but a new set of sound Bishops must be put in their places, and they should all receive such respect and rights again, nothing but heresy being changed.

NOTE 916.—The Apostatic Conventicle and Handful of which John of Antioch was the leader had presumed to deprive of communion the Third Ecumenical Synod.

NOTE 917.—This and other facts show that John of Antioch and the Orientals did hold the opinions of Nestorius, as the Ecumenical Council accuse them in this document of doing.

NOTE 918.—See note 915 above.

of their having dared to preoccupy and deceive your pious ears (919).
And we pray your Imperialness devoted to God that the most holy
and most dear to God Bishops, Cyril and Memnon, may be given
back (920) to the Holy Synod, for they have not been at all condemned by the Canons, and that the faith be preserved unshaken;
even that faith which has been written on your soul by the Holy
Ghost" [and] "has been handed down to you from your ancestors,
and has been explained very clearly in the records of what was done
some time ago by us against Nestorius and reported to you; for the
faith of the Three Hundred and Eighteen most holy Fathers who
met in Nicaea lies forth in those Records (921); and all the Action
on those matters is sufficient on the one hand to refute the impiety of
our adversaries, and, on the other hand, to show the Orthodox Faith,
which faith till now, ye have been zealous to guard. But if it seems
good to your Mightiness to make an exact examination of the differences between us and the Schismatics, we pray your Headship (922)
to send to the Holy Synod persons whom your Mightiness may approve, so that by that means your Christ-loving Imperialness may
personally gain full information and assurance in regard to all things"
(923).

ORTHODOX DOCUMENT V.

COPY OF AN EPISTLE OF CYRIL, ARCHBISHOP OF ALEXANDRIA, WRITTEN
TO THE CLERGY AND PEOPLE (924) OF CONSTANTINOPLE.

[CONTENTS]: *Cyril tells what was done at Ephesus after the arrival there,*

NOTE 919.—Literally, "*snatch away your pious ears.*"

NOTE 920.—Or "restore," ἀποδοθῆναι.

NOTE 921.—That is in the Records, that is Minutes of Act I., in which the Creed of the 318
is recited and made a norm of Definition on Nestorius' case. See Chrystal's *Ephesus*, Vol. I.,
pages 50-154, and 154-178. See also Act VI. above,

NOTE 922.—Greek, τὴν ὑμετέραν κορυφήν, that is, "your pre-eminence."

NOTE 923.—I have translated the above from *Coleti's Concilia*, tome III., col. 1280-1292, but
have compared readings in tome V. of the *Collectio Regia* (Paris, 1644), pages 745-747. I have
also looked over Mansi and Hardouin to some extent.

NOTE 924.—Greek, τὸν λαόν, that is, "*the laity*" of the Christian Church there. For in
accordance with Christ's command in Matthew xxviii., 19, 20, to disciple and baptize all
the nations whole cities, aye, perhaps, nations, men, women and children, were already in
the New Covenant.

by the command of the Emperor, of Count John, for matters were now clear (925) (926).

"THE HOLY SYNOD was very much troubled when it heard that the most magnificent and most glorious Count John did not report all things rightly, and that, as a consequence, those there (927) are even taking counsel (928) to exile us; as though the Holy Synod had admitted the uncanonical and lawless deposition which had been wrought by John and the heretics who are with him (929). Mark therefore that another (930) Report has been made by the Holy Synod, which states that it was even grieved at the Imperial letter (931), and that we have not admitted that the three have been deposed (932); and mark especially that the things enacted impiously and lawlessly by those" [heretics] (933) "are pronounced invalid, and that on the other hand our enactments are confirmed. For the Holy Synod, even by its first Report, taught that they (934) had rendered invalid the things which had been done un-

NOTE 925.—The contents are not in Coleti, but are given in col. 141, 142 of tome 77 of Migne's *Patrologia Graeca* from which we translate the above Epistle.

NOTE 926.—I have rendered "quid modo paretur," by *"for matters were now clear,"* but it may also be translated, *"in regard to what is now being prepared;"* or, *"in regard to what is now prepared."*

NOTE 927.—That is, persons in Constantinople, probably including the Emperor, who alone had the power to exile; and it must be remembered that he had been Cyril's enemy from the start, and the enemy of the Orthodox Synod till after its dispersion, and that in an edict above he had in his illogical and secular or probably even heretical way of looking at things, even accepted the action of the Apostatic Conventicle of John of Antioch and his friends against Cyril and Memnon, and at the same time the action of the Orthodox Synod against Nestorius. His action was one of the silliest attempts ever made to blink the vitally important doctrinal points involved in the controversy, and to mix oil and water; but by God's mercy and to the glory of his truth it failed. But about this time Theodosius II. exiled Nestorius, and was probably taking action to exile Cyril and Memnon likewise. For in an edict just before he had specifically said that he would not recognize them longer as Bishops; see it on pages 285-287 above; compare John's Epistle to the Emperors on pages 287-292. On the Epistles or Edicts of the Emperor to the Ecumenical Council see pages 295, 269, above.

NOTE 928.—Or, *"are even determined,"* βούλεσθαι.

NOTE 929.—John of Antioch and his Apostatic Conventicle are meant.

NOTE 930.—It seems to be the Document next above here.

NOTE 931.—The Emperor's edict to the Synod, which admits the action of the Apostasy in deposing the Orthodox Cyril and Memnon, as well as the Action of the Third Ecumenical Synod in deposing the heretic Nestorius. See note 927 above.

NOTE 932.—See the note last above.

NOTE 933.—John and his Apostatic Conventicle.

NOTE 934.—That is, the Holy Synod. The collective noun, "*Synod,*" is now changed to the plural, with reference to the Orthodox Bishops who constituted it. Their first report is in this volume, pages 3-14; their second is on pages 114-124. But the first or former Report here meant seems to be that on pages 163-167. Acts IV. and V., to which it refers are on pages 138-162. The last mentioned Report is the first since those Acts, the above being the second since then. The other two were on preceding Acts, Acts I. and II. of the Ecumenical Synod, the first after Act I. and telling its decisions and the second after Acts II. and III., that is, after and on the arrival of the Roman Legates and the assent of the then West, expressed in

canonically by those" [heretics] (935) "and that they hold us as in communion and fellow-bishops with themselves, and that they would not depart from that judgment. And though the aforesaid most magnificent man, has kept doing unnumbered things to this very day, so as to bring it to pass that John might come into communion" [with it], "and that those with him might come to" [and co-sit with] "the Holy Synod, it would not endure even to hear of such a proposition (936), but all" [of the Synod] "persisted saying, *It is impossible for us to agree to that, unless what has been uncanonically done by them be abrogated and unless they prostrate themselves to the Synod, as persons who have erred, and anathematize in writing his* (937) *dogmas;* and all the Synod stands to those determinations. So the aforesaid most magnificent man, when he failed in that matter, contrived another thing also and asked it of the Synod, that is that it should give him a Forthset (938) of faith in writing, in order that he might make them also (939) assent to it and subscribe it, and then report" [to Constantinople], "saying, *I have joined them together in friendship for they had only human* (940) *grievances against each other.* The Holy Synod understanding that thing, again rose up to the last man, saying, We *do not insult ourselves. For we have not been summoned*" [hither] "*as heretics, but we have come to establish the faith which had been put away; and we have established it; and the Emperor does not now need to learn the faith, for he knows it and was baptized* (941) *in it.* Therefore that effort in favor of those from" [the Diocese of] "the East did not succeed either. And know ye another thing also, that is that when they set to work to compose a Forthset (942) of faith, they quarrelled with each other, and they are yet in that quarrel. For some of them consent to say that the Holy Virgin is *Bringer-Forth of God* (943) but join with it the expression *Bringer Forth of Man* (944) also; whereas others

---

a Western Council mentioned in that Report, and by Celestine of Rome, the chief see of the then only locally Christianized Occident, who had no legates in Act 1., though Cyril of Alexandria was his place holder.

NOTE 935.—By John of Antioch and his small faction.
NOTE 936.—Literally, "*of such an expression.*"
NOTE 937.—Nestorius' or John's. They were the same in effect.
NOTE 938.—Or, "*an Exposition,*" ἔκθεσιν πίστεως.
NOTE 939.—John of Antioch and his Man-Serving Conventicle of the Apostasy.
NOTE 940.—Count John, like his Master, the Emperor Theodosius Junior, utterly failed to grasp the vastly important theological points involved, and seems to have wished to report as above, because he knew it would please him. He wished, like the Emperor, to resolve the whole matter into a non-theological, and purely *personal* matter between two parties of Bishops, Cyril being at the head of one, and John of Antioch at the head of the other
NOTE 941.—Literally, "*dipped,*" βαπτισθείς. Trine immersion is witnessed to by Tertullian of the second century and the third; and by a crowd of writers afterwards as being the custom of their times, including Cyril's.
NOTE 942.—Or, " *Exposition of faith,*" ἔκθεσιν πίστεως.
NOTE 943.—Greek, Θεοτόκον.
NOTE 944.—Greek, ἀνθρωποτόκον. This was Nestorius' position about the time of the Third Ecumenical Synod. See the letter of his mentioned and quoted and epitomized

utterly refuse, and say that they are ready to have their hands cut off rather than to subscribe such an expression. And they every where act unseemly showing themselves to be heretics. Let all be informed of these facts, and especially the most God-revering and most holy Archimandrites, by your God-Reveringness, lest the aforesaid" [Count John], "on his return" [to Constantinople], "may, in order to gratify the ears of certain persons (945) say or state what is false instead of what is true (946). And let not your God-Reveringness shrink, nor grow weary of its sweating labors in our behalf, for it (947) knows that it (948) commends itself both to God and to men. For here also by the grace of the Saviour, those of the most God-Revering Bishops who never knew us, hold themselves in readiness to lay down their lives for us, and come to us with tears, and say that they have the wish to be exiled with us and to die with us. And we are all in much distress, both because we are kept under guard by soldiers, and because they sleep before our sleeping-rooms, and we especially are" [so distressed]. "And all the rest of the Synod is wearied out and

---

above, page 277. He was willing to use the expression "*Bringer Forth of God*," provided the other, "*Bringer Forth of Man*," were used with it. Though the Orthodox used both, nevertheless *Bringer Forth of Man*, inasmuch as it confessed in effect nothing more than that Christ came into the world a man, was inadequate to defend the doctrine that the eternal Substance of God the Word was in the Man brought forth before he was brought forth, in his being brought forth and ever after, and inasmuch as by not expressing God the Word's Incarnation, it might be used in a wrong sense, that is to favor the error that Mary brought forth nothing but a mere man, and so lead to *Man-Service*, that is, *creature-service*, by paganizers, therefore Cyril and the Synod insisted on the other expression. But John of Antioch and some of his party represented in the Apostasy, about this time gave up the quarrel as to the use of the expression *Bringer Forth of God*, and bent all their endeavors to maintain what the Third Synod had condemned, *Man-Service*, against Cyril's Twelve Chapters which condemn it. Nestorius' Epistle to Scholasticus, in which he admits the expression *Bringer Forth of God* after his first censure of it, if not rejection of it, and his denial of the Incarnation, had got him into trouble, is found on pages 277-285 above. See also page 309. Theodoret on pages 361, 362, shows how Nestorius' utterances were remembered against him by the Emperor at last. Nestorius shows his dislike for the expression *Bringer Forth of God* in his Epistle to Cyril, which was condemned by the Third Synod; see page 101, vol. I. of Chrystal's *Ephesus*, and under *Nestorius' Heresy* I., pages 637-639, in that volume, and under Θεοτόκος, on page 711; under ἀνθρωποτόκος, on page 696, and Χριστοτόκος, on page 766. See also Nestorius' other heresies on pages 639-644, all which were more or less connected with his denial of the Inman. Indeed, that was their root error.

NOTE 945.—Probably the Emperor and such as he.

NOTE 946.—Literally, "*some things for other things*," this being a euphemism for the idea of the text.

NOTE 947.—That is, "*your God-Reveringness.*"

NOTE 948.—That is, "*your God-Reveringness.*" The Orientals of the fifth century abounded in the use of such complimentary expressions, some times not wisely nor well; for they were sometimes what are condemned in God's word, that is, flattering titles. Perhaps as to this particular instance being faulty, all would not agree. It is certainly non-New Testament and unnecessary and Byzantine.

suffering and the most (949) are dead; and, finally, those who are left or selling their things because they have nothing to pay their expenses with," (950), (951).

ORTHODOX DOCUMENT VI.

COPY OF AN EPISTLE WRITTEN BY MEMNON, BISHOP OF EPHESUS, TO THE CLERGY OF CONSTANTINOPLE.

"What we endure daily in Ephesus for the sake of the true faith doxy can not be told in words. For trouble unceasingly succeeds the confession and power of the Faith affords us much courage to be things nobly. For the most magnificent Count Caudidian some times

NOTE 949.—The language here is very strong: καὶ οἱ πλείους ἀπέθανον. If it be taken literally it implies that the durance and hardships of the sound Bishops at Ephesus must have been such as to constitute most of them martyrs for Christ. But probably Cyril means only that most of those of them who were taken sick at Ephesus died there.

NOTE 950.—The unselfish and self-sacrificing stand of the Orthodox Bishops at Ephesus, at the risk of life and exile, is worthy of all commendation, and of imitation by all prelates in a future surely coming Seventh Ecumenical Synod, if there be need of such self-sacrifice. Alas! how few of the persons claiming to be Bishops to-day in any part of the Christian world are sound and faithful. The great bulk of them are in the Roman Communion, the Greek, the Nestorian, and the Monophysite, and are all creature invokers and cross worshippers, and nearly all of them worshippers of other images also, and paganizers and blasphemers on the Eucharist, and therefore condemned by Ephesus. And while the Bishops of the Anglican Communion, if true to their formularies and to the six Synods, are free from those soul-damning errors, nevertheless they can not be moved to crush those heresies, but permit their own colleagues, like King of Lincoln, and Grafton of Fond du Lac, to go scot free when they fail to do their vowed to God duty to banish such errors from God's flock, and they suffer clerics to officiate who are ruining the souls of poor simple women with such deplorable and destructive paganizings. But what better can be expected of a man, if he has been elevated to the episcopate as some or many have, because he is a Freemason, though he be unlearned and utterly unfit for the office. Alas! for such a wretched and unfaithful watchman when he comes to stand at God's bar and to render an account of his dread stewardship.

NOTE 951.—I have translated the above document from col. 141-144 of tome 77 of Migne's *Patrologia Graeca;* and have compared to some extent the form of it in *Coleti Conc.*, t. III., col. 1202, 1203; and in the Paris edition of the Councils, tome v. (A. D. 1644), pages 748-750. I have looked over Hardouin and Mansi to some extent.

NOTE 952.—Memnon deserved well of the whole Church, for he exerted himself greatly for the triumph of God's truth. Above in the sixth of the Documents on the Synod of the Apostasy, between Acts VI. and VII. of Ephesus, p. 263, it is said by John of Antioch that forty of the Bishops of the Third Ecumenical Synod were Asiatics under Memnon. See Coleti's *Concilia*, III. col. 1240. Those, with the fifty brought by Cyril of Alexandria, as mentioned in the same column, outnumbered the whole Synod of the Apostasy, and were nearly twice its number. As to Memnon's relations to the throne of Constantinople, it seems to have been about what the relations of Western sees out of Italy had been forced to become to Rome about this time. For Philip, a presbyter of Constantinople, as quoted in col. 1463, 1464, tome 77 of Migne's *Patrologia Graeca*, said in the Second Act of the Council of Chalcedon, that Memnon had been confirmed by the throne of Constantinople, a remark, by the way, which shows that the

the soldiers against us (953), and fills the city (954) with trouble, and at the same time, by his guards, deprives us of the privilege of bringing in (955) any necessaries. But he permits many of those of Zeuxippus (956) who are standing by the deposed Nestorius, and are supported for that purpose, and a large multitude of rustics from the ecclesiastical possessions, to pour down insults on us and on all the Holy Synod, and acts by means of them in pouring down the insults. And the presence of the Bishop of the Antiochians (957) assists both the aforesaid disorder and the daily deceiving of the simpler sort by the most magnificent Count Irenaeus. For the Holy Synod, having learned that he (958) was about to arrive, by way of honoring him and of fulfilling the proper duty towards the priesthood (959) sent some of the most dear to God Bishops

see of Constantinople was then beginning to exercise the power which was afterwards given to it by the twenty-eighth canon of the Fourth Ecumenical Synod in the great civil Dioceses of Thrace, Asia, the head of which was Ephesus, and Pontus. Indeed before the year 431 and the Third Synod, the Bishop of Constantinople, as the ruler of the capital see of the Eastern Empire, exercised sway approaching or reaching the Patriarchal and by canon III. of the Second Ecumenical Synod was made first prelate of all the East, and by canon VI. a Patriarch. Compare on that Socrates' statement in book v., chapter 8 of his *Ecclesiastical History*, that it had constituted the Patriarchates, though at the same time in canon II. and VI. the Synod forbids Bishops to go out of the civil Diocese, to which they belong, to ordain, unless invited. But as Wiltsch has shown, even before the Fourth Synod A. D. 451, the Bishop of Constantinople had exercised sway in other civil Dioceses of the East, and in that Synod had three of them put under him, as stated above. Indeed his sway increased in the Eastern Empire with about equal speed with that of Rome in the Western, and in the eighth century it acquired rule in Italy in what had been the original Patriarchate of the Bishop of Rome. Both Constantinople and Rome as equals, the one of the East and the other of the West, acquired dominion, each by the same means, the ambition of its Bishop and the favor of its Emperors. See on those matters under *Constantinople* in the index to volume I. of the English translation of Wiltsch's *Geography and Statistics of the Church*, especially sections 97, 98, 99, pages 147-154, and section 258, pages 434-438. In the middle ages, after the conversion of Russia, Servia, Bulgaria and Roumania, and till the discovery of America, the sway of the Patriarch of Constantinople covered more territory than did that of the Roman Bishop, though on account of his many idolatries, he was cursed with the loss of dominion in the East and in Egypt and in North Africa, and in Europe, as the Roman see was in parts of the West, both of them to the cruel Mohammedan, Arab and Turk.

NOTE 953. Or, "*threatens us with the soldiers*."

NOTE 954.—Ephesus.

NOTE 955.—Or, "*deprives us of the privilege of procuring any necessaries.*" Starvation into submission seems to have been the policy of the Emperor and his officers against the Orthodox Bishops. See the preceding document, where Cyril states that most of the Bishops of the Orthodox Synod had died, or that most of those of them who had been sick had.

NOTE 956.—The Latin translation in Migne here speaks of "*the inhabitants of Zeuxippus*'" and so makes it a place.

NOTE 957.—John of Antioch.

NOTE 958.—The same prelate.

NOTE 959.—*Priesthood*, (τῇ ἱερωσύνῃ) is here used for the priesthood par excellence, that is, the episcopate; a very common use of the term among the ancients, though all Christians are priests, (I. Peter i: 5-9; Rev. i: 6) that is, *performers of sacred actions*. So in the Old Testament though all the Israelites are termed priests (Exod. xix: 6), nevertheless the expressions "*priest*" and "*priesthood*" are often applied in an excellent sense to the sons of Aaron. And as leadership and certain functions under the Mosaic Covenant were prerogative to the Aaronic

with most religious Clerics also to meet him. So it did the two following things, that is it both gave him the due honor and made known to him that he ought to be on his guard against having any intercourse with Nestorius, because he had been deposed by the Holy Synod on account of the impiety which he had contrived. But not being permitted by the soldiers, who were following him in the way, to reach him, they nevertheless followed and went to the house where he stayed; and persevered many hours, and were not permitted to have any intercourse with him, and" [et] "remained and suffered insults. But after many hours, it seemed good to him (960) to send for the most God-Revereing Bishops and the most religious Clerics, and he led them in through the soldiers. But when they had informed him of what had been done by the Holy Synod, he permitted the most magnificent Irenaeus, and the Bishops and Clerics" [who were] "with him to lay unbearable stripes upon our Fellow-Ministers and the Clerics, so that they had experience of perils also (961). So after those things were done, the most God-Revereing Bishops who had been sent, came into the Holy Synod and showed their stripes, and narrated what had been done, for the Records of the transaction, the Holy Gospel lying forth" [before them] (962), "and they roused the Holy Synod to indignation. And by

ministry, so under the New and and Better Covenant of Christ leadership and certain functions are prerogative to the higher and more spiritual ministry established with greater powers and more blessed promises, and, let us remember, with greater responsibilities. See further page 650, vol 1. of Chrystal's *Ephesus* under *Priest, Priesthood, and Priestly*.

NOTE 960.—John of Antioch.

NOTE 961.—This shows the spirit and the conduct of that Count Irenaeus who figures so largely and prominently and often as an opponent of the Third Ecumenical Council; and the course of the Bishops of John of Antioch's Nestorian, Man-Serving faction. For such men to complain of persecution afterwards seems inconsistent enough. They began it and continued it so long as they had the Emperor and the secular powers in their favor, and never gave it up until they were compelled to. By similar means in the hands of their Persian rulers the Nestorians of that land banished Orthodoxy or put its martyrs to death. Gibbon, in chapter XLVIII. of his *Decline and Fall of the Roman Empire* (page 258, vol. v., (London 1854), Bohn's seven vol. edition) tells us that *"the Nestorians"* of Persia were favored by the Zoroastrian rulers of Persia because they opposed the Orthodox, and that *"they were encouraged by the smile, and armed with the sword of despotism,"* and that though some there *"were startled at the thought of breaking loose from the communion of the Christian world,"* nevertheless *"the blood of seven thousand seven hundred Monophysites or Catholics confirmed the uniformity of faith and discipline in the Churches of Persia."* The followers of Nestorius therefore while complaining of persecution were themselves bloody enough persecutors where they had the power, only they, as the willing tools of an Anti-Christian tyrant, shed blood to maintain denial of the Christian doctrine of the Inflesh and to establish their own Anti-Christian Man-worship, whereas the Orthodox, like the reforming kings Hezekiah and Josiah, used force in strict consonance with God's Word and His law, aye, with the prediction in Revelations xi: 15, and as God's ministers to maintain his Gospel and all his truth (Rom. xiii: 4) and to crush such infidelizings and paganizings, lest they might bring God's curse on the realm, as creature worship is sure to do.

NOTE 962.—Migne's *Patrologia Graeca*, tom. 77, col. 1405: καὶ τὰ γεγενημένα διηγησάμενοι, ἐπὶ πράξεως ὑπομνημάτων τοῦ ἁγίου Εὐαγγελίου προκειμένου, εἰς ἀγανάκτησιν διανέστησαν τὴν ἁγίαν σύνοδον. Anciently the Eucharist does not seem to have been re-

way of chastising h'm a little they deprived him (963) of Communion, and the deprivation of Communion was made known to him. For we had learned that a certain anonymous and unsubscribed document had been put forth in a certain part of the city, which shows his disorderliness and his uncanonical judgment; and he daily calls upon the venerable senate (964) and the most illustrious men (965), and asks, as a matter as to which they are under the law of necessity, for votes from them that he may ordain some one in my place; so that all the inhabitants of the city, being Orthodox, have occupied the houses of prayer, and abide in them, in order that his recklessness and uncanonical audacity which he had published by his notices stuck up, may not be turned from a mere report into an accomplished fact (966). Wherefore, he having gone up also into the holy John the Evangelist (967), and having indicated that

---

served on the communion table, at least not before Synods. For, as Cyril shows elsewhere in this work, the Orthodox did not believe in the actual presence of the Substance of God the Word, nor in the actual presence of the substance of His humanity in the Eucharist, but only of God's sanctifying grace and the symbols, bread and wine, there; for the substance of His Divinity and of His humanity are both locally present in heaven alone *until the restitution of all things*, Acts iii: 21. Compare Acts i: 11, and vii: 55, 56. See his doctrine and the decision of the Third Synod on the Eucharist told in note 606, pages 240-313, vol. 1. of Chrystal's *Ephesus*.

With that Ecumenically approved view of the Lord's Supper agrees the presence of the Gospels here, and the fact that the testimony of the messengers of the Council is made so much of here, as showing that their witness was given under the most solemn circumstances. There is no reason, however, to charge them with performing the idolatrous act of giving relative service to the Gospels, for that is not mentioned and did not come into use till corruptions came, and it was one of them. Whenever we swear we should not do more than lift up the hand to God Himself in the heavens. We should not, on such a solemn occasion, anger Him by committing the idolatry of book worship, and call him to witness it.

NOTE 963.—Or, "moderating themselves a little in regard to him, they deprived him of communion." John of Antioch is meant by *him*.

NOTE 964—The "*senate*" here referred to seems to be that of the city of Ephesus, and the *illustrious men* seem also to be those of that city, for no others could vote in an election for Bishop of the place.

NOTE 965.—See the last note above.

NOTE 966.—As elections of Bishops were made or assented to in churches ordinarily, John and his faction wished to get one at their disposal for that purpose, and the Orthodox, knowing that, were just as anxious to keep him out of them. And by the canons, Memnon was the sole supreme arbiter and ruler, subject to his co-provincial Synod, of all the property of the church in his episcopal jurisdiction, that is, in his *paroecia* or parish. By Canons IV. and VI. of Nicaea and by Canon II. of the Second Ecumenical Council, John of Antioch had no right to ordain a Bishop for Ephesus which was out of the civil diocese of the East, but was in that of Asia, which had never been under Antioch. Its Patriarch was Memnon then. Afterwards, by Canon XXVIII. of Chalcedon, it came more definitely under the sway of Constantinople.

NOTE 967.—That is, as men say now, "into the church of St John the Evangelist." The evil custom of naming churches after creatures had then begun. It afterwards produced bitter fruits in the way of invoking saints. A future Ecumenical Council should abolish it; for it is unnecessary, and is much associated still in creature serving communions with creature service. The Jews, even though blind in other respects, teach us a lesson of greater faithfulness in one respect, and that is in not naming any of their synagogues after

he was under obligation to ordain there (968), he made a sedition and a trouble in the place, for he had gone up moreover with a multitude of disorderly persons who were armed, so that he even half-killed some of the beggars (969) who were there, and" [then] "out of his envy (970) against the Holy Synod he reported (971) that he had been insulted (972) by those who were there. Deign therefore, most devout" [brethren], "to put forth every effort to publish both the madness and the uncanonical judgment of John and of those who are with him, before the most magnificent Counts (973), who are daily troubling the city and the Faith, go up hence" (974) [to Constantinople], "in order that they may not by their deceptions adulterate the facts which relate to the Faith" (975).

---

the saints of the Old Testament. It is prerogative to God to have all Churches named after Him, for they are His. The saints would feel grieved at the custom of naming places of prayer after them if they knew of it. It should be said, however, that John the Apostle was buried in the Church which bears his name, and that some have held that the Virgin Mary was buried in the Church which bears hers; on this last point I hope to publish an article which I have written.

NOTE 968.—Of course John was out of his own jurisdiction, and had no right to depose Memnon, nor to ordain a successor in his place. The sole authority at that time to do that was an Ecumenical Synod, and Memnon was in communion with it; and John and his creature-worshipping conventicle were suspended from all communion by it. But John and his small faction were usurping the functions of the Ecumenical Synod of sound Bishops in that matter, and were justly resisted as malefactors. On the other hand, the deposition of Nestorius was accepted even by the Emperor, and in accordance with the wishes of the Ecumenical Synod a sound successor, Maximian, was put into his place by the canonical authorities.

NOTE 969.—Or, "*some of the poor*" ($\pi\tau\omega\chi\tilde{\omega}\nu$) *who were there.*"

NOTE 970.—Or, "out of malice" ($\phi\theta\acute{o}\nu\omega$).

NOTE 971.—Or, "*out of his malice against the Holy Synod, he made a report as though he had been insulted*" [or, "*maltreated*"] "*by those who were there.*" See John's reports, pages 260-268 above. They are Documents VI.-IX. above of the matter on the Apostatic Conventicle, between Acts VI. and VII. of Ephesus. They are from John and those who were with him, that is the Apostatic Conventicle. This affair of an attempted ordination in Memnon's place in St. John's Church, is colored by those heretics to suit their own aim to excite sympathy. They suppress all mention of some of the facts here reported by Memnon. I have epitomized them above.

NOTE 972.—See the last note above.

NOTE 973.—Candidian and Irenaeus are mentioned in this very letter. Count John was sent from Constantinople afterwards to the Synod.

NOTE 974.—Or, "*return hence,*" that is to the Emperor at Constantinople, for he had sent them.

NOTE 975.—I have translated the above Document from columns 1464, 1465, tome 77 of Migne's *Patrologia Graeca*. It is also in tome III. of Coleti's *Conc.*, col. 1293-1296, and on pages 750-752 of tome V. of the *Collectio Regia* (Paris 1644). I have also looked over Hardouin and Mansi to some extent.

ORTHODOX DOCUMENT VII.

"A Report on the Subscription of the Emperors."
{In the marginal Greek in Coleti and in the *Collectio Regia*, I find the following on this Document.

"*Copy of* A REPORT *sent by* THE HOLY SYNOD *to the* MOST REVERENT EMPEROR THEODOSIUS."
The Latin in the same margins adds:

"REPORT OF THE HOLY SYNOD TO THE EMPERORS FOR THE RESTORATION OF CYRIL AND MEMNON." Another lection in the Latin as stated by Coleti, is "EPISTLE OF THE WHOLE COUNCIL TO THE AUGUST ONES," *that is*, "TO THE EMPERORS."]

"TO THE MOST REVERENT AND CHRIST LOVING EMPERORS, THEODOSIUS AND VALENTINIAN, VICTORS, POSSESSORS OF TROPHIES, EVER AUGUST ONES; THE HOLY AND ECUMENICAL SYNOD, GATHERED BY THE GRACE (976) OF GOD, AND THE COMMAND OF YOUR MIGHTINESS IN THE METROPOLIS OF THE EPHESIANS" (977) [*sendeth greeting*].

"Your Mightiness did not suffer the true faith to be undermined by the doctrines of Nestorius, who with the Jews brings as a reproach against the Master Christ (978) the human sufferings which He endured for us and for our salvation; but your Piety loathing (979) such words against Christ, commanded us to be gathered from almost the whole world (980) in the metropolis of the Ephesians (981), for your Piety wished the dogmas of the religion (982) of the Fathers and of the Apostles to be settled and fixed firmly. Wherefore, we having come together, confirmed, by a decree in common, the faith set forth on this matter (983) by the Three

---

NOTE 976.—Literally, "*by the favor* (χάριτι) *of God*.
NOTE 977.—That is, Ephesus.
NOTE 978.—Literally "*the Master Anointed*," that is Christ, (τῷ δεσπότῃ Χριστῷ.)
NOTE 979.—Or, "*abominating*." βδελυξαμένη.
NOTE 980.—Literally, "*from almost the whole world under the sun*."
NOTE 981.—Ephesus.
NOTE 982.—Or, "*the piety*," τῆς εὐσεβείας.
NOTE 983.—The First Ecumenical Synod in condemning Arius for making God the Word *a creature* and for worshipping him *as a creature*, may be justly said to have condemned by *necessary implication*, and *a fortiori* all worship to any one less than God and hence all

Hundred and Eighteen who were gathered in Nicaea in the time of the Constantine of the blessed memory (984); and" [besides] "we deposed from the priestly (985) grade Nestorius, for we had detected him bringing in innovations into that faith by tricks of words, and injuring the sense of piety (986) by alien sophisms; for we wished to bar out his doctrine which, like a sort of pestilence, was feeding on the Churches. Moreover, inasmuch as we find that some of the Bishops also have been already shaken, and hold the same opinions as he does, and have been deceived and carried away by his blasphemy, we have deprived of Communion all who hold the same errors, until they leave that corrupt doctrine, and acknowledge the universal and apostolic faith, by relying on which, from the beginning, we are all saved. But we decreed those things to set right

worship to Christ's humanity, and, *a fortiori*, to any other creature less than that humanity.
That is enough. I will not adduce as proof a doubted document ascribed to that Synod and to a council of Ephesus against Paul of Samosata, which is still preserved. It forbids specifically giving any worship to that humanity. I will only remark that whatever be thought of its genuineness, its testimony accords with Ephesus. On it elsewhere hereafter.
Furthermore the sense of the Creed of Nicaea is that God the Word, not merely by His Spirit, but in His own divine and eternal Substance descended into the womb of the Virgin Mary, took flesh and put on a man in her and came forth in that man into this world again by birth out of her womb.
Besides the Synod impliedly condemned Nestorius' views on the Eucharist, and approved Cyril of Alexandria's. See what is quoted on the discussion between them in note 606, vol. I. of Ephesus. And Theodoret's presentation of the then Antiochian views on that topic shows that they involved service to a creature. See on that in this note below. On the worship of Christ's humanity by the Nestorians and the definition of the Universal Church against it, see volume I. of Chrystal's *Ephesus*, note 183, pages 79-128; note 664, pages 323-324, note 679, pages 332-362; and against the Nestorian plea of *relative worship* of it and the many decisions of the Universal Church against it, see note 949, pages 461-463. See also note 156, pages 61-69, and note 582, pages 225-220. For the doctrine that God the Word is the sole Mediator by His Divinity and by His humanity see note 688, pages 363-406.
And on the decisions of *Ephesus* on the Eucharist see note 606, pages 240-313, and note 599 pages 229-238. Compare note E, pages 517-528; note 692, page 407, and note 693, page 407-408.

NOTE 984.—Or, *"Constantine of blessed memory;"* though the Greek is literally rendered above. As above the intention may be to distinguish and approve his kindness to God's Church, as contrasted with others who were pagans, and persecuted it.

NOTE 985.—That is, *"episcopal"* here; ἱερατικοῦ βαθμοῦ is the Greek.

NOTE 986.—Nestorius depraved the sense of Christian piety and its Creed of Nicaea by making that Creed teach denial of the Incarnation of the eternal Substance of God the Word in the womb of the Virgin, and service to a creature, that is to the man put on by God the Word, and *cannibalism* in the Eucharist. Hence he was justly deposed, for he erred on fundamentals.

(987) those who have now been dragged under in that error (988), and we expected their repentance; they are a little more than thirty in number. For some among them were both liable to the canons on other charges, and had taken to themselves the most reverent Bishop of the Antiochians, John, who also himself was liable to accusation for his great dilatoriness" [in coming to the Holy Synod]: "while others are convicted of other heresies, and some of them were already deposed also. They did not" [however] "look towards repentance, but being assembled to make a stand in favor of Nestorius, they dared to write a" [verdict of] "deposition against the leaders of the Holy and Ecumenical Synod, and reported it to your Piety as though it had been done by all the Synod. Your Mightiness having received that deposition, commanded it to be firm, for your Mightiness supposed (989) that it had been enacted by the Synod, and not against the Synod by those who hold the opinions of Nestorius and as an act of revenge on their part against us for deposing Nestorius, when they could utter no accusation against the leaders of our Holy Synod. For they dared to deceive your dear to God ears, so that the" [verdict of] "deposition enacted by them against the Synod should be admitted; though it was not enacted lawfully nor canonically, nor did many enact it. Wherefore, also the Holy Synod has overturned (990) by lawful and canonical action, the things done by them outrageously and unreasonably. Wherefore we all betake ourselves to the Mightiness of your Piety, and beg that those things which have been done against Nestorius and those who hold the opinions of Nestorius may have their own proper force, and that those things which have been un-

---

NOTE 987.—Or, "*to correct*" ἐπὶ διορθώσει.

NOTE 988.—Or, "*subverted by that error*," or, "*swamped by that error*," τῶν ἐπαχθέντων τιν ἐν τῇ πλάνῃ.

NOTE 989.—Or, "*thought*," νομίσαν.

NOTE 990.—That is, "*nullified*," ἀνέτρεψε, for as being an Ecumenical Synod and so as representing the whole Church it could do that with authority, by God's New and Better Testament. Compare Matt. xviii.:17; Matt. xxviii.: 19, 20; John xiv: 16, 17; I. Tim. iii: 15. Whereas, John's Conventicle represented only a part, and as the issue proved, not a very large part of it, and only a corrupt part at that.

lawfully done against the leaders of our own Synod by those who avenge Nestorius because they hold his (991) opinions, may remain ineffective and inoperative; for they have not been enacted in an orderly and canonical manner, against persons convicted of faults, but have been audaciously put forth against the Holy Synod, for the sake of revenge alone, by those who hold the opinions of Nestorius. For since the vote of the Holy Synod against Nestorius, was reasonable and fair, and your Mightiness admitted it on the ground that Nestorius had preached plain impiety, your Mightiness certainly sees at once that it is a thing fair and reasonable that the things done against the Holy Synod by those who hold the opinions of Nestorius should remain utterly ineffective and without authority; for they are unfair and unreasonable, and spring from no other cause than revenge alone for what the Holy and Great Synod did against Nestorius. We therefore beg your Mightiness to relieve us at last (992) from this oppression (993), and to command that the leaders of this Holy Synod, the most dear to God Bishops, Cyril and Memnon, be given back to us. For it is a thing fair and reasonable, now that Piety (994) has been vindicated (995) and those who injured it have been made to cease, that those who have co-struggled with us for the faith should enjoy honor with us, and not be condemned with those who have been condemned for their unrighteous blasphemies against the Lord Christ.

"I, Juvenal, Bishop of Jerusalem, have subscribed these petitions.

"In like manner did all the Bishops as they stand in the Minutes" (996) (997).

NOTE 991.—Literally, "*because they hold the opinions of that man.*"

NOTE 992.—Greek, λοιπόν. Or, "*therefore.*"

NOTE 993.—Or, "*this distress,*" τῆς θλίψεως. It was both.

NOTE 994.—Or, "*religion,*" τῆς εὐσεβείας.

NOTE 995.—Surely this expression is justified by the Acts of the Third Ecumenical Synod, for it had not only condemned the infidelity of denying the real Incarnation of God the Word, but also those forms of Nestorian Man-Service in worshipping the man put on by God the Word, any and every where, and the cannibal views on the Eucharist enumerated by that heresiarch.

NOTE 996.—Or, "*in their standing in the Acts,*" or, "*in the series of the Acts.*" The Greek is ἐν τῇ στάσει τῶν ὑπομνημάτων ἐπίσκοποι. The Latin is "episcopi in commentariorum

ORTHODOX DOCUMENT VIII.

"A SYNODICAL EPISTLE TO THE CLERGY OF CONSTANTINOPLE (998).

"THE HOLY SYNOD GATHERED BY GOD'S GRACE (999) AND THE DECREE (1000) OF THE MOST REVERENT EMPERORS IN THE METROPOLIS OF THE EPHESIANS (1001). *to the beloved and most longed for Fellow-Ministers, who sojourn* (1002) *at Constantinople, and to the most religious Presbyters and Deacons of the same Constantinople*

"To those who are situated in so heavy a sea (1003) of affairs," [as we are], "and who are so much warred against from every side, and who are not at all permitted to look at the gentle and serene face of the most reverent and Christ-loving Emperors, from whom alone we could hope for release from our troubles," [to such as we, we repeat], "what other consolation can be thought of than with our own members to bitterly lament our" [sorrowful] "circumstances. And ye have exhibited zeal for piety in all things, and are members of the Ecumenical Synod (1004). Therefore let your

---

serie recensiti " See the Greek in col. 1300 of tome III. of Coleti. and the Latin in col. 1299 id.

NOTE 997.—I have translated from the Greek, as in col. 1296-1300 of tome III. of Coleti's *Concilia* and have to some extent compared the *Collectio Regia*, tome v., Paris, A. D. 1644, and have looked over Hardouin and Mansi to some extent.

Mansi here adds, in a note, col. 1443, 1444 of tome IV. of his *Concilia*. "*In the Greek Codex Regius* 524, *and in the ancient Version which both Ant, Contius edited, and which some manuscripts exhibit. Julian*" (Juvenal?) "*subscribes alone.*"

NOTE 998.—The marginal note in col. 1300 of tome III. of Coleti, here is, "*Epistle written by the Holy Synod to the Bishops, Presbyters, and Deacons in Constantinople.*"

NOTE 999.—Literally, "*by God's favor.*"

NOTE 1000.—Or, "*oracle,*" or, "*Godly decree,*" or, "*Godly utterance,*" Greek θέσπισμα.

NOTE 1001.—Ephesus.

NOTE 1002—There seems as early as this to have been nearly always a number of Bishops at Constantinople, and during the Synod it sent representatives there.

NOTE 1003.—Greek, ἐν τοσαίτῃ τρικυμίᾳ . . . πραγμάτων.

NOTE 1004.—"*And ye, exhibiting zeal for piety in all things,*" [are] "*members of the Ecumenical Synod ,*" [and so share our lot and can sympathize with us].

Whenever a Christian contends for the Incarnation, anti-creature-serving decisions of Ephesus, or any other Orthodox Ecumenical Synod, he is doing the same blessed work as

Piety understand that our abiding in Ephesus amounts to nothing more than prisons" [to us], "and that accordingly we have been shut up in it for the three months time, and that we are not permitted to send any persons by sea, or by land, without peril and without fear, to the pious Court or to any other place (1005). For as often as it has been possible for our missives to be delivered" [to those to whom they were sent,], "those who carried them through unnumbered dangers (1006) could be safe only by altering their appearance at one time in one way at another in another. And the cause of our being so kept under guard is that all things regarding us may be lyingly reported" [by them] "to the most religious Emperor. For some, as we learn, tell the pious ears" [of the Emperor] "that we are making seditions (1007) while others have dared to report that our Ecumenical Synod has deposed the in all things most dear to God and most holy Archbishop of Alexandria, Cyril, and the most holy and most dear to God our Fellow-Bishop Memnon (1008), and still others have perchance had the audacity to add the statement that we have permitted ourselves to come to friendly terms with

---

those who sat in it and in that sense is a member of it. But the Ecumenical Synod had sent Bishops of its own assembly to the Emperor, and they were at Constantinople. See the English translation of Hefele's *History of the Church Councils*, vol. III., pages 78, 79, 87, 90, 91, 102, 106, and 116.

Furthermore, every Bishop holding to the vi. Ecumenical Synods is eligible to a seat in any Orthodox Ecumenical Synod. And the Ecumenical Synod, in earlier times, before the division into East and West, was always considered the highest court of appeals for the whole Church, though it was not called together by the Emperors except on great and emergent occasions, just as the Synod of the civil diocese was its highest court of appeal at first for it, and recognized as such in Canon VI. of the Second Ecumenical Synod, though it met only seldom as there provided.

NOTE 1005.—Surely this was oppression of the Orthodox. Noble was their stand against creature worship and cannibalism and idolatry on the Eucharist.

NOTE 1006.—Or, "*through ten thousand dangers.*"

NOTE 1007.—This falsehood is asserted as truth in the Nestorian documents above epitomized. See for example in the *Report of John and his Conventicle to the Emperor*, pages 263 264 above, and their context, and the answer to that slander in *Memnon's Epistle to the Clergy of Constantinople*, that is Orthodox Document VI. above, pages 428-432.

NOTE 1008.—The Synod of the Apostasy had so reported. See the Nestorian Documents above particularly pages 248, 250, 263, 264, 268, 270, 272, 276; compare 285-287, 289, 290, 293-295, 296-303, 360, 377.

the Sanhedrim (1009) *of the Apostasy of which John, the Bishop of the city of the Antiochians, is leader.* And the strict watch and the great war against us comes from the desire to keep these facts from being known. Therefore being in not a little deprivation of resources," [and difficulty], "we have hastened to write to your God-Revering-ness, for we know that inasmuch as ye hold the rank of genuine children to the Ecumenical Synod, and do not permit the Orthodox faith to be at all betrayed, that ye will prostrate yourselves with much entreaty, and with tears and with this letter to the most religious and Christ-loving Emperor, and tell him of all the things done against us. For we have not condemned the aforesaid most holy and most dear to God Bishops Cyril and Memnon (1010) but deem them worthy of the greatest glory and of crowns, for they alone and first, before all the rest" [of us], "were moved with godly zeal and made use of every means to cut off the preacher of the impiety (1011), the most impious Nestorius, and to purge the Churches of such defilement (1012). And now we will not suffer ourselves to be separated from the Communion of the aforesaid most holy Bishops, but deem it the greatest gain to be exiled with them (1013). And

---

NOTE 1009.—Or "Little Synod" or "Conventicle."

NOTE 1010.—The Apostasy had reported that the Synod had so done, for they represented themselves as the Synod to the Emperor, till their cheat in that matter was detected. See the note last above.

NOTE 1011.—Greek, τῆς ἀσεβείας. And surely infidelity on such a point as the Incarnation, and on that of worshipping God alone, is "*impiety*," and so are Cannibalism in the Eucharist, and wafer, and bread and wine worship, God's Word every where being witness.

NOTE 1012.—All such heresies as those mentioned in the last note above, are *defilements* in the worse sense, God's Word being witness. The Church will not be free from "*spot or wrinkle or any such thing*" (Eph. v: 27), till it gets rid of them.

NOTE 1013.—Noble words nobly stuck to. How unlike the wretched so-called Anglican and American Bishops of our days, who prefer ease and fat salaries and honors to doing their vowed duty, and who let the heretical clergy infidelize by denying the Incarnation and the inspiration of Holy Writ, or idolatrize by bringing in the worship of creatures, not only of Christ's humanity, but also, by invocation, of angels and saints, and by holding to real substance presence of Christ's Divinity and humanity in the Lord's Supper, and to their worship there, and that, too, when all those infidelizings and idolatrizings are condemned by God's Word, and following it, by the Third Ecumenical Synod, and by the three after it, and by their own Thirty-nine Articles and Homilies. For the eternal damnation of the poor souls of simple men and still simpler women entrusted to them, what can they say when Christ says to them, What have ye done with my sheep? Where are my

we have decided not to receive the *Sanhedrim of the Apostasy* into Communion, but we have all, even with one voice, anathematized before the Church both John the Bishop of Antioch and those who are with him; in the first place because they would not permit themselves with us, to co-depose the preacher of the impiety, Nestorius, and moreover, have not at all ceased to consort with him (1014), and to talk and argue for him; and in the second place (1015) because they made that most lawless and alien to the canons attempt to outrage and spitefully insult the aforesaid most holy Bishops, and dared to co-deceive the pious ears of the most Christ-loving Emperors; and thirdly (1016) because they have not at all forsaken the opinions (1017) of Nestorius. For all those reasons indeed, having once cut them off from all Church communion, and having stripped them of every priestly (1018) function, we have separated them, and we are determined rather to be deprived of our Churches, (which God forbid!), rather than to come into communion with them again, until they shall, in an especial manner, correct their faults aforesaid (1019). And we make these things known to your

---

Note 1014.—This was contrary to the law of the New Testament (Matt xviii: 17; I. Tim. vi: 3 to 6; Titus iii: 10; compare II. Thess. iii: 14, 15, &c.), and that of the Christian Church in the Ecumenical and in the local canons. The design of such withdrawal of fellowship was to admonish the sinner thus bound on earth and so bound in heaven (Matt. xviii: 18; John xx: 23; I. Cor, v: 3 to 6; II. Cor. ii: 10; I. Tim. i. 20), of his lost estate, and so to warn and convert him; and at the same time to minimize, and if possible to do away with all his influence in the Church, to corrupt and ruin souls. Every organization must have discipline. And Christ, therefore, has not willed his Church to be lacking in that respect. The fact that it has some times been *abused* should not prejudice us against its due use, for without it a Church sinks into doctrinal and moral anarchy.

Note 1015.—Or, "*then*," or "*in the next place*." Greek, ἔπειτα δὲ.

Note 1016.—Greek, μετὰ δὲ τοῦτο, which may be rendered "*besides that*."

Note 1017.—Literally, "*the mind*," or "*way of thinking*," (τοῦ φρονήματος τοῦ Νεστορίου).

Note 1018.—The word ἱερατικὴν is here used probably, as is quite common in old writers, for "*episcopal*." See notes on that use of the term elsewhere in this work. See under *Priesthood* in the *General Index* to vol. I. of Chrystal's *Nicaea*, and under *Priest, Priesthood*, and *Priestly* on page 650, vol. I. of his *Ephesus*.

Note 1019.—Nobly said again. How many of the so-called Bishops of the Christian world would be willing to sacrifice their support and honor as those Holy Ghost moved Bishops at Ephesus were? But they felt their responsibilities and "*had respect unto the recompence of the reward*," Heb. XI., 26.

Piety also that you may regard them in the same way (1020). Be exhorted therefore in regard to these things, and tell the most religious and Christ-loving Emperor, and ask in behalf of all the Synod that those who have not been at all condemned by the Canons be given back to us, that is the most holy and most dear to God Bishops Cyril and Memnon; and ask him moreover to show mercy upon us and at last to deliver us from this specious prison, and if indeed we are worthy to see the face of the most religious and most Christ-loving Emperor, ask him to cause that" [favor] "to be granted to us; but if we have been judged unworthy of that" [favor], "ask him to let us at least return to our own Churches, that we may not all perish here, some wasting away by disease and others from sadness (1021). Furthermore, in order to avoid the labor of a large crowd's appending their subscriptions" [to this document], "we have deemed it sufficient that it be signed by the hands of the presidents" (1022) (1023).

"*A Monition*" [or "*Reminding*"] (1024) "*sent to the Constantinopolitan Clergy with the Report* (1025).

We are being killed by the heats, for the atmosphere is heavy

---

NOTE 1020.—That is as suspended from communion, and so by Church law and that of the New Testament to be treated *as the heathen man and the publican* till they repented, Matt. xviii; 15-19.

NOTE 1021.—Greek, ὑπὸ ἀθυμίας

NOTE 1022.—Greek, τῶν προεδρῶν. We should expect their names here, but they are not given either in Coleti or in the *Collectio Regia*. I infer that Juvenal of Jerusalem was one of them, both from his rank in the absence of Cyril and Memnon and of the occupants of the other great Eastern sees, and because his name is signed to the document next above this.

NOTE 1023.—I have translated the above document from the original Greek in Coleti's *Concilia*, tom. III., cols. 1300, 1301, and have corrected one or two typographical errors in it by it as in tom. v. of the *Collectio Regia* (Paris A. D. 1644), pages 756-759. I have looked at it to some extent in Mansi and Hardouin, as I have also the Memorial after it above as in them.

NOTE 1024.—This document is found only in Latin in Coleti, Mansi, Hardouin and in the *Collectio Regia*; and seems to be an appendix to the document which it here immediately follows. Or does it belong to one before it? Its heading in Latin is "Commonitorium cum Relatione directum clero Constantinopolitano."

NOTE 1025.—Hardouin here states, "An old edition adds '*From the Synod*.' "I suppose the report here meant to be the last document above which is a Report, though it is headed "*A Synodical Epistle to the Clergy of Constantinople*," in Coleti.

(1026), and almost daily some one is buried, so that all the servants (1027) languishing and growing feeble are sent home, and the rest

NOTE 1026.—Ephesus was unhealthy then as now.

NOTE 1027.—That is the men-servants (pueri) of the Bishops. If they were single, the common sentiment of the Church was against their having female servants. Canon III. of the First Ecumenical Synod forbade them to have any women living with them except close relatives and such as were above suspicion. And the whole Church from the beginning generally preferred fit single men for that office. In so doing it acted in accordance with the example of Christ, who, so far as appears, chose only one of His apostles, Peter, from the married; and invited those who had left all to follow him to remain single, if they could, for the kingdom of heaven's sake (Matt xix; 12). Of course such rare cases as Bp. Bull, who was married, deserve an episcopate, for they have the requisite learning, and soundness in faith, and self-sacrifice; but all Church History teaches, that while such of the lower clergy as can not contain should be allowed to marry, nevertheless *a learned and sound monk* ordinarily makes the best Bishop. Such were nearly all the Apostles including Paul, and nearly all the greatest Fathers, and such were Ridley and Latimer, and, unless the report is a mistaken one, such were Sancroft and the other Bishops of the Church of England who went to incarceration in the Tower in the reign of James the Second and saved Church and State from the idolatry of Rome and from subjugation to it, when its married Bishops cowered and avoided the conflict, as its married Bishops suffer their Church doctrines to be trampled under foot by enemies within it now. In brief, Church History teaches that the New Testament system is the best in practice. It is to choose the bulk of the Bishops from the sound and learned and chaste monks; but nevertheless not to debar a few married men of equal learning and soundness from that high function; and while inviting before ordination, in Christ's words, every man to receive the higher exhortion of becoming a *eunuch for the kingdom, of heaven's sake* (Matt. xix: 12) *if he can receive that saying*, nevertheless to admit to the deaconship and the presbyterate men who have never been married but once, and to permit no second marriage to any Bishop, Presbyter or Deacon. In case they marry again let them become laics, according to the ancient rule. For Paul, by the Holy Ghost, forbids to ordain any man even deacon who has been *the husband of more than one wife* (I. Tim. III: 12. Compare I, Tim. III: 2, and Titus 1: 6.) as that passage has been generally understood from the beginning, and his language contemplates that the married clergy should be married *before* entering orders. But if those who cannot receive Christ's precept of the single life be forced to remain without wives, they will keep concubines, as the whole history of the Roman church proves, and damn their own souls and corrupt their people. A law that would permit the proportion of married men in the episcopate now that there was in Christ's day, say about one twelfth or one sixth of the whole order would be closest to Christ's example in this matter. But it should not be put into the hands of the married lower clergy or the people to trample under foot the virginal and celibate teaching of Christ and his single Apostles Paul and John (Matt. xix; 10-13, I. Cor. VII. all of it; and Rev. XIV. 1-6.), for when left to themselves they are in our day apt to forget it and in their selfishness and ignorance to fill the episcopate with married men almost wholly, to the decay of discipline and the growth of heresy and the wreck of their communion as in the Church of England to-day, and in its American daughter, the Protestant Episcopal, in both which ruin comes through the weakness and dodging of the duty of enforcing order on the part of married Bishops, who are content, if they can get their bellies full of food and drink and a good fat salary and rich wives for their sons and good matches for their daughters, to be moved by their families to let God's work take care of itself and to leave the wolves of infidelity and

of us, all being Bishops (1028), are in these" [painful] "circumstances. Wherefore it is a reasonable thing for your Reverence (1029) to go to the Christ-loving Emperor and to say that the Synod is oppressed by those who forbid a termination" [of its labors] "to be granted to it, in order that they (1030) may be absolutely (1031) killed by feebleness and lassitude. But your Reverence ought to know that although they (1032) may struggle so hard

---

Roman creature-service to tear and rend the sheep of their flocks. Their wives and daughters are not theologians, and importune them to avoid conflict with the powers and agents of what is evil, and they generally do so to the eternal damnation of their own souls as well as to the ruin of their flocks. There is no greater sham or curse to a Church than a wholly married episcopate; except it may be the sham of putting unlearned and heretical monks given to the spiritual whoredoms of invoking saints, which is creature-worship, and to the worship of the wafer or bread and wine in the Eucharist, to image and cross worship, and to other idolatries, into the episcopal office. Both parties should be deposed and excommunicated, among the latter Bishop King of Lincoln and Bp. Grafton of Fond du Lac and all single Bishops, Presbyters and Deacons of their kind. Some writer has said that all the Archbishops of Canterbury after Parker to Wake were single. However that may be, with the exception of the unworthy celibate Laud, they were reputable men. He is deserving of condemnation for violating his own ordination vows by putting images into Churches again, and by imitating the mediæval idolatrous Romish Church. He did all that rather than to follow the New Testament and the doctrine, discipline, rite and custom of the first three centuries, and of the VI. Ecumenical Synods which he did not thoroughly know. And he persecuted and imprisoned faithful men. Now such men must never be chosen because they are single, but, if there be no sound and learned and otherwise fit single men let sound monogamous men be chosen, for the preservation of Scriptural Orthodoxy is the chief thing.

And let no one of the Deistical sect of the Freemasons be chosen, nor any one for any motive of nepotism or earthly relationship, or from any other unworthy reason, and if any such have been chosen let them be at once deposed. The only motive that should be allowed to operate is to choose the men best fitted to promote the glory of God the good of the Church and the upbuilding and salvation of souls.

The New Testament nowhere forbids a single cleric of any order to marry even after ordination, nor does any canon of the four Ecumenical Synods, nor any enactment of the Six. Yet some local canons of the fourth century and the fifth do, but not wisely, for the result has often been concubinage and whoredom and shame. Paul, after he had become an Apostle even, implies in I. Corinthians ix, 5, that he might marry if he would, but would not, preferring the single life. But of them more anon, if God will, in the proper place.

NOTE 1028.—Latin, "et alii omnes episcopi."
NOTE 1029.—"The Bishops, Presbyters and Deacons in Constantinople."
NOTE 1030.—The Bishops of the Ecumenical Synod.
NOTE 1031.—Latin, ut absolute languore necentur. Hardouin reads *absumpti*.
NOTE 1032.—The Emperor's representatives at Ephesus. John of Antioch and his party seem not to have made any complaint on that score till they saw their efforts to save Nestorian heresies failing of their intended result. See their documents above.

against us that we may all die, nevertheless nothing else shall be done besides those things which have been decreed by us, with Christ our Saviour's help" (1033).

ORTHODOX DOCUMENT IX.

"COPY OF AN EPISTLE WRITTEN BY THE ARCHBISHOP CYRIL TO THE MOST RELIGIOUS BISHOPS IN CONSTANTINOPLE, THEOPEMPTUS, AND POTAMON AND DANIEL IN REGARD TO THE INTRIGUES FROM WHICH HE SUFFERED FROM THE TRUMPED UP CHARGES IN THE LETTERS OF NESTORIUS AND JOHN (1034).

"CYRIL *to Theopemptus, and Daniel, and Potamon, beloved and Fellow-Ministers; joy* (1035) *in the Lord.*

"Many slanders have been made and sent thither (1036) against us. One is that many followed us from the city of the Alexandrians from the bath (1037). Another is that nuns have come forth" [thence with us] (1038), "and it is reported that the slanderers have asserted that Nestorius suffered his deposition by my contriving and not by the intention of the Synod. But blessed be the Saviour who has refuted those who say such things! For when my Lord the most magnificent and most glorious Count of the divine largesses came into the city of the Ephesians (1039), he condemned those who talked such foolish things, because he found nothing of truth in them. But he perceived that the Holy Synod is contending for the faith of its own motion, and not to gratify me nor anyone else, but that, moved by godly zeal and not being able to bear the blasphemies of that man (1040), it condemned him by a vote.

NOTE 1033.—As is said above, I have translated the above "*Monition,*" or "*Commonitory,*" from Coleti, and have looked at it in the *Collectio Regia* also.

NOTE 1034.—The Greek of the end of the above sentence is corrupt, and so I have followed the Latin.

NOTE 1035.—Or, "*greeting in the Lord.*"

NOTE 1036.—Literally, "*Many slanders have gone thither against us,*" that is to Constantinople. See some slanders in the Nestorian Documents above, pages 241 and after.

NOTE 1037.—Does this mean employees of a public bath in Alexandria, or was one part of that city called "*the Bath*" (τοῦ βαλανείου).

NOTE 1038.—Monks, like Cyril, are of course vastly injured by charges of undue intimacy with women, and so his enemies meanly lied about him on that score, though it does not appear that they charged him with fornication. And we may be sure that when Count John, the agent of his enemy the Emperor Theodosius, found nothing of fault in him to gratify his master with by reporting it to him, there was none.

NOTE 1039.—That is, Ephesus.

NOTE 1040.—Nestorius.

Nevertheless when the letter of the most pious and Christ-loving Emperors was read, in which it was said that the deposition" [from the episcopate] "of the three (1041) must be received, we were taken into custody, and so remain, not knowing what will be the outcome. But we thank God, not only when we are counted worthy of being made prisoners in fetters (1042) for His name's sake, but also when we are called upon to endure all things besides. For that thing is not without its reward. But the Synod has not suffered itself to commune with John (1043), but stands firm in resistance saying: *Behold our bodies! Behold our Churches! Behold our cities! Ye have authority! But it is impossible for us to commune with the Orientals* (1044) *till their deceitfully contrived enactments against our Fellow-Ministers, which are the issue of their own false accusing, are abrogated*" [by them], "*and they confess the right faith also. For they are convicted of uttering and holding and confessing the dogmas of Nestorius. So all our objection and resistance*" [to them] "*rests on those things* (1045). Let all the Orthodox pray for us. For as the blessed David says, '*I am prepared for the scourges*' (1046), (1047)."

NOTE 1041.—Nestorius, deposed by the Ecumenical Synod, and Cyril and Memnon by the Apostasy. The Emperor had committed the folly of receiving the action of the Apostasy against Cyril and Memnon as valid, an act which shows either his ignorance of the facts, or his lack of any due appreciation of the all-important and vital doctrines involved. See this edict on pages 285-287 above. It is there followed on pages 287-292 by an Epistle of Count John to the Emperor, which shows what sadness and opposition the Orthodox manifested at the deposition of Cyril and Memnon.

NOTE 1042.—Greek, δεσμῶται.

NOTE 1043.—John of Antioch.

NOTE 1044.—That is, the Bishops of the Patriarchate of Antioch, John's jurisdiction, for it was the part chiefly infected with Nestorian heresies.

NOTE 1045.—Noble and self-sacrificing language, and worthy of the apostolic men who were contending for the worship of God alone in accordance with Christ's own teaching in Matt. iv: 10.

NOTE 1046.—Psalm xxxvii. 18, Septuagint.

NOTE 1047.—I have translated the above document from the original Greek in col. 1304 of tome III. of Coleti, and have in places compared pages 760, 761 of tome V. of the *Collectio Regia*, and col. 144, 145 of tome 77 of Migne's *Patrologia Graeca*. I have also glanced at it as in Hardouin and Mansi.

ORTHODOX DOCUMENT X.

"Copy of a letter written to the Holy Synod in Ephesus by the Bishops found in Constantinople, on the twentieth day of Mesori (1048), Indiction XV.

"*To the most holy* (1049) *and most dear to God Bishops*" [or "*Archbishops*"] (1050) "*and Fathers who are gathered by God's grace* (1051) *in the metropolis of the Ephesians*" [*that is*] "*to Celestine* (1052), *Cyril, Juvenal, Firmus,* (1053), *Flavian* (1054), *Memnon* (1055), *Herenian, Theodotus, Acacius, and all your Holy and Ecumenical Synod* (1056), *from the Bishops found in Constantinople, joy in the Lord.*

"We ought to have been present with your Holiness, not only with our souls, but also with our bodies, and to share the distress of your trials, and with

---

Note 1048.—This, according to the marginal note here in Coleti, was August 13, 431. On the Egyptian months see page XIII. of the Introduction in the Oxford translation of *the Festal Epistles of St. Athanasius*. There were thirteen months in the Egyptian year.

Note 1049.—The text here has παναγίοις "*all holy*" in Coleti, but his margin has ἁγιωτάτοις, which the Latin "sanctissimis" in the parallel column follows. The former title, and indeed both are Byzantine Anti-Biblical and blasphemous.

Note 1050.—The margin in Coleti here has ἐπισκόποις, which the Latin in the parallel column, "episcopis," follows. It may well be the truer reading; for most of the prelates at Ephesus were not Archbishops but Bishops suffragan. Indeed the term *Archbishop* was not given at first even to all Metropolitans, but only to the chief of them; see in proof under ἀρχιεπίσκοπος in *Sophocles' Glossary of Latin and Byzantine Greek*, and in his *Greek Lexicon of the Roman and Byzantine Periods*. Indeed as yet the term *Bishop* was a common appellation of prelates of all grades, as we see by the Acts of this very Synod of Ephesus.

Note 1051.—Literally, "*God's favor*" (χάριν).

Note 1052.—Celestine is mentioned with the rest as being considered, like every Bishop, a member of the Ecumenical Synod, and as having a vote in it like the rest; and he is mentioned first according to the Oriental principle set forth in substance in Canons III. of I. Constantinople and XVII. and XXVIII. of Chalcedon, that Ecclesiastical precedences should follow the civil rank of cities, because Rome was the old capital.

Note 1053.—Firmus of Caesarea in Cappadocia, seems to be meant. It was the Patriarchal see of the Diocese of Pontus. Compare Canons II. and VI. of the Second, Ecumenical Synod, and the remark of Socrates in book v. chapter 8 of his *Ecclesiastical History* on the establishment of Patriarchs by that Council. Compare id., book VII. chapter 31.

Note 1054.—Flavian, Bishop of Philippi in Macedonia is meant. He was place holder for Rufus of Thessalonica. Thessalonica was the chief see of the Diocese of Eastern Illyricum.

Note 1055.—Memnon of Ephesus, the chief see of the Diocese of Asia [Minor.] From what is said on page 463, vol. I. of the English translation of Wiltsch's *Geography and Statistics of the Church*, it would seem that Caesarea, Thessalonica and Ephesus are mentioned in the order of their relative precedence in the Ecclesiastical Notitia at that time, or in about that order at that time.

Note 1056.—Or, "*all the Holy and Ecumenical Synod to which you belong.*"

you to be crowned with the prizes (1057). But since the war against the Holy Synod has been extended even to us, and those who go from this very place are not allowed to travel by sea, and are not permitted to go by land, on account of those who lie in wait on the roads (1058), and we can do nothing, we have for our part contributed our tears and prayers; and inasmuch as we can not reach your Holiness, we have made use of our readiness and zeal for you as hands, by co-deposing those whom you have deposed, and by arousing the saints of the Anointed One (1c59). Moreover, we have not been useless to those here, for we have strengthened the people (1060) and kindled the zeal of most" [of them], "and have also rendered the aid of our services to the priests in whatsoever things seemed good to them. But forasmuch as these are small things and only what those who are absent" [from you] "can do, we have also taken courage to write this very epistle, for we deemed blessed your sweating labors for piety, and we address to each one of the Holy Fathers separately, and to all of them in common, the commendations" [uttered] "of (1061) the holy Prophets and of the Fathers. For as Fathers holy and worthy of the heavenly calling (1062), ye have been reckoned as sheep for the slaughter, for ye have been slain all the day long for Christ (1063), and a·e destitute, maltreated and oppressed, though the world is not worthy of you (1064). But, by an epistle, give us counsel as to what is to be done; in order that if we ought to go to the Holy Synod, and with you endure throughout what remains in the way of struggles, we may do it. But if ye command us to remain here (for, by the help of the God who is to be worshipped (1065), reports

---

NOTE 1057.—Greek, τοῖς ἄθλοις. That is the rewards to be reckoned of grace that is of favor, and not of debt, for faithful service to God, and to His Church, and to the deathless souls of men. Compare the expression "*prize of the high calling,*" etc., in Philip iii: 14. See also I. Cor. ix: 24.

NOTE 1058.—Or, "those who come from that very place" [Ephesus] "are not allowed to travel by sea, and not permitted to come by land, on account of those who lie in wait on the roads." The rendering in the text agrees with the Latin translation, though the Greek is so indefinite as to bear either meaning. Yet the context would seem to favor the rendering in the text, and so would perhaps an expression in the document next following this.

NOTE 1059.—That is "*Christ's saints,*" as it may be rendered, and as it means, for "*Christ*" means "*Anointed*"

NOTE 1060.—That is "*the laity,*" τὸν λαὸν.

NOTE 1061.—Or, "by."

NOTE 1062.—Heb. iii: i.

NOTE 1063.—Rom. viii: 36, Psalm xliv: 22.

NOTE 1064.—Heb. xi: 37, 38.

NOTE 1065.—Greek, διὰ τὸν προσκυνητὸν Θεὸν. This may be rendered to the same effect "*by the help of the adorable God.*" The peculiar kind of adoration meant is, however,

are brought to us of useful things even from the most dear to God and most religious Emperor), make that clear, so that we may not be longer consumed by the very great anxiety we are under" (1066).

ORTHODOX DOCUMENT XI.

AN ANSWER OF THE HOLY SYNOD TO THE SAME BISHOPS WHO HAD BEEN FOUND IN CONSTANTINOPLE.

"To the most religious and most dear to God Fellow-Ministers, Eulalius, Eutrechius (1067), Acacius, Chrysaphius, Jeremiah, Theodulus, Isaiah; THE HOLY SYNOD ASSEMBLED BY GOD'S GRACE (1068) AND A DECREE OF OUR MOST RELIGIOUS AND CHRIST-LOVING EMPERORS IN THE METROPOLIS OF THE EPHESIANS (1089) wish joy in the Lord (1070).

"It is not at all unnatural that those who are so disposed as your letter to us has shown you to be, should contend on our side with

---

bowing, the most common act of religious service, and so here used for them all. Cyril and the Council had contended that God alone (not the Man put on by the Word) could be bowed to, that is worshipped. See vol. I. of Chrystal's *Ephesus*, note 183, on pages 79-128; note 664, pages 323-324; note 679, pages 332-362, and against the Nestorian *relative worship* of Christ's humanity, page 461, note 949; note 156, pages 61-69, and note 582, pages 225, 226.

The definitions of the whole Church against the worship of Christ's humanity are summed up in the note matter under Head II. on pages 108-112 of vol. I. of Chrystal's *Ephesus*. There and on page 461, text and note 949 there, the whole Church has again and again, aye often, condemned the attempted dodge of *relative worship* for that error of *Man-Worship*, that is *Creature-Worship*.

All worship of an alleged presence of Christ's humanity and of an alleged presence of His Divinity in the Lord's Supper, and the Cannibalism of eating the former there, and what St. Cyril of Alexandria terms the *impossibility* of eating the latter there are condemned by Cyril and the Universal Church in note 606, pages 240-313 of vol. I. of Chrystal's *Ephesus*. See also there under *Man Worship*, pages 631-635, and Nestorius' Heresy 2, *Man-Worship* on pages 639-641, and his heresy 4, one nature Consubstantiation page 642, and his Heresy 5, his worship of the alleged real substance presence of Christ's humanity in the Eucharist, page 642, id.

NOTE 1066.—I have translated the above from col. 1304. 1305 of tome III. of Coleti; and have to some extent compared the same document as on pages 761-763, tome v. (Paris 1644) of the *Collectio Regia*. I have also glanced at it as in Hardouin and Mansi.

NOTE 1067.—Or, "Eutrochius."

NOTE 1068.—Greek, κατὰ χάριν θεοῦ.

NOTE 1069.—*Ephesus*.

NOTE 1070.—Or, instead of *"wish joy in the Lord,"* *greeting in the Lord."*

their souls and their bodies and should deem common" (1071) [to themselves also] "the toils which we have here endured. And in" [wrestling] "contests eager spectators bring not a little aid to the contestants, by suggesting to them to use some of the wrestler's arts (1072) and by exciting them to victory, and by impressing on them what those who struggle for glory should do. But your God-Reveringness has devised what is greater than that art by strengthening us by your prayers and by propitiating God for us, to the end *that we may not be tried more than we are able to bear* (1073), and that though tried we may overcome those who try us (1074). And ye have shared with us the care of the labors. For those who are at a distance, as they learn what is being done, usually suffer more from anxiety than do those who are engaged in the contests themselves. So it is a sufficient consolation for us to learn that the devices of the enemies against us are not unknown, but that their presumptuous actions against the Holy Synod have reached even you. For we know that, through your God-belovedness, every one of them will pass on to the ears of the most religious Emperors, and that we shall be released from these difficulties, when ye (1075) make clear to them both the madness (1076) of John of Antioch and of those who are with him, and those things which they have dared to do unlawfully" [and] "contrary to the canons against the most dear to God and most holy Bishops, Cyril and Memnon and against the Holy Synod. For we reckon that the dear to God and most pious Emperor knows nothing of those things

---

NOTE 1071.—Greek, κοινούς.
NOTE 1072.—That is, "wrestlers' *tricks*,' τῶν παλαισμάτων.
NOTE 1073.—I. Cor. x; 13.
NOTE 1074.—The favorers of Nestorius and his heresies.
NOTE 1075.—One or two words in the Greek here are corrupt. I follow a reading in Coleti's margin on one word; that is his substitution of ὑμῶν for the corrupt ἡμῖν of the text. The Latin rendering there in the parallel column agrees with ὑμῶν, and the English translation above.
NOTE 1076.—Greek, ἀπόνοιαν.

clearly (1077). For those who have roused (1078) war against us
could not have so far prevailed against us as to induce him to think
that we who were wronged were deserving of no pity, but that we
should be subjected to accusations as though we had done wrong,
though we had not roused ourselves to execute any" [mere] "revenge
(1079) against those who did us wrong. We deem the matters which
have hindered your Holiness from coming hither, a sufficient excuse
for you. For we are now held fast together, in a state of strict siege
both by land and by sea, so that we cannot make known to your
Holiness the things which have been done (1080). And there was
need of your tears and prayers (1081) that each one of us who have
not yet reached the end" [of this business] "may have the same
judgment on the matter and persevere in refusing to come to"
[wicked] "terms with them (1082) though the rulers (1083) are using great violence to drive us to it (1084). And as we share your
good-will in this affair, we know also that ye share both the labors

---

NOTE 1077.—Or, "*has known nothing*," hence, it means, *knows nothing now*; Greek, εγνωκεναι.

NOTE 1078.—Or "*rouse.*"

NOTE 1079.—The Ecumenical Synod, up to the session in which it made its canons, had not deposed any of the Nestorians except Nestorius himself, no, not even John of Antioch, but had only suspended the Bishops of the Apostasy from communion and from the exercise of Episcopal functions; though, as having an overwhelming majority of the Ecumenical Synod they could, before that, have deposed them all, and might righteously have done so. And when at last they did depose them, they acted not from any spirit of revenge but from the behests of solemn duty as God's watchmen and discipliners against soul-damning error. They could not have done otherwise without being so derelict in the performance of their obligations as to be justly deposed in time and eternally damned for all eternity. For they stood as the teachers of the hundreds of millions of the Universal Church in future ages, against infidelity on the Incarnation and against creature-service.

NOTE 1080.—Or, "according to the marginal reading in Coleti, "*are being done.*"

NOTE 1081.—Literally "*prayer.*"

NOTE 1082.—John of Antioch, and his Nestorian Synod of the Apostasy.

NOTE 1083.—The representatives of the Emperor at Ephesus, the Counts sent from Constantinople, and the soldiers and the rest who were under their orders.

NOTE 1084.—Greek, πολλῆς ἀνάγκης εἰς τοῦτο τῶν ἀρχοντων ἡμᾶς συνελαυνοίσης. The term ἀνάγκης, "*necessity*" shows us what sort of measures were made use of to force the Bishops of the Ecumenical Synod to a deathful and damning compromise with soul-damning error. The attempt was made to *necessitate* them to that sinful course but it failed.

Answer of the Synod to Bishops at Constantinople. 451

and the prizes (1085). And as we know what took place regarding those who loved the holy martyrs, so we see the same thing in the case of your God-lovedness (1086). For though ye are outside of the contests (1087), nevertheless ye have been deemed worthy of the crowns" [given for good conduct in them] "because ye are in favor of those who are suffering wrong, and condemn those who have risen up against them (1088); so that your (1089) absence" [from us] "does not seem" [to us] "to be a defect, because ye agree with all our judgments. And what we have learned that ye have done in increasing the zeal of the people and in rousing them to boldness against the enemies, is not a little in the way of help towards victory, and is, besides, a very great thing in the way of consolation" [to us]. "It remains, therefore, that ye stay in that place (1090) and make known to us the affairs there, and bring the things from us to the knowledge of the most godly Emperors and of the Holy Church. For that will be a greater help" [to us] "than for you to come to us and to endure miseries with us who are besieged. Moreover, as we reckon that the things sent before have not come to your knowledge, we have sent again to your God-Reveringness copies of the same matters; and we have reported" [matters] "again to the most religious Emperors. And let it be your God-Reveringness' care to get information; in order that, if they have given any answers, they may be reminded of the things reported" [to them] "and that if that has not been done, their Piety may now at least learn of those things as to which some of

---

NOTE 1085.—Greek, τῶν ἄθλων, that is the heavenly "*rewards*" for *contending earnestly for the faith once delivered to the saints*, Jude 3. In the document next above to which this is an answer, the Bishops found at Constantinople had expressed a desire for them.

NOTE 1086.—Greek, τῆς ὑμετέρας θεοφιλίας.

NOTE 1087.—Or, "*remote from the contests*," that is remote from those undergone by the Orthodox Synod at Ephesus.

NOTE 1088.—Or, "*the insurgents*," or, "*the rebels*," (τοὶς . . . ἐπαναστάντας), that is John of Antioch and his fellow unbelievers and creature-servers. The blessings mentioned above as given to the sympathizers with and defenders of the Orthodox doctrines of the Third Ecumenical Council in Cyril's age, belong to all their class in every age.

NOTE 1089.—Coleti's text has typographical errors here and there, which I correct from the more accurate *Collectio Regia*, which has here ὑμᾶς where Coleti has wrongly ἡμᾶς.

NOTE 1090.—That is, Constantinople.

the plotters against us were before" [this] "eager and active" [to ensure] "that their God-belovedness (1091) should be ignorant of them. We pray that ye may be strong in the Lord, beloved and most longed for brethren (1092)."

ORTHODOX DOCUMENT XII.

A Prayer and Supplication by the Clergy of Constantinople for the Holy Synod in Ephesus, addressed to the Emperors, Theodosius and Valentinian.

"Forasmuch as we know that your Piety has made much account both of the holy churches of God and of the pious faith which is preached in them and which has been handed down to us from (1093) the Fathers, and that your Piety knows how we have labored for it before, and how great praise moreover belongs to your piety for your zeal on its behalf; we make bold therefore to tell your Christ-loving ears of the present trouble also of the churches, For the aim of our profession, most religious Emperors, in addition to setting forth other laws" [of God] "enjoins upon us the duty of obeying all rulers and authorities, so long as that obedience may seem to be profitable to the souls" [of men] (1094). "But whenever it passes the limit of what is useful and profit-

---

Note 1091.—That is the Emperors. It has seldom been the case in history, never in the case of any other of the Six Ecumenical Synods, that the Orthodox had to struggle against such heavy obstacles as had this Third Council, which has been so unjustly, and wickedly, and unwisely blamed. The action mentioned above in keeping the Emperors ignorant of the facts, and in using all the powers of the State to crush the Synod and Orthodoxy, and especially its chief champions, Cyril and Memnon, would be deemed scoundrelly in the case of a Synod in our day. But for God's help that iniquity would have succeeded.

Note 1092.—I have translated the above Document from col. 1105-1108 of tome III. of Coleti's *Concilia*, but have corrected errors in it from vol. v. of the *Collectio Regia* (Paris, 1644), pages 763-766. I have also looked at it to some extent as in Hardouin and Mansi.

Note 1093.—Or, "*out of the Fathers*," ἐκ πατέρων. The translation in the text above would include all that was handed down in the faith and customs in doctrine, discipline, and rite *from the beginning*, and what was handed down in the writings of the Fathers also: the translation in this note would mainly or wholly refer to the latter though without denying the former.

Note 1094.—Titus III; 1: Matt. xxii; 17-22: Mark xii; 13-18: Luke xx; 19-27: Acts IV; 18-21: etc.

This was a noble position to be taken by the clergy of Constantinople; and they deserve the more credit for it, because the government being absolute, and the monarch a sympathizer with Nestorius and seemingly to some extent with one or more of his heresies, they ran the risk of being deprived of their liberties, their orders, and even their lives if

able, then the expounders (1095) of God's laws exhort us (1096) to speak freely to your Summitness (1097) also. And especially if the imperial Dynasty is also ornamented with the matter of Orthodoxy, we reckon that fact as on the side of correct deeds, and glory in it exceedingly, so long as they may continually sing to us" [the words],"*I was speaking before kings*" [or "*Emperors*"], "*and was not put to shame*" (1098); and so long as by those words they may urge us not to fail to imitate that boldness of speech on like occasions. And we, therefore, being persuaded that the present is a fit time for us to use that boldness of speech, by this Supplication make known our judgment to your Piety. As to the pretended deposition" [from the episcopate] "enacted against the most holy and most dear to God Bishops Cyril and Memnon, by those who have split off from the Holy Synod (1099) of whom the majority are heretics, and without a city (1100), and excommunicated (1101) our decision is that if your Mightiness should be persuaded by the authority of the authors of that vote" [of deposition] "to ratify it and to approve their authority and to admit that vote, which is without any reason and is of no force in any respect, and is puerile, inasmuch as it was not enacted piously at the first by any person who belonged to the Holy Synod, which" [alone] "has the authority to hear and decide such cases (1102) and because the sentence of conviction" [passed against Cyril and Memnon] "was not for any of those things which are

---

he chose. Who of us in these modern times in so-called free lands dares to stand up against creature-serving monarchs and the unbelieving multitude of nominal or radical Protestants who wish to deprive God's orthodox and spiritual minister of his rights and to subject him to their humors and caprices, and in fact to make him their slave. and to compel him to deny the plain teachings of the New Testament which set forth such doctrines as the Trinity, the Atonement, a hell of fire and brimstone, and baptism for the remission of sins? And, much more, who of us would dare to stand up before a creature-invoking and Man-worshipping monarch and protest against his sins to his face.

NOTE 1095.—Greek, τῶν θείων νόμων ἐξηγηταί. From what follows below, this expression seems to include the writers of Scripture if it does not primarily refer to them.

NOTE 1096.—Or "*warn us*," or "*command us.*"

NOTE 1097.—Greek, τὴν ἡμετέραν κορυφήν. The Latin rendering in Coleti here is vestrum apicem.

NOTE 1098.—Psalm CXVIII: 46, Septuagint version: our CXIX· 46.

NOEE 1099.—John of Antioch and his conventicle of the Apostasy.

NOTE 1100.—As episcopates were commonly named from cities as now, therefore to have no city was really to have no real episcopal jurisdiction, but only the title.

NOTE 1101.—As in the case of laics, so in the case of clerics, there were two kinds of excommunication, one *lesser* which simply *suspended* from communion but did not depose the Bishop or other cleric but only inhibited him from performing any ministerial function; and another and a *greater* excommunication which excluded a man entirely and utterly from the Church. This last would, I suppose, not be inflicted on a Bishop, Elder, or Deacon, till he had been first deposed.

NOTE 1102.—The Church from the beginning held that if a decision on doctrine, discipline, or rite was to bind the whole church, it must represent the decision of the whole

prohibited to the priesthood" (1103): "[if your Piety, we say, approves that vote, we repeat], "then" [our decision is that] "we are all ready, with that forwardness of soul which befits Christians, to share the perils or the aforesaid most devout men, and not to shun any dangerous trials, for we deem that a fitting tribute of appreciation on our part for their perils for the faith. Every one of us therefore having so purposed, we earnestly entreat your Divinity (1104) and demand (1105) what we are persuaded is a just thing, namely that ye confirm the vote of those who are the majority (1106), both in authority as it respects the sees" [represented] "and in accuracy as it respects the power of examination as to the right faith, who voted on the same side as did the most holy man" [Cyril] "and they have shown to your Mightiness that their sentiments are right and" [we earnestly intreat and demand moreover] "that ye will not permit all the inhabited world to be thrown into confusion together by listening to the false pretext of peace and to avoid some small part of the" [Diocese of the] "East seeming likely to separate, for, as to that matter, if it is persuaded that the provisions of the canons shall prevail, there is no design on the part of any portion of it to rend itself off from unity (1107). For inasmuch as" [Cyril] "the Teacher of the Ecumenical Synod, on whose side all have voted as is evident by their own statements, has suffered some one of those things which

---

church *assembled* in Ecumenical Synod by its Bishops, or in the local decisions of the whole Church *distributive*, that is by the bulk or majority of its local Synods and of the Bishops who composed them, acting in strict accordance with God's Word as understood by the primitive Church, and witnessed to by its faith and practice from the beginning.

NOTE 1103.—That is, the episcopate, (ἱερωσύνη). On that topic see other notes in this work. under *Priesthood*, page 462, vol. 1. of *Nicaea*. and under *Priest* and *Priesthood* and *Priestly* on page 650, vol. 1. of Chrystal's *Ephesus*.

NOTE 1104.—Greek, τὴν ὑμετέραν θειότητα, literally, in the mouth of a heathen flatterer, "*your divinity*;" but in the mouth of a Christian who admitted no divinity but the Eternal Trinity, it was very wrong. For the term is a relic of the old pagan Roman worship of their Emperors, and its use to a creature is against God's Word and is impliedly anathematized by Anathema VIII. of Cyril's XII. which were approved by the last four Ecumenical Synods. See in proof Chrystal's *Ephesus*, vol. I, pages 204-208, note 520. and pages 331, 332 and notes 676 677 678, 679 and 680 there.

NOTE 1105.—Or "*ask*," ἐξαιτοῦμεν.

NOTE 1106.—That is the Third Ecumenical Synod, the *majority* as opposed to the small *minority* in the Conventicle of John of Antioch at Ephesus.

NOTE 1107.—He who refused to receive the decisions of an Ecumenical Synod which set forth the doctrine held from the beginning, by that fact became a heretic, and a schismatic also when he separated from the said Synod. Indeed the decisions of the Six Ecumenical Synods themselves depose every cleric and excommunicate or anathematize every laic who does not receive them. Of course this would not apply to any one who rejected a spurious so-called Ecumenical Synod, which set forth a faith which had not been from the beginning and which contradicts any of the VI. Ecumenical Synods, like, for instance, the Robbers' Coun-

A Supplication of the Clergy of Constantinople for the Synod. 455

are not befitting according to the order of the canons (1108), and that too after your Piety had reasonably and fairly renounced communion with such things, and had therefore (1109) gathered a Synod, that thou mightest not rob (1110) it of the authority guaranteed to it by its own laws; it is therefore clearly evident that your Piety should not ratify to his (11..)wn injury the outrage and insult perpetrated against the rest of those who vote on the same side" [as Cyril, (1112)]: "for in that case it will necessarily follow that all the Bishops of he inhabited world have been deposed with the aforesaid most devout men; and furthermore it will come to pass that men will suspect that Arius and Eunomius were Orthodox, inasmuch as the most holy Bishops Cyril and Memnon have been made by deception and trickery (1113) to suffer, undeservedly and

---

cil of A. D. 449, or the idolatrous conventicle, held at Nicaea in A. D. 787, which creature servers call the Seventh Ecumenical Synod. Indeed he who receives such a new faith separates himself from the old faith which was from the beginning. Hence the maintainers of the council of A. D. 449 are anathematized by the whole Church, as are those who maintain that of 787 also by the Six Synods.

NOTE 1108.—The reference is to the uncanonical and farcical deposition of Cyril of Alexandria and Memnon of Ephesus by the Conventicle of the Apostasy.

NOTE 1109.—Or, "*for that reason*," διὰ τοῦτο.

NOTE 1110.—Or, "*deprive,*" ἀποστερήσῃς. It would, of course, have been a robbery on the part of the secular powers if they had deprived the episcopate, that is the apostolate (compare Acts i: 20, with Acts i: 25) of their God-given power of deciding church dogma, discipline and rite. This is another praiseworthy utterance of the Constantinopolitan clergy in favor of the Church's liberties, liberties which, it should be added, Theodosius II. had attempted to trample under his feet when he ventured to nullify the decisions of the Third Ecumenical Synod in the case of Nestorius, and to put on a level with their decisions the unauthorized and rebellious enactments of the small conventicle of the Apostasy by receiving their deposition of Cyril and Memnon, and by imprisoning those two confessors of the truth, and trying to bully and force the Synod into the path of heresy.

NOTE 1111.—Or, "*its.*" If we render by *his*, the change from the "*your*" above to *his* is accounted for by the fact that Theodosius was practically the only acting Emperor, owing to the extreme youth of Valentinian.

NOTE 1112.—Or, *on the same side as the Emperor.*

NOTE 1113.—Or, "*by roundabout means.*" The meaning seems to be that the Apostasy by passing off on the Emperor their own deposition of Cyril and Memnon as that of the Third Ecumenical Synod had so cheated him and got him to approve it. The clergy say truly in effect that to approve the enactments of a spurious Ecumenical Synod is really to bring the authority of the genuine Ecumenical Synods under suspicion. The reception of the Synod of Irene and Tarasius of A. D. 787, has had that effect upon hundreds and millions of minds, and has to this hour, and will till it and its paganism and creature-service be formally condemned, as it certainly will be in a future free and really Seventh Ecumenical Synod. Similar has been the result of all those Synods in the West and all those in the East, which have been held since the Sixth Ecumenical Synod, and which, like it, professed to be Ecumenical whereas they contradicted and condemned impliedly or expressly all the definitions of the Third *against the worship of a human being* (ἀνθρωπολατρεία) and

unlawfully (1114, and unbefittingly, the same penalty as did Nestorius who was deposed with good reason for his impious teaching. Do not therefore, O Christ-loving Emperors, suffer the Church which has nursed you to be torn at all," [the Church] "which without any toil on your part raises trophies to your Mightiness against the enemies, nor show that the times of your reign are a season of martyrdom; (1115) but keep now to the affection of your ancestors for the Church, and as each of them obeyed the authority of the Synod of the holy Fathers (1116) held in their own times (1117) and by legislation fortified the de-

against *cannibalism* in the Eucharist ($\dot{a}\nu\theta\rho\omega\pi o\phi\alpha\gamma ia$), and its concomitants of the real substance presence of Christ's flesh and blood in that rite and their worship there, and the later and comparatively new fangled blasphemy of the real presence of the substance of Christ's Divinity in the rite and its worship there, a heresy and blasphemy condemned by Cyril the Orthodox as well as by Nestorius the heretic; see in proof Chrystal's *Ephesus*, vol I., note 183, on pages 79-128 Finally, no man of logical mind and Orthodoxy who knows well and fully believes all the doctrinal decisions of the Six Ecumenical Councils can receive any other Synod which contradicts them or any of them, be said Synod that of the Vatican of 1869, 1870, that of Trent, A. D. 1545-1563, that of Ferrara-Florence, in A. D. 1438-1439, the other Western Councils of Basel, Constance, Vienne, the two of Lyons, the four of Lateran, and that of Constantinople, A. D, 869, and all others, including the image breaking assembly at Constantinople of A. D. 754, because it sanctioned the worship of creatures by invocation, &c., though it acted in perfect consonance with the VI. Synods in smashing the images; and the Greek Conventicle at Jerusalem in A. D. 1672.

NOTE 1114.—That is *"uncanonically,"* and *"wickedly,"* ($\dot{a}\theta\acute{e}\sigma\mu\omega\varsigma$).

NOTE 1115.—Theodosius II. in his persecution of Cyril and the Orthodox Synod was fast travelling that way.

NOTE 1116.—Is *"the Synod of the Holy Fathers"* here meant the First Ecumenical, held in the time of the Emperor Constantine? Is it not rather the Second Ecumenical which was held in the time of Theodosius I, the grandfather of Theodosius II, while the latter's father Arcadius was also living? Constantine the Great was not one of the *"ancestors"* ($\tau\tilde{\omega}\nu$ $\pi\rho o\gamma \acute{o}\nu\omega\nu$) of Theodosius II, to repeat the term used in this Document, and hence the reference must be to the Second Ecumenical Council, not to the First. This is the first, and so far as I have seen, the only Document *relating* to the Third Ecumenical Synod which alludes to I. Constantinople. And even this is not a Document of the Third Council itself, but only a Document which bears on its history. Yet we can readily see that the clergy of Constantinople then regarded as authoritative that Second Council which had made their see the first in the Eastern Church, and the tenor of the passage above would serve to show that they deemed the laws of the Empire and the Emperor to agree with them. But there seems to have been a disposition of some of the greater sees of the East not to bend their necks under the see of Constantinople by allowing its new claim to the right of appellate jurisdiction over them, just as we find chief sees of the West, as for instance Carthage and Arles resisting the then new and anti-canonical claim of Rome to the right of appellate jurisdiction over them. But as from what Gibbon calls the *"final and permanent division of the Roman Empire"* by Theodosius I. between his two sons about A D 395. (See chapters XXIX XXVII and XXXII of his *Decline and Fall of the Roman Empire*: pages 307, 308, 482 and 269 of vol. III. in Bohn's seven volume edition), the Empire of the East was one nation, and the Empire of the West another, it was natural on the principle of having a national Church independent of every other national Church except so far as keeping to the decisions of the Ecumenical Synods and to all the doctrine, discipline, and rite of the whole Church from the beginning is concerned,

cisions which had been set forth by them (1118) and thoroughly taught respect for them; so do ye also be forward in soul to devise the same things for the Holy Synod which has now been assembled by you (1119). So that ye may

that Constantinople should be the chief see of the Eastern Empire and Rome of the Western and that, as in secular matters an appeal always lay from the provinces to Rome; so for convenience sake and for the sake of guarding the national ecclesiastical unity, and its independence *under the Ecumenical canons* from the encroachments of foreign prelates who might use their religious influence to undermine the national secular authorities, should the older system of the Church be changed and an appeal allowed from the ecclesiastical provinces and Dioceses consisting of several provinces, in the Italian, that is Western Empire, to Rome; and likewise from the ecclesiastical provinces or Dioceses of the Greek or Eastern Empire to Constantinople. Up to I. Constantinople such a thing as an appeal from a Patriarch to any thing but an Ecumenical Synod was not permitted by any Ecumenical Canon. Its canon III. even is not definite on the point, but canons IX., XVII. and XXVIII. of the Fourth Ecumenical Council are precise and clear on the matter, at least so far as Constantinople and the Eastern Empire are concerned.

Rome, less favored than Constantinople by the Ecumenical Canons, had no right of appellate jurisdiction outside of Italy at the farthest. Nevertheless by influencing the secular power in Rome to intervene for her, and by the claim of a divine right to override the canons of the whole Church she secured it for in the West for long; though that claim is plainly negatived in the canons of the first four Ecumenical Synods. But as the ages rolled on and new Christian nations arose in the West, many of them shook off the Roman-Italian yoke, as all outside of Italy will in time; as in the East new nations have risen, like Russia, and Servia, and Bulgaria for instance, and have shaken off the Constantinopolitan-Greek yoke. In time the principle embodied in anons IX., XVII., and XXVIII. of the Fourth Ecumenical Synod which in effect and in reality permits an appeal in every nation to the Bishop of its capital from every province and every Diocese consisting of several provinces in that nation, will become universally accepted. The only appeal allowed beyond that will be to an Ecumenical Synod. That principle embodied in those canons saved the Greek sees from subjugation to Rome, and preserved to them their language in the service and their rights in the Church. And so will it do for every other people who embody the principle of allowing no appeal beyond the Bishop of their own capital and his Synod composed of several Bishops from different parts of his nation, as now, for instance, in Russia, except such appeal be to an Ecumenical Synod.

Every nation in those three Dioceses of Thrace, Asia Minor, and Pontus, subjected to Constantinople by canon XXVIII. of Chalcedon and every nation of the former Eastern Empire should, if it becomes independent, act on the principle of no appeal except to an Ecumenical Synod outside of the national church, and so forbid any appeal to Constantinople or any other local foreign appeal, which implies any right to Appellate Jurisdiction for said foreign power outside of its own jurisdiction.

Of course in saying all this, it is admitted that an appeal not in the Canons I think but which has been from the beginning, that is the appeal to the whole Church *distributed in sees, for advice, and opinion* is still allowed as much as ever, provided, of course, the sees appealed to hold to the VI. synods and are anti-creature invoking and anti-image worshipping and Orthodox in every respect. See in Chrystal's *Nicaea*, vol. I., under *Appellate Jurisdiction* and *Rome* in the *General Index* and under the same terms, and under *Appeal* also in Chrystal's *Ephesus*, vol. I., *General Index*.

NOTE 1117.—See the note last above.

NOTE 1118.—That is the decisions of the Second Ecumenical Synod.

NOTE 1119.—The Third Ecumenical Synod, which Theodosius II. had opposed after he called it together.

purely and piously reap the fruits of its hymns of thanksgiving for your reign, and that we may send up to the Master Anointed (1120) sincere prayers for the duration of your Mightiness, most pious and Christ-loving Emperors (1121).

ORTHODOX DOCUMENT XIII.

A MANDATE MADE BY THE HOLY SYNOD FOR THE MOST RELIGIOUS BISHOPS WHO WERE SENT BY THE HOLY SYNOD ITSELF TO CONSTANTINOPLE TO PLEAD ITS CAUSE AGAINST THOSE FROM THE" [Diocese of the] "EAST:

"*To the most dear to God and most God-Revering Presbyter Philip holding the place of Celestine the most holy Bishop of the Apostolic See of the greatest Rome* (1122), and to the most **God-Revering Bishops, Arcadius, Juvenal, Flavian, Firmus, Theodotus, Acacius,**" [and] "Evoptius (1123), THE HOLY AND ECUMENICAL SYNOD GATHERED BY THE GRACE OF GOD AND A DECREE OF THE MOST RELIGIOUS EMPERORS, IN THE METROPOLIS OF THE EPHESIANS, wisheth joy in the Lord.

"Forasmuch as we have been permitted by the most religious and Christ-loving Emperors to send ambassadors on behalf of all the inhabited world assembled together, which through those assembled with us in the metropolis of the Ephesians, has undertaken the

---

NOTE 1120.—That is, "*to the Master Christ*," (Χριστῷ).

NOTE 1121.—I have translated the above Document from columns 1308-1312 of tome III. of *Coleti's Concilia*; and have compared in places, pages 766-769 of tome V. of the *Collectio Regia*, (Paris A. D. 1644). I have also glanced at it to some extent as in Hardouin and Mansi.

NOTE 1122.—Rome on the Tiber, as being the ancient capital of the Roman Republic, was termed "*the older Rome*" and "*Great Rome*," and "*Greatest Rome*" as here (τῆς μεγίστης 'Ρώμης). Constantinople was the new Rome as it is called in canon XXVIII. of the Fourth Ecumenical Synod, and in canon III. of the Second. As has been often said the only reason assigned for Rome's and Constantinople's ecclesiastical preeminence is their preeminence in the civil secular notitia as secular capitals.

NOTE 1123.—Of these eight names the first two were from the patriarchate of Rome, Juvenal from what was then beginning to become the patriarchate of Jerusalem, Flavian from the patriarchate that is Diocese of Macedonia, Firmus from that of Pontus, Theodotus from that of Pontus, Acacius from that of Pontus, and Evoptius was from Ptolemais in Egypt; and every one of these six Orientals was either a Diocesan Bishop, that is, a Patriarch or a Metropolitan, unless Evoptius perhaps be excepted, though from the article on him in

Mandate of the Synod to its Embassy to Constantinople. 459

struggle on behalf of the right faith, we have by a vote (1124) made your God-Reveringness" [such ambassadors], "as before Christ (1125) entrusting to your hands the Embassy for Orthodoxy, and for the holy Fathers and Brethren the most holy and most devout Archbishop Cyril and the most dear to God Bishop Memnon; and by way of providing for the safety of them both and of ourselves and of you also, we have handed this Mandate to you, so that we may know for what things we have sent you, and that your God-Reveringness may know that ye ought not to do any thing at all beyond (1126) those things. Before all things, therefore, it is necessary that your Holiness should know that ye must in no way admit to the Communion John of Antioch and the little Synod of the Apostasy (1127) who are with him; because they are not willing with us to co-condemn (1128) Nestorius, the preacher of the impiety, and because, moreover, they are pleading his cause up to the time of your

---

Smith and Wace's *Dictionary* of *Christian Biography* where it is stated that he "succeeded his elder brother Synesius, as Bishop of Ptolemais, the chief city of the Libyan Peutapolis c [irca] A. D. 430, compared with the article on *Synesius* in *McClintock* and *Strong's Cyclopaedia*, where his church is spoken of as, "the metropolitan Church of Ptolemais," I judge that he was a Metropolitan. Bingham's *Antiq. of the Christian Church*, book IX, chap. VIII, sect. 1, gives a list of ten provinces in the Diocese of Egypt of which Libya Pentapolis was one.

The Mandate of the Conventicle of the Apostasy is addressed to an embassy of eight also, nearly all of whom were from the patriarchate of Antioch. See above, page 806. Compare page 387.

NOTE 1124.—This shows that there was a session of the Ecumenical Synod, the minutes of which are now lost. And other enactments of the Council exist, the minutes in relation to which are not extant. There were probably several sessions whose results only have come down to us. The Acts of Ephesus which we have are therefore only a part of the whole. Such sessions, if later, must have been more or less under the surveillance of the secular representatives of the Emperor, for they seem to have kept them from assembling except when the Emperor permitted them to, as he did in the matter of sending delegates to Constantinople.

NOTE 1125.—Literally, "*before the Anointed One*," that is "before Christ."

NOTE 1126.—Or, "*contrary to those things*," παρὰ ταυτα. If one of those eight ambassadors of the Ecumenical Council, Acacius of Melitine did say that Divinity is liable to suffering as John of Antioch and the rest of the Nestorian embassy to Constantinople in a letter to their own Conventicle at Ephesus (pages 373-375 above) assert that he did, he certainly went far beyond and contrary to this Mandate, which is really a letter of instructions. But that accusation being from convicted and prejudiced heretics should not be received on their testimony alone.

NOTE 1127.—Greek, τὸ . . . τῆς 'Αποστασίας Συνέδριον; which may be rendered

setting out" [hence] (1129), "and, because, contrary to all the Canons, they have dared to condemn the most holy and most dear to God Archbishop Cyril, and the most holy and most dear to God Bishop Memnon, and because, above all, they yet strive together for the dogmas of Nestorius, and some among them are Celestians (1130), and furthermore are deposed, and they have dared to slander the Synod of the inhabited world as though it were heretical. (1131) But if any necessity be brought forward (1132) by (1133) the most religious Emperor, (since it is necessary to obey the authority of Christ-loving and pious Mightiness so far as we can), if the aforesaid" [John of Antioch and his party] "should be willing to subscribe to the deposition of Nestorius, and by written statements ask pardon of the Holy Synod for their headlong and rash acts against our Presidents, and both to anathematize first of all the dogmas of Nestorius and to cast off (1134) those who plainly hold and have held the same dogmas, and, together with us, labor to have the most holy Archbishops Cyril and Memnon given back to us, we give charge to your Holiness, (those things being done), to promise the communion to them, and to write to us, in order that, we consenting with you, the peace with them may be perfect. But ye are not to promise them communion unless the Holy Synod get back its own Presidents (1135). And we wish your Holiness to

---

also' "*the Sanhedrim of the Apostasy*," and "*the Conventicle of the Apostasy*."

NOTE 1128.—That is, to condemn, in company with the Orthodox Synod, Nestorius, etc.

NOTE 1129.—From Ephesus to Constantinople.

NOTE 1130.—Another name common in the East for the Pelagians. Canon IV. of Ephesus, and its Synodical Epistle condemn them and depose all clerics guilty of their heresies.

NOTE 1131.—That is, as though the Ecumenical Synod itself were heretical, as the Greek here shows clearly the meaning to be.

NOTE 1132.—That is to impose on the Ecumenical Synod. It is worthy of note that though the Ecumenical Synod are dealing with an Autocrat in whose power they were, they refuse to compromise with John's party but exact a condemnation of heresy and of favorers of heresy before they will admit him or his party to communion. So should we do with all creature worshippers and with all deniers of the Incarnation, aye, so must we do.

NOTE 1133.—Or, "*from.*"

NOTE 1134.—Greek, ἀποῤῥίψασθαι.

NOTE 1135.—Greek, τοὺς προέδρους ἑαυτῆς, that is Cyril and Memnon.

know that if any of these commands be neglected (1136) by you, the Holy Synod will neither admit what ye may do, nor hold you as in communion" [with itself].

"I, Berinianus, Bishop of Perga, giving mandates, have subscribed.

"And all the most God-Revering and most holy Bishops who are fore-arranged in the order (1137) in the Acts subscribed.

"These written statements in refutation on those matters (1138) being given by the Holy Synod, and the persons aforesaid being sent as charged with the mandate; the other party, that is that of John" [of Antioch] "sent also persons charged with their mandate to Constantinople (1139), (1140)."

ORTHODOX DOCUMENT XIV.

"*Copy of* A REPORT *sent*" [to the most pious Emperors (1141)] *by* THE HOLY SYNOD *through Juvenal, Firmus, Flavian, Arcadius, Theodotus, Acacius, Evoptius, Bishops, and*" [through] "*Philip a Presbyter* (1142).

"To the most religious and most dear to God and Christ-loving Emperors, Theodosius and Valentinian, Victors, possessors of trophies, Ever-August Ones; THE HOLY SYNOD COLLECTED BY GOD'S

NOTE 1136.—Or, "*overlooked,*" παροϕθείη.

NOTE 1137.—Or "*who are forearranged in their position*" (or "*in their standing*") "*in the Acts.*" See *Ephesus*, vol. I., pp. 21-30, 489-503, and this vol., pp. 187-193 and 225-234.

NOTE 1138.—That is, in refutation of the falsehoods contained in the Nestorian statements above from John of Antioch and his Synod of the Apostasy.

NOTE 1139.—See above, pages 306-398.

NOTE 1140.—I have translated the above Document from columns 1312, 1313 of tome III. of Coleti's *Concilia*, and have corrected it from pages 769-771 of tome V. of the *Collectio Regia* (Paris A. D. 1644.) I have compared somewhat Hardouin and Mausi.

NOTE 1141.—"*To the most pious Emperors*" is not in the Greek, but is in the Latin translation in Coleti.

NOTE 1142.—All these were of the Eastern part of the Church except the Roman legates Arcadius and Philip. Evoptius, that is, Euoptius, was Bishop of Ptolemais in Pentapolis. See *Ephesus*, vol. I, pages 27, 406 and this vol., pages 191, 230. His utterances are strongly Orthodox on pages 152 and 173.

GRACE (1143) AND THE DECREE OF YOUR MIGHTNESS, IN THE METROPOLIS OF THE EPHESIANS" (1144) [sendeth greeting].

"All the purposes (1145) of your Imperialness are to be praised, and display much zeal for piety, O Christ-loving Emperors; and for that reason, we all in common, and each separately, send up prayers to the Master Christ for the perpetuity of your Might, and ask that your Christ-loving Headship (1146) may be perpetually preserved to the inhabited world. And since moreover, Your Piety has now inclined to our petitions and, through the most magnificent and most glorious Count John, has exhorted (1147) the Ecumenical Synod, to send most dear to God Bishops, whom it approves, to your Mightiness and to state fully all our matters before your face, we" [therefore] "necessarily thanking your Christ-loving Imperialness, have selected the most holy and most dear to God Bishops, Arcadius, Juvenal, Flavian, Firmus, Theodotus, Acacius, Evoptius, and Philip a Presbyter of Rome, who manages the place (1148) of the most holy and most dear to God Bishop of the Apostolic See of the Great Rome (1149), Celestine; and by this letter we present them to your Serenity, and ask that they get both gracious looking and hearing.

NOTE 1143.—Or "*favor*." Greek. κατὰ θεοῦ χάριν.

NOTE 1144.—That is Ephesus.

NOTE 1145.—Greek, πάντα μὲν τὰ τῆς ὑμετέρας βασιλείας, ἐπαινετά. The Latin renders this by, Omnia quidem, Christianissimi Imperatores, Majestatis vestrae studia et laude digna sunt; but in some things his *efforts* or *purposes*, though well meant by him, were very evil as, for instance, his Acts done in error against the Third Ecumenical Synod and against God's truth which it promulgated.

NOTE 1146.—Greek, τὴν φιλόχριστον ὑμῶν . . . κορυφήν. The language is that of subjects to Autocrats whose intentions they charitably deemed well meant; and who were the head, not of the Church, but of the Roman empire, "*the inhabited world*" meant above.

NOTE 1147.—Or, perhaps better, "*has commanded*," παρεκελεύσατο.

NOTE 1148.—Greek, διέποντα τὸν τόπον; that is, *fills the place of*, or *represents* the Bishop of Rome. Cyril had done that himself in Act I. of the Council, by delegation from Celestine. My impression, from the uniformity of the extravagant and flattering and therefore insincere and Anti-New Testament titles given to the Emperor, his Counts, and other secular officers, and to all the Bishops, is that their use was bound on the Council and on all, as was the rule later in the stilted and degenerating Byzantine autocracy.

NOTE 1149.—Old Rome as the old seat of Empire was great Rome; Constantinople was New Rome, and at first was smaller than old Rome.

Report of the Synod to the Emperors Introducing Their Embassy. 463

"Moreover, knowing that your Christ-loving and devoted to God soul (1150) makes much of serving the Christ (1151) who fights for and saves you, and that your soul (1152) honors through all things His Priests (1153), because He has said, '*He that heareth you, heareth me, and he that receiveth you, receiveth me,* (1154), we therefore make bold to add information to the (1155) letter in regard to those things which have grieved us. For we came to the city of the Ephesians for no other reason than to thoroughly examine regarding the faith, in accordance with your pious decree. And inasmuch as the abominable dogmas of Nestorius have troubled its long (1156) unmoved serenity, we, as was seemly, having deliberated and counselled on those matters on the fifteenth (1157) day after the day decreed and fore-appointed, summoned Nestorius who has thoroughly troubled the Churches by his own dogmas. But inasmuch as he was held fast by an evil conscience, he refused to come and meet us. So having thoroughly examined the impious dogmas which have been set forth by him in writing on the putting on of a body by the Master, Christ (1858), we both anathematized those very dogmas and their father (1159) and made him an utter alien to the episcopal dignity. But John of the city (1160) of the Antiochians (1161), having at long last made out to arrive on the twenty-first

---

NOTE 1150.—Or "*souls,*" for it means both Emperors, though the Greek here is in the singular after its own idiom in such a case often. It is ψυχὴν.

NOTE 1151.—Literally, "*the Anointed,*" τὸν . . . Χριστόν.

NOTE 1152.—Literally, "*that it,*" that is the soul just mentioned of the Emperors "*honors,*" etc.

NOTE 1153.—Greek, ἱερεῖς, that is *Bishops* here.

NOTE 1154.—Matt. x; 40; Luke x; 16.

NOTE 1155.—That is, the letter above, that is the Mandate.

NOTE 1156.—Greek, ἐξ αἰῶνος, or *its Serenity unmoved for an age.*

NOTE 1157.—The Greek says *the sixteenth,* but that means the fifteenth in our idiom; for they counted in the day from which they started to number and that on which they stopped, but we omit the former.

NOTE 1158.—Literally, "*the Master Anointed,*" Greek, περὶ τῆς ἐνσωματώσεως τοῦ Δεσπότου Χριστοῦ.

NOTE 1159.—Nestorius.

NOTE 1160.—Or "*the Church.*"

NOTE 1161.—That is Antioch.

(1162) day after the aforesaid fore-appointed day, as though he would punish us for our zeal for the faith, gathered a little more than thirty about himself; of whom some were Celestians (1163), and others had been deposed long before; and then he made a movement against our leaders; and though those zealots for Orthodoxy," [we mean] "the most holy and most dear to God Archbishop Cyril of Alexandria, and our most holy and most dear to God Bishop (1164) Memnon, had neither been accused before him nor summoned in accordance with the order of the Canons, he" [nevertheless] "pilloried them by hanging on them the insult and outrage of" [an attempted] "deposition, and deceived and got a snap-judgment from your pious and dear to God ears (1165) by representing that the Holy and Ecumenical Synod took part in that injustice against them (1166). Therefore the Holy and Ecumenical Synod, in which co-sits both Celestine the most holy and most dear to God Archbishop of our (1167) Great Rome, and all the Western Synod (1168), by the most holy Bishops sent by it (1169) to

NOTE 1162.—In the Greek idiom it is counted the *twenty second*. See note 1157 above.

NOTE 1163.—That is, Pelagians, on whom see the circular letter of Ephesus and its Canon IV. below. Compare its condemnation of the Pelagians after or in Act V. in the Letter of the Council to Celestine of Rome and its ratification of the local condemnations pronounced against them before; pages 168-182, above, especially pages 177-182.

NOTE 1164.—The margin in Coleti here has "*Fellow-Bishop*," συνεπίσκοπον, instead of "*bishop*," ἐπίσκοπον.

NOTE 1165.—Literally, "*has snatched away your pious and dear to God ears*."

NOTE 1166.—That is, against Cyril and Memnon.

NOTE 1167.—The margin in Coleti and the *Collectio Regia* has here "*of your*," instead of "*our*," (ὑμῶν for ἡμῶν).

NOTE 1168.—The expression "*all the Western Synod*" seems here to be used for only a part of the West, for Africa and Illyricum are mentioned below as different from it seemingly. So *East* and *Eastern* were often used in the Orient for the patriarchate of Antioch and its people. How much of the West is meant here by "*all the Western Synod*" is not clear. Britain, was then of little account, and Spain and Gaul were then, and especially the former of less civilization than Italy, and the former was under the barbarians, and indeed was more or less afflicted by them, as indeed was Britain. Italy was some times called Hesperia, that is, the West. And Germany and the Scandinavian countries were still pagan, as was all or nearly all of the north of Europe. Britain was then not under Rome.

NOTE 1169.—By "*the Western Synod*," perhaps the Synod of the Bishop of Rome's jurisdiction in Italy is meant, perhaps an extra-canonical Council of all Italy. The Bishops sent by it were Arcadius and Projectus. Noteworthy is the fact that the Third Synod in the above Document XIV. speaks of them as sent to it not by Celestine alone but by "*all the Western Synod*."

us, and in which co-sits also both all Africa (1170) and Illyricum; having acted canonically (1171), has decreed that both John the leader of the Sanhedrim of the Apostasy (1172) and those who are with him shall be aliens from all ecclesiastical communion, and has stripped them of all priestly power and function, and has also nullified (1173) all those things which have been uncanonically done by them. And we sent before this to your Headship, an account of those things which we have done regarding them (1174); and now again both by this letter and by the Bishops sent" [by us], "we grasp (1175) with outstretched hands your pious knees (1176) and beg that those things which have been done as the result of deception and getting a snap-judgment against the holy and most dear to God Bishops Cyril and Memnon, and which, according to the Canons, have no validity, may be utterly null and void (1177), so that the Synod may not be headless, and so that both we and all the Priests (1178) of Christ (1179) in the world may not be afflicted

---

NOTE 1170.—The Diocese of North Africa, under the Autocephalous see of Carthage. Illyricum was also another great Diocese, practically autocephalous probably. At least the above language would seem to imply it. See Chrystal's articles in the N. Y. Church Journal for 1870 on the attempt in century v. of Rome to acquire appellate jurisdiction in Carthage and Latin Africa, and their resistance to it. On Illyricum and its relation to Rome and on the extension of Rome's sway in the West and the means by which it was procured, see Smith's Gieseler's *Church History*, volume 1., section 94, pages 377-396. Compare what is said on the Eastern patriarchates in section 93, pages 371-377, id., and sections 20 and 21, pages 109-127, in volume 2, id., and on Thessalonica and Eastern Illyricum in *Wiltsch's Geography and Statistics of the Church*, English translation, volume 1., pages 128-133, and 462-470.

NOTE 1171.—The meaning is that the Ecumenical Synod had canonically summoned John of Antioch to appear before it and answer, before they condemned him, a regular act which the Conventicle of the Apostasy had violated in its deposition of Cyril and Memnon and in its excommunication of the other Bishops of the Ecumenical Council.

NOTE 1172.—Greek, αὐτόν τε τὸν ἔξαρχον τοῦ τῆς Ἀποστασίας συνεδρίου Ἰωάννην.

NOTE 1173.—Literally "overturned," ἀνατρίψασα.

NOTE 1174.—See the Report of the Orthodox Council to the Emperors on pages 3-14 above and that on pages 163-167, and that on pages 399-405.

NOTE 1175.—Or, "touch," ἁπτόμεθα.

NOTE 1176.—A position of earnest suppliants, in the East, such as the Ecumenical Synod in their earnestness against infidelity and creature service were.

NOTE 1177.—Greek, πάντῃ ἀργεῖν.

NOTE 1178.—That is here, Bishops.

NOTE 1179.—Greek, τοῦ Χριστοῦ ἱερεῖς, literally, *"priests of the Anointed One."*

ceaselessly with unbearable sorrow for our Presidents (1180); but that we may obtain our requests, and so send up with" [all] "the Churches in the inhabited world, the usual prayers to the Master, Christ (1181), that your Christ-loving Mightiness may be long (1182) granted to us as a favor. For the slander concocted against them (1183) both by John of the city (1184) of the Antiochians and by those who are with him, looks towards us all who are of the same faith as the aforesaid (1185) and co-priest (1186) with them; because of the fact that both all the Western Synod bear witness to their correct and unblamable faith, and because we, having been fully satisfied on that matter, have loudly proclaimed in writing in the Acts, both that they are Orthodox and that they hold to the judgment of our holy Fathers as it regards the dogmas of the Apostolic and Universal Church. We beg therefore, your Mightiness release us ourselves from bonds. For we have been bound with those who have been bound for being brethren and Presidents (1187) of our Holy Synod" (1188).

NOTE 1180.—Greek, τοῖς προέδροις; Cyril and Memnon.

NOTE 1181.—Greek, τῷ δεσπότῃ Χριστῷ.

NOTE 1182.—Or "*perpetually*," δι' αἰῶνος.

NOTE 1183.—Cyril and Memnon.

NOTE 1184.—Or "*the Church.*"

NOTE 1185.—Cyril and Memnon.

NOTE 1186.—Greek, καὶ συνιερατεύοντας αὐτοῖς, that is, they co-ministered with Cyril and Memnon in episcopal offices, notwithstanding the farcical attempt of John of Antioch and his little Conventicle to depose them.

NOTE 1187.—This certainly implies that Cyril and Memnon had been put into bonds to bully them into acquiescence with Nestorian errors. The Greek of this part reads, Δεόμεθα τοίνυν τοῦ ὑμετέρου κράτους, λύσατε καὶ ἡμᾶς αὐτοὺς τῶν δεσμῶν. Συνδεδέμεθα γὰρ τοῖς δεδεμένοις, ὡς ἀδελφοῖς καὶ προέδροις τῆς ἁγίας ἡμῶν Συνόδου, Coleti *Concilia*, tom. III., col. 1317.

There seems here to be a reference to Hebrews XIII., 3: "*Remember them that are in bonds as bound with them.*" Compare also Colos. IV; 18, "*Remember my bonds;*" Heb. x; 34: "*Ye had compassion of me in my bonds,*" etc.

NOTE 1188 —I have translated the above Report of the Third Ecumenical Synod from the Greek in col. 1313-1317 of tome III. of Coleti compared with pages 772-775 of tome V. of the *Collectio Regia*. I have compared somewhat Hardouin and Mansi also.

DOCUMENT XV.

EPISTLE OF ALYPIUS TO CYRIL.

"*To the most holy and most dear to God and chief worker in sacred things,* (1189) *Cyril;* ALYPIUS, *a presbyter*" [of the Church] "*of the Apostles, wisheth joy in the Lord.*

"Blessed is the man whom first God shall deem worthy to see with eyes of love thy dear to God and holy head wearing the crown of martyrdom confession (1190). For thou, most holy Father, hast trodden with watchful eye the way of the holy Fathers, and hast taught those who were going lame in both knees to walk erect to the truth (1191). Thou hast put on the boldness of speech of Elijah (1192), and thou alone hast taken to thee the zeal of Phinehas (1193). Thou hast stopped the mouth of the poison darting dragon (1194), and thou hast overturned much-eating Baal (1195); and thou hast rendered ineffective and of no force his vain hope of patronage procured for him by

---

NOTE 1189.—Greek, καὶ ἀρχιερουργῷ Κυρίλλῳ The margin here in Coleti suggests ἀρχιεπισκόπῳ Κυρίλλῳ instead of the last two words above.

NOTE 1190.—Greek, τῆς ὁμολογίας τὸν τοῦ μαρτυρίου στέφανον.

NOTE 1191.—Greek, καὶ τοὺς χωλαίνοντας ἐπ' ἀμφοτέραις ταῖς ἰγνύαις ὀρθοποδεῖν πρὸς τὴν ἀλήθειαν ἐδίδαξας.

NOTE 1192.—Compare his bold rebuke to Ahab for his service to creatures in I. Kings XVIII.; 8 to 20, and to the people for the same sin in what there follows: and again in I. Kings XVII; 1: and again in I. Kings XXI; 17 to 25, against Ahab and Jezebel.

NOTE 1193.—He is commended by God for his zeal against the idolatry and creature-service of Israel at Shittim in the matter of Baalpeor, and against the men guilty of it, and against the heathen women who led them into it. He used the javelin to suppress it and them. See Numbers XXV., 1 to the end of the chapter; and Psalm CVI; 28 to 32. Cyril was such a crusher of creature worship but on a wider and broader field.

NOTE 1194.—Nestorius and his infidel and his creature serving heresies seem to be here meant by Alypius. For instances of the simile, see Deut. XXXII; 34, 33; Rom. III; 13:. James III; 8; etc. And Alypius by "*dragon*" refers to the fact that all creature worshipping and all infidelizing heresies come from the old serpent, the author of all error. See under '*dragon*'" in *Cruden's Concordance* and the Definition of the Sixth Ecumenical Synod where similar language is used of Pope Honorius' Monothelite heresy and where it is ascribed to "*the author of evil,*" and where also "*impieties of Nestorius*" are condemned.

NOTE 1195.—Or, "*voracious Baal.*" The reference is to the Apocryphal book, "*The History of the Destruction of Bel and the Dragon,*" where the anti-creature serving hero, Daniel, refuses to worship the image of Bel, that is Baal, and exposes the cheat and lie of his priest in asserting that Bel ate the large supply provided for him by the pagans; which was "*every day twelve great measures of fine flour, and forty sheep, and six vessels of wine.*" See it verse 3, etc. The same book tells how Daniel refused to worship a brazen image of a dragon, and destroyed it.

money (1196), and thou hast made the contrivance of the golden image (1197) to become dead. And what sort of a mouth full of spiritual perfumes (1198) will be able to express the praises due thy zeal! For thou hast become a perfect imitator of the blessed Theophilus, thy uncle (1199); and hast also put on the witness of the blessed Athanasius (1200). For just as he escaped the plots (1201) of the lawless heretics which were like sunken rocks (1202) having repelled them by his prayers (1203); so also thy Holiness by thy pure and con-

---

NOTE 1196. This seems to refer to Nestorius' having secured patronage by money, perhaps from Scholasticus the Emperor's chief chamberlain, which finally failed him, or from others. Here Alypius charges Nestorius or some one or more of his party of using *"money"* to procure patronage for their heresies, the very thing that they accused the Orthodox of doing for Orthodoxy; see on that pages 362, 383, 396, 397 and 398 of this volume.

NOTE 1197.—Daniel, chapter III., all of it. This is another slap at Nestorius' creature-service. Alypius was evidently among those godly men, who groaned in spirit over the increasing creature service of the times, and hailed with rapturous joy, the light of Cyril's teaching against that darkness and gloom, even his stand for the truth taught by Christ himself that *God alone is to be worshipped* (Matt. IV; 10), and that to serve a Man with the Trinity is to substitute a worshipped Quaternity for a worshipped Trinity. The Church gloriously established the true doctrine against such error before the break into East and West, and no after attempt can upset it, or put anything else in its place. See on Nestorius' Tetradism, and his worship of a Quaternity Chrystal's *Ephesus*, vol. I. pages 89-96, and indeed the whole of note 183, pages 79-128, of which that place forms part and under *Tetradism* on page 656, id.

NOTE 1198.—Literally, *"perfumed unguents."* Greek, μύρων.

NOTE 1199.—Here long after Theophilus' action against John, Bishop of Constantinople, commonly called Chrysostom, we find him mentioned with honor, as he deserved to be. And John is accused of invoking creatures, and if he did, Theophilus might well condemn him. But see more fully under *Chrysostom*, page 439, vol. I. of Chrystal's *Nicaea*, and page 581, vol. I. of his *Ephesus*. On some points, if what is written of him be true, he was a heretic. See in those places. Indeed it would be difficult to find one of the Antiochian School to which he belonged who was not more or less affected by the heresies of its chief teachers, Diodore of Tarsus and Theodore of Mopsuestia. It was no wonder therefore that St. Cyril of Alexandria and the Third Synod and the Fifth condemned them.

NOTE 1200.—Athanasius was the great leader of the Church in the fourth century against the Arian doctrine of creature service, and, in showing that we must worship Christ as Eternal and Uncreated God, he incidentally shows that if he were a mere creature he could not be worshipped at all; hence he shows impliedly, that all religious service is prerogative to the Divinity alone. See the English translation of his *Select Treatises against the Arians*, passim. (Oxford, A. D. 1844). See also to the same effect, Chrystal's *Nicaea*, vol. I., pages 217-240, and Athanasius' utterance against *Cannibalism* in the Eucharist and for, in effect, the figurative view, as against Consubstantiation, in Chrystal's *Ephesus*, vol. I., pages 274-276, note matter.

NOTE 1201.—Or, *"devices,"* τὰς συσκευάς.

NOTE 1202.—*"Sunken rocks,"* on which a vessel may strike and be lost unless its pilot watch. Greek, ὡς σπιλάδας.

NOTE 1203.—Literally *"by the prayers."*

scientious life, hast made to cease the fabrications of the lawless One (1204) just as though they had been weak blasts. For so the blessed Athanasius also, after many false accusations had been made against him by heretics, proved them to be stale lies, and by a decree of exile accepted an abiding in a foreign land, because those who then held sway had devised it against him; and the more their impure mouths fabricated false accusations" [against him] "so much the more pure and resplendent was he proved to be in his long suffering, and he shone forth eminent by those victories" [won againt such false accusations] (1205). "And by those conflicts having woven for himself the crown of the good witness bearing he established the doctrine of the *Same Substance* (1206) trod under foot the heterodoxy of Arius, and raised up Orthodoxy, and exalted the holy throne of the Evangelist Mark (1207). And thou thyself having made use of those things, hast walked in the steps of that holy man. I pray therefore, most holy Father, that I may be deemed worthy to see with my own very eyes thy holy face, and to lay hold on thy knees, and to enjoy" [the sight of] "a Confessor" [of the faith], "crowned with crowns in a time of peace (12c8) Moreover all things relating to us, how we have spoken boldly, having confidence in thy prayers and in the prayers of the holy Fathers (1209), and whatsoever we have done, will the beloved Deacon Candidian tell" [thee] "who also delivers the letter of my Littleness to thy Holiness. I salute all the Holy Synod of those who are crowned with the crown of bearing a good testimony, with thy Holiness. Mayest thou be in good health and strength and of good cheer, eminent in the Lord, and contending for the truth" [which has been] "graciously granted to us by (1210) God" (1211).

NOTE 1204.—II. Thess. II; 8 where the words, ὁ 'ἄνομος rendered "*That wicked*" in the King James version mean "*The Lawless one,*" in the Greek.

NOTE 1205.—See the Church Histories as to the slanders against Athanasius, put forth by the Arians. See also for details on the slanders, Professor Bright's article *Athanasius* in vol. I. of *Smith and Wace's Dictionary of Christian Biography*, especially pages 183, 188.

NOTE 1206.—Greek, τὸ ὁμοούσιον 'ἔστησε.

NOTE 1207.—That is, the see of Alexandria, his own and Cyril's.

NOTE 1208.—As distinguished from the long Arian struggle which had been a time of war, Alypius' language of abasing himself before Cyril by embracing his knees is not in accordance with Peter's rebuke to Cornelius in Acts x. 25, 26, nor, let us hope, in accordance with Cyril's feelings. Such language and customs were already occasionally used, I presume, but wrongly.

NOTE 1209.—That is, those of the Third Ecumenical Synod.

NOTE 1210.—Or "*from God.*"

NOTE 1211.—I have translated the above Document from the Greek in columns 145-148 of tome 77 of Migne's *Patrologia Graeca*; and have compared it as in col. 1317-1320 of tome III. of *Coleti's Concilia*, and as on pages 776, 777 of tome v., (A. D. 1644), the Paris edition (the *Collectio Regia*) of the Councils. It is the last of these Documents between Acts VI. and VII. in that Paris edition. I have looked at it somewhat as in Mansi and Hardouin.

DOCUMENT XVI.

A DIVINE LETTER (1212) TO THE HOLY SYNOD IN EPHESUS, RELEASING ALL THE BISHOPS" [and dismissing them] "TO THEIR OWN HOMES, AND REINSTATING THE MOST HOLY" [men] "CYRIL AND MEMNON IN THEIR OWN CHURCHES (1213)."

"We, preferring in honor the peace of the churches to every other business, wished to bring you together, not only by our secular officers, (1214) but also by our own personal action (1215), for we believed it to be a thing impious

NOTE 1212.—This document exists in an ancient version in chap. XXXIII. of the *Synodicon* of Irenaeus, as Baluze informs us, as given in note *a*, col. 1319, tome III. of *Coleti's Concilia*. The Greek for "*divine letter*" above is θεῖον γράμμα, and I suppose it was written at the emperor's dictation or by a copyist following the then customary and I suppose legally *enforced* style of address, enforced, I presume, like the worship of the emperors' images, by imperial edict. For the flattering and wicked way of speaking of a sinful man as a *god* and his letters, palace, etc. as *divine* continued from the custom of the pagan Romans, and was wickedly used by them and to them as above. The custom is indefensible and inexcusable. So Tertullian and the Ante-Nicene Christians held. See vol. I. of Chrystal's *Ephesus*, page 8, note 6; page 19, note 20, and pages 505-512, note B. See Sophocles' *Glossary of Later and Byzantine Greek* under θεῖος. See also in his *Lexicon* under that word and under θειότης. And we must remember also the stress they were under, an example of which we have just mentioned, and which will be found in the honor and worship claimed by the emperors for their images to which some sinfully acceded, while others resisted nobly. See the references in note "*n*," page 405 of the Oxford translation, (A. D. 1844 edition) of "*Select Treatises of St. Athanasius, Archbishop of Alexandria, in Controversy with the Arians*." I do not feel sure whether that worship and the use of such titles was not exacted of them, though that does not excuse them. Jerome on Daniel III. condemns strongly that worship.

NOTE 1213.—In the *Synodicon*, chap. XXXIII., col. 631, tome 84 of *Migne's Patrologia Graeca*, the heading is quite different from the above. There it reads (translated) as follows:

"*A sacred letter of Theodosius. After the* protest of John and the other Bishops who were retained in Chalcedon while the Emperor entered into Constantinople with the opposing party, this *sacred letter was sent to the Bishops who had convened with the Bishop* of Alexandria, *the text of which, after the preface, is as follows.*"

NOTE 1214.—The Greek here in Coleti is διὰ τῶν ἡμετέρων ἀρχόντων. The Latin translation in the *Synodicon* of Irenaeus, col. 632 of tome 84 of Migne's *Patrologia Graeca* is "per judices nostros." The object of sending the secular officers was to make them judges in certain matters between the Bishops. Such officers were the Counts Candidian and John. But the Orthodox Bishops very properly resisted their interference when they usurped the God-given rights of the episcopate in attempting to decide matters which involved doctrine.

NOTE 1215.—The Greek is δι' ἑαυτῶν. The Latin rendering in the *Synodicon* is "*per nos ipsos.*" Theodosius seems to refer to his efforts to bring the parties together at Chalcedon and at Constantinople, when he should have considered the matter settled by the decisions of the Bishops in the Universal Synod, and should have recognized the fact that he, as a mere layman, could not reopen the question again, nor in any way usurp the functions and authority of an Ecumenical Synod, the very thing that he was trying to do, without, in his unwise and ignorant and probably heretical egotism, seeming to notice it.

An Imperial Letter to the Synod. 471

and unworthy of our own reign that the Churches should be divided and that we should be negligent and not do all things whatsoever are possible" [to unite them]. "But since it has not been possible for you to be united, and your Piety was unwilling to come to a discussion (1216) regarding the matters in dispute, we have decreed that the Oriental Bishops (1217) shall go away into their own countries and Churches, and that the Synod in Ephesus shall be dissolved (1218); that, furthermore, Cyril shall go into Alexandria, and Memnon shall remain in Ephesus (1219). Only we inform your God-revereingness (1220) that so long as we live we shall never be able to condemn the Orientals (1221). For they have not been convicted in our presence, for no one wished to dispute with them (1222). If therefore there is any wish for peace, choose it without quarreling and make it known to us. But if there is not, at once fix your thoughts on your departure, in accordance with what we write; we are not at fault, but God knows those who are at fault (1223)."

At this point we find the following note in Latin in the *Synodicon* at the end of chapter XXXIII. of it.

NOTE 1216.—Literally, *"to come to words,"* εἰς τοὺς λόγους . . . ἐλθεῖν, that is, *"to a discussion."* The Emperor wished the delegates of the Ecumenical Synod at Chalcedon or Constantinople to consider the decisions of the Ecumenical Synod at Ephesus as null and void and to begin to discuss them anew, and practically to let him, an unlearned layman, decide all the matters involved as supreme Judge, a thing which he had no right to impose on them, and which they had no authority to grant. The time for the Nestorian party to discuss was when they were summoned to attend the sessions of the Ecumenical Synod before it decided, when however they refused. In the Mandate given them by the Ecumenical Synod the Orthodox legates to the Emperor were practically sternly forbidden to insult by any such course the decisions of the whole Church, fairly rendered with the Christ-promised aid of the Holy Ghost to guide them.

NOTE 1217.—That is, John of Antioch and the other Nestorianizing prelates of his diocese of the Orient, of which Antioch was the head and capital.

NOTE 1218.—"Liberatus, chap. VI: *"And after that he"* [the Emperor] *"commanded all the Bishops to go away, each to his own region."* Baluze's note in col. 1319, tome III. of Coleti's *Concilia*.

NOTE 1219.—"*Hence it is clear that this Letter was given forth after that epistle which had been written by the Holy Council to the Emperor Theodosius after the arrival of John, Count of the Sacred Largesses, which is published above:*" Baluze, note in col. 1319, tome III. of Coleti.

NOTE 1220.—Greek, τῇ ἡμετέρᾳ θεοσεβείᾳ.

NOTE 1221.—That is, the Bishops of John of Antioch's Patriarchate of the Orient.

NOTE 1222.—For the very good reason that when Theodosius II. wished that to be done, the matter in dispute had been fairly, fully, and forever settled by the Third Ecumenical Council; and no one had any just reason for regarding them as otherwise and as unsettled, and for so denying the authority of the Orthodox Council. Theodosius II. was probably a Nestorian at heart, at least on Man-Worship, at this time.

NOTE 1223.—Oh! the blindness of the Emperor and his wondrous self-sufficiency. He had been and was guilty; for he had favored Nestorius and practically condemned Cyril of Alexandria and Orthodoxy before the Third Council met; and after it had condemned

"This imperial letter was sent the last of all. It was sent after the blessed Cyril, Patriarch of Alexandria, had already returned into his own city (1124)."

Nestorius and his heresies, he had, with criminal effrontery, assumed to undo their work and to nullify that voice of the whole Church speaking with the promised aid of the Holy Ghost, promised. moreover, by Christ Himself, and to threaten the Orthodox Bishops, and to recognize the condemned heretical party of John of Antioch and his suffragans as either the whole Ecumenical Synod, or as, at least, a part of it; and to imprison the leaders of the Ecumenical Synod, and never to release them till after the voice of the Church was raised in their defence and till further persecution might have been unsafe for himself.

NOTE 1224.—Col. 632, tome 84 of Migne's *Patrologia Graeca*; where more matter on the above document may be found in the notes, as to works in which it is published, etc. This document xvi. is not in the Paris edition of the Councils here, in tome v., pages 777, 778. I have also glanced at it as in Hardouin and Mansi.

Of the foregoing sixteen Orthodox Documents, the following are emanations from the Third Ecumenical Synod: Documents I, IV, VII, VIII, XI, XIII, and XIV, and, as being of Ecumenical authority, should all have been in coarser print in the text than the others, and all of them are except the first. The rest are individual utterances, valuable, but not sealed with the imprimatur of the whole Council.

The indexes to this volume will appear at the end of the next and final tome of these Acts, and will be indexes for both these last volumes.

www.ingramcontent.com/pod-product-compliance
Lightning Source LLC
Chambersburg PA
CBHW021417300426
44114CB00010B/531